President Washington's Indian War

The Struggle for the Old Northwest, 1790–1795

by

Wiley Sword

UNIVERSITY OF OKLAHOMA PRESS : NORMAN AND LONDON

BY WILEY SWORD

Shiloh: Bloody April (New York, 1974)

President Washington's Indian War: The Struggle for the Old Northwest, 1790–1795 (Norman, 1985)

Firepower from Abroad: The Confederate Enfield and the LeMat Revolver (Lincoln, Rhode Island, 1986)

Sharpshooter: Hiram Berdan, His Famous Sharpshooters and Their Sharps Rifles (Lincoln, Rhode Island, 1988)

Embrace an Angry Wind, The Confederacy's Last Hurrah: Spring Hill, Franklin, and Nashville (New York, 1992)

Library of Congress Cataloging-in-Publication Data

Sword, Wiley.
President Washington's Indian War.

Bibliography: p. 384.
Includes index.
1. Indians of North America—Wars—1790–1794. 2. Northwest, Old—History—1775–1865. 3. St. Clair's Campaign, 1791. 4. Wayne's Campaign, 1794. 5. Indians of North America—Northwest, Old—Wars. I. Title.
E83.79.S95   1985   977'.02   85-40481
ISBN: 0–8061–1864–4 (cloth)
ISBN: 0–8061–2488–1 (paper)

The paper in this book meets the guidelines for permanence and durability of the Committee on Production Guidelines for Book Longevity of the Council on Library Resources, Inc. ∞

2   3   4   5   6   7   8   9   10   11

For my sons, Greg and Andy,
and their generation—
that they may better understand
the promise and the responsibility

Contents

Illustrations

Maps

Preface

Perhaps it will seem shocking to read that the heartland of the United States is conquered territory. Contrary to the popular conception that the lands of the midcontinent were essentially unclaimed, vacant, and merely there for the taking, the occupation of mid-America by white civilization required a costly and prolonged war.

The Old Northwest Territory (embracing modern-day Ohio, Indiana, Illinois, Michigan, and Wisconsin) was long the domain of various Indian nations, whose existence depended on the land in its natural state. Since these lands represented the strategic key to the continent, their possession was crucial to the destiny of the rival native and Euro-American civilizations.

Following the Revolutionary War, the hue and cry among United States citizens was for westward expansion, resulting from the enormous pressures within the developing new nation. Specifically, the vital land mass extending west of the Appalachian Mountains to the Mississippi River, bordered on the south by the Ohio River and on the north by the Great Lakes, beckoned for white settlement. Yet the energetic Indian opposition imposed severe obstacles to the influx of encroaching white settlers.

Far from the rather inept military force depicted in popular literature, the Indian confederacy's army defending the region was an effective fighting force in 1790. In combination with their British allies, they were quite capable of changing the course of history.

In retrospect, the United States–Indian War of 1790 to 1795 seems as vicious and as bitterly fought as any conflict in our nation's past. Possibly the worst defeat at the hands of Indians in the history of the United States Army was suffered during the course of this war. General Arthur St. Clair's defeat on November 4, 1791, was a rout so complete that more than two-thirds of the entire army and its dependents became casualties.

Although this war was fought over terrain that today is regarded as among the most tranquil and commonplace of our various states, its bloody history is at odds with the lack of publicity that it has received. Frequently dismissed as a rather disjointed sequence of skirmishes and random encounters, the contest was, in reality, a five-year struggle crucial to securing and sustaining American nationalism. Moreover, in historical perspective, this wilderness conflict looms as the decisive confrontation in the Indian–United States wars that spanned two centuries.

As a result of this contest the Indian civilizations were compelled to yield control of the vital midcontinent, which ultimately sealed the fate of the unconquered tribes west of the Mississippi River. While the United States thereby secured many vital natural resources and the base essential for further territorial expansion, the Indians were largely deprived of any hope of an independent existence. Confronted by a radically altered environment, and crushed by the overwhelming weight of the whites' numbers, the original Indian civilizations in North America were largely relegated to a vanquished and dismal status.

Somehow, despite the millions of words written about American wars, from the Revolution to Vietnam, historians and scholars have often neglected this conflict. "Perhaps no war in the history of the U.S. has been so overlooked," wrote the noted historian Richard C. Knopf. Indeed, this book is the first comprehensive history of the United States–Indian War of 1790 to 1795.

As the very first war under the United States Constitution, the contest was both a catalyst for national development and the Indian peoples' ruin. Accordingly, this book is intended to present objectively a truly remarkable and significant American story. Serving neither as an indictment of our past nor the glorification of a lost cause, it is an effort at reasoned investigation and analysis.

Since nations, like individuals, reflect all of their endeavors, we can look with justifiable pride to the relative progress in human existence represented by the development of the United States of America. Yet, if we are to shape the future wisely, a discerning knowledge of our past is important.

Time, it would seem, reveals little change in the basic confrontations of past and future generations. As surely as the all-perfect society has yet to exist, it is unlikely that various nations will cease to impose on the rights of others. Equally foreseeable is the role of human attitudes, which serve as the fulcrum of mankind's destiny. As surely as the traits of human character know no bounds of nationality, this book is largely a chronicle of our imperfection both as a nation and as individuals.

May we therefore read with reason and understand therefrom mankind's inalienable responsibility for the respect and improvement of all human life.

WILEY SWORD

Birmingham, Michigan

Acknowledgments

The fruition of such a complex project as the writing of this book requires the assistance of many people and institutions. For the generous cooperation of the following individuals and organizations (listed in alphabetical order) I am particularly grateful. Beth Bamberger, Sue Sutton, Bloomfield Township Library, Bloomfield, Michigan; Joseph Oldenburg, Burton Historical Collection, Detroit Public Library, Detroit, Michigan; John Dann, Arlene Shy, William L. Clements Library, University of Michigan, Ann Arbor, Michigan; Anna DiPiazza, History and Travel Section, Detroit Public Library, Detroit, Michigan; Connecticut Historical Society, Hartford, Connecticut; Dr. William Phenix, Fort Wayne Military Museum, Detroit, Michigan; Historical Society of Pennsylvania, Philadelphia, Pennsylvania; Huntington Library and Art Gallery, San Marino, California; Ray Mahoney, Michigan State Library, Lansing, Michigan; National Archives, General Services Administration, Washington, D.C.; Gary J. Arnold, Charles A. Isetts, Ohio Historical Society, Columbus, Ohio; Brian Discoll, Charles MacKinnon, Public Archives of Canada, Ottawa, Ontario, Canada; Nelda Hinz, Saginaw Public Library, Saginaw, Michigan; Irene Bakewell, Wayne State University Library, Detroit, Michigan; Wisconsin Historical Society, Madison, Wisconsin; U.S. Army Field Artillery Center and Fort Sill Museum, Fort Sill, Oklahoma.

Special thanks are due Katharine Price for her skilled cartography and the staff of the University of Oklahoma Press, especially George Bauer, John Drayton, and Sarah Morrison.

I would also like to thank those who helped prepare the manuscript for publication: Lauri Walker, Karen Cameron, and Cheri McEvoy.

Last but not least, I would acknowledge the patience of my wife, Marianne, who tolerated the many hours of research and writing.

President Washington's Indian War

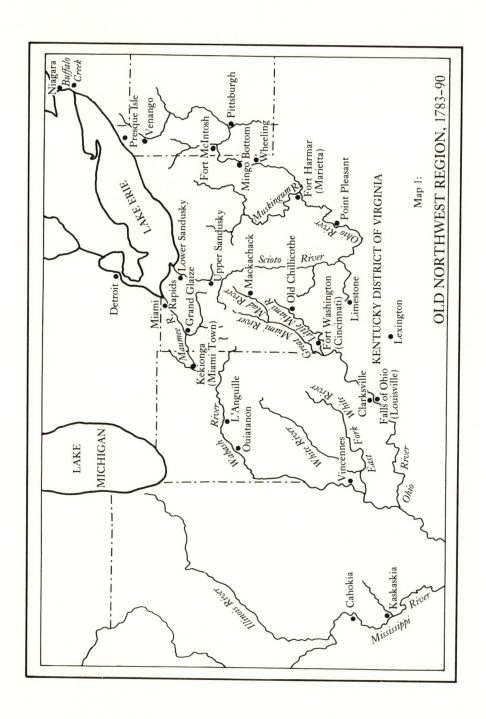

OLD NORTHWEST REGION, 1783–90

Map 1:

1

River of Many White Caps

IT was a magnificent view. The river Oyo, as the Indians called it, spread in a wide corridor of sparkling blue, gliding through a verdant timberland of walnut, cherry, and oak. Interspersed among the stately oaks and sycamores were sugar maples, groves of beech and poplars, and stands of tall hickory. Vines of grape and wild honeysuckle spread from tree to tree and carpeted the rich earth. There were islands, almost too numerous to count, intensifying the mild current that swirled briskly by.[1]

Back from the riverbank, uneven, forbidding hills of dark timber swelled in profusion, with stands of hardwood and conifers spreading into the wide bottomlands. It was, indeed, a vast wilderness, thought one observer, where soon "the people of Virginia and elsewhere . . . , exploring and marking all the lands that are valuable," would strive to settle. This early traveler was none other than George Washington, on a surveying journey to mark bounty lands in 1770.[2]

The river that Washington observed was destined to become one of the most historically and strategically important waterways in North America. To the French, who had first explored it in 1669, it was La Belle Rivière ("the beautiful river"). The Indians knew it as Ohiopeekhanne ("the White Foaming River," or more properly, "the River of Many White Caps"). To modern America it is the Ohio River, the principal commercial watercourse of the middle western United States.[3]

The Ohio was of great importance to the nation because it ran westward. From the impressive confluence of the Allegheny and Monongahela rivers in western Pennsylvania, the Ohio spread in a quarter-mile-wide water highway and flowed 981 miles before emptying into the mighty Mississippi in southern Illinois. It served, moreover, as the watershed of 200,000 square miles of America's heartland, accounting for nearly one-fourth of the water reaching the Gulf of Mexico at the mouth of the Mississippi River. To be sure, the Ohio beckoned as a prime, expedient means of transit in the years immediately following the American Revolution.[4]

Near the turn of the eighteenth century a river traveler recorded his satisfaction at the Ohio's modern appearance: "The settlements on each side of the Ohio are extensive, and much of the land is . . . cultivated. The appearance of the rising towns and the regularly disposed farms on its banks is truly delightful. . . . No scene can be more pleasing . . . than this, which presents to view a floating town, as it were, on the face of a river."[5]

3

Thus the Ohio gave rise to a great crisis. Less than twenty years after George Washington's survey of the wilderness river, a virtual flood tide of settlers descended the Ohio to claim western lands. At the diplomatic close of the American Revolution, Great Britain, by the Treaty of Paris in 1783, had ceded a vast expanse of North American wilderness to the fledgling United States. Included in this wilderness domain were the seemingly endless "Black Forests" of the Ohio country. It was a magnificent stroke of good fortune—and also nearly an invitation to disaster.[6]

Burdened with an immense war debt from the Revolution amounting to nearly $40 million, and cognizant of the claims due its veterans by the individual states, the financially burdened Confederation Congress looked to the new western lands as a solution to the new nation's problems. By the sale of vast forested tracts the federal war debt might effectively be reduced. Land grants to the several states might underwrite much of their public obligations. Moreover, the considerable produce emanating from settlements in the Kentucky and Ohio regions could be marketed in the East, alleviating critical shortages.[7]

The practical means to fulfill that ambitious program were obvious. "The Ohio River," wrote George Washington in 1784, "embraces this commonwealth from its Northern-most to its Southern limits. . . . The Western settlers have no other means of [going or] coming to us but by long land transportation and unimproved roads. . . . [In order] to fix the trade of the Western country to our markets. . . . The way is plain. . . . It is to open a wide door, and make a smooth way for the produce of that country to pass to our markets."[8]

Through General Washington's "wide door" passed settlers by the hundreds, and an impressive flow of commerce. In little more than a month during the winter of 1785, thirty-nine boats, with an average of ten settlers each, passed down the Ohio. At Fort Harmar, opposite Marietta, in the latter half of 1787 an observer counted in passing 146 boats bearing 3,196 persons, 1,371 horses, and 165 wagons. The following year the immigration was even greater. By November, 1788, 967 boats carrying 18,370 people, 7,986 horses, 2,372 cows, 1,110 sheep, and 646 wagons had cruised down the Ohio. Once begun, the inexorable westward pressure of Neo-European civilization had reached a floodtide.[9]

Yet the movement west was to precipitate a costly war, one of the most brutal this nation has known. For good cause, the influx of white civilization had been largely on the Kentucky side of the Ohio River. In fact, the Kentucky District of Virginia had grown significantly from the first meager attempt at settlement in 1775 to a population of 73,677 in 1790. Thriving communities, such as Louisville, Lexington, and Harrodsburg, could boast of many stores and sizeable gristmills. The popular clamor for admission to the Union as a new state soon was so great that Kentucky was voted entry in 1791. Yet there remained too much wilderness, and not enough merchandise and commerce. Since travel was difficult, many new roads were needed. The ground had to be cleared for dwellings and crops, and the earth was to be mined for minerals. White civilization persisted in devouring the land. What had existed for centuries, progress now would drastically change. An unfulfilled destiny lay before the land and its peoples.[10]

4

Across the Ohio River the many Indian inhabitants looked upon the new civilization with great bitterness and anger. Kentucky had been for them a bountiful hunting ground, the "ancient country" of their ancestors; "a beautiful country of prairie and forest" filled with "deer, elk, bear, and otter"; and a land of "large rivers, [and] of rapid waters filled with fish." By 1790, however, it was virtually closed to them forever.[11] Following a disastrous battle near Point Pleasant, Ohio, in 1774, the Kentucky tribes gradually had yielded the vast hunting grounds south of the Ohio to the white settlers. Although during the years of the Revolution there had been much bloodshed throughout the wilderness, the frontier settlements in Kentucky had survived. In the postwar westward land rush the overwhelming numbers of the new settlers ensured permanent possession of the Kentucky country by the Long Knives.

After the Kentucky confrontations the Indians' prospects became more and more forlorn. As surely as the face of the land was changing, so did the outlook for the survival of Indian civilization. The conflicts seemed unavoidable and basic because the worlds of the white settler and the Indian were not compatible. Where before the beaver had dwelled in plenty, the white man had driven them away by clearing the rivers and improving the creeks for transportation. The bison were slaughtered for food and clothing; the elk and bear had thinned greatly. Even the deer were reduced in considerable numbers. The vast Kentucky countryside was no longer a great hunting ground. It was becoming domestic farmland.

Although the dispute continued, the ultimate fate of Kentucky was never in doubt. Soon only a legacy of bitterness remained, and with it a determination on the part of the Indians to resist to the ultimate any further encroachments on the once vast wilderness empire of the Algonquian and Iroquois civilizations—the beautiful Ohio country. "Look back and view the lands from whence we have been driven to this point," warned a tribal council in the early 1790's. "We can retreat no farther, because the country behind hardly affords food for its present inhabitants, and we have therefore resolved to leave our bones in this small space, to which we are now [reduced]."[12]

By the guarantee of the British in 1768, all land north of the Ohio River was to remain Indian territory indefinitely. Yet by 1790 there already had been bold transgressions of this last red domain in the East. White settlements north of the Ohio were established at Marietta, Steubenville, and Cincinnati. Lesser farming communities, such as Gallipolis, North Bend, Columbia, Belpre, and Waterford, were continually springing up as the result of post-Revolution land speculation.[13]

Thus the course of the future had become manifest. The ancient prophecy of the chieftain Metacomet was about to be fulfilled. This sage, better known as King Philip, had foreseen in the seventeenth century the serious threats to all native peoples from white civilization: "Brothers . . . you see the foe before you—that they have grown insolent and bold—that all our ancient customs are disregarded; the treaties made by our fathers and us are broken, and all of us insulted; . . . Brothers, these people from the unknown world will cut down our groves, spoil our hunting and planting grounds, and drive us and our children from the graves of our fathers . . . and enslave our women and children."[14]

5

More than a century of relations with the white immigrants from across "the great waters" had affirmed that prophecy. Relatively few populous Indian nations continued to dwell in the magnificent upper Ohio and Great Lakes country: the Shawnees, the Miamis, the Delawares, the Wyandots, the Iroquois League (Six Nations), the Ottawas of the Great Lakes region, the Chippewas, the Potawatomis, the Cherokees, and the Wabash Confederacy (the Wea and the Piankashaw tribes). These were all that remained of the once mighty Woodland Indians.[15]

The challenge was taken up by the Shawnee war chief Captain Johnny in May, 1785. Should the dreaded American Long Knives attempt to cross the Ohio River and settle on the Indian side, he warned, "We shall take up a rod and whip them back to your side of the Ohio." The great Shawnee leader Tecumseh, just emerging as an able warrior, later spoke of the crux of the problem from the Indian perspective: "At first they [white men] only asked for land sufficient for a wigwam, now nothing will satisfy them but the whole of our hunting grounds, from the rising to the setting sun."[16] His view of the future was ominous: "My people . . . are determined on vengeance; they have taken up the tomahawk; they will make it fat with blood; they will drink up the blood of the white people."[17]

Inevitably there would be war—a great, decisive contest between the Indian and the white civilizations—for the land, the one coveted asset possessed by the Indians, which was essential to both societies although they utilized it in incompatible ways.

2

Seeds of War

"THE Indians," wrote a white captive forced to live as an Iroquois warrior for four years, "are a slovenly people in their dress. They seldom ever wash their shirts, and in regard to cookery . . . are exceedingly filthy." Notorious for their barbaric and savage treatment of white captives, and pagan in their religious beliefs, the North American Woodland Indians were not merely scorned and abused but frequently regarded as little more than animals by their white contemporaries. "[They are] more brutish than the beasts they hunt, more wild and unmanly than that unmanned wild country which they range rather than inhabit," wrote an early observer.[1]

Tecumseh succinctly stated the prevalent American attitude: "They do not think the red man sufficiently good to live." In a later generation the motto "The only good Indian is a dead Indian" would become almost a sportive, if crude, jest. However, it was merely a manifestation of what had long been understood.[2] Genocide was the unmistakable, if inadvertent, consequence of the forward thrust of colonial American civilization among the native populations. Although there were whites who proffered their friendship to, and had compassion for, the Indians, the results of such attitudes were always beyond the course of individual relationships. It was ultimately a question of which of the two opposing cultures would prevail: "They must either change their mode of life or they must die. . . . That is the alternative," asserted an Ohio senator regarding the Indian problem shortly before 1900.[3]

The bitter tragedy was that the agony of more than seven generations between 1750 and 1900 was largely perpetuated by ignorance: a general preponderance of the people on each side failed to recognize the basic nature of the opposing population. The ways of white society contrasted so sharply with red culture that complete dominance by one or the other society was inevitable. Despite this for more than one hundred years the innumerable treaties between Indians and whites largely ignored that central problem, merely postponing the final, decisive confrontation. Then, when the bitter conflicts were eventually terminated by demeaning and outright capitulations, the tribes' mandated acceptance of white dominance eliminated the overt threat that they had presented as rival, native peoples. Sadly, too few among the white victors understood that this peculiar tragedy would result in the demise of native civilizations that personified the very virtues that their own society ardently proclaimed. Freedom and a free spirit had long characterized American Indians.

7

One who was perhaps in the best position to assess the merits of the respective cultures, an Indian who was educated and assimilated into white society, once wrote: "When nature is at her best, and provides abundantly for the savage, it seems to me that no life is happier."[4] The basis for the Indians' simple existence was nature, and as astute students of the natural order, they exhibited a keen awareness of their environment.

This basic Indian principle—an abiding respect for life—was founded on a rigid code of self-discipline and personal responsibility. As a white captive of the Iroquois observed: "No one can arrive at any place of honor among them but by merit. . . . It would appear to the Indians a most ridiculous thing to see a man lead off a company of warriors, as an officer, who had himself never been in battle."[5] Among the various Indian standards of conduct were many refined ideals, such as kindness, polite behavior, love, humility, and reliance on a common bond. The obligation to uphold principles such as absolute honesty was great within the various tribes.[6]

Despite those strong virtues, which were largely unpublicized at the time, there were certain Indian peculiarities that brought into sharp contrast the irreconcilable differences between Indian and white societies. For example, many Indians considered certain wildlife, such as eagles and owls, as minor deities who were engaged in communicating the deeds of men to the gods. Some even worshipped the evil spirit, out of fear of dire consequences. "If there is any such thing now in the world as witchcraft," thought one white man, "it is among these people."[7]

Many Indians were also highly susceptible to omens and mysterious occurrences. An owl perched in a tree about a camp at night required the offering of a sacrifice, such as the burning of tobacco, so that the bird might have a good report to carry to the gods. The abject terror created by natural phenomena such as solar or lunar eclipses was further cause for derision by the white man.[8]

Yet, most of all, the frequent reports of barbaric cruelty toward prisoners cast the Indians in the role of "savage beasts." By Indian custom an enemy captive was considered to have forfeited all rights to life. This practice was based on the strong tribal belief that as individuals they were responsible only for their conduct toward their own people. Indians often considered that they owed nothing to others, except to return in kind the treatment that they received.[9]

In periods of extended warfare, such as ravaged the eastern wilderness after the mideighteenth century, much bitterness and a strong quest for vengeance was evident among contending Indian and white elements. Nonetheless, for practical reasons, the Indians often acted humanely and with great compassion when they were the victors. "It is a custom of the Indians," wrote a former female captive of the Shawnees, "when one of their number is slain or taken prisoner in battle, to give to the nearest relative [of the victim], a prisoner . . . or the scalp of an enemy. On the return of the Indians from conquest . . . the mourners come forward and make their claims. If they receive a prisoner, it is at their option either to satiate their vengeance by taking his life in the most cruel manner they can conceive of, or to receive and adopt him into the family in place of him whom they have

8

lost. . . . Unless the mourners have but just received the news [of a relative's death] . . . and are [unduly influenced by] grief, anger and revenge, or, unless the prisoner is very old, sickly, or homely, they generally save him, and treat him kindly. But if their mental wound is fresh, their loss so great that they deem it irreparable, . . . no torture, let it be ever so cruel, seems sufficient to [give] them satisfaction."[10]

Indeed, it was following massacres or other brutal deeds by whites that the Indians perpetrated their most inhumane and vicious tortures on captives. Barbara Leininger, a Delaware captive during the French and Indian War, was compelled to witness the extreme cruelties inflicted on two white prisoners after a surprise raid by Colonel John Armstrong on the Indian village of Kittanning in Pennsylvania. Most of this village had been burned to the ground by Armstrong's men after many of its residents had been killed and their bodies mutilated, including a prominent chief and some of his family. Returning to their razed village, the Delawares in a frenzy put to death the two captives, who had attempted to escape with Armstrong's raiders. One victim, "an English woman," was tied to the stake, while Barbara Leininger looked on with horror: "First, they scalped her. Next they laid burning splinters of wood here and there upon her body. Then they cut off her ears and fingers, forcing them into her mouth so that she had to swallow them. Amidst such torments this woman lived from nine o'clock in the morning until toward sunset, when a French officer took compassion on her and put her out of her misery. An English solider . . . who deserted and joined the French, had a piece of flesh cut from her body, and ate it. When she was dead, the Indians chopped her in two through the middle, and let her lie until the dogs came and devoured her."

The other white captive, an Englishman, was later burned alive. "His torments," wrote Barbara Leininger, "continued only about three hours, but his screams were frightful to listen to. It rained that day very hard, so that the Indians could not keep up the fire. Hence they began to discharge gunpowder at his body. At last, amidst his worst pains, . . . the poor man called for a drink of water. They brought him melted lead, and poured it down his throat. . . . He died on the instant."[11]

Tales of such macabre tortures were related by repatriated prisoners, and being highly publicized and often enlarged or distorted among the white settlers, they aroused a bitter hatred of the red men. Retaliatory murders of Indians, often of innocent tribes, prompted further depredations on both sides, until mutual distrust and malice permeated the entire frontier. By the middle 1780's this terror so influenced Indian attitudes that abhorrence and distrust of the white man was ingrained among the yet unconquered tribes.[12]

Centuries of relations with white civilization had created this widespread distrust. Even the Indians' white allies, the British, often were regarded with suspicion. "You may perhaps think me a fool," warned a Delaware chief during the Revolutionary War, "but . . . who of us can believe that you can love a people of a different color from your own, better than those who have a white skin like yourselves?" "We people of one color are united, so that we make but one man that has but one heart and one mind," admonished a Shawnee chieftain in 1785.[13]

9

The continual abrading of raw emotions had translated into a maelstrom of conflicting interests and racial malice. Thus during the crises, when the Indians' ultimate fate was being determined, there was little compassion among the whites in their conquest of the supposedly inferior society of the Indians. "Shall the liberal bounties of Providence to the race of man be monopolized by one of ten thousand for whom they were created?," argued a prominent American statesman. "Shall the lordly savage not only disdain the virtues and enjoyments of civilization himself, but shall he control the civilization of a world? . . . No." Another orator, President Andrew Jackson, touched nearer than he perhaps realized to the essence of the problem — white attitudes: "What good man would prefer a country covered with forests and ranged by a few thousand savages to our extensive Republic, studded with cities, towns, and prosperous farms, embellished with all the improvements which art can devise or industry execute, occupied by more than twelve million happy people, and filled with all of the blessings of liberty, civilization and religion."[14]

Sadly, Jackson's statement reflects how little the white men had come to understand the ways of those who coinhabited this vast continent. Further, it was ample evidence that our forefathers had, if need be, a willingness to compromise justice for the sake of progress—long a classic ingredient of wars among mankind.

3

The Lion in Winter

THE British, according to American Secretary of War Henry Knox in 1790, were guilty of "rank injustice" and flagrantly unfair behavior in refusing to implement the terms of the peace treaty of 1783 ending the Revolutionary War. Another American, Major John F. Hamtramck, a veteran army officer, fretted that "nothing can establish a peace with the Indians as long as the British keep possession of the upper forts (Detroit—Michilimackinac—Oswego—Niagara), for they certainly are daily sowing the seed of discord betwixt the measures of our government and the Indians."[1]

For more than a decade following the Revolutionary War, the hostile presence of the British loomed as a dreaded spectre throughout the Old Northwest. More than an outgrowth of the Revolution, the British cold-war policy was a remarkable attempt by colonial interests to recoup the indiscreet blunders of the treaty makers of 1783 in ceding the English claims to the vast Old Northwest Territory. Perhaps by virtue of Colonel George Rogers Clark's conquest of the Illinois country in 1778–79, the American Congress had laid claim to the approximately one quarter million square miles of wilderness that now comprise five states: Ohio, Illinois, Michigan, Indiana, and Wisconsin. To the briefly tenured, but crucially circumstanced, British ministry of William Fitzmaurice (Lord Shelburne) had fallen the task of concluding a peace with the rebellious colonies. Embroiled in an international conflict and thoroughly sick of the American war, the comparatively liberal Shelburne ministry had acceded to the United States claim largely because of the impracticality of cheaply and effectively defending the forested domain from incursions by the French, the Spanish, and the Americans. Moreover, an incorrectly charted map drawn by John Mitchell in 1755 had been the basis of the formal peace negotiations of 1782–83. Since the Mitchell map depicted the ceded Northwest Territory as significantly smaller than its actual size, the Shelburne cabinet's estimation of what was being yielded to the Americans was proportionately in error, as was quickly recognized by the British colonial establishment.[2]

"My apprehensions of a shameful peace are too well founded," wrote an embittered Loyalist, the former British mayor of Albany, New York. Another British official thought the terms of the provisional treaty "certainly beyond their [the Americans'] most sanguine hopes or expectations." Several English fur merchants were equally adamant in their objections to the treaty, believing the actual deliverance of the Northwest posts would prove a "fatal moment."[3]

Alexander McKee, the noted British Indian Agent. Courtesy of William Clements Library, University of Michigan, from the original painting in the possession of Raymond W. McKee.

The boundary terms of the peace agreement were so controversial to the British commander at Detroit that he deliberately concealed them from the Indians for fear of upheaval. Negotiated in Europe without representation from, or even reference to, their Indian allies, the Treaty of Paris ending the Revolutionary War forced the British to relinquish an enormous tract of land, most of which was actually Indian country. Great Britain's claim to this wilderness domain had rested upon the final conquest of the French during the French and Indian War of 1754 to 1763. Yet the French had been merely commercial tenants of the lands, not primary exponents of an alien occupation and settlement.[4]

The Indian tribes had tolerated this essentially practical arrangement for purposes of mutual trading advantage, even with the British in control. American dominance in the vast midcontinent, however, had a more sinister connotation of usurpation and despoiling of the lands. Moreover, the continuing intrigues of Great Britain in North America served as an uncertain, disruptive influence. At the root of the matter was the commercially valuable fur trade controlled by the British. General Frederick Haldimand, the British commander in Canada, anticipating that the several forts on soil claimed by America ultimately would have to be given up, established contingency plans calling for the construction of new forts "on the opposite side [of the boundary] for the security of the fur trade." When the season of 1783–84 produced an unusually large volume of pelts, Haldimand cautioned his subordinates to avoid aiding the Americans in their efforts to penetrate the Indian territory.[5]

As the British colonial government well understood, if the extensive English fur trade was to be maintained, the British must remain in control of the Northwest Territory. The key to physical control obviously was possession of the military posts within the territory, and the means of retaining possession was quickly seen to lie with those who actually occupied the land— the Indians.[6]

Although at first compelled to consider the imminent evacuation of the "Upper Country Forts," the British military authorities under General Haldimand began actively to conspire for their retention. When pressed by American military commanders for their evacuation, Haldimand, a rather harsh Swiss professional, even refused to allow American Major General Friedrich von Steuben to visit those posts in 1783, saying the instructions he had thus far received from the king declared only "a cessation of hostilities." Haldimand was soon further encouraged in his policy of continued nonbelligerent resistance to American occupation of the Northwest posts by the receipt in November, 1784, of secret instructions from a more conservative ministry in London to make no withdrawals until ordered to do so.

The basic intent of those instructions may have been to put as much pressure on the fledgling United States government as political and practical circumstances would allow. The newly independent thirteen colonies were as yet a small Atlantic Coast nation weak in international influence and unproven in domestic credibility. Should the United States government fail to survive, Great Britain, by having retained possession of the posts would own the Northwest by default. Moreover, by enlisting the aid of the various Indian nations, the British might thwart the advance of American settle-

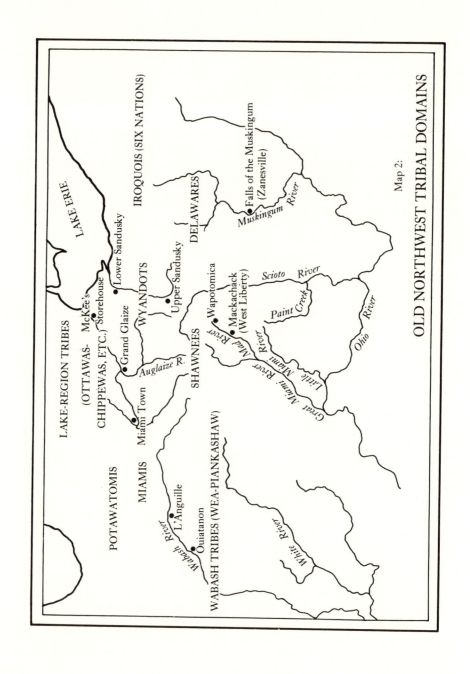

LAKE ERIE

LAKE-REGION TRIBES

(OTTAWAS-
CHIPPEWAS, ETC.)

McKee's
Storehouse

Lower Sandusky

Grand Glaize

WYANDOTS

Upper Sandusky

IROQUOIS (SIX NATIONS)

DELAWARES

Falls of the Muskingum
(Zanesville)

Muskingum River

Auglaize R.

Miami Town

SHAWNEES

Wapotomica

Mackachack
(West Liberty)

Scioto River

Paint Creek

Ohio River

POTAWATOMIS

MIAMIS

L'Anguille

Ouiatanon

Wabash River

WABASH TRIBES (WEA-PIANKASHAW)

White River

Great Miami River

Little Miami River

Mad River

Map 2:

OLD NORTHWEST TRIBAL DOMAINS

14

ments, confining the United States to the eastern seaboard. Protection of the important fur trade would be assured for many years, and considerable leverage could be exerted for fulfillment of the treaty terms required of the Americans, such as repayment of individual debts owed British citizens and the restoration of rights and property to Loyalists.[7]

Crucial to the implementation of these plans were the Ohio-country Indians. British strategy required the utilization of the red men as instruments of policy. Without regard for humanitarian or idealogical considerations, the Home Office generally regarded the Indians as British chattels, useful as warriors or fur procurers as circumstances might warrant.[8]

To that end the British had long since established a strong Indian Department charged with the responsibility of managing the various tribes. Throughout the Revolution the department had acted with considerable success. Relying on a staff of competent if unsavory operatives, such as the renegade Simon Girty and his immediate superiors, Matthew Elliott and Alexander McKee (who were both defectors from the American side), the British had established a clear dominance in the Northwest Territory by the end of the Revolution. Except during the brilliant campaigns of George Rogers Clark in 1778 and 1779, the British and their Indian allies had generally controlled the war in the West, establishing a supremacy that was in marked contrast to the failures of the British military establishment along the eastern seaboard.[9]

This success of the British Indian Department in the West had long been founded on a technique of subtle and substantive coercion. Besides promising to "provid[e] for the needs of as many [natives] as remain faithful and grateful" and threatening dire consequences to those who failed to support the king, the Indian agents reduced their professional relationships to the simplest terms. In formal councils the Indians were always treated as inferiors. For example, they were addressed as "children" while the representative of the white civilization was termed their "father." "Which of the two [white] fathers do you prefer?" demanded a British officer during the Revolution. "The one who, attentive to your wants, . . . is watching your safety and taking care of your days [British], or he from whom you have received no favors, who does not even know you except by the evils which he is [attempting] to make you feel [American]."[10]

Considerable dissension and variance of opinion had been prevalent among the Indians in the early years of the war, but as the Revolution progressed, the majority of the Northwest tribes became British partisans, particularly the yet-powerful Six Nations of the Iroquois. Largely responsible for this was the enormous outpouring of gratuities that obligated the Indian tribes and made them more dependent on the British. The gifts ranged from silk handkerchiefs to scalping knives, from looking glasses to rum.[11]

Yet the matter of Indian presents soon got out of hand. Knowledge of the bountiful British gifts, enhanced by counter offers of presents from the Americans, caused the Indians to descend in swarms upon the British posts. In a single five-month time span in 1781, four major Indian councils were conducted by the Indian Department at Detroit, involving ten separate Indian nations. It is little wonder that Major Arent Schuyler de Peyster

15

suggested to an assembled council that he had "as many children as the sands of the sea to supply."[12]

The inevitable, if subtle, consequence of these transactions was the growing dependence of the Indians on white civilization, particularly on the British. "[They] absolutely depend upon us for every blanket they are covered with," asserted General Haldimand, the British commander in Canada, who urged that pressure be brought to bear to diminish Indian Department expenditures while achieving greater results.[13]

Having thus obtained considerable leverage, the British continued to exert pressure for greater control and efficiency. Major de Peyster reported in October, 1780, that "no goods are given to people [Indians] who are altogether inactive," and that having "stretched the cord to the utmost extent," he would resort to such methods as sending away "200 Potawatomis empty handed until they perform a service pointed out to them."[14]

The Indians, cajoled and baited by oratory and presents from white agents, soon began to fall deeper and deeper into a state of reliance on the British. "They cannot [adequately] hunt to furnish themselves while they have a part in the war," advised a British commander in 1781.[15] Some perceptive Indian observers foresaw that the diminishing self-sufficiency of the tribes would result in their ruin, but so long as active warfare continued, most Iroquoian and Algonquian nations made few attempts to resist British overtures. Although it was not yet apparent, the heavy wartime reliance on the British for weapons, merchandise, subsistence, and merriment would considerably hasten the demise of the Indian cultures. Even the British, who were so calculating in the management of their Indian allies, soon began to lose the very control of Indian affairs that they sought to achieve.

By far the greatest difficulty in dealing with the Indians, and the most tangible evidence of their degeneration, was their widespread drunkenness. Strong liquors had long since been introduced by the traders, who found rum a desirable bartering medium. The Revolution had only heightened the problem. In order effectively to deal with the Indians, especially in matters involving military operations, the British were compelled to resort to the distribution of copious quantities of rum. Unfortunately, most Indians did not often drink in moderation. When liquor was available, it was consumed until the supply was exhausted, or until the principals lay in a drunken stupor. Intoxication was an exhilarating experience to many Indians, yet their inability to handle strong spirits subjected them to derision and fraudulent activities. "It required but a very small quantity of whiskey to cause a very large drunk among the . . . red men," wrote a Michigan pioneer. "Rum is their God," disgustedly announced another frontier observer.[16]

Thus traders bartering for furs continually resorted to rum to appease the Indians' demands, and some used liquor to cheat or deceive them. To the military the Indians' demands for liquor were a constant irritation and detriment to their effective deployment. For want of "a keg of rum" reported de Peyster in 1780, he had seen Indian war parties refuse to go out.[17]

The specter of an "insatiable [Indian] monster" became an outright dilemma to the British once the war had ceased. The fur trade still was to be protected, and the encroachment of the Americans into the Ohio country was to be avoided if possible. Yet of necessity British expenses had to be curtailed drastically. As the Indian Department had to be reduced, sufficient funds for Indian subsistence were lacking. Meanwhile, the Indians, although unvanquished in battle, had to be persuaded to put down the tomahawk and negotiate with American territorial commissioners, who would attempt to annex much of their land. Moreover, there was a growing schism in the British ranks over the value of the Indians as allies. On numerous occasions during the war the Indians had disrupted organized British expeditions, and many military commanders looked upon them with disdain.[18]

Contrasted against those views were the unceasing efforts of the Indian Department to provide for and to retain influence with the peoples who, in effect, had been wards of the British government. A serious complicating factor was the intensifying Indian discontent with the British, which had begun to be manifest even before the war ended. "They are thunderstruck at the appearance of an accommodation so far short of their expectation from the language that has been held out to them," wrote General Haldimand in October, 1782.[19]

At a Detroit council an Indian earnestly pleaded: "Although our services should no longer be wanted, we yet hope you will supply our wants. Our women and children are almost naked. . . . We are informed that instead of prosecuting the war, we are to give up our lands to the enemy. . . . In endeavoring to assist you it seems we have wrought our own ruin." When an outraged Ottawa chief announced in 1783, "I believe all of you have been telling us lies," the British commandant felt helpless to retain influence.[20]

The Indian Department was increasingly pressed for information on what disposition would be made of the Indians, harassed and threatened by tribes demanding provisions and presents, and ordered by the king's ministers to restrain, and yet achieve greater control of, the unruly Indian elements. Thus the hard-pressed department could but offer excuses and resort to stopgap measures in order to stall for time. Although they believed that the Indians had been greatly "spoiled" during the war by the vast "treasures" given them, and since they were faced with an austere budget, British agents were compelled to borrow heavily from traders' stocks, and to occasionally issue pork for "the use of the savages" that was "unfit for the use of His Majesty's troops."[21]

The effect of such actions was further to confuse, frustrate, and divide the various Indian nations. Throughout the Revolutionary War the Indians largely had complied with British policy. A new spirit of independence, if not defiance, now began to emerge, however.

With the advent of peace in 1783 the Indians were faced with a great dilemma. Citing the "miserable situation in which we have left this unfortunate people," the British commander at Niagara reported in May, 1783:

The Indians, from the surmises they have heard of the boundaries, look upon our conduct to them as treacherous and cruel. They told me they never could believe that our king could pretend to cede to America what was not his own to give. . . . That [in 1768] a line had been drawn from the head of Canada Creek (near Fort Stanwix) to the Ohio; that the boundaries then settled were agreeable to the Indians and the Colonies, and had never been doubted or disputed since; that the

Indians were a free people subject to no power on earth; that they were the faithful allies of the King of England, but not his subjects; that he had no right whatever to grant away to the States of America their rights of properties without a manifest breech of all justice and equity, and they would not submit to it. They added . . . that they had no wish or inclination to go to war with the English, their allies, or with the Americans, their neighbors. . . . [Thus] they would not be the aggressors, but they would defend their own just rights or perish in the attempt to the last man. They were but a handful of small people, but they would die like men, which they thought preferable to [the] misery and distress if deprived of their hunting grounds. That if it was really true that the English had basely betrayed them by [relinquishing] their country to the Americans without their consent, or consulting them, it was an act of injustice that Christians only were capable of doing, that the Indians were incapable of acting so.[22]

This "very strong language," as the British conceived it to be, was hard evidence of the imminent crisis in postwar British Indian policy. The British decision and its manner of implementation, accordingly, were to have a profound effect upon the course of America's expansion westward.

Unfortunately, the Indians' new-found spirit of sophistication and independence was inconsistent with the realities of their physical existence—that is, their significant dependence on the very civilization that they sought to oppose. Although the British might fear the consequences of losing the Indians' allegiance, that allegiance was not essential to their survival in North America. The various Indian nations, on the other hand, were confronted with a civilization that was progressing beyond all limits—one that they could not, in a practical sense, avoid. Essentially, the question was which white power the tribes would support in the altered circumstances after the Revolution.[23]

With the French all but vanquished in North America, and the Spaniards struggling to hold onto the territories that they nominally held along the Gulf Coast, the Indians' only viable trading partners, besides the British, were the Americans. Although the Americans had been their dreaded enemies for much of the Revolution, there was at first considerable interest and much hope among the Indians regarding bargaining with the "thirteen council fires." Throughout the Revolution, American Indian agents had sought to enlist the aid of the Indians of the Old Northwest, or at least to ensure their neutrality. Tactics such as those utilized by the Virginia commissioners in 1778 were commonplace. "My children! . . . Come now to look for what you want and you will find all that is necessary for you," proclaimed the Virginians. "We are not doing like your [British] father giving you a little rum; with us it is as water, we make it ourselves. You may believe that we are numerous and that we will make an end of your father, who is at Detroit. We regard him as a fish which we are about to take on the end of a line."[24]

The American policy, however, proved to be generally inept. Once control of the Saint Lawrence River was lost following the abortive invasion of Canada in 1776, the American colonies were unable to compete effectively with the British in volume and cost of Indian goods. The Indians were thus faced with a choice of supporting an established government, whose reign had been long and successful, or the ill-equipped rebels against the lawful authority of the land. Their preference was obvious. The political ideology of colonial versus self-government was irrelevant and of little concern compared to the practical considerations. Effectively enticed by British presents, and naturally aligned with the interests of the fur traders rather than the settlers, the Indians soon demonstrated their allegiance during the Revolution.[25]

At the end of the war the majority of the Algonquian and the Iroquoian tribes east of the Mississippi River were under British influence. Therefore the Americans turned their efforts largely to reestablishing diplomatic relations with the Six Nations, by which means some authority might be asserted. In an effort to persuade the Iroquois nations to reject the British and submit to their new American landlords, the United States agent for the Middle Department said in August, 1783:

Brothers [a title of equality rather then the subordinate "children" normally used], the chiefs and warriors of the Six Nations have been a long time drunk and possessed with the evil spirit. —They are now getting sober and coming to themselves. . . . They have broken in pieces and destroyed the chain of friendship which your wise ancestors made with ours. . . . They joined with the English to make dogs of us. They have found themselves mistaken, and have themselves submitted to become dogs to the English. Brothers, the Great Council of the United States, which we call Congress, has determined to treat all the Indian as brethren, and will appoint some wise persons to call upon each nation in order to make a new chain of friendship.[26]

Reports of the "designing, hypocritical" Americans, "eternally sending messages and private emissaries to our Indians," already had begun to plague the British by mid-1783. Aware of their vulnerability, the British began to intensify their planning, in order to forestall the councils that were quickly called for by American Indian agents. When Ephraim Douglass, an American commissioner, arrived among the British Indians with a proclamation of peace, including details of the preliminary treaty's provisions about cession of Indian territory, the British acted quickly to suppress this "effrontery and impudence."[27] Douglass, perceived to be a shrewd, capable diplomat who spoke "several different Indian dialects," was considered too dangerous to be allowed ready access to the Indians. Shuttled from Detroit to Niagara to Oswego by British escorts, he was effectively dissuaded from his mission of contacting the Indians.

Responding to the urgent entreaties of many of his subordinates, Sir John Johnson, the British superintendent of Indian affairs, authorized a grand Indian council af Lower Sandusky (present-day Fremont, Ohio) in early September, 1783. This vast gathering of thirty-five nations, with the obvious undercurrent of dissension among the tribesmen over the British peace terms, was a most significant meeting, crucial to the Indians' formulation of postwar policy.[28]

Fully aware of the stakes involved, the British Indian Department had worked diligently but covertly to lay the groundwork for the grand council, in order that they might exercise complete control. Much like the intraparty machinations before a modern political convention, the British utilized leverage, compromise, psychology, and promises of rewards in varying amounts to achieve their objectives. Indeed, their basic strategy utilized their longtime allies, the still-powerful Iroquois nations, to set precedents for the other tribes.

At an exclusive precouncil meeting at Niagara during July, Sir John Johnson had explained the implications of the peace treaty to the Six Nations, who were regarded by the other Indians as their "elder Brethren." In a give-and-take atmosphere Johnson traded his assurances of continued British patronage for guarantees of a land grant on Canadian soil and aid in the establishment of a grand alliance (or confederacy) among the Indians.

Thereafter the rum flowed freely, and Alexander McKee, who would be the principal British agent at the formal Sandusky council, soon obtained the desired promises of support from various Great Lakes tribes.[29]

At the general Sandusky council, which began September 5, 1783, the Indians followed the British bidding almost without a hitch. McKee explained that peace had been declared. Then, reading from a prepared text by Sir John Johnson, he declared that he would "take the tomahawk out of their hand, though he would not remove it out of sight or far from them, but lay it down carefully by their side, that they might have it convenient to use in defense of their rights and property if they were invaded or molested by the Americans."[30]

Concerning the controversial boundary settlement, McKee told the Indians: "You are not to believe, or even think that by the line that has been described, it was meant to deprive you of an extent of country, of which the right of soil belongs to you. . . . Neither can I harbor an idea that the United States will act so unjustly or impolitically as to endeavor to deprive you of any part of your country under the pretext of having conquered it."[31]

In summation, McKee held out the prospect of continued patronage, including the generous distribution of presents, a large quantity of which had been shipped aboard the schooner *Faith* for the occasion. Matters proceeded so smoothly, with the Six Nations' delegates supporting the British position, that the council was concluded on September 8, following a general agreement among the Indians.[32]

Having achieved virtually all that was desired, McKee could soon boast to Sir John Johnson that the meeting had been of great service in removing the Indians' doubts and uneasiness. Moreover, a matter of great importance to the Indians, their general confederacy, had been agreed upon. From then on, the various tribes were "to speak and act like one man," so that, as McKee told them, "A single breath which rashly blows can have no effect in turning you aside from the straight path laid before you by your Father."

McKee thus had presented a fundamental strategic concept. Yet all but overlooked by the Indians was another crucial aspect of the Sandusky council: the mutual commitment between the principals.[33] The Indians had agreed to remain faithful British allies and to unite in the common interest, though the extent of the British commitment to the allied tribes remained unexplained. Many Indians took it for granted that the British would actively support their attempts to resist American territorial aggression, despite earlier warnings by some British authorities of less-than-full military cooperation. Newly promoted Lieutenant Colonel de Peyster had ominously warned the Shawnees in July, 1783, that open hostilities with the Americans must be an "affair of your own," for "as your Father has already made peace with the Americans, . . . he is bound in honor to keep peace and can afford you no assistance if you foolishly bring mischief upon yourselves."[34]

Thus no overt military commitment was to be required of the British under any circumstances, a point not well understood by the tribes. Being generally satisfied by British promises—"to their utmost expectation," according to McKee—they would proceed to negotiate with the Americans over boundaries and cessions of land. Instead of negotiating from strength, however, the foundation of their support was the British self-interest, which was often undefined and always changing.[35]

As the crisis in Indian affairs intensified, British equivocations would become increasingly evident. Indeed, they were manifest from the beginning. Although the Indians pleaded, "You will not allow your poor children to be crushed under the weight of their enemies," the British regarded their situation in a different light.[36] "With respect to our Indians," wrote a British officer in 1783, "[they] get this day from the King's stores the bread they are to eat tomorrow, and from his magazines the clothing that covers their nakedness; in short, they are not only our allies, but they are a part of our family."[37]

While the British regarded the Indians as their personal dependents and managed them accordingly, the natives were not sufficiently important to them to warrant going to war. The Americans, with whom the Indians had to negotiate, meanwhile, regarded them as cruel, merciless savages. Thus the tribes of the Old Northwest were inadvertently courting ruin. In dire circumstances, and in their hour of greatest need, the Indian leaders were basing all their hopes and aspirations on the rhetoric of a nation that, when crisis arose, had always regarded only its own self-interest.

To more politically sophisticated peoples it might have been an ominous sign that the very articles of peace between Great Britain and the United States had made no mention of, nor any provisions for, England's Indian allies who were compelled to suffer a common fate with Britain in the Revolutionary War. The legacy had become manifest. It only remained now for the consequences to be enacted.

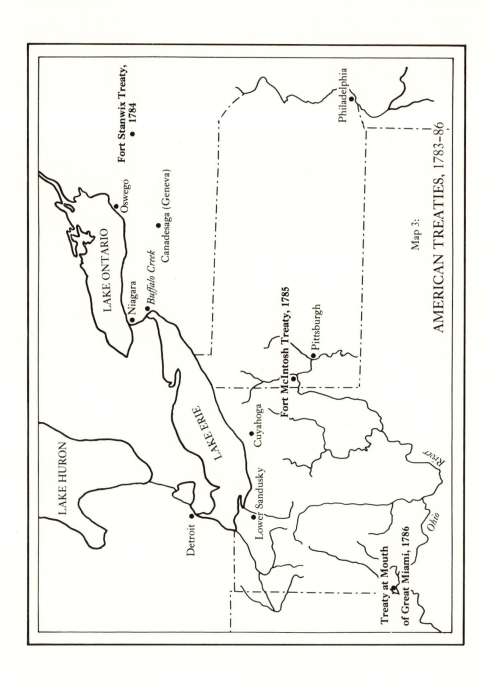

Map 3: AMERICAN TREATIES, 1783–86

LAKE HURON

LAKE ONTARIO

LAKE ERIE

Fort Stanwix Treaty, 1784

Philadelphia

Oswego

Canadesaga (Geneva)

Niagara

Buffalo Creek

Fort McIntosh Treaty, 1785

Pittsburgh

Cuyahoga

Detroit

Lower Sandusky

Treaty at Mouth of Great Miami, 1786

Ohio River

4

"Nothing but the Soil They Live On"

IT is with pleasure we announce to you that we are the commissioners sent by Congress, who is the great council of the United States of America, to kindle a council fire at this place, where we may smoke the calumet together, undisturbed by evil thoughts. [We are to] renew the friendship and brighten the chain of alliance with you and our faithful brothers, and give peace and good counsel to those who have been unfortunately led astray by evil advisers. We therefore wish you to put away all evil thoughts and cleanse your hearts and minds that we may begin the good work.

With this glowing rhetoric the United States commissioners, Oliver Wolcott, Richard Butler, and Arthur Lee, opened the proceedings of the council that was to produce the Treaty of Fort Stanwix in 1784.[1] This precedent-setting treaty was to be both the most important Indian-policy enactment since 1768 and the precursor of Indian-American relations in the generation to come. Yet, from the very beginning, there was an aura of contrivance and disruption about the council at Fort Stanwix on the banks of the Mohawk River near present-day Rome, New York.

The proud and eminent Six Nations, spokesmen for the Indians allied with Britain, had organized the council for early September, 1784, after lengthy negotiations with Congress. Following the concept generally agreed upon among the tribes at Sandusky in 1783, the negotiations were supposed to proceed on behalf of the Indian grand alliance so that the entire confederacy would speak in a united manner to the Americans. With great difficulty Captain Joseph Brant, the impressive and articulate Mohawk war chief, had brought about an assembly of the western nations' delegates at the British post at Niagara earlier in September. However, the American commissioners had not then been ready.[2] While the days of September slipped into October, the western Indian delegates, particularly the Wyandots, had become restive and had returned home. Sickness also had dissipated the Indian ranks, and when Brant had returned to Niagara late in September, he had found only a few Shawnees remaining among the Six Nations' delegates.[3]

Finally, on October 2, 1784, the American commissioners arrived at Fort Stanwix. They were disappointed to find there only a few Iroquois warriors, who were awaiting the arrival of their sachems and chiefs belatedly en route from Niagara. That delay was a harbinger of recurring troubles that would plague the treaty council. During the lengthy interim, what was intended to be a solemn, businesslike gathering assumed a carnival atmosphere. A swarm of sutlers, traders, and vendors, who had gathered especially for the occasion, circulated among the tribesmen and kept them intoxicated.[4]

At last, on October 11, the newly arrived delegation of Mohawks led by Aaron Hill and a few Shawnees were present to witness the inception of serious negotiations.[5] With their tribesmen "well disposed for peace," and believing that the commissioners' opening remarks were a reaffirmation of Congress's intention "to be friends with all the Indians," the Six Nations' delegates settled back to listen to the "good counsel" of their new white fathers.[6]

It is apparent they were psychologically unprepared for the thunderbolt that smote them. First the commissioners read the terms of the peace treaty with Great Britain, so that the Indians might understand that the United States had absolute sovereignty over the Northwest Territory and was "therefore the sole power to whom the nations living within those limits are hereafter to look for protection." It was further emphasized that in the peace treaty "no mention is made by the King of Great Britain of any Indian nation or tribe whatever, but that he has left those tribes to seek for peace with the United States upon such terms as the United States shall think just and reasonable."[7]

Having set a tone designed, in effect, to break the Indians' spirit and make them suitably contrite, the commissioners terminated the proceedings by asking the Indians to propose a land boundary to which the United States could agree. Further councils were delayed for nearly a week while the commissioners allowed the consternation and bewilderment among the Indian delegates to grow and fester.[8]

By October 17, when negotiations resumed, the Iroquois, accustomed to being feted for their friendship, were reduced to an unfamiliar defensive status. "We are free and independent, and at present under no influence," protested Aaron Hill. "We have hitherto been bound by the Great King, but he having broken the chain and left us to ourselves, we are again free and independent. . . . We have a right to treat for peace."[9] Another orator, the Seneca leader Cornplanter, followed with a plea for mercy, proposing a retention of the Ohio River boundary that had been agreed upon at Fort Stanwix in 1768 and reaffirmed at the first Treaty of Pittsburgh in 1775.[10]

For two days the Indians were kept waiting. At last, on October 20, when the commissioners replied to the Indians' proposal, it was evident what the Americans' basic attitude had been and would be. In a forthright declaration of sovereign power, and with obvious contempt for the Indians, the commissioners shattered the pretense of amicable relations:

"You must not deceive yourselves, nor hope to deceive us," they admonished:

You are mistaken in supposing that having been excluded from the United States, and [by the] King of Great Britain, you [have] become a free and independent nation and may make what terms as you please. It is not so. You are subdued people; you have been overcome in a war which you entered into with us. . . . The Great Spirit who is at the same time the judge and avenger of perfidity has given us victory over all our enemies. We are at peace with all but you; you now stand out alone against our whole force! When we offer you peace on moderate terms, we do it in magnanimity and mercy. If you do not accept it now, you are not to expect a repetition of such offers. Consider well, therefore, your situation and ours.[11]

As if that blow were not heavy enough, the commissioners further cast aside the cloak of earnestness about the negotiations and revealed that, indeed, they had never intended to negotiate a treaty of agreement at the council, but had sought to impose articles of surrender. "We endeavored to make the terms on which you were to be admitted into the peace . . . appear to spring from your own contrition for what you had done, rather than from a necessity imposed by us," they announced. "Yet on neither of these points [immediate delivery of white prisoners and a proposed boundary acceptable to the Americans] have you given us the smallest satisfaction. . . . We shall now . . . declare to you the condition on which alone you can be received into the peace and protection of the United States."[12]

What followed was the presentation of a land policy that had to result in either war or capitulation. The Indians' interests were no longer to be regarded except for such superficial appeasements as it was hoped might prevent a costly war. In fact, the great schism between white and red was to be further accentuated by the modification of existing physical boundaries. Rather than substantiating aboriginal rights to what was commonly known as "Indian Country," the American post-Revolution land policy required an admission by the Indians that the United States were "the sole and absolute sovereigns of all the territory ceded to them" by the Treaty of Paris, 1783.[13]

In retribution for the hostility of the Six Nations during the Revolutionary War—which had been "without the smallest provocation on our part," said the commissioners—all Iroquois claims to lands west of New York and Pennsylvania were to be relinquished. Moreover, the Six Nations were to be confined to certain areas of those states, subject to the approval, of course, by the state treaties yet to be held.

This was necessary, said the commissioners, because of the Americans' great "numbers and their wants." "Our warriors must be provided for," they admonished. "Compensations must be made for the blood and treasures which they had expended in the war. The great increase of [our] people renders more lands essential to their subsistence." "By right of conquest," the Americans asserted, "they might claim the whole of the British cessions, yet [we] have taken but a small part." This was "peace on moderate terms" offered in "magnanimity and mercy," warned the commissioners. Therefore the Indians were to "be wise" and "answer . . . accordingly."[14]

The Six Nations felt whipsawed, stunned, and now thoroughly intimidated. Aaron Hill of the Mohawks could but plead that the red nations had been "misunderstood." Even Cornplanter skittishly thanked the Americans for being candid, then acquiesced in the American demands.[15]

On October 22, 1784, the Treaty of Fort Stanwix was formally presented, and the various chiefs of the Onondagas, Mohawks, Senecas, Oneidas, Cayugas, and Tuscaroras slowly trudged forward to place their mark on the historic document.[16]

As if matters were not sufficiently difficult for the Iroquois, the Pennsylvania and New York state commissioners also concluded treaties with the Six Nations at Fort Stanwix after the Continental Congress council was ended. By these treaties the Iroquois were required to cede all of their hunting grounds in Pennsylvania and much of their land in New York. Aaron Hill and Cornplanter were then promised "two good rifles of neat workmanship" for "their services at the late [land] purchases."[17]

Once a full realization of what had occurred became widespread, there was great bitterness among the Iroquois. For years afterwards the Six Nations chiefs who had been involved in the Fort Stanwix negotiations were subjected to severe criticism within their own tribes. In 1786 a Six Nations council at Buffalo Creek refused to ratify the Fort Stanwix Treaty and denied the authority of the individual delegates there to cede any Indian lands.[18]

In fact, the immediate effect of the Fort Stanwix treaties was further to divide the Iroquois nations in their allegiance and perspective. The Mohawks, under Joseph Brant's influence, turned more openly to the British and sought a land grant on Canadian soil. The Oneidas and Tuscaroras, who had been on good terms with the Americans during the war, remained so, their lands being secured for them by the Fort Stanwix Treaty. The Senecas, Cayugas, and Onondagas remained on American soil, and became increasingly complaisant to the United States, being by close proximity those most certain to suffer in the event of hostilities.[19]

Although it was not yet apparent, the once imperial Iroquois confederacy, beset by internal dissension and reduced to a conquered-nation status by American diplomacy, had abdicated their once-powerful role as the dominant spokesmen of the Old Northwest Indians. Inevitably, if ever so slowly, the leadership in Indian politics passed to the nations on the west, especially the as-yet unconquered Shawnees and Miamis.[20] Of further importance, and severely damaging in the eyes of the Western Nations, was the unfortunate precedent that the Six Nations had set at Fort Stanwix in negotiating independently of the entire Indian confederacy. By mutual agreement at the Sandusky council of 1783 the Indians were to "be all of one mind and one voice." Joseph Brant had been instrumental in organizing the confederacy, and his indignation at what happened at Fort Stanwix was great. Evidently, what Brant had expected from this meeting with American commissioners was the promotion of peace and a renewal of friendship "in [an] honest manner." Talking of their "double face . . . business," Brant warned the Americans in a letter that he no longer trusted their motives and that his Mohawks would be permanently alienated by such tactics.[21] Yet the damage had already occurred. Much bitterness was promoted among the western tribes not only toward the Americans but also eventually toward Joseph Brant and the Six Nations. In the months and years ahead this internal bickering would severely damage the Indian confederacy and aid American schemes to divide and conquer.[22]

The Continental Congress's Indian policy had been founded, ironically, on the premise of avoiding open hostilities that would have impeded American postwar development. An important influence in the formulation of that policy was George Washington, who was not only the "father" of our country but also an acknowledged Indian expert and the owner of a vast tract of wilderness along the Ohio River. Once American sovereignty in the Old Northwest was assured by the articles of the peace treaty of 1783, Washington was asked by Congressman James Duane of New York for his view. Writing to Duane on September 7, 1783, Washington elaborated in depth on the matter, providing the foundation for what was to become a formal ordinance of Congress on October 15, 1783. First and foremost, Washington foresaw that "the settlement of the western country, and making a peace with the Indians," were so interrelated that "there can be no considerations of one without involving those of the other." Because of the rapidly increasing population, it was necessary to provide for white settlement of the western lands, and the Indians had to be persuaded to yield a portion of their country. "Care should be taken," advised Washington, "to yield nor to grasp at too much." Fundamental to that objective was the calculating strategy proclaimed by Washington. Citing the high cost of an Indian war versus the "cheapest . . . least distressing way of dealing with them" (the purchase of their lands), he relied on a gradual, programed encroachment on the Indian country to achieve settlement and thus to make "our barriers formidable, not only [among] ourselves, but against our neighbors [British and Spanish]." "As the country is large enough to contain us all," reasoned Washington, "I have very little doubt . . . that they [the Indians] would compromise for a part of it."[23]

The direct result, said Washington, would be an orderly, lasting settlement of the western lands, as the Indians "will ever retreat as our settlements advance upon them." Likening the savage to the wolf, "both being animals of prey, though they differ in shape," Washington summarized his remarks by cautioning Congress that "there is nothing to be obtained by an Indian war, but the soil they live on, and this can be had by purchase at less expense, and without . . . bloodshed."[24]

This remarkable declaration of private opinion was to find its way into formal interior policy. James Duane headed the congressional committee on Indian affairs, and he embodied Washington's suggestions in an ordinance that was submitted to Congress on October 15, 1783. "For imperial aggressiveness and outright effrontery," wrote the modern historian Randolph C. Downes, "This document takes a front rank in the annals of American expansion. To the Indians it could mean nothing less than an open declaration of war."[25] Included in the ordinance were further elaborations on Washington's views, requiring the yielding of all white prisoners regardless of circumstance and a boundary line pushed west almost to the modern Indiana and Michigan state lines, if possible.[26]

In their tragic naiveté the congressional committee members declared that, should perchance the Indians be dissatisfied at the new lines drawn, disclosure of the damages suffered at their hands would tend to "suppress any extravagant demands." In order to reward the Indians for compliance, the peace commissioners might provide some "coarse goods," consisting of government surplus clothing and other articles from the "public magazines," for distribution following a concluded treaty. "The public finances do not admit of any considerable expenditure to extinguish the Indian claims upon such [ceded] lands," said the committee by way of explanation.[27] Blithely thinking such a policy would preclude a costly Indian war while preventing British intrigues among the natives, Congress looked ahead to the rapid conclusion of peace negotiations and the opening of the western lands to settlement.

Since the Fort Stanwix treaty had already proved so successful to American designs, the commissioners were encouraged in their policy of mandate diplomacy. Indeed, although Congress had originally intended to conclude only a single treaty, because of the cost and time involved, it was readily apparent that the separate-treaties concept was serving American purposes well.[28]

So confident were the American commissioners following the Fort Stanwix Treaty that they did not feel it necessary to go to Cuyahoga, the intended site of the next treaty, deep in the country of the Wyandots and the Delawares. Instead, several interpreters were sent into the interior in December, 1784, to induce those tribes to convene at nearby Fort McIntosh, which was at the mouth of Beaver Creek only about thirty miles northwest of Pittsburgh. Once the Indians were present, the rum began to flow in prodigious quantities, causing Arthur Lee to remark in derision, "[I do not] believe that one coming from the dead to tell them that there was a place of happiness [Heaven] without rum, would gain any credit."[29]

In bitterly cold weather the treaty negotiations opened on January 8, 1785, with a now-familiar assertion of American dominance. For all practical purposes, in fact, the subsequent negotiations paralleled those of the Fort Stanwix Treaty, adding impetus to the declaration that the Six Nations had surrendered, and by concluding a separate peace, voiding the Indians' concept of a grand confederacy.

Despite protestations from the Delawares—such as, "I think that . . . the country is mine; and as our children grow up, we will tell them that the country is ours"—the Americans again succeeded in imposing their terms.[30]

On January 21, 1785, the subdued chiefs of the two assembled nations placed their marks on the dictated articles of treaty, thereby acknowledging the American claims. By the formal terms of the Fort McIntosh Treaty the Wyandots and Delawares were confined to a reservation encompassing a portion of northern Ohio, and they were required to give up three chiefs as hostages until all American prisoners were released. In return, because of the "humane and liberal views of Congress," goods such as liquor, kettles, blankets, paint, lead, and gunpowder (which had been "spoiled" from long storage) were given to the Indians. Tents, which some Indians requested, were refused because they were "too expensive."[31]

Like the unexpected cession by Great Britain of so much wilderness territory in 1783, the treaties of Fort Stanwix and Fort McIntosh were a mild surprise to the American statesmen. George Washington confided that he "did not expect such a [large] cession of territory" and remarked, "These people have given, I think, all that the United States could reasonably have required of them." So eager was Congress to promulgate these treaties that legislation was quickly passed (in the form of a land ordinance in 1785) providing for the surveying into seven ranges and the public sale of much of the "purchased" Indian lands.

Yet, as the astute Washington and others soon recognized, the critical test of Indian submission to American territorial expansion was yet to come. Still to be dealt with were the least tractable of all the formerly hostile Indians, the Western Nations. Particularly troublesome among those tribes were the Shawnees and Miamis, who were both truculent nations even then involved in warfare with Kentucky settlers.[32]

Continuing in the spirit of their recent successes, the American Indian commissioners nonetheless looked forward to a practical resolution of the Indian problem. Richard Butler wrote in his journal before the opening of the Shawnee treaty, "We have determined [it] shall be the last we need."[33]

In order to assemble the Indians of the western alliance, including the Shawnees, Miamis, Potawatomis, and Wabashes, formal invitations were sent in the summer of 1785. Therein the commissioners requested that the Indians meet in October at the confluence of the Great Miami and Ohio rivers, near modern-day Cincinnati, for the purpose "of holding a general treaty of peace."[34] By late October, 1785, the commissioners themselves were on hand, witnessing the construction of three rude blockhouses and a council house, and providing for the expected imminent arrival of the Indians.

The western Indians, however, had long since perceived what was intended at the mouth of the Miami. News of the Fort Stanwix and Fort McIntosh treaties had spread rapidly among the tribes, creating great indignation. The Shawnees replied to the American commissioners in November, 1785, saying, "to take our chiefs prisoners, and come with soldiers at your backs," was not the way to make a lasting peace. Further, the Shawnees stated that they were aware "of your design to divide our councils," and they would consent to a meeting no sooner than the spring of 1786 at Detroit, where a confederated council might be convened under British auspices.[35]

Butler and the other commissioners accordingly grew more restive. Although they continued to maneuver for a council of some significance, and they tendered various invitations, only a few straggling Shawnees were present by mid-December. Some Wyandots and Delawares, on hand by American invitation as a moderating influence, were continually drunk. Finally, on December 28, Butler dispatched his last messenger, the Delaware chief Wingenund, to the Shawnee towns.[36]

Thereafter, on January 14, 1786, an advance delegation of Shawnees arrived, followed a few days later by a larger band. Although they represented only a very minor portion of the Shawnee nation, adverse circumstances had accounted for their sudden attendance. Beyond the persuasion of Wingenund, these Shawnees from the Mackachack region were in dire need of provisions, especially tobacco and corn. Although the Miamis and most of the Shawnees continued to shun the council—because of British influence, said the commissioners—by late January, 318 Shawnees were present, enough to justify the conclusion of a treaty.[37]

In order to provide a proper reception for "this proud little nation," the commissioners arranged for the firing of a salute by an honor guard consisting of a sergeant and twelve men. As the echo of gunfire rolled across the timbered hills, the Indians were ushered into the council house, which was adorned with the flag of the thirteen states, while the drum beat "an American march."[38]

In fact, the entire treaty was to proceed as orchestrated by its American designers. Once the formal business began on January 28, matters proceeded rapidly to a climax. When the Shawnees protested the imposed American boundary, because it would make them live on mere "ponds," "leaving them no land to live or raise corn on," the younger Indians, observed Richard Butler, "appeared raised [in spirit] and ready for war." Chief Kekewepellethy (Tame Hawk) demanded justice, speaking with ardor: "As to the lands, it is all ours. You say you have goods for our women and children; you may keep your goods, and give them to the other nations, we will have none of them." Then, when he finished his speech, Kekewepellethy delivered a string of black wampum, symbolic of hostility.[39]

According to an acquaintance, Richard Butler was a man not lightly to be trifled with. Of strong Irish stock, he had served through the Revolution as a frontline Pennsylvania officer under "Mad Anthony" Wayne. A self-proclaimed Indian expert, based on his former experience as an Indian trader, the often-arrogant Butler had but little compassion for the Indians. Terming their position "unwise and ungrateful," Butler chided: "We have told you the terms on which you shall have it [peace]. These terms we will not alter, they are liberal, they are just."[40] Declaring an ultimatum of "peace or war," Butler then took the Shawnee's string of black wampum and "dashed" it on the council table, before stalking out of the meeting. George Rogers Clark, not to be outdone, pushed the wampum off the table with his cane, taking care to trample on it with his foot, as he too left the council.[41]

That afternoon Butler and the other commissioners were called back to the council house by the Indians. Goaded by the Wyandots and Delawares, who had reminded them of the terms of the Fort Stanwix and Fort McIntosh treaties, and placed in an untenable position by the American ultimatum, the Shawnees relented. Kekewepellethy suffered the indignity of delivering the capitulation statement. Imploring that he had been "misunderstood," he meekly told the commissioners, "Brothers, everything shall be as you wish. . . . We agree to all you have proposed."[41]

At last, satisfied that the Indians were sufficiently contrite, the commissioners two days later concluded the council, which was to be known as the Treaty at the Mouth of the Great Miami. The Shawnees by now were so awed that they gave six hostages rather than the required three. Too, the new boundary was imposed without further question. This restricted the Shawnees to a parcel of land adjacent to the Wyandot and Delaware reservation in the northwestern corner of Ohio and northern portion of Indiana.[43]

The signing occurred on a Wednesday, February 1, 1786. When the ceremonies were concluded, Richard Butler wrote in his journal that tobacco, drink, and other gifts had been distributed. Then, while the commissioners and chiefs drank and retired to dinner, "liquor was given to the Indians and they got drunk." "This business [the treaty] was conducted with great care," said the smug Butler, "and gave the Indians perfect satisfaction."[44]

5

Frontier Justice

IN July, 1786, a unique proclamation was distributed throughout the Kentucky district announcing the "implied contract between settlers of this country to support and defend each other against our relentless and common enemies." At stake, continued the document, were "the lives of ourselves, our wives, and helpless infants," who without prompt action "will most probably fall prey to savage barbarity."[1]

Ostensibly an appeal for defensive aid from the settlers of Jefferson County to their adjoining neighbors, this document was far more sinister than merely an overwrought vilification of the Indians of the present-day northern Middle West. Following in the wake of recently concluded peace treaties, it was a direct call to arms, a tacit admission of the futility of anything other than a military solution to the Indian problem. As a sort of manifesto by the Territory of Virginia, District of Kentucky, it was to lead to the first major confrontation between Indians and whites since the end of the Revolutionary War.

In 1786, Jefferson County comprised a large area of land bordering on the Ohio River, including the Louisville region. Its inhabitants regarded the prevention of Indian incursions as so unlikely a prospect that year that they had attempted to organize the settlers of other Kentucky regions for widespread military service.[2] By signing the July, 1786, proclamation, County Lieutenant William Pope and others implied that the security of the Kentucky country might be ensured by mutual support for the common defense. Yet a covert and integral part of the Jefferson County appeal to arms remained undisclosed. What were actually contemplated were offensive operations—preemptive strikes not only to disrupt the threatened Indian raids but also to avenge the recent wrongs suffered at the hands of marauding "savages." Because of the temper of the people, the publication of such propaganda was well calculated to facilitate overt, full-scale hostilities against the menacing tribes.[3]

For months the Kentucky counties bordering on the Ohio had been in turmoil. Small parties of Indian raiders from the Wabash country had ravaged the settlements, burning outlying homesteads and annihilating several large families. Punitive raids by a handful of local frontiersmen had only intensified the red incursions. Now there was a prospect of even greater depredations because of the recent successes of Indian "banditti."[4] Kentucky County Lieutenant John May wrote: "Scarcely a week has passed . . . without some person being murdered. All the Indians on and about the

31

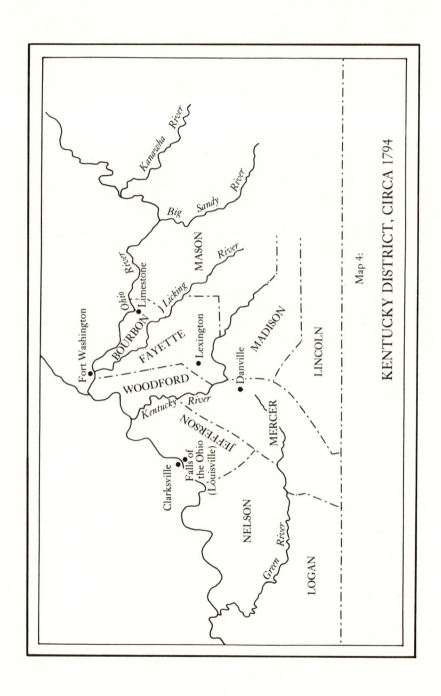

Map 4:

KENTUCKY DISTRICT, CIRCA 1794

32

Wabash are for war, and news is just received . . . that there are several hundred of them at this time out at war."[5]

Immediately after circulation of the Jefferson County proclamation in July, news was received of the massacre by Indians of all eleven members of the Captain James Moore family and the burning of their dwelling.[6] In the aftermath of such grisly incidents there had been repeated outcries by the Kentucky settlers for greater protection. Noting that the federal government offered no immediate support, and that under Virginia law the District of Kentucky had no power to order militia out of the state, General George Rogers Clark wrote that season to Governor Patrick Henry, "I don't think that this country even in its infant state, bore so gloomy an aspect as it does at present."[7]

When, in spite of mounting pressure for direct action, the Virginia Council still dawdled in indecision, the Kentucky settlers proposed an expedition of their own. At a special meeting held in May, 1786, a "voluntary campaign" had been agreed upon, to proceed in August against the Wabash Indians despite the lack of official sanction by Virginia's government. Thus the Jefferson County proclamation of July, 1786, was intended not only to rally popular support but also to recruit the personnel necessary for a strike at the Indians' homeland.[8]

This threat of imminent unregulated action by the increasingly unruly frontier settlers produced the desired effect in Virginia. Yielding to the demands of the Kentuckians and the advice of his senior militia commanders, Governor Henry belatedly sent new instructions authorizing the district's ranking officers to "concert some system for their own defense."

Armed with this tacit approval for "a regular campaign," Kentucky's militia commanders quickly organized a high-level council.[9] At the assembly on August 2 field officers from every county in the District of Kentucky resolved unanimously that an expedition against the Wabash and other Indians was "justifiable and necessary." General Clark, of whom one field officer said "his name alone would be worth a half a regiment of men," was appointed to command the army, which rendezvoused at Clarksville (opposite Louisville) on September 10, 1786.[10]

Clark's attitude and his rationale for the expedition were reflected in a letter to Governor Henry that he wrote during May. Citing the "certainty of a war already commenced" by the Wabash Indians, he portrayed a gloomy outlook for Kentucky that could be improved only by attacking the red enemy. "Such an example would have a great and good impression on those Indians already treated with [Shawnees] as fear would cause them to be peaceable, when presents make them believe we are afraid of them," reasoned Clark.

Despite his appointment as a congressional Indian commissioner and his role at the Great Miami peace treaty fewer than six months earlier, Clark's attitude was typical of the frontier philosophy of Indian management, which was to intimidate the red man, or as the frontiersman put it, "to keep them in awe."[11]

Estimating the enemy warriors of the region to number about fifteen hundred, Clark set as the target of his forthcoming campaign the Wabash

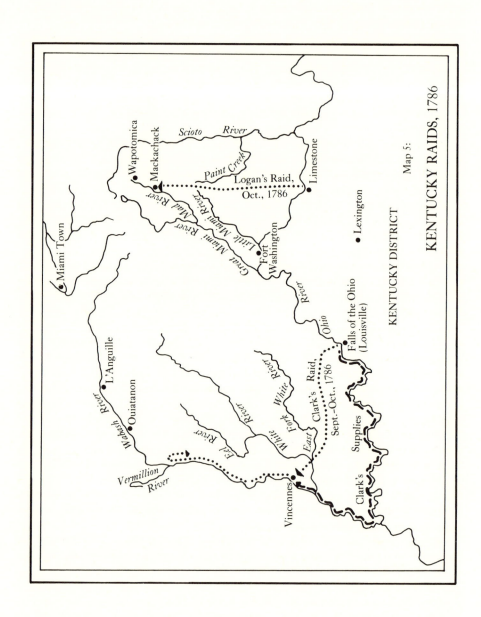

KENTUCKY RAIDS, 1786

Map 5:

KENTUCKY DISTRICT

Logan's Raid,
Oct., 1786

Clark's Raid,
Sept.–Oct., 1786

Wapotomica

Mackachack

Scioto   River

Paint Creek

Limestone

Lexington

Miami Town

Great Miami River

Little Miami River

Mad River

Fort
Washington

River

Ohio

Falls of the Ohio
(Louisville)

L'Anguille

Wabash River

Ouiatanon

Eel River

White River

White

Fork

East

Vincennes

Vermillion   River

Supplies

Clark's

34

country, which was the particular domain of the Weas (near modern-day Lafayette, Indiana), the Piankashaws (near Vincennes, Indiana), and the Miamis (at Fort Wayne). The most troublesome among these Wabash River tribes were the belligerent Miamis, whom George Washington termed "mistaken people" noted for "their robberies and murder."[12]

During the Revolution the Miamis had often raided extensively in Kentucky, acting under the direction of British Indian Agent Alexander McKee. In continuing to contest the occupation of their former hunting grounds, they had maintained a hostility with the Kentuckians despite the white men's peace of 1783. For the Miamis the central question was entirely independent of the white man's quarrels; it was possession of the land, their inherent birthright.[13]

Under the able leadership of their principal war chief, Little Turtle, who was the son of a Miami chief and a Mohican squaw, the Miamis had remained unyielding in their resistance to white settlement. So determined were they and their confederates, the Weas and the Piankashaws, "to exterminate all the Americans who might be in these lands" that a war party of about four hundred and fifty Indians had appeared before Vincennes in July, 1786, fully intending to fight. By a combination of "speeches," threats, and presents the French magistrate at Vincennes had managed to dissuade the Indians temporarily, but the situation remained dangerous, he said, because of "the number of [American] outlaws" at Vincennes, who were constantly stirring up trouble with the Indians. He thus appealed to George Rogers Clark for help on July 22.[14]

In organizing his expedition to the Wabash, Clark planned to utilize about two thousand militiamen. Because many of the frontier residents were notorious for shirking their responsibility, the judges of the Kentucky District ruled that Governor Henry had authorized impressment of supplies and troops. Thus, each of Clark's militia captains was required to furnish his quota of men and supplies, by impressment or otherwise. At least one officer was later court-martialed for "irregular" behavior in supplying the army. Several citizens and unwilling draftees later gave depositions of what actually had occurred. Descending upon the homestead of one Philip Eastin, a Kentucky militia lieutenant had the recalcitrant inductee tied to a horse's tail. Forced to walk behind the horse, which frequently was prodded, Eastin constantly fell down and was dragged for considerable distances. Others were accorded similarly harsh treatment. One man was required to perform more than two months' service on one day's notice.[15]

Beset by a variety of logistical problems, Clark's army of about twelve hundred men was ready to advance no sooner than mid-September. So anxious was Clark to campaign during temperate weather that he forsook awaiting a shipment of critically needed lead from the mines. Instead, ammunition was cast from impressed pewter dishes, cups, and other meltable articles.[16] Finally, on September 17, "the most formidable force yet collected in the West under American arms" moved forward from Clarksville.[17]

Yet, almost at the last moment, there had been a major change in plans. On September 13, Benjamin Logan, a veteran frontiersman who nominally had been second-in-command of Clark's army, was detached to "march against the Shawnees' towns." Ostensibly this separate mission was a justified retaliation, based on the premise that the Shawnees "have violated the treaty with the United States held at Miami," said Clark.[18] Actually, the Logan expediton had derived as much from apprehension and grand strategy as from injuries suffered. One of Clark's ranking officers, Colonel Levi Todd, wrote on August 29, 1786, "We have some hopes that the Indians may demand protection from the British, . . . [and] if this is refused, as we may expect, a coolness, or perhaps a quarrel, may arise between them."[19]

Clark hoped to rid the Kentucky frontiers of the growing Shawnee menace by a simple stratagem. "Their attention is on me at present," he advised Logan, implying that Logan's secondary force might easily wreak havoc among the exposed Shawnee villages and thereby further accomplish his overall "defensive" program. Simply stated, Logan's raid was merely an extension of Clark's strategy of keeping the Indians "in awe," with the hoped-for bonus of embarrassing British-Indian relations.[20]

Long the traditional enemies of the Kentucky frontiersmen, the Shawnees recently had been blamed for a rash of attacks among the settlements. An American spy, Cadet Philip Liebert, had been sent that spring as a goodwill messenger among the tribes on the Great Miami and had found "the Shawnees in general not well disposed to the Americans." Liebert reported, however, that only a few of the Shawnees were joining with some marauding Cherokees in carrying out frontier raids. Undoubtedly, a large portion of the Shawnee nation was then hostile, if not actually engaged as belligerents, but a sizeable number, particularly those sects who had attended the treaty council at the mouth of the Great Miami, were generally peaceable. "The nation is divided," advised a principal Shawnee chief in midsummer, saying that he desired the Americans to have patience, as he was striving to live up to the terms of the Great Miami Treaty.[21]

Thus what was planned as a punitive raid against hostiles actually operating against Kentucky had expanded into a two-pronged general campaign involving the northern Indians at large. Unfortunately, as one historian has noted, the Kentuckians habitually made little distinction between Indian tribes, attacking friends and foes alike. Moreover, because of the circumstances of the Logan raid, the innocent would suffer a fate comparable to that of the hostiles.[22]

While Benjamin Logan and his officers were busily engaged in recruiting their Shawnee-expedition troops, many of whom also were impressed by severe methods, George Rogers Clark was advancing into the Illinois country. Ill-fated almost from the beginning, Clark's column marched for the site of his old Revolutionary conquest, Vincennes, instead of going directly to the upper Wabash where most of the Indians' towns lay.[23]

By the time Clark had reached this first destination, there were signs of his impending failure. Many of the army's supplies had been sent on keelboats by a roundabout water route down the Ohio and up the Wabash. Because the water was low in the Wabash, there was an excessive delay, and in the unseasonable heat many perishables spoiled.[24]

Now short on provisions, Clark pushed on, after having waited nine days. Already there was talk among the rank and file of going home. It was by now well known that the Indians had been alerted and were concentrating on the upper Wabash to meet Clark's advance. Deep in enemy territory and facing the prospect of fighting what one officer considered "a body of the finest light troops in the world," the drafted Lincoln County men began to lose their incentive. Clark was under heavy criticism for the want of provisions, and it is unlikely that his reportedly frequent drunkenness inspired confidence. By the time the column approached the mouth of the Big Vermillion, about the first week in October, a mutiny was in progress. When an estimated three hundred men from Logan County deserted en masse, Clark was compelled to fall back to Vincennes and garrison that village. With his expedition ruined, and the bulk of his column streaming back to Kentucky in "vile disorder," Clark could but endure the storm of criticism unleashed upon him.[25]

Benjamin Logan's "secondary" expedition, meanwhile, was to effect much of what Clark had sought. In fact, it made an indelible impression on the subsequent course of Indian-American relations. Logan's column was mostly mounted and included some of the more notable Indian fighters and prominent figures on the frontier, including Colonel Daniel Boone, Lieutenant Colonel James Trotter, and Major Simon Kenton. Departing from Limestone about October 1, 1786, Logan's 790-man strike force marched almost due north toward the well-known Mackachack towns of the Shawnees, which were located along the Mad River in present-day Logan County, Ohio.[26]

Ironically, just as Logan's raiders were about to depart, intelligence from "Indian country" had been forwarded to American Commissioner Richard Butler: "There is one town of the Shawnees, called Mackachack, that has done all in their power to keep the Shawnees from going to war." This communication was not received until after Logan's column had marched; thus the Kentuckians maintained as their objective perhaps the most peaceably inclined town of the entire Shawnee nation.[27]

On the evening of October 4, Logan's column was approaching its destination, now only about sixty miles distant. During the night a deserter stole an officer's horse and defected to the enemy. In the morning word spread through camp that the deserter had fled to warn the Indians. Logan promptly dispatched three of his best woodsmen, including Simon Kenton, to pursue the turncoat. While Logan prepared to make a forced march with his entire army, Kenton and the other scouts set off in a desperate race to catch the deserter before he could abort the surprise attack.[28]

Ahead, in the first Shawnee village, Mackachack, the unsuspecting inhabitants were preparing for a grand council of the confederacy, which was to take place after many of the principal warriors had returned from the Wabash country. Already present were deputies from the Six Nations, the Delawares, and other nations, the most prominent of whom was Captain Joseph Brant of the Mohawks, who had just returned from a visit to London. Residing at Mackachack was the aged Moluntha (Shawnee King), a principal chief.[29]

Moluntha had been one of the signers of the Great Miami Treaty and was regarded by some as friendly to American interests. Indeed, throughout that summer he and many other Shawnees had acted with moderation, despite their belief that they had been cheated by the Americans at the last treaty. Moluntha even had corresponded with the Americans at the mouth of the Great Miami, professing friendship and asking them to be patient.[30]

On the morning of October 6, 1786, a lone white rider appeared on the outskirts of Mackachack bearing aloft a white handkerchief. It was the deserter, who barely had outdistanced Logan's scouts to the Indian village. The man was met in town by several Indians, who refused to believe his excited warning that the Kentuckians were coming. By one account he was roughly pulled off of his horse and eventually tomahawked. Many chiefs, including Brant, and nearly four hundred warriors were said to be absent, hunting with Blue Jacket on the Wabash. Thus the Shawnees appear to have made no effectual attempt to defend their village.[31]

Nor should they have felt the need for defense. As a nation the Shawnees had the assurance of the American commissioners at the Great Miami that they were "included among the friends of the United States." As late as May, 1786, the Shawnees had received a pledge that "the Thirteen Great Fires were determined to hold fast the chain of friendship." Accordingly, the aged Moluntha hoisted the "thirteen stripes" on his sixty-foot lodgepole to receive the approaching Americans in friendship.[32]

At noon the advance of the Kentucky army made its appearance on the prairie that separated two large Indian villages. Logan's force already had been divided into three columns. The left, under Colonel Robert Patterson, was to attack satellite villages on the left bank of the Mad River; while the center, under Logan, and the right wing, under Colonel Thomas Kennedy, would strike directly for Mackachack. Logan, fearing that some of the Indians' captives might be killed by mistake, had given specific orders not to kill anyone within the towns who surrendered. "Spare the white blood" was the way the men understood it, however. Indians were to be treated as the men pleased during the fighting.[33]

When they were within three quarters of a mile of their objective, Logan's horsemen saw "the savages retreating in all directions, making for the thickets, swamps, and high prairie grass." Logan drawing his sword and waving it high about his head, shouted for his men to charge.[34]

With Boone and Kenton leading the advance, Logan's and Kennedy's mounted columns thundered across the prairie in pursuit of the fleeing Shawnees, who were on foot. Among the first to be caught were the slower Indian women. Colonel Kennedy, swinging an old Scottish broadsword that he had spent nearly half a day grinding down to a proper size, swiftly felled one running woman with a savage blow to the head. Another, who put up her hand to ward off Kennedy's heavy sword, had three fingers cut off and suffered a fractured skull. Later this woman was discovered to be a white captive. The other women remaining in the cluster fell upon their knees for mercy, and Kennedy marched them back to Mackachack at sword's point.[35]

Meanwhile, scattered fighting had broken out in the vicinity of the town. Here the few warriors who were present were putting up a desperate, but ineffectual, resistance. It was quite surprising to a sixteen-year-old Kentucky youth who had been anxious to try himself in battle that the encounter was so ridiculous. "I was disappointed . . . that we should have little to do," wrote this youthful volunteer.[36]

The Indians, not suspecting Logan's intent, had been totally unprepared for combat. Moluntha, who at first had attempted to flee, surrendered himself with his wives and children, being unable to run swiftly because of his advanced age. Dressed in a cocked hat and an elegant shawl, and carrying a large peace pipe, he now advanced to meet the onrushing Kentuckians. Bewildered by the sudden commotion, he could but shake hands with the soldiers who gathered about him. Then he pointed to the American flag flying from his lodgepole.[37]

In a few minutes the scattered fighting ended, and thirteen bedraggled prisoners were rounded up, including the famed six-and-one-half-foot Grenadier Woman, sister of the great chieftain Cornstalk. Among the ten Indian warriors estimated to have been slain were several delegates of the Six Nations and an Ottawa chief.[38] A crowd gathered around the prisoners, and Moluntha passed his pipe and pouch of tobacco among his captors.

Shoving his way through the assembled throng came a man notorious for his hot-headed actions, Captain Hugh McGary. McGary had in great measure been responsible for the disastrous rout of the Kentuckians at Blue Licks during the Revolution. Then a major, he had impetuously pursued a large Indian raiding party, disregarding the decision of Daniel Boone and his other commanding officers to await reinforcements. Shouting that all who were not cowards should follow him, McGary had plunged his horse into the Licking River, hot on the trail of the marauding Indians. By blind impulse and with unreasoning enthusiasm, the bulk of the Kentuckians had followed him across, where, a mile beyond the river, the entire party had fallen into a major ambush. In a brief fight the Kentuckians were routed, losing about sixty killed and seven prisoners of their 180-man force. McGary, however, had escaped unscathed.[39]

Still burning for revenge four years later, McGary approached the aged Moluntha. "Were you at the defeat of the Blue Licks?" he demanded. Moluntha, evidently not understanding English well, merely agreed benevolently, saying yes as if to appease the agitated white man. McGary instantly seized a small belt axe and in one blurred motion struck Moluntha with the poll, knocking the old man to the ground. Then, turning the edge, McGary savagely swung again, burying the blade in the side of Moluntha's head.[40]

Immediately, a furor ensued. McGary, after scalping the dead chieftain, was pommeled to the ground, though he escaped the angry crowd. Benjamin Logan, having ordered that all prisoners be spared before the attack, was furious and relieved McGary of his command. Still sputtering that, "By God, he would chop him down or any other man who should attempt to hinder him from killing them [the Indians] at any time," McGary strongly berated Lieutenant Colonel James Trotter when the angered Trotter told his men to shoot down any man who killed an Indian prisoner.

Emboldened by their easy success, some of Logan's men now began to plunder the empty huts, while others seized upon the few warrior prisoners. One Indian, a Delaware who had come to Mackachack to marry a young woman, had offered no resistance, but was taken to an Indian cabin and made to stand on a stool with a rope tied around his neck. The rope was tautly suspended from a roofpole so that, if the Indian tipped over the stool, he would hang himself. Thus the unfortunate warrior was left standing for hours.[41]

Already plagued by insubordination and want of proper discipline, Logan's militia soon suffered considerable embarrassment. As several detachments of raiders formed to attack other Indian towns some miles distant, Mackachack was fired. A few men then began rummaging through the underbrush near the town for hogs that had been seen running loose. Soon thereafter a lone Shawnee hunter, carrying the carcass of a deer on his back, came into close proximity, before seeing that the upper village was on fire. Shot at by several Kentuckians, the Indian disappeared into the tall prairie grass. Captain William Irwin, leading a troop of horse, now appeared and charged through the high grass toward the spot. Missing the Shawnee on the first pass, Irwin wheeled about too abruptly. The Indian fired, killing Irwin outright. When the horsemen again swept through the prairie grass without uncovering their elusive target, another man was shot. Charging toward the last telltale cloud of smoke, a half dozen dismounted riflemen got to the Indian before he had fully reloaded his rifle. Firing at point-blank range, the Kentuckians put five balls into his breast, abruptly ending the duel. In the Shawnee's hands they allegedly found the rifle of a militia officer killed earlier that summer.[42]

Having lost two good men to a lone warrior, the militia soon attacked and burned a third Indian village, Wapatomica. Alerted by the fugitives from Mackachack, this town was nearly deserted when the Kentuckians arrived. Yet a determined stand by a handful of warriors wounded several more Long Knives, and ten Indians were later found dead in this village, including Shade, a principal Shawnee chief. Here one warrior allegedly was burned at the stake in retribution for Indian cruelties, small bags of gunpoweder being tied around his body for added effect.

Systematically proceeding from one village to the next, Logan's Kentuckians burned eight large villages and destoyed all the crops in two days of devastation. The Shawnees, scattered and disorganized, had deserted these villages almost without resistance. Among the estimated two hundred dwellings consumed in flames was the storehouse of the British trader and Indian agent Alexander McKee, whose "laced cocked hat" was carried off in triumph by the Kentuckians.[43]

Aware that their raid was about to end, Logan's militia hastily prepared to depart. They had plundered the Indian towns of nearly every valuable that could easily be transported (Indian trophies always "sold high": twelve dollars for a "worthless gun," five dollars for a small brass kettle, one dollar for a useless knife, said a militia participant). Still vengeful, the Kentuckians then determined to settle accounts with their lone remaining warrior prisoner.[44]

The Delaware would-be bridegroom was untied and led to a log outside of his cabin prison. Seating the Indian on the log, a man positioned immediately behind swiftly executed him with one downward blow of a tomahawk. Lest the returning Indians discover that he had been murdered in cold blood, several militiamen shot the corpse to make it appear that he had been killed in battle.

Having scalped all of the fallen Indians, men and women alike, the Kentucky militia then buried their own three dead beneath an Indian hut, which they fired to keep the Indians from finding the graves. On October 8, confident that he had fulfilled the intent of his mission, Logan withdrew. Within a week he was back at Limestone, where the raiders dispersed.[45]

At a cost of three men killed and three wounded, Logan's raiders had extracted eleven warrior scalps, twenty-six women prisoners, two children, and four "rescued" whites from the Shawnee nation. Moreover, according to Logan's report, ten Shawnee chiefs had been killed; and even more important, fifteen thousand bushels of corn had been destroyed, and all of the Indians' livestock butchered or driven off. Yet, though it was hailed as a great success by some Kentucky citizens, the raid generally was recognized as barren of important results, and to many of the men who had been impressed and inexpertly led, it had been obnoxious.[46]

Indeed, the central objective, to strike terror into the Indians, had been only momentarily achieved. Instead of intimidating the Shawnees and diminishing the prospect of frontier raids, the attack merely intensified the Indian problem. As early as December, 1786, a frontier army officer observed an upswing in Indian raids, saying, "There are more Shawnees now on the south side of the Ohio River than have been discovered at one time for two years past."[47]

For the Shawnees the Logan raid had been a stunning disaster because many of their provisions and most of their dwellings and been destroyed. The following winter was a nightmare for many Indian families. One, for example, was reduced to a bare subsistence, consisting of mostly "raccoons, . . . with little or no salt, without a single bite of bread, hominy, or sweet corn." In the spring the tribesmen returned to their burned-out villages to begin anew. Then, once the maple sugar season ended, the Shawnees withdrew to the comparative safety of the Maumee River valley in northwestern Ohio. Some Shawnees even departed from American territory entirely, migrating across the Mississippi River to live under Spanish rule.[48]

In a strategic sense, however, the Logan expedition proved to be an important cohesive factor within the Shawnee nation. From that time on the Shawnees showed little equivocation in their attitude toward the American objectives. Embittered by this "ill treatment" at the hands of their professed benefactors, nearly all Shawnees abandoned thoughts of reconciliation with the Americans. Thereafter they would be hostile until subdued by force of arms. Moreover, while driving the Indians further into the British camp, Logan's raiders had failed to diminish in any meaningful quantity the number of Shawnee warriors, most of whom had been absent at the time of the attack. Armed and equipped by the British at Detroit, they would later develop into formidable opponents, indeed. In fact, the general Indian confederacy was even strengthened by the events of October, 1786, for thereafter the Shawnees were among the most active and ardent supporters of the grand-alliance concept.[49]

The council of the Shawnee towns planned for October was only temporarily disrupted, for on November 28, 1786, a grand conference of the confederated tribes was held at Detroit. Present were delegates from the Six Nations; the Huron, Wyandot, Delaware, Shawnee, Ottawa, Chippewa, Potawatomi, Miami, and Cherokee tribes; and the Wabash Confederacy.

Here the central spokesman for the grand alliance, Joseph Brant, proclaimed in an eloquent speech, "The interests of any one nation should be the welfare of all the others."[50]

Yet Brant was soon confronted by various schisms. The Wyandots and the Delawares, having ceded some territory north of the Ohio River, began to be more open in their support for conciliation with the United States on liberal terms. These tribes, soon to be joined by the Senecas and others, comprised the political right wing of the confederacy. Essentially they were the nations who would be most exposed to danger in the event of war with the Americans. Being in close proximity to existing settlements they were likely to be the first to suffer.[51]

Diametrically opposed to the views of that faction were the Shawnees, the Miamis, and the Wabash tribes. These were the hard-core belligerents, or left wing, of the confederacy. As generally westernmost nations they were ardent advocates of the Ohio boundary line, insisting that it be kept inviolate. Logan's raid, which occurred less than two months before the Detroit council, had served greatly to polarize the Shawnees, adding materially to the left wing's strength. Bitterness, outrage, and demands amounting to an ultimatum spilled forth from these Wabash and Maumee nations at the beginning of the council in November. Yet, under Brant's reasoned guidance, when the council was concluded on December 18, a diplomatically worded, though firm, "speech" was sent to the U.S. Congress, asking for a new overall treaty early in the spring of 1787, and denying the validity of the separate treaties formerly concluded.[52]

Thereafter, immediately following the confederated Indian council, a summit conference was requested with the British to determine the extent of their support. This central question had plagued the Indians' leadership since the close of the Revolution, three years earlier. Chief Joseph Brant, in fact, had made a special trip to London in the winter of 1785–86 to resolve the crucial question. His conference with Lord Sidney, the British secretary for colonial affairs, had been cordial, but had produced no tangible commitment. Lord Sidney had merely shrouded in ambiguity the prospect of armed intervention on behalf of England's "Indian allies." Furthermore, he had suggested that the unified tribes act with "temper and moderation" while showing a "peaceable demeanor."[53] Accordingly, because Brant was still troubled by the lack of British commitment, he pressed the issue in 1786 at postcouncil negotiations with the British officials at Detroit. These officials, of course, merely reiterated the official British policy line, which was no answer at all.[54]

At the close of the Detroit conference in December the Indian leadership could, nonetheless, rejoice in the declaration of their collective position and also in the fruition of the grand alliance as a viable, working entity. Soon thereafter, early in the spring of 1787, it even seemed that substantial progress had been achieved in obtaining an overt British commitment of support.

In the middle of 1786 a new and yet familiar figure in British colonial administration had been reappointed as governor of Quebec. He was Sir Guy Carleton, who had been the Revolutionary War commander in Canada.

Effective, though aging at sixty-two, he was looked upon as a favorable change from the often austere and condescending Sir Frederick Haldimand. In fact the able, Irish-bred Carleton had been created Lord Dorchester before his arrival in Canada toward the end of 1786. Once he had assumed his new post, Dorchester sought to implement instructions from the Home Office that merely foresaw a "further advantage" in active Indian assistance, "should [the Americans] carry their threats into execution of attempting to gain the forceable possession of the [ceded] posts." Unfortunately for the Indians, Sir John Johnson, the British Indian agent, soon distorted that underlying rationale by advising Brant that the forts on ceded American territory were being held "chiefly, if not entirely," for the Indians' benefit. Intoned Johnson: "What security would you then have [if the British gave up the posts]? You would be left at the mercy of a people [Americans] whose blood calls aloud for revenge."[55]

This message was of the strongest import to the Indian leadership. It virtually committed the British to holding the forts, as they expressed it, "for your [the Indians'] sakes." So long as the British garrisons occupied the forts, it was tangible evidence, Johnson seemed to say, of the crown's commitment to the Indians. Inherent in the British possession of the forts was the risk of armed conflict with the Americans, hence the implied willingness to support the Indian confederacy militarily.[56]

The Indian leadership eventually accepted that argument almost without reservation. Johnson's statements implied that the British would ultimately provide support though they warned that "he [the King] cannot begin a war with the Americans because some of their people encroach and make depredations upon parts of Indian country."[57] Accordingly the Indians anticipated that, as the support of the British officials began to materialize, the prospects for equitable negotiations with the Americans would increase. Therefore, backed by the prospect of active support by the British military, the Indian confederacy might apply some leverage in treaty negotiations.

At that very time, in the spring of 1787, important events bearing directly on the Indian question were taking place in Congress. Work had already begun on the organization of the vast "Indian country" into the Northwest Territory—work expressly designed to infuse white civilization into the region. It was an irreversible effort, wrought of necessity and ostensibly justified by the post-Revolutionary Indian treaties. Already a premature influx of settlers had descended upon the lands, vying for the choicest sites. A host of others awaited merely the awarding of the land grants. What was about to occur had long been a foregone conclusion. It would be one of the great land sales of the century, if not of all time.[58] Nearly everybody, in fact, knew that the lush Ohio lands were about to be opened for public settlement, and nearly everybody, it seemed, wanted part and parcel. Nearly everybody knew, that is, except the people most affected by the forthcoming land rush—the Indians.

South of these soon-to-be-divided lands, an obscure event satisfied the Kentuckians that the matter of the Logan Shawnee-towns raid was closed. On March 21, 1787, Captain Hugh McGary was brought to trial in court-martial proceedings arising from the murder of Moluntha, the Shawnee King.

The matter had been so sensitive that Benjamin Logan, in requesting the court-martial, had suggested a change of venue, as otherwise "justice might not be done." McGary, accused of murder, disobedience of orders, disorderly conduct, and insubordination, was tried by a court consisting of thirteen Kentucky militia officers, seven of whom were captains. The findings were returned the same day. McGary was held guilty of murdering Moluntha, not guilty of disobedience of orders, guilty of behaving in a disorderly manner, and "in part guilty" of insubordination. His sentence was passed immediately. In a loud, clear voice the presiding officer read, "suspended [from rank] for one year."

High atop the Fayette County courthouse, the thirteen-striped flag that once had been Moluntha's flapped in the breeze, a visible trophy of Kentucky's burgeoning prowess.[59]

6

By Act of Congress

IT is difficult to perceive that there ever was a greater impetus for legislative action during the formative years of our nation than in the spring and summer of 1787. Secretary of War Henry Knox, reporting to Congress, defined much of the crisis that was at hand that April. Citing the "usurpation of the public lands [of the Northwest Territory]," Knox warned that such would eventually serve "to wrest all the immense property of the Western territory out of the hands of the public," because the sheer numbers of the intruders would make their forcible removal impractical.[1]

Indeed, some seventy families of American squatters had occupied lands in theWabash valley in 1786, and the rapid influx of others was expected to create dangerous precedents in the settlement of western lands, as well as intensify difficulties with the Indians.[2] Moreover, the very lands being illegally occupied by these squatters were intended to extinguish Revolutionary War debts, particularly debts to Continental Army veterans who had been promised land grants in payment for their services. "These unfortunate men now consider the lands promised them as their only resource against poverty in old age, and therefore are extremely anxious to receive immediately their due," Knox pointedly wrote.[3]

The secretary was encouraged by the repeal of the requirement in the 1785 Land Ordinance forbidding distribution or sale of lands until the "seven ranges" had been surveyed. Yet, noting the slow progress made toward the distribution, he cited the numerous complaints from veterans over a "four years delay." Already hounding the representatives of Congress were numerous land speculators and agents, including Samuel H. Parsons, the former Indian commissioner, who was now a director of the Ohio Company. Parsons, eyeing the estimated 3 million acres due the army veterans, submitted a formal proposal for the purchase of western lands at a price of up to $1 million on behalf of the Ohio Company, a group composed mostly of Revolutionary War officers who had organized in 1786 for this purpose. Parsons' proposal was not approved, and the seething agitation for disposal of the western lands continued.[4]

In this crisis Knox well understood the significance of the burgeoning difficulties with the western Indians. Exposed to increasingly severe raids along the frontier, the Kentucky settlements were vehemently demanding protection, and as a result pressure continued to emanate from the settlers' parent state, Virginia. Because the hostile Indians dwelled within the federal government's new western territory, the governor of Virginia even went so far

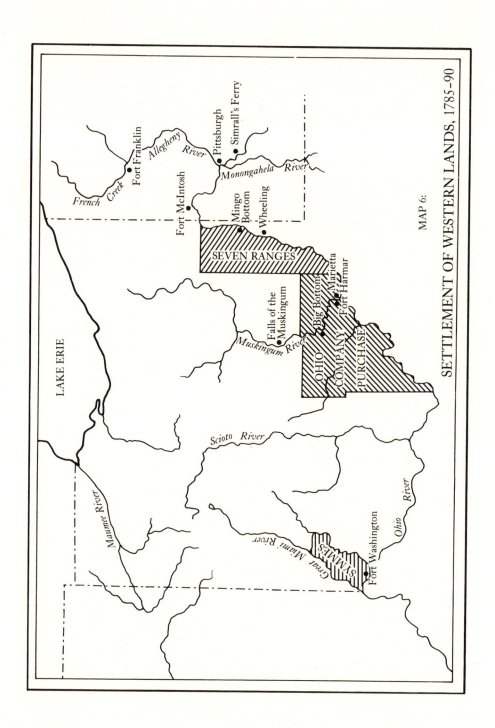

MAP 6:   SETTLEMENT OF WESTERN LANDS, 1785–90

LAKE ERIE

Fort Franklin

Allegheny River

French Creek

Pittsburgh
Simrall's Ferry

Fort McIntosh

Monongahela River

Mingo Bottom
Wheeling

SEVEN RANGES

Falls of the Muskingum

Big Bottom
Marietta
Fort Harmar

OHIO COMPANY PURCHASE

Muskingum River

Scioto River

Maumee River

Great Miami River

SYMMES

Fort Washington

Ohio River

as formally to petition Congress early in July, 1787, for pacification of the region.[5] Unfortunately, as the secretary of war understood, the small corps of federal troops located nearby on the Ohio River was far too weak to be effective for this purpose. A force of fifteen hundred men would be required, he said, but because of "the depressed state of the [federal] finances," only about five hundred troops were then available. Knox thus warned that the "whole western territory is liable to be wrested out of the hands of the Union by lawless adventurers, or by the savages."[6]

A further difficulty was that the nation's financial system had broken down entirely, and the government tottered on the verge of bankruptcy. Loans from foreign or domestic sources were nearly unprocurable, requisitions on the various states for funds were unfulfilled, and efforts to impose a national tax had failed.[7]

In this time of grave crisis on all fronts, the Confederated Congress at last responded to the mounting pressure by enacting legislation in July, 1787, that was intended to spare the nation from disaster. With startling political dispatch, a combination of compromises and temporary coalitions produced one of the most important ordinances of the nation's formative years.

It had long been recognized that the practical solution of these many difficulties involved the development of the Northwest Territory, which would thereby be incorporated among the productive, contributing elements of the nation. Yet for months a congressional committee created for the purpose of drafting an ordinance for the organization and government of the western territory had labored unsuccessfully. Then, on July 9, the political climate was much altered. A new committee was appointed, and serving as chairman was Congressman Edward Carrington of Virginia, who also headed the important Committee on Lands, which was charged with making recommendations for the disbursement of the public domain.[8]

The new committee worked with a discerning awareness of the aims of the federal government, as well as private interests headed by Manassah Cutler of Massachusetts, who had replaced Parsons as the chief negotiating agent for the Ohio Company. Carrington and his committee drafted, introduced, read, amended, and saw passed the Ordinance of July 13, 1787, in four days. This historic document provided for the government of the new territory under a governor and three judges, until a sufficient population would justify the formation of no fewer than three, nor more than five, states within the region. Included in the ordinance was a fundamental bill of rights, provisions for education, and the prohibition of slavery.[9]

By establishing a viable means of self-regulation and autonomy, the Northwest Ordinance of 1787 represented a strong inducement to legitimate settlement. Most important, however, the legislation cleared the way for the sale of large tracts of land to private interests, which would provide the hard-pressed Treasury with additional revenue. Certainly the sense of imminent crisis provided a strong impetus for the legislation, but commercial motives were deeply interrelated.

Without the adept maneuverings of the Ohio Company that summer to purchase 1.5 million acres, the extensive political alignments necessary to push through this major legislation probably would not have existed. In combination with the secretary to the Board of the Treasury, William Duer; the president of Congress, Arthur St. Clair; and the chairman of the Land Committee, Edward Carrington; Manassah Cutler arranged what was to be the nation's first large-scale real-estate deal.[10]

Ingratiating himself with the influential Carrington and other important southern congressmen, Cutler, a northeasterner, provided the practical means for the accomplishment of what the powerful Virginia faction considered "necessary measures in the Western Country." Interrelated with the suppression of the Indians, and the fulfillment of the large land grants to Virginia's veterans, were significant financial objectives that the Virginia faction knew would be served by the opening of the Northwest Territory. Among the state's financial motives was a reduction in the high cost of defending the Kentucky frontiers, particularly in militia expenses. Because the federal government was considered unlikely to assume any past or future costs involving direct actions initiated by state authorities, Virginia's strategy was to push the outermost frontier settlements into the Northwest Territory, thereby forcing the federal government to assume the defensive burden. There appears also to have been an attempt to purchase at depreciated values existing continental certificates, in speculation that they would either rise in value or could be redeemed at face value in government land. This was discussed by Arthur Lee, a Virginian member of the U.S. Board of Treasury, in a letter to Governor Edmund Randolph on May 20, 1787, wherein Lee urged the purchase of federal securities "speedily and secretly."[11]

In the key matter of administrative personnel, Manassah Cutler obligingly agreed to accept St. Clair as governor of the territory if Samuel Parsons was made first judge and if another director of the Ohio Company, Winthrop Sargent, was appointed secretary. St. Clair, a personal friend of Carrington's, accepted the governorship after having been persuaded by friends that it would be a lucrative position providing ample means to support his large family. Cutler, who originally had supported Samuel Parsons for governor, confided in his diary that matters went much better once St. Clair was endorsed for the post.[12]

By making the land purchase more palatable to a powerful eastern faction, Cutler also struck a deal with William Duer of the Treasury. Duer, an immigrant Englishman who had become wealthy and influential during the Revolution, was not above using his office for personal gain. Indeed, of the estimated 5 million acres sought, Duer's Scioto Company, which included General Rufus Putnam, would obtain options on 3.5 million acres. Moreover, in contrast to the Ohio company, which proposed to pay $500,000 down at $1.00 an acre upon the signing of the contract, the Scioto Company would merely speculate, being granted an option to purchase land at the same price. Cutler's Ohio Company would therefore write the entire contract, with the Duer interests operating as a silent partner until the actual sales of the Scioto land tract began.[13] Cutler later wrote, "Without connecting this speculation [the Scioto Company], similar terms and advantages could not have been obtained for the Ohio Company."[14]

Although there was opposition, particularly to the granting of special favors to private interests, the Cutler-Duer-Carrington coalition prevailed.

An offer made on July 21 was cleared by the Land Committee with minor alterations. Aware that the entire matter was about to be submitted to Congress for final approval, Cutler wrote a letter to the Board of Treasury on July 26 warning that, should his offer be refused, he was prepared to negotiate with the individual states for large tracts of their existing land, thereby removing the Ohio Company as a prospective large purchaser of the western country.[15]

Cutler's coup occurred the very next day. Congress, guided by a coalition of powerful political interests and responding to the crisis atmosphere, passed the resolution on July 27—"without the least variation," Cutler noted in his journal.[16] The issue thus was swiftly settled. Congress, having "purchased of the Indian inhabitants" and acquired from the various states cessions of western land claims, would now sell for a dollar an acre large tracts of the virgin black forests of the Ohio country. On October 27, 1787, the formal articles of indenture with the Ohio Company were concluded, and $500,000 in depreciated Continental certificates were added to the public coffers as a down payment.[17]

Ironically, because of the depreciated value of the currency and a one-third discount allowed "for bad lands and incidental changes," the Ohio Company's purchase yielded the United States a net revenue of about nine cents an acre. Moreover, the Ohio associates failed to make the balance of their payments, and Congress doled out to the company an additional 214,285 acres for military warrants—as well as 100,000 acres for donation lots to existing settlers. Of further misfortune, the shareholders of the Ohio Company ultimately divided the title to this "unappropriated land" among themselves, requiring later settlers to purchase their lots from private portfolios.[18]

Even worse, the Scioto Company of William Duer (and of "many of the principal characters in America," according to Manassah Cutler) utterly failed to provide any revenue at all, although it was soon engaged in fraudulent land sales to Frenchmen of land that the company did not own in the Northwest. When these nearly six hundred French immigrants arrived in 1790, Duer and two associates contracted to purchase from the Ohio Company about 200,000 acres upon which the Frenchmen might settle. Yet Duer and his associates again defaulted in payment, voiding the entire arrangement. The swindled French settlers at Gallipolis were then confronted with the prospect of repurchasing their lands from the Ohio Company at $1.25 an acre. Finally, in 1795, to relieve the situation, the federal government had to allot these distressed French immigrants a tract of land.[19]

As private speculators well knew, the heavy initial cost would prohibit individual settlers from acquiring land ($640 plus fees was the minimum purchase allowed by the government). As was to be expected, some congressmen argued that such a system served the financial interests of the government by favoring large speculative purchases.[20] Accordingly, with the prospect of huge resale profits on land acquired for less than ten cents an acre, there was much speculation, particularly among the favored clique in Congress. John Cleves Symmes, a New Jersey chief justice and congressman, effected a contract for 1 million acres in October, 1788. Yet Symmes too proved a financial disappointment to the federal government. Only partial payment was received, and Symmes sold land beyond his specified boundaries, ultimately acquiring the title for more than 300,000 acres.[21]

Unaware that their lands were being divided at the very time their petition for redress of "illegal" treaties was under consideration, the Indian confederacy waited in vain for word from Congress. Coincidentally, the "speech" agreed upon at the December, 1786, council first arrived in New York on July 18, 1787, while the Cutler land negotiations were underway, and after the Northwest Ordinance had been passed.[22]

The initial congressional reaction to the Indians' petition thus was merely a repetition of the procrastination and the divide-and-conquer strategy of the recent past. Yet, recognizing the economic catastrophe inherent in an outright war for control of the disputed lands, and aware of the dire need to secure the regions for settlement, Congress mandated a modification of former policy. Accordingly, as presented in an August 9, 1787, committee report, the means of achieving American objectives was refined to what became known as the "purchase" policy. Instead of dictating to the tribes on the basis of a superior-versus-inferior civilization, the report recommended what was supposed to be a more humane and just policy whereby lands were to be "fairly" purchased from the tribes. In this manner the United States government would be treating the Indian peoples with good faith and would impart to them the supposed blessings of civilization (that is, the white man's methods of agriculture).[23] Such a policy was accepted by the executive branch and ostensibly was adopted by many leading congressmen as the guiding principle in Indian affairs. The accompanying rationale of greater respectability and morality was offered as the premise for concluding future treaties.

This whole matter, of course, was an enormous charade. Any prospect of fairly dealing with the Indians by "purchasing" their lands paled under the overt declaration in the 1787 Northwest Ordinance, which committed the United States to possession and development of the very lands in question. The United States, in fact, would tell the Indians which tract was to be "sold" and what would be paid for it, according to the existing national circumstances. That the Indians might refuse to "sell" was simply regarded as implausible. In fact, ultimately they would be *required* to dispose of all needed lands. Despite its superficial alteration of Indian policy in 1787, the federal government failed to acknowledge its underlying objectives, thus rendering the entire era of purchase diplomacy meaningless.[24]

Congress's true intransigence in Indian policy was evident in the instructions that were belatedly sent to Governor St. Clair during the autumn of 1787. In effect, this was the long-awaited response to the Indian confederacy's petition from Detroit. Yet because of the calculating designs of Congress, the message was indirect and shrouded in secrecy. St. Clair was told to examine "the real temper of the Indian tribes" and proceed accordingly. If their attitude was found to be "hostile," St. Clair was to hold a general treaty "so that peace and harmony" might ensue.[25]

Again congressional rhetoric had supplanted a willingness to engage in substantive bargaining, for St. Clair was also advised that no change would be permitted in the boundaries established during the recently concluded treaties, unless the change was "beneficial," that is, unless it secured more land for the United States. St. Clair was also instructed: "Every exertion must be made to defeat all confederations and combinations among the tribes. . . . You will use every possible endeavor to ascertain who are the real head men and warriors of the several tribes, and who have the greatest influence among them. These men you will attach to the United States by every means in your power."[26]

Committed inflexibly to the retention of the boundaries decreed by the government and to the political manipulation of Indian leaders, St. Clair was expected to implement promptly congressional policy, including perhaps the conclusion of an important new treaty, with a total appropriation of $14,000.[27]

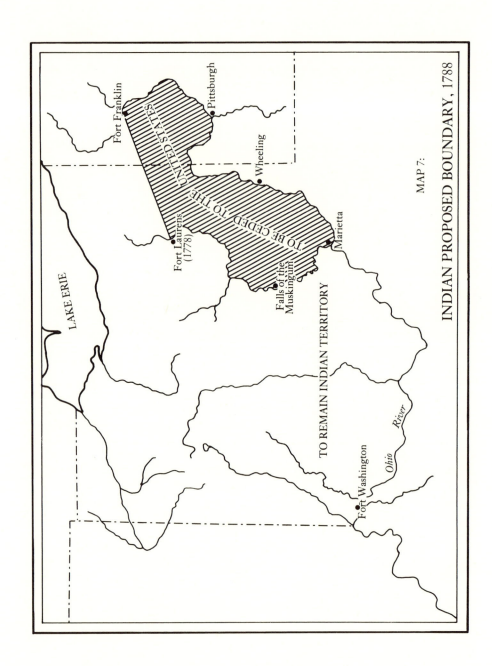

MAP 7: INDIAN PROPOSED BOUNDARY, 1788

52

7

The Course of Empire

JOSEPH Brant and Arthur St. Clair seem to have shared a similar burden at the beginning of the negotiations involving western lands in 1788. Upon their initiatives depended the attainment of the respective Indian and American objectives. Enormous internal pressure, long building among the factions on both sides, had created a crisis-charged atmosphere that increased with each frustrating delay on the diplomatic front.

The Kentucky District, beset by a variety of restrictions on military activities imposed by Virginia, continued to bombard Congress with angry complaints and demands for action. Encouraged by their success in the previous session, speculators in western lands were clamoring for a solution to the Indian problem, so that settlement of the ceded lands might begin in earnest. Then too there was the monetary crisis; adequate funding of the nearly bankrupt Treasury depended in a large measure upon rapid development of the Old Northwest lands.[1]

In 1762, Arthur St. Clair had been a self-assured British officer with considerable experience during the French and Indian War. Once described as "tall and graceful," his dignified appearance had been enhanced by long, flowing chestnut hair and a fair complexion. Yet he had lost much of his youthful verve in the intervening twenty-six years. Having emerged from the Revolution as an American major general, St. Clair was worn and somewhat discredited by his controversial abandonment of Ticonderoga in 1777. Now corpulent and severely afflicted by the gout, his hair graying, he had resigned his position in Congress to manage the destiny of the western lands without the slightest knowledge of the Indians' perspectives on the situation. Described by one frontiersman as "minister looking," this aging man was from the first subject to suspicion and distrust.[2]

St. Clair's opposite number, Joseph Brant, was a younger man of proven leadership and recognized talent. Educated in white schools, this prominent Mohawk chieftain had become so proficient in the English language that he had helped translate several religious works into his native dialect. A convert to the Anglican church, he had been intimately involved in the British fortunes throughout the revolutionary era. His sister Molly was the mistress of the British Superintendent of Indian Affairs, Sir William Johnson, and Joseph had been appointed Johnson's secretary, even earning a captain's commission in 1775.[3]

During the war years the name of Joseph Brant had become one of the most feared on the frontier. Involved in raids in upstate New York and

Joseph Brant, the famous Mohawk leader. Courtesy of Burton Historical Collection, Detroit Public Library.

throughout the frontier, Brant's Iroquois warriors had spread so much destruction and achieved such success as to earn their leader a colonel's commission, despite his Indian lineage.

Yet, in the decade following the conclusion of peace, many doubts had been cast upon Brant's leadership. Rival Iroquois factions, under Cornplanter and other leaders, openly denounced Brant and separated themselves from his sphere of influence. Mellowed in his perspective toward the Amer-

54

icans, Brant at times seemed equivocal. The strident position of radical elements, such as the Shawnees and the Miamis, contrasted sharply with Brant's counsel, and already in 1788 an undercurrent of restlessness pervaded even moderate Indian factions.[4]

With the peace initiative resting squarely in the hands of the United States emissaries, there were extended delays in achieving important results. St. Clair had journeyed alone to Fort Pitt, back to Philadelphia, and then on to New York during the winter of 1787. Yet he had been unable to obtain substantive information on the attitude of the Indians, information required by Congress before the initiation of a treaty. Noting that an Indian council assembled at Buffalo Creek had broken up for want of an American answer, St. Clair promised to "get . . . at the bottom of their designs," while proceeding with plans for a treaty at the falls of Muskingum River in May, 1788.[5] Meanwhile, Brant, in quandary over American procrastination, warned that a conference of all the Indian nations of the confederacy planned for the spring of 1788 would settle on "decisive measures."[6]

Ironically, both Brant and St. Clair were, in fact, involved in an enormous charade. While each floundered in political detail and diplomatic maneuver, momentous events with irreversible consequences already had diminished any prospect of a mutually satisfactory settlement. By 1788, without bothering to await the outcome of the intended treaty, hordes of white settlers had begun to descend upon the beautiful Ohio country, with the express approval of the federal government. Although the Indians might protest this "illegal" invasion, thousands of white settlers were soon to occupy the Indian side of the Ohio River, and the history of red-white relations had demonstrated that such settlements could not be uprooted. The dispute between rival civilizations thus was reduced to one highly visible, basic issue: the land. In fact, it was now evident that the possession of the land must determine the Indians' destiny. Moreover, because the last important vestige of Indian lands east of the Mississippi was at stake, the Indians truly had little choice but to fight or to surrender.[7]

Although the whites were an important new influence in the region, white encroachments on Indian lands in the Ohio country had been initiated covertly during the preceding decade. As early as December, 1781, the American commander at Fort Pitt had reported a well-organized scheme whereby immigrants crossed the Ohio River into Indian lands. At that time it appeared that "the best and cheapest means of protecting the frontiers" involved an "invasion [by settlement] of the Indian country" by the people of Westmoreland County, Pennsylvania. Only the possibility that these settlers might establish an independent government or come under the control of the British dissuaded officials from sanctioning the scheme. Then, with the advent of peace between Britain and the United States, increasing numbers of immigrants had journeyed into eastern regions of the Ohio country.[8]

Since this widespread immigration was founded on several illegal but practical arguments, there was much early indecision and controversy over the handling of the matter by various federal authorities. At first it was claimed that by making slight improvements upon a tract of land, a settler might legitimately claim title. These "tomahawk" improvements were often just that, the mere marking of individual boundaries by the blazing of a prominent tree with an axe.[9]

Another premise of settlement, equally indefensible under the law, was a sort of eminent-domain philosophy at the popular level. "I do certify," wrote an early advertiser and organizer of Ohio land speculation, "that all mankind . . . have an undoubted right to pass into every vacant country." This was one of the more revealing manifestations of the "course of empire" spirit that pervaded the post-Revolutionary era. The idea that lands were available for the taking might be censurable in a variety of ways, but to the American people it was a practical resolution of the enormous pressures toward westward expansion and national development. Legalities have a way of becoming distorted in the face of massive popular movements. Because the opposing Indians represented a rival and supposedly inferior civilization, there was little remorse among whites in fulfilling what they regarded as their manifest destiny.[10]

Predictably, there had been adverse governmental reactions to the unauthorized settlement of the "Ohio lands," though more for practical than for moral reasons. George Washington established much of the federal land policy when he wrote in September, 1783, that a proclamation should be issued making it a felony for any person to settle beyond the Indian boundary.[11]

On September 22, 1783, Congress passed such a resolution to "prohibit and forbid all persons from making settlements on lands inhabited or claimed by Indians without the limit or jurisdiction of any particular state." Yet, because the resolution provided no penalty nor any practical means of enforcement, it was virtually ignored.[12] Little attempt was made to prevent or discourage the new immigrants until late in January, 1785, when the American commissioners, on their way to the Treaty at the Mouth of the Great Miami, asked the federal commander at Fort McIntosh to "drive off persons attempting to settle on the [Ohio] lands of the United States." The reason for this was, of course, the impending negotiations with the more belligerent western tribes, who still resented even the decade-old settlements in Kentucky.[13]

Ensign John Armstrong, who led a twenty-man army detachment seventy miles down the Ohio River in April, 1785, found settlers moving into the Ohio lands "by forties and fifties." Many of these immigrants he regarded as "a banditti whose actions are a disgrace to human nature." Noting that many seemed to be fugitives from justice, he suggested "speedy" measures to enforce the laws regarding settlement.[14] Thereafter, Armstrong's commander, Colonel Josiah Harmar, was authorized to move his command from Fort McIntosh down the Ohio to a point between the Muskingum and the Great Miami rivers, where they might effectively police the region. Late in 1785, therefore, Harmar sent a detachment to construct a stockade on the west bank of the Muskingum at its confluence with the Ohio. "This position at Muskingum will answer the valuable object of removing the intruders from the public lands," he had written in October of that year. Soon known as Fort Harmar, this formidable log stockade stood two stories high, with artillery emplaced to sweep the land approaches.[15]

Theoretically, American land policy was unequivocating. Lenience in regard to the squatters was "to be out of the question." An officer proceeding to garrison the fort was ordered to "burn or destroy any remaining cabins" along the route.[16] Subsequently, throughout 1786 and early 1787, various army detachments ranged the Ohio River valley destroying illegal homesteads. But even though much land below the mouth of the Muskingum soon was considered cleared, Harmar continued to have trouble, particularly at Mingo Bottom near present-day Mingo Junction, Ohio.[17]

Indeed, faced with a virtual floodtide of settlers descending the Ohio, Harmar despairingly reported the mounting difficulty of policing the lands, citing as evidence an officer's record of the number of immigrant boats passing the garrison. "From the 10th of October 1786 until the 12th of May 1787," Harmar wrote, "177 boats, 2689 souls, 1333 horses, 766 cattle, and 102 wagons have passed Muskingum, bound for Limestone and the Rapids [Louisville]." Because these immigrants ostensibly were bound for the legal Kentucky settlements, Harmar was powerless to interfere, though some later were found crossing the Ohio into Indian country.[18]

The Indians meanwhile had actively joined the effort to rid the Ohio and Indian lands of white settlers, unhindered by United States countermeasures. Although the Americans had claimed by conquest these specific Ohio lands, settlement had been forbidden until approved by Congress. As a consequence of that technical restraint, neither the government nor the army responded to Indian attacks north of the Ohio.[19]

Operating with relative immunity, Indian raiders spread death and destruction with increasing intensity. In fact, by mid-1786 the combination of Indian incursions and harassment by army patrols had been so effective that the lower Ohio's north shore was partially clear of squatters. Most of the illegal settlement thereafter was centered in the region immediately west of Pennsylvania, among the more peaceable Senecas and Wyandots, and at Vincennes, in the remote Wabash country.[20]

However, after the great governmental crisis of 1787 prompted the sale of vast tracts of the Ohio wilderness, a far greater invasion of settlers was imminent. Moreover, these settlers were coming with the express approval of the United States government.

St. Clair, who was to provide the requisite governmental stability and security for the legal settlements, understood that the success of these ventures depended upon "a solid peace with the Indians." Yet the illogic of his task was glaring. He was committed by congressional instructions not only to the implementation of the post-Revolutionary American-decreed Indian boundaries but also to the physical exploitation of the Ohio land through settlement.[21]

However, the western tribes with whom St. Clair was to deal were committed to reestablishing the old 1768 treaty boundary, the Ohio River, which would have protected intact their last domain. Since de facto settlement of part of the disputed lands had already been achieved, the Indians were forced to contest the status quo—a position that put them beyond the realities of white political objectives. Hostilities, initiated on a small scale, had intensified between settlers and Indians in proportion to white encroachments on Indian lands. That St. Clair or Brant could settle by diplomacy what had already become a contest of arms was as unrealistic as it was naïve.

The United States Army, at first a moderating influence in the dispute, thus would soon be thrust into an unfamiliar and compromising role. With the advent of the first Ohio Company settlers in 1788, the army's circumstances were much altered. Fort Harmar, built to protect the Ohio lands from the intrusions of white settlers, had been selected as the location of the first large-scale legal settlement under the Northwest Ordinance of 1787. As the very symbol of protection of the new western immigrants, Fort Harmar was but one of the many ironies in the westward course of America's empire.

8

"They Must and Will Have Our Country"

THE winter of 1787–88 was remembered as one of the severest on the upper Ohio, and the ensuing spring was cold and wet. Yet in mid-February, 1788, a bedraggled party of forty-eight pioneer immigrants arrived at Simrall's Ferry (present-day West Newton, Pennsylvania) preparatory to making the final journey to their new Ohio lands. These hardy souls—New Englanders from Massachusetts, Rhode Island, and Connecticut—were the vanguard of the Ohio Company settlers organized to exploit the Manasseh Cutler purchase of 1787. Their transportation was an agglomeration: a river schooner of forty-five tons, traditionally named *May Flower*; a ferryboat of three tons, named *Adelphia*; and three log rafts. Belatedly they sailed for their new homes early in April led by the crusty, self-taught Revolutionary brigadier Rufus Putnam, who had been chosen as their superintendent. Traveling without incident, the small party landed at the mouth of the Muskingum River opposite Fort Harmar on a rainy April 7, 1788. Determined to establish the first permanent white settlement in the Ohio country, the newcomers set to work felling trees and clearing the ground under the watchful eyes of the army garrison. Within days a cluster of log houses with shingled roofs sheltered the pioneer families, and construction was begun on a stockade.[1]

By midsummer it was apparent that the settlers' enthusiasm and industry had virtually assured the success of their colony. Noting that "a spacious city" had been laid out, a federal lieutenant observed that "these people appear the most happy folks in the world, greatly satisfied with their new purchase." Even the often skeptical General Josiah Harmar was early impressed by the new settlers, saying, "they are industrious, and quite a different set of people from these frontiersmen."[2]

On July 2, 1788, having erected for security a two-story stockade, called Campus Martius, about a half mile north of their settlement, the directors of the Ohio Company confidently proclaimed their new venture Marietta, in honor of the famous French Queen Marie Antoinette. New immigrants were arriving nearly every week, and the influx soon became so great that by September, 1788, the population numbered 132 persons, nearly all of whom were former New Englanders.[3]

Thus far no difficulty had been encountered with Indians. Although several families chose to reside within the Campus Martius stockade, they were considered timid souls. Indeed, the flourishing nature of the Marietta settlement was fully evident upon the arrival of Governor Arthur St. Clair in July, and with the subsequent establishment of civil government in the territory.[4]

In fact, a new impetus was already evident for further expansion. Estimating that "upwards of seven thousand" immigrants had passed down the Ohio since the establishment of Marietta, Rufus Putnam ardently sought the open sale of Ohio Company lands, reflecting that many of these passing immigrants would have settled on the Muskingum if they could have obtained lots. Thereafter plans were laid for new settlements at such outlying locations as Belpre, Waterford, and Duck Creek.[5]

Land development was already such a sensation on the frontier that there was keen competition among the settlements for the increasing multitude of white settlers. Congressman John Cleves Symmes of New Jersey, who envisioned huge profits in land speculation, had initiated a calculating scheme for the settlement of land between the two Miami rivers. By arranging for the purchase of one million acres in his name, Symmes became a major broker in parcelling out Old Northwest land to developers. Ten thousand acres were sold to Major Benjamin Stites and others, who promptly organized a party of about twenty immigrants and journeyed to the site of their purchase in November, 1788. The Stites party founded Columbia, which was soon a bustling village near the mouth of the Little Miami. Another party was led by Matthias Denman and Robert Patterson to a tract of land that they purchased from Symmes opposite the mouth of Licking River, where they were to become the founding fathers of Cincinnati. Originally named Losantiville, this settlement was but seven miles from Columbia and was first populated by "twelve or fifteen" pioneers who braved floating ice and freezing weather to locate on the site late in December, 1788.[6]

Despite the successful initial occupation of the Ohio lands, and the development of logistic self-sufficiency, the immigrants were still confronted with a serious threat to their security. The Indian menace was the focus of considerable attention among the growing number of land developers, plus the sizeable number of moderate red men who were fearful of hostilities with the Americans.

To the Indians the growing controversy over a unified bargaining position reflected the considerable political disarray among the various red factions, and it posed a severe threat to the effectiveness of the Indian confederacy.

Already there were bands who despite their wishes were resigned to a vanquished status and sought peace at any price. Adamantly opposed to what they considered such "backward" Indians were the as-yet-unconquered western Algonquian nations. Representing the essence of a vibrant native people, they were still willing to risk all if necessary in a decisive confrontation. A third, moderate faction, allied with British interests and reflecting a conservative viewpoint, was the pivotal coalition composed mostly of dissident Iroquois and Great Lakes tribes thus far uncommitted to peace or war.

Due to the considerable strength of these various factions, within post-Revolutionary Indian civilization in America fundamental policy enactments had become a protracted internal ordeal. Led by the articulate Joseph Brant, who well understood the efficacy of the white society, the moderates ardently sought compromise as a basis of Indian unanimity. Brant's personal views were nonbelligerent, but he sought to attain Indian objectives through a common front, utilizing the threat of widespread hostilities as bargaining leverage. Particularly galling to Brant was the American position that the Indian lands were conquered territory which the British had ceded to the United States as the price of peace.[7]

Since it was apparent to many tribesmen that the Americans would not be denied in their annexing of land, among the most outspoken of Brant's red opponents were the tribal leaders who favored peace at any price. Particularly difficult to persuade to the common cause were the Senecas, led by Brant's great rival, Chief Cornplanter. Cornplanter had ardently sought to secure favored-nation status with the United States. "As for the Five Nations [led by Cornplanter], most of them have sold themselves to the devil—I mean to the Yankees," bitterly complained Brant in 1788. Fort Franklin, on French Creek near Venango, Pennsylvania, had been constructed in 1787 ostensibly to protect the Senecas, further securing that tribe's attachment to the United States. A council among the Six Nations at Canadesaga, near Geneva, New York, early in 1788 had broken up in a quarrel, and these Senecas, with other allied Indians, generally refused to support the so-called confederacy.[8]

On the opposite side of the spectrum, and just as intransigent in their attitudes, were the Shawnees, Miamis, and Kickapoos. Brant had particular difficulty in restraining these headstrong nations, all of which were generally in favor of "open war with the Americans," he said.[9] Miami and Shawnee raiding parties had already begun intensified operations in mid-1788, striking hard at the Kentucky settlements, where they were particularly successful in stealing horses. Moreover, the passage of considerable time since the Indian ultimatum of December, 1786, had worked against Brant's moderating influence, and when the American proposal for a treaty at the Falls of the Muskingum became known early in 1788, there was still considerable dissension over what policy the Indians should pursue.[10]

In view of the recent white settlements in the Ohio country, Brant and the other moderates realized that some modification of the Ohio River boundary would have to be made if an accommodation was to be reached with the Americans. Consequently, Brant led the fight to yield "a small part" of Indian country, and the boundary line fixed, "rather than enter headlong into a destructive war."[11]

As Brant correctly foresaw before the Indians' policy-setting grand "council at the Miamis" opened in mid-October, 1788, the western nations were outraged by this suggestion. In fact, at one point during the council the Wyandots presented the Miamis with a large string of wampum, "taking hold of one end of it and desiring them [the Miamis] to hold fast by the other." Not only did the Miamis refuse this gesture of unity, but also when the Wyandot delegation then placed the wampum over the shoulder of the principal Miami war chief, Little Turtle, "recommending to them to be at peace with the Americans, and to do as the Six Nations and the others did," Little Turtle tilted his shoulder and let the wampum fall to the ground, without making any answer. The insulted Wyandots then stalked out of the meeting, leaving the Miamis to their own council.[12]

With his grand Indian confederacy already verging on collapse, Brant and the moderate faction now encountered further difficulty—this time from the very interests they had sought partially to appease, the Americans.

Early in 1788 the Indian confederacy learned of the belated American decision to convene the council that the Indians had requested to settle boundaries. The date of this council was then fixed tentatively for May 1, 1788. Yet a series of long delays and unforseen events had postponed the treaty. St. Clair, the American principal, was handicapped by a general lack of experience in Indian affairs. After his belated arrival at Fort Harmar on July 9, 1788, the governor showed befuddlement over Indian internal affairs and a naïve estimation of the Indian character. Within a few days of his arrival at Fort Harmar, an incident involving actual warfare betrayed St. Clair's limited perspective. Instead of investigating the circumstances of what was obviously a skirmish, St. Clair rashly proclaimed the conflict an example of the Indians' "perfidity" and stated that he had lost faith in their character. This incident, a minor affair by any military standard, was to become a substantial impediment to the conclusion of a meaningful treaty, and reflected the American territorial administration's want of expertise.[13]

Late in May, Governor St. Clair, then at Fort Pitt, had authorized the shipment of a large boat laden with provisions for the intended treaty to the proposed site of the council, the Falls of the Muskingum, about seventy miles north of Fort Harmar. Because the level of the Muskingum River was falling, it was thought best that the goods be transported to the council site, as the river would "soon be so low that it will be impossible for loaded boats to ascend it." St. Clair requested that an army escort be provided, which would not only provide security but also be able to construct a council house.[14]

Under the command of Ensign Nathan McDowell, this escort, consisting of a sergeant, a corporal, and twenty privates, proceeded up the Muskingum on June 13. By June 29 two separate log houses, one for the men and the other for McDowell, had been erected; and construction of the 12-by-46-foot council house was begun. This structure was completed on July 6, and thereafter the detachment busied itself in idly clearing away the brush and chatting with the small hunting parties of Indians (mostly Delawares) who almost daily came to trade their skins and obtain provisions.[15] Discipline seems to have been rather lax, and in order to prevent an embarrassing accident, McDowell instructed his sentinels not to fire when challenging an approaching person but merely to retire to the guard post should they fail to halt.[16]

Between daylight and sunrise on July 12 a war party of about ten or twelve Chippewa Indians approached McDowell's campsite from upriver. Being undetected, they silently landed their canoes within eighty yards of the log houses. Then with a sudden yell one group of Indians sprang at the drowsy outposts, while the others dashed into the camp proper. Most of the soliders' muskets were unloaded, and many of the sentinels' arms failed to discharge due to damp powder. Before much resistance could be organized, two privates were killed, and three wounded. As the Indians paused to scalp their fallen victims, including a dead Negro servant, the scattered soldiers dashed into their log hut and began a random answering fire. After a few minutes the fighting ended, with the Indians vanishing into the brush. One warrior, shot in the midst of the camp, was found dead, and two others were presumed wounded.[17]

McDowell, shaken and fearing a renewal of the attack, had his men sling wet clay against the cracks in the cabin's log walls, seeking to provide better protection. When a friendly Delaware came in shortly after the skirmish, he was promptly sent as a runner to Fort Harmar with news of the incident. Appropriately named George Washington, the Delaware messenger arrived at Fort Harmar with his grim dispatch on July 13, throwing the garrison immediately into an uproar. St. Clair, who had been in the Northwest Territory less than a week, was infuriated by what he termed an insult and an indignity to the United States. He immediately resolved to remove the provisions and garrison from the Falls of the Muskingum. Moreover, in his rage he determined to make a major alteration in the plans for a treaty. "After such an insult," he fumed, "to meet the Indians at the place [Falls of the Muskingum] . . . I thought inconsistent with the dignity of the United States." Immediately, he dispatched a formal message to the mouth of the Detroit River that chastised the Indian nations for disrespect and "unprovoked hostility." "The flag of the United States has been fired upon," St. Clair angrily wrote, "and (what is perfidious beyond comparison) when a small party of soldiers were sent to watch the council fire, kindled at your request; to build a council house for you to meet in, and to take care of the provisions sent there to feed you, you have fallen upon them, and killed them. . . . In the name of the United States I require an immediate explanation of these transactions, and demand satisfaction and the restitution of the prisoners [several soldiers were reported by McDowell as missing]. Until these are made, as there can be no confidence, it will be improper we should meet one another in council." To emphasize his anger, St. Clair related that the council fire at the Falls of the Muskingum was permanently extinguished: any treaty would have to be held at an American site.[18]

While George Washington, the Delaware messenger, was sent to recall McDowell's detachment, another runner went to the Wyandot towns bearing St. Clair's formal message, which was to be forwarded by that tribe to the Indians' council. Included was a string of black and white wampum, a tacit reminder to the Indians of St. Clair's ultimatum of peace on American terms or war.[19]

Ironically, on July 16, three days after sending the Indians notice of the canceled treaty, St. Clair received the further instructions of Congress on concluding a treaty, as well as notification of the appropriation of additional monies. Secretary of War Henry Knox, in a covering letter, talked of the great anxiety of Congress "for quieting all disturbances among the Indians" and "accomplishing effectually the public expectations."[20] St. Clair, somewhat embarrassed, later awkwardly reflected that "tamely submitting to one injury usually invites a greater," and that accordingly he had resolved to "maintain and defend" the national honor.[21]

Meanwhile, the McDowell party had abandoned the Falls of the Muskingum camp and embarked for Fort Harmar. Arriving on July 20, the party landed with six Indian prisoners, who were said to have been participants in the action of July 12.

According to McDowell, two days after the skirmish a party of six Chippewa warriors and four squaws had come in for provisions. Their actions and countenance had aroused suspicion, and an army cartridge box was found in their possession. McDowell secretly determined to take them as prisoners to Fort Harmar. On July 19, when preparing to leave, he invited the unsuspecting Chippewas and some Delawares on board the army boats for an issue of flour. After the Indians had gathered in a group to board the waiting boats, McDowell had his men seize the Chippewas and put the warriors aboard under guard. Although they protested their innocence, saying the cartridge box had been found in the woods, a Delaware was found who reportedly contradicted this story. McDowell and an army contractor further asserted they could positively identify one of the Chippewas as the killer of one of the soldiers. At Fort Harmar, St. Clair had the Indians put in irons, but eight days later two escaped by slipping their shackes while passing a cornfield on their way to an outdoor privy. Thereafter the remaining four prisoners were confined behind bars, with irons on their wrists and legs.[22]

St. Clair's handling of the whole affair, which began as an isolated attack by a handful of Indian banditti, not only placed the entire treaty negotiations in jeopardy but also had a disruptive effect on the Indians in general. The two escapees soon spread word that the remaining four prisoners had been murdered by the Americans. St. Clair, now under pressure from the administration for a rapid peace, soon began to despair of an early answer from the Indians to his ultimatum of July 13. In mid-August he learned that his message had not gone forth from Sandusky until late July. Since it was known that the Indian nations had not yet assembled in general council, he correctly presumed an answer would not be forthcoming until all were present.[23]

Moreover, reports confirmed that Chippewas alone had carried out the Falls of the Muskingum attack, and that this war party had crossed Lake Huron near Detroit and ultimately had sold one of their prisoners to a merchant at Michilimackinac. Thereafter St. Clair's attitude was one of growing uneasiness toward Joseph Brant and the Indian confederacy.[24]

Late in October more disquieting reports arrived. It was said that the Indians in their grand council on the Miami River had resolved to insist on the Ohio River boundary and would go no farther to hold a treaty than the Falls of the Muskingum. This news generally paralleled a series of reports of recent violence in other frontier areas. Late in July Lieutenant William Peters with an escort of thirty soldiers had been attacked by Indians near the mouth of the Wabash River and severely defeated. Peters had lost eight men killed and ten wounded, plus a boat laden with provisions. Late in September Lieutenant John Armstrong's party had been fired on while sailing down the Ohio near the mouth of the Scioto River. One man had been wounded in the cheek. In October an army lieutenant at Fort Harmar learned that a soldier recently captured by Indians near the Rapids of the Ohio had been killed and mutilated in a ghastly manner. "Not content with scalping him," the officer complained, "[they] cut him in four quarters and hung them up on the bushes."[25]

All of this information served to disgust and alarm St. Clair and the army's commander at Fort Harmar, Brevet Brigadier General Josiah Harmar. Believing that the Indians were "hatching a great deal of mischief," Harmar, like St. Clair, anticipated the imminent commencement of widespread hostilities by the more-western tribes, if not by the general Indian confederacy.[26]

Ironically, just at the time when St. Clair most despaired of a prompt meeting with the Indians in a significant council, a sudden break in the impasse occurred. On November 7, 1788, an advance party of prominent Six Nations warriors and chiefs, including Captain David and the son of Joseph Brant, arrived at Fort Harmar for a brief visit. Captain David bore a friendly message from the Indian confederacy, which had only recently concluded the grand Council of the Miamis. This significant missive quickly raised American hopes for a successful and general treaty. Yet by an incredible display of inept diplomacy, the prospect was soon dashed.[27]

Joseph Brant had partially succeeded in his determined attempts to bring the various nations at the Council of the Miamis to a unified position on the American boundary problem. Despite the refusal of the Miamis and some of the more belligerent Shawnees, Brant had worked out a tentative compromise involving certain preconditions for a treaty. Aware of the burgeoning American settlements north of the Ohio River at Marietta, Brant had persuaded the confederacy to yield a portion of those Indian lands, provided that the Americans would provide some evidence that they would negotiate fairly. Thus in the letter that Captain David delivered, the Indians asked for restoration of the Falls of the Muskingum council site as an indication by the Americans that bargaining in good faith would occur. (Some Indians evidently feared a repetition of the high-handed American tactic of taking hostages at the council, or even an attempt to poison or introduce disease among the red men).[28]

St. Clair, however, was in a surly mood, then being "very ill with the gout." Although aware of the many divisions among the various tribes of the confederacy, he was nonetheless totally oblivious of the hard-wrought compromise that Brant had forged by his moderating influence.[29]

Without hesitation he responded to the Indians' request arbitrarily and harshly, denying any change in location from Fort Harmar, which had been now designated as the new treaty site. This policy, as St. Clair had earlier explained, was enacted because after the "insult" of the federal troops at the falls, meeting the red men at that site would be an affront to the dignity of the United States. Moreover, he had no wish to meet the Indians "quite unprotected" by adequate fortifications, being obviously distrustful of their motives.[30]

Captain David, carrying St. Clair's reply, arrived at the principal camp of the Six Nations about November 15. On November 19 the "Indian chiefs of the Six Nations and Western Confederacy" responded in a biting commentary: "From the misconduct of a few individuals who live at a great distance . . . and are little concerned with a union with you [a reference to the Chippewa raiding party that had attacked McDowell's detachment at the Falls of the Muskingum], you have extinguished the council fire." "We look upon [this] extremely hard," they continued, "particularly as we have been exerting ourselves for several years past to bring the whole of the Indian nations of this country to agree to come to some terms of peace with the United States."

Stating that they had done everything in their power, the Indians admonished that since it had been mutually agreed at the Miami council that the nations would go no further than the Falls of the Muskingum for the treaty, they accordingly would not participate.[31] The Indians then revealed the full extent of the compromise that the moderates had been able to obtain at the Miami conference. Essentially, the heart of the entire issue was the adjustments that the Indians were willing to make in the "Ohio River boundary" as a concession to peace. In a carefully worded text the chiefs explained what they would concede as evidence of their earnestness: "Brothers, as it is our wish to live in peace with all men, [and] to avoid further trouble, we propose to give to the United States all the lands lying on the east side of the Muskingum [embracing most of present-day eastern Ohio and western Pennsylvania]." Accordingly it was the firm position of the Indian confederacy that that was the boundary line beyond "which we cannot exceed." Citing the lateness of the season, the Indian spokesmen then appealed for a prompt answer.[32]

Arthur St. Clair, still unwilling to make any compromise, was unappreciative of the moderation that the Indians exhibited in yielding a portion of the Ohio River boundary. In decisive language his reply, written in late November, flatly denied the Indian proposals as "altogether inadmissible." Furthermore, the American territorial governor accused the Indians of being under undue British influence. They had received many presents as payment for the British cession of their territory, he asserted.[33]

Upon receipt of St. Clair's answer most of the Indians, and Joseph Brant in particular, were outraged. The chiefs of the Six Nations immediately responded in a speech heavy with sarcasm. Noting that "you must and will have our country," the chiefs concluded, "we now tell you we have our feeling and our spirit and must leave the event to the will of the Great Spirit, to whom we look up for justice."[34] Stating that the large tract of land that they were willing to yield gratis "must convince every person that peace is our wish," the Indians closed with a not-so-subtle mockery of the American greed for territory. Acknowledging the American right to the military posts ceded by Britain in 1783, the Indians asked, "What then is the reason you do not take them, which we acknowledge is yours, agreeable to the treaty of peace between the British and you?"[35]

Joseph Brant apparently was even more indignant in his actions and words. Since the Indians had been reported as in great want of provisions following their Miami council, most of the tribes had been "hunting their way" toward the Falls of the Muskingum. Brant's party had apparently moved within sixty miles of Fort Harmar when he received St. Clair's final message. According to some Wyandots, Brant threw the American governor's letter into the fire, saying it was a very bad speech, and immediately moved off with his tribesmen to meet the delegation of Shawnees, Delawares, and Miamis, who were said to be two days distant and en route to the treaty.[36]

From Licking Creek on December 8, 1788, Brant wrote his final communication to St. Clair, advising that the Shawnees, the Delawares, and the other tribes whom he had met were "of the same opinion" that "nothing more can be done than what we have offered" unless the general confederacy should later agree to it. As a further warning against any more "little treaties" with individual nations, Brant admonished that "no business of consequence is to be transacted without the unanimous consent of all concerned," and accordingly, little attention would be paid to what any individual Indians might do.[37]

Abruptly, five years of anguished diplomacy was thus concluded. Although Arthur St. Clair immediately intensified preparations to hold a face-saving treaty at Fort Harmar with the American-aligned Senecas and other pacified Indian factions, the aging governor had effectively alienated the vital moderate tribal leaders. The result was an increasingly troublesome awareness that there could be no middle ground in the controversy. While Arthur St. Clair busily prepared for the expected arrival of the peace-oriented Indians, Joseph Brant and the Mohawks, the Shawnees, the Miamis, and some Delawares dispersed to their homelands, determined to resist this American "backwardness."

St. Clair, when he learned of Brant's "evil work" in removing his tribesmen and the other western nations, remained characteristically naïve. Believing he had disrupted their general confederacy, St. Clair wrote on December 13, "I do not . . . consider [Brant's and the others' absence] as any great misfortune, because I believe the consequence will be the dissolution of the general confederacy which he and the British had taken so much pains to form."[38]

On the contrary, the leadership of the Indian confederacy had now passed into more belligerent hands. Although some nations remained alienated from the policies of the majority, the polarization of the confederacy had been furthered by St. Clair's actions. Instead of partially appeasing the confederacy's left wing, and thereby nurturing a moderate Indian faction, St. Clair had unwittingly strengthened the hostile elements, and materially complicated the government's strategic military problem.[39]

Indeed, the confederacy had been gleaned of its more pacific elements. The tribes who obligingly were about to proceed to council at Fort Harmar were now so removed from the mainstream that they could be of little practical consequence as a quieting influence.

Adding to the miseries of a continually deterioriating situation was St. Clair's growing realization that the western territory, "instead of proving a fund for paying our national debt," was becoming "a source of mischief and increasing expense."[40]

As a crowning touch, soon thereafter new instructions arrived from Secretary of War Knox delineating the seriousness of the Indian problem from a governmental perspective. St. Clair was explicitly warned of "the evils attending an Indian war," either partial or general, and accordingly, the governor was to utilize "every honorable expedient to avoid so injurious event." Asserting that "a protracted Indian war would be destruction to the republic in its present circumstances," Knox then asked that St. Clair "make a solid arrangement" for assembling the northern and western nations as soon as possible.[41]

To Brevet Brigadier General Josiah Harmar, his chief military subordinate, Knox was even more specific: "I most sincerely hope some expedients may be devised for avoiding an Indian war. This event would at present be embarrassing beyond conception. It has been with the greatest difficulty that money has been obtained for the recruits, clothing, and stores which have been forwarded during the present year. If an Indian war should arise, it is greatly to be apprehended that it must languish for want of money. In this case it might be protracted to such a length as to produce extreme distress and disgrace."[42]

Perhaps it was fitting irony that Knox's letters were written on the same date, December 8, 1788, that Joseph Brant had penned his somber refusal to capitulate to American designs.

9

This Is the Road to Hell

THE Ohio River had been choked with ice through the first week in March, but on March 10 the heavy ice broke up with a tremendous roar. One observer reported that the swirling waters of the river then rose twenty feet in three days. To the isolated immigrants at Fort Pitt this thaw meant the welcome opening of the riverboat season. Within a few days the Ohio was dotted with flatboats and keelboats that were bound downriver for the Ohio and Kentucky countries despite the drifting masses of floating ice.[1]

Aboard one flat-bottomed Kentucky boat that March was an English merchant, Thomas Ridout, who was journeying to the western country to collect debts from persons who had immigrated to Kentucky. Moving with a five-mile-an-hour current, the flatboat proceeded night and day, stopping only briefly at well-known landing spots. Ridout recorded that after the boat passed Fort Harmar the weather became very pleasant, with the trees bursting forth in leaflets.

The river, said Ridout, flowed in a "majestic stream, . . . and the moon being now full and the nights serene and clear, added greatly to the [enjoyment] of our journey." By the morning of March 21, which was Good Friday, the young Englishman was completely enamored with the beauty of this magnificent wilderness. Happily Ridout busied himself in calculating the distance by his traveling compass to the "Big Bones" site where mastodon skeletons had been unearthed for the British Museum.[2]

Around a bend in the Ohio, Ridout suddenly saw an abandoned flatboat jammed into the bushes on the Indian side of the river. It appeared to be the same rivercraft that had departed from Limestone in the Kentucky District only a few hours before Ridout's party. To the horror of the onlooking passengers a large canoe suddenly put off from shore filled with Indians "almost naked, painted and ornamented [for] . . . war."

In a blurred remembrance of what next occurred, Ridout later portrayed an Indian assault so swift that no resistance was offered. The Indian boarding party clambered aboard brandishing knives and tomahawks and "yelling and screaming horribly." One warrior, painted black, seized Ridout and claimed him as his property. Ordered to strip, Ridout saw his hat, long coat, and waistcoat appropriated as spoils of war. Quickly taken ashore, he was treated with considerable civility, yet made to join a group of white prisoners, which then numbered ten men. Since the war party had been composed mostly of Shawnees, Ridout was allotted to that tribe.[3]

Departing the following day for an Indian village on the Wabash, said to be five days distant, Ridout was compelled to endure the hardships of captivity. Loaded with a thirty-pound bundle pack and stripped of his pants and shoes, he was furnished only with a breechclout and a pair of moccasins. At night his hands were placed in a small leather bag which was secured at the wrist so tightly with a throng that by the morning he was unable even to bend his fingers, both hands being swollen and black. On one occasion sleet fell following a cold and driving rain, yet Ridout said "the agony I suffered in my wrists, hands and arms, made me insensible to almost everything else."[4]

Bedraggled, and partially crippled so that he "could scarcely stand upright," Ridout finally arrived in the Indian village. Held for ransom rather than chosen for death, Ridout was more fortunate than a Virginia youth of about twenty, named Mitchell. At an Indian village on the White River, Ridout observed the fate that befell many of the captured "Shemanthe" (meaning Virginians, or Big Knives). Young Mitchell was driven out of a hut naked, "his ears having been cut off, and his face painted black." For three hours, during which sounds of the victim's dreadful shrieks and groans pierced the air, Ridout cowered in an Indian hut, fearful that his own fate soon might be the same. At last the Indians returned, firing their guns, and with large sticks began beating their wigwams. With relief Ridout learned that this was to drive away the evil spirit of the prisoner whom they had burned at the stake, rather than any menacing gesture toward the remaining captives.

Taken eventually to Detroit, Ridout was later ransomed into the custody of a British officer. Just how fortunate Ridout had been was revealed by the entries recorded on the back of his diary. Of the six prisoners whose fate he learned, only Ridout and one other man had escaped death at the hands of the Indians; several in fact had been burned at the stake.[5]

Another traveler during the same period of Ohio River Indian raids was Charles Johnston, an attorney from Botetourt County, Virginia. Johnston was en route to Kentucky with his wealthy employer, John May, who was then involved in litigation of western land claims. Both had set out in mid-March from Point Pleasant aboard a "wretched ark," in the company of four other persons, including two sisters, Peggy and Dolly Flemming.[6]

On March 20 their keel boat was passing in the vicinity of the mouth of the Scioto when a lookout spotted a pall of smoke on the Ohio shore. Two bedraggled white men soon appeared and from the riverbank pleaded for the keel boat to land and take them aboard. They shouted that they had been captured by Indians and had escaped, and that they were in great danger of perishing from cold and hunger. Having been warned that decoys were operating along the Ohio to lure unsuspecting boats into an Indian ambush, the May-Johnston party continued their passage in midriver. Persisting in their cries of distress, the two white men ran along the shore opposite the boat, pleading in desperation to be rescued from falling again into the hands of the merciless savages.

Persuaded by the two sisters and the boy friend of one that the danger of Indians was exaggerated, the travelers agreed to attempt a rescue. Since the boat had already outdistanced the men on shore, it was agreed that the boat would briefly put in to the riverbank and discharge the boy friend, who would look for Indians.[7]

In crossing the current, the keel boat lost considerable distance and time, allowing the two white men nearly to catch up. As soon as the boat touched shore, the youth jumped out—only to meet face to face with an onrushing party of Indians. While only the swiftest Indians were yet present, the main party was observed rapidly approaching along a path bordering the river. After firing a volley at the nearest Indians, the boat's occupants attempted to shove the heavy keel boat back into the current. Yet the water was so high and the brush so thick along the riverbank that the boat was soon hung up on the branches of a large tree. While the occupants desperately struggled to free the craft, most of the lagging Indians came up to within sixty feet of them, and raising a "horrible war whoop," poured a well-aimed fusillade into the boat. Dolly Flemming was instantly killed by a ball that struck her in the corner of the mouth. Another passenger, Skyles, was seriously wounded. May, Johnston, and Peggy Flemming ducked down beneath the high sides of the boat, leaving only their terrified horses exposed to the close-range musketry. Frightened by the deafening noise and the pungent smell of powder, the animals thrashed about wildly until shot by the Indians. Even after they fell, their dying agonies made the bottom of the boat unsafe from their spasmodic kicks and thrashing. When the last horse had fallen, the firing ceased, and John May incautiously rose, taking off the nightcap that he still wore in order to wave it as a token of surrender. Instantly, a volley of shots rang out, and May slumped into the bottom of the boat, a rifle ball through his forehead. Only Peggy Flemming and Johnston remained unhurt as the Indians rushed toward the boat. While those on shore stood with leveled rifles, about twenty Indians plunged into the water and waded out to the boat, tomahawks in hand. Johnston, realizing his hopeless situation, rose and hastened to help the boarding party clamber over the side. "When they entered, they shook hands with me, crying out in broken English, "How de do! How de do!" said Johnston. After some momentary confusion as they searched the boat and appraised their capture, the Indians poled the boat ashore, and Johnston and others were removed as prisoners. Immediately, said Johnston, the Indians swarmed over the boat appropriating the booty and scalping the dead. A fire was soon kindled, and Johnston was made to remove most of his clothes. Joined by the boy friend, who had been captured ashore, Peggy Flemming, and the wounded Skyles, Johnston reflected in horror, "Already my imagination placed me at the stake, and I saw the flames about to be kindled around me."[8]

The next morning, in the company of the two whites who had hailed his boat, Thomas and Devine, Johnston was made to go to the riverbank in order to decoy a canoe containing six men. Devine readily encouraged the canoeists to land, saying that they had been stranded by a boating accident and needed an axe to repair their craft. When the unsuspecting canoemen put across the river, they were fired on at point-blank range by the Indians. Four of the canoeists were instantly killed, and the remaining two wounded. Swiftly the Indians retrieved the canoe and brought the wounded men ashore, where they were promptly tomahawked. After the corpses were scalped, all were dumped into the Ohio River like so much driftwood.[9]

Satisfied with the results of their brief foray, the Indian war party, consisting of about fifty Shawnees, Delawares, Wyandots, and Cherokees, divided their prisoners and plunder and dispersed. Johnston was awarded to a Shawnee chief and later was taken to Upper Sandusky, where he was ransomed by a Canadian trader. Peggy Flemming, claimed by the Cherokees, was similarly ransomed after a grueling ordeal. Skyles, Johnston's wounded companion, eventually escaped from the Shawnees and made his way to Detroit, where he was saved by several of the British garrison. Only the youthful boy friend failed to survive. Taken to the Miami Villages, he was burned at the stake amid all the tortures the Shawnees could devise, then "devoured" by the Indians, one of whom allegedly claimed his flesh was sweeter than bear's meat.[10]

The Ridout and Johnston incidents were but two of the myriad of "depredations" along the Ohio River during the period of undeclared war between 1788 and 1790 (Ridout's capture occurred in 1788, Johnston's in 1790). Although isolated examples, they reflected a peculiar transition that had gradually occurred in frontier warfare. By the late 1780's the flood tide of immigrants to the western lands had so populated Kentucky that lethal Indian incursions south of the Ohio River by large war parties were no longer practical. By 1788 most of the Indian forays into the interior were of a limited nature, involving perhaps the stealing of horses and the killing of an occasional isolated settler. After such raids the warriors generally scurried back across the Ohio River as soon as possible, often just ahead of the strong pursuit that was certain to develop. As an alternative to the Kentucky raids, the hundreds of immigrants passing down the Ohio River provided many vulnerable targets of opportunity, without the risk associated with operations amid the populous white settlements.

Although the intensifying guerilla warfare was an ominous new trend, Indian attacks had long been prevalent on the Ohio River, dating back to the Revolutionary period. Captain David Rogers, commanding some Virginia troops, had been ambushed on the Ohio near the mouth of Licking Creek in October, 1779, losing fifty-seven out of seventy men and $600,000 in Spanish coin. With the subsequent widespread migrations to western lands, the sheer numbers of whites decreed that the prospects for Indian success lay more than ever in stealth and cunning. Indeed, during the entire period of hostilities between American pioneers and the Algonquian and the Iroquois civilizations there are few more classic examples of Indian guile than the Ohio River raids. White decoys, Indians speaking English and dressed as whites, wild-game calls, and seemingly abandoned or disabled rivercraft were among the various ploys utilized with considerable success.[11]

Despite mounting Indian successes, the targets of opportunity seemed unceasing during the peak river season between April and November. Often manned by inexperienced travelers who were poorly armed, the clumsy and frequently overcrowded rivercraft were particularly vulnerable to direct attack. Soon many immigrants traveled in miniconvoys of two or three rivercraft for added protection. Yet, as indicated by the bodies frequently floating past Limestone, sudden disaster remained a constant hazard of travel on the Ohio.[12]

Aware of the foreboding significance of this mass influx of colonists, the Indians displayed little remorse in carrying out their depredations. In an atmosphere of mutual hatred, unavenged murders, and long-suffered injustices, bitterness and rancor spilled over into atrocities that further intensified the conflict. Each new barbarity seemed to beget a more brutal and unreasoning attitude in the participants on both sides.

The spectacle of a drifting Kentucky boat at Limestone in 1788 was enough to rouse even the most insipid spirit. Amid the dead horses and scattered debris from an Indian attack lay a dead woman with a bawling infant futilely attempting to suckle at her breast. In the following spring a father and one of his young sons emerged from the woods to tell another shocking tale of Indian atrocity. The man, Captain Ashby, lived in the Kentucky District and had been attacked in the company of his family while on the Ohio below the Great Miami. Although assailed by an overwhelming Indian war party in canoes, his older son, Jack, had fought valiantly, wounding or killing two of his attackers with a clubbed rifle and a skinning knife even as they had boarded Ashby's flatboat. Finally killed during the struggle, Jack Ashby had been split open, and his heart had been removed and later roasted and eaten by the Indians in view of the captive parents. Regarded by the Indians as a means to infuse the prowess and courage of a brave fallen enemy, this custom nonetheless was a revolting atrocity to the family, several of whom had escaped to tell the story.[13]

Gross brutality was characteristic particularly of many of the younger warriors, whose hot-headed passion for war was notorious. In fact, increasing ferocity, evidenced by dismemberment and gross mutilation of fallen whites, began to characterize frontier Indian attacks in the late 1780's and early 1790's. Responding in kind, the American pioneers demonstrated a cruel viciousness of their own.

So embittered by Indian raids were the settlers of one Kentucky county that they decided to poison their red foes. Noting that Indian raiders had frequently utilized several evacuated cabins, which had been robbed of "wheat, corn, potatoes, etc.," these frontiersmen connived to impregnate foodstuffs "with arsenic or any other suitable poison" in order to kill the marauders. The *Kentucky Gazette* of March 15, 1788, contained notice of this scheme, warning "all persons not to touch any article left there."[14]

Daniel Morgan, an early pioneer living on the west fork of the Monongahela, earned the somewhat revered sobriquet "Savage Morgan" by his intense hatred of red men. Morgan was particularly fond of displaying a razor strap that he had fashioned of an Indian's skin. In fact, men like Hugh McGary, who had murdered Moluntha, were all too common along the frontier, being consumed by their unreasoning hatred of the Indian. The treacherous McGary on one occasion pretended to befriend a lone Indian encountered on the trail. Gaining the Indian's confidence, he savagely brained the red man with a large club once his fellow traveler's back was turned.[15]

The blind, unreasoning hatred of all the red race, in fact, was so prevalent that it threatened to disrupt even the convening of the pacifist-faction Indians at Fort Harmar in the fall of 1788. Reports that "several vagabonds in the neighborhood of Wheeling mean to fire upon these Indians on their passage down the Ohio to this post," caused Josiah Harmar to detach an army escort from Fort Pitt in order to bring the Seneca delegation safely to the treaty site.[16]

Despite the attitude of mutual distrust and enmity that was spilling forth in the virulent, expanding warfare along the frontier, and though hampered by the absence of the moderate Indians who had been alienated by his indiscreet diplomacy, Arthur St. Clair announced the advent of the treaty at Fort Harmar on December 13, 1788. "It will not, however, be a very general meeting," St. Clair sheepishly advised a congressional officer.[17]

Of the twenty-seven chiefs and sachems who ultimately signed the treaty, the missionary John Heckewelder is said to have observed that only four were principal chiefs. Composed largely of Senecas, Wyandots, and Delawares, the Fort Harmar Indian contingents were mostly Americanized tribesmen of a motley sort. One army officer, familiar with Indians, described the Senecas as "indolent, dirty, inanimate creatures, [the] most of so of any Indians I had seen."[18]

After the arrival of about two hundred Indians on December 13, the proceedings in council began two days later amid bitter cold weather. Aware that the various tribes present were quarreling among themselves, St. Clair deceitfully sought to intensify this discord by attempting to hold them accountable for actions of the Indian confederacy. Moreover, not content merely to manipulate people who obviously had become wards of the United States government, St. Clair proceeded to dupe and humble these destitute red men. It was even suggested at one point that, if war broke out, these "treaty" Indians might want to join with the regular troops or militia in chastising their red brethren.

When the crucial subject of the treaty was finally discussed (settlement of the boundary issue), the Indians were so intimidated and distraught that they could but plead for mercy, while tamely suggesting that the recent offer of the general Indian confederacy be accepted (that is, the so-called Ohio River boundary less the large tract that the confederacy had agreed to cede east of the Muskingum River).

Compassion for friendly Indians was obviously not to characterize St. Clair's treaty, however. Modified only by the governor's estimation of practical limitations, the imposition of American will was quickly and easily achieved. St. Clair announced that no changes from the American-dictated terms of the earlier Fort McIntosh treaty would be permitted.[19]

Thus on January 11, 1789, two separate federal treaties were laboriously concluded, one with the Iroquois and the other with the "Wyandots and more westerly tribes." The reason for this, St. Clair later told the president, "was a jealousy that subsisted between them, which I was not willing to lessen by appearing to consider them as one people."[20]

Speaking with suitably bombastic oratory, Arthur St. Clair belatedly brought to a close the anguished treaty of Fort Harmar by announcing that, although they had just signed a treaty of peace and friendship, many innocent Indians were likely to be attacked in the woods by whites who "cannot distinguish [among Indians]." Therefore, to avoid such incidents, he said these Indians should become spokesmen for the whites, "to oblige those [hostile] people to be at peace."[21] An American army officer who had observed most of the proceedings candidly remarked, "This was the last act of the farce."[22]

From start to finish, the treaty had required less than a month. The total cost of the treaty goods had been $3,000, which represented the "utmost possible economy," according to St. Clair's assessment. The results, reported the governor, were "as favorable . . . as could have been expected." "I am persuaded their general confederacy is entirely broken," he advised President Washington. "Indeed, it would not be very difficult . . . to set them at deadly variance." Since General Harmar concurred, saying that the treaty would have a "good tendency at last to divide the savages in their councils," the proceedings were regarded as of substantial consequence by the Washington administration, especially with regard to the embarrassment of Joseph Brant.[23]

In contrast to this unfounded American optimism were the grim views of the Indian confederacy. Meeting in general council later in 1789, the new leaders of the united tribes, the Shawnees, related how they had been en route to meet with the Americans to fix a permanent boundary when they were "disappointed" by St. Clair's ultimatum. Chiding some of the tribesmen present (the Senecas) for having attended the boycotted treaty, the Shawnees dismissed the Fort Harmar proceedings by saying "the lands belong to us all [the confederacy] equally, and it is not in the power of one or two nations to dispose of it." "We now declare," announced their spokesman, "that we mean to adhere strictly to the confederacy, by which only we can become a people of consequence. . . . We are united and must turn our faces to those encroachers."[24]

In fact, just how seriously the aborted general treaty was regarded by the Indian confederacy is revealed by the terse correspondence of Sir Guy Carleton, First Baron Dorchester, the British governor-general of Canada. Writing to Lord Sidney in June, 1789, Dorchester warned, "[The Indians] seem now to be determined to remove and prevent all American settlements northwest of the Ohio. They have dispatched war pipes to the different nations, and sent a large deputation from the Wabash and Miamis to Detroit to announce their determination for war, and demand a supply of ammunition."[25]

While it continued to be general Indian policy to oppose white encroachments at the negotiating level, no mutual consent was now necessary for any one tribe to strike the enemy.

Indeed, at the practical level the Wabash tribes, including the Shawnees, already were seriously committed to fighting the "Kentucky people," and in the spring of 1789 an unprecedented warfare of even greater scope and savagery was apparent. Violence, always a fact of life on the frontier, seemed to assume a new viciousness in the bloody aftermath of the Fort Harmar Treaty. Murders, scalpings, the stealing of horses and even of livestock, and the most dreaded fate of all, Indian captivity, were prevalent throughout the entire frontier. A tabulation of depredations in Kentucky for fewer than three months in mid-1789 revealed seventeen settlers killed, fifteen wounded, and five taken captive. Also, the previously inviolate "legal" settlements in the Ohio country suffered their initial losses. Among these were several prominent incidents; a Captain King was murdered in May, 1789, while attempting to establish a colony at Belpre; and five relocated settlers were massacred at Drunkard's Creek near present-day Marietta, Ohio.[26]

One unfortunate soldier from the garrison at Fort Knox was found horribly mutilated in mid-June, 1789, following a skirmish with Indians on the Wabash. The lieutenant who reported the incident observed that he had been "shot in two places with balls, and was scalped; had two arrows sticking in his body, his heart taken out, and his privates cut off."[27]

White captives, who often had been spared for use as slaves or as a bartering medium, increasingly were put to death. Horrible tortures, such as those endured by Charles Builderback in June, 1789, were ominously more frequent. Builderback, while attempting to round up some of his cattle grazing on the Indian side of the Ohio, was captured along with his wife by the Shawnees. Unfortunately, he was recognized by his captors as the man who had begun the infamous Moravian massacre in 1782. Builderback was then a militia captain and had drawn the dubious honor of executing the first lot of peaceful Christian Indians arbitrarily condemned to death by a vengeful Pennsylvania colonel. With the Indians lined up shoulder to shoulder and facing the wall of their mission prison, Builderback had systematically murdered thirteen Indians with a large cooper's mallet before his strength gave out. In all, ninety-six Christian Delawares—thirty-five men, twenty-seven women, and thirty-four boys—had been killed and scalped in perhaps the worst atrocity of the western fighting during the Revolutionary era.[28]

For Builderback, now a captive, there was swift retribution, once his identity became known. After separating him from his wife, the Indians horribly mutilated this "big Captain," apparently cutting off various organs before ending his misery with the blow of a tomahawk.[29]

The emotional drain on white pioneers who observed the aftermath of such tortures was enormous. In fact, it served as an effective psychological deterrent to many settlers, some of whom abandoned the country. The severe trauma of the Indian mutilations of prisoners perhaps can best be documented by the sufferings endured by one young white man, who was put to death in view of a fellow captive by the Shawnees. Having cut holes in the victim's cheeks, the Indians threaded a small cord through the wounds and fastened the thong to a sapling. Two Indians, each having heated a gun barrel red hot, seared his naked body, one driving the suffering victim in agony around the tree, where he was met by the other who prodded him back again. The onlooker said the friction of the cords on his torn cheeks and the burning agony of the heated gun barrels was torment indescribable. Yet it was only a beginning. Next they ripped the scalp from his head and applied flaming ashes and hot coals to the bare skull. Once the effect of this had diminished, they slit open his abdomen and separated one end of his bowels which they fastened to a tree. Applying red hot irons to his body, they forced him to move around the tree until all his intestines were drawn out. Still alive, the youth was next castrated by slicing off his penis and testicles. Helpless, a bloody,

76

lacerated hulk, by now nearly insensible to pain, the victim was finally killed by thrusting a red-hot gun barrel onto his chest until it burned through into the heart.[30]

Probably it was the knowledge of such tortures that compelled one forlorn Indian captive during the 1780's to carve on a large beech tree in modern-day Hocking County, Ohio, "This is the road to hell."[31]

By 1789, with so many emotionally charged participants, both red and white, actively conspiring to wreak vengeance on one another, there was ample opportunity for increased violence. In fact, the lingering malice of the whites in the Kentucky District precipitated another brutal and disastrously unfortunate raid into Indian country in midsummer, 1789. Again, the net result was a further embarrassment in federal-frontier relations. Major John Hardin, a prominent frontier leader and a veteran Revolutionary officer though not yet forty years of age, was selected to command this raiding party, which was organized in Kentucky late in July, 1789. Hardin's mission ostensibly was to interdict the Indian war parties from the Wabash region, which had been moderately successful of late in marauding the Kentucky settlements. With a volunteer force of 220 Kentuckians, Hardin marched for the Wea Towns on August 3. On August 9 his scouts discovered a hunting party of about twenty-two Shawnee men, women, and children, who were peacefully camped with fires kindled and their horses put out to pasture. When this news was received, the Kentuckians' vanguard impetuously rushed forward to attack, without waiting for orders. In a blundering, poorly conceived assault three Shawnee men, three squaws, a boy, and an infant were killed before the remainder escaped. Proceeding on to Vincennes, Hardin's raiders were soon strutting about the town displaying the grisly scalps of their victims, while the federal commandant seethed with rage.[32]

"It is very mortifying to see the authority of the United States so much insulted," wrote Major John Hamtramck, who was powerless to intervene, having only a small, sickly garrison. Moreover, as usual, the Kentucky timing had been most unfortunate. By considerable exertion Hamtramck had previously succeeded in convincing many of the Wabash tribes to suspend hostilities with the whites. Now he glumly foresaw that "this Kentucky affair will end everything." Unable to control his rage, the doughty major strongly denounced this "provocation" of the Indians, who he feared would not only require that Kentucky "pay for it" but also the village of Vincennes.[33]

The basic rationale of United States Indian policy was, of course, absurd, requiring as it did the pacification of the Indians at a time when the military generally were too weak to control either the Indians or the whites. The woeful inadequacy of federal influence in this situation was vividly portrayed by the many complaints of the Kentucky militia. Hard hit by a series of retaliatory Indian raids in the fall of 1789, and frustrated by the meager results of their own improvised forays into Indian country, many frontier leaders openly denounced the role of the federal government. "It is inexplicable to some why the Indians attack our frontiers with such fury, destroying all where they come," wrote a Kentucky official in 1789, "when at the same time we are told the Governor of the Western Territory made peace with the Northern Indians last winter. . . . Will not Congress adapt some effectual measures before long respecting Indian affairs?"[34] Observing that the Indians were very troublesome and the people dispirited, one Kentucky officer asserted, "It is impossible for them [Federal troops] to afford the smallest security to the people of Kentucky"; in fact, he said, they were "no security whatever."[35]

The course of subsequent affairs thus had become increasingly obvious by the autumn of 1789. Enormous pressure was building on the federal government to take physical control of the situation. Though Secretary of War Knox might assert, "The injuries and murders have been so reciprocal [between Kentuckians and Indians] that it would be a point of critical investigation to know on which side they have been the greatest," the ultimate recourse was never really in doubt. As surely as the frontier people had little inclination to differentiate between the so-called friendly and hostile Indians, most red men now were convinced that Americans were invariably treacherous and deceitful, be they Kentuckians or federal officials.[36]

With so little basis for a substantive dialog, because of the mutual lack of credibility, there remained but one obvious, bloody solution to the great conflict of the red and the white civilizations.

10

An Eagle Untethered

O N Thursday, April 30, 1789, George Washington, resplendent in "a full suit of dark brown cloth" and wearing "a steel hilted dress sword," stood on the balcony of Federal Hall in New York City and was inaugurated as the first president under the new Constitution of the United States. In his inaugural address Washington said: "The magnitude and difficulty of the trust to which the voice of my country [has] called me . . . overwhelm[s me] with despondence." Only a few days earlier he had stated his feelings were not unlike "those of a culprit who is going to the place of his execution; so unwilling am I . . . to quit a peaceful abode for an ocean of difficulties." One modern historian has well concluded that "Washington upon taking office was confronted by demands more complex and critical than were to be posed any incoming President until the day of Lincoln's inauguration."[1]

Among the most crucial of the new administration's problems was the inability of the federal government effectively to deal with the threat of a strong external force. For five years the American military establishment had languished in a weakened and impoverished state. Suspicious of any central-ized authority backed by a large standing army, the Confederation Congress had purposely created a weak federal military organization, which was in-tended solely to police the frontiers, garrison the British forts when they were surrendered, and guard the public stores. For the general defense in time of war, a well-regulated militia was regarded as the primary expedient. Even Secretary of War Knox concluded that "a small corps" of federal troops was sufficient, saying, "An energetic national militia is to be regarded as the capital security of a free republic, and not a standing army forming a distinct class in the community."[2]

Yet the utter impracticality of the Confederation's system of regulating the regular army was vividly demonstrated during the tenure of that govern-ment. By an act passed June 3, 1784, the Congress had allowed only the establishment of a single 700-man regiment furnished in entirety by four states (Pennsylvania, New Jersey, New York, and Connecticut). Further, Congress had exercised direct operational control of the army, requiring the secretary at war to carry out its instructions. Interstate quarreling over policy was frequent and was encouraged by the practice of political patronage, which allowed each state to appoint and promote its own officers in the federal corps. The pay of the troops was so low ($6.67 per month for a private, without subsistence or forage) that the legal quota of the First American Regiment was still unfilled in 1789. Army recruiting officers had resorted to

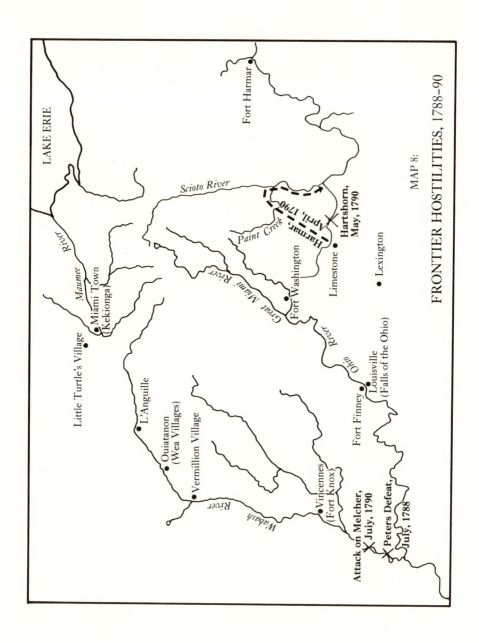

LAKE ERIE

Miami Town
(Kekionga)

Little Turtle's Village

Maumee River

L'Anguille

Ouiatanon
(Wea Villages)

Vermillion Village

Wabash River

Vincennes
(Fort Knox)

**Attack on Melcher,
July, 1790**

**Peters Defeat,
July, 1788**

Scioto River

Paint Creek

Great Miami River

Fort Washington

Harmar, April, 1790

**Hartshorn,
May, 1790**

Limestone

Lexington

Ohio River

Louisville
(Falls of the Ohio)

Fort Finney

Fort Harmar

MAP 8:

FRONTIER HOSTILITIES, 1788–90

80

enlisting drunks, drifters, and other undesirables from the city slums in order to fill the ranks. A congressional survey in 1788 found that the lure of food and warm clothing, in fact, was the greatest inducement to enlistment. This, of course, was an ample indication of the former civil status of the average soldier.[3]

It was no accident that the decline of public confidence in the Confederation government generally coincided with the demise in reputation of the federal army. Desertions, pillaging, poor morale (often created by a lack of provisions), and inefficiency were some of the many problems plaguing the military establishment in 1789. Yet the stronger system of government under the Constitution fortunately provided the basis for reform. The new Congress had created the War Department as one of the executive branches of the government on August 7, 1789. Under the new centralized system the president was empowered as commander in chief to appoint officers and to call forth the militia to execute the nation's laws, to suppress insurrection, and to repel invasion. Control of the army was vested directly in the executive branch, though Congress retained authority to determine the size and nature of the armed forces.[4]

Nonetheless, only about 672 men actually were in service in 1789, this being the pitiful force with which the power and authority of the United States was to be implemented in the Northwest Territory. Considering the complexity of the foreign and the domestic affairs upon which the stability of the entire government rested, there have been few occasions in American history when so much depended upon so few.[5]

The use of military force in resolving the national crisis had been contemplated by George Washington long before his inauguration. Yet Washington was beset by a variety of difficult circumstances requiring great caution and patience. As the president of a weak nation in a hostile world dominated by European powers, he was committed to peace and conciliation where possible. War, even on a limited scale, would impose unacceptable financial and political burdens upon the young nation.

Spain, concerned about American expansion westward, had refused to recognize the independence of the United States and had even laid claim to the Ohio valley, denying the legality of the British cession of 1783. Moreover, Spain still controlled two thirds of the western country, which it had received in the French cession of lands west of the Mississippi in 1763. Furthermore, it had arbitrarily closed the vital Mississippi River to American trade. Thus enormous pressure was brought to bear on the frontier settlements in Kentucky, for which the most practical outlet of western commerce was New Orleans via the Mississippi River. Agents of the Spanish government were already active among the frontier leaders, even employing bribery to bring about a separation of western settlements from the American alliance.[6]

Meanwhile, the English, angered by Spanish seizure of British ships off Vancouver Island, had threatened Spain with an immediate war and had served that nation with a strong ultimatum. Believing that a foreign war was likely, American officials warily anticipated that British troops marching down the Mississippi would perhaps capture Spanish New Orleans and thus reassert English control over the western territory. Even France, which had aided American independence, retained an active interest in the western lands, supporting Spain as the caretaker of the French colonial empire in North America.[7]

Equally serious was the prospect of American involvement in a foreign war. This danger was ever present because of the intrigues of frontier characters such as Dr. James O'Fallen, who threatened to lead a force of Kentucky volunteers to seize Spanish possessions. The status of the American military establishment was therefore of much consequence. The military, in fact, represented the only practical means to assert federal authority and to establish governmental credibility amid this maelstrom of foreign and domestic designs.[8]

Because of the "considerable alarm in the public mind," Washington resolved in June, 1790, that it would be necessary to punish "certain banditti of Indians from the northwest side of the Ohio." Yet the army that was to attempt this was so incapacitated by congressional neglect that, a year earlier, the brigadier-general commandant had written that he could not muster 300 or 400 rank and file. "In our present scattered state, miracles cannot be worked," was the way General Josiah Harmar had put it.[9]

Indeed, the post-Revolutionary history of the United States Army was a sad chronicle of frustration and impotence. From the very beginning in 1784, problems in discipline and sagging morale had weighed heavily on the army's capabilities. Boredom, insufficient rations, irregular pay, and severe discipline often caused soliders to flee the ranks, despite the threat of harsh punishment if they were caught. Terming desertion "the greatest crime," General Harmar even threatened at one point to cut off the ears of deserters.[10] Whippings of fifty to one hundred lashes on a bare back were frequent for minor offenses ranging from stealing musket balls to sleeping on duty, and the rigors of such discipline caused much disaffection. One sentinel at Fort McIntosh in 1785 was sentenced to receive one hundred lashes for allowing a theft to occur, that being the same penalty meted out to the thief who was caught.[11]

Moreover, supplies and equipment were frequently lacking. During 1788, Captain Jonathan Heart at Fort Franklin north of Pittsburgh had had his men cut off their coattails to use for patches on their threadbare uniforms. Then during the cold weather, with ice covering the river and preventing the receipt of supplies, the men had had to eat condemned flour in order to survive. So many had failed to reenlist in the spring of 1788 that the officer in charge had had to return to New England to recruit sufficient men to garrison the fort.[12]

Finally, with the reorganization of the central government in 1789, came the means to revitalize the bedraggled military establishment. On April 30, 1790, Congress enacted a new law expanding the authorized strength of the army to 1,216 rank and file. Yet the penny-wise congressmen at the same time attempted to effect substantial savings by reducing the soldiers' pay scale. The pay of a private, for example, was reduced from four dollars per month to two dollars, after deductions for clothing and hospital stores. Even the officers were subjected to a slight decrease. The immediate response within the regular ranks was one of outrage and demoralization. "Are you determined to break up the Army?" wrote a disgusted federal officer on learning of the pay reduction.[13]

The inconsistencies were, indeed, glaring. Having inherited a variety of logistical, materiel, man power, and morale liabilities, the United States Army in 1790 was being asked to resolve one of the nation's most difficult problems, pacification of the frontier by force. The enormity of the task was appalling, and the crucial element of time was fleeting.

Ironically, the mounting impetus to resort to arms had originated from an attempt to avert a military confrontation by one of the more moderate American officials, Secretary of War Henry Knox. Although Knox had opposed the initiation of widespread hostilities, as early as May, 1789, he had foreseen that some military action would be necessary in the West. Expressing his desire to establish a fort at the Miami Villages, "the next best position to the possession of the [ceded but not yielded] posts at Niagara and Detroit," Knox admitted that the undertaking would require a much greater force than the United States could field in 1789 because of economic considerations. Instead, less than a month later, Knox had recommended to Washington "a conciliatory system" by which progressive settlement would destroy the Indians' land base (and ultimately their cultures) while the United States pressed the British to surrender their ceded posts. These actions would "awe" the Wabash Indians while facilitating the establishment of a base of active operations, Knox said.[14]

Meanwhile that summer, Governor Arthur St. Clair, reporting in person to the president on the recently concluded Fort Harmar treaty, had asked for a major policy decision, in light of "the constant hostilities" between the Wabash Indians and the Kentuckians. St. Clair said at the time, "It is not expected, sir, that the Kentucky people will, or can, submit patiently to the cruelties and depredations of those savages; they are in the habit of retaliation." Estimating that the Kentuckians would march through federal territory to carry out these retaliations, St. Clair had predicted "The [Federal] government will be laid prostrate." He had then asked for formal congressional approval of his power, in the case of hostilities, to call upon the militia to act with regular troops in "carry[ing] war into the Indian settlements." This, he had advised, would "justify me in holding a [threatening] language to the Indians which might obviate the necessity of employing force against them."[15]

Thus, while Knox had sought some conciliation of the Indians in order to facilitate massive immigration of American settlers, St. Clair had stated that this was impractical because of hostilities that were already occurring. In fact, St. Clair said, the only way to deal effectively with the red men was to use military force.

President Washington had responded in September, 1789, by dumping the matter into the hands of Congress with the recommendation that "some temporary provision for calling forth the militia" be enacted. In doing so, Washington placed much confidence in the judgment of Arthur St. Clair, though Washington's policy had been and would be to avoid an Indian war "by all means" consistent with frontier security and national dignity. Congress, of course, had quickly passed on September 29, 1789, the requisite authority to utilize the militia for protection of the frontiers.[16]

Washington, however, remained reluctant to yield to the building pressures for overt action against the Indians. In a carefully prepared letter of instructions to St. Clair, who was about to proceed to the Illinois country to establish civil government and adjust land claims, Washington asked the governor to investigate whether the Wabash-region Indians "are most inclined for war or peace." St. Clair was to impress upon those natives the United States's "reasonable desire that there should be a cessation of hostilities as a prelude to a treaty." Only if the Indians should continue open hostilities, and if the president could not be advised in time, might St. Clair call up 1,000 Virginia and 500 Pennsylvania militia to act with the federal troops for "offensive or defensive" operations. Furthermore it was necessary that St. Clair and General Harmar agree "conjointly" on such action. Above all, Washington had said, it was to be the guiding principle of the governor's conduct that war with the Wabash Indians was to be avoided.[17]

So informed, St. Clair had departed in December, 1789, en route to Kaskaskia and Cahokia, where he planned to fulfill the civil portion of his mission. Arriving on January 2, 1790, at Fort Washington, near the Symmes settlement, St. Clair exercised his influence in renaming Losantiville as Cincinnati after the Society of the Cincinnati, of which the governor was an original member. Then, from the Falls of the Ohio, on January 8, St. Clair issued a "speech" to the Indian tribes on the Wabash, ostensibly in compliance with the Washington administration's request for a treaty with the hostiles. This document, however, actually was little more than an ultimatum consistent with St. Clair's intention to obtain a peace by using strong language that threatened military action. At one point the governor asserted, "I do now make you the offer of peace; accept it or reject it as you please."[18]

By thus reaffirming the mandate diplomacy that had long characterized American peace negotiations, St. Clair was shunting what Washington had intended as an earnest attempt to initiate a substantive dialog with the Wabash nations. In fact, St. Clair's underlying attitude seems to be characterized by an offhand remark that he made at this time about an attempt then being organized to negotiate with hostile southern tribes. Such, he said, would be "a wild goose chase."[19]

In dispatching these "propositions of peace" to the Wabash tribes, St. Clair, still painfully afflicted with the gout, saw fit to forward his speech by an intermediary, whom he anticipated would probably be a French trader from Vincennes.[20] Thus, despite the importance of this mission, with peace or war hanging in the balance, St. Clair chose to rely on indirect correspondence rather than personal negotiation and direct communication. Only when the Indians had assembled at Vincennes according to his instructions, would St. Clair consent to meet them.

Almost from the beginning there were unforeseen complications and delays in this Wabash initiative—ominous signs that it was to be an abortive effort. At Vincennes the post commandant, Major Hamtramck, decided to wait until the Indians returned from their winter hunts before relaying St. Clair's speech. Finally, in mid-March, 1790, a friendly French resident and justice of the peace, Pierre Gamelin, was dispatched with duplicate documents in French and English. He got no farther than the Vermillion Villages before he was insulted and his life threatened. Severely intimidated, Gamelin promptly returned to Vincennes. Yet Hamtramck, believing the Indians might have resented this particular interpreter, soon dispatched Gamelin's cousin Antoine, who was an Indian agent, trader, and local notable. Departing from Vincennes on April 5, Antoine Gamelin also ran into Indian opposition. Some Kickapoos fumed that St. Clair's words were menacing, particularly his peace ultimatum. This response caused the alarmed Gamelin to exclude that section in his translations thereafter. Proceeding from village to village, he finally arrived at the Miami Villages on April 23.

There Gamelin was told by Blue Jacket, a principal warrior of the Shawnees: "From all quarters we receive speeches from the Americans, and not one is alike. We suppose that they intend to deceive us." Accordingly, Blue Jacket said, no direct answer would be given until their British "father" at Detroit could be consulted. Also, many tribesmen felt that the United States's offer of peace was intended "to take away by degrees" the Indians' lands, and the new white settlements north of the Ohio River were cited in that regard. Therefore, unless the Americans respected Indian rights by clearing those lands, there never would be a proper peace.[21]

Thus the matter was concluded. Gamelin returned to Vincennes after about a month bearing nothing in the way of a positive answer. The negative response was immediately construed by the American officials to be so much Indian perfidy. Major Hamtramck promptly reported to General Harmar on May 16: "Those excuses [that the British must be consulted] are unfavorable omens, for they certainly are acquainted with each other's sentiments. I think that a war seems inevitable."[22]

St. Clair, who had journeyed to Kaskaskia and Cahokia and was bogged down in land claims among French residents (whom he termed "the most ignorant people in the world"), received the news of Gamelin's failure about June 1. Immediately upon reading Gamelin's journal and Hamtramck's dire assessment, he decided that "the utmost expedition was necessary" to organize a punitive expedition. Hastily he departed for Fort Washington on June 11, but because of the unfavorable level of the rivers his arrival was delayed until July 11.[23]

Subsequently, the gout-ridden St. Clair admitted that, because of mounting pressures and responsibilities, he was then "more plagued and vexed than ever I was in the same time in my life." Having brought Robert Elliot, the army contractor, up from the Falls of the Ohio, the governor sat down to confer with General Josiah Harmar on July 15, 1790. Both men were intent on "punishing" the Indians.[24]

Since March, Harmar had chafed under the constant depredations by Indians along the Ohio River. In fact, he had already seen fit to lead what was intended as an ambitious foray against the "nest of vagabond Indians who had infested the river . . . near the mouth of the Scioto." James Wilkinson, who was later to play a prominent part in the conquest of the Old Northwest, had written to Harmar suggesting that such an expedition "may perhaps give you a little eclat at these dull times." Harmar had readily agreed to the plan, and on April 15 he had sailed with 120 regular troops aboard barges from Fort Washington. After landing at Limestone (present-day Maysville, Kentucky), Harmar was joined by about 200 Kentucky militia under Brigadier General Charles Scott, with whom he agreed to sweep overland in the direction of the Scioto.[25]

Unfortunately for Harmar and the Kentuckians, that scheme had been virtually for naught. Beginning April 20, five days had been consumed reaching the Scioto, which is five miles above Painted Creek, and no fresh sign of Indians had been discovered. The militia then had begun clamoring to go home, and Harmar's bedraggled men had finally arrived at the mouth of the Scioto on the afternoon of April 27, with little to show for their two weeks' effort.[26]

Thereafter Harmar's attitude was increasingly belligerent and irascible. "The Indians have been and still are damned troublesome," he told one friend in June. "I am in full hopes that the new government will give me the materials to work with, and the next year be prepared for a general war with them."[27]

When Harmar met with the territorial governor on July 15, he was in ready agreement with St. Clair's proposal of an offensive campaign against the Shawnees and Miamis. The two principals, whose joint concurrence had been required by Washington for the initiation of any major military action, were, in fact, so anxious to effect a campaign during that season that immediate orders were issued for calling out the militia.[28]

The basic plan concocted by St. Clair and Harmar involved two separate thrusts. The primary column, consisting of about 1,200 Kentucky and Pennsylvania militia and about 300 federal regulars led by General Harmar, was to strike directly for the Miami Village (present-day Fort Wayne, Indiana) from Fort Washington. Meanwhile, a secondary column of about 400 Kentucky and Vincennes militia and 100 federal troops, commanded by Major John Hamtramck, would proceed from Vincennes to attack the Wea or Vermillion villages along the Wabash River, so as "to divert the attention of the Miamis to the quarter." In order that this diversion might succeed, Hamtramck's force was to move on September 25, preceding by about a week Harmar's advance.[29]

Although, less than a year before, St. Clair had petitioned President Washington for authority to "justify me in holding a language to the Indians which might obviate the necessity of employing force against them," he now opted for an offensive military campaign of limited preparation, a campaign that required the timely coordination of widely scattered and inexperienced forces as the basic premise of success. For a man who had been a major general in the Continental line during the Revolution and was originally trained as a British officer, this was indeed a rather dubious effort.[30]

Meanwhile, six hundred miles away in New York, a significant decision had been reached by the highest officials of the nation, entirely independent of the St. Clair–Harmar agreement.

For months backwoods merchants, citizens, and civil and military officials had been badgering Congress and the administration for federal action against Indian depredations along the frontier. George Washington's good friend Harry Innes, who was also the district judge for Kentucky, had convincingly branded the Indians as aggressors in his letter of July 7, 1790, to Secretary of War Knox. Innes claimed that, since his arrival in Kentucky in November, 1783, 1,500 persons had been killed or taken captive, and that "upwards of 20,000 horses" had been stolen, along with loss of merchandise and other personal property amounting "to at least £15,000." Innes warned that the frontier people, seeing no prospect of relief, were about to take matters into their own hands by raiding Indian villages in federal territory.[31]

Such a large volume of complaints had continued to pour in during the spring and early summer of 1790 that Secretary of War Knox had been moved to approach the president with the problem. On the basis of these Kentucky protests and letters from General Harmar, Knox obtained Washington's permission to attempt an offensive expedition. In his instructions to Harmar, dated June 7, the suddenly hawkish Knox ordered his senior military commander "to extirpate, utterly, if possible, the said [Indian] banditti." This, he said, was to be "a standing order," until accomplished.[32]

Admittedly, Knox's decision to order offensive action was partly political. He explained to the president that this thrust would not only "strike terror into the minds of the [hostile] Indians" but also would be "highly satisfactory to the people of the frontiers." Since Washington was well aware of the importance of retaining Kentucky's allegiance to the federal government, he made little objection to the scheme.[33]

What had started out in the spring of 1790 as a pacific overture to the Wabash-region Indians, by midsummer had become an armed crusade against a handful of marauding red men. That a general, large-scale offensive into Indian country in quest of "banditti" might be regarded by the Indian confederacy as aggression of the first magnitude, involving American desecration of Indian lands and rights, apparently was ignored by the federal planners. This promised to be a fatal oversight in the rapidly deteriorating Indian situation. The offensive was to change the course of American history.

Through all the post-Revolutionary mistakes in Indian diplomacy and interior affairs the American military had been the entity least involved. Yet suddenly the army was now being asked to save the situation, even though it was ill prepared to accomplish such a mission. Despite these circumstances Josiah Harmar had written in November, 1789, with considerable pride, "If the word *march*! is given by proper authority, a speedy movement shall be made against the savages." Such comments reflected the general frustration that had long prevailed among a corps of men who had endured political neglect and considerable abuse at the hands of hostile Indians without effective means of retaliation.[34]

The army's will to fight, in fact, was the one beneficial influence that sustained the pitiful corps in its approaching hour of crisis. The chance to retaliate had long been sought by army leaders, and a growing bitterness, occasioned by the long-standing defensive posture, was responsible for a certain eagerness that now pervaded the frontier posts. "I live in hopes to have ample revenge of them [the Indians] at some future period," Josiah Harmar had written in 1789.[35]

Moreover, several new embarrassments further intensified the smoldering anger of the soldiers even as plans were being made for an offensive campaign. For example, in July, 1790, Ensign Jacob Melcher, returning from Tennessee to Vincennes, was fired on while cruising along the Ohio, and three men in his party were killed. Fully convinced that warlike Indians were lurking everywhere, Melcher reported "the waters are fairly alive with savages."[36]

Thus, on the eve of the offensive, the army high command seethed with new resentment. Josiah Harmar even began avoiding the word *Indians* in his personal correspondence, referring to them instead as "merciless villains" and "treacherous . . . savages." By mid-1790 he had become so deeply committed to active operations that he had advised a friend in Philadelphia: "Affairs wear a gloomy aspect with the savages. I expect nothing else but a general war with them must take place." Arthur St. Clair also fueled the growing enmity by observing, "Every day, almost brings an account of some [Indian] murder or robbery." They "are now actually gone to war," he proclaimed, later adding that their conduct was an outrage to humanity and that, accordingly, they were to be humbled and chastised.[37]

Almost at the very time when St. Clair and Harmar were concluding their plans for an autumn offensive, a delegation of Potawatomi and Miami Indians arrived at Vincennes to discuss peace, in accordance with St. Clair's earlier speech—to which the tribes had agreed to respond later. Major Hamtramck fairly bristled with anger. The Indians, he said, had seen fit to pay no attention to St. Clair's peace offer in the spring; therefore the governor had returned to the Ohio Country. If the Indians really wanted to make peace, they must bring in all their prisoners. Then he might consider them to be sincere.

The delegation went away much dissatisfied, reported Hamtramck, who confided to General Harmar, "I would have deceived them [about the American war plans] by making peace with them but it could not be done without giving them goods—that I did not choose [to do]."[38]

Although the actual breach had been long in coming, the controversy would not now be denied. All of the bitterness, rancor, and enmity would thus spill forth, until the lifeblood of the native peoples was virtually drained.

Perhaps with fitting irony, Major Hamtramck now declared, "It certainly was high time that such a thing [war] take place."[39]

11

Forth into the Wilderness

JOSIAH Harmar seemed an unlikely choice to lead the most important military campaign since the Revolutionary War. An orphan at three months of age, he had been reared by a Quaker aunt and educated in a Society of Friends school. Yet the cosmopolitan influence of Philadelphia, and perhaps a natural quest for adventure, had influenced the rather straightlaced Harmar to enroll as a captain in the Pennsylvania line in 1775 at age twenty-two. Competent but unspectacular as a combat officer, Harmar had emerged from the Revolution as a brevet colonel, later becoming the private secretary of Thomas Mifflin, the president of Congress. In 1784, Pennsylvania had been allotted the largest quota of troops (260) for the new First American Regiment and thus was entitled to select the lieutenant colonel-commandant. Mifflin had arranged Harmar's appointment, much to his thirty-year-old protégé's surprise.[1]

Firm in his concept of discipline and order, Harmar remained urbane and refined in his personal tastes. After his marriage to comely Sarah Jenkins of Philadelphia in October, 1784, he and his bride had journeyed west to share the rigors of frontier duty. By 1789 such luxuries as two Windsor chairs and six Windsor side chairs were included among their furnishings, providing a curious contrast to their rough-hewn garrison abode. Harmar also imported casks of madeira wine, the "best" cognac, and lime juice from Philadelphia.[2]

If critical assessment were made of Josiah Harmar as commander of the frontier army in 1790, his considerable urbanity may have rendered him somewhat suspect as an Indian fighter. A brevet brigadier general at thirty-seven years of age, he was nonetheless a textbook soldier who carried the Prussian Baron von Steuben's manual of regulations (1779) with him during field operations. Although mass-encounter techniques had proved ineffective during the Revolution's Indian campaigns, Harmar continued to train his soldiers in formal methods, even requiring that artillery, with its cumbersome train, be readied for his upcoming Indian campaign.[3]

Almost from the beginning, Harmar had experienced difficulty in developing the logistics of the fall, 1790, offensive. The center of activity, and his base of operations, was the recently erected Fort Washington, which guarded the Symmes settlements at and near Cincinnati. Harmar had transferred his headquarters from Fort Harmar to this site in January, 1790, even before the new structure's completion. Built of hewn timber and of planks from dismantled Kentucky boats, the structure stood two stories high, and

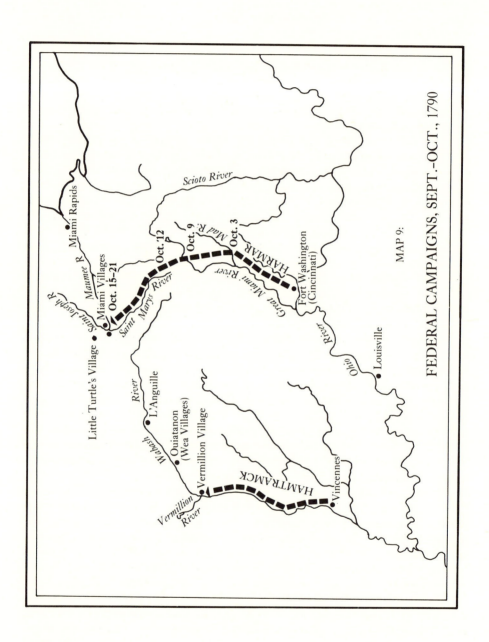

Little Turtle's Village •

Miami Rapids

Maumee R.

Saint Joseph R.

Miami Villages
Oct. 15-21

Saint Marys River

Oct. 12

Oct. 9

Mad R.

Scioto River

Oct. 3

HARMAR

Great Miami River

Fort Washington
(Cincinnati)

Wabash River

L'Anguille •

Ouiatanon
(Wea Villages) •

Vermillion Village •

Vermillion River

HAMTRAMCK

Vincennes •

Ohio River

Louisville •

MAP 9:

FEDERAL CAMPAIGNS, SEPT.-OCT., 1790

was fashioned in a square with four blockhouses at the angles. Harmar said he thought it proper "on account of its superior excellence" to name the fort after the president.[4] Yet, because of the fort's newness little military equipment and few provisions were available at the site. General Harmar complained in February, 1790, "We have been on the point of starvation here ever since my arrival."[5]

Harmar's difficulties with the army's system of contracting provisions, clothing, and minor equipment were long standing. One of his post commanders in the eastern region had been so angered by the private contractors in January, 1790, that he had reported, "Our situation is such that the contractors disregard our complaints: for this reason I am determined not to complain if I starve to death."[6]

St. Clair's distrust of one of the principal contractors for 1790, Robert Elliot of the firm of Elliot and Williams, had caused the governor to bring this supplier to the mid-July conference with General Harmar. Harmar, immediately upon the agreement to march, had charged Elliot with delivering 800 horses, 17 horse masters, 130 horse drivers, 1,200 bags of flour and corn, 200 felling axes, 200 spades, 350 knapsacks, and 350 haversacks, among other articles to be available upon demand. Elliot assured both officials that all would be provided except for the flour, which he believed would be impossible to get.[7]

As he had anticipated, Harmar by mid-August was fully involved in preparing even the most minute details of the campaign. Particularly vexing to the commander were the difficulties with many of the basic materials required. Major John Doughty at Fort Harmar, who had been instructed by his general to make cartridges for small arms, found he had no rifle powder. Instead, he proposed to utilize cannon powder for such arms, though it was too coarse. Even lead, to be cast into ball for small arms, was in short supply because of a recent allocation to the Chickasaws. Eventually, by improvisation, Doughty was able to manufacture "2100 dozen new musket cartridges with a bullet and three buckshot in each," providing the basic ammunition for the campaign.[8] Also, since cannon were desired on the campaign, "for use against houses into which they [Indians] may throw themselves for security," Major Doughty had two six-pounder cannon remounted and a five-and-one-half-inch howitzer prepared for field service.[9]

Harmar, who was obviously struggling in his attempt to gather the requisite munitions and supplies at Fort Washington, belatedly received the welcome information from Secretary of War Knox that two tons of the best musket and rifle powder was being forwarded. Furthermore, advances amounting to about $33,000, for "extra services" required in the quartermaster's and commissary departments, were said to be en route to the contractors.[10]

Many such details had of necessity been arranged by Governor St. Clair, who had journeyed to New York in August to confirm arrangements for the raid. Full approval had been given for the expedition by the administration, including authorization for enlargement of the primary strike force by militia units if the governor so desired.[11]

All but overlooked in the hastily projected campaign were the ramifications of any substantial increase in the size of the operation. Whereas Secretary Knox had advised the governor of Virginia on July 20 that 100 federal troops and 300 militia would be utilized to raid the Shawnee and Cherokee banditti, a month later an expedition five times the original size had been approved, and further increases at St. Clair's discretion were authorized. Since the nominal number of federal regulars available remained constant, any increase in the force of necessity would be drawn from the militia. In fact, ostensibly under the command of federal authorities, the militia already comprised about 80 percent of Harmar's force. Such reliance on that often-maligned and unpredictable force boded only ill consequences, according to many regular officers.[12]

Throughout the past decade the militia had become the butt of regular-army derision. Officers, such as Major Erkuries Beatty had grown so disdainful of the Kentucky militia that he had written disgustedly, "I don't know which is the worse, the Indians or the people of this country." Harmar's adjutant, Ebenezer Denny, found the civilian population of Vincennes so alienated by the antics of visiting Kentucky militia that, he said, "they viewed us [regulars] as belonging to another nation; [and] called us the real Americans."[13]

Perhaps General Harmar best expressed the prevailing opinion among the regular army when he wrote in 1788, "It is my wish that not a single officer of the regiment may ever have the mortifying disgrace of being subjected to militia command." Later he confided to a subordinate, "No person can hold a more contemptible opinion of the militia in general than I do."[14]

Still, Harmar was a reasonable man: he understood the practical limitations of his regular force. Effective militia performance was so essential to his mission that he adopted an almost conciliatory tone toward these military amateurs. "One mind" was the motto he professed to regulars and militia alike in appealing for the unity that he earnestly sought.[15]

Ordered forth from Virginia's Kentucky District, and from Pennsylvania, 1,500 militia were expected to assemble at Fort Washington and at Fort Steuben at the Falls of the Ohio by mid-September, 1790. Although Kentucky militia detachments began to arrive at Fort Washington in September as requested, a devastating surprise was in store for Harmar and his officers. Instead of experienced frontiersmen, the militia appeared to be mostly levies and substitutes totally unfamiliar with military life. "They appear to be raw and unused to the gun or woods," wrote a dismayed army officer.[16]

An ordnance officer observed that one militiaman carried a rifle without a lock and another displayed a weapon devoid of the stock. When the officer asked why they even bothered to bring such arms, they replied that they had been told in Kentucky that the federal government would repair their old arms at Fort Washington.[17]

While through the middle of September the Kentucky militia continued to pour in to Fort Washington, one regular officer estimated that two-thirds of them were filling the muster rolls in name only. "Their whole object seemed nothing more than to see the country without rendering any service whatever," he reported.[18]

As the overworked artificers worked diligently to repair the militia arms, Harmar awaited only the arrival of the last major segment of militia, the

Josiah Harmar, commander of the ill-fated United States Army campaign of 1790. From an etching of a painting by John Trumbull, courtesy of William Clements Library, University of Michigan.

Pennsylvania troops who were en route with Major Doughty's regulars from Fort Harmar, before initiating the advance.[19]

On September 22, 1790, Governor St. Clair arrived from New York, bringing word of the Pennsylvania militia's imminent arrival. Yet, as St. Clair warned, there was to be further disappointment. On their arrival on September 25, Harmar discovered that, instead of the 500 well-armed troops who had been sought, there were only about 300 Pennsylvania militia a great many of whom were "hardly able to bear arms—such as old, infirm men and young boys." Incredibly, the Pennsylvanians' arms were worse than the Kentuckians. Indeed, many men had no muskets at all. Major James Paul, their deputy commander, apologetically confided that many were substitutes who probably had never fired a gun. Most were so awkward, said Paul, that they could not remove their gun locks in order to oil them, nor did they even know how to affix flint in the jaws of the gun hammer.[20]

As if the necessity of arming and equipping these untrained soldiers was not a sufficient burden, quarreling erupted over seniority and the command structure in the militia. Ever the politician, though known to be a dubious fighter, Lieutenant Colonel James Trotter of Kentucky disputed the overall militia command with Colonel John Hardin, his apparent senior. So many of the Kentuckians demanded, officers among them, that Trotter should command or they would go home that General Harmar found it necessary to effect a compromise. By prolonged negotiation it was decided that Colonel Trotter would directly command the three battalions of Kentucky militia, and Lieutenant Colonel Christopher Truby would lead the one Pennsylvania battalion, while all four battalions would be under Colonel Hardin's jurisdiction. Although it was alleged that the militia matter was thus settled to their mutual satisfaction, a considerable enmity remained.[21]

So many varied pressures had already encumbered Harmar's attempts to organize the expedition that the detailed instructions brought by Governor St. Clair from New York did not unduly dishearten him. As was to be expected, the Washington administration was apprehensive of any failure and warned that the expedition was "not only of great importance in itself" but also involved "remote considerations." Accordingly, Harmar was to make rapid movements to "astonish" the enemy, yet be cautious and guard against surprise. Even the tactical utilization of small arms was decreed; the secretary of war advised Harmar that as many as possible of the rifle-armed militia were to be resupplied with smooth-bore muskets, as rifles "are certainly not good arms in a close fight."[22]

Perhaps most distressing was an astounding decision that had been made at the executive level, threatening the very security of the expedition. Because of the delicate international situation and the necessity of avoiding a war with Great Britain, Secretary of War Knox had instructed St. Clair in August to send a messenger notifying the British of the Indian offensive "at a proper time." He was to assure them that the United States was not preparing to march against the ceded posts but merely organizing a raid against the Indian "banditti." As if communicating news of the impending strike to the Indians' professed "father" were not risk enough, the peaceful Indians with whom St. Clair had treated were to be informed also.[23]

While at Marietta in mid-September, St. Clair had complied with this directive. His letter to Major Patrick Murray, presumed to be the British commandant at Detroit, expressed "assurance of the pacific disposition" of the United States toward Great Britain. Specifically, St. Clair stated, "the expedition about to be undertaken is not intended against [any British] post . . . , but is on foot with the sole design of humbling and chastising some of the savage tribes whose depredations are become intolerable." Having presented this "candid explanation," St. Clair then rather sheepishly asked the British not be betray this confidence or aid the hostiles in any way. Since the garrison at Fort Harmar could not spare a commissioned officer to deliver the message, St. Clair chose the son of a territorial official, who was also instructed to report on British activity at Detroit. Meanwhile, messages also were prepared to the more peaceful tribes (the Wyandots and the Senecas), announcing the punitive nature of the raid.[24]

When Washington later learned what had transpired, he was most displeased. Terming the warning to the British "unseasonable," the president, as an old military officer, regarded St. Clair's announcement as premature. Harmar too must have had grave reservations about the matter. Although his potential opposition initially had been estimated at "200 fighting men," St. Clair had already revised the estimate to "1,100 warriors" in the Wabash region, more than enough to cause serious concern. Warnings had already arrived from various outposts that the Indians had learned of the forthcoming raid. Thus a critical tactical aspect, the element of surprise was in jeopardy.[25]

Encumbered by burdens inherent and imposed, threatened by the approach of inclement weather for campaigning, and mindful of the dissension smoldering among the militia, Harmar initiated his army's advance on September 26, 1790. St. Clair reported that this decision had been prompted by the impatience of the militia—a clear indication of the loss of practical control by federal authorities. Accordingly, Harmar abandoned the prospect of adding other militia reinforcements who had been ordered from Kentucky to replace the missing quota from Pennsylvania.

On September 26, Colonel John Hardin was told to take all of the militia and advance twenty miles north, opening a road for the artillery and securing better feed for the oxen. Part of Hardin's troops moved off and camped four miles away that night in a pouring rain.[26]

Harmar, who elected to remain near Fort Washington until Tuesday, September 30, because of the rainy weather, about this time received perhaps the cruelest blow of all: notice that his character had been severely impugned at the highest levels. In a secret letter dispatched Spetember 3, 1790, Secretary of War Knox advised Harmar that it had been reported with some credibility that "you are too apt to indulge yourself to excess in a convivial glass." This report had reached Washington, said Knox, and there was considerable doubt about Harmar's "self-possession." Accordingly, Knox wanted the general to understand that the outcome of the expedition would be of much importance not only to the government but also to Harmar's career. "It will be the foundation of your future professional prospects," warned Knox. If the campaign should fail because of Harmar's drinking, Knox promised, the officer's reputation "would be blasted forever."[27]

It was a further burden that Harmar also had to endure a lengthy tirade from Arthur St. Clair, which included in the additional instructions some rather remarkable advice. St. Clair wrote that there was a "savage ferocity about the militia," and therefore it would be "unnecessary" and "perhaps improper" to restrain it.[28] The tenor of his letter was unmistakable: Harmar was to chastise the Indians and their French and English trader allies severely. "They should be made to smart" for their treachery, St. Clair put it. Vengeance, therefore, was to be a primary objective. The Indians' corn, expected to be hidden in the traders' houses, was to be destroyed; open plunder of the traders' merchandise by individuals was preferred over general confiscation; even Indian peace overtures were not to disrupt these punitive operations unless they were of a general nature and backed by the security of hostages. St. Clair further directed that these wanton depredations were to be made to look like acts unavoidable in "wars carried on against savages," so that the British would not perceive them to result from a national policy of retribution.[29]

Having received the last of the expected supplies, Harmar put his regular troops in motion at 11:00 A.M. on Thursday, September 30. The weather was fine, and the regulars covered seven miles in the wake of the militia, who had pushed ahead after constructing at least one small log causeway for the artillery. Although the country was at first said to be hilly and difficult for the artillery, the terrain soon became level and rather open. Harmar thus was able to march rapidly northeast along the old trace that had been used by George Rogers Clark in October, 1782, to raid the Shawnees at Old Chillicothe (modern-day Piqua, Ohio).[30]

By October 3 he had joined Colonel Hardin with the militia about thirty miles from Fort Washington, near modern-day Xenia, Ohio. The combined forces now numbered 1,453 men, including 1,133 militia organized into five battalions and two battalions of regular troops numbering 320. For security Harmar arranged his command into three columns on the march. Each flank component was to maintain about a forty-yard distance from the trace. Scouts proceeded ahead of the main column along the trace, followed in the rear by the ponderous procession of pack horses and cattle.

At each evening's bivouac a defensive square was formed to provide security. Baggage, horses, cattle, and stores were herded into the center, around which a line of sentries was stationed. Yet "due to the carelessness of the militia," who were supposed to hobble the horses but often did not, said a federal officer, many horses broke loose and strayed through the lines after dark in search of better forage. So many pack horses were lost that a federal major considered it a deliberate scheme on the part of the drivers to lose many of these emaciated animals, then collect an inflated indemnity along with daily pay for their services. Patrols finally had to be sent out at daylight each morning to round up as many of the strays as could be found, before the army moved away.[31]

The character of the army's march thus seemed more to resemble a herd of elephants trampling through the underbrush than the stealthy approach of a raiding column intent upon surprising their enemy, as earlier envisioned by Knox.

96

Yet as the army approached the Miami River (near modern-day Piqua, Ohio) on October 9, about ninety miles from Fort Washington, there had been no sign of surveillance by the Indians or their recent presence. Several riding horses had turned up missing on the morning of October 4 and supposedly had been stolen by Indians, but there was no proof of that.[32]

On October 10, after two days of rainy weather, Harmar's advance came to the "Big Miami," a meandering river about forty yards wide. Drawn up on the opposite shore was an abandoned Indian canoe. When the scouts investigated, they found the skin of a freshly killed bear cub cut up into small pieces and stuck on various stumps. Veteran Indian fighters immediately knew the chilling significance of this find. The Indians were not only watching the progress of Harmar's column closely, but had left a warning that many white scalps were in danger of being taken.[33] Harmar's adjutant tersely reported that a half pound of powder and one pound of lead were soon issued to each rifleman, and twenty-four buck-and-ball cartridges were allotted to each musket-armed infantryman.[34]

The army was now in a country of sprawling lakes, meandering streams, and dense undergrowth. Several abandoned traders' lodges were passed on October 11 and 12 near modern-day Saint Marys, Ohio. Then early in the morning of October 13 a patrol of horsemen on a routine search for stray packhorses encountered two Indians who evidently had been sent to spy on the American army. One made his escape into a swamp, but the other was ridden down and captured. The captive was said to be a Shawnee warrior about twenty years of age, and was soon brought into camp and closely interrogated. The Indians, said the prisoner, had anticipated making a stand before the Miami Villages, but had given that up and were making preparations to evacuate their villages and burn them.[35]

At a council of war later that day, Harmar determined to detach one of the mounted columns on the following morning and strike the Indians before they might get away. A French trader accompanying the expedition as a guide, who had lived at the "French Store" nearby, said it was little more than a half day's ride to the Miami Villages from that point. As most of the mounted troops were in the one battalion of Kentucky militia, Harmar planned to utilize a 600-man detachment under Colonel Hardin to carry out the mission. Only a small detail of about fifty regulars under Captain David Ziegler would be sent along to provide support.[36]

Once word of the raiding detachment spread through camp, excitement pervaded the ranks. Hardin reported that some of his officers were so eager to go along that they drew lots to choose the participants. Even among the plodding infantry, who would march behind as rapidly as possible, there was considerable excitement. The packhorses were tied up that night so that the army might start as rapidly as possible in the morning.[37]

The day of Thursday, October 14, dawned rainy and cold. Hardin, instead of marching at daylight, was unable to depart until 10:30 A.M., a mere half hour in front of the rest of the army. Although it was estimated that only about thirty-five miles remained to be traveled, Hardin's guides evidently got turned around in the underbrush and driving rain. When they camped that night, it was found they were only about four miles ahead of the main column.[38]

What had begun as a day of much promise thus had ended in frustration, and for more reasons than were then apparent. Unknown to Harmar, October 14 also had been a day of negative consequence about 150 miles to the southwest, where Major John Hamtramck's command of militia and regular troops had sought to divert the Indians' attention from Harmar's column.

Hamtramck had remained at Vincennes until September 30 because of the slowness of the militia, who failed to arrive until the twenty-ninth. Then he had marched north along the Wabash River with 330 men, only about fifty of whom were regulars from the Fort Knox garrison.[39]

Estimating that his red enemies in the vicinity of the Wabash numbered about 750, Hamtramck had reason to be somewhat intimidated even before beginning to march. His instructions were to raid Vermillion, L'Anguille, or the Wea Towns. Yet, since the specific site was left to his own discretion, Hamtramck had chosen the Vermillion village at the mouth of that river as his initial objective. Upon his arrival there on October 10, however, "nothing but empty houses" were found, the Indians having abandoned it completely.[40]

Hamtramck then anticipated moving on to the Wea Towns, but his command already was in such disarray that a serious controversy soon occurred. Although Hamtramck had not seen a hostile Indian on the march, his troops now threatened mutiny. Some of the militia had deserted while en route to the Vermillion village, and when news spread through camp of the proposed Wea raid, eleven more Kentuckians departed. Most of the remaining militia wanted to go home, giving the shortage of rations as an excuse.[41]

Hamtramck, who had recently been sick, had little confidence that he could keep the unruly militia with him, and he feared to use stern measures for fear of outright mutiny. Should he push on, Hamtramck anticipated "a severe drubbing" at the hands of the Indians, who were said to be lurking nearby. A courier dispatched to Vincennes came back after being chased by Indians.[42]

About October 14, Hamtramck broke camp for the return to Vincennes, worried that he had failed in his attempt to divert the Indians from Harmar's column. To add to his misery, the Indians managed to steal many horses during the return journey. On their arrival at Fort Knox about October 26, the troops were without meat or flour and were forced to live on corn and what little game the hunters could kill.[43]

Perhaps even more ominous were the events at British Detroit on and about October 14. Return J. Meigs, Jr., the young attorney who had been selected to deliver St. Clair's message of September 19 to the British, had arrived at that post during the second week in October after a harrowing journey. Threatening language and false reports of American defeats had greeted his arrival at almost every Indian village en route. Received at Detroit with great coolness, Meigs was given an answering letter by Major John Smith, the commandant, on October 14.[44]

Smith wrote that the military preparations by the Americans had caused no "uneasiness" at Detroit, nor had the Indians received any encouragement or assistance in committing depredations along the Ohio. Furthermore, Smith cited the recent return of about eight American citizens who had been captured by Indians and ransomed by British authorities as an example of England's peaceful demeanor.[45] (Included in this party of released prisoners was Charles Johnston, the attorney from Botetourt County, Virginia, whose ordeal is described in Chapter 9.)

This communication by Smith, of course, was intended as a deception. Certainly, the British were very deeply concerned about the Harmar expedition, and Major Smith immediately sent messages to the British traders at the Miami Villages, warning them of imminent danger. Messengers and observers were also quickly dispatched from Detroit to the Miami Towns in a flurry of activity during the second week in October. They were to report on the American expedition and aid and advise the Indians in their resistance to the greatest extent possible.[46]

Josiah Harmar, who optimistically reported "fine, clear weather" beginning on the afternoon of October 15, remained oblivious to the increasing difficulties that lay ahead. In obviously buoyant spirits, Harmar recorded on Saturday, October 16, the encouraging news he had just received by an express from Colonel Hardin with the advance detachment: "The savages have evacuated their favorite Miami Village and towns. . . . They have left . . . a great quantity of corn and vegetables behind."[47] Not far distant, an able Shawnee warrior reflected on the crisis that confronted his people. Blue Jacket, war chief of the Shawnees, said: "We as a people have made no war, but as a people we are determined to meet the approaches of an enemy, who come not to check the insolence of individuals, but as a premeditated design to root us out of our land. . . . We and our forefathers and our children were and are bound as men and Indians to defend [this land], which we are determined to do, satisfied we are acting in the cause of justice."[48]

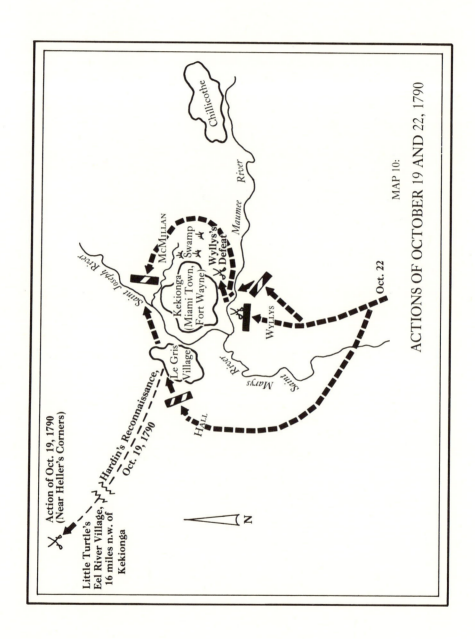

Chillicothe

Maumee River

McMillan

Swamp

Wyllys's Defeat

Kekionga (Miami Town, Fort Wayne)

Saint Joseph River

Wyllys

Le Gris Village

Hall

Saint Marys River

Oct. 22

Action of Oct. 19, 1790 (Near Heller's Corners)

Hardin's Reconnaissance, Oct. 19, 1790

Little Turtle's Eel River Village, 16 miles n.w. of Kekionga

N

MAP 10:

ACTIONS OF OCTOBER 19 AND 22, 1790

100

12

They Fought and Died Hard

KEKIONGA was perhaps the major strategic center of the western tribes in the Old Northwest. The Miami chief Little Turtle called it "that glorious gate through which all the good words of our chiefs had to pass." Known to the Americans and the English as the Miami Village, or the Miami Town, Kekionga served as the hub of six other nearby Indian villages. Its strategic location at the confluence of the Saint Marys and Saint Joseph rivers, which combine to form the Maumee, ensured its importance as a commercial entity even into the twentieth century, when the community became known as Fort Wayne, Indiana. At Kekionga the British had established one of their primary fur trading posts in the region, where a dozen or more traders vied for the peltry brought in by the Indians.[1]

Called by the Americans "that nest of villainy the Miami Village," Kekionga had long been eyed as the center of Indian hostilities. For years frontier officers had complained of depredations attributed to the Indians of the "Miami Towns." Senior American officials were so obsessed with the negative influence of the villages, that they had long contemplated erecting a fort at the Kekionga to "awe" the Indians and to present "a respectable appearance" to the British. Major Hamtramck at Vincennes readily foresaw the strategic implications of such a project. Recognizing the Miami Village as the vital communications link of the Northwest Territory, because it controlled the flow of traffic between the Wabash and the Lake Erie regions, Hamtramck stated that a Miami post was next best to possession of the British fortifications at Niagara and Detroit. Yet, because of the lack of troops to garrison and supply any fort "in the heart of Indian country," and the want of money to increase the regular army, Secretary of War Knox said that establishment of a Miami post was "not to be undertaken." Thus Harmar's offensive remained mostly tactical. His raiders would simply destroy the Miami Village, reducing the Indians to poverty, and thereby inhibit their ability and incentive to wage war.[2] Further, the British traders at Kekionga were to be harshly treated for aiding and abetting the red enemy. "It is the traders who are every day inducing the Indians to go to war; they [the Indians] return to their villages with plunder and horses, which the traders get of them for rum or a little nothing," complained an American officer in 1790.[3]

As Arthur St. Clair had anticipated, there was little point in attempting to restrain the Kentuckians from acts of retribution during the raid. Long anticipated and sought, massive vengeance was not only the frontiersmen's objective but also their virtual obsession.[4]

101

Kekionga, as a British businessman and official observed in the spring of 1790, was "a very pretty place" and also a community of some refinement. While he visited the Miami Villages for four months, John Hay, the twenty-four-year-old son of a former lieutenant governor of Detroit, found the town replete with charming women, strong religious traditions, and a minisociety that featured a grand ball and gala parties. Hay, a bachelor, found delight in playing the flute and singing to the accompaniment of a fiddle while the daughters and wives of the British traders smiled approvingly. One entry in his journal records a festive party where the traders and their women danced the minuet, and the men wore "very fine fur caps" decorated with black ostrich feathers and cockades made of white tinsel ribbon. Hay remarked that his feet were so swollen from performing the "Dance Ronby" that he had no inclination for further dancing. During another evening's celebration he got so "infernally drunk," along with two local traders, that he later discovered, "Mr. Abbott gave me his daughter Betsey over the bottle." Like many later-day miscreants, Hay awoke the following morning "damnation sick . . . in consequence of last night's debashe."[5]

Kekionga had its more serious moments, however, as Hay well observed. During his stay he found one Shawnee warrior displaying a rather unusual trophy on his bundle pack. Hay observed that "it was quite dry, like a piece of dried venison, with a small stick run from one end of it to the other." Upon inquiry Hay found the object to be a white man's heart taken from an American settler in Indian country.[6]

There were also frequent war dances, during which the Shawnees and others swung sticks to which white men's scalps were affixed. At the end of his visit Hay seemed thoroughly weary of Kekionga with its "rascally scrambling trade" and drunken sprees. "Everyone tries to get what he can, either by foul play or otherwise," he wrote in obvious disgust.[7]

To be sure, Kekionga was a surly and frequently a dangerous frontier community. Yet even the white prisoners and soldiers who came there found the village "beautifully situated" amid vast fields of corn, fruit trees, and "a few pretty good gardens." Hundreds of wigwams and log houses had been erected in the vicinity, mainly on the north section of land across the Maumee River. Directly opposite Kekionga, west of the Saint Joseph River, lay a smaller village of the Miami tribe. A large Shawnee village, called Chillicothe, stood two miles down the Maumee on the north shore.[8]

For nearly two months word of the impending American raid had circulated through Indian country, yet there remained considerable disarray in the Indian ranks. Advance intelligence, partially supplied through British informants at Sandusky on the Lake Erie shore, suggested that the Americans, about 3,000 strong, would soon attempt to establish posts at the Miami Town and the Miami Rapids (the British trading base on the Maumee near modern-day Toledo, Ohio). Because of the customary indecisiveness of the various Indian parties, plus the equivocation of a few Wyandots and Delawares who seemed "inclined to remain neutral," few defensive preparations had been made in the vicinity of the Miami Towns before mid-October. About all that had been accomplished was the manufacture of an added quantity of bows and arrows to compensate for the shortage in firearms.[9]

Finally, during the second week in October, news that a powerful American army was on the march toward the Miami Villages compelled the Indians to react. Recognizing that the warriors available from the Miami Towns were too few to confront Harmar's column, the Indian leaders sent runners throughout the Old Northwest asking for the assistance of other nations. Yet, as the British Indian agent at Detroit foresaw, the other tribes were much too dispersed to collect at the Miami Villages in the short time remaining.[10] Aware of the close proximity of Harmar's column, the Indian leadership was compelled to make a painful decision on October 13. Although one of the British traders said that it was astonishing to see the alacrity with which other Indians were assembling to help fight the Americans, only about six hundred warriors were present, not enough to defend Kekionga.[11]

With reluctance, on October 14 the Indian leaders ordered an evacuation of the Miami Towns, including Kekionga. The British and French traders were ordered to remove as much merchandise as possible, but the Indians confiscated all of the traders' powder and ball in the crisis. Also, the local cattle herd was slaughtered, to prevent its falling into American hands, and more than one thousand bushels of corn, recently harvested, were hidden in trenches beneath the Indians' log huts. Then, on the morning of October 15, when nearly everyone had left, the vast Indian village of Kekionga was fired to prevent it from sheltering the enemy.[12]

Thereafter, the Indians' initial plan, to attack the American rear guard and stampede their cattle during the night, had to be abandoned after the rapid approach of a mounted detachment of Kentucky soldiers. Although the rainy weather of the past few days had cleared, the prevailing mood among the stream of refugees and Indian dependents trudging toward the Miami Rapids on the afternoon of Friday, October 15, was as black as the pall of smoke that hung over the smoldering village of Kekionga.[13]

Colonel John Hardin's Kentucky militiamen had ridden hard on October 15, covering more than twenty miles of thick brush and swamp forest to reach their objective. About three o'clock that afternoon Hardin's riders splashed across the shallow waters of the Maumee and rode into Kekionga. Amid the still-smoldering log houses and wigwams was the unmistakable debris of a hasty evacuation. Gardens of vegetables, with vines of large pumpkins, lay untouched. A vast panoply of cornfields stretched as far as the eye could see along the Saint Joseph and the Maumee.[14]

Hardin's militia quickly dispersed through the abandoned town, rushing among the few log cabins still standing in search of plunder. A disgusted federal officer observed that all was chaos within a few minutes. Even the discovery of two Indians hiding under the riverbank across the Saint Joseph failed to halt the pillaging.[15]

When it was discovered that other Indian villages nearby were not so completely destroyed, the militia "ran from town to town in search of plunder, contrary to orders"—reported a regular-army captain. So many looters were wandering about, laden with all manner of trinkets and trophies, that another federal officer estimated that "one hundred and fifty warriors might have beat us off the ground."[16]

103

From the tenor of the dispatch that Hardin sent back to Harmar that afternoon, it was apparent there was much elation within the American ranks over this bloodless victory. Hardin was later praised for his "zeal and alacrity," though Harmar was very sorry "the villanous [British] traders" got away.[17]

On October 16, Harmar hastened his march with the main army, making about ten miles in fine, clear weather. The remaining seven miles were covered the following morning, and by one o'clock in the afternoon of October 17, Harmar's troops had joined with Hardin's detachment at Kekionga.

As had Hardin earlier, Harmar soon had great difficulty restraining the militia, en masse, from indiscriminate pillaging. Finally, he had to post general orders forbidding such unsoldierlike behavior, and he ordered the collecting of the "kettles and every other article already taken" so that a fair distribution might be made.[18]

The absence of the Indians had so emboldened the militia that parties of thirty and forty men were roaming the countryside, uprooting nearly every potential Indian cache. The self-serving quest for hidden treasure seemed to absorb nearly everyone, especially after six brass kettles were unearthed containing thirty-two silver dollars. Soon it was found that the Indians, in order to conceal their gathered corn, had dug holes about the village sites, filled them to capacity, and then replanted the bushes and shrubs earlier removed, to camouflage the locations. A regular army sergeant later recalled how he roamed through the hazel thickets poking aside the leaves and brush looking for "hidden treasure."[19]

General Harmar by now had become so assured that he contemplated marching on to the Wea Towns along the Wabash. He even ordered that a formal council be convened to consider this move. Indeed, the Indians had been unaccountably dormant in abandoning without resistance the Miami Towns, which had long served as their operational headquarters. Yet Indian dogs and a few stray cattle had wandered into the villages from the nearby woods, and this was taken as a positive sign that the Indians were close by. Perhaps, it was suggested, the Indians were badly demoralized.[20] Then, on the night of October 17, between fifty and one hundred packhorses and a few cavalry mounts were driven off by Indians. The loss of so many packhorses was severe, and all thoughts of advancing to the Wabash were promptly forgotten.[21]

Harmar already had decided to send out a reconnaissance detachment of 300 militia and federal troops on October 18, having learned from an old Frenchman who was found about the towns that the Indians were scattered in the woods. He said they were unable to fight the Americans because insufficient assistance had come from other tribes.[22] Although Colonel John Hardin of Kentucky had solicited the assignment, his rival, Lieutenant Colonel James Trotter, was named instead. Hardin said Trotter coveted the mission because he had been promised a command and wanted the glory.[23]

Trotter's reconnaissance in force was announced for the early morning of October 18. His orders were to take three day's provisions and uncover the enemy if possible. Since women's and children's moccasin tracks had been

Little Turtle, the brilliant Miami chieftain. Courtesy of Burton Historical Collection, Detroit Public Library.

discovered leading northwest toward "the Kickapoo towns," it was thought best to scout in that direction. Trotter put his forty-man detachment of light horse in the vanguard. They had proceeded only about one mile when a lone mounted Indian was discovered along the path. After a swift and overwhelming pursuit, this Indian was shot and killed. Then, as the pursuers were making their way back to the column, another mounted warrior was discovered, he being presumed to be a second vedette. As if on a sportive fox chase, the cavalry and even the mounted officers bolted forth to ride the second man down, leaving their waiting infantry without orders for nearly a half hour.[24]

Once this second Indian had been dispatched, Trotter decided to set up an ambuscade, believing perhaps that the recent firing would attract other Indians. The long wait proved fruitless, however. Then, when a stray Kentucky cavalryman galloped in, obviously frightened, Trotter learned that the man, who had been separated during the earlier Indian chase, had encountered fifty mounted warriors in the woods and had barely escaped with his life. Trotter than broke up the ambuscade and cautiously withdrew. For the next few hours he marched in various directions, ostensibly searching for the Indian war party. Finally, about sunset, the firing of a six-pounder cannon at Kekionga was interpreted by Lieutenant Colonel Trotter to mean his detachment was being called in. Accordingly, he turned about and marched for the army camps, arriving at dusk.[25]

Harmar that day had completed arrangements for the transfer of the army to nearby Chillicothe, a more convenient base of operations that would provide greater shelter. Trotter was said to be content with the two scalps that he had taken, but Harmar and, particularly, John Hardin were displeased. Word was already circulating among the militia and regulars that, if Trotter had proceeded farther along his original path that morning, he would have found the Indians' camp and defeated them. Hardin was especially chagrined at the meager results of the patrol, saying that the character of the militia had been impugned. Angrily he asked permission of Harmar to re-execute the same mission personally the following morning. Since the object of Trotter's reconnaissance, to uncover the enemy or their camps, had not been accomplished, Harmar agreed to Hardin's proposal.[26]

Hardin, anxious to redeem the reputation of his militia, departed from camp about 9:00 A.M. on October 19, passing northwest along the same trail that Trotter had taken earlier. Hardin, not being as popular with the men as Trotter was, had intended to take the same size detachment out with two day's rations, yet Harmar's adjutant observed that the militia moved off with great reluctance. When they were a few miles from camp, he estimated that about a third of the militia had deserted and returned to camp.[27]

In all, about 180 men marched with Hardin, thirty of whom were regular troops under Captain John Armstrong. Proceeding in fine October weather, Hardin's advance came to the site of a recently abandoned Indian camp, presumably that of the war party that had been reported in the woods the day before. Hardin now was about five miles from Kekionga, and he halted the column momentarily.[28]

A half hour later, Hardin's column abruptly moved off again, leaving behind a militia company under Captain William Faulkner, who were somehow forgotten in the rush to press forward. It appears that Major John Fontaine of the cavalry had ridden ahead with a few scouts while the column was halted and had discovered fresh sign of Indians. Fontaine said that they seemed to be retreating, and Hardin ordered an immediate pursuit.[29]

Hardin's anxiety quickened when three miles ahead they came upon two Indians on foot, obviously taken by surprise. Although these warriors threw off their packs and escaped into the underbrush, Hardin seemed confident that he would soon overtake the enemy. At this point it was remembered that Faulkner's company had been left behind. Major Fontaine with a few cavalry went back to bring them up.

Hardin's depleted column now was strung out in single file for nearly a half mile along the trail. Captain Armstrong, in the van with his regulars, reported that a gun had just been fired up front, possibly as an alarm signal. A few yards ahead he noticed tracks where a horse had moved down the trail and then had retreated. Hardin paid no attention. With obvious contempt, he said the Indians would not stand and fight. Impatient to get at the Indians, the colonel rode ahead, in the very forefront of the column.[30]

Ahead lay a small meadow bordered by heavy timber, with a swamp on one side. At the far end of this opening a fire had been kindled, and trinkets and other Indian property were scattered about. Hardin rode ahead with some of his cavalry, distracted by the fire and the plunder lying about. Soon the militia began to gather around the fire, eager to snatch up what they could.

At that instant the trap was sprung. Colonel John Hardin had incautiously approached the village of perhaps the most capable Indian leader then in the Old Northwest, Little Turtle of the Miamis. Although the still-absent Sauks and Foxes had forbidden the Miamis to attack the Americans without them, Little Turtle could not ignore the threat to his Eel River village, which was about sixteen miles northwest of Kekionga. The crafty chief had carefully hidden in the timber immediately beyond the fire, aided by not more than 150 warriors with muskets leveled.[31]

Their first fire, a rolling fusillade, came from the right, striking down several militiamen, including the son of General Charles Scott. In shock the militia and regulars recoiled to the left, only to take a point-blank volley from other Indians hidden in that direction.

All instantly became chaos. The rear of the column had not yet come up, and the militia bolted to the rear, Hardin among them. Many threw down their muskets without firing a shot. Captain Armstrong and the regulars attempted to form a line in the meadow, but so many militia broke through their ranks that this line was thrown into disorder.

Farther behind, the single-file column of militia infantry now refused to advance and support Armstrong's wavering line. Instead, they wildly ran from the field. Armstrong noticed that only nine militiamen remained with his thirty regulars. Although they had had a swaggering air of confidence only moments before, Hardin's militia detachment was already scattered in utter panic.[32]

The regulars, however, stood their ground, firing into the underbrush that surrounded them. Little Turtle, seeing the disorder among the soldiers, boldly ordered an immediate charge. Out of the underbrush poured the Miamis, with a few Shawnees and Potawatomis. The advance warriors brandished tomahwaks, and once the regulars had expended the single round of buck and ball from their ponderous Revolutionary War muskets, there was no time to reload. The soldiers stood the charge of their enemy with fixed bayonets. Amid the screaming, dying men and the swirling gun smoke, Armstrong saw his men bayonet the onrushing Indians. The fighting was soon hand to hand, and the hideous yells of the savages could be heard for nearly a mile. Armstrong saw one of his few remaining men fall, and realized that his command would soon be annihilated. Desperately, he sprinted through the smoke toward the adjacent swamp and plunged into a pond. Ensign Asa Hartshorne, the only other officer, ran into the nearby timber, attempting to escape. There he tripped over a log, behind which he quickly concealed himself. Thus Hartshorne avoided detection, though most of the scattered remnants of his regulars were chased down by the Indians and slaughtered.[33]

The contest was short but bloody. In a few minutes' fighting, twenty-two regulars and all but a few of the nine militiamen with Armstrong were slain. Armstrong, who lay hidden in the swamp for the three remaining hours of daylight, watched in horror as the Indians swarmed over the dead soldiers, shrieking and yelling as they scalped and plundered the torn bodies. With tears in his eyes Armstrong later recalled how his men had fought with their bayonets and sold their lives dearly while the "dastardly" militia had run away. "They fought and died hard," said Armstrong. It was perhaps a rather humble beginning for the modern United States Army, yet a proud combat tradition was rapidly emerging.[34]

A mile or so in the rear, along the same Indian trail that Hardin had used earlier, Major Fontaine and Faulkner's missing company trudged toward the sound of the fighting. Around a bend in the trail rode two cavalrymen, each with a badly wounded soldier behind the saddle. "For God's sake," they cried, "retreat. You will all be killed! There are Indians enough to eat you up."[35]

Moving cautiously ahead, the detachment, about seventy-five strong, passed a small creek. Once on the other side, they met a horde of badly frightened militia, who gasped that they were just ahead of the Indians, who could be heard yelling and firing nearby. Faulkner's troops "took to the trees," forming an irregular line across the trail. The militia quickly streamed past. Yet none but four mounted officers led by Colonel Hardin bothered to remain with the new line. A few Indians now came up, halting about ninety yards distant. With Faulkner's troops growing more anxious by the minute, Hardin and the others tarried until they were convinced no further stragglers would come in. Then they resumed their retreat.[36]

It was after dark when the bedraggled remnant of Hardin's patrol reached the new army camps at Chillicothe. Hardin was said to have broken down in tears when he related to General Harmar how the "cowardly behavior" of his militia had led to a complete defeat. Immediately Harmar ordered a six-pounder cannon fired at hour intervals throughout the night to guide the stragglers in. Then he began to count the casualties.[37]

To his chagrin, Harmar found that nearly three-quarters of the federal troops and about one hundred militia were missing, in addition to perhaps a hundred arms. Rumors of a great massacre by the Indians began to spread through the camp, creating panic among the militia. Harmar was so dumbfounded by the affair that he could not answer Hardin when that officer pleaded to go back to the battlefield with another detachment the following day.[38]

Harmar's bewilderment turned to outright rage the next morning when Captain Armstrong stumbled into camp with his account of the militia's cowardice. The irate Armstrong reported not only that the Indians had been less than one hundred strong but also that many were armed only with tomahawks. Never again would he willingly fight alongside or under the command of any militiamen, proclaimed Armstrong.[39] Without delay General Harmar published general orders announcing that, should there be a repetition of yesterday's "shameful cowardly conduct" by the militia, he would "order the artillery to fire on them."[40]

In a single, unaccountable turn Josiah Harmar had seen his prospects for an easy conquest of the Miami Villages dashed. Moreover, the recent fiasco had so demoralized the troops that he could put little confidence in his preponderantly militia army. Major Paul of the Pennsylvania militia said that he was sure that his men would not fight, and that, accordingly, Harmar should not put any faith in them. Even the subordinate officers were reporting widespread panic among the ranks, with signs of a potential revolt.[41]

On October 20, Harmar told Hardin that his request to return to the battlefield was denied. In fact, considering the mood of the army, Harmar feared that such a mission might do more harm than good. The sight of so many mangled bodies, he speculated, might further demoralize the troops. Moreover, since his objective was to destroy all of the Indian villages, Harmar believed that this should be accomplished before something happened to prevent it.

Beyond that, he had already decided to begin preparations to return to Fort Washington. His provisions were running low, and the loss of so many packhorses had crippled the army's transportation.[42]

Overnight, the entire complexion of Harmar's expedition had been altered. Where there had been an eager quest for vengeance and a reckless disdain for the enemy, now only a cold, uncertain fear prevailed.

The army began its task of widespread destruction in earnest on the morning of October 20. Five Indian villages, ranging in size from about twenty to sixty huts, were razed. Even Chillicothe, which had been occupied on October 19, was fired. Vast piles of corn, beans, pumpkins, and hay and fencing were consumed in the conflagration. When the work was completed, Harmar estimated that his men had destroyed or consumed twenty thousand bushels of corn, in ears. More satisfyingly, he was convinced that the "total destruction of the Maumee [Miami] towns" would break up the Indians' base of operations.[43]

During the day on October 20 several Indians had been observed lurking about. In one incident, several of Major Fontaine's horsemen had managed to approach undetected on the flank of two Shawnees who were watching

Harmar's raiders burn a village. After an exchange of shots, both Indians were killed, and the head of one, later identified as Big Shawnee Ben, was brought to camp. It appears that afterwards Fontaine's horsemen perpetrated a grisly prank. Since the Indian had been so intent on watching the village burn, the Kentuckians propped up his headless corpse and left him sitting across a log facing the ruins, in evident mockery of his curiosity. A few days later many Kentuckians would have cause to regret such atrocities.[44]

At dawn on Thursday, October 21, Josiah Harmar's general orders announced that the departure of the army from the Miami Towns was to begin at 10 o'clock that morning. "Having completely effected" their objective, said Harmar, the army could now return to Fort Washington. Yet his instructions for the march suggest a retreat from a demoralizing defeat. "It is not improbable . . . the savages will attempt to harass the army," he warned, threatening once more to turn the artillery on any troops who ran away.[45] Ebenezer Denny recorded that the army marched eight miles that day, finally making bivouac in beech and swamp oak land near where it had encamped on October 16.[46]

According to Colonel Hardin, who was still smarting over his defeat, he that day suggested to General Harmar the propriety of making a quick foray back to the Miami Villages to surprise any Indians who had returned to salvage buried provisions. Harmar was skeptical at first. Then, during the evening, several scouts, including the Indian expert Daniel Williams, came in and reported that about 120 Indians had returned to Kekionga several hours after the army's departure. Williams, who had watched from his hiding place until nearly dark, said that the Indians had seemed perfectly at ease and secure in their reoccupation of the village.[47]

Harmar admittedly was looking for some means to embarrass the red enemy, believing that the Indians would severely harass his retreat unless checked. Inwardly, he must also have been anxious to retaliate for the drubbing that his troops had taken on October 19. That night he wrote in his journal of his impromptu decision to send a strong detachment back to the ruined towns, "in hopes that [they] may fall in with some of the savages."[48]

Because of the fiasco on October 19, Harmar was at first determined to rely on his regular troops to conduct the mission—they would be steadfast, he said. Major John Palsgrave Wyllys of Connecticut, an officer experienced in the Revolution, would have command. Yet, because only about sixty regulars could be spared, it was quickly perceived that some militia would be needed. Ultimately, Harmar, Wyllys, and the solicitous Hardin agreed that four hundred men would go out, including three hundred of the best militia infantry, plus forty horsemen under Major Fontaine. This time Hardin would serve under Wyllys, while still exercising command of the militia. According to Daniel Williams's estimate, little more than a hundred Indians might be encountered, yet a federal officer reported that the morbid prospect of falling victim to a savage enemy already had some of the designated militia so frightened that a few of them had begun to cry.[49]

By Wyllys's order, the raiders were to assemble at midnight and immediately march for Kekionga. Yet it was about 2:00 A.M. before the column got underway.[50] Since the weather was mild, and the night clear with a bright moon, they proceeded without serious incident until they were within an estimated two miles of Kekionga. There Wyllys called a meeting of the senior officers to review his plans.

To trap the unsuspecting enemy amid the ruins, Wyllys ordered Major Horatio Hall to make a circuitous march westward across the Saint Marys River with about 150 Kentucky infantry. They would then angle back toward the east, enabling Hall to fall on the rear of Kekionga merely by crossing the shallow Saint Joseph River. Meanwhile, Major James McMillan with the remainder of the Kentucky infantry would circle Kekionga from the east, crossing the Maumee below the village to cut off escape in that direction. Only Major Wyllys, with his sixty regulars aided by Major Fontaine's forty cavalrymen, would strike directly for Kekionga, hoping to drive the Indians north into the waiting militia pincers. Nearly all agreed that this was a most viable plan calculated to surround the savages and inflict maximum punishment on them.[51]

After Hall's command, led in person by Colonel Hardin, was detached and en route, Wyllys with Fontaine's and McMillan's troops resumed the march north toward the Maumee. Streaks of light were visible on the horizon, and as the attack was to commence at daybreak, Wyllys hurried on, anxious to surprise the enemy.

Across the still-dark landscape, an estimated two hundred warriors and headmen of the Shawnees, Miamis, Ottawas, Sauks, and Delawares had begun to file from Kekionga along the main trail, passing noiselessly into the underbrush. Among the throng was a twenty-nine-year-old half-blood Miami, the son of a French trader, who was destined one day to become the principal chief of his nation. Like the rest of his tribesmen, Jean Baptiste Richardville was said to be elated with the prospect that lay ahead that morning. Despite the destruction of their Miami Village homes and a shortage of provisions and ammunition, the Indians were in high spirits. On October 20 they had held a general council, during which it had been decided to continue to fight the Americans. Should the red families need provisions, some newly arrived Sauks and Foxes urged that their enemies' bodies and horses would serve the purpose.[52]

During the night of October 21 the Indians had learned that the American Army, which that day had retreated into a swamp, had after nightfall sent a detachment back to the Miami Towns—to bury their three-day-old battlefield dead, it was supposed. This American design had been well scouted, for Indian spies had carefully watched the movements of Harmar's troops night and day. Although the rapid approach of the American detachment had not allowed sufficient notice to gather all of the warriors in the vicinity, enough were present to provide a formidable reception.

Again the Miamis would fight under Little Turtle, the mastermind of the Eel River action that had proved so successful on October 19. That skillful tactician had once more devised a simple but effective plan to fight the dread *shemanthe*—the Americans. It would begin with the favorite Indian stratagem, an ambuscade.[53]

Major John Palsgrave Wyllys, resplendent in his large Continental-style cocked hat, was a man of stern countenance. Once arrested for having three deserters shot without due process, Wyllys had an austere reputation as an officer. Certainly, he was a man to be reckoned with. That morning, the evidence suggests, he was seething with anger. As he had painstakingly elaborated to the militia commanders, Wyllys's plan to trap the Indians depended upon the simultaneous coordination of attacking columns. McMillan's right wing, which had the farthest to travel, had been designated to begin the attack at first light. Then both of the remaining segments were to press forward. Yet daylight had already filtered into the forests as Wyllys approached the main ford across the Maumee at Kekionga. Although the sun had not yet risen, Wyllys and his men could see across the river on the west where Hall's column was advancing.

Hall, it appears, when crossing the Saint Marys River, had discovered a lone Indian, apparently a scout, who had promptly fled. Immediately, some of Hall's militia had run after him, firing their guns as the warrior ran for higher ground. Before he had escaped, the Indian had whirled and returned their fire, striking a rifleman in the thigh.[54]

This noise evidently carried to Wyllys's troops just as they approached the Maumee ford, evoking the federal major's ire because of the premature discovery of his column. In the western sky the red glow of an autumn sunrise filled the horizon. Wyllys, who had been sickly much of the fall and seemed to have a premonition that "the last sad accident" would befall him, hurriedly pushed ahead.[55]

At the ford the banks of the Maumee were said to be about eighteen feet above the riverbed, which on this morning ran with "a fine, transparent stream" less than a foot deep. Wyllys's troops, with Major Fontaine's horse in the forefront, splashed into the shallow stream. About seventy yards distant the opposite riverbank lay couched in shadows. There was a mellow, almost vernal warmth to the air, suggestive of a fine Indian-summer day.[56]

Major Fontaine's horsemen reached midstream. Stretched out behind them, Wyllys's slow-moving column of infantry were just emerging from the forest.

Peering down the barrels of their flintlock muskets, many of which were American surcharged arms that they had picked up on the Eel River battlefield, a contingent of Little Turtle's Miami and Shawnee warriors lay concealed along the riverbank above and below the ford. No one was to fire until the Americans were fully exposed. Now their fingers tightened on the triggers.

Private John Smith of Fontaine's Kentucky cavalry looked up to see the opposite riverbank erupt in a sheet of flame. Horses and riders were struck down as if by some whirlwind force. A crossfire of musket balls and buckshot rent the air, as what had been a quiet river was suddenly a cauldron of yelling, cursing men and braying mounts.

The terror of that moment was never to be forgotten. Smith was struck and fell into the river. Yet the water was not deep enough even to cover the bodies. Prostrate mounts, some still thrashing, and dead and wounded cavalrymen littered the Maumee in such profusion that, Smith observed, the water ran dark with blood. An Indian eyewitness wrote that so many horses and cavalrymen had fallen "one upon the other" that the river was, indeed, strewn from bank to bank.[57]

Recovering from the awesome shock, Major Fontaine, who was miraculously unscathed, shouted for his men to charge and then spurred his horse "with the fury of a mad man" toward the hostile shore. Without faltering, Fontaine drew his brace of pistols and rode among the Indians, emptying his pistols in their faces. He then looked about as he drew his sword. Only one man, George Adams, had followed him across. "Stick to me," Fontaine cried, before Adams saw him slump in the saddle. Nearly a dozen Indians had fired at the two Kentuckians. Adams hastily swung his mount back into the river, escaping with five wounds. Fontaine was last seen draped over the neck of his horse, desperately wounded.[58]

Due to the confusion, Major Wyllys had been momentarily unable to organize an effective counterattack. His regulars were still coming up, and the Kentucky horses were badly scattered. During the impasse, Major McMillan arrived on the scene. He had gone farther to the east than Wyllys, where he was supposed to sweep across the Maumee, forming the easternmost pincers of the attack. Yet McMillan had swung back to the river immediately on hearing the firing. Coming up on Wyllys's right, McMillan was now beyond the flank of all but a few of the Indians who formed the easternmost portion of the ambuscade. Charging directly across the Maumee, McMillan's infantry easily gained the opposite shore under a moderate fire. Being outflanked, the Shawnees and Miamis promptly got up and ran from the weeds and bushes, taking a heavy volley from the Kentuckians as they dispersed.[59]

What next occurred was long to be remembered in the annals of the Indian fighting army. With the Indians scattering in obvious confusion, the Kentucky horse regained their composure and dashed after the routed red men. McMillan's troops joined in the chase too. Soon the wildly yelling Kentuckians could be heard pursuing the fleeing red enemy north, past Kekionga and a large morass that began a half mile north of that site and ran west into the Saint Joseph River.[60]

Major John Wyllys with his sixty regulars hastened to follow in the wake of the departed militia. Crossing the Maumee, they began to file past the ruins of Kekionga, visible in the distance. Here a large, desolate cornfield earlier razed by the American army sprawled around them.

Suddenly, a "hideous yell" shattered the air. Out of the adjacent underbrush poured the largest body of Indians yet seen in the vicinity of the Miami Towns.

Little Turtle not only had duped the American Army into chasing his river-deployed decoys, he also had caught an isolated segment in the open plain where there was little cover to mask their vulnerability.

Wyllys barely had swung his men into line to meet the onrushing enemy when Captain Joseph Asheton, posted on the right, sent word that another war party was streaming toward his exposed flank. Wyllys desperately attempted partially to change front in that direction. A portion of his men were scrambling toward a rising section of ground covered with hazel and low oak bushes when the original Indian line opened fire.[61]

The segment remaining with Wyllys now was enshrouded in smoke. The regulars stood their ground, firing point-blank into the oncoming warriors. There was a great volume of yelling and firing. Within a span of three minutes, said an eyewitness, the Indians were among Wyllys's men in the cornfield, fighting hand to hand. The regulars fought with their bayonets, having no time to reload their single-shot flintlock muskets. The Indians used tomahawks and spears, fighting with great fury.

Captain Asheton caught a glimpse of Wyllys sitting on the ground with his hand grasping his breast, surrounded by Indians. When a regular-army sergeant next saw Wyllys's large cocked hat being flaunted and worn by an Indian, they knew their commander's fate.[62]

Asheton and the others, fighting along the brush-strewn rising ground on the right, also were in immediate danger of being overrun. As best they could, they ducked from bush to bush, endeavoring to escape in the swirling smoke and confusion of the moment. Yet the Indians swarmed over their position, and, said Asheton, the federal troops "became an easy sacrifice."

Bitter over their lack of support and badly beaten, the few survivors scattered to escape capture, most fleeing in the direction that the militia had taken. In all, the brief action had come close to being a massacre. Ten regulars survived the fighting that day, after a casualty loss of 83 percent. A senior militia officer later observed that the debacle was to be compared with the old Blue Licks disaster.[63]

North of Kekionga, Major James McMillan had found little action beyond chasing the few scattered warriors remaining from the initial encounter. Hearing heavy firing back in the direction of the main ford, McMillan soon reformed his Kentuckians and started south. They had gone but a short distance when they met the few survivors of Wyllys's command. A portion of the Indians were observed close behind, and McMillan rushed into position beyond a narrow creek. Evidently the number of militia at this point out-numbered the pursuing Indians. When some red warriors tried to force their way across the creek, they were met by hand-to-hand fighting, with the regulars in the forefront. A militia officer said that the fighting here was "helter skelter." The line momentarily receded, then surged forward again.[64]

Although the Indians fought with desperation, they were driven toward a bend in the Saint Joseph River, across which Hall was seen to be approaching. Down the banks of the river plunged the Indians, with a mixed assortment of regulars and Kentuckians in close pursuit. The Saint Joseph here was extremely shallow; one Kentuckian said it was five inches deep, and the banks about twenty feet apart.[65]

One of Hall's men, approaching from the west, saw a desperately resisting Indian tomahawk a regular at the river's edge. Raising his rifle, he brought the warrior down with a single shot. Caught between the two rapidly closing militia detachments, the Indians already had begun to scatter in confusion. A regular observed with much satisfaction several of his comrades driving their bayonets into the hapless Indians as if they were "gigging" fish. Later Sergeant David Morris recounted the story of an old Indian who had been trapped in midstream, apparently with two of his sons. The youths were hit first, and the old Indian dropped his gun and dragged them one at a time from the stream. "He drew them both to shore, sat down fearlessly between them, and was himself instantly killed," wrote Morris.[66]

In a few minutes the firing slackened, then sputtered to a halt. Although the evidence is conflicting on this point, it was said that those Indians who had escaped from the river cut their way through Hall's men, throwing a portion of that line into confusion. Within a few minutes the last of the red men vanished into the underbrush.[67]

It was as yet only midmorning when the survivors looked about them. One militiaman estimated that the fought-over ground was littered with forty dead Indians. Later the Indian body count was upped to one hundred killed. Ultimately it reached "about 200" in St. Clair's correspondence.[68]

In intensity the fighting had been quite serious. Hall's, McMillan's, and Fontaine's Kentuckians were found to have lost about sixty-eight men missing and presumed killed and twenty-eight wounded, which represented a 27 percent casualty rate. Too battered and bloodied to consider other action, the Kentucky militia and regular remnant withdrew to the Kekionga ruins, leaving their slain where they had fallen. There they discharged, cleaned, and reloaded their muskets and rifles, occupying about half an hour before beginning their retreat toward Harmar's distant encampment.[69]

Thereafter about a dozen Indians hovered about the flanks of the departing column, occasionally sniping at the retreating soldiers. The dire nature of the withdrawal was amply revealed by the loss of a wounded federal lieutenant, Ebenezer Frothingham, who was left sitting beside the riverbank, deathly pale, saying that he was mortally wounded and could go no farther. Indeed, within a mile or so along the southward trail, the retreating column had broken up into fragments, and squads of men began pressing forward in mounting disorder.[70]

At eleven o'clock that morning a bloodied and badly frightened Kentucky cavalryman, one of Fontaine's men, reached Harmar's encampment. He had been in the fight at the ford, he said, where Wyllys's regulars had been cut off and badly mauled. Although Harmar wasted little time before sending out reinforcements, it was decidedly a half-hearted effort. Major James Ray of the Kentucky militia was told to gather what men he could and advance to meet Wyllys's survivors. He was able to persuade only about thirty men to go, and ultimately they marched only several miles before meeting Colonel Hardin with his retreating column. Hardin told Ray that his troops, in fact, had worsted the Indians, and he asked the major merely to wait until the remainder of the militia came up and then to withdraw to camp.[71]

At the army's main bivouac Hardin found Harmar and immediately related an exaggerated account of the fighting. Hardin left the impression that the detachment had performed wonders that day and the militia had fought and behaved "charmingly." Harmar, from this account, thought "the savages [had] never received such a stroke before." The Great Kanawha victory over the Shawnees in 1774 was said to be a farce in comparison to this day's work.[72]

Yet the regulars in camp had noticed the considerable disorder among the returning militia, and they began to express growing skepticism. One regular officer observed that the militia had not lost so many men as the regulars.

Another, a federal ensign, said that he had heard both the Kentucky officers and men say that ten federal regiments should not keep them in this country; that they were determined to go home. So panic-stricken were these returning militia that they appeared to be nearly in revolt. Ebenezer Denny, the army's adjutant, was convinced that, if the enemy made an attack upon their camp that evening, the militia were so terrorized that few of them would stand. Thus the entire army would have been stampeded.[73]

Again the chilling rumor of a great slaughter of federal regulars by the Indians spread through camp. Even General Harmar conceded that the detachment had been "terribly cut up." Adjutant Denny, commenting on the probable number of militia deserters and their "ungovernable disposition," blamed Hardin's men for the want of better results.[74]

That evening, as the wasted stragglers continued to pour into camp, Harmar's "After Orders" were as follows:

The General is exceedingly pleased with the behavior of the militia in the action of this morning. They have laid very many of the enemy dead upon the spot. Although our loss is great, still it is inconsiderable in comparison of the slaughter made amongst the savages. Every account agrees that upwards of 100 warriors fell in the battle; it is not more than man for man, and we can afford them two for one. The resolution and firm determined conduct of the militia this morning has effectually retrieved their character, in the opinion of the General. He now knows that they can and will fight. . . .

The general begs Colonel Hardin . . . . Together with the officers and privates of the militia . . . to accept his thanks for the bravery displayed by them on this occasion.[75]

At that very time, on the battlefield near Kekionga, Private John Smith of the Kentucky cavalry was able to crawl out of hiding and painfully make his way away from the horrid scene. Smith, too badly wounded to escape during daylight, had lain near the riverbank in the tall reeds until evening. Although he was exceedingly thirsty, the waters of the Maumee were so dark with the blood of his comrades that he would not drink them.

In the afternoon Smith had heard the Indians approach the river and strip and scalp the dead. They were highly exultant, Smith noted, and their excited shrieks and yells "sounded like the chattering of a parcel of black birds."

Smith, and the other battle-wise participants who had borne the brunt of fighting that day, found little cause to rejoice in the aftermath. They were well convinced that the affair had been, indeed, "a complete rout" of the Americans.[76]

13

The Miami Moon

THE evening of October 22, 1790, remained balmy, a continuation of the fine Indian-summer weather that had prevailed during the previous three days. In the camp of the elated Indians three surviving American prisoners who had been taken that day were closely interrogated by their captors. Sullen and despondent in defeat, these men evidently were so badly frightened that they provided generally accurate military information to their enemies. The American army consisted of no more than 1,500 men, they said, and was endeavoring to effect a retreat to rejoin Governor St. Clair with only seven days' provisions left. The flower of their army had been slain, they acknowledged; and they corroborated the account of two prisoners taken in the fight of October 19 (who had since been put to death) that the Americans contemplated the establishment of an American fort at Kekionga, from which an attempt on Detroit would be made the following spring.[1]

Wearying of their prattle, the Indians executed these prisoners in retribution for the curel desecration of Indian victims earlier in the campaign.[2] Yet the importance of the additional information was quickly perceived by the Indian leaders. Blue Jacket and other principal warriors now urged an attack on the dispirited American column before it could escape. Seven hundred Indians were available for the purpose, they advised—a formidable body. In the next few hours a plan was formulated and agreed upon, requiring that the Indians merely await further movements by the Americans from their bivouac. Then the united tribesmen would attack and separate an advanced segment, who they anticipated might be stampeded through the remainder. This perhaps would lead to the complete dispersal of the column.

Messengers were sent that night to the British trading post at Grand Glaize, urging all Indians who had gone there for provisions to return immediately to the Miami Towns. The next action was expected to be "decisive," the messengers asserted.[3]

As the evening progressed the sky remained clear, and the full moon, visible in autumn splendor, shrouded the landscape in an ethereal light. Yet about seven o'clock there was a seemingly ominous event. The sky suddenly darkened, and an obliterating shadow crept across the face of the moon. It was a lunar eclipse, lasting for nearly two hours, the first such occurrence in many months. To the onlooking superstitious Indians, it was an awesome happening. The Ottawas, in particular, were greatly affected by it. Their conjurers interpreted the eclipse to be of negative import; if another action took place, they warned, the Ottawas would lose great numbers of warriors.

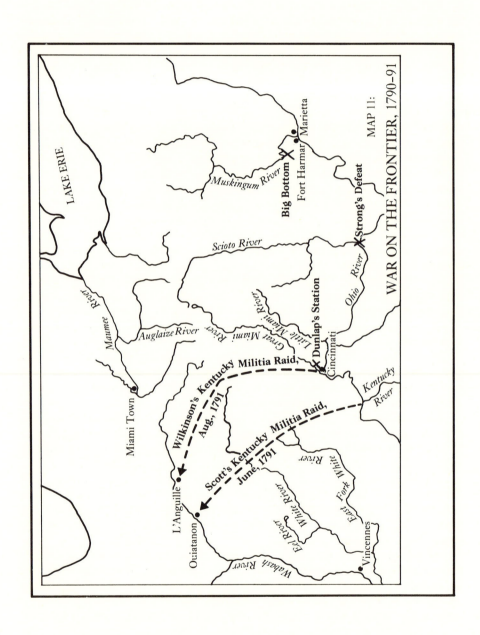

MAP 11: WAR ON THE FRONTIER, 1790–91

118

That night the entire tribe abruptly withdrew from camp without consulting the other nations. Amid a growing consternation within the remaining tribes, other factions began packing their belongings and leaving the encampment. Rumor and contagious example had so decimated the Indian ranks by daylight that Blue Jacket said only a few Shawnees and Miamis were present to carry out the plan, aborting the entire operation. "We were obliged to suffer the Americans to retreat without further molestation," reported Blue Jacket with some bitterness a few days later. Noting that the Americans were known to be retreating "in great confusion," he implied that, if the Indians had attacked in concert, a total and decisive victory would have resulted.[4]

Ironically, Blue Jacket's opinion was shared by those who were in perhaps the best position to estimate the postcombat status of Harmar's army. Adjutant Denny later testified that, "had the enemy made an attack . . . that evening, or the morning following, the militia were so panic struck that very few of them would have stood; the consequences that would have happened stared every person with horror; the sick and wounded, and all the stores, artillery, etc. would have fallen, a prey to the savages."[5] Indeed, on the night of October 22, Harmar consolidated his lines, drawing his men into a more compact formation in case the Indians, though "sorely galled," might "hover about our encampment."

On the following morning, with the march scheduled to resume at eight o'clock, Harmar proceeded with the forward elements of his army, until he learned somewhat later that sufficient litters for all the wounded had not been made. Colonel John Hardin with the rear guard, meanwhile, remained in camp until 10:00 A.M., when his column was finally ready to march. Thus, purely by chance, Harmar strung out his army, providing the Indians with the ideal opportunity to execute their avowed plan. Yet, because the moon had mysteriously darkened only hours earlier the Indians' opportunity to achieve an enormous victory had all but vanished.[6]

Harmar's column, nonetheless, was confronted by serious difficulty in their attempt to regain Fort Washington. Like some ponderous pilgrimage, the march proceeded very slowly, in part because they had to carry much of the baggage by backpack due to the loss of so many horses.[7]

By Monday, October 25, the warm days had been superseded by what Harmar termed "cold, disagreeable weather." A driving rain turned to snow that night, and though provisions were plentiful, the horses had to be fed with flour to keep them going.[8] Thereafter the troops plodded homeward in often rainy and bleak weather.

At one point Harmar had to order the federal troops to parade with fixed bayonets to quell a threatened mutiny by the militia. When the dispirited army marched into Fort Washington on November 3, it was on the verge of being ungovernable. Harmar had already been talked out of taking action against the insubordinate militia officers for fear it might break up the army and inhibit future operations. In fact, he was persuaded by Hardin to issue complimentary orders discharging the militia with "honor and reputation."[9]

Still, nothing could hide the deepening enmity between the militia and the regular military establishment. Adjutant Denny summarized the festering bitterness, recounting what "an arduous task [it had been] to keep the militia in order or within reasonable bounds at any time."[10] For their part, many of the militiamen complained of the "dreadful slaughter" of their friends and associates in the "unfortunate" federal campaign. Harmar was singled out for specific criticism because he had abandoned the wounded and dead on the battlefield and had not personally taken part in the fighting. Rumors that he drank excessively, so much that he was incapacitated in critical situations, were widely circulated. Almost before the forwarding of Harmar's preliminary dispatches, it was apparent that controversy and great indignation would prevail in the aftermath of his initial federal campaign.[11]

The country at large had first learned of the army's several encounters with hostile Indians after the arrival of a special messenger detachment from Harmar's army at Fort Washington about October 29. Although the detachment had been waylaid and scattered by a war party near modern Piqua, Ohio, the first three men to arrive said that five of the Indian villages had been destroyed, with as many as 200 warriors killed. Federal casualties were reported as "considerable," however.[11]

St. Clair immediately forwarded this information to Secretary of War Knox and proclaimed Harmar's expedition an entire success. Yet the news of a severe American defeat preceded Harmar's actual return, most likely via militia deserters. A petition from representatives of seven Virginia counties was forwarded to the governor of that state early in November asking for additional means of defense in light of the recent disaster. "The Indians, flushed with victory, will doubtless fall on our frontier as soon as the weather permits," it said.

While Harmar was busy writing his official report, in which he asserted "the headquarters of inequity [Kekionga] were broken up," a floodtide of resentment was building among the western populace.[13] One civilian immigrant at Muskingum observed sagaciously that "the prospects of peace on our frontier seems to me to be vanished for the present." Also he noted that in the "total defeat" of Harmar's troops the Indians had acquired important supplies, including 200 to 300 small arms, 400 packhorses, and all of the clothing and equipment of the slain.[14]

At the Symmes settlement (Cincinnati), John Cleves Symmes listened to the accounts of the returning soldiers and concluded that the campaign would have a drastic negative influence on the further settlement of his western lands. "But for the repulse of our army," he said, "I should have had several new stations advanced further into the purchase by next spring, but I now shall be very happy if we are able to maintain the three advanced stations [Dunlap's, Ludlow's, and Covalt's]. The settlers at them are very much alarmed at their situation. . . . Moreover, I expect that the panic running through this country will reach Jersey and deter many prospective settlers."[15]

Symmes's choice of the word "panic" was ironic, for the man who was soon to bear the brunt of the gathering storm in the aftermath of the federal raid seemed oblivious of the widespread disaffection at first. Josiah Harmar repeatedly talked of the great stroke that the Indians had been dealt, and he had begun contemplating further offensive action. Then on November 20 he received a candid letter from James Wilkinson in Kentucky, who asked for the general's version of the campaign, "to enable me to do you justice, and to stem the current of prejudice poured forth against you from almost all quarters in this country."[16] Indeed, as Secretary of War Knox had warned in September, Harmar was soon to learn that his entire career was in jeopardy. Knox's letter of January 31, 1791, revealed the extent of the administration's disenchantment with their 37-year-old commandant:

The general impression upon the result of the late expedition is that it has been unsuccessful; that it will not induce the Indians to peace, but on the contrary encourage them to a continuance of hostilities, and that, therefore, another and more efficient expedition must be undertaken. It would be deficiency of candor on my part were I to say your conduct is approved by the President of the United States, or the public. The motives which induced you to make the detachments on the 14th, 19th, and 21st of October last, and without supporting them . . . , require to be explained. . . . I further suggest to your consideration . . . to request the President of the United States to direct a court of inquiry, to investigate your conduct in the late expedition.

Harmar's shock, at what some of his officers later termed "cruel treatment" resulting from militia-inspired "falsehoods," was obvious. Although he later vigorously defended his conduct and complained to Colonel Hardin that, "instead of . . . censure, we merit applause," the youthful general's fate had long since been sealed.[17] George Washington, responding to a preliminary report from Secretary Knox, bitterly denounced Harmar as early as November 16. Citing his experience that "the report of bad news is rarely without foundation," and his forebodings of "a disgraceful termination under the conduct of Brigadier General Harmar," Washington virtually mandated the Pennsylvania officer's removal as field commander by his pointed remarks. The president wrote: "I expected little from the moment I heard he was a drunkard. . . . And I gave up all hope of success as soon as I heard that there were disputes with him about command. . . . My mind . . . is prepared for the worst;—that is—for expense without honor or profit."[18]

Washington, it appears, had already decided to replace Harmar with Arthur St. Clair, who with political acumen had hastened up the Ohio River to Philadelphia on November 8. St. Clair's postcampaign assessment of the status of the frontier was essentially optimistic, yet couched in ambiguous and often evasive rhetoric. After his arrival at the seat of government, a series of private conferences with the administration during December resulted in the acceptance of many of St. Clair's hypotheses for future actions on the frontier.[19]

In mid-March, 1791, Secretary of War Knox informed Harmar that Arthur St. Clair had been appointed and confirmed as major general commanding. Another of Harmar's informants suggested that Richard Butler would be made a brigadier general and second-in-command. Subsequently, the distraught Pennsylvanian refused to take any further active role. "General Harmar seems determined to quit the service," wrote Adjutant Denny upon his return to Fort Washington, "[He] has positively refused going on the [forthcoming] campaign, and takes no command."[20]

Although his friends urged him to remain in the service, Harmar concluded as early as May, 1791, promptly to resign after completion of a court of inquiry that he had requested in March. Thus Harmar's professional experience and organizational ability were to be lost to the army entirely.[21]

It was not then anticipated that the administration's remedial action might contribute further to the demise of the military. Yet, as a result of the general indignation over the 1790 campaign, a man of equally questionable performance was chosen to implement by force of arms the pacification of the frontier. It was in terms of military administration perhaps the lowest ebb of the Washington regime, for blame had been disproportionately focused on an individual rather than the existing United States army system. Through this premature rush to judgment a nearly fatal vulnerability was perpetuated in the military establishment. As the veteran soldiers on the frontier understood all too well, they were badly misused, underpaid, and underfed. In fact, the government's neglect was so prevalent that the frontier army was totally unpaid for 1790. As fast as their enlistments expired, the seasoned regulars began quitting the service. This exodus amounted to more than a hundred troops from Fort Washington alone in the sixty days following Harmar's return.[22]

What was painfully obvious to Josiah Harmar, that the administration's reaction to his campaign had been largely misdirected, was to contribute to perhaps the severest defeat of a major American army in the history of the Indian wars.[23]

While American reassessments following the initial federal Indian campaign tended to be superficial, the British response was equally faltering, being shrouded in indecision and miscalculation. Even before the arrival of Harmar's returning column at Fort Washington, an Indian delegation headed by Blue Jacket of the Shawnees had arrived in Detroit, seeking substantive British assistance. If the Indians' position had been precarious before Harmar's offensive, the Old Northwest tribes were now so critically circumstanced that they required a strong British commitment. Blue Jacket, speaking in formal council with Major John Smith, the British commandant of Detroit, declared that, in consideration of the Indians' alliance with the British during the Revolutionary War, they had been promised "not to be forsaken." "We now, Father, call for your assistance," said Blue Jacket, who sought not only provisions and material but also active aid in the form of "your young men," who were needed to organize the Indians and re-establish the Miami Villages.[24]

Because Blue Jacket's speech was delivered to a subordinate British officer, Major Smith could only offer words of friendship and compassion. Being privately "fearful the Indians will be very pressing for provisions this winter," Smith then promptly referred the matter of widespread support to Quebec, saying he was "very anxious to receive some instructions" from Dorchester.[25] By the time this communication was received and analyzed in Quebec, however, more than two months had elapsed. Dorchester finally responded late in January, 1791, advising his frontier commanders that essentially the status quo must be preserved. "There is no power in this country to begin war," he advised. "We are at peace with the United States and wish to remain so." Guided by instructions from England dating back to 1789 and mid-1790, Dorchester merely reflected the official Home Office position that, although it was desirable to secure the attachment of the Indians "both on commercial and political grounds," the very large expense involved perhaps made that a marginal effort. The preservation of peaceful relations with the United States was of paramount importance. Any active support of the Indians that might provoke a British-American confrontation thus was to be avoided.[26]

Britain would have difficulty maintaining this policy, said Dorchester, only if the United States attacked the disputed posts—Detroit, Niagara, Michilimackinac, and Oswego—as the British prisoners taken during Harmar's campaign had predicted. In that case, Dorchester observed this would be considered a beginning of hostilities on the part of the United States. "And war must be repelled by war," he warned.[27]

As a secondary consideration, Dorchester did seek to preserve normal relations with the Indians, even allowing the issuance of certain munitions under authority granted by a 1787 ministerial instruction. That document had provided for distribution of sufficient ammunition to allow the Indians to defend their country but not enough "to incite them to any hostile proceedings." Obviously an ambiguous guideline, this decree had been calculated to maintain British flexibility in retaining influence among the red men, as was deemed expedient by the Canadian governor.[28] Dorchester's strategy was thus obvious: until the Colonial Office responded from England to the recent developments, he would attempt to sustain normal relations with both sides.

Unfortunately, Dorchester's largely desultory actions avoided the realities of the situation. By 1791 the prolonged political confrontation of the preceding decade had evolved into an active war. The great issues dividing the Indian and American civilizations could not be resolved by negotiation. Not only was the destiny of an allied civilization at stake, but also Britain's stature as a dominant force in America. The quasi-neutrality of the British thus was ill advised, merely allowing Indian affairs to drift in an uncertain direction.

Strategically, the United States was most vulnerable at this time.[29] The enormous potential growth and influence of the young nation might be retarded if the land base so vital to its subsequent development was restricted. For that reason, although politically divided, the Woodland tribes represented a significant threat on the North American continent. They were the current occupants of the land mass that was in dispute, and they were determined to defend it. Although outnumbered overall and destitute of military resources, within the sparsely occupied frontier country the Indians were as yet unvanquished and represented a formidable force. With the material and technical assistance required to fight a sustained wilderness war, which was adaptable to their particular fighting skills, they might have established a separate buffer state. Such a result would have been largely contingent on active intervention by the British—if not in an outright military commitment at least by the exertion of intense political leverage sustaining a successful Indian resistance.

Furthermore, indecision worked against the interests of the British by allowing their former enemies, the Americans, latitude of maneuver. Indeed, procrastination and indecision contributed as much to the further decline of

British influence in North America as did the American military operations that had precipitated the crisis of 1791.[30]

Dorchester's letter of January 23, 1791, to the Foreign Secretary in England, Lord Grenville, reported the crucial turn of events in Indian affairs. The British governor of Canada was apprehensive about the effect on the fur trade of the posts in Indian country that intelligence reports had suggested the United States would establish.

Yet, being committed to the status quo, Dorchester demurred on further specifics, leaving it to his superiors in England to initiate any change in policy.[31]

Obviously Dorchester's letter was a particularly important communiqué, calling for reappraisal of British postwar Indian policy. Unfortunately, the letter was so delayed en route that its impact was restricted. Because of the severe winter weather, navigation had ended for the season, and the dispatch had to be sent to Halifax, Nova Scotia, for forwarding to England as the weather permitted. The tenuous, unsatisfactory line of communications in times of crisis thus was explicitly delineated. As late as March 7 the British foreign secretary had received no communications from Dorchester since November 10, 1790. Accordingly, the instructions that were forwarded to Dorchester early in March (which he received in mid-1791) had been prepared without full knowledge of Harmar's campaign. As a result, during 1791, British Indian policy was based largely on outmoded information. On March 7 Foreign Secretary Grenville advised Dorchester that the prospect of hostilities involving Indians and the United States was alarming: "Every measure" was to be taken "for the conciliation of differences and the establishment of tranquility." The "good offices" of the British might be useful in accomplishing that goal, said Grenville, especially since Britain's evacuation of her ceded forts might be utilized as an inducement to the Americans to bargain in earnest.[32]

Amazingly, because of the horrendous communications lag, an answer to Dorchester's crucial letter of January 23, 1791, was not forthcoming for nearly eight months, until September 16—far too late for the implementation of any operational orders before the second major Indian-American military confrontation, which also began in September.[33]

Ironically, the September 16 instructions dispatched from England in response to news of Harmar's campaign reaffirmed what the Indians had long suspected: they were regarded as a trifling, expendable commodity by Britain's policy makers. The communiqué issued by Grenville's new replacement, Secretary of State Henry Dundas, was evidence of a subtle yet important change in the Indians' status. Dundas inferred that they were to be considered no longer as allies but as a separate neighboring entity, toward which, in view of current British interests, it was necessary to observe "the strictest system of neutrality." Dundas warned that Great Britain was "in no degree" to become involved in "these unfortunate [Indian] disputes," though His Majesty's "attention and regard" for the tribes might be shown in attempting to secure for them their hunting grounds through negotiation. This, reasoned Dundas, might "enable them to procure a comfortable existence" and might maintain the fur trade that was said to be so valuable. Only if the United States was so rash as to attack the disputed posts would the Indians be regarded in a different light.[34]

Intended to be of moderating influence, this avowed British policy of neutrality represented, in the final analysis, perhaps the worst possible option. It established no alliance or real basis of friendship with the United States, nor did it otherwise provide for the retention of England's power base in North America by preserving Indian control of the important mid-continent.

This critical situation required a fundamental choice. Yet the British made no forthright decision or commitment. Ultimately, the result was a serious erosion of British influence in North America, and it was soon apparent that their diplomacy was mistaken. Indeed, the actions of British Indian Department officials and subordinates in discharging their field responsibilities suggested just how difficult the establishment of a uniform British Indian policy was during the 1790–91 delay in communications. Since no authoritative word was immediately forthcoming on Britain's ultimate commitments, responsible British officials were required to interpret generalized instructions in resolving specific situations. Predictably, there was great variation in the perspectives and the attitudes of the individuals involved in British-Indian relations. Most significant were the operational officers directly charged with managing Indian contacts. By an odd circumstance, three of the most influential British Indian agents were American defectors to the British side during the Revolution. As disgruntled outcasts, regarded as traitors by their former Pennsylvania associates, Alexander McKee, Matthew Elliott, and Simon Girty were strongly anti-American in their sentiments.

McKee, a former Indian agent and trader out of Pittsburgh during the 1770s, had risen to become the British Indian agent at Detroit, where he eventually earned the rank of colonel. Like his assistant, Matthew Elliott, McKee had resided among the Shawnees and lived with a common-law Indian wife. His personal interest in the preservation of British influence among the Indians was demonstrated by his long residence at the foot of the Miami Rapids.[35]

The extent to which these agents subtly encouraged Indian hostility is shown by Simon Girty's renewed employment in his former Revolutionary War role as military adviser to the Indians. Of all those whose names were vilified on the frontier following the revolution, it is unlikely that anyone was more generally despised among the Americans than Girty. He and Elliott and McKee had long been the preeminent British Indian operatives. The three had defected together in March, 1778, but Girty, because of his cunning and his intimate knowledge of the Indians, was particularly effective as a leader in combat. In 1756, at about the age of fifteen, he had been captured by a French-led Indian war party and had been forced to witness the execution by torture of his stepfather. Yet, when released three years later under the terms of a frontier treaty, Girty was said to be more Indian than white in his habits. He had lived with the Senecas, and although he was illiterate, his extensive knowledge of native languages led eventually to his employment in the Indian trade as an interpreter. Appointed as a second lieutenant in a Pennsylvania militia company, after a dispute over rank he resigned his commission and defected to the British nearly three years after the beginning of the Revolutionary War.

A strong-willed and embittered man, Girty was driven by a professed morbid hatred of the American enemy. In 1782, American Colonel William Crawford was horribly tortured and burned to death at the stake. It was alleged that Girty was gleefully present and his involvement earned him the designation of "fiend" and "white savage."

Although ostensibly Girty was only an interpreter in the British Indian Department, he often served as a frontline military adviser. During the Revolution he was particularly active in Indian raids throughout the frontier, being deeply involved in the bloody Blue Licks disaster. As a dreaded, vulgar man, Girty had even emerged from the war with an $800 price on his head. Two of his brothers, James and George, also joined the British Indian Department during the war. They too earned for the Girty name a particular infamy among frontiersmen.[36]

At the time of Harmar's raid in 1790, Simon Girty was absent on a clandestine mission in the vicinity of Pittsburgh, Pennsylvania. After reporting the information that he obtained during his trip at Detroit early in November, Girty proceeded toward the Miami Villages, where the Indians had been gathering in considerable strength for the past several weeks. Alexander McKee had reported that the various tribes did not consider themselves adequate of going to war without British support. McKee thus dispatched Girty as an adviser in what was to become the first Indian offensive of the new war.[37]

Although the winter weather was not normally associated with active warfare, the Indians had decided, probably with tacit British Indian Department approval, to carry out retaliatory raids on white settlements in the Ohio country.[38]

The two obvious targets for their hostilities were the Symmes tract in and about Cincinnati and the Ohio Company lands around Marietta, which were the principal white settlements north of the Ohio. Late in December several Indian raiding parties set forth to terrorize the fringes of these white settlements.

The largest and most imposing of the two war parties consisted of nearly two hundred Maumee region warriors under the Shawnee Blue Jacket. Led by their war counsellor Simon Girty, these raiders were directed to proceed from the upper Maumee River to the headwaters of the Great Miami and strike at the Symmes purchase in the Ohio's western regions. During the first week in January, 1791, Blue Jacket's warriors passed along the still-navigable waterways to the advanced Symmes outpost at Dunlap's Station, about seventeen miles north of Cincinnati.[39]

The new year of 1791 had brought little warning of impending danger to the approximately thirty-five residents of Dunlap's Station, who included a thirteen-man federal garrison. The weather, being generally clear and frosty, had not inhibited the daily routine of clearing and surveying the adjacent lands. On the morning of January 8 a four-man surveying party on the west banks of the Great Miami was fired on by about eight Indians in an ambush. One man was instantly killed, and another, Abner Hunt, was thrown from his horse and captured. The remaining two surveyors managed to escape. Making their way to Dunlap's Station, the survivors reported the incident on Sunday, January 9. No undue alarm was taken, however, for it was presumed that a small raiding party, intent on stealing horses, had chanced upon the surveyors.[40]

It had rained throughout that day, and all of the local settlers remained in the rather-flimsy blockhouse, which was unprotected on the side fronting the Great Miami.

During the night of January 9, Lieutenant Jacob Kingsbury was up much of the night, joking with some of his men. At about sunrise on January 10 only the sentries and Kingsbury were awake when the cry of "Indians!, Indians!" rang out. As the startled settlers sprang to arms, Blue Jacket's entire war party surrounded the stockade. Rather than launch a sudden surprise attack, the Indians had decided first to demand the surrender of the garrison. Abner Hunt, bound and tethered, was pushed forward to ask for its capitulation.

Kingsbury, bluffing, said through this intermediary that they had been expecting the Indians for several days and were well prepared, having plenty of men, ammunition, and provisions. He was informed in turn that Girty was present, though hidden from view, and that the Indians were prepared to starve the garrison out if necessary. The unsuccessful termination of these negotiations resulted in a heavy volley of gunfire from the Indians, and the siege was begun.[41]

Throughout the morning the bright sunshine and mid 30-degree temperatures contributed to spirited resistance by the small garrison. Several pauses for parleys with the bedraggled Hunt revealed the increasing belligerence of the red warriors. Kingsbury was told that, unless he surrendered, the Indians would storm the stockade and burn it down. In midafternoon, with an overcast sky and falling temperatures, a sudden assault with fire arrows aborted—one warrior who attempted to carry a firebrand toward the wall was killed as he ran forward.

Hunt, in his occasional parleys, now pleaded that he would be tortured to death unless Kingsbury gave up. Although his men mocked the Indians during their attacks, Kingsbury realized he was in serious difficulty. From the appearance of the Indians, who had heavy packs on their backs and several packhorses laden with heavy loads, he concluded they were prepared for a siege. His men had expended much of the twenty-four rounds of ammunition available to each of them, and lead was so scarce that the women were casting pewter spoons and plates into rifle balls. Although only a few men had been wounded, Kingsbury realized he would soon need help.[42]

After nightfall the surveyor who had escaped from the ambush on January 8 attempted to slip through the Indian lines, but he failed to find a way out. About midnight the psychological wear on the morale of the garrison was heightened by a ghastly proceeding. Abner Hunt, stripped naked, was dragged within two hundred yards of the stockade and spread-eagled on the ground. His wrists and ankles were secured, and an excruciating torture began in full view of the appalled garrison.

A fire was kindled so near that it scorched Hunt, and live coals were periodically thrust into incisions that were made in his limbs. Amid his tortured screams the Indians circled in a derisive war dance, "whooping and yelling." Finally, wearying of the affair, they kindled a fire on Hunt's naked abdomen with firebrands, allowing him to suffer a lingering death. An eyewitness reported with revulsion, "His screams of agony were ringing in our ears during the remainder of the night, becoming gradually weaker and weaker, til toward daylight, when they ceased."[43]

Hunt's torture produced a new sense of urgency, and about 3:00 A.M. two men slipped into a canoe and quietly made their way across the Great Miami. Hastening overland in the direction of Cincinnati, they encountered an unexpected apparition about six miles from Fort Washington.

Marching with all speed for Dunlap's Station was a 96-man contingent of federal troops and local volunteer militia summoned from Cincinnati and Columbia. By chance a hunter, named Cox, had heard heavy firing near Dunlap's Station on January 10 and had surmised that it was under Indian attack. His arrival at Fort Washington that evening had prompted an emergency call-up of the militia and the dispatch of the regulars as a relief party.

Most of the command was mounted, and with the two scouts in the lead the relief party hastened for Dunlap's Station,[44] where smoke from the smoldering ruins of fired cabins had greeted the eyes of Kingsbury's garrison that morning. Later the Indians had resumed their sporadic firing, only to disappear suddenly about 8:00 A.M.

Although immensely relieved, Kingsbury's garrison soon learned that their stout defense had resulted in a hollow victory. After the arrival of the Fort Washington relief column about midmorning, an assessment of damage was undertaken. It was soon found that all the settlers' cattle, corn, and other possessions had been destroyed, and their homesteads burned. So few provisions remained that almost immediately a majority of the settlers decided to abandon the site and go back to the Ohio. Eventually, the entire outpost was given up, providing a bitter sequel to the congratulatory orders that Kingsbury received from Harmar praising his "spirited defense."[45]

Of equal impact, and even more embarrassing to American land-development interests, were the consequences of the easternmost Indian foray.

A war party of only about twenty-five Wyandots and Delawares had moved undiscovered down the west bank of the Muskingum River on New Year's Day, 1791. On the afternoon of January 2, from a ridge opposite Big Bottom, thirty miles north of the Muskingum's confluence with the Ohio, the Indian raiders reconnoitered the recently constructed blockhouse on the east bank, where a company of about thirty-six Ohio Company associates had initiated a settlement the previous autumn. Mostly young, unmarried men who were recent immigrants to the western country, they had carelessly constructed a blockhouse of large beech logs. Not yet chinked and daubed, it was also devoid of an outer palisade. Even more incautiously, they had omitted to post sentries or plan for their defense in the event of an attack. They presumed that merely the cold winter weather would inhibit any hostilities on the part of the Indians until spring.[46]

Toward dusk on that Sunday evening of January 2 the settlers were preparing dinner. Thirteen persons occupied the main blockhouse, including one woman and two children. Twenty rods north of the blockhouse stood a small cabin with four men inside. Another small log structure lay below the blockhouse, which contained two settlers.

Crossing noiselessly on the ice, the red warriors reached the east bank of the Muskingum and split into two groups. Smoke was pouring from the open chimneys, and the aroma of frying meat wafted in the air. The air was still, even the settlers' dogs being inside by the warm fire.

At the north cabin the four men looked up from their supper to find their small structure suddenly filled with Indians. Almost in a friendly manner, recounted a survivor, the Indians made them aware that they were now prisoners and bound them with thongs.

There was no such cautious behavior at the main blockhoue. The unbarred door was suddenly flung open, and a volley of gunfire poured into the structure. One man was killed instantly, and several others took severe wounds. So stunned by the sudden attack were the survivors that they hardly attempted to reach their muskets, which were standing nearby in the corners.

As the Wyandots and Delawares poured into the room brandishing tomahawks, the portly wife of a Virginia hunter swung her small axe at the Indian securing the door. The blade struck him in the cheek and sliced downward into his shoulder, inflicting a severe wound. The woman was quickly killed by a tomahawk blow, and the shrieking Indians fell on the hapless settlers.

There was no further resistance, as the Indians slaughtered the remaining occupants. Two of the Virginia woman's children were killed, and blood spurted onto the walls and gathered in pools on the blockhouse floor. A frightened youth, the son of a prominent Ohio Company associate, attempted to escape by springing up a ladder into the loft and from there onto the roof. He was on the roof, begging for his life—"for God's sake, spare me, I am the only one left," he said—when the Indians watching outside shot him down. Only the youth's brother, a lad of sixteen, managed to hide under some bedding in the corner of the room until he was later discovered by Indians ransacking the premises. His life was spared, and he joined the four other prisoners secured in the north cabin.[47]

Fortunately for the two occupants of the lower cabin, the gunfire alerted them of an attack. They fled into the woods just ahead of the Indians, who found their supper still hot on the table.

Their grisly work completed, the Indian war party plundered the buildings, piled the white carcasses in a heap in the blockhouse, and attempted to burn the structure down by ripping up the flooring and setting it afire. Since the green beech logs would not easily burn, only the interior was gutted, leaving the charred walls and blackened, disfigured bodies to greet the relief party that arrived on January 4.

Burdened by their five prisoners and their severely wounded comrade, the Indians proceeded north, where they eventually reached McKee's storehouse at the foot of the Maumee rapids. At a trifling cost, their rather minimal winter foray had managed not only to break up the Big Bottom settlement but also to achieve an important strategic impact.[48]

Tactically, both raids were very limited successes. Indeed, the Dunlap's Station attack was an outright failure. Yet the midwinter Indian offensive significantly altered the course of frontier history. Thereby, the forward

129

thrust of white expansion could no longer be readily continued in the Old Northwest. It was all too evident to the would-be settlers, whose lives and property were at stake, that the imminent danger of Indian attacks precluded further American expansion until a military solution was achieved.

That bitter truth was reflected in the multitude of long, grievous complaints that were soon directed at the federal administration in Philadelphia. "Unless [the] Government speedily sends a body of troops for our protection," warned Rufus Putnam of the Ohio Company, "we are a ruined people." Observing that several other advanced settlements had broken up after news of the Big Bottom massacre, Putnam told President Washington that the expected destruction of that outlying settlements' corn, forage, and cattle by the red enemy would allow no means of sustaining people there: "As to new settlers, we can expect none in our present situation; so that instead of increasing in strength, we are likely to diminish daily. If we do not fall prey to the savages, we shall be so reduced and discouraged as to give up the settlement."[49]

There was an important lesson here: the Indians no longer had to achieve an absolute military success to halt the tide of white civilization. Merely by denying the Americans access to the land, they could smite their enemies where they were the most vulnerable. So long as control of the vital countryside was maintained, an Indian confederacy could hope to persevere in successful resistance. Ultimately, their strategy must be not so much to strike military objectives but to wreak havoc on the real enemy of a native civilization, the encroaching white civilian populace. Indeed, for both Indians and settlers, the scales were heavily weighted in favor of that side that most effectively played upon its opponent's weaknesses.

As Secretary of War Knox understood after Harmar's unsuccessful campaign, the strategy utilized in this first offensive had been no solution to pacification of the frontier. He had but to look at the comments of Rufus Putnam and others to understand what had occurred. "This event [the Big Bottom attack] clearly provides that the expedition against the Shawnees will not produce peace, but on the contrary, a more general and outrageous war," said Putnam. Another Marietta resident added his observations, saying, "I can say with propriety that it [Harmar's raid] has not had the deserved effect—for in place of humbling, it only irritated—and instead of a *partial* [conflict], it has produced a general war."[50]

If Knox had any doubts about the altered status of the frontier, the people who observed the aftermath of the two January Indian attacks did not. Across the crushed and mutilated body of Abner Hunt, whose brains had been beaten out by these very instruments, lay crossed war clubs, the Indian declaration of war. At Big Bottom the handful of militiamen who attempted to bury the unrecognizably burned corpses of their fellow settlers in the frozen ground found a similar war club dangling in a conspicuous location. It was, said one Ohio-country resident in melancholy candor, the advent of a truly critical situation.[51]

14

The Town Destroyers

PRESIDENT George Washington, in his message to Congress of December 8, 1790, elaborated a basic, profoundly significant view of the frontier. Observing that the District of Kentucky's desired admission to the Union was "a very important transaction," Washington enumerated the "aggravated provocations" directed against American frontier settlements. It was essential, he said, that "the aggressors [the Indians] should be made sensible that the government of the Union is not less capable of punishing their crimes, than it is disposed to respect their rights and reward their attachments."[1]

Washington's statements reflected an all-important policy guideline of his administration. While peace with the Indians was desired if at all possible, of even greater importance was America's expansion westward—of which the securing of Kentucky by the federal government was a fundamental aspect. In deciding between conflicting alternatives, there was but one all-important consideration: the United States must and would promote its manifest destiny by expanding and procuring vital resources in the West.[2]

This fundamental precept was soon expressed in specific plans that were submitted for congressional approval after the unsuccessful Harmar campaign of 1790. Secretary of War Knox advised Congress on January 22, 1791, that it must consider the cost versus the objective. Pacification of the frontier would consolidate United States territory and provide the basis for future expansion. Knox thus reasoned that the cost of pacification must be borne. "The inhabitants request and demand protection; if it not be granted, . . . sentiments of separate interests will arise," he admonished. Declaring that "it is true economy to regulate events instead of being regulated by them," Knox asserted, "Affairs cannot remain where they are." An active war was underway in the Old Northwest, and it seemed "indispensable that another expedition must be made against the Wabash Indians."[3]

Having committed to the conquest of the vast Ohio country by force, Knox then elaborated the method to accomplish that task. First, "a strong post and garrison" at the Miami Village (Kekionga) was necessary. To achieve that, Knox said, a substantial expedition involving three thousand troops would be required. By expanding the regular army from its authorized 1,216 men to 2,128 noncommissioned officers and privates, and by further relying on short-term levies and militia rangers, the Secretary of War estimated that a sufficient force might be organized. Knox thought that the considerable cost, about $100,000 for the new regulars alone, would be

131

Cornplanter, the United States–aligned Seneca chief. Courtesy of Burton Historical Collection, Detroit Public Library.

justified because the expedition would "effectually dispos[e] the Wabash and other hostile Indians to peace."[4]

Left unsaid in this unfolding of strategic design was the enormous logistical problem of implementing such a program. While it was a matter of some complexity to obtain the enabling funds from Congress, it was infinitely more difficult to carry out the plan. Indeed, because of the impoverished, weakened status of the military establishment, interim plans of a different nature were promptly implemented.[5]

The fallacy of the United States being involved offensively in an Indian war without the physical means to wage that war was never more apparent than in the early months of 1791. Fearing a loss of initiative, the administration decided to pursue certain "desultory operations" involving diplomatic parleys and militia raids until the main campaign could begin. Although officials also hoped for beneficial consequences, these preliminary measures were intended largely as delaying tactics until a sufficient, "decisive" force of arms could be brought to bear.[6]

Foremost among these interim plans was the peace initiative assigned to Colonel Thomas Procter, which served as an adjunct to a scheme that was designed to limit the potential Indian enemy. President Washington intended Procter's diplomatic offensive to be of consequence in preventing a widespread Indian war, as opposed to the localized "present war against the [western] Indians." Senator Rufus King of New York had warned Washington early in 1791: "You are sensible that almost every person here is interested in our Western lands. Their value depends upon the settlement of the frontiers. These settlements depend on peace with the Indians; and indeed the bare possibility of a war with the Six Nations would break up our whole frontier. . . . I presume it will be the case that all prudent means will be used to keep the Six Nations quiet."[7]

King thus delineated an important, if covert, objective of the federal Indian commissioners: to keep the Iroquois nations from joining with the hostile elements. In fact, to improve relations between the Six Nations and the United States, leaders of the friendliest of the Iroquois factions, Cornplanter's band, had been invited to Philadelphia in the fall of 1790.

Cornplanter, a "principal warrior" known also as Captain O'Beel, is believed to have been the son of an English or Dutch trader and a full-blooded Seneca woman. In 1790 he was said to be more than fifty years old. At the head of a delegation of three Seneca chiefs and various councillors of his political allegiance, he arrived in Philadelphia about November 1, 1790, to confer with the great chief of the Thirteen Fires, Honandaganius—President Washington.[8] After a visit of some three months, his delegation left Philadelphia early in February, 1791, laden with presents and supplies. Their ready submission to American sovereignty had been carefully noted by the government. In fact, the direct result of their sojourn was to heighten American interest in involving the Six Nations as a moderating influence on the frontier. Within a month of Cornplanter's departure a new message was prepared for the Senecas, reflecting the matured federal plans for 1791. Henry Knox advised them that an emissary was being sent to give the western Indians "a solemn warning of their fate," should they continue their hostilities. In view of Cornplanter's recent visit, the Senecas were requested to "immediately set out" with this representative, gathering some of the friendly Wyandots and Delawares along the way to add impetus to their mission of persuasion. Colonel Thomas Procter, the American emissary, was a former Revolutionary War artillery officer, who had served with General John Sullivan in his 1779 campaign against the Iroquois in western Pennsylvania. Procter was furnished with various speeches, of which one, "offering of a desire to save you from ruin," was intended for the Miami Indians. To comply with what was, in effect, an American ultimatum, the hostiles were instructed, "Call in your parties, and fly with your head men to Fort Washington [Cincinnati]" for a treaty.[9]

This utilization of friendly Six Nations elements was intended to produce political leverage by implying an Indian-American combination of strength. That such a stratagem would evoke contempt rather than credence along the frontier was soon evident, once Procter's mission was underway.

Colonel Procter's instructions were to complete his mission to bring the Miami-region Indians to a treaty no later than May 5. At that date he was to be at Fort Washington, he was told, "whether you succeed or not."[10] As he well understood, his mission remained secondary to the forceful intimidation of the Indians. In fact it was for that reason that he was to complete his peace initiative by May 5. Offensive operations would begin in May against the hostiles unless the results of his mission precluded an offensive.[11]

Accompanied by a French officer who had served in the Massachusetts line during the Revolution, Captain Michael Gabriel Houdin, Procter arrived at Cornplanter's village on the headwaters of the Allegheny on April 6, 1791. Upon his arrival he learned that Cornplanter had been forced to take sanctuary with the American garrison on French Creek (at Fort Franklin), about 130 miles distant. Proceeding there, Procter found the Seneca chief and 180 tribesmen of his faction fearing for their lives.

It seems that Cornplanter had been subjected to a harrowing experience at the hands of disorderly frontier elements. Proceeding from Pittsburgh toward Fort Franklin via the Allegheny early in April, he and some of his tribesmen had been compelled to put to shore under the guns of a Pennsylvania militia detachment. Although a federal noncommissioned officer was aboard their large garrison boat, which was loaded with provisions for Fort Franklin and with many of the Indian treaty goods from Philadelphia, this property had been seized, along with several canoes in which the Senecas were traveling. The garrison boat had drifted away, but the canoes with their considerable property had been taken to Pittsburgh and sold as captured property. Meanwhile, the Senecas, including Cornplanter, had fled into the underbrush.

When Procter found them at Fort Franklin on April 8, the greatest possible anxiety filled their minds. Although Procter finally persuaded a portion of them to accompany him, they would not go directly to the Miami country. Instead, they directed that Procter travel to Buffalo Creek, where a full council of the Six Nations might consider the recent attack.[12]

So disgusted were many of the Senecas over the loss of their militia-plundered merchandise that several canoe loads of the tribesmen deserted on the first night out. Subsequently, among the various Six Nations delegates at Buffalo Creek on April 27, Procter began to understand the dubious nature of his mission. It was soon apparent to him that the Buffalo Creek Indians, including many Senecas, were British-oriented, being but thirty-five miles from the English post at Niagara. Also, Procter noticed that these Indians were better clothed and supplied than their more southern brethren. The Farmer's Brother, an important Seneca chief, even proceeded to greet Procter while dressed in the coat of a British colonel, "red faced with blue . . . and equipped with a pair of the best epaulets." When the sachems and chiefs learned a Six Nations delegation was wanted to help bargain with the hostiles, there was an immediate furor.[13] Some of the Six Nations spokesmen were so antagonistic—saying that one half of their nations were not for peace—that Procter threatened them with a reduction in future presents and a bad report to the secretary of war about their inopportune delays and disrespect.[14]

Finally, after nearly a month's delay, the politically divided Iroquois agreed to send a six-chief delegation with Procter to the western country. Yet, as Procter soon discovered, the entire plan was to be aborted. So much time had elapsed that it was now necessary to travel by water to reach the Miami country. The British controlled navigation in the Great Lakes region, however, and their cooperation was needed to charter a merchant vessel to transport Procter and his Indian escorts. When, on May 16, Procter sent a request to the British commandant at Niagara to charter an adequate vessel on Lake Erie, his request was refused. "His unfriendly denial" put a stop to the further continuance of his mission. The designated time for his arrival at Fort Washington had long since passed, and on May 21, Procter departed for Philadelphia, after telling an assembled Indian council that the British action in denying passage was "replete with envy . . . towards the United States."[15]

What had been regarded as an unpromising bid for peace by the federalist administration had turned out to be precisely that. Yet Procter's mission had materially added to the discord and uncertainty perplexing the Iroquois nations. During Procter's stay at Buffalo Creek a message had arrived from Colonel Timothy Pickering of the United States, requesting the Six Nations' presence at the Painted Post on the Tioga River (modern-day Athens, Pennsylvania) on June 16 for a general treaty to "brighten the chain of friendship." Although that sounded innocuous, the true purpose of the intended treaty, revealed in official correspondence, was "to draw the Six Nations to a conference at a distance from the theatre of war, in order not only to prevent their joining therein, but also, if necessary, to obtain some of their young men to join our army."[16]

It was soon apparent that the Six Nations had been intimidated by the thinly veiled muscle flexing of Procter and St. Clair, on the one hand, and the olive-branch diplomacy of Pickering offering the prospect of numerous presents, on the other.

Because many of the Six Nations resided on ceded lands in a central location, competing British and American interests impinged on their immediate status. Befuddled by the variety of diplomatic initiatives, they resolved to take the path of least resistance. They would neither join the hostiles nor accept American sovereignty, preferring instead to remain British wards. Thus, during the supreme crisis in red and white relations on this continent, most of the Six Nations did virtually nothing. Ironically, their fate had turned full circle, for they were abdicating the very role that the Iroquois League had assumed long ago, utilizing political and military means to achieve a preeminent status as leaders of the native civilization. It was indeed a requiem for a once mighty and proud people.

While the status of the easternmost frontier was uncertain during the initial months of 1791, the western lands were embroiled in a full-scale war. Even before Major General St. Clair's departure for the Old Northwest early in March, 1791, the War Office had begun planning to inhibit the Indians' offensive capabilities until the main expedition could get underway. Yet, predictably, the tribesmen seized the initiative and struck the first blow.

Throughout March, 1791, the weather had been rainy and mild. River traffic, generally immigrants' and traders' boats going downstream, had been brisk along the Ohio. Early in the month word had passed among the frontier settlements that a party, headed by Captain David Strong of the regular army, was preparing to head upstream. At the rendezvous Strong found that he had so many men, fifty-three, that all would not fit with their belongings aboard the large boat that he had provided for the journey. By having some of the men walk on shore, while the remainder rode in the boat with the baggage, Strong was able to accommodate nearly everyone. Composed of a polyglot collection of discharged soldiers, traders, civilian merchants, and veterans on furlough, Strong's party finally sailed upriver about March 22. On the twenty-seventh they were about eight miles beyond the mouth of the Scioto River. Twenty-six men were walking along the Kentucky shore, where the danger of Indian attack was believed to be much reduced.[17]

In a narrow bottomland bordered by rising ground immediately ahead, Strong's luck abruptly ran out. A war party of about thirty Indians had concealed themselves in the brush and lay waiting there. Suddenly they opened fire from ambush, shouting and yelling amid the frightening din.

So panic-stricken was the shore party that they offered very little resistance. Many of the frantic Kentuckians plunged into the water to escape the onrushing Indians. A survivor on the boat later related that he fired five times at Indians tomahawking white men at the river's edge, before the boat drifted downriver and out of range. Only one man was said to have been hit in the boat, but they later learned that twenty-three of the twenty-six men ashore had been massacred.

That night Strong's shaken survivors drifted back to Limestone, Kentucky, where a relief party was soon organized. Under the command of Colonel Alexander Orr, nearly three hundred Kentuckians proceeded up the Ohio about April 1, burdened with additional grim news. Word of the Indian depredations along the Ohio had spread like wildfire throughout the Kentucky frontier, but the news of marauding Indian raiders in the vicinity of the Scioto had not yet reached the eastern regions. Scattered parties of immigrants thus continued to pass downriver.[18]

During this one bloody week in March the Indians had captured the fifty-foot pirogue of a local trader, a Captain Hughes, whom they killed. Using this craft, they then emerged at the mouth of the Scioto to attack a keelboat containing Captain William Hubbell and eight others. Hubbell took a wound in the right arm, and six of his party were injured, but his boat gradually outdistanced the Indian pursuers, who soon turned their attention to a second keelboat floating a short distance behind.[19]

As Hubbell's craft drifted out of sight, its occupants saw the Indians converging upon the second keelboat, which seemed to be making little resistance. Aboard the boat, they knew, was a noted frontier character, Jacob Greathouse, and his wife, together with about a dozen immigrants. They later realized with a shudder that Greathouse, a former hunting companion of Simon Kenton's and an inveterate foe of the red man, had been linked to the murder of the famous Mingo chief Logan's family in 1774. His brother Daniel had been primarily involved in that massacre, which had initiated the sanguinary Lord Dunmore's War, but the names of both Greathouses were notorious on the frontier for bloodthirsty Indian slaughter. Should Greathouse fall into the hands of the red enemy, especially of Mingo warriors, his fate was certain to be horrible if his identity was discovered.

As revealed in the journal that a British-allied observer kept among the Miamis that spring, the war party then operating on the Belle Rivière, the Ohio, was largely comprised of Shawnees, Cherokees, and Mingos. Two Canadian traders were also along, including "La Chapelle" (Lacelle), formerly of the Miami Towns, who could identify names on any paper that might be captured.[20]

Alexander Orr's relief party, knowing that only Hubbell's boat had subsequently landed at Limestone, arrived in the vicinity of the Scioto about the first week in April. Proceeding to the site of Strong's encounter, they found about twenty dead white men, many mangled and defiled to the point where they were unrecognizable. One observer noted that the vermin in the woods had eaten the flesh off the corpses so that mostly bones remained. Only one man was found fully intact. He had fallen into the water along the bank, partially hidden from view. Thomas Ireland secured his fine Pennsylvania-Kentucky rifle, engraved with a "square compass" on the patch box. Then they buried all the remains in a shallow grave.

Across the Ohio on "the Indian side," Orr's men next found the abandoned fifty-foot pirogue that had belonged to the trader Hughes. The bottom of the vessel was stained with enough blood to fill a barrel, thought one observer. Nearby, three dead Indians were discovered by the odor of their rotting flesh. A hole had been gouged out under an uprooted tree, and the dead warriors placed therein, with a few clumps of dirt thrown over them. "Though they smelled badly," said a Kentuckian, "old Joe Lemon went and scalped them."[21]

On their way home Orr's men made their final, grisly discovery. A little below the mouth of the Scioto, Greathouse's abandoned keelboat was found. It had been more than a week since his boat had been waylaid, and the disheartening sight was more than many hardened frontiersmen could bear. Strewn in disarray were the decomposing remains of human beings and animals, intermixed with broken furniture and disassembled wagon parts. A thick mass of feathers from broken feather ticks carpeted the scene. One eyewitness remarked that the remains were so disfigured and consumed by vermin that they could not tell a man from a woman in most cases. Due to the warm weather, the pungent odor of rotting flesh was almost unbearable. A short distance away, however, the frontiersmen found the most gruesome sight of all. Jacob Greathouse and his wife had been separated from the other prisoners, stripped naked, and tied to separate saplings. The Indians then had made an incision in their abdomens and unfolded part of the large intestine, which they fastened to the saplings. Greathouse and his wife each had been driven around the sapling, perhaps with willow switches, until their entrails were wound around the tree in a hideous mass. Thus the Greathouses had died, victims of an atrocity that would long be remembered along the frontier by vengeful whites.[22]

Several weeks later a party including Simon Kenton set an ambush at Snag Creek, where several sunken Indian canoes had been discovered, indicating that a war party had crossed the Ohio into Kentucky. Before the whites' ruse was uncovered, five natives were killed as they approached the north shore, after raising their canoe and recrossing the Ohio. Among them was a blue-eyed renegade, identified as Bill Frame, who was shown no special mercy. Their riddled bodies were scalped and mutilated, and the head of one dead Indian, identified as the Shawnee youth captured by Harmar and set free after his campaign, was severed and stuck on a tall pole as a grisly reminder of white vengeance.[23]

The frontier was already aflame with a bitterness reminiscent of the Revolutionary War years when Arthur St. Clair wrote in May, 1791, to Henry Knox of the late-blooming American plan to counter Indian raids along the Ohio frontier. Several offers of monetary rewards for Indian scalps were now being circulated. One Ohio-country resident boasted, "We . . . have by subscription raised £50 per scalp for the first Indian [brought in], £30 for the second, and £20 for the third." The various methods that were used to cope with the red menace, such as turning loose in the woods dogs trained to scent Indians so that they could track down marauding war parties, suggested the fear that permeated many frontier communities.[24]

"We who are yet alive are crowded into small forts, uncomfortably lodged in wet and dirt," complained a distraught frontier settler in the spring of 1791. "There is not cleared ground about the forts sufficient to raise bread for our children. For this reason many are moving to the old settlements over the mountains, and several hundred have it in contemplation . . . to move to Spanish Territory—where they will live in peace and have their interests more attended to." Bitter complaints, that the government had taken the means of defense out of the hands of the people, were commonplace along the frontier.[25]

It was just such budding dissension that St. Clair sought to deter in the arrangements that he made for a limited thrust against the Indians while his main column was building strength for a late-summer campaign. St. Clair said that the raid that he planned (a part of the delaying tactics intended by the administration to keep the hostiles off balance) was, in fact, "calculated expressly to gratify the people of Kentucky." Despite his lingering difficulties with the gout, the governor found it essential that he hasten to Lexington early in May to confer with the designated commander, Brigadier General Charles Scott of the militia.[26]

About May 8, Scott met with St. Clair to review plans for the raid. Despite intense bickering among jealous militia colonels over commands, Scott had been able to fill the maximum quota of 750 designated for his force. Now the entire body of mounted militia was ordered to proceed to the mouth of the Kentucky River for muster and final preparations.[27]

On May 19, Scott began transporting his men across the Ohio near the mouth of the Kentucky, and by May 23 he was ready to proceed north. No information had been received from Colonel Procter about an Indian peace treaty, and further delay was considered unwise, lest the militia's term of service expire in midcampaign. On the afternoon of May 23, Scott took up the march, proceeding north in threatening weather.

Scott's instructions, issued by Secretary of War Knox on March 9, required that "surprise and sudden attack" be the objective of the expedition.[28] Yet, as early as April 1, the red men had gleaned from a white prisoner that there was "another army preparing to visit the Indian country." Then, in May, urgent requests from the Shawnees and Miamis to come forth caused hundreds of Indians to proceed toward Kekionga, according to the British agent, Alexander McKee.[29]

McKee later reported that 1,057 Indian fighting men had hurried from the Grand Glaize trading post to the Miami Towns to await the coming of the Americans. McKee estimated their force to number nearly 2,000 men, including the warriors already at Kekionga and in its vicinity. Even Joseph Brant, who was present at the Miami Rapids, felt "obliged by every tie of friendship to join them [the western nations] in defense of their country." He too moved forward to the Miami Villages.[30]

Accounts reaching the Miami Villages on May 29 reported that the American column consisted of militia, with no artillery. They were said to be at the portage of the White River, and a prisoner taken by the Indians reported that several hundred cavalry from Kentucky were involved. An anxious, expectant atmosphere now prevailed at the Miami Towns, and McKee felt compelled to send a pirogue laden with ammunition and provisions in response to Indian demands.[31]

Unknowingly, the large concentration of red fighting men gathered at the Miami Towns were waiting in vain. A major miscalculation had occurred when the Indian scouts had initially reported the American column proceeding north. Instead of following the route used last autumn by Harmar's troops, the Kentuckians, by design, had suddenly swerved away and were striking northwest for the Wabash region. Thus Scott's instructions had been well calculated to avoid a major confrontation.

The Wabash had been targeted as the raiders' objective largely because the federal government sought to demonstrate the vulnerability of Indian villages in even the most remote regions. Moreover, there was an ulterior motive in suddenly striking an unsuspecting Indian village, revealed in Knox's original instructions: "[You] . . . are to proceed to the Wea, or Ouiatanon towns . . . to assault said towns . . . , capturing as many as possible, particularly women and children." The utilization of these non-combatant prisoners would soon be obvious: Taking care to treat his captives with humanity, Scott would deliver them to a United States military post for safe keeping; then leverage could be applied to bring the hostiles to treaty by offering them the recovery of their women and children.[32]

This insidious scheme, tantamount to extortion, was furthered by an incredible stroke of good fortune. Only two days before Scott's approach to the Wabash villages, 500 warriors of the region had departed for the Miami Towns to help fight the Americans. This was only the beginning of a series of unlikely events that soon occurred.

On June 1, Scott's vanguard was crossing a broad prairie near the Wabash River. Ahead lay their objective, the important Wea village of Ouiatanon (four miles from modern-day Lafayette, Indiana). While traversing the prairie, a lone Indian on horseback was discovered nearly two miles distant, yet the detachment sent in pursuit failed to overtake him. Aware that his column had been uncovered, Scott pushed rapidly on, and at about 1:00 P.M. he entered a grove of timber, beyond which two small Indian villages were observed. Since speed was all-important, Scott detached sixty mounted infantry and a troop of horsemen under the ever-aggressive Colonel John Hardin to attack the two small villages, while Scott made a dash at Ouiatanon, which was said to be five miles ahead.[33]

Guided by the smoke of distant campfires, Scott's column rode rapidly for the main Indian village. Once they rounded a high point in the woods, Ouiatanon appeared shimmering in the midafternoon sunshine on low ground bordering the Wabash. Ouiatanon had been quiet that day before the arrival of Captain Bull, the warrior who had discovered Scott's column on the prairie. Since the principal warriors were absent, only a few fighting men remained, along with many old men, women, and children. Desperately these Weas had attempted to evacuate the town, crossing the rain-swollen Wabash in canoes to the Kickapoo village on the opposite shore. The last of the Indian families were preparing to embark when the crackle of gunfire announced the appearance of Scott's Kentuckians.

In grim remembrance of his son lost in Harmar's campaign, Scott hastened to carry out his orders. First, a lone hut containing two rearguard warriors was overrun, and its occupants killed. Then Scott's militiamen rushed to the rising ground overlooking the Wabash, where the Indians, "in great confusion," were seen attempting to get across the river in canoes. Scott sent Lieutenant Colonel James Wilkinson with a battalion rushing down to the riverbank to fire into the crowded craft. "A well directed volley," said Scott, "virtually destroyed all the occupants of five canoes." Later a body count revealed nearly thirty victims. Somehow only about six prisoners had been taken once the firing ended.[34]

About sunset, however, Colonel Hardin arrived in camp with welcome news and a multitude of prisoners. First, they had attacked a small Wea village of nine families, where they had killed six Indians. The sound of the firing had carried to a larger village nearby, causing the occupants, again mostly old men, women, and children, to come and see what they supposed was a war party returning with prisoners. Hardin's men rushed upon them before they could get away. Fifty-two captives, nearly all women and children, were herded forward to Ouiatanon under the muzzles of Hardin's rifles, causing Brigadier General Scott to exult that the Indians had fled before the American Army, leaving their wives and children to his mercy.[35]

After burning several Indian villages, including Kethtippecanunk at the mouth of the Eel River (later Prophetstown, Illinois), and destroying their crops, Scott liberated sixteen of the "weakest and most infirm" prisoners, sending them off to find their scattered tribesmen with his offer of peace terms. This message proclaimed that the United States had "no desire to destroy the red people, although they have the power"; therefore, the captive Indian women and children would be carried off and deposited at the United States military post at the mouth of the Miami. "If you wish to recover them," said Scott, "repair to that place by the first day of July . . . , determined with true hearts to bury the hatchet and smoke the pipe of peace. They will then be restored to you."[36]

Satisfied that he had fulfilled his mission, Scott withdrew from Ouiatanon on June 4, long before news of his attack had reached the Miami Towns. By June 15, Scott was at Fort Steuben on the Ohio, where he delivered forty-one prisoners to the federal commandant.[37]

At Kekionga it was nearly mid-June before the assembled throng learned of Scott's raid on Ouiatanon. Meanwhile, the building impatience and the uncertainty regarding the American designs had produced considerable disarray in the Indian ranks. Because of the enormous logistical burden of feeding so many Indians, several sizeable elements had withdrawn. The Sauks and Foxes, wanting food, had gone home about June 1. Some Wabash-region Indians had heard of an American force going to Vincennes and had started back toward their villages on June 2. This contingent found the ruined villages near Ouiatanon shortly after Scott's departure. Although they followed Scott's trail, the Americans, being mounted, moved too rapidly to be intercepted. At Ouiatanon the warriors found their once-picturesque village in a shambles. One principal chief of the Wabash confederacy, known as Wasp, had been killed and his body skinned.[38]

When news finally reached the Miami Towns of what had happened, there was much indignation. Greatly concerned about their inability to sustain a defensive concentration, the Indians now advised the British that, if they were not better supplied with ammunition and provisions, they must disperse, and that they would be angry with the English, "who [first] put the axe in their hands."[39]

This warning was not lightly regarded by the British Indian Department. Alexander McKee wrote to Lord Dorchester in June that the Indians were so agitated by Scott's recent attack that he feared but "little attention will be now paid to any [peace] proposals." Since this was directly contrary to Dorchester's recent orders to obtain the specific terms on which the Indian confederacy would agree to peace with the United States, McKee promised to intensify his efforts. Yet, while the senior British officials conspired to obtain the terms that might form a basis for direct English mediation, their subordinate Indian officers continued in their unofficial tactical support of the war effort.[40]

McKee, in particular, was active in arrangements for provisioning and supplying the western nations, and he sought to inspire more overt British military involvement. Additional quantities of corn were requisitioned under the guise of providing for the assembled nations who would debate peace terms. McKee even found an opportunity to suggest that a British military post, garrisoned by "not . . . less than 100 regulars and 50 militia," should be erected at the Miami Rapids. The British Indian agent said that this would prevent Detroit from falling by surprise attack to an invading American army and, furthermore, was the key to defending the entire region.[41]

Aroused by the renewed British interest in an equitable settlement of the conflict over their lands, the Indians, as yet "in high spirits," sat down to a council with McKee during the first week in July. To be determined was the fundamental question of a "reasonable" boundary with the Americans that would be the basis for peace. Only the Shawnees and the Miamis were adamant in their attitude, said Joseph Brant; they avowed that no equitable terms could be obtained from a people "so wicked."[42]

At this very time, while the Indians debated terms for a negotiated settlement, a letter from Arthur St. Clair to the military committee of Kentucky arrived in Lexington, wherein St. Clair professed "very great pleasure in congratulating you upon the success of the late expedition (Scott's)" and announced new plans for "another expedition of the same nature." This second raid would be of very great use, said St. Clair; the upper Wabash towns might be attacked with very beneficial consequences. The "public interest" required offensive action, he continued, since it would be "some time before the . . . more systematic operations of [my] campaign can be put in motion."[43]

Soon there was further evidence that consistency, both in word and in deed, was greatly wanting in American frontier policy. As the pitifully few Wea tribesmen understood, when they later arrived at Forts Washington and Knox, there still was little to rely on in the often-ambiguous federal peace rhetoric, especially if American objectives were not to be served. Invited to a treaty to reclaim their wives and children, the Weas could but look with despair at the helpless, miserable prisoners incarcerated at Fort Washington, while the federal government refused to consider their release. They were even told by one post commander that, since they had acted more like children than men, peace would be denied to them; all of the Wabash tribes would have to come in before amnesty could be granted. "The United States would no more be deceived by such perfidious promises [of Indian friendship]," they were warned. Such had become the plight of the distraught Weas that a captured Indian youth, named Billy, was even required to accompany the American Army to serve as a messenger during St. Clair's forthcoming campaign. It seemed that the nearly forgotten prophecy of the ancient chieftain Metacomet (King Philip) had been further validated. Metacomet had long warned that the "people from the unknown world [Europe]" would not only drive off the Indians and despoil the land but also "enslave our women and children."[44]

Thus saddened, the handful of Wea tribesmen wandered away from the federal posts, unaware that fate would soon inflict an even greater humiliation on their American enemies, including, ironically, many white women and children.

Henry Knox, United States secretary of war. Courtesy of William Clements Library, University of Michigan.

15

A Disaster in the Making

IN mid-March, 1791, Arthur St. Clair was summoned to a meeting with President Washington at his Philadelphia office. At that time St. Clair was newly appointed a major general in command of the United States Army, yet continued to draw his annual salary as governor of the Northwest Territory. Washington had some rather somber reflections for his handpicked commander. St. Clair had been selected, the president advised, for his knowledge of the Old Northwest, including of the military resources there, and because of the president's "full confidence" in his military abilities, based on St. Clair's Revolutionary War experience. Yet Washington had some specific counsel, "as an old soldier" and one whose early life had been particularly involved in Indian warfare (for example, at Braddock's Defeat): "General St. Clair, in three words, beware of surprise; trust not the Indian; leave not your arms for the moment; and when you halt for the night be sure to fortify your camp—again and again, General, beware of surprise!"[1]

St. Clair's instructions, issued on March 21 by the secretary of war, covered more than 4,500 words detailing "principles of your conduct." Knox, by Washington's order, was particularly careful to define St. Clair's primary objective: "to establish a strong and permanent military post" at the Miami Village as a means of "awing and curbing the Indians in that quarter." This, warned Knox, was of paramount importance. Even a potential peace with the Indians was not to interfere.[2]

With Harmar's unsuccessful attempt in mind, Knox elaborated on the refinements of the military means available to accomplish St. Clair's task. First, an additional regiment of regulars would be recruited from the New England states to garrison the new post and strengthen the meager southern detachments. This unit was to be known as the Second United States Regiment, and would increase the permanent military establishment to 2,128 rank and file. Since the War Department estimated the opposing hostiles along the Wabash River at 1,100 warriors plus perhaps 1,000 additional, "more distant Indians," Knox decreed that a 3,000-man army would be superior to all opposition. To achieve that, 2,000 "levies" would be recruited to serve for only six months. These men, in effect, would be short-term soldiers; they were accorded a United States designation in order to achieve "a pride of arrangement and discipline." Yet they would remain on a temporary footing so that they could be discharged once their mission was completed. The reason for such a system was threefold, according to Knox: their officers might be selected by the federal government; they would be more effective than the unruly militia; and hiring them would be more economical than requisitioning state troops. To round out the program, if circumstances prevented the assembling of 3,000 effectives for the campaign, St. Clair was authorized to call up the militia of Pennsylvania, Virginia, or the Kentucky District.[3]

Paramount in these revised 1791 plans was the reliance merely on an enlarged force to achieve the American objectives. The quality of the army was not under particular scrutiny; it was presumed that the incidental discipline imposed by federal officers would triumph over the "undisciplined Indians." Most ominous was the lack of assessment of the enemy's capabilities. In the rush to achieve superior strength, the efficacy of the Indians as a fighting force under their proven and sagacious military leaders was all but ignored.[4]

Assured by the secretary of war that all arrangements for the campaign would be expedited in Philadelphia, Arthur St. Clair left that city for the Old Northwest on March 23. While en route to his Fort Washington headquarters, the self-assured American commander wrote to the "friendly" Senecas that it was the United States' intention to make "strong war" on the Shawnees and the Miamis. At the same time, he warned the Ottawas of the "vengeance" that the western Indians would experience. Supremely confident of his military ability as a result of his service from 1757 to 1783 "under some of the first generals in the world" (James Wolfe and George Washington), St. Clair talked openly of the hostiles' "utter destruction," saying that "ruin will surely overtake them."[5]

Yet, barely a few days distant from Philadelphia, St. Clair was seriously stricken with his frequent affliction, the gout. For nearly a month he languished near Pittsburgh, accomplishing little. When he finally arrived at Fort Washington in mid-May, the major general found that the nucleus of his expedition, the veteran regulars, had dwindled to seventy-five soldiers ready for duty at headquarters. In fact, in the entire eastern region embracing Forts Knox (Vincennes), Steuben (Falls of the Ohio), and Harmar (Muskingum), only 189 additional noncommissioned officers and privates remained.[6]

Josiah Harmar, who was disgusted with the impoverished state of the military and awaited only the convening of his court of inquiry before resigning, said that the garrison at Fort Washington was "exceedingly weak" because of the refusal of veterans to re-enlist under the revised enactment of 1790 requiring a reduction in pay. Secretary of War Knox reported in January, 1791, that, of 420 men whose enlistments expired during 1790, only 60 had re-enlisted. Further, the entire western contingent of regulars was unpaid for 1790 as late as April, 1791.

Newly appointed Lieutenant Colonel–Commandant John Doughty of the Second United States Regiment was so distraught over the financial discrimination between military and civil service—"one being regularly and generously rewarded and the other not"—that he refused the command and resigned from the army.[7]

Thus St. Clair was confronted by a discontented and diminished force of regulars that was intended to serve as the basic fiber of his expedition. Summoning the distant garrison at Vincennes, as well as those from the Falls of the Ohio and Fort Harmar, St. Clair was able to consolidate his First United States Regiment at Fort Washington in mid-July. Together they numbered 299 men, all that remained of his former experienced military personnel.[8]

Later St. Clair offered his troops' inexperience as an excuse for their inefficiency. Yet it should have been self-evident almost from the beginning that the quality of the army would be contingent upon the caliber of the recruits and their discipline and training.[9] Since the widespread lack of public support had resulted in a large deficiency of recruits, Knox reported a deficit of 300 men, or approximately one-third of the First Regiment's full strength; and about 550 soldiers or 60 percent of the Second Regiment's complement. Even before St. Clair's campaign began the regulars were short nearly 50 percent of their authorized and anticipated strength. Besides being admittedly inadequate in numbers, the appearance of the regulars at the Fort Washington base of operations caused an astute veteran officer to observe that they were largely urban riffraff. Some were former prisoners, others were inveterate drunkards, all had been hastily thrown together and sent West totally unfamiliar with army methods and frontier life. The burden of the forthcoming campaign was thus clearly to fall on what first had been intended as only an auxiliary force, the United States levies.[10]

As conceived by the War Department, the six-months levies were to be a large, sustaining force providing numerical superiority without the disadvantages of militia. All two thousand levies were to be recruited in New Jersey and Pennsylvania (one regiment) and Maryland. As a separate corps they would establish St. Clair's latitude of maneuver. Then, once the campaign ended, it was anticipated that the discharged levies would replenish the regular troop strength. A six-dollar bounty would be paid to those who enlisted in the permanent military establishment.

Again the same miscalculation of popular support was evident in the levy recruitment as in the plans for the regular military. In his final accounting, Knox calculated that of the 2,000 levies sought only 1,674, or about 84 percent of the quota, were enlisted. Thus, with the deficiency of regulars, a crisis was precipitated by the shortage of a total of about 1,000 men.[11]

When a serious shortage became evident as early as mid-June, Knox began urging St. Clair to recruit additional troops on the frontier, including militia. Knox specifically suggested that St. Clair obtain a force of up to 750 mounted Kentucky volunteers or militia. St. Clair, however, delayed acting decisively upon the matter for several months. Finally, about September 1, he made a curious and significant decision. The secretary of war had urged him to use volunteer *mounted* miltia, in the belief that they would be more effective than the usual drafts of infantry and thus worth the additional expense. St. Clair opted instead for a three-month draft of 1,160 rank and file of ordinary militia. He reasoned that the mounted militia would be inappropriate on an expedition of slow and tedious advances requiring the construction of interim posts. As the final deterrent he cited the expense of paying mounted volunteers four shillings per day, versus the three dollars per month granted to infantry draftees.[12]

Unfortunately, the unpopularity of St. Clair's decision was later to be reflected not only in the poor militia turnout but also in the service that they rendered. The same unruly and inept elements were to be conscripted who had failed Harmar during his campaign. By calling out the militia infantry, St. Clair fatally weakened an army already characterized by inexperience and diminished numbers.

It was perhaps in the critical element of timing that the army's increasing confusion and disorganization first became manifest. St. Clair had initially expected the main portions of the levies and the regular recruits to arrive at Fort Washington early in the summer. According to his original instructions, St. Clair's column was to have been intact by mid-July, allowing the beginning of an offensive movement later that month. These plans were necessarily revised in mid-July to allow for a September 1 projected march. Little more than a month later, Knox acknowledged that the "unfortunate" delay in transporting troops down the Ohio to Fort Washington would further retard the start of the expedition. The president was by now very upset with the various delays; he warned the secretary of war that "languor and want of success" would produce dishonor for all concerned.[13]

Since St. Clair was unwilling that his expedition be carried beyond a nominal distance from Fort Washington before his entire force was present, the onus soon fell on Major General Richard Butler, the man designated to organize the recruiting and forwarding of troops from the East. A rather austere and self-centered politician-general, Butler had emerged from the Revolutionary War with a reputation for valor in the Pennsylvania line. Eventually the right connections made him the United States superintendent of Indian affairs for the Northern District and caused him to be appointed major general commanding the six-month levies. Not yet fifty and disheveled in appearance, the Irish-born Butler had proceeded to the task of raising the levies under the admonition of Secretary Knox that he was the "pivot upon which all things turn."[14]

Butler began to understand the complexity of this undertaking when he arrived at Fort Pitt on May 22.[15]

Here the chronic inefficiency of the entire military system was soon evident. Clothing, tents, provisions, and transportation were lacking, and although Secretary of War Knox promised "all the stores for the campaign" would be forwarded by June 1, Butler complained repeatedly thereafter of the want of articles such as canteens, camp kettles, shoes, and knapsacks. The pack saddles, when received, were "large enough for elephants." Butler soon found himself also short of provisions, a problem that was accentuated by the want of money in the hands of the contractor's agent to purchase foodstuffs.

In all, the situation was a bitter indictment of army logistics under the contract system, causing the harassed Butler, who had taken sick in the middle of June, bitterly to denounce the entire supply operation.[15]

At the root of the matter was a familiar bane of the American political process, internal corruption and want of personal integrity high in the government's administration. William Duer, an unscrupulous New York financier, had been reassigned the original contract for provisioning the army in January, 1791. A familiar face on the congressional and financial scenes during the Revolutionary War years, Duer seemed now to be an emerging giant among the nation's entrepreneurs. A rakish and immensely ambitious man in his early forties, he boasted important connections in the highest circles. Washington had been his friend from the time of the Conway Cabal incident during the Revolution, and the president had given the bride away at Duer's marriage to Catherine ("Lady Kitty"), daughter of William Alexander ("Lord Sterling"). In September, 1789, Duer had joined his close friend Alexander Hamilton to serve the new administration briefly as assistant secretary of the Treasury. His relationship with Henry Knox was also intimately cordial.

As the army contractor in 1791, Duer was responsible to Knox for provisioning the army. Yet as the recipient of more than $75,000 in advances from the Treasury for the purchase of army supplies, Duer was financially able to participate in a favorite activity, land speculation. Already under severe monetary pressure for liabilities incurred in stock speculation, Duer, on April 28, 1791, with a fresh $15,000 in his pocket from a Treasury advance on the army contract, proceeded to loan $10,000 to his good friend Henry Knox, who was also interested in land speculation. Together they concluded a secret partnership to speculate in New England lands, from which it was anticipated enormous profits would ensue. With their enterprise at least partially funded from the monies advanced on the army contract, Knox and Duer engaged the erstwhile Revolutionary War brigadier and Boston crony of Knox, Henry Jackson, to act as their agent in dealing with the state of Massachusetts. Duer and Knox wanted to purchase four million acres of state land in Maine (which was part of Massachusetts in 1791), anticipating that immigrants could be brought from abroad (particularly, French dissidents) to purchase much of the tract at inflated prices. Duer had used his leverage in the Ohio Company purchase to extract an option on Old Northwest lands, which, in turn, were the basis for Duer's Scioto Company's fraudulent sale of Ohio lands to French emigrants. Since Duer had already achieved some success in such ventures, Knox had confidently complied with Duer's "operations," which involved tactics such as the use of influence to achieve special favors. For example, the purchased Ohio lands were to be exempt from taxes for ten years. All of these devices, assured Duer, "will make the speculation solid and productive."[17]

Indeed, Duer and Knox were so heavily involved in arranging the details of their land speculation from April to July, 1791, that frequent trips and meetings were required on this special project. On July 1, 1791, the initial articles of agreement were signed with Massachusetts for two million acres of Maine lands at ten cents an acre. Ultimately, the two officials contracted for another tract of one million acres at twenty cents an acre, plus other Massachusetts lands, for a total obligation of about $500,000.[18]

The net result of these activities, of course, was that Duer grossly neglected the army contract. Not only did he give insufficient time and attention to organizing and maintaining a viable supply system, but also, worse still, he siphoned off the funds advanced for procurement of flour, beef, and other provisions to the land speculation. Duer's appointed agents, who were on site at Fort Pitt and other locations, received little or no funds to purchase needed supplies. Hence, when the various merchants refused to grant further extension of credit, there was an abrupt stoppage in provisions. General Butler complained loudly and bitterly in June, 1791, causing Knox to advise Duer, "For God's sake, put the matter of provisions on the frontier in perfect train." When it became obvious that Duer had long neglected his army responsibilities, Knox, in July, warned his partner, "I hope in God you have made other and more effectual [arrangements] or you will suffer exceedingly."[19]

This, of course, was in private correspondence. Publicly, Knox was covering up for his associate as much as possible, saying that perhaps Duer's subagents were failing to give him full information on their needs. Knox even went so far as to favor Duer in supplying shoes to the army, which were not in his army contract; and late in July he wrote to his field commanders assuring them of Duer's continued activity.[20]

As if Knox's complicity in the insufficient provisioning of his troops was not sufficiently worrisome, the lumbering 300-pound secretary of war suffered further embarrassment in the performance of his friend Samuel Hodgdon, the newly appointed quartermaster. Hodgdon was among the men whom Henry Jackson, Knox's agent, termed a "number of suckers" hanging about the secretary of war looking for lucrative government jobs. Hodgdon had served during the Revolution as commissary general of military stores, having been mustered out in June, 1784. As recently as October, 1790, he had scurried about Philadelphia looking for a residence for Henry Knox after the transfer of the seat of government to that city. Despite his former experience as an officer in the army supply system, Hodgdon was nonetheless short on ability and often was careless in his business transactions. Although appointed quartermaster on March 3, 1791, and entitled to the same pay as a lieutenant colonel–commandant, he tarried at Philadelphia until June 4, more than a month past the date that Knox had first established for his departure to join the army.

Ostensibly, Hodgdon was preoccupied in Philadelphia with ordering, gathering, and making arrangements to transport the needed military stores to Fort Pitt. Yet if one scrutinizes the long list of items forwarded in mid-June, Hodgdon's singular lack of judgment and even of common sense is apparent in the procurement of construction and land-clearing tools. The army was to cut its way through the wilderness of the Ohio country, building several interim posts en route to its main objective, the establishment of a strong fortification at the Miami Village. Yet Hodgdon forwarded only fifteen axes, eighteen broadaxes, twelve hammers, and twenty-four handsaws— certainly an insignificant quantity. Furthermore, he relied, for the sake of thrift, on reprocessed gunpowder "manufactured from damaged public powder." Hodgdon was so penny-pinching, even in the contracts that he made for new equipment, that he often procured merchandise of shoddy quality.[21]

Once on the scene at Fort Pitt, Hodgdon, who carried $20,000 in government funds, became bogged down in various minutiae. Knapsacks that he had ordered in Philadelphia were neither "painted" (weatherproofed) nor strapped, necessitating their completion before being shipped to the frontier. The Philadelphia-purchased packsaddles were found so odd-sized that new trees had to be fashioned at Fort Pitt. Even worse, the supply of shoes on hand for the levies was so minimal that two thousand pairs had to be ordered from Philadelphia late in June. Hodgdon's wanton carelessness in basic procurement ultimately resulted in the purchase of William Duer's shoes, which just happened to be on site to fill a critical need. Ultimately, these were found to be of such poor quality as "to last not more than four days" in many cases.

Overall, the extended delays in forwarding troops and materiel evoked the wrath of nearly all concerned. Arthur St. Clair, of course, was furious. Beginning in August, he complained bitterly to Knox. Hodgdon, who was still at Fort Pitt, was openly denounced for sending forward an assistant "that is incapable of anything and is constantly drunk." Despite repeated orders from St. Clair to proceed to Fort Washington, Hodgdon remained at Fort Pitt until the last week in August.[22]

In late July and early August "the unfortunate detention of the troops on the upper . . . Ohio" came into sharp focus with the return to Philadelphia of President Washington, who had been in the South. Washington was soon angered by what he regarded as the "unnecessary and improper" delay in forwarding troops down the Ohio. Beginning late in July and continuing weekly, Knox reminded Butler and Hodgdon of the president's extreme "anxiety" over the delay. With each passing week the pressure on Knox seemed to mount, and his correspondence became increasingly blunt. Finally, Knox had to admonish his friend Hodgdon, "You ought personally to have been at headquarters long ago."[23]

Beginning in mid-August, detachments of levies and regulars finally began moving with some frequency down the Ohio. Yet, because a drought had diminished the water level, it was mid-September before all of Butler's troops were present at Fort Washington. Among the last to embark at Pittsburgh, on August 26, were Samuel Hodgdon and Richard Butler. Their arrival at St. Clair's headquarters on September 10 was greeted with anything but enthusiasm from the major general commanding. On that date, they were present exactly two months beyond the time originally set for the beginning of the major offensive.[24]

By this time an ill-tempered St. Clair had instructed Israel Ludlow, now an agent of William Duer, to purchase up to 800 horses for use in carrying the army's provisions. Because of the urgent time schedule, Ludlow thought it necessary to purchase 656 packhorses at a cost of more than $17,500, which was charged to Duer's account. Since the terms of Duer's contract required the contractor to furnish all of the transportation involved in provisioning the army, St. Clair estimated that he was justified in assigning the cost of the 635 horses actually delivered to Fort Washington by September 15 to Duer. Of course the evasive Duer refused to accept these bills, saying Ludlow had no authority from him to buy horses, because "another arrangement" had been made. Ultimately the United States Treasury was required to pay the bill.[25]

St. Clair had been delayed for three days by incessant rains on his second journey to Kentucky about September 1. He returned to Fort Washington on the ninth to find many of Butler's troops present at last. At this point, however, the army's and St. Clair's personal ill fortune were only beginning.[26] By St. Clair's order, in mid-August the advance contingents, includ-

151

ing Major Hamtramck's regular detachment from Vincennes (which had been present at Fort Washington since July 15), had moved from Fort Washington to Ludlow's Station, about six miles north. There, St. Clair reasoned, "tolerable pasture" would be found for the horses. Actually, the move was largely intended "to deprive them [the soldiers] of the means of intoxication, which was very plentifully supplied at Fort Washington—"this was reported by the House committee that later investigated the campaign.[27]

Rather belatedly, St. Clair responded to President Washington's urging to begin construction of his interim posts. Instructions were given to Major Hamtramck to march to the banks of the Great Miami and begin "a small fort," once the surveyor had completed marking the route. The distance forward from the Ludlow's Station camp was about eighteen miles, but on September 10, when St. Clair rejoined the advanced troops, he found that due to the recent heavy rains the troops had been unable to march until September 8, and construction of the fort had not yet begun.[28]

In all, about fourteen weeks had elapsed since the arrival of the first troops intended for the campaign, back on June 13. Even though his undisciplined soldiers had been abruptly thrown together without any sort of combat preparation or training, St. Clair expressed optimism in his correspondence with Henry Knox, once Butler's troops were present. In one letter St. Clair said to tell President Washington "nothing has been left undone." In another he talked of bringing the campaign to "a speedy and happy issue," proclaiming, "I do not now see anything that is likely to impede us any further." On September 23 he again wrote, "All seems now as if it would go well."[29]

That very week, the long-awaited court of inquiry requested by Josiah Harmar met and conferred its opinion after ten days of testimony and deliberation. Richard Butler, president of the court, proclaimed it was their unanimous verdict that General Harmar's conduct had been "irreproachable." In fact, read Butler's statement, "Brigadier General Josiah Harmar merits high approbation."

Vindicated, so he believed, by this cursory investigation of the 1790 campaign, Harmar promptly packed his baggage and, with his family, ascended the Ohio River to retire to civilian life. Before he left, he conversed with a few of his army friends about the forthcoming campaign.[30] "[He] predicted a defeat," said Ebenezer Denny:

[This] was founded upon his experience and particular knowledge of things. He saw with what material the bulk of the army was composed; men collected from the streets and prisons of the cities, hurried out into the enemy's country, and with the officers commanding them totally unacquainted with the business in which they were engaged. . . .

"It was a matter of astonishment to him that Arthur St. Clair . . . should think of hazarding, with such people, and under such circumstances, his reputation and life, and the lives of so many others.[31]

Before Harmar left, he had frequently revealed the extent of his bitterness and disgust to Denny, who was so moved that he talked of resigning and going home with his former general. "You must," countered Harmar, "go on the campaign—some will escape, and you may be among the number."

As Denny tersely noted in his journal a few days later, about twenty-five men, led by a sergeant, had deserted already.[23]

With the days becoming shorter, and the weather rapidly changing (on September 11 the first frost of the season occurred), the army seemed to seethe with uncertainty and misgiving. Yet Arthur St. Clair continued his inane correspondence with Secretary of War Knox, even professing an eagerness to meet the Indians in battle, as "the troops seem to be in perfectly good disposition for it."[33]

Such were the elements of a major disaster in the making.

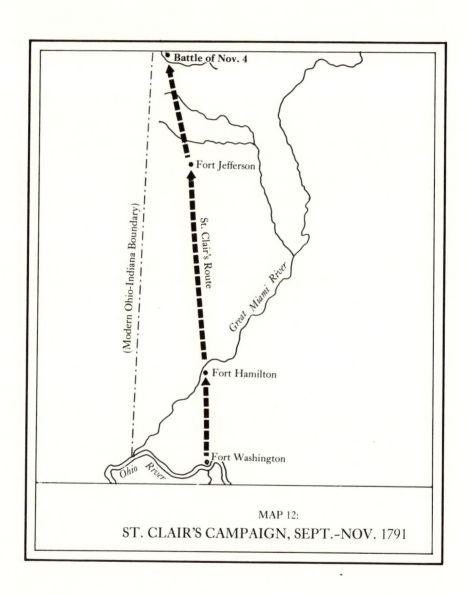

Battle of Nov. 4

(Modern Ohio-Indiana Boundary)

St. Clair's Route

Fort Jefferson

Great Miami River

Fort Hamilton

Fort Washington

Ohio River

MAP 12:

ST. CLAIR'S CAMPAIGN, SEPT.–NOV. 1791

154

16

March into Oblivion

JAMES Wilkinson was only thirty-four years of age in 1791, yet his reputation as a frontier leader seemed to surpass even that of George Rogers Clark. Wilkinson had become a brevet brigadier general at the age of twenty, having served as aide-de-camp to Major General Horatio Gates at Saratoga and later as clothier general of the Continental Army. A brilliant orator and an accomplished politician, Wilkinson was looked on as a man of extraordinary ability. Yet his shortcomings often exceeded his attributes.

Vain and pompous in manner, the former Marylander was so excessively ambitious that he frequently compromised even basic loyalties. Imbued with the scruples of a hardened convict and the cunning of a New York speculator, Wilkinson was the sort of man who is only as trustworthy as his pure self-interest will dictate. Despite his flashy, ostentatious, and often outspoken style, he had a long history of intrigue and scandal. Having been implicated, for example, in the Conway Cabal affair, which had involved an attempt to remove Washington during the Revolution, he had escaped serious difficulty only by adept political maneuvering.[1]

Following his resignation as clothier general, because of gross irregularities in his accounts, Wilkinson had immigrated to Kentucky in 1784. As a merchant dealing in speculative commodities, his success in transporting bacon, tobacco, and flour down the Mississippi to New Orleans in 1787 earned him enormous prestige on the Kentucky frontier as a man with connections. It also resulted in a clandestine and highly irregular "understanding" between Wilkinson and the Spanish governor at New Orleans, by which Wilkinson claimed a Spanish "pension" including a $6,000 initial grant and the rights as the sole American trading agent on the Missisipi. The price for this lucrative arrangement had been Wilkinson's help as a secret agent in influencing Kentuckians to separate from an American alliance and form a state under Spanish protection.[2]

Although Wilkinson had thus materially compromised his loyalties, he soon became involved in American military affairs, with an eye toward achieving even greater frontier prominence. As a Kentucky-militia lieutenant colonel under Brigadier General Charles Scott during the Ouiatanon Towns raid of May and June, 1791, the often hard-drinking Wilkinson had inveigled an appointment as the commander of the second "desultory" raid ordered by St. Clair late in June.[3]

Wilkinson's raid was occasioned by the protracted delay in organizing the main expedition against the Miami Villages, and was directed against

L'Anguille, another of the Wabash-region villages allegedly so troublesome to Kentuckians. By St. Clair's instructions, Wilkinson was to take with him not more than 500 mounted volunteer militia and, through surprise, seize and destroy the Indian village, taking as many prisoners as possible. As Scott had accomplished so successfully in his Ouiatanon raid, Wilkinson sought to deceive the Indians about his real objective by feinting in the direction of the Miami Towns before veering northwest toward L'Anguille. The Kentucky lieutenant colonel anticipated that his entire force would thus be brought into action in a sudden surprise attack, providing, by maximum stealth, success without a hard fight.[4]

Proceeding from Fort Washington with 523 rank and file on August 1, 1791, Wilkinson's column, fully mounted, traversed about seventy miles in two and one-half days. On August 5, in "cool, temperate" weather, Wilkinson began his direct approach through the unbroken wilderness. On the morning of August 7, after losing his way, he at last brought his men to the vicinity of L'Anguille.[5]

Hastily charging across the Eel River into the village, the Kentuckians rounded up thirty-four prisoners, mostly women and children. Six warriors were killed, at a loss of two militiamen dead and another wounded. After deploying work details to cut down the standing corn, which was "scarcely in the milk," and burn the clustered huts, Wilkinson bivouacked for the night. Although he intended to proceed to the Kickapoo villages the following morning, his men now feared Indian retaliation and were reluctant to advance farther into the enemy's country. Wilkinson was soon compelled to return to Kentucky via the trace that Scott had used in June, stopping en route at the deserted village of Ouiatanon, where more corn was destroyed.[6]

Boasting of his men's "usual good conduct," Wilkinson prepared an inflated report of his operations, asserting that he had destroyed "the chief town" of the Wea nation. More pointedly, he claimed the accolades that would be due a bold and successful commander, particularly the "favorable consideration of Government." President Washington was so pleased by his glowing report, a copy of which Wilkinson had deliberately forwarded to the government in Philadelphia, that a special congratulatory message was issued thanking Wilkinson for his "zeal, perseverance, and good conduct." Moreover, within a few months a commission was issued to Wilkinson by Secretary of War Knox, appointing him lieutenant colonel–commandant of the Second United States Regiment.[7]

Wilkinson had been most fortunate, indeed. Again extraordinary circumstances had intervened that allowed the raiders' column to escape unscathed. At the time of the attack on L'Anguille the Indians had only recently dispersed to their various villages after the grand council held by Alexander McKee early in July at the Miami Rapids. Early in August another "policy" delegation was en route to Quebec, and the lapse in significant activity until their return had provided an atmosphere of false security. Moreover, a severe sickness, possibly influenza, had so incapacitated "nearly all" of the Indians of the Miami region that a British-based observer wrote, "every day two or three are buried, and how can . . . they go to war and who shall fight?" Even the element of blind luck had gone against the Indian defenders of

Arthur St. Clair, the plodding general who led the American army to defeat on November 4, 1791. From an engraving of a pencil drawing from life by John Trumbull, courtesy of William Clements Library, University of Michigan.

L'Anguille. According to the lone white captive recovered by Wilkinson's men in the village, the male inhabitants were so randomly dispersed that only eight warriors had been present at the time of the attack. Sixty fighting men had gone east to reconnoiter across the Wabash, while others were absent purchasing ammunition at the French Store near Vincennes and digging roots in the woods.[8]

Stung by the loss of so many of their women and children, the tribesmen were in despair, but the immediate reaction of the general confederacy was outrage. Complaints were renewed that the Indians on the Wabash had been attacked at the very moment when the confederacy was deliberating "pacific measures" (this was a reference to Dorchester's conference in Quebec). Again there seemed to be a glaring want of credibility in American motives. As the missionary David Zeisberger noted in his diary, the whole country was now so alarmed that the hostiles even began sending messages among Zeisberger's Christian Indians, virtually demanding that they too prepare to fight the Americans.[9]

In early September red-painted tobacco, the traditional Indian summons to war, was circulated among the Detroit tribes following the news of St. Clair's initial advance from Fort Washington. A great gathering of the confederated tribes had been planned for September 1 at the Miami Rapids to hear of the returning delegates' conference with Dorchester. Wilkinson's raid, followed by intelligence of St. Clair's advance to the Great Miami, occasioned an even greater concentration of Indians than had been expected.[10]

In late September an observer near Detroit reported a steady stream of transient warriors "going to war." McKee, in fact, became increasingly apprehensive about provisioning so many natives. In July the several thousand Indians present had consumed five hundred bushels of corn, which originally had been intended to serve as the season's supply for the Miami Towns. Throughout the late summer McKee had requisitioned increased supplies, and by midautumn, with perhaps 3,000 Indians present, the drain on British provisions was so excessive that he again pressed for greater aid.[11]

The whole purpose of the Dorchester administration's preoccupation with placating the Indians was to achieve a unilateral agreement among the red nations on the terms by which they would return to peace with the United States. This great object of British policy was proclaimed throughout 1791, and it was the apparent reason why Dorchester had granted an extended conference to the deputation of Indians from the July council at the Miami Rapids.

On August 15 and 17, at the very time when Wilkinson's raiders were returning from the Wabash, a substantive private council was convened at the Castle of Saint Louis in Quebec. Among those present were Lord Dorchester; Lieutenant Governor Alured Clarke, who would soon assume the reins of government temporarily during Dorchester's imminent journey to England; and Joseph Brant, with six chiefs of various Indian nations.[12]

When the central issues were raised, Brant spoke solemnly, asserting that the Indian confederacy had concluded "to ask that a British fort be built at the Miamis Rapids for their mutual protection." Beyond that, the Indians sin-

158

cerely asked to know, "in case of another attack, which we have great reason to expect shortly, how far we can be assisted—that we know what to depend upon." As for their willingness to settle the dispute peacefully: if the United States would grant the crucial Ohio River boundary (exclusive of the section east of the Muskingum), the Indians would abide by those terms and make peace.[13]

Dorchester, pleased that the Indian leadership had defined their collective terms for a nonbelligerent settlement, ordered additional provisions and supplies to be issued. He also directed an inquiry into the feasibility of reestablishing military posts at the Miami Rapids and Kekionga. As for overt British involvement, Dorchester urged only a negotiated settlement, saying "we have no power to begin a war." Otherwise, he promised the Indians to "represent your wishes to the King, your father," during his upcoming visit to England. Having perhaps further obscured the British intentions in the Indians' minds, Dorchester sailed for Europe late in August. He was not to return until September, 1793, following an absence of more than two years.[14]

Conveyed by the ship *Nancy*, the Indian delegates were so plagued by inordinate delays in returning to their villages that they did not arrive at Detroit until the middle of October. As they candidly discussed with some residents near Detroit, they had been led to expect an answer from the king in the spring; meanwhile, if the United States agreed to the Ohio boundary and sent no army into Indian country, they would "make peace with the Americans" as suggested by Dorchester.

On Monday, October 17, the deputies departed from Detroit for the Miami Rapids, carrying their news of the British-inspired program. Yet as Alexander McKee tersely reported a few days later, the delegates had already missed the grand gathering of the assembled tribes at the rapids. Because of the approach of an American army toward the Miami Towns, the entire assembled council had gone forward to defend the Miami Villages en masse. As McKee now dutifully reported to his superior, all thought of a negotiated settlement "is now laid aside."[15]

In mid-August the Miami-region Indians had been so destitute of provisions that they had consumed corn planted on the Miami before it was mature. Yet by midautumn, in consequence of McKee's initiative, they were not only well provisioned but also adequately supplied with war materiel that was brought from the eastern ports to Detroit in late September. The intrigued McKee thus observed, "It appears probable that a few days will determine the affairs of one or other [the Indians or the Americans] for this season."[16]

Major General Arthur St. Clair had anticipated originally that Wilkinson's raid would coincide generally with the main army's advance and create a "collateral movement." Although he was disappointed in the extended delay in forming his army that prevented its advance until nearly three weeks after Wilkinson's return, St. Clair was nonetheless elated with the Kentuckian's expedition. Unaware that the raid had triggered a sequence of events that boded ill for his expedition, he blithely continued his ponderous preparations for the forthcoming offensive.[17]

Throughout the summer the army had become increasingly impatient and frustrated at the continual delays, but by mid-September, with Butler's levies finally present, there was at last an expectant atmosphere.

With the transfer of the army to Ludlow's Station and then twenty miles forward to the camp on the Great Miami, the weather had steadily improved. Throughout most of September and into October the temperatures were generally mild, ranging in the sixties and seventies, with moderate rain. The troops, camped in an estimated 300-acre prairie of tall grass along the banks of the Great Miami, found that there was abundant game of many kinds and that the rivers were filled with fish. Discipline was generally lax, and soldiers frequently strolled beyond the camp limits in a casual manner, unarmed and indifferent to the danger of lurking Indians.[18]

The objective of the bivouac at the Great Miami was, of course, to establish St. Clair's first place of deposit, a "50 yards square" fortification soon designated Fort Hamilton in honor of the secretary of the Treasury.

About September 11 the construction of the fort had begun, under the direction of Major William Ferguson of the artillery. In two weeks an irregular, five-sided stockade with four blockhouses was erected, enclosing a barracks for one hundred men and several storehouses. Since it was about twenty-three miles north of Fort Washington (within a day's march), St. Clair seemed gratified that his first communications link had been established.[19]

After his departure to join the army in the field on September 18, St. Clair, in tolerable health and spirits, had dispatched a message to Secretary of War Knox that everything was in order to commence an effective campaign. No sooner had he arrived at the Fort Hamilton site, however, than matters began rapidly to deteriorate. The mutterings of the malcontents among the soldiers were daily growing louder. Because of heavy fogs between daylight and 7:00 or 8:00 A.M., the army frequently formed in line of battle until the danger of attack had passed. With the appointment of new staff officers, an even sterner discipline was imposed. The late September rains dampened nearly everyone's ardor, and an officer recorded in his orderly book that the country was unhealthy—he was the only captain well enough to do duty in his regiment, and even he was suffering from a severe cold.[20]

St. Clair was present with the army only long enough to make arrangements for the next forward advance, then he returned to Fort Washington on October 2. On his arrival there the major general was disappointed to find only about 300 Kentucky conscripts present, who were badly officered and poorly equipped. In fact, the proportion of officers to privates was so unbalanced that the entire force had to be reorganized.[21]

Although their commander, Lieutenant Colonel William Oldham, assured St. Clair that perhaps 300 more Kentuckians would soon arrive, the major general disgustedly sent the militia forward immediately to join the army on October 5. Their arrival in camp was heralded by the usual sarcasm, especially among the regulars. Remembrance of Harmar's ill-fated expedition was deep-seated, and an undercurrent of skepticism ran through the army, especially when it was observed that many of the militia conscripts were old and "by no means woodsmen." The impact of the militia, which was understength by about 450 men, was of such negative consequence that no regular duty was assigned to them because of their unreliability. The militia, far from being a sustaining force, thus seemed to harken only to turmoil and rebelliousness. Accordingly, the regular officers kept a wary eye on them.[22]

At Fort Washington, in a final communiqué before setting forth to rejoin the army for the general advance, St. Clair advised Henry Knox that his command now numbered about 2,300 men. Should the rest of the militia join up, said St. Clair, "it will make the matter [the expedition's success] pretty certain." Meanwhile, from the nearly completed Fort Hamilton, the army had marched north on October 4 under Major General Richard Butler, leaving behind a garrison mostly of "convalescents or men improper for actual service."[23]

Richard Butler had long criticized the aristocratic St. Clair for "know[ing] little about managing Indians," but already he had found it necessary to alter a basic campaign directive regarding the order of march. After fording the waist-high and rapidly flowing waters of the Great Miami, the army, using St. Clair's method of carving two narrow and parallel roadways through the wilderness (separated by some two or three hundred yards), had managed only a mile and a half on the first day. The adjacent timber was heavy, and for the first time the troops' strength began to wane due to the imposing obstacles of their late-season wilderness campaign. Wet and cold from an intermittent rain, the men found that the axes that they had been issued were so improperly tempered that they rapidly dulled at the cutting edge. Too, there were only ten men assigned to each work detail, with relief granted every two hours. Even the promise of an extra ration of liquor, "as an encouragement to industry," failed to speed the road-cutting process.[24]

Butler, exasperated over the protracted movement of the army over the two parallel roadways, ordered that a single path be cut instead, at least twelve feet wide to accommodate the artillery and baggage. Still, the timber and underbrush were so thick that the infantrymen had "to cut their way at every step." Only three miles were gained on October 5, and the terrain was found so difficult that by October 8 the army had covered only about twenty-two miles in five days.[25]

That evening Major General St. Clair and his staff returned to the army from Fort Washington. St. Clair was immediately disgusted by the laboriously slow progress. He promptly termed the movement under Butler as being of "very gentle" marches. The personal relationship between Butler and St. Clair, decidedly cool following the delay on the upper Ohio, now assumed a new acerbity. Butler attempted an explanation, giving his reasons for changing the order of march and apologizing for doing so. St. Clair, however, was abrupt and icy in his response. The change was not satisfactory, he exhorted, since a defensive line of battle could not as easily be formed, and in his opinion it was more efficient to open "three roads of 10-12', than one of 40'." Deeply offended by St. Clair's attitude, Butler withdrew from other than a perfunctory contact with headquarters and purposely avoided his commander's presence.[26]

Moreover, other schisms were festering in the army's command, expanding the undercurrent of friction and partisanship among the officers. No basis for seniority had been established between Colonels William Darke and George Gibson of the levies, and this caused a heated dispute to occur between the two. Ultimately, Darke was given seniority based on his previous regular-army service, but the roughhewn Darke seemed already to have earned the enmity of many regulars for his lack of professionalism.[27]

Equally vexing to the regular establishment was the presence of a civilian, Winthrop Sargent, as the army's adjutant general. His austere disposition, haughty demeanor, and stern demands were the bane of the regular line officers, and even St. Clair admitted Sargent was "very obnoxious" to them. Once regarded as the best-dressed man in the Continental Army—his field kit included pewter plates made by Paul Revere—Sargent had been hand-picked by his friend and associate in the civil administration of the Northwest Territory, Arthur St. Clair. St. Clair, in fact, had obtained special permission from Henry Knox for Sargent's appointment; there had been no provision for the office of adjutant general. All of this was very unsettling to the regular officers, many of whom resented such a politically inspired intrusion.[28]

St. Clair, while chagrined to find his officers bickering among themselves, was even more alarmed to find that the army was in dire physical condition. On October 8 he discovered that the expected quantity of rations were not on hand at Fort Hamilton, contrary to the assurances of his quartermaster and the contractor's agent. In a blistering letter to Duer's agent, St. Clair warned that, "by the day after tomorrow I shall not have an ounce [of provisions] unless some arrives in the meantime." "Take notice," he cautioned, "that the want of drivers will be no excuse to a starving army and a disappointed people."[29] Despite such pointed remarks, the logistic capabilities of the contractor failed materially to improve. By October 12 the army was so impoverished, having only three days' supply of flour, that St. Clair ordered a halt to erect another fort. By then his column had advanced sixty-eight and one-half miles from Fort Washington.[30]

Crucial in the rapidly deteriorating supply situation was the serious deficiency in horses. Despite the procurement of the 656 packhorses charged against the contractor's account in mid-September, barely a month later the dwindling number of the contractor's horses was traceable, St. Clair believed, to the negligence and incompetence of Duer's horsemaster. Described as "a man who had never been in the woods in his life," the horsemaster, W. Dunn, was so inexperienced that he attempted to feed the horse herd by scattering forage along the ground, rather than fashioning troughs from tree bark. The horses were said to be much injured by "kicking each other and fighting over it." Also the cavalry horses, which had been brought from Fort Pitt aboard the crowded riverboats, had been turned loose in the woods without bells or hobbles. About seventy of them were later found missing, and St. Clair exploded with wrath when the horsemaster told him that he did not know bells were necessary to locate the animals. Said St. Clair in disgust, "he should have carried a bell himself, for he never would have found his way back [out of the woods] again."[31]

St. Clair assigned Captain Jonathan Snowden of the regulars to help manage the horses, but in mid-October not enough healthy animals were on hand to carry sufficient provisions. The autumn frosts by then had killed much of the natural forage. Already weak and emaciated, the contractor's horses, said one soldier, died so rapidly that nearly every prairie and swamp was littered with their carcasses.[32]

By October 19, St. Clair was so alarmed that he assigned nearly all of the three hundred army-owned baggage horses to the contractor's task of provisioning the army. As a result, much of the troops' baggage, including spare clothing and all personal effects that could not be carried in a knapsack, had to be left behind.[33]

Although the weather had been favorable for nearly a week before October 14, during that evening it began raining incessantly. For four days the deluge continued amid falling temperatures, the rain turning to hail on the seventeenth. As might be expected, the effect on the army was nearly disastrous.

St. Clair had selected a site on a rather low, rounded gravel knoll, about five miles south of modern-day Greenville, Ohio, for the location of his new fort of deposit. Although he said that the site was "proper enough" for a post, his men thought the location too accessible to the enemy. It was surrounded by small knolls and was susceptible to have the supply of water cut off because the fresh spring that issued nearby was about 100 feet distant.[34]

When the men began to clear the timber for the stockade on October 14, it was found that only eighty axes were available. Then it was discovered that Quartermaster Hodgdon had on hand only one crosscut saw and a single frow. With the onset of high winds, followed by a storm front, progress became exceedingly slow. Except for the two hundred men assigned to the work detail, the army mostly languished in their light tents of Russian sheeting, buffeted by the cold winds and drenched by the steady rain. The small tents had been procured because Knox had instructed that "the nature of the campaign [rapid marches during the summer] will render it very improper that heavy tents should be used." Termed by the men "truly infamous," these cheaply made tents had been fashioned of crocus on their flap ends, which would not keep out the rain. Soaked to the skin, the troops could but endure in misery until the storm clouds finally broke on the morning of October 18. Under cloudy skies and in chilly temperatures the work details labored to lay the rafters on the new fort, beginning at midday on the nineteenth. Yet so many men were sick from exposure and insufficient rations that St. Clair feared the entire campaign might soon be aborted.[35]

Indeed, the levies were found sloshing about the marshy campground with their new clothing, procured under Hodgdon's contracts, in tatters. The coats and hats were particularly inferior, and their shirts shrank so that they were almost useless. The shoes purchased from Duer's stock continued to fall apart at the seams. Moreover, there now was uncertainty about fixed ammunition, since "many hundred dozens" of musket cartridges had been soaked by the rain in the leaky storage tents.

To make matters worse, the wilderness road had turned into a morass, and travel was exceedingly difficult. The procurement of provisions now was so uncertain that even the aloof Adjutant General Sargent expressed concern. Despite the arrival of about 6,000 pounds of flour by packhorse on the evening of October 18, the food situation remained critical. Except for 240 bullocks on hand, it was found that this flour represented the entire stock of provisions for the army and its camp followers, in all about 2,700 persons. St. Clair successively put the entire column first on single rations of flour, then on half rations of one-quarter pound on the twenty-first. In fact, with a ration of one-quarter pound of flour per man scheduled for issue on the twenty-second, the entire supply would be expended.[36']

At this point the army was in such dire straits that St. Clair ordered most of his baggage horses returned to the rear for provisions. The major general now faced the grim prospect of an outright failure. Some of the troops, especially the militia, were so mutinous that they ceased to perform even minimal duties. Moreover, the soldiers' general attitude was that of outrage. "We were almost starved to death," wrote a young regular lieutenant of the breakdown in the army's subsistence. "Does any man suppose that a pound of poor beef, a quarter of a pound of flour, and no liquor, would inspire adventurous bravery," an incredulous infantryman later wrote.[37]

Many of the Virginia levies were so angered by the deteriorating conditions of their service that they clamored for immediate discharge, claiming their six-month term had expired. St. Clair wrote an impassioned letter to Henry Knox on October 17, stating that he was on the point of losing the entire Virginia battalion. The dispute raged on whether they had agreed to serve for six months from the date of their enlistment or from the date of their arrival at the point of rendezvous. Finally, St. Clair allowed the discharge of dozens of men, including an entire Virginia company on October 20.[38]

Beginning early in October and continuing with frequency throughout the march into the wilderness, desertions had been reported from both the regular army and the militia. With the difficulties of the third week in October, however, the number of desertions had increased significantly. Men like John Oneil and John Wade, two Irishmen who professed former loyalty to the British king, made straight for Detroit after abandoning the American army, carrying with them important military information. Four regulars of the First Regiment were found to be missing between October 14 and October 17, and on the night of October 21 at least a dozen militia vanished.[39]

St. Clair, seeing his army rapidly disintegrating, was greatly angered by what he considered to be irresolute, unjustified behavior. "Persons that cannot look greater difficulties than those in the face with patience, and even pleasure, should never think of being soldiers," he later wrote. On October 22 the general was moved to an act of extremity. He imposed the death penalty on three soldiers in order to restore a measure of discipline. Two artillerymen, who had been caught attempting to desert to the British forts on the night of the seventeenth, and a levy private, who had shot a comrade and threatened an officer, were hung on October 23 with the entire army drawn up to watch.

After a general crackdown on misdeeds of all sorts, including fifty lashes imposed on each of two men found sleeping on duty, the army gradually appeared to quiet. Thereafter the attitude seemed to prevail that pardoning serious offenders was "mistaken clemency." St. Clair, in fact, later reported that so many punishments had been inflicted that his orderly journal read mostly as a "book of pains and penalties." It was thus ironic that a private of the First United States Regulars, William May, who had been caught attempting to desert at the same time as the two executed artillerymen, was pardoned after pleading guilty and was sent back to duty with his unit. May's subsequent behavior was to prove of considerable importance in the war.[40]

The respite in the turmoil following St. Clair's stern attempt to discipline his troops proved to be only momentary, however. On October 21 the long-dreaded hard frost had occurred. Ice was found to be nearly a half-inch thick in the camp kettles that morning, and what remained of the forage that had been gathered daily for the horses by an infantry detail was mostly destroyed. That afternoon snow flurries swirled in the strong breeze, and St. Clair, aware that he was further losing control of his campaign, made another hard decision.[41]

The fort that had been nearly ten days under construction was by now well roughed in. It was a square structure with 114-foot sides protected by four bastions, and containing barracks and storehouses; St. Clair considered it strong enough to withstand attack. Yet, since the forage in the immediate area had been consumed or destroyed, a change in locale seemed "absolutely necessary." St. Clair was further prodded to action by the unexpected appearance of Richard Butler at headquarters. Butler had come to request permission to take 1,000 picked men and advance to the Miami Town in order to establish a post there. The season was so far advanced, warned Butler, that he doubted the objective of the campaign could be met in any other way. Although St. Clair said "he had liked to have laughed in his face" and sent Butler away humiliated for suggesting that the army be divided (Butler was probably reminded of Harmar's sad experience in detaching various columns), the incident further quickened the commanding general's anxiety. With the arrival of about sixty straggling Kentucky militia on the afternoon of October 22, bringing with them a packhorse convoy carrying about 1,600 pounds of flour and a small drove of cattle, St. Clair immediately ordered a forward movement.[42] Since this flour was sufficient for only a few days, instead of the fifteen days originally anticipated, Quartermaster Hodgdon was sent back to Fort Washington on the twenty-first for a further supply.

Arthur St. Clair was increasingly nagged by the fear that his army would break up after the expiration of the six-month levies' term of service. Noting that nearly all of the levies would begin leaving about November 3, St. Clair wrote that he hoped to get them into action before that date. Even more important was his covert design to get them deeper into Indian country, where "the men will find themselves so far [advanced] that it will be obviously better to go forward than to return [because of the danger of being attacked in a small body]."[43]

Thus, impelled by reasons of weakness rather than strength, St. Clair's army was ordered to resume the offensive on October 24. Two field guns were to remain at the new stockade—which the major general named Fort Jefferson on October 24—with a garrison of about 120 men, mostly invalids and the sick. Then, at 9:00 A.M. on October 24, under cloudy skies, the long column of troops and their sixty-odd camp followers, who included wives and children, began the last leg of their wilderness trek. Deposited in the unfinished confines of Fort Jefferson was all of their baggage, including even vital munitions and military stores. Since the column was now without packhorses, only the tents and a few tools could be transported by the four-ox teams.[44]

More ominously, Arthur St. Clair, who had been suffering from what he termed "rheumatic asthma," was stricken by the gout in his left arm and hand. On October 24 he was so ill that he found it difficult to keep up with the army, which marched only five and one-half miles that day. On October 25 the army was ordered halted to await the receipt of further provisions, without which, St. Clair asserted, his troops could not bear to march. When he learned that afternoon that 13,000 pounds of flour would arrive on October 27, St. Clair decreed a halt until the thirtieth.[45]

Having marched less than six miles from Fort Jefferson, the army thus was allowed to languish without adequate supplies and equipment for five days during damp weather in an unpleasant and improvised bivouac. The semblance of order that had been briefly restored by the harsh execution of the deserters now dissipated in a rash of desertions.

The small quantity of flour expected on the twenty-seventh failed to arrive, and the last of the flour rations were issued that day. An officer glumly wrote that he no longer felt that it was practicable to continue the campaign under the conditions—"forage entirely destroyed; horses failing and cannot be kept up; provisions from hand to mouth." Too sick to take any effective preventive action, St. Clair noted that his Virginia battalion was rapidly melting away. In fact, nearly all of the levies were riotous now, and a great clamor was building for immediate discharge.[46]

On October 28 the expected seventy-four-horse convoy of provisions finally arrived. Since a portion had been taken en route by the equally deprived garrison at Fort Jefferson, the quantity of flour received was only enough for four days. Of further significance, a few extra horses in the convoy were found to be laden with new clothing for the First Regulars. By St. Clair's direction these clothes were offered to the ragged levies whose terms were about to expire, but only if they would enlist in the regular service. "[This] is not openly complained of by the officers . . . ," wrote St. Clair, "but it is certainly, privately, by some of high rank, and the measure of tempting them with warm clothing [is] condemned." Nonetheless, about forty levies were induced to enlist on this pretext alone during the next few days.[47]

Although a small quantity of flour was now on hand, St. Clair, being "so very ill," continued to keep his army in camp. A fatigue party of about 120 men was sent out on October 29 to open a road, and a small detachment of newly arrived Chickasaw Indian scouts, under their chiefs Piamingo and Colbert, were dispatched on an extended reconnaissance patrol.

At last, on Sunday, October 30, the army was once again put in motion. Although seven miles were covered that day in warm, windy weather, that night a strong gale blew down limbs and dead trees amid frightening bolts of lightning. "With the darkness of the night and in an enemy's country, [it] occasioned some concern," noted an uneasy officer. To the unfortunate St. Clair expedition it was yet another harbinger of the greater difficulties that lay ahead.[48]

Word was received that night that 212 packhorses had arrived that day at Fort Jefferson, laden with provisions. St. Clair therefore decided to remain halted on the thirty-first. The provisions on hand would be expended with the issues of that day, and he anticipated that the vital supplies would reach the army more rapidly if it remained halted. Yet the effect was only further to disrupt his expedition, for at this point the continuing embarrassment in logistics precipitated a major crisis.[49]

St. Clair had breakfasted on the thirty-first with Lieutenant Colonel Oldham of the militia. Oldham was on his way back to camp when he was informed by one of his men that half of the militia had deserted in a body and were determined to plunder the expected convoys of provisions. Hastening back to St. Clair's headquarters, the badly shaken Oldham warned the major general that perhaps the entire militia contingent would soon follow. St. Clair immediately ordered the First regulars under Major John Hamtramck to march in pusuit of the deserters with the objective of saving the vital provisions that were enroute. He hoped that this would further induce the remaining militia to stay—since the First Regiment would thus be interposed between the army and home.[50]

Belatedly, word was received that, instead of half of the militia deserting, only about sixty Kentuckians had gone off, after complaining that they were underfed and insufficiently provided for. Although fully one-third of the militia had formed with the intention of marching home, several officers had persuaded many to stay. Only the most disgruntled had marched away, "swear[ing] they will stop the pack horses with provisions."[51]

St. Clair reasoned that two supply convoys were then enroute. It was known that the first of these, under Captain Thomas Brenham, had been within a few miles of the army at Fort Jefferson on the thirtieth. The second contractor's convoy was presumed to be within twenty miles, on the basis of instructions given to Hodgdon on the twenty-first. Since only a small portion of the militia had left camp, the urgency of their pursuit by the regulars was now somewhat diminished. Hamramck therefore was allowed to provision his men by killing and butchering sufficient beef for six days before marching.

Because of that delay in readying his force of approximately 300 men, it was late in the evening before Hamtramck marched. By that time Brenham's packhorse convoy had already arrived in camp bearing about 32,000 pounds of flour. Since there was little expectation that he might bring the militia deserters back, Hamtramck's mission now involved only the second convoy, whose location or existence was unknown. Adjutant General Sargent wrote in his journal: "This movement may have a further good effect upon the militia that are in camp and be the means of keeping them to their duty; but however necessary it may be, I have to regret that we are hereby deprived for a time of a corps of 300 effective men . . . which must be estimated as the best in the service." Another soldier, a lieutenant, noted that the army had now dwindled to about 1,200 regulars and levies, with an additional 250 Kentucky militia on hand.

It was of further concern to an informed few that the army was now so deep in Indian country that it had to stand on permanent alert. The men were instructed to sleep at night minus only their coats, vests, and shoes. Yet virtually nothing was known of the enemy, of his plans, location or strength. As St. Clair candidly wrote on October 21: "I think my force sufficient, though [I have] no manner of information as to the force collected to oppose us. It seems somewhat extraordinary that they should have allowed us to be here so long in the interior of their country and never looked at us, nor stolen a horse, for though we have lost a few, I have no reason to think they were taken away by the enemy."[52]

St. Clair's conception of a minimal risk facing him was based on his long-standing assumption that his force would be numerically superior and better disciplined than the Indians. This involved rather circumspect reasoning—that, since they had not attempted to molest his column during their eighty-mile march into the wilderness, the Indians had failed to gather a force sufficient to resist the American army. Therefore, St. Clair said, they either would desert their towns on his approach or, more probably, sue for peace.[53]

During the first few days of November the army's high command continued to regard the occasional sightings of warriors by outlying sentries and hunting parties merely as chance encounters with roaming Indian hunters. Even the mysterious disappearance of outlying sentries failed to evoke undue alarm, it being "uncertain" whether they had deserted or had been captured by the enemy. With each progressive march farther north into the wilderness, encounters and Indian sightings seemed to increase, yet these were largely dismissed by the ranking officers as random incidents. Several brief skirmishes with a few Indians had failed to produce a prisoner.

Frustrated by a lack of intelligence, St. Clair had sent out the twenty Chickasaw Indians, who had been persuaded to join the American Army to fight their traditional enemies, the Wabash tribes (although this delegation originally had arrived at Fort Washington as emissaries to Congress). The Chickasaws, who left camp on October 29, were told to wear a handkerchief tied about their heads with a single red plume within, so that they would not be mistaken for the enemy. Their orders were explicit: "to take a prisoner" even it if required ten days.[54]

As late as November 1, St. Clair continued to regard the Indian presence as insignificant. "The few Indians that have been seen were hunters only, who we fell upon by accident," he reassuringly wrote in a dispatch to Knox.[55]

Just how obtuse his reasoning had become was revealed by an imminent-combat alert that the British military adviser Simon Girty sent to his superior, Alexander McKee, on October 28. The Indian leadership, under Little Turtle and Blue Jacket, in fact, had been receiving a constant stream of information, including important intelligence from deserters and prisoners as well as warrior scouts sent to spy on the American army. Already the Indians had decided to advance against the American column. Although only ten warriors from the Six Nations were present, fighting men totaling 1,040 effectives had arrived from various other tribes. Aware of their white enemy's strength, location, and plans, this formidable Indian force had advanced from the Miami Village October 28, at which time a distance of only about seventy-five miles had separated the opposing forces. Said Simon Girty, in obvious anticipation of the impending fight, "The Indians were never in greater heart to meet their enemy, nor more sure of success—they are determined to drive them to the Ohio."[56]

Winthrop Sargent recorded in his journal on November 1 that the army had inexplicably remained halted that day. Except that St. Clair was writing dispatches to the War Office, no reason for the delay was stated. Colonel Darke, however, had another explanation: "Our commander is so exceedingly afflicted with the gout that all the men that can possibly get in reach of him are scarcely enough help to him on and off his horse and, indeed, now a litter is made to carry him like a corpse between two horses." While professing his health was "considerably improved," St. Clair admitted that he had been so unwell during the past week that he was incapable even of writing. Furthermore, the skies had turned cloudy, an ominous sign of an approaching weather front. As St. Clair all too well understood, the army could not travel encumbered with even a semblance of its normal baggage. Many of the remaining packhorses available for heavy transportation had been afflicted by an undiagnosed and contagious hoof disease, and they were rapidly dying. To lighten the horses in preparation for the following day's march, a quantity of heavy articles were ordered left behind. This small deposit, St. Clair now reasoned, could also serve as a rallying point "in case of disaster."[57]

Others who feared the consequences of continuing the campaign were further alarmed by the events of November 2 and 3. On the second, the army marched about eight miles through low, swampy terrain that one observer thought would be almost impassable in wet weather. The leaden gray skies that had loomed overhead all day began emitting rain about three o'clock. Within an hour the rain turned to a light, constant snow.[58]

Throughout the night and into the morning the intermittent snowfall continued, and while not enough had accumulated to cover the ground completely, the shivering troops awoke on November 3 amid a frigid wilderness. The commander of a levy regiment wrote that so many officers and men were sick with colds that his officer son had to stand guard, despite a severe viral infection–because all of the other captains in his battalion were similarly afflicted.[59]

The army marched at nine o'clock on the morning of November 3, and as the long, winding column trudged through the "wet, sunken grounds of woodland," Lieutenant Colonel Darke placed several letters in the hands of one of his lieutenants, Rawleigh Morgan, who was soon to return to Virginia with a contingent of discharged levies. Darke, who was thoroughly disgusted with the campaign, revealed his misery in a lengthy letter to his wife:

My dear: [We] have been since that time [August 29] crawling through Indian country. For an excuse for our idleness . . . we have built two sorts of forts—though in fact we have been very busy doing nothing. . . . In this rapid manner we move to catch the Indians—83 miles [advanced] in better than two months. I expect we shall soon return as most of the levies' times will be out this month; and many other reasons—the food being all killed with frost long since in this cold country, and the horses dying every day; [also] I think bad management in every department. . . . I in short expect by the last of this month we shall begin our march back, which if we perform as slowly as we seem to advance, will take us til

March to see Fort Washington again. But I imagine . . . when the men's times are out they will be . . . anxious to return, and instead of a mile and a quarter a day, [they] will march 25 [miles], and that we shall be at Fort Washington in one week from the extent of our scandalous expedition. . . . I expect we shall march . . . early on [tomorrow] towards the Indian towns, where we, I believe, shall not find an Indian. . . . , Your loving husband, William Darke.[60]

17

A Mouthful of Earth

THE afternoon of November 3, 1791, remained cold, and during an interim halt some of the troops had kindled a large fire. Presently Major General St. Clair came up and began to converse with several of his officers about their location. It was presumed, St. Clair was heard to say, that the army had now passed the tributaries of the Miami River and was about to cross over the ridge separating the Saint Marys from the Miami. St. Clair, accordingly, ordered a halt for the day, intending to bivouac amid the adjacent thick timberland.

Shortly after that order was given, however, Adjutant Denny and Quartermaster Hodgdon rode up, having just completed a reconnaissance several miles ahead. Noting that the small nearby creek—termed a "limestone run" by one officer—provided "no good water," Denny urged St. Clair to proceed with the troops to the high ground that he had just reconnoitered two miles distant. The forward site had a "pleasant, dry ground," Denny reported, and was on the bank of a stream about twenty yards wide, presumed to be a branch of the Saint Marys River.

Although it was midafternoon and the army had already covered about six miles, St. Clair ordered the march continued to this better campground.[1] By about four o'clock the advance elements, a party of militia rangers, had arrived at the designated location. Here the stream, shallow enough to ford, meandered across their path. Proceeding across it, the Kentuckians soon discovered an old Indian camping ground so extensive that one officer remarked that it must have been a general meeting place. Along the riverbank nearby, the militia also found the fresh tracks of about fifteen Indian horses. As Lieutenant Colonel Oldham immediately reported these presumably marked the passing of an enemy reconnaissance patrol. "The first that has been about us," he said (the other sightings still were thought to have been merely hunting parties).[2]

It was almost dark before the rear of the army arrived at the relocated campsite, which was along the nearly fifteen-foot-high eastern riverbank. No attempt was made to establish a defensive perimeter or throw up rude breastworks, "the men [being] much fatigued." In fact, one wagoneer reported that it was about eight o'clock before they were able to cook and eat their "scanty mess of provisions."[3]

Because the high ground, estimated at six or seven acres, was bordered on all sides by low, swampy terrain, the campsite was "barely sufficient to encamp the army." When both lines had formed, with Butler's levies on the

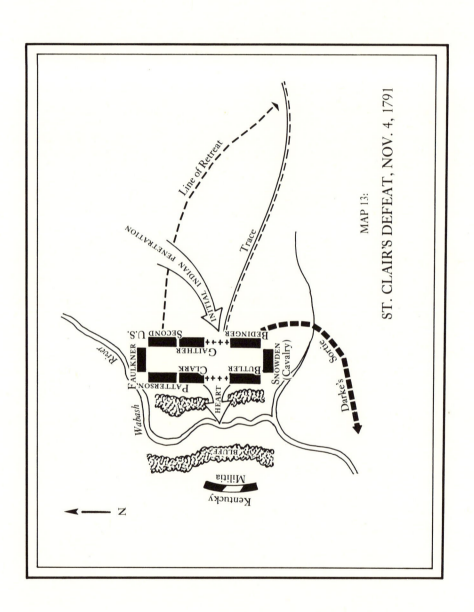

MAP 13:

ST. CLAIR'S DEFEAT, NOV. 4, 1791

west nearer the river, and Darke's men and the Second United States Regiment in the rear and higher on the riverbank, they were separated by a gap of only about seventy yards. Beyond that Faulkner's company of riflemen were posted on the right flank on the north, and a troop of horses were sent to the left on the south. The outer perimeter was then established a few hundred yards distant by a network of about 220 sentries. Laid out in the general shape of a rectangle about four hundred yards long and seventy yards deep, the encampment provided insufficient ground for the militia. Accordingly, following the new practice of posting the militia ahead of the army to prevent desertions, they were sent across the riverbottom three hundred yards to a "high, extensive flat of open woods" amid the old Indian camps. Here the militia rangers were deployed a short distance in advance as outguards.[4]

Meanwhile, in the main camp four pieces of artillery each were parked in the center of Butler's and Darke's levies, pointing west and east respectively. Yet no breastworks were fashioned for these guns, possibly because St. Clair had recently discouraged the cutting down of trees—which made movement about the camp "extremely inconvenient." Elsewhere within the hollow square formed by the levies and regulars, the several hundred servants, noncombatants, and camp followers pitched their tents, mostly on open ground. Chilled by the cold and exhausted by the day's unusually long march, the army at last consumed their meager rations and bivouacked for a restless night's sleep.[5]

As darkness fell, sporadic shots from the pickets sounded while St. Clair, who was so ill with the gout that he was unable to be up past midevening, discussed the following morning's plans with several of his officers. Believing that the army was camped only about fifteen miles from the Miami Village, St. Clair told Major Ferguson that he would halt here until the First United States Regiment returned. Accordingly, construction of a slight log enclosure would begin in the morning to hold knapsacks and every other nonessential item. This, St. Clair anticipated, would facilitate the army's unencumbered approach to their objective.

As for the several shots that they had heard from the direction of the outlying sentries, they were regarded without undue concern. It was presumed that the guards had discovered a few lurking Indians intent on stealing stray horses. By ten o'clock St. Clair was in bed, while several of his staff officers went to the headquarters tent of General Butler to review the following morning's plans.[6]

Edward Butler, the youngest of the three Butler brothers serving with St. Clair's army, had been considered too young to fight in the Revolution. While of his prominent family Richard and Thomas had emerged from the war with considerable laurels, Edward was now perhaps the most aggressive of the three. A twenty-nine-year-old captain and company commander in his brother Thomas's battalion of Pennsylvania levies, Edward was of strong Irish stock and frequently was outspoken.

Angered by the random firing at the sentry posts, Edward went to the tent of his regimental commander, Lieutenant Colonel George Gibson, and said he thought a small patrol might succeed in catching "some of the rascals" who were attempting to steal the army's horses. These horses had been hobbled and turned loose in the woods because of the scarcity in forage. "We were under the necessity of either turning them out to feed, or suffering them to starve," the adjutant general later admitted. In fact, it already had been reluctantly conceded that some of these animals probably would be lost to the prowling enemy.[7]

Present at Gibson's tent at the time was Captain Jacob Slough. Slough, an ambitious young man, was another of Gibson's company commanders, but St. Clair thought that he lacked "steadiness." When he heard of Butler's plan, Slough asked to lead such a patrol. After arranging for the mission with the adjutant general, Butler handpicked about twenty-three volunteers from his own regiment and returned to his brother's tent, where the party was to meet for instructions.

The men were mostly sergeants, Slough observed, and Major General Richard Butler invited him into his tent for a glass of wine and some advice. Warned by Butler that he was to be very cautious, Slough marched from camp shortly after ten o'clock. On his way out he stopped at the tent of the militia commander, Lieutenant Colonel William Oldham. Oldham, restless following the day's activities, was lying down with his clothes on, and he warned Slough of his fear that the army might be attacked.[8]

The night was exceedingly dark despite the patches of snow, and Slough only advanced what he estimated was about a mile along the Indian path leading beyond the militia camp. He then deployed his men in two detachments, one on either side of the trail, where they lay prone in a thicket with muskets cocked, waiting and watching.

Only a few minutes had passed before six or seven Indians were discovered within fifteen yards, approaching upon Slough's left. A volley of shots rang out from the hidden levies, and at least one Indian was seen to fall before the remaining enemy disappeared at a run.

Slough had his men reload their guns and remain in place. Again an eerie quiet pervaded the thicket.

Fifteen minutes later an Indian war party approached, larger than before. They passed at a distance of about forty-five feet, stopping to cough as if they were attempting to cause Slough to fire and betray his position. "I thought they meant to waylay me," Slough later wrote. He was soon further alarmed to discover another large war party moving through the brush on the other side of the path, beyond his second detachment.[9]

Once those Indians had passed, Slough and several of his subordinates, each obviously shaken by this close call, quickly agreed to return to camp. Instructing his men to retreat single file along the path and not to fire their guns if attacked, but to resort only to the bayonet, the anxious Slough began to move back toward their encampment.

Nearly out of breath with fear and excitement, Slough and his patrol finally streamed back into the militia camp about midnight. Slough went directly to Lieutenant Colonel Oldham's tent, where he told the Kentuckian of his harrowing experience, saying that he too believed the army would be attacked in the morning. Immediately Oldham sent Slough to inform General Butler of what he had seen. Yet evidently he made no further plans to send out a daylight patrol that had been ordered by St. Clair, presuming that the Indians already had been discovered.[10]

Richard Butler had thus far spent a restless night. Evidently troubled by a variety of problems, including a recent sickness, Butler had, a few hours earlier in opening a bottle of wine, half jokingly remarked to his companions, "Let us eat, drink, and be merry, as tomorrrow we may die."[11] Unable to sleep, he stood by the campfire when Slough approached. Speaking in guarded tones so that the sentry might not hear, Slough warned Butler of what he had seen. Butler listened intently but evidently did not speak. If the general thought it prudent, continued Slough, he would personally go and report to Major General St. Clair.

Butler paused in thought for a moment. Then he told Slough, no, the captain was fatigued and had better go and lie down, implying that he would inform St. Clair himself.

Exhausted, and convinced he had now fulfilled his mission, Slough returned to his tent and flung himself down to sleep, not even bothering to remove his clothes.[12]

Richard Butler, long aware of St. Clair's notorious wrath while suffering with the gout, and still smoldering over the army commander's recent snide remarks and callous treatment of him personally, chose to return to his tent with Slough's message undelivered. He later remarked that St. Clair had treated all his proposals with contempt.

In the sky above the army's woodland encampment the winds shifting from the northeast to the northwest had cleared away the lingering cloud cover. The morning of November 4 would be clear and cold, and since no ground fog would form, the men might be dismissed early from their routine call to arms in order to collect the scattered horses.[13]

Me-she-kin-no-quah was not yet forty years of age, yet the renown of this Miami chief already was nearly legend throughout the Ohio Indian villages. Although better known among the English traders as The Little Turtle, the stature of the war chief who had defeated Harmar's columns was anything but small among his tribesmen. Standing about six feet tall, with a "sour and morose" countenance and fond of wearing reams of silver on his ears and clothing, Little Turtle presented an impressive, if forbidding, appearance. A sensitive and profound man, he was revered by his contemporaries as a leader of extraordinary wisdom and courage. When confronted by the recent military invasion of Indian lands, Little Turtle had perhaps considered the sentiment of another native leader, the Ottawa chief Egushawa, who said, "I do not yet see the means of obtaining peace but by war; for our enemy confide in their superior numbers and strength and not on God, who made them and us—nor on the justice of their cause."[14]

On October 28, Little Turtle of the Miamis and Blue Jacket of the Shawnees had led their assembled strike force forward from the Miami Village to meet the Americans. Advancing about fifty miles in four days, they had awaited St. Clair's approach in the vicinity of the upper Wabash River, amid terrain that was deemed some of the wildest in the region. Since their series of camps lay within two and a half miles of the American army's bivouac on the night of November 3, 1791, there is evidence that Little Turtle, the overall commander, was laboring under great difficulty in controlling his impetuous young warriors. Many were found roaming through the woods within earshot of the American encampment, gathering up wandering cattle and packhorses that had been set loose in the woods to forage for what food they could find. Fearful that this activity might alert the Americans of an impending attack, Little Turtle apparently spent a strenuous night attempting to restrain these warriors.[15]

Before daybreak, however, the final plans were laid. The Wyandots and a handful of Six Nations tribesmen were to fight on the right; the Shawnees, Miamis, and Delawares would attack the center; and the so-called Lake Indians, mostly Ottawas, Chippewas, and Potawatomis, would advance toward the left. Deployed in a half-moon formation that allowed rapid encirclement of the American camp, Little Turtle's warriors, 1,040 strong, were in position before daylight. Among those present was Simon Girty, ostensibly as an observer, but actually serving among the Wyandots as a war leader. Girty's quest for vengeance was strong, and he is said to have uttered "fiendish" exultations of revenge.[16]

As might be expected, the importance of the impending action was understood by all. Because the Indians were fighting in defense of their land, homes, and way of life, they were full of ardor. Emotionally aroused and fully confident of success, they now awaited merely the coming of daylight.[17]

Reveille in the American camp, the shrill echo of the fife and the roll of the drum, sounded about a half hour before daylight on November 4. Perhaps fifteen minutes later, the usual morning assembly was called, but since Lieutenant Colonel Darke complained that his men were suffering from the cold, and the scattered packhorses had to be found and prepared for a resupply mission to Fort Jefferson, the men were dismissed from parade just as the first glimmer of daylight filtered through the woodlands.[18] At the advanced militia camp, the outlying sentries were gathered about their campfires. Some were chatting with the horse guards, who were starting to round up the wandering animals.

Objects were not yet distinguishable beyond a few hundred feet in "the gray of morning." Robert Bradshaw, a militia ranger, was standing near a campfire, talking with a comrade, when he saw what appeared to be several dozen Indians "dodging around among the trees in front of us." Thinking they were a war party intent on surprising and capturing the outpost, he quickly raised his rifle and fired at the nearest enemy. The smoke from his rifle had not yet cleared, said Bradshaw, when a terrific volley of gunfire, followed by an appalling yell, rose from the underbrush. Out of the surrounding timber poured a multitude of "painted" savages, dashing straight for the ranger outpost and the militia camp. Bradshaw turned to run, and stumbled over the body of the man he had been chatting with only a few moments before. With a shudder, Bradshaw saw that he had been shot through the temple.[19]

Another ranger, William Kennan, also had fired and had dropped flat into the grass to reload. Then, discovering the overwhelming numbers of the enemy, he threw aside his empty gun and fled, just ahead of a pursuing

Richard Butler, St. Clair's second-in-command, who met death on the battlefield. Courtesy of William Clements Library, University of Michigan.

Indian. Dodging through the timber as rapidly as possible, Kennan scrambled over a fallen tree and down into the Wabash riverbed, narrowly eluding several pursuers. Out of breath, he soon stumbled into the main encampment amid utmost confusion.[20]

In front of the militia camp men already were seen running in all directions, pursued by an estimated 300 Indians. One Kentucky ensign, who at the first fire had rushed forward with a detachment of eleven men, saw his men halt, then scatter in panic when they saw the oncoming Indians. Robert Bradshaw, in attempting to fall back upon the militia camp, in the half-light came upon a ragged line of militia, who fired randomly at the yet-distant red warriors, then broke up in disorder. Badly scared, they fled for their lives into the nearby thirty-foot-deep bottomland that separated their outlying camp from the main army. In a few minutes the entire 270-man militia force had scattered in confusion, said Bradshaw.[21]

Close in pursuit, the red warriors now began "screeching . . . with such an appalling effect" that many of the Kentuckians became bewildered and ran aimlessly about, falling easy prey to their adversaries.

Bradshaw stumbled as best he could through the timbered bottomland, chased by a youthful warrior brandishing an uplifted tomahawk. Unable to outrun his pursuer, he attempted to avoid the blow aimed at the back of his head by quickly falling down. In an instant, the Indian tripped over the Kentuckian's foot, lost his grip on the tomahawk, and went sprawling to the ground. Bradshaw leaped upon him with a drawn hunting knife before the warrior could regain his feet. "[I] drove my hunting knife through his throat, severing his jugular [vein]," the desperate ranger later remembered. Without pausing to recover his weapon, Bradshaw raced off again, chased by a horde of yelling Indians. After being struck by a musket ball that carried away a portion of his ear, the blood-spattered ranger finally splashed across the Wabash and staggered into the main camp, more frightened than injured.[22]

In the drowsy encampment of Arthur St. Clair, Major Thomas Butler had been talking that morning with one of Captain Slough's soldiers, who had participated in the previous night's patrol. Visibly worried by the soldier's report of having sighted many Indians, Major Butler angrily reflected that Slough should have taken a prisoner. A few moments later a scattering of shots was heard, followed by a peculiar noise that made men stop and listen in puzzlement.

Nearby Winthrop Sargent had just returned from the militia camp, where he had reprimanded Lieutenant Colonel Oldham for not ordering out the reconnaissance patrol requested by St. Clair during the previous evening. Sargent now heard a din that he thought resembled a multitude of horse bells suddenly clamoring. Another officer in camp said the sound was "the damnedest noise imaginable," what he supposed was "ten thousand cow bells." Others said it was a confused kind of noise, like the howling of wolves. All too suddenly it was realized that the tumult was the Indian war cries. Soon the furious beating of drums sounded the alarm throughout St. Clair's camp.[23]

Officers, some still eating breakfast, raced from their tents to form their men. Although arms and equipment were readily at hand from the recent morning assembly, the bewilderment and inexperience of the troops inhibited formation of a regular line of battle. Only about five minutes passed between the initial firing in front of the militia camp and the appearance of the fleeing Kentuckians. They came running through the "rich sugar tree bottom," dashing "helter-skelter" into main camp, said an officer. The three battalions of levies attempting to form the front line were immediately thrown into disorder by these wild-eyed men rushing past. Yet on the militia sped, continuing through camp until they burst through the second line of troops, who were also forming, even carrying with them a few of Major Henry Gaither's Maryland levies.[24]

Damning the militia for their "ignominious flight," Winthrop Sargent suddenly appeared among the front line. The militia's conduct "was cowardly in the most shameful degree," raged Sargent, and he hastened to restore order among the levies. Bayonets were ordered fixed, and with soldiers still rushing into line, the ragged front rank of infantry raised their muskets to fire at the oncoming enemy.[25]

It was shortly after 6:00 A.M., estimated an officer, and in the east the sun had begun to rise in a serene and cloudless sky. Illuminated by these filtered rays, the shrieking, irregular line of Indian warriors seemed to fill the bottomland. Hard on the heels of the last few retreating militiamen, the foremost warriors had sprinted to within sixty yards of the levies' front line, and their painted faces loomed in terrible perspective. Suddenly, an ear-shattering roar erupted from the high ground fronting the east branch of the Wabash. Enveloped by a thick cloud of gunsmoke, the levies peered beneath the obscuring haze—only to discover the enemy still pressing onward. Spontaneously dropping down behind logs and stumps to return the soldiers' fire, the red foe dodged from tree to tree, shooting into the standing ranks of infantry with telling effect.

The artillery fronting the Wabash, the four 6- and 3-pound smooth-bore guns under Major William Ferguson and Captain Mahlon Ford, by now had joined in the action, creating a tremendous din with their blasts of round shot and canister. Yet the cannon, which were believed to have a terrible effect on Indian morale, in truth seemed only of a momentary benefit. A war chief on horseback wearing a red coat, possibly Blue Jacket of the Shawnees, was seen through the swirling smoke, rallying his men. As the Indians later explained, the soldiers were occupying the crest of the high ground, and their fire was too high. The charges of canister shook the trees as high as thirty feet above the heads of the Indians, and the blanket of thick gunsmoke so obscured the soldiers' vision (soon drifting within three feet of the ground), it was necessary at times to stoop below the layers of smoke to see anything. Under this sulphurous, murky cover the Indians had already begun to execute their tactic of encirclement. Glimpses of war-painted tribesmen moving swiftly through the underbrush to the right and left were reported almost from the first fire. As the gathering, telltale crescendo of gunfire moved in rapid succession among the outer perimeter, a sobering awareness began to settle upon the army. Beset by an enemy variously estimated at between "upwards of a thousand," and twenty-five hundred warriors, St. Clair's stunned troops soon perceived that they were fighting a pitched battle with a merciless foe inside a restricted perimeter, from which there was now no escape. As the harried aide-de-camp Ebenezer Denny aptly remarked, their underestimated foe had within a few minutes "completely surrounded the camp, killed and cut off nearly all the [outer] guards," and now advanced in relentless fashion from tree to tree under the cover of the smoke from the soldiers' guns. "The Indians seemed to brave everything," wrote Denny, "and when fairly fixed around us, they made no noise other than their fire, which . . . [was] very constant, and . . . seldom failed to tell."[27]

The approach of the battle within the hollow-square zone largely occupied by the noncombatants "always reminded me of one of those thunderstorms that comes up quickly," wrote an army wagoneer. Here was found "a scene of the wildest confusion," observed the militia ranger Robert Bradshaw. The women and children were in a state of shock and excitement bordering on stupefaction. "Some were running to and fro, wringing their hands and shrieking out their terrors," noted Bradshaw, while others "were standing speechless, [being] statues of horror . . . with eyes fixed upon the not very distant scene of strife." Some women were found kneeling in prayer— "calling on Heaven for protection," continued the ranger—yet many were simply "sobbing and groaning in each others arms." Others who had collapsed from fright now "lay upon the ground as if dead."[28]

Contributing to the chaos were many of the routed militiamen, who had been kept within the confines of the encampment by the encircling enemy and now began to plunder the officers' tents. Most of these men had not yet eaten, and a few were shot by hostile fire while attempting to scavenge breakfast. So many bewildered, dispirited men were found loitering among the tents that even Arthur St. Clair attempted to force them back into the ranks. At one point, a staff officer saw the general draw his pistol and threaten a soldier with death if he refused to fight. Yet nearly lame with the gout, St. Clair quickly found he was unable to stem the tide of spreading confusion, the men already being insensible with shock and despair.[29]

For St. Clair the agony of the day was already a nightmare. Unable to move without excruciating pain, the portly, grey-haired general evidently had been so crippled by the gout that he remained in bed, undressed, at the time of the initial onslaught. Dressed only in "a coarse cappo coat" and a three-cornered hat, he attempted to mount the first of four personal horses that had just been retrieved from the woods. This animal, a young horse, was much frightened by the firing nearby and bolted with each new discharge. Though three or four men steadied the horse and attempted to boost St. Clair into the saddle, they could not manage it. Then, before St. Clair was able to mount, the horse was shot in the head and instantly killed.

Another steed was quickly brought up, and after disentangling the saddle and trappings from the first horse, the men prepared it to receive its rider. Again, before St. Clair could be lifted in place, the animal and the servant who held his reins were killed. Saying he could wait no longer, St. Clair finally shuffled off toward the firing line.[30]

The focal points of the fighting, front and rear, as observed by a participant, centered around the artillery, which was in action near the middle of each battle line. St. Clair, his gray hair flowing in large locks from beneath his beaver hat, soon hobbled among the artillerymen. Here a musket ball grazed the side of his face, cutting off a portion of a lock. "My pains were forgotten," wrote St. Clair, who later remembered that he was able to walk thereafter with considerable energy.[31]

Directing the artillery of the Wabash line was the doughty Major William Ferguson, who had intended to construct the light log structure ordered by St. Clair, but instead this morning was fighting for his life. Although his cannon appeared to be bravely manned, one observer noted that their fire seemed generally ineffective, because the Indians lay concealed behind stumps and uprooted trees, presenting few targets of opportunity.[32]

Indeed, the galling hostile fire was rapidly decimating the cannoneers, who were without cover. William Wells, a youthful white captive turned Indian war leader, said his party of Miamis, firing from cover immediately beneath the knoll, piled the white corpses almost to the height of their cannon. Included among the early casualties was Major Ferguson, struck down with a mortal wound. Said General St. Clair, who saw the growing carnage before moving to the left, "it became necessary to try what could be done by the bayonet."[33]

Less that a month after his appointment as major general commanding, St. Clair had been instructed by Henry Knox in a fundamental theory of American military science. Announced Knox, "It is to be presumed that disciplined valor will triumph over the undisciplined Indians." This maxim, accordingly, had been adopted by St. Clair as the basis for his campaign. Only ten days before the surprise attack along the Wabash, St. Clair had published a rather remarkable battle order, defining the proper means of engaging the red enemy. "Discipline has often been found superior to numbers, even sometimes 10 to 1," read the order. "[The soldiers therefore] are to depend wholly on their arms and good behavior for their safety—that [is] if they stand and fight like soldiers, certain victory will be their reward. . . . It has been often proved that the savages if violently attacked will always break and give way—and when once broke, for the want of discipline, will never rally."[34]

Threatened by heavy enemy pressure against the left sector of his encampment on November 4, St. Clair attempted to restore this flank by ordering a bayonet charge, in the prescribed manner of disciplined maneuver. Viscount de Malartie, St. Clair's volunteer aide, had been sent to the left with orders for assault, but Malartie, riding St. Clair's spare horse, had been wounded, and the horse killed in the attempt.[35]

Ironically, in the absence of orders, the commander of the rear echelon, Lieutenant Colonel Darke, finding the enemy "growing more bold and coming to the very mouths of our cannon," also had ordered a charge with fixed bayonets soon after the investment of the rear line. The Indians "were all around us, as thick as bees," observed a worried officer. Prevailing upon several officers of the Second United States Regiment to lend their assistance, Darke said about three hundred men were hastily gathered, many of them being regulars. Captain Alexander Trueman with twenty-six horsemen, all that could be mounted of his seventy-five cavalrymen, also hurriedly formed for the charge. Although Darke nominally commanded, Major Jonathan Heart of the Second Regiment took charge on the right.[36]

With a yell, the men rushed forward, veering southwest in the direction of a small creek, since known as "bloody run," then across the Wabash into the bottomland south of the militia camp. Although the cavalry immediately became tangled in the undergrowth and fell behind, one of the men following the charge said the Indians were driven "clear out of sight." Benjamin Van Cleve, a wagon master with the army, reported that the red warriors in front got up and ran to the right into a small, log-filled ravine. In all, an estimated three to four hundred yards were traversed before the winded soldiers came to a halt.[37]

The Indians in this sector were said to be Wyandots, fighting under the eye of Simon Girty. At a distance of about thirty yards, they dodged behind trees and uprooted stumps and continued to snipe at Darke's troops, who were now broken into several fragments.

From the direction from which the charge had originated, sudenly came the sound of heavy shouting and firing. A nearby "woodsman and hunter" suggested to Darke that the Indians had closed up behind the sortie, and that they were attacking the void left in the defensive perimeter. "If we return and take those Indians with their backs to us," said the man, "we will have them in a severe fix." "Lead the way," shouted Darke, and the levies and regulars began to withdraw toward the sound of the raging conflict.[38]

"I have often heard . . . officers call the Indians . . . undisciplined savages," wrote an experienced former captive. "[This] is a capital mistake, as they all have the essentials of discipline. They are under good command, and punctual in obeying orders; they can act in concert, and when . . . they go into battle, . . . each man is to fight as though he were to gain the [victory] himself." Furthermore, a basic tactical premise of the Indians was to attempt to kill the enemy's officers at the first fire. "[They] see that they first shoot the officers," reported another woodsman who had lived among the Shaw-nees, "and then, . . . the soldiers will all be confused, and will not know what to do. . . . They say the English people [white men] are fools, they hold their guns half man [waist] high, and then let snap—we take sight . . . and not only shoot with a bullet, but with big swan shot [a ball and six buckshot]."[39]

This fundamental difference between eighteenth-century American and Indian military science was never to be more vividly demonstrated than within the few hours following the attack on that frigid November morning. Running back toward the smoke-shrouded encampment, Darke's troops found the southernmost sector in a shambles. In their absence, a horde of Little Turtle's warriors had overrun the rear line of artillery and captured many of the noncombatants' tents. The dead lay in piles about the smolder-ing guns, said an eyewitness. One soldier estimated there were about thirty officers and artillerymen scattered on the ground by the guns. "It appeared that the Indians had not been in a hurry," he said, "for their hair was all skinned off."[40]

Indeed, one veteran soldier looked upon the scene and saw "horrors . . . which can never be obliterated from my mind." The position had been in the hands of the enemy for only five or ten minutes, estimated a soldier, yet the atrocities were widespread. Wounded men had been scalped while still alive and flung on still-burning campfires. The groans of the dying and mutilated were terrible, thought a wounded militia ranger, who sped on, ignoring pleas for help and water.[41]

Elsewhere, the Indians had fallen upon the milling cluster of women and children. The atrocities inflicted on them badly shocked a young lieutenant of the second regulars: Women lay scattered in disarray, "some of them cut in two, their boobies cut off, and burning with a number of our officers on our own fires."[42]

Yet Darke and his mixed command had little time to ponder the circumstances. They had barely reached camp when the Indians "swarmed like bees" about them. "They were so thick we could do nothing with them," wrote a rifleman. Having fired an estimated fourteen times, he found the cock on his rifle lock had loosened so that it was nearly inoperable. Also, the gunpowder seemed to be weak, in that several Indians seemingly struck by his rifle balls were not brought down.[43]

In contrast, so many of Darke's men were falling, the ground being relatively open at this site, that one of his men ran to his side and said that they all would be shot if they did not move. "Charge, then," said Darke, and a cluster of men with fixed bayonets rushed toward the center of camp.[44]

It was probably at that point that St. Clair was compelled to go to the left, sending in advance a detachment of Lieutenant Colonel Gibson's levies in order to avert a total collapse of the entire flank.

Advancing at the run among the scattered Indians, Gibson's men momentarily eased the pressure on Darke's troops. Fighting briefly hand to hand, the two adjacent detachments struggled to regain a portion of their encampment. "The Indians fought like hell hounds," said a participant. Darke took a painful flesh wound in the thigh, and his son, a captain, was shot in the face, the musket ball fracturing his jaw. When one of Darke's riflemen shot an Indian through the hips, the warrior attempted to crawl away on all fours. Lieutenant Colonel Darke, his sword flashing, then ran after the struggling enemy and "struck his head off." "[Darke] is most passionately intent upon Indian killing himself," later reported a staff officer, but disgustedly added, "[he is] inadequate to performing it by battalion, or even by platoons."[45]

To Darke's men the chaos here reflected the "helter-skelter" nature of the fighting. "I wish I could describe that battle," a rifleman later wrote, "but I have not the power. . . . It seems like a wild, horrid dream in which whites and savages . . . were all mixed together in mad confusion, . . . melting away in smoke, fire, and blood amid groans, shouts, yells, shrieks—the flashing of steel and crackling of firearms—all blended into one loud, continuous roar." The sensation was of bewilderment, he added, with a "half stupefied" awareness of extreme danger, as if one were dangling by a slender thread over a great chasm.[46]

Although the red foe were driven back, and the encampment momentarily cleared, the incoming fire remained constant, reported an officer. Soon a milling cluster of men began to crowd together in the middle of camp. These troops, mostly levies, were so distraught and bewildered that they "ran in a huddle," said Lieutenant Colonel Darke. All the exertions of their officers to get them in some order seemed to be in vain.[47]

As a veteran staff officer reported with candor, the Indians continued to utilize a superior mode of fighting. Covered as they were behind logs and trees, and continually changing position so that they seldom fired twice from the same spot, "it is almost impossible to find them out, or to know [where] to direct your fire," he later wrote. American officers, meanwhile, conspicuous by their dress, were being singled out and shot with appalling rapidity. Further demoralized by the loss of these officers, the leaderless, confused group of stragglers drifted from one side of the encampment to the other, sustaining heavy casualties at every step. Embittered by what he regarded as disgraceful, unthinking refusal to fight, William Darke ranted that these levies—"a bad set of men, not fit to be soldiers," said another officer—were "as well out of this world as in it."[48]

The Second Regiment of United States regulars, observed Winthrop Sargent, had received little formal instruction, and being such a new unit, they had hardly even fired a blank cartridge before November 4. Although decimated by Darke's charge, the Second remained the only sizeable body of infantry available to face the crisis that was then unfolding along the front line facing the Wabash. Here the mounting pressure on the thin blue line near the artillery had produced a near massacre. So many dead men lay about the smoking cannon that volunteers were called to serve the guns. It soon appeared that the cannon would be overrun by swarms of Indians, many of whom had worked their way forward to within a few yards of the muzzles. In desperation another bayonet charge was ordered to save the artillery. The Second regulars were led forward by Major Heart. Major Thomas Butler— already wounded in the leg, but propped up on horseback so that he could continue to fight—joined with his battalion of Pennsylvania levies.[49]

If a more forlorn charge was ordered that day, it was not to witness such an enormous sacrifice of life. Charging directly into the center of the Indian "half moon," Heart's and Butler's men were devastated by a tremendous fire. Heart was almost immediately shot and killed. Butler, on horseback, was such an easy target that he was hit before the charge carried forty paces. In fact, every officer of the Second regulars except three was lost, and one of the survivors was badly wounded. "The ground was literally covered with the dead," wrote the appalled Lieutenant Ebenezer Denny.[50]

Then, as the charge carried forward, the Indians seemed to "skip out of reach of the bayonet" with ease, turning to fire on their pursuers as the opportunity allowed. When the charge had carried a short distance beyond the Wabash, the pace slowed. Scattered fire from both flanks soon halted the advance, and the handful of survivors, aware that the Indians were rapidly closing behind them, turned and ran. Lying on the frozen ground with one leg broken and the other bleeding from a severe wound, Major Thomas Butler could but ponder his uncertain fate as the few retreating men streamed past him and disappeared into camp. It was not yet nine o'clock but already the army seemed on the verge of collapse—thought a soldier who witnessed the "pale and frightened" men running in all directions through the standing tents. St. Clair's assertion that disciplined valor would prevail had been severely refuted. Now the army could but rely on their instincts for survival.[51]

In the midst of his camp Arthur St. Clair stood and looked at the devastation about him. The firing had inexplicably ceased for a few minutes, and

184

St. Clair told his aide Denny how pleased he was that the savages at last had been repelled. Yet this eerie calm was shattered after only a few moments. "It was like the interval of a tornado," a participant later explained, for it preceded an even "deeper horror."[52] Indeed, the renewed enemy pressure was enormous and immediate on the front line facing the Wabash. Here Richard Butler, the ostracized second in command, had been stalking up and down the line with his coat off, gesturing, and urging his men to hold firm. Painfully wounded during the earlier fighting, Butler's arm now hung in a sling. Someone had caught a stray horse in camp and apparently offered it to the portly Butler during the renewed fighting. Amid the swirling gunsmoke Butler mounted, evidently seeking to inspire his dwindling corps of levies by personal example. Now a conspicuous target, he almost immediately fell with a severe wound in his side. Four soldiers rushed to the stricken general and carried him away in a blanket to the tents of the Pennsylvania battalion in the middle of camp.[53]

Butler's body wound was so painful that he apparently asked to be propped up in a sitting position, supported by two knapsacks. Thereafter an officer found him calm despite the constant small-arms fire that swept through the nearby tents. When Captain Edward Butler later came up carrying the seriously wounded Major Thomas Butler, it was already apparent that the position would be overrun. The Indians were so close that arrows were falling about the rows of tents, fired from within the camp perimeter.

Miraculously, Edward had found and rescued his middle brother during the brief interval following the last bayonet attack. Yet there was only enough time for a terse discussion of what to do. Richard, now weakened by loss of blood, and too heavy to be easily carried, told Edward to save Thomas. "I am mortally wounded," he moaned. "Leave me to my fate and save our brother."

There was little opportunity for argument. Although both Edward and Thomas protested, Richard ordered them to go. Groggy, and "so nearly dead" that he seemed insensible to the great pain in his side, General Butler gave his ring, sword, and watch to Major Gaither, and asked for a loaded pistol with which to defend himself to the last. One of his flintlocks was cocked and placed in his hand, then the cluster of officers sped from the scene.[54]

On the firing line the dazed, benumbed soldiers were fighting mostly on their own initiative. So many officers had been shot that of the entire regular artillery crew, not an officer was yet alive except one, Captain Mahlon Ford, who was desperately wounded. Lieutenant Colonel Oldham of the militia also was down, with a mortal wound. Moreover, the severely cold weather already had exacted a heavy toll in fighting efficiency, and one rifleman admitted his fingers became so cold that he had to put the rifle balls in his mouth to keep from dropping them. Ammunition was running low; to keep firing, the men had to salvage discarded cartridge boxes, Also, many of the vintage Revolutionary War weapons had been disabled. One soldier found that after a few shots the bands fell off his musket. "The men, being thus left with few officers, became fearful," wrote an exasperated eyewitness. "[They] gave up the fight, and to save themselves for a moment abandoned entirely their duty and ground, and crowded in toward the center of the field."[55]

Much of the army already had broken up in disorder as the onrushing warriors of Little Turtle and Blue Jacket charged directly at the few remaining cannon yet in action. Standing at one of the guns was captain Nicholas Hannah of the levies, who with a single volunteer had remained to fight. Following a final blast at point-blank range, Hannah jammed his bayonet into the vent and broke the tip off, spiking the piece. Ensign Bartholomew Schaumburgh of the First regulars, in camp as a baggage guard for the recently detached unit, manned his gun to the last, barely escaping with his life.[56]

In an instant the artillery was gone, and the Indians raced on, passing among the advanced rows of soldiers' tents. "The whole army ran together like a mob at a fair," wrote the anguished William Darke, who added that had it not been for the exertions of a few remaining officers, "[they] would have stood there til all were killed." Adjutant General Winthrop Sargent stared in disbelief as the milling, bewildered men refused to fight: "They were very much depressed . . . and huddled together in crowded parties . . . where every shot from the enemy took effect. It was in vain that their surviving leaders used threats, entreaties, and almost every other means that could be devised, to [bring] them to the appearance of order." St. Clair's army had ceased to exist in form, reported Lieutenant Denny. It was now merely a frightened rabble. Denny saw the Indians take more deliberate aim from close range. They killed so many men that the scene seemed horrible beyond description.[57]

St. Clair, convinced his army was overwhelmed by superior numbers, at last sought to effect a retreat. His command had been pushed back to the extreme northeast corner of the encampment, and the incoming fire from all directions disclosed that they were, in fact, completely surrounded. Although a few soldiers had managed to break through the enemy lines to escape along the wilderness road constructed by the army, that route now seemed well covered by the Indians.[58]

Despite this, a hasty attempt to gain the road was organized by some of Darke's levies and the remnant of the regulars. Charging in the direction of the abandoned artillery of the rear line, they swept across ground littered with the dead and dying. "The freshly scalped heads [of our men] were reeking with smoke, and in the heavy morning frost looked like so many pumpkins [in] a cornfield in December," thought a frightened noncombatant. Another participant, Lieutenant Micah McDonough of the Second regulars, here saw a scalped captain of levy regiment "sitting on his backside, his head smoking like a chimney." As McDonough raced past, the captain weakly gasped, was the battle almost over?[59]

The charge toward the road failed to break through. Darke said that he had difficulty controlling the frightened mob, and evidently enough soldiers failed to get the word so that the attempt aborted for want of strength.

The situation now was truly desperate, wrote Winthrop Sargent. The enemy pressed in even closer and were shooting the soldiers down "at pleasure from behind trees," while the terrified troops "could scarcely be led to discharge a single gun with effect." "Both officers and men seemed confounded, incapable of doing anything," said another eyewitness. "The only hope left," wrote the forlorn aide-de-camp Denny, "was that perhaps the savages would be so taken up with the camp as not to follow [their advantage]." Earlier, during the rush toward the road, a rifleman had glimpsed a large body of Indians swarming among the noncombatants' tents, "busy at their work" of slaughtering the remaining women and children. As St. Clair later understated, the troops seemed to realize they had "a dreadful foe." Thus he sought to excuse the panic that ensued.[60]

Despairingly, St. Clair sent word to Darke that he must attempt to break out with some of the survivors, if at all possible. Darke could hardly get anyone to listen to him. A drummer sounded retreat, but in the confusion and noise, nobody seemed to understand what to do.[61]

Finally, George Adams, a veteran of Harmar's campaign, shouted to several men of his regiment. "Boys, lets make for the trace"; and with fixed bayonets, a handful of men rushed forth. The movement gained momentum as various frightened soldiers, many of them without guns, fell in behind.[62]

"There was no alternative," said Ebenezer Denny. "Delay was death." Those among the wounded who could hobble along went too. The other remained behind. The retreat "was done without form," wrote a regular, "every man for himself." To another observer who soon joined in the rush, it was like being amid "a drove of bullocks" as the army ran pell-mell toward the woods.[63]

By design the charge had been directed nearly east, not near the road but into the timber north of it, along a parallel course. The Indians here were surprised by the sortie, and most scattered to the right and left, opening a path through the forest. "The stoutest and most active now took the lead," said Lieutenant Denny, "and those who were foremost in breaking the enemy's line were soon left behind."[64]

Arthur St. Clair, disheveled, his long gray hair hanging in strands about his torn coat, was nearly exhausted. Captain Alexander Trueman of the cavalry had managed to save only a few horses, and a worn-down packhorse, barely able to move "much beyond a walk," was appropriated for the general. Somehow, St. Clair was shoved onto the animal's back although so pained by the gout that he later wrote, "I would sooner have suffered a thousand deaths" than endure "quick motion." Thus he was led from the field, a beaten, disconsolate man.[65]

Aided by the momentary lapse in the Indians' pursuit, the shattered column streamed through the woods utterly in flight. It was 9:30 A.M., and Winthrop Sargent heard the distant sound of sporadic firing in the abandoned camp. There was little doubt, said Sargent with a shudder, what had occurred. Those among the immobilized wounded, so long as they could pull a trigger, had chosen to fight to the last.[66]

Richard Butler—who had once imposed a humiliating treaty on the Shawnees, asserting that the English king had given away the Indian lands, and that he (Butler) would decree the terms on which peace might be restored—had been greatly weakened by the loss of blood. With a cocked pistol in his hand, he now lay propped up against a "large sprawling oak tree," cold and alone, awaiting the inevitable.

Two warriors, said to be Shawnees, approached through the lingering haze of gunsmoke. Butler raised his pistol and fired once. He was reportedly attempting to grasp a second gun, when the blade of a tomahawk ripped through his skull, abruptly ending his life.[67]

Later identified by Simon Girty as an important officer, Butler was scalped and his heart cut out, to be divided into as many pieces as there were tribes in the battle and eaten. His corpse was then left for the wolves and ravens. Butler's words had become tragically prophetic, beyond what even he had foreseen. He had said in 1787, "We plainly tell you that this [Ohio] country belongs to the United States—their blood hath defended it, and will forever protect it." Etched on the finely polished Toledo blade of Richard Butler's sword, now being removed from the battlefield to prevent its capture, was a rather remarkable inscription: "No Me Sacque Sin Razon—No Me Enbaines Sin Honor" ("Draw me not without just cause. Sheath me not without honor").[68]

There were many tragic consequences enacted along the banks of the Wabash that day. Perhaps most indicative of the deep-rooted Indian resentment of American designs was the often-brutal treatment of the wounded white captives found lying on the battlefield. Although many of the more able-bodied were saved, to be sold to the English or kept as slaves, horrible and pitiless torture was inflicted upon captive soldiers and noncombatants alike. Heads, body extremities, and sexual organs were severed and mutilated. Persons still living were sometimes tossed on campfires to burn in excruciating pain. At least one female captive was spread-eagled, and then stakes "as thick as a person's arm" were driven through her body."[69]

Delirious with triumph, the Indians swarmed over the encampment, ransacking tents and enemy bodies, breaking into officers' baggage, and rummaging through letters, personal effects, and camp equipment. Indeed, to the Indians, astonished at the magnitude of their victory, the spoils of the American encampment were enormously alluring. Scattered over seven acres lay the debris of an entire army. Two traveling forges, two baggage wagons, 384 common and 9 horsemen's tents, an estimated 1,200 muskets and bayonets, 163 felling axes, and a variety of other booty littered the ground. Included among the eight cannon captured were two howitzers allegedly taken from the British general Cornwallis in 1781. These and the other guns soon were divided among the principal tribes involved in their capture, including three cannon that were presented to Simon Girty by the Wyandots. Yet, because there was no means nor a suitable trail by which to remove them north to Kekionga, all ultimately were buried or hidden in nearby creeks or the Wabash River.[70]

Among the more interesting finds were the diaries and correspondence of many of the American leaders, nearly all of which were eventually passed on to the British. Simon Girty was later observed with a pair of silver-mounted flintlock pistols thrust into his belt that were perhaps obtained from Butler or another unfortunate United States officer. In fact, according to one account there was so much booty that the Indians were forced to abandon some of the equipment. Oddly enough, the intense lure of this plunder saved many white fugitives: Though at first several hundred Indians had pursued the retreating

Americans, many soon returned to the shattered encampment to claim their share of the spoils. When several kegs of liquor were found, some Indians began drinking heavily. Soon the major portion of the warriors had all but forgotten the remnant of St. Clair's army fleeing through the nearby forest in utter panic.[71]

"The retreat [of our troops]," wrote the distraught Arthur St. Clair, "was, you may be sure, a very precipitate one. It was, in fact, a flight." Winthrop Sargent and Ebenezer Denny were even more candid in their disgust. Said Sargent: "The conduct of the army after quitting the gound was in a most supreme degree disgraceful. Arms, ammunition and accoutrements were almost all thrown away, and even the officers in some instances divested themselves of their fusees." Denny observed, "Such a panic had seized the men that I believe it would not have been possible to have brought any of them to [fight] again." Denny, mounted on a strong horse, attempted to reach the front of the flying mob to halt their flight and compact the mass. Yet ultimately he was unable to consolidate more than a small portion of the troops, despite forcibly jamming the road with a half-dozen stout men who had been instructed to move slowly.[72]

Contributing to the difficulty was the rapid pursuit of the soldiers by a determined handful of warriors, estimated by an officer to be not more than twenty individuals. The Indians gave chase and kept up their horrid yells, wrote an eyewitness, causing many of the men to throw away their guns and knapsacks and race ahead "with all their might."[73]

One harried fugitive found that because so many bayoneted guns had been thrown away by the troops ahead of him, he had difficulty avoiding being stabbed as he ran through the brush.[74]

Another soldier, William Kennan, burdened by a personal friend who had a broken thigh and was desperately clinging to his back, saw that several Indians were so close in pursuit that death was certain for both unless the friend let go. There was no choice, said the able-bodied Kennan; his companion must drop off. Yet compulsively the wounded man clung to Kennan's back, frozen with fright. A warrior brandishing a gleaming tomahawk was within twenty yards, said Kennan. Desperately he reached for his hunting knife and slashed at the companion's fingers. The man let go with a groan and rolled to the ground. The man was tomahawked before Kennan had gone thirty yards farther.[75]

Although Arthur St. Clair had designated Major Clarke to provide a rear guard, this effort soon collapsed in chaos. Clarke somehow became separated from his men, and thereafter the battalion broke up in disorder. For about a mile and a half, the extended stream of soldiers blindly groped through the timber before finally striking the wilderness road recently constructed by St. Clair.[76]

The scene here was incredible. Exhausted, bedraggled men stumbled forth as if in a stupor. Several horses still with the column were burdened with two and sometimes three persons.

Panic had completely seized some of the survivors. One of Butler's levies saw an exhausted woman abandon her infant by the roadside that she might better escape from the Indians. This woman, Catharine Miller, known also as "Red-headed Nance" because of her long, flowing auburn hair, was later found crying as she stumbled forlornly along the wilderness road. One of only three women known to have escaped that day, Nance later bemoaned the loss of her child, which allegedly was recovered by the Indians and raised in a Sandusky village.[77]

Tragedy mixed with irony seemed to prevail everywhere during the retreat. Captain Samuel Newman of the regulars, who on one occasion had been the only captain healthy enough to perform duty in his regiment, had survived the fighting that morning, though wounded in the arm. Now he was so weak that during the forced trek he lay down and told his companions to leave him. Refusing to abandon him to the Indians, his friends found a stray packhorse and put Newman on the animal's back. Shortly thereafter a pursuing warrior fired a musket ball into Newman's back, killing him instantly.[78]

Although the Indians finally ceased their pursuit after a distance of perhaps four or five miles, the panic and chaos continued. When Ebenezer Denny again tried to organize some of the troops, he found it hopeless, the men being in "the most miserable and defenseless state." "How fortunate that the pursuit was discontinued," later wrote Denny. "A single Indian might have followed with safety upon either flank."[79]

Ahead, the burgeoning fear had already carried through to the elements of the army not engaged in the fight. Major John Hamtramck, with the veteran First United States Regiment, had been unsuccessful in escorting the expected supply convoy. A detachment sent to within nineteen miles of the Miami River had found that the contractor had not yet dispatched the supplies. Returning to within a few miles of Fort Jefferson on the night of November 3, Hamtramck's troops passed that post early the following morning. In the distance, the men could hear the firing of cannon. Puzzled, Hamtramck ordered his men to load and to fix bayonets before proceeding to rejoin St. Clair. After breakfasting at a creek six miles beyond Fort Jefferson, Hamtramck continued several miles farther before encountering several militiamen who informed him the army was "totaly destroyed." Shaken and uncertain of what to do, Hamtramck belatedly decided to retreat to Fort Jefferson, sending ahead only a lieutenant with a small detachment to learn what had happened. Hamtramck reasoned that if the army were defeated, Fort Jefferson would be the nearest point of refuge and it must be secured. Yet, as Lieutenant Colonel William Darke later observed, Hamtramck thus abandoned the retreating men, many of whom were wounded and might easily have been saved.[80]

Thus for St. Clair's shattered army, defeated and routed, with nearly two-thirds of its personnel and all of its equipment lost, the walk back to Fort Jefferson was an excruciating ordeal. Ice "as thick as a knife blade" filled the ruts, and slushy snow lingered in the shaded areas. "I was worn out with fatigue," wrote a soldier whose feet were cut and swollen from "splashing through the ice without shoes." Others, having limped from the battlefield following the earlier actions, were found crawling and staggering along the road with the blood oozing from their scalped heads. William Darke, his wounded thigh so sore and stiff that he could scarcely move, and having gone without food for a day, found the agony of the retreat beyond description. Perhaps the most pathetic example of suffering endured on the long march was Major Thomas Butler. With one leg broken and the other mangled by a gunshot wound, Butler had been carried from the field bleeding profusely. When at last a moment was gained to look at the major's wound, his brother Edward ripped up his own linen shirt and staunched the flow, barely in time to save Thomas's life. Carried by hand, alternating between three stragglers and Edward, Thomas found each step such agony that he cried out to be placed on the ground and allowed to die. At last a lone mounted dragoon was persuaded to take the wounded major behind him. Yet in a congested spot, crossing a deep rut, another horse jostled Butler's mount, nearly knocking him off and reopening his wounds. Ahead the lack of medicines and facilities at Fort Jefferson necessitated a continuation of the painful trek. Not until six days later, at Fort Washington, did Thomas Butler receive adequate treatment.[81]

On the battlefield, during the waning hours of November 4, the victorious forces of Little Turtle and Blue Jacket reveled in the enormity of their accomplishment. At a cost of twenty-one killed and forty wounded, they had virtually annihilated a larger American army. Later the Indians would boastfully allude to the multitude of soldiers' corpses left rotting on the field, saying that they had truly "feasted the wolves . . . with the carcasses of enemies."[82]

Among the elated multitude of Indian combatants, the evening of November 4 would long be remembered. Some captured bullocks had been slaughtered, and after feasting and drinking, clusters of warriors roamed through the desolated encampment. Some had dressed in the uniforms of dead officers, with silver epaulets sparkling in the light of the campfires and captured watches dangling from their earlobes. Many of their women, who had come to the battlefield, now found their arms weary from taking the scalps of white men. In fact, Richard Butler's scalp was carefully dried and preserved, so that it might be sent to Joseph Brant to chide him for his absence, with the warriors of the Six Nations.[83]

Amid the shrieking, exultant warriors and shattered wilderness campground, St. Clair's army lay cold and unmoving, occupying only in death the land that they had sought to conquer. In mock tribute to the greed of these white men, who already had usurped so much land and yet sought more, the Indians had crammed earth into the mouths of the American slain. Perhaps now the symbolism would be recognized. Urged a tribal chieftain: "Let us war on, like men, forever."[84]

18

"This Moment May Never Return"

THE American arms never met with such a defeat," wrote a despairing survivor of the November 4 fight. "Be assured," he added, "its a pleasure for me to . . . inform you that I am alive and well, although such a great number of my acquaintances and friends have lately changed their place of abode—and that without the hair on their heads." Another participant, an officer, recorded in his journal, "The fortunes of this day have been the cruelest . . . and will blacken a full page in the future annals of America."[1]

Once the battered remnant of St. Clair's army reached Fort Jefferson, it was evident that more than half of the army had been killed or wounded. St. Clair forlornly acknowledged that the battle was "as unfortunate an action as almost any that has been fought." The retreat from the battlefield had been a flight—a "disgraceful business," he said. The rout continued for twenty-nine miles, to the very walls of Fort Jefferson. An officer of the garrison there wrote that, with straggling soldiers streaming through the gates in broken clusters throughout the late afternoon and evening of November 4, the chaotic scene at the fort was horrid beyond description. One soldier staggered in without his scalp, his skull crushed in two places by a tomahawk. Reflecting the utter misery of this ordeal, one private said he was virtually out on his feet and "could hardly [stay] awake."[2]

Yet there was little respite for these forlorn, defeated men. Having gone without food for nearly twenty-four hours, it was found they could not be supplied from the Fort Jefferson stores, simply becasuse there was so little on hand. The garrison itself was reduced to a single day's flour ration (300 pounds) and was entirely without meat. It was expected that the Indians would soon invest Fort Jefferson and cut off the convoy of provisions that was en route from Fort Hamilton. Arthur St. Clair, convening an urgent council of the senior officers present, plaintively asked what could be done. The council soon resolved that all but the badly wounded and a small garrison should immediately retreat—both to escape further mauling from the enemy if they besieged the fort and to obtain more quickly the provisions that were en route.[3]

Accordingly, at 10:00 P.M. on November 4, with stragglers still wandering in from the woods, St. Clair put his exhausted soldiers on the road behind the First Regiment, and the all-night trek began. The route was mostly through a "beech [tree] swamp," wrote a bedraggled private, who continually stumbled over logs and roots in the darkness, barely able to keep going. Shortly before daylight even the austere Adjutant General Winthrop Sargent admitted that the army "could not possibly be pushed farther"—the men had traveled seven miles and seemed to be at the limit of their endurance. A halt was ordered, and at daylight it was estimated that the straggling column stretched for more than five miles, completely dispersed and vulnerable to an attack.[4]

Meanwhile, men like Lieutenant Colonel William Darke—overwrought with fatigue, anger, and shock—already had resolved to take matters into their own hands. Darke, still infuriated by the alleged cowardice of Major John Hamtramck of the First Regulars in retreating to Fort Jefferson on November 4 without covering the defeated column that was fleeing from the battlefield, refused to trust anyone. Although his two sons remained at Fort Jefferson desperately wounded, Darke obtained a mount after midnight and went galloping after St. Clair's departed column. Darke believed that he might perhaps prevent Hamtramck from interfering with the forwarding of the supplies that were enroute to the Fort Jefferson garrison. After passing along the straggling column, belatedly he met the supply convoy, which was already in turmoil following the news of the disaster. Darke said that he had to persuade St. Clair to allow sixty regulars to escort fifty horseloads of provisions forward to Fort Jefferson, otherwise the drivers would have refused to proceed. As it was, the sixty-six remaining packhorses retreated with St. Clair's column to Fort Hamilton. Darke swore mightily all the way back to Fort Jefferson, some eighteen miles. His wounded thigh was so swollen that it seemed nearly as large as his body and as hot as fire.[5]

At Fort Jefferson the miserable, wretched conditions persisted, despite the arrival of Darke with provisions sufficient for about three weeks. Many of the wounded remained within the uncompleted 114-foot-square structure, suffering from the lack of medical care and nourishment. "No medicine, nor [proper] nourishment,—not even a quart of salt" was on hand, wrote an officer. One by one, the wounded began to die, including Lieutenant Colonel George Gibson on November 12. With an occasional wounded straggler still wandering in, the situation had so deteriorated by late November that there was talk of an imminent evacuation. Only a few days' provisions remained on hand. Word was spread that a large Indian force had been sighted on the wilderness road within fifteen miles of the stockade, and it was feared that Fort Jefferson would soon be besieged. William Darke, unable to move his wounded sons, in frustration finally set out for Fort Washington, loudly damning the army's commanders for their lack of exertions to relieve the exposed outpost.[6]

To Arthur St. Clair the fatigue of his forced march to Fort Washington, about seventy miles in three and a half days, was so debilitating that upon his arrival he immediately took to bed. He was not even to leave his room for more than two weeks. The army's return to Fort Washington had been such a painful ordeal that the straggling column had ceased to function as a military force. Mob rule had prevailed with increasing intensity, reaching a new height as the troops approached the banks of the Ohio River.[7]

The soldiers' morale was at the nadir. Therefore their "ignominious flight" had proceeded unchecked. Drenched by a cold, intermittent rain, the pitiful, beaten column sullenly tramped into the confines of Fort Washington at noon on November 8. Soon it was found that nobody had provided even for so much as shelter in the event of an emergency. Sufficient room for more than the normal garrison was lacking, and the troops were directed to a bivouac along nearby Deer Creek. There the bedraggled infantry men found few tents, provisions, or equipment. All had been lost in the defeat of November 4. The officers then "quit their men," announced the army's adjutant general, and found houses in the town to shelter them. The resulting chaos nearly rendered the army inoperative.[8]

By the morning of November 9 many of the demoralized soldiers had abandoned their bivouac area and were milling through the villge of Cincinnati. "Every house in this town is filled with drunken soldiers and there seems one continued scene of confusion," reported Adjutant General Sargent.

Virtual anarchy prevailed among the levies and militia. "The levies were lost forever," wrote the chagrined Sargent. "Their time of service was near expiring; all relation between officers and men [was] forgotten, and not even the semblance of duty acknowledged."[9]

By now the levies were so ragged and devoid of equipment that they were half-naked. Finally, they were promised clothing from the Fort Washington stores, but by St. Clair's decree, only if they consented to have the cost of it deducted from their pay. In the vital matter of pay, moreover, St. Clair steadfastly refused to allow any disbursements, because the records of the levies' enlistment had been lost on the battlefield. Also, many had thrown away their arms, for which they were to be charged. Furthermore, scoffed St. Clair, if paid, these men had no use for their money other than to buy whiskey. Asserting that they were the "kind of men" who were unaccustomed to discipline and disliked labor, St. Clair reasoned that he was really doing them a favor in holding back their monies.[10]

Meanwhile, the weather continued to deteriorate. There were heavy showers of rain, then freezing cold winds. By November 15 snow had fallen, and the men, although finally supplied with some flimsy tents from the government stores, were still without blankets, warm clothing, and camp equipment.[11]

Desertions were occurring at a phenomenal rate, and many of the released men were found selling their discharge vouchers showing an unspecified amount due them. These, reported St. Clair in disgust, were bartered in town for whatever was offered, which was usually whiskey. Some got only one quart for their voucher.[12]

Despite all of the chaos at Fort Washington, by the second week after St. Clair's return, the situation seemed to be much worse at the interior forts. Of the remote Fort Jefferson virtually nothing was known, and it was presumed this stockade was under siege by the enemy. For relief St. Clair belatedly authorized a fifty-man escort with a packhorse convoy on November 10. Major David Ziegler followed on the eleventh with about one hundred men of the First United States Regiment. It was not known whether they could get through, however, and for further relief the outer forts would have to await the arrival of a Kentucky mounted militia force that was then organizing.[13]

To make matters worse, the small reconnaissance party of friendly Chickasaws who had gone out on October 29 returned and reported encountering a lone warrior in the vicinity of the Miami Towns. This warrior, not suspecting that he was among enemies, had boasted to them that he had been in the fight of November 4, in which only 700 warriors had fought against the Americans. He had then so elatedly recounted the fight that the Chickasaws angrily shot him down in the middle of his story. Among the last words spoken by the warrior was a remark that his "arm was quite weary with tomahawking [white men]."[14]

On November 9, Arthur St. Clair took a pen in hand and began a most difficult letter to the secretary of war announcing the utter defeat of his army. There never had been, nor has there been since, such a disaster at the hands of hostile Indians. In fact, St. Clair's defeat remains one of the worst defeats of a major United States army at the hands of Indians, dwarfing even the Custer debacle on the Little Big Horn in 1876. A staggering 55 percent of the American combatants had become casualties within only a few hours. The dead and missing numbered 630 by Adjutant Denny's count, and in the Second United States Regiment three-fourths of the entire unit were lost. Of the approximately 1,400 persons who had been present, less than 500 remained uninjured, and many of the survivors were noncombatants. The officer corps was reduced by half. Sixty-nine of the 124 commissioned officers present were reported killed, wounded, or missing. More than 280 wounded still cluttered the outpost forts and the Cincinnati camp. Still to be considered were the massive losses of equipment and war materiel, valued at nearly $33,000.[15]

Arthur St. Clair had not eaten a normal meal in nearly a month. Sustained only by "bread and tea," he could "neither eat, drink, nor sleep." Ruefully he began his letter to Secretary of War Knox, "Yesterday afternoon the remains of the army under my command got back to this place, and I now have the painful task to give you an account."[16]

British Indian agent Alexander McKee, discrediting early reports of the Indians' overwhelming military success, at first had refused to believe what he regarded as exaggerated accounts of the action. A few weeks later, however, McKee was so thoroughly convinced of the Indians' enormous victory that he fairly exuded enthusiasm. "The astonishing success of a few Indians . . . who have opposed and destroyed the whole American force," he wrote elatedly, "will probably cause a more numerous collection of Indians [in the spring] . . . than ever before known in this part of the country." A constant stream of prisoners and veritable reams of captured documents had convinced McKee of the major Indian triumph, and he set to work preparing further military assistance for the "brave, and warlike race of people."[17]

By November 12 the first news of the battle had reached the Detroit area, and at Niagara news of a "universal" rout of the American army caused the British greatly to exult. Soon it was reported that the two American forts built by St. Clair had been surrounded by the Indians and, being stocked with but a few provisions, must soon surrender. Indeed, immediately following the tumultuous victory celebration on November 4 and 5, the Indian leadership had proposed that they move quickly against these vulnerable forts.[18]

Yet, as in the aborted pursuit of Harmar's disorganized column the preceding year, another combination of circumstances impinged on the exploitation of the huge Indian victory.

In the summer of 1791 the Indian crop yields had not been sufficient to sustain the Maumee- and Wabash-region tribes. The continual rains that had hampered St. Clair's army during their initial advances had also severely flooded the vast cornfields adjacent to the Indian towns on the upper Maumee River, and a large portion of that crop had been lost. Moreover, the gathered Indian army had required so many provisions during October that it had nearly exhausted all supplies. With adverse weather rapidly developing, the Shawnees, Miamis, and Delawares, in particular, were compelled to disperse, Alexander McKee said—in order "to hunt for the support of their families—at a time when their services were wanted . . . to reduce the forts." Thus by mid-November much of the Indian force had scattered, and reports were rife of small parties of warriors returning to their villages throughout the Old Northwest.[19]

Before this vast concentration of Indians had entirely broken up, a momentous grand council had been convened on the banks of the Ottawa River, near what is now Lima, Ohio. To be determined, in the light of their recent defeat of the American invasion, was the tribes' future policy toward the United States. Should the general confederacy continue the active war? Or should they attempt to negotiate on the basis of the recent stunning victory?

"Gushgushagwa," perhaps Egushawa of the Ottawas, an old war chief renowned for his fearless spirit, began the debate with a ringing denunciation of the white enemy: "I do not yet see the means of attaining peace on honorable terms, but by war—for our enemy confide in their superior numbers and strength, and not on God, who makes them and us; nor on the justice of their cause. I am of the opinion . . . you ought not to give peace to your enemy until they ask it, or until they retire out of your country."

Exhorting the assembled throng to continue the fight, the aged chieftain concluded by alluding to the great recent victory: "If a despised banditti can do this, what may you not do, united as you will now soon be? . . . "It is not a time to talk or think of peace! . . . It is only a time to act like men and as warriors!"[20]

Drained of emotion, Gushgushagwa sat down, and another chief, Yeshiva, rose to speak on behalf of the peace faction. "Why strive in vain against the influence of this evil spirit?" he demanded. "You may possibly beat your enemy until you teach him your own manner of warfare. What then will be the consequence?" Stating that the whites were too numerous for the Indians to achieve a lasting military victory, Yeshiva pleaded that every effort should be made to reach a peaceful solution, especially in view of the British offer to mediate.

The warriors continued to debate with ardor, and uncertainty about the proper policy increased. No one was able to predict what the American attitude might be, should negotiations be renewed. With the British exerting pressure for a political settlement, perhaps, as was suggested, the twice-beaten Americans could be brought to reasonable terms.

When the council broke up, it had concluded nothing—only that a great gathering would be held at the foot of the Miami Rapids in the spring, which would properly consider the course of action to be taken.[21] Only the Miami tribe, frustrated by the ruinous logistics that had hampered the war effort during the past year, concluded to take important action. Kekionga was distant from most of the Great Lakes region and from the Algonquian nations who would comprise an Indian army. To facilitate a rapid concentration of Indian forces and reduce their vulnerability to a surprise attack, the Miamis decided to abandon their villages permanently and to move close to the British trading base at the Miami Rapids. The improved accessibility to British provisions was expected to be an important advantage in the future resistance to American invasions.[22]

Although it has been long neglected by historians, this council on the banks of the Ottawa contributed significantly to the ultimate destiny of the red people. At a time when the Indian belligerents had seized the initiative militarily, that hard-won advantage was allowed to dissipate through indecision. Thus time was allowed to become a compromising element.

The Indians could hope to maintain their power only by sustained and unrelenting physical control of the disputed territory. Although their enemy had been temporarily shorn of much of his military protection, the Indians chose to ignore this vulnerability. They were not realistic to hope that a viable negotiated settlement could then be reached. The Americans had not been conclusively beaten, and the external forces impinging on both sides, from London and Philadelphia, required a final, determinant solution. Because the Indian peoples could no longer hope to compete numerically, their prospects for success lay in the rapid application of maximum offensive pressure. In the winter of 1791, because the United States had expanded its frontier beyond its power to defend it, an enormous opportunity existed— but only at that precise time.

In the inexorable ebb and flow of war, one achieves control by managing events rather than being managed by them. In the decision to do nothing, like the British equivocations earlier about the extent of the support that that nation would give the Indians, the Ottawa River council had established a dangerous precedent. From now on the destiny of red civilization was to drift in an infinite and capricious sea of uncertainty.

The direct consequence of the proceedings in the Maumee River region during the fall and winter of 1791, wrote Alexander McKee, was to make the resident Indians "more and more attached to the British interest in due proportion to the extreme hatred and antipathy which they bear their [American] enemies." The movement en masse from the Miami Towns was a case in point. Settling near the confluence of the Auglaize and Maumee rivers, about fifty miles from McKee's trading post at the foot of the Miami Rapids, the relocated Shawnees, Miamis, and Delawares were so dependent on British supplies that they soon pleaded extreme poverty. "We and our women and children are almost starving for want of provisions," wrote the chiefs at the Glaize early in the spring of 1792. "We are very sensible of the goodness of our father at Detroit, who last year supported our families when they had nothing to eat, and we hope now for the same consideration, our situation . . . being rather worse." Slowly, yet inevitably, the Indians were being brought to a state of extreme reliance on their British benefactors, a condition that was accentuated by the escalating hostilities with the United States.[23]

To the British the supreme moment in the Indian fortunes in the Old Northwest had brought with it a sense of burgeoning importance. "The Americans must be severely hurt at this blow," thought a British observer late in November, 1791, who speculated, "They would [now] probably listen to any reasonable terms." "Perhaps this can only be effected by the influence of the British Government," he surmised. "[Then] we should secure our posts, [and] the trade and the tranquility of the country." Yet official word of St. Clair's defeat did not reach the Home Office in Whitehall, England, until about June, 1792, nearly seven months after the event.[24]

While inordinate delays in transmitting diplomatic communications thus usurped precious time on the political front, the British posture at the operational level continued warlike. Reports from Alexander McKee in January, 1792, advised that the hostiles were gathering "to reduce the forts" and secure the cannon left on the battlefield. "The minds of whites [British agents] and Indians are filled with war," wrote an apprehensive missionary near Detroit on January 15, 1792.[25]

Meanwhile, unresolved logistical difficulties, particularly the critical shortage of food, continued to hamper any serious attempt against the exposed wilderness forts. McKee was compelled to order 500 bushels of corn during January, just to get the transient Miami Town families through the winter.[26] A rash of sickness further complicated any planned military operations, and by early spring the unusually deep snow had so inhibited hunting that the Indians were reduced to begging again from the British.[27]

Although one might have anticipated, as a fruition of the Indians' ascending fortunes in war, the establishment of an imposing and politically capable native force, even the operational capabililties of the Indian army became uncertain in the spring of 1792. Moreover, since some factions were fomenting internal discontent because the British were not providing greater material aid, there was talk of a red revolt. According to several accounts, speeches from the Spaniards along the Mississippi urged the Indians to "plainly see that the English are deceiving them in putting them off with vain promises— that they are as much their enemies, under the mask of friendship, as the Americans." The British, proclaimed the Spanish messages, merely "furnish[ed] them with ammunition and set them on as they would a parcel of dogs wishing them to destroy each other—while they themselves sit spectators." The resulting confusion, said Alexander McKee, caused some among the tribes, who now were destitute of adequate subsistence, to talk seriously of emigrating south of the Illinois country, "where they can live at peace [under Spanish rule]."[28]

Yet the desire for preeminence remained intact within the British Indian Department. Additional corn and "other provisions" were soon sent to partially alleviate the shortages. Thus the British expected that the Indians would assume the offensive with the advent of good weather in the late spring. Encouraging speeches were received from the Shawnees and Delawares, who proposed to commence operations in 1792 with the seige of Fort Jefferson. If successful, the tribesmen exulted, "we will send our answer [to proposals of peace] by the prisoners [taken]."

A British observer now lamented, "I wish our peacemakers of [17]83 had but known a little more of this country." Optimistically, he wrote, "Perhaps this is the important moment in which the unfortunate terms of that peace may be altered." Then, hesitating in view of the imposing obstacles involved in perpetuating the American defeat, he cautiously added, "Perhaps this moment may never return."[29]

On December 13, 1791, the *Maryland Journal* had proclaimed that an express had arrived on December 12 from the District of Kentucky bringing news of the defeat of the army under General St. Clair. The remnant of the troops were said to be "cooped up and almost starving" in Fort Jefferson. "BLOODY INDIAN BATTLE," blazoned a Boston broadside, which was printed with two rows of twenty black coffins over that headline. "This is a fatal stroke to the United States," said an "eyewitness" in an account printed in a Maryland newspaper.[30]

Thus the American public was informed of the stunning disaster of November 4. As early as mid-November, private correspondents had picked up the news in Kentucky, and they hastily sent it east in terse dispatches that progressively shocked and alarmed the nation. Incomplete accounts of the "remains of the army," beseiged in the outpost forts and reduced to eating "the flesh of pack horses," had Kentucky's populace so alarmed that, according to one correspondent, "all the leading characters are turning out" to relieve the army. Yet on November 24, Adjutant General Sargent disdainfully wrote that he had no doubt that the projected Kentucky expedition "must fail." Instead of the 1,500 volunteers expected, only about 200 had come forward to Cincinnati with Brigadier General Charles Scott. In fact, several days later Sargent reported that these Kentuckians had gone home.[31]

Arthur St. Clair, meanwhile, wrote to Henry Knox that the country between Forts Hamilton and Jefferson, for ten or twelve miles, was now under water following a snowfall of considerable depth. The small relief detachment under Major David Ziegler, who barely managed to get through the deeply mired roads and nearly unfordable rivers, found the Fort Jefferson garrison of 116 men reduced to the necessity of eating "horse flesh and green hides."[32]

Word of the dire plight of the army, of course, quickly spread throughout the frontier. Demands from the alarmed citizens at Marietta caused St. Clair to reapportion his meagre troops in that sector.[33] At Pittsburgh the inhabitants looked upon the recent developments as the prelude to a catastrophe of the first magnitude. "The late disaster of the army must greatly affect the safety of this place," asserted a committee of citizens. Fearing the involvement of the Six Nations in the hostilities, and pleading a "defenseless situation" along the entire Pennsylvania frontier, the citizens demanded an adequate garrison, more arms, and additional ammunition for the common defense.[34]

Immediately, of course, these accounts and petitions were passed on to the east in order that the "general government" might act. Previous orders given by St. Clair for the transfer of the Pittsburgh garrison had to be countermanded; special authorization was given to the militia commanders to call out scouts and ranger companies, and a blockhouse was ordered erected at Fort Pitt.[35]

St. Clair's expedition had been conceived as a punitive expedition to establish physical control over the territory ceded by the British, so that those lands might be incorporated into the productive regions of the nation. Instead, the expedition had only enormously increased expenses by expanding the war.

From the west came anonymous and highly derogatory comments by experienced officers and officials, published in a variety of newspapers, that further inflamed the public outrage. An unnamed soldier stated that it was madness for the United States to think "an insignificant, undisciplined army, badly provided, will conquer the formidable enemy they are now at war with." "The army must be remodeled," demanded another veteran officer, who remarked that under the United States's present unfortunate policy the men enlisted at two dollars per month were of such poor quality that they merely enriched the enemy with plunder. "What a pitiful establishment!" he concluded in disgust.[36]

At Fort Washington, St. Clair's aide-de-camp candidly wrote in his diary of the despair and disillusionment within the military establishment: "The remains of our wretched and miserable army are encamped in front of the fort. The weather is cold and wet with snow." Although he had been so pained by the recent ordeal that he attempted to banish all remembrance from his mind, Lieutenant Ebenezer Denny was selected to carry the fatal news to the administration in Philadelphia. So sick of the military life that he was soon to refuse a promotion to captain and resign his commission, Denny departed for Philadelphia on November 19. Although at that time he wrote that St. Clair "has scarcely had his head off the pillow," the major general proposed soon to follow. Thus, St. Clair, politically cognizant of the burgeoning controversy in Philadelphia, laboriously began his trek to the "Atlantic country" nearly three weeks later.[37]

Instead of a triumphant return to the seat of government, adorned by the "honest fame [which] has ever been the strongest passion in my breast," St. Clair, broken in health and charged with gross mismanagement of his army, could expect to endure only the bitter wrath of defeat.[38]

19

A Matter of Commitment

THE president of the United States was entertaining guests at dinner, wrote an observer of the Philadelphia scene in 1791, when an urgent dispatch arrived from the War Department. Although the president wished not to be disturbed, his ubiquitous private secretary, Tobias Lear, entered to whisper the news of the courier's presence. Leaving the dinner table to read the important intelligence, Washington returned after a brief absence and graciously continued in the evening's festivities.

It was much later, after the guests had departed, that Washington spoke freely. In the presence only of Lear, the president then fairly exploded with rage. "It's all over," he began, his voice rising with pent-up emotion. "St. Clair's defeated—routed, the officers nearly all killed. . . . Here," he continued with even greater vehemence, "yes, here on this very spot I took leave of him. . . . You have your instructions, I said, from the Secretary of War. I . . . will add but one word—beware of a surprise! You know how the Indians fight us." "He went off with that as my last solemn warning," continued the infuriated Washington. ". . . And yet!! to suffer that army to be cut to pieces, hacked, butchered, tomahawked by a surprise—the very thing I guarded him against!! Oh God, Oh God, he is worse than a murderer! How can he answer to his country? The blood of the slain is upon him—the curse of widows and orphans—the curse of Heaven!"

Bellowing invectives and gesturing wildly, Washington damned Arthur St. Clair with a fury that completely intimidated and awed Tobias Lear. Finally collapsing upon a sofa, the president sat silent, his reddened face draining of emotion. At last, he spoke again. "This must not go beyond this room," he admonished. "General St. Clair shall have justice. . . . I will receive him without displeasure, I will hear him without prejudice, he shall have full justice."[1]

Perhaps a little more than a week later, Lieutenant Denny arrived with St. Clair's official report. The young officer was promptly taken to see the president, and, obviously, Denny felt some trepidation. Yet after a breakfast with Washington's family present, he and the president talked in depth of the late campaign, and Denny later recorded that he was received with "attention and kindness." Only among his friends was Denny regarded as something like a specter—having "escaped from the dead," he was seemingly a curiosity "little better than one of the savages."[2]

By the time St. Clair had laboriously journeyed to Philadelphia, arriving about mid-January, the storm brewing over his conduct had already carried beyond the executive branch. Yet he too was treated to "a very gracious reception" by the president, St. Clair later wrote.[3]

Washington, it appears, was already looking beyond any individual responsibility to the source of the problem—an outmoded military system. Early in 1792 he drafted a dispassionate memorandum assigning certain causes to the November 4 defeat. Principal among these was the lack of necessary commitment, as demonstrated by the short enlistments of the levies who had been a major part of St. Clair's force. Thus, although he privately faulted St. Clair for a lack of intelligence and improper tactical deployment, Washington publicly utilized the "unfortunate affair" to press Congress for major revisions in the military establishment—the essential reform that he sought.[4]

St. Clair was the recipient of a charitable letter from the secretary of war late in December, but he found on his arrival in Philadelphia that he was to be shunted from further military command. Although he pleaded with Washington to be allowed to retain his commission as major general until a court of inquiry could be convened, the president refused, saying that was impracticable. Even in his pursuit of an army inquiry or court martial St. Clair was to remain frustrated. There were no other active officers of equal rank "to form a legal court." Only in the resolution of the House of Representatives, appointing a special committee to investigate St. Clair's expedition, was the prospect of public redress afforded. St. Clair, as the former president of Congress and the friend of influential members of the House, may have had a covert role in that committee, which his close friend Thomas Fitzsimons chaired. Several other members were also known to be former cronies of St. Clair's.[5]

This development was of immediate concern to the president. Indeed, the investigation was a potential source of embarrassment to the entire administration. A congressional body threatening to pass judgment on a coequal branch of the government was not only unprecedented but also dangerous. The Hamiltonian faction was most vulnerable, since Knox, Duer, Hamilton, and others were involved in a potential scandal of major proportions. It was imperative that the situation be handled adroitly.

Washington convened one of the first full meetings of his "cabinet," which debated the issue extensively. Ultimately, they resolved to turn over to the congressional committee all appropriate documents, while retaining the authority to withhold papers that might "injure the public."[6]

The committee sessions in the following weeks included some rather heated testimony. St. Clair asserted that "a deep cabal" had formed against him among his officers and that his army had been beaten only after an "obstinate struggle against a greatly superior force." Whitewashed by the initial report that the special committee presented on May 8, 1792, St. Clair exulted that his detractors had "darkened" themselves sufficiently, although he was forced to resign his commission as major general.[7]

As was to be expected, the bitterness of the allegations concerning the 1791 campaign remained undiminished, and the intense controversy continued for years. Affronted by the preliminary report of the House committee, the Knox-Hamilton faction lobbied arduously to change the report's substance. At the commencement of the second congressional session Knox's request for a reopening of the investigation was approved. Subsequently, the committee was restructured, and a second, or revised, report was submitted in February, 1793, acknowledging that certain "mistakes" had been in the original. Subsequently, the revised report was "tabled" by the House of Representatives, and the committee discharged. Although St. Clair was extremely disappointed, he was unable to obtain further action on the report.[8]

St. Clair, who was allowed to remain as governor of the Northwest Territory, continued to suffer deteriorating health, and he was frustrated in his attempts to regain a position in Congress. Ultimately, in 1802 he was cashiered from his post by President Thomas Jefferson, following his opposition to Ohio's statehood. Reduced to poverty when his farm near Ligonier, Pennsylvania, was sold to satisfy personal indebtedness in 1810, an infirm and all-but-forgotten Arthur St. Clair died a pauper at age eighty-four, eight years later.[9]

For the harassed administration of George Washington, the winter of 1791–1792 was a nightmare of unabated crisis. Not only were explanations and reassurances demanded, but important decisions had to be made. Paramount among the Indian difficulties loomed the necessity of a basic revision in policy. The United States had either to accede to the Indian claims and negotiate a settlement or to proceed with a military solution.

Senator Benjamin Hawkins of North Carolina, who had negotiated treaties with the Creeks and Cherokees in 1785, raised a fundamental question in a letter to Washington that winter. Asserting that the recent fiasco in the West was the "harvest" of "the feeble efforts" to negotiate a peace, Hawkins complained that "we seem to have forgotten altogether the right of the Indians." "I am for peace," he declared, stating that the Indians would part with their country only at the cost of their lives, and "as long as we attempt to go into their country . . . we shall be at war."[10]

Hawkins's letter posed the basic alternatives that had caused the Indian confederacy to defer an offensive campaign. For nearly two years the Indians pondered whether the Americans' attitude would be revised following significant military failures. Yet George Washington essentially had resolved this fundamental issue in his own mind within a few weeks of learning of St. Clair's defeat. His conclusions reflected not only his sense of a manifest destiny and his intuitive grasp of the strategic alternatives but also his inner fiber. Writing a memo based on Benjamin Hawkins's observations, Washington expounded the fundamental concept that was to prevail: "We are involved in actual war!" he wrote. Were the objectives sought by the nation to be obtained by active operations or passive restraint? "Defensive [policies] are not only impracticable against such an enemy, but the expense attending them would be ruinous," Washington reasoned. Because he believed that the defeat of November 4 had really been due to lack of commitment, under the president's revised concept there would be no repetition of the 1791 failure. The requisite manpower and resources would be provided to reach an optimum solution. In the determination to persevere, there also would be no hasty rush to an uncertain victory. Time would be utilized as an ally of the United States Army. Specifically, the composition of the force to be raised would be adapted to the nature of the fighting. A combination of knowledge, skill, and discipline would be emphasized in forming an efficacious military force. As a fighting instrument, the army would be prepared to meet the enemy and win under adverse circumstances.[11]

On December 26, 1791, "in obedience to the commands of the President of the United States," Secretary of War Knox presented the administration's formal plans to resolve the crisis in the Northwest Territory. Observing that "an Indian war of considerable extent has been excited," Knox stated that "it is by an ample conviction of our superior force only, that the Indians can be brought to . . . peace." "The pride of victory is too strong at present for them to receive the offers of peace on reasonable terms," he continued. "Since they would probably insist upon a relinquishment of territory, to which they have no just claim," Knox said that "a strong coercive force" was required.[12]

The military establishment was to be increased to 5,168 men, rank and file, who were to serve for three years maximum. The military's pay was to be liberally increased and the cavalry service would be expanded. An entire regiment of riflemen was to be recruited, and mounted militia would be employed for protective duties. Even a contingent of friendly Indians would be utilized as scouts and spies. Altogether this expanded program would cost a total of $1,026,477.05, which was a staggering sum for the time and nearly double the original estimate for 1792.[13]

A month later, when the program was brought before the House of Representatives, it provoked a bitter floor fight, as expected. Speakers for drastically cutting the bill urged that the frontier whites were most probably the aggressors, citing that the Indians had made no attempt to invade United States territory. In rebuttal two staunch Federalists from Virginia stated that the inveterate bitterness on both sides made any prospect of a lasting peace unlikely. "It is too late to inquire whether the war was originally undertaken on the principles of justice or not. We are actually involved in it, and cannot recede," they proclaimed.[14]

The issues had been defined, and the fate of the military appropriations bill was decided after a challenge to a key segment of it, the section authorizing three additional regiments for three years' service. By a vote of 34 to 18 the House passed the measure intact, providing the basis for the Senate's approval. The bill was then enacted March 5, 1792.[15]

Washington had won a major victory. The mood of the public had been reflected in the mandate of Congress. The United States now might make a total commitment to victory and utilize sufficient resources to achieve its objectives. The message that the two Virginia congressmen had proclaimed would be amplified to one and all: "We are able, abundantly able to do it . . . —we can yet raise both men and money sufficient to defend the nation."[16]

By the terms of the new act the president was authorized nearly all of what he had sought. The army was to be recruited to full strength; it would be expanded by three regiments for three years. A squadron of light dragoons was added. Pay was increased for nearly everyone, including a one-third increase for privates to three dollars per month net. A bounty of eight dollars was offered to new recruits and veterans alike. Even a special force of cavalry was authorized for emergency service at the president's discretion.[17]

In rapid succession, Washington soon was able to realize even greater military reforms. Because of the imminent threat to the Kentucky and Pennsylvania settlements in particular, an aroused Congress authorized what Washington had long sought: a uniform, federally controlled militia, in which practically every white male between the ages of eighteen and forty-five in the United States might be enrolled. Now the president could call out such troops to repel invasions by foreign nations or Indians or to suppress insurrection.[18]

To pay for these new forces, Congress also devised stringent laws for the taxing of spiritous liquors. This proved to be an unpopular and highly controversial action, though it was mandated by the crisis at hand. Ultimately, two years later, the smoldering furor and outrage of the western residents resulted in the so-called Whiskey Rebellion, and military force was required to quell an open insurrection.[19]

After the flurry of enabling acts by Congress, the president still faced a crucial military question—that of determining a successor to the vanquished Arthur St. Clair. Washington was plagued by doubt and indecision in this important selection. First, he took the matter to his cabinet, after preparing a list of sixteen former generals from the Revolution. His candid comments on the list provided no clear-cut choice to be commander of the army. Several, like Benjamin Lincoln and Lachlan McIntosh, were regarded as too old and infirm. Others of higher reputation were dismissed because of various circumstances. Daniel Morgan, the famed Virginia rifleman, was illiterate, intemperate, and in poor health. Charles Scott of Kentucky and George Weedon of Virginia were heavy drinkers. Baron von Steuben was a foreigner. William Moultrie was largely unknown to the president. Mordicai Gist and Jedediah Huntington seemed to lack ability.[20]

One whose name stood out for initiative and zeal, Anthony Wayne of the Pennsylvania line, was considered vain, "too indulgent to his officers and men," and perhaps overly aggressive. Perhaps the most impressive name on the list, Charles Pinckney of South Carolina, was considered by Washington to be of such junior rank that few veteran soldiers would serve under him.[21]

In all, it was a frustrating selection. Washington arranged and rearranged the names, attempting to determine who might agree to serve under whom as a subordinate general. Privately, he admitted that his choice was not even written on the list: Henry Lee, "Light Horse Harry" of revolutionary fame, who was energetic and not yet forty, though governor of Virginia. Washington considered Lee extraordinarily qualified for the command, and he later wrote the governor, saying he was "strongly in your favor." Yet the matter was inherently political, Washington observed. Few senior, experienced officers would consent to serve under one who was only a former colonel, and should there be another disaster, the weight on the president's shoulders would be "too heavy to be borne."[22]

The selection then narrowed to the least detrimental choices. "I never was more embarrassed in [making] any appointment," Washington privately wrote; and while various factions lobbied sometimes frantically for their candidate, Washington drew a curtain of seclusion about the proceedings.[23]

Finally, in mid-April, 1792, a commission as major general in the United States Army was issued to the man who under "all circumstances . . .

appeared most eligible," said Washington. He was Anthony Wayne, forty-seven years old, the barrel-chested, fire-eating former Pennsylvania infantry commander, who by chance also happened to need a job.[24]

Wayne's checkered career since leaving the army in 1783 had been anything but productive. Although involved in farming a war grant of 847 acres in Georgia following several years of undistinguished service in the Pennsylvania General Assembly, by 1790 he was wallowing in debt. He had even attempted unsuccessfully to obtain a seat in Congress, because he feared that he might be jailed as a debtor, and congressmen were then immune from such prosecution. Ultimately, Wayne was forced to sell his Georgia lands and slaves at a depreciated value. In January, 1791, afflicted with the gout and despondent over unpaid taxes, he was able to gain election as the United States Representative from a rural Georgia district. Unfortunately, there was fraud in the balloting, and although Wayne claimed the seat of James Jackson, once his personal friend, Jackson succeeded in contesting the election. By the unanimous vote of the House of Representatives on March 16, 1792, Wayne's election was declared illegal and the seat vacated.[25]

Thwarted as a Congressman, Wayne evidently lobbied unsuccessfully for several federal appointments, including the post of surveyor general. Washington, however, seemed to favor the politics of Wayne's selection as commander of the army. Virginia already was regarded as too dominant in the administration. The appointment of a well-known Pennsylvania officer with strong ties to the South would broaden Washington's political base. Wayne's former rank as a brevet major general would further facilitate the appointment of experienced subordinates.[26]

Wayne was nonetheless a very controversial choice. Imbued with a natural love of military life, he was a man of action and not a profound thinker. A stickler for good appearance—he was sometimes referred to as "Dandy Tony"—Wayne was an emotional, ambitious person who had left a trail of broken friendships and had figured in unethical business transactions. Although he was a heavy drinker with a reputation for headstrong valor, Wayne's Revolutionary War record nonetheless suggested that he was a conservative strategist and a strong disciplinarian. Known to be brave to a fault, Wayne was also exceedingly vain. In typical fashion he had once written to the president, flattering him upon his inauguration, only to seek a federal appointment from him in the next paragraph.[27]

In substance, Wayne was a man of strong contrasts. He was blessed with extraordinary ability, yet his liabilities would weigh heavily upon his efficacy as commander of the army. Washington wrote that he hoped "time, reflection, good advice, and above all, a due sense of the importance of the trust which is committed to him, will correct his foibles, or cast a shade over them."[28]

Although Senator James Monroe had argued fervently against Wayne's confirmation, and letters of protest had filtered in after the announcement of the appointment, "Mad Anthony" Wayne, of the jutting jaw and piercing hazel eyes, was duly installed. Although Wayne refrained from gloating, there was heavy irony in the appointment. St. Clair, whom he replaced, had been his arch rival and enemy during the Revolution. Wayne had been repeatedly required to serve under the obtrusive St. Clair, and then after the war he had been installed as vice-president of the Pennsylvania Society of the Cincinnati with St. Clair as the president.[29]

Because Wayne had operated in the shadow of more imposing generals, there was an element of uncertainty about his "possessing abilities equal to the conduct of regular and extensive operations." The British minister at Philadelphia, George Hammond, confided that Wayne was "unquestionably the most active, vigilant and enterprising officer in the American army," but that he was purely a soldier, lacking in civil ability and prone to rashness; in all, more of an "active partisan" than an army commander.[30]

Uniformly, however, Washington, Hammond, and many others under-estimated the man and his nature. Anthony Wayne was above all a de-termined and ardent competitor. Given the means to accomplish a task, he would win by finesse or by brute force, by deception or by direct assault, but inevitably he would find a way to persevere until the object was at hand. Moreover, Wayne was from the beginning specifically committed to the war with the Indians: "I have always been of the opinion that we never should have a permanent peace with those [hostile] Indians until they were made to experience our superiority," he wrote in December, 1791. Determination and purpose thus combined to make Anthony Wayne a far more capable and formidable soldier than the public imagined. Militarily there would be no equivocation or vacillation from him. He would not lose sight of the task ahead despite any temporary setbacks. Even his rather-hackneyed nick-name, "Mad Anthony," belied his real personality. Allegedly, an inveterate deserter, who happened to live in the same Pennsylvania county and knew Wayne, had bestowed the sobriquet in 1781. When General Wayne had refused to intercede on the deserter's behalf, the man had fumed that Anthony must be mad—hence "Mad Anthony." Although the name stuck, the popular interpretation seems to have suggested a mental imbalance, perhaps involving reckless, daring escapades.[31]

Wayne was not to be denied by any unfair assessment. He would devote his considerable energy and talent to one unalterable purpose: training a capable and effective professional army. Once that task had been achieved, the result would speak for itself on the battlefield. Although the storm of controversy continued over his selection, nearly all agreed on one fun-damental truth: "In a warfare of the kind in which he is engaged," wrote Hammond, the British minister, "much will depend upon the personal qualities of the commander in chief."[32]

That sentiment had profound implications for the idle Indian army. Time now was no longer to be the ally of the red man.

20

Desultory Operations

OBSERVING that "the present partial Indian war is a remnant of the later general war [the Revolution], continued by a number of separate banditti," Henry Knox reasoned that since the Indians were flushed with recent victory, "it would be altogether improper to expect any favorable result" from peace efforts. A "strong coercive force" was indispensable, announced Knox, "to terminate this disagreeable war as speedily as possible." The army to be raised would be "disciplined according to the nature of the service" and would have to be adequate in stength to defeat the greatest probable combination of Indian enemies.

Knox well understood that considerable time would be required to satisfy those requirements. Of necessity, there had to be interim plans. Knox characterized the calculating strategy implemented in 1792 as "desultory operations."[1] Of primary importance was the isolation of the hostiles to prevent the once-powerful Six Nations from joining with them, or the estimated 15,000 members of southern Indian tribes from being drawn into an expanding war. As a diversion a major peace initiative, involving multiple overtures, was to be utilized deftly to obtain the time needed to recruit and train the army. These overtures would also serve to satisfy the substantial pacific faction in the eastern states who were clamoring for a moderate Indian policy. Should these interim activities unexpectedly produce a peaceful settlement, Knox thought that would serve well to convince the world that the United States was acting with "perfect humanity and kindness."[2] "If they [the hostiles] will not . . . listen to the voice of peace," wrote Washington in support of a militant posture, "the sword must decide the dispute, and we are, though very reluctantly, vigorously preparing to meet the event."[3]

In fact, the voice of peace of which the president spoke was to be manifest not only as a bellwether of the Indians' attitude but also as a divisive stratagem. The Six Nations, already reduced to a vacillating and politically divided status, were to be further manipulated in the role of the devil's advocate. In the name of civilizing these British-oriented tribes and duly impressing them with the power of the United States, certain chiefs had been invited to Philadelphia at the time of the Painted Post Treaty in June, 1791. In late December, 1791, this effort was expanded when the British-supported Buffalo Creek Iroquois were assembled at Philadelphia for a carefully orchestrated meeting with the pro-American Senecas from the Allegheny country. Invitations were sent to The Farmer's Brother and other

Buffalo Creek Seneca chiefs; also to the much-used Cornplanter, and several other friendly chiefs who were asked to come along.[4] Although the British Indian agents at Niagara were dubious, and they urged their charges not to go, fifty sachems and warriors of the Buffalo Creek region finally were persuaded to attend by Samuel Kirkland, an American representative among the Six Nations.

After arriving in Philadelphia on March 13, 1792, this delegation was feted by the government for more than a month, during which time the American desire for a reasonable accommodation with the hostiles was repeatedly expressed. The Six Nations were asked to send a delegation to the expected "great council of Western Indians" to be held that summer along the Maumee.

Minus two of their number, who died in Philadelphia during the proceedings, the Buffalo Creek delegation dutifully returned to their villages, prepared to carry the message of the United States's sincere intent to "do what is right" in making peace. Yet, because of their "frequent counseling and dilatory manner of conducting business," Knox was later to lament that they made no effort to go among the hostiles until mid-September, diminishing the effectiveness of this diplomatic endeavor.[5]

By far a more serious attempt at diplomatic persuasion was the Americans' intense courtship of their former nemesis during the Revolutionary War, the Mohawk chief Joseph Brant. Although President Washington had commented unfavorably on Brant little more than a year before, reports of the Mohawk leader's "friendly sentiments" had been increasingly rife. Following a rather inane correspondence with his old friend Samuel Kirkland over the possibility of a visit to Philadelphia, Brant was suddenly urged in the strongest terms to come to the seat of government in January, 1792. Kirkland even resorted to outright flattery, for Brant was told that he was much too important to "be crowded into the company of all the old chiefs and dragged along promiscuously with them." Indeed, Henry Knox was moved to extend a personal invitation to Brant late in February.[6]

Brant's responses were duly measured. In reply to Knox he wrote that, although favorably inclined, he wished to obtain approval from the western tribes so that he might speak as a duly deputized negotiator rather than as an individual. Brant's calculating grasp of political reality was self-evident. Having acknowledged the transfer of leadership to the Shawnees in 1788, he obviously viewed the American invitation as a means of reasserting his influence on behalf of the Indian confederacy, believing that his moderate policies would best promote "such desirable ends as civilization and peace making."[7] In May, 1792, he acknowledged receipt of a reply from the Miami region, and although the message was evasive, "after weighing matters maturely," Brant decided to leave promptly for Philadelphia.

Brant had noted that the Americans were the solicitors in this peace initiative, and he therefore anticipated that he might encounter a more reasonable attitude among their negotiators. Beginning his journey about June 1, Brant hoped "to form an idea of their intentions, and how far a peace is likely to take place." On that basis, he said, the Indians could decide "whether to prosecute the war or to make a peace, one of which must be the case."[8]

After his arrival in Philadelphia on June 20, Brant reported that he was offered one thousand guineas in advance and double the pension-and-a-half of a military officer that he was receiving from the British, if he would act as an agent on behalf of American peace initiatives. "Afterward I was offered the pre-emption right to land to the amount of £20,000, . . . and $1500 per annum," he said. Brant promptly refused on the grounds that such was "inconsistent with the principles of honor" and duty to his people.[9]

Although these offers of personal fortune were unavailing, Henry Knox soon was convinced that Brant would serve the United States's interests well. The Mohawk chieftain was indoctrinated that the hostiles were "entirely mistaken as to the object of the war" and that the United States desired only those lands that had been ceded by fair treaty; otherwise the country was the Indians' own. Brant seemed to agree to express those views to the great council on the Maumee.

Despite these impressions, he had immediately realized the fallacy of the American proposal. After his return to Niagara in July, the perceptive chieftain warned that the United States insisted on a boundary in accordance with the Fort Harmar Treaty of 1789. Although the Americans offered additional compensation, should that purchase be deemed "under value[d]," Brant said that he had argued heatedly with the American officials that "nothing but a new boundary would have the effect desired." In requesting that a pair of flintlock pistols be purchased in England for him by a friend, Brant now ominously remarked, "Pray send them as soon as possible as I may have occasion for them."[10]

Since the season was already so advanced the Americans could expect little result from their diplomacy. Henry Knox soon learned that Brant had taken sick and was delayed in journeying to the Miami country.[11] Burdened by the prospect of multiple failures in diminishing the intensity of the war, the secretary of war was very frustrated during early August, and he commented bitterly that it would be unfortunate "if all our overtures fail."[12]

Indeed, the news through midsummer of other peace initiatives was equally dismal.

In January, Knox had sought a direct approach to the hostile Indians by dispatching two agents, Peter Pond and William Steedman, in the guise of traders to mingle among the Indians in the Niagara and Detroit regions. Although they were to attempt to convince the Indians to "ask a peace of us," Pond and Steedman were also to serve as spies, gathering military information and learning of the enemy's plans. This scheme had been quickly frustrated on their arrival at Niagara. The British, "not knowing their business," had refused to let Pond and Steedman proceed, obviously suspecting clandestine activities.

Next, in February, the War Department had instructed Lieutenant Colonel Wilkinson at Fort Washington to send "confidential agents" from Vincennes and Cincinnati to the hostiles, inviting the chiefs to Fort Washington for a council.[13]

Less than a month later Knox, apparently having misgivings about the dispatch of such unofficial emissaries to the hostiles, concluded to send yet another flag to the Indians by official means. Captain Alexander Trueman, the energetic Revolutionary War veteran from Maryland who commanded St. Clair's cavalry during the November 4 fight and escaped with a slight wound, had been in Philadelphia for testimony at St. Clair's inquiry. Slated for promotion to major, Trueman was prevailed on to accept what was obviously a dangerous undertaking. On April 3, 1792, Knox instructed him to proceed to the Miami Villages via Fort Washington, carrying a dispatch signed in the name of the president of the United States promoting a treaty for "the great object of peace."[14]

Both of those efforts not only proved futile but, even worse, cost the emissaries their lives. Freeman and Gerrard, the two messengers sent by Wilkinson about April 3, apparently fell in with a hunting party of Indians en route to Kekionga. Although they carried a speech from Wilkinson professing peace, they and a third young man were taken prisoner. By one account, they were spared until, while en route to the Auglaize towns, "they made so many inquiries of the Indians relative to the distances of Indian towns and names of waters they crossed," that their escorts concluded they were spies and killed them.[15]

William May, the private of the First United States Regiment who had been caught attempting to desert during St. Clair's Wabash campaign but had been pardoned, soon was sent on their trail in the guise of a deserter. Ordered to learn what had happened to Freeman's party and then to return, May traveled for more than a week before discovering the three corpses, scalped and stripped, in the woods. Captured a few hours later by a party of Mingos, May was beaten and condemned to death before being spared by Simon Girty, apparently on the condition that he would guide a war party against the American outposts. Ultimately, he was put to work aboard a British schooner servicing McKee's storehouse at the Miami Rapids. Then, in September, 1792, May was allowed to go to Niagara, where he finally made his way overland to Pittsburgh, bringing with him much useful information on British and Indian operations.

May, judged "a very knowing [and] intelligent fellow" by Anthony Wayne, was able to provide a detailed account of what had befallen Alexander Trueman's ill-fated peace mission.[16] Traveling by riverboat down the Ohio, Trueman had arrived at Fort Washington in mid-May. In conjunction with Colonel John Hardin of Kentucky, who had led the notorious raid on Mackachack in 1786 and had participated in Harmar's disastrous Miami Towns campaign, Trueman was to proceed via a separate route on a dual diplomatic mission. Hardin would travel to the Wyandot towns on the Sandusky River to induce the chiefs and sachems to journey to Philadelphia, or failing in that, to prod them into going to the Maumee region, where Trueman might be found.[17]

Trueman, for his part, was enjoined to carry the primary message of the government to the Maumee River. Newly promoted to major and dressed in full military uniform, Trueman had begun his journey on May 20. In the company of a body servant, William Lynch, and his interpreter, William Smalley, Trueman is believed to have proceeded to within sixty miles of the Auglaize villages by about May 29. During that day the party met an Indian hunter accompanied by his son, who joined with them in journeying north.

211

Toward evening the Indians became uneasy and stated that they were going to leave, for fear that the white men would overpower them during the night. Evidently, Trueman told the Indians that they might tie one of his party so that the numbers would be equal. Lynch, the servant, was soon securely tied. Regarding this conduct as foolish of the Americans and strong evidence of their weakness, the Indian next raised his gun and shot Trueman dead. Lynch, being bound was easily tomahawked, and Smalley, who briefly escaped into a swamp, was finally induced to come out on the assurance that his life would be spared. After scalping "the great captain" and throwing him into the water, the Indians hastened on with Trueman's papers and their captive, arriving at the Auglaize villages about June 3.[18]

Having departed on the same date, John Hardin and a companion suffered a nearly identical fate. Evidently mistaken for spies, both were killed, although the messages that they had carried soon found their way into McKee's hands at the Miami Rapids.

By mid-July reports from Vincennes began to reach Fort Washington that the peace flags had been fired on and at least four men had been killed. Within a few weeks the news was confirmed; it being reported with certainty that Hardin and Trueman had fallen "victims to savage ferocity."[19] Henry Knox, while refusing to give up the ruse of attempting to negotiate a treaty, now had to despair of an imminent military solution. Early in August he wrote, "The season of the year is too far advanced, the number of recruits too few, and the undisciplined state of the army such as to preclude any great expectations of . . . important movements this season." Stating that every preparation must be made for offensive operations as early in the spring of 1793 as the weather would allow, Knox cautioned that "another conflict with the savages with raw recruits is to be avoided by all means."[20]

Forced into a continuance of the uniformly unsuccessful peace overtures, Knox admitted that his remaining hope rested with the moderate Indian faction, who had proposed to arrange a peace. The dismal situation had evolved further after the failure of yet another American emissary, the third in as many months. Belatedly appointed a brigadier general, after several other nominees had refused to accept the commission, Rufus Putnam, a moderate in Indian affairs, had been assigned to supplement Trueman's peace mission by formalizing the truce that the earlier emissaries were supposed to arrange.[21]

Delayed at Marietta until June 26, Putnam belatedly arrived at Fort Washington on July 2. There he learned that the Indians had attacked some hay cutters on June 25 near Fort Jefferson. With a shudder, he realized that in a speech to the Indians he had originally stated that he would be at the same site on that day: "I conceive there [is] great reason to believe that myself was the . . . object of that [attack]," he wrote in obvious alarm. Learning too that Trueman and Hardin had probably been murdered, the suddenly skittish brigadier decided to go to Vincennes to conclude peace with the Wabash nations and thus remove those Indians from possible participation in the war. After considerable delay he sailed west from Fort Washington in mid-August.

Although later sustained by Henry Knox in the decision to shift his peace initiative to the Wabash region, Putnam thus assumed a secondary role in dealing with tribes who had already manifested an intention to keep the peace. In fact, the great council at the Maumee, which Putnam regarded as hostile, had not yet even begun to meet. Henry Knox lamented in a letter to Anthony Wayne after receiving the news of Putnam's change in plans, "Our remaining hope of the hostile tribes to be acquainted with our pacific overtures must rest upon the Senecas, Captain Hendricks, . . . and Captain Brant."[22]

Hendrick Aupaumut, alias Captain Hendricks, was an individual perhaps to be regarded as much with curiosity as with confidence. He was one of the few remaining Stockbridge Indians, a remnant of the ancient Mohican tribe of Massachusetts. Ravaged by war, pestilence, and famine through nearly three centuries of close contact with whites, Aupaumut's people had dwindled to an insignificant few by the close of the American Revolution. Yet he himself stood in marked contrast to Indian tradition, looking more to the assimilation of red men into the white society than to the perpetuation of a separate existence. Noted for his spirit of cooperation with American interests, Aupaumut had been engaged to attend the grand council on the Maumee as an unofficial spokesman for American interests.

Although Hendricks' party encountered severe weather en route to the Miami Rapids, they finally arrived there on July 13. While the council had not yet been convened because of "a sore famine" in the various villages along the Maumee, Hendricks observed that he was the only one to speak favorably of the United States in several precouncil gatherings.

Indeed, he was soon discredited by Alexander McKee, who derisively asserted that Aupaumat was a spy sent by the Big Knives to estimate the numbers of the hostile Indians. Hendrick was so ineffectual that he was repeatedly reduced to a defensive posture. At length, he felt compelled to write a rambling manuscript about his journey, in which he acknowledged that the end result of all his effort was that "they brought my name at naught."[23] While he privately despaired of a peaceful solution, Henry Knox was increasingly pressured by "the opinion of probably the great majority of the citizens of the United States" favoring a peaceful settlement. In September, 1792, he concluded, "The [peace] offer being made, we must wait for the issue." Knox was particularly troubled by the adverse public opinion regarding a military solution, of which one of the more embarrassing manifestations was the refusal of two of the four officers recently selected to serve as brigadiers under Anthony Wayne to accept their commissions. Daniel Morgan and Marinus Willett had both declined to serve. Willett's refusal was tantamount to a glaring indictment. "It has been uniformly my opinion," he wrote, "that the United States ought to avoid an Indian War. . . . The intercourse I have had with these people, [and] the treatment I have myself received . . . make me an advocate for them. To fight with them would be the last thing I should desire." Willett's comments seemed to reflect a widespread popular reliance on the peace efforts, especially since no major offensive action had been undertaken by the victorious red enemy.[24]

Knox, however, stung by the murders of the American peace emissaries, continued to complain to the president of the "misfortune, disappointment, or delay" in the efforts to achieve a peaceful settlement. Committed to a toughening of the United States military posture while seeking to appease popular opinion, Knox calculated, "If it shall then appear upon a fair experiment that peace is unattainable but by a sacrifice of national character and national justice, it is presumed that public opinion will support the war in a more vigorous manner than at present."[25]

Thus the prospects for a successful outcome of the war seemed to depend on not only applying adequate force but also managing the popular will. Henry Knox was explicit in his resolve: "I confess, in confidence, my apprehensions that the Indians will require more than we can grant consistent with any sort of dignity, and that therefore we ought to strain every nerve in making all sorts of preparations . . . as shall effectually accomplish our objects of bridling and punishing the refractory tribes."[26]

This underlying concept was to endure even with the advent of a dramatic new turn of events regarding a peaceful solution. There was after all the burning fear of which Washington had written in August, 1792, "That it [the war] may be a concerted plan between certain powers to check the growth of this rising country is far from improbable—diabolical as it may seem."[27]

The Indians, it appears, were unwittingly reduced to an untenable bargaining situation. By looking to the resolution of what they viewed as a practical matter—the fair use of the Ohio country lands, as determined by their needs and the whites'—they had perpetuated a major miscalculation. In effect, the Indian confederacy continued to regard the issue as physical, whereas the essence of the matter from an American perspective was perhaps an allegory—an unfulfilled destiny.

21

Toward an Uncertain Fate

WILLIAM WELLS was an extraordinary young man. Captured by the Eel River Miamis at about age thirteen, he had lived as an adopted son of Me-she-kin-no-quah, the Little Turtle, for nearly nine years. Known as "Blacksnake" among the Indians, Wells had been accorded "perfect liberty to go where he pleased" as a trusted warrior. After the bloody fighting on November 4, 1791, in which Wells had participated with distinction, the young man, then nearly twenty-two, had returned to his village, Ke-na-po-co-mo-co. Then, in mid-June, 1792, he visited Fort Knox (Vincennes), evidently as an interpreter for a small party of Wea Indians, who had once more come forth to regain members of their families who had been held prisoner since Charles Scott's and Wilkinson's raids a year before. At the fort Wells by chance happened to meet his long-separated white brother. It was a most fortuitous meeting for the United States. Not only was Wells persuaded to return to Kentucky with his brother, but also he was soon in demand as an interpreter and Indian expert in the employ of the United States government.[1]

The Weas whom Wells had accompanied had been sent from Vincennes to Fort Washington by Major Hamtramck, who sought permanently to separate such dissidents from the hostile Miamis. Hamtramck regarded them as merely interested in getting back their families, who were held prisoner at Fort Washington. Nonetheless, he had conducted preliminary negotiations for a truce at Vincennes and had suggested to Rufus Putnam that a formal treaty would likely keep them peaceful.[2]

Putnam sought to promote such an arrangement by scheduling a full treaty with all of the Wabash tribes at Fort Knox. Because "Vincennes under the existing circumstances presents the most eligible point for negotiation," Putnam engaged William Wells as an interpreter and scheduled the treaty for about September 20, 1792. Supplied with enough blankets, shrouds, leggings, and shirts to supply seven hundred Indians, Putnam began his journey by river to Vincennes on August 17, anticipating that the gathering would prevent "most if not all" of the Wabash tribes from joining the hostiles.[3]

After his arrival on September 12, Putnam hastened to favorably impress some early arrivals by delivering a conciliatory speech and releasing the long held women and children prisoners. Putnam observed that this had a great influence on the Indians and produced in them a suitably contrite demeanor for the council meetings, which began on September 24.[4]

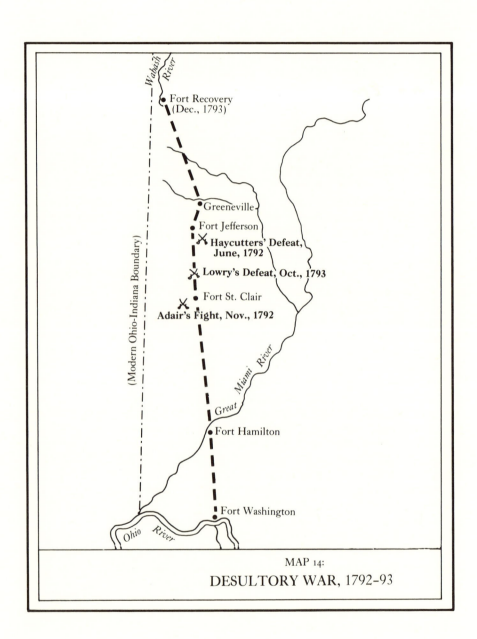

Wabash River

● Fort Recovery
(Dec., 1793)

(Modern Ohio-Indiana Boundary)

● Greeneville

● Fort Jefferson

✗ **Haycutters' Defeat,
June, 1792**

✗ **Lowry's Defeat, Oct., 1793**

● Fort St. Clair

✗
Adair's Fight, Nov., 1792

Great Miami River

● Fort Hamilton

Fort Washington

Ohio River

MAP 14:

DESULTORY WAR, 1792–93

With Wells present, paid one dollar per day as an interpreter, a total of 686 Indians, including 31 chiefs, sat through the four days of proceedings. Represented among the Indians were the Eel River, Wea, Potawatomi, Piankashaw, Kaskaskia, and Kickapoo tribes. Their spokesman was an energetic young chief of the Kaskaskias, John Baptist Ducoigne.[5]

Ducoigne spoke of the fair weather, a good omen for the treaty. The sky was clear, he said, adding that all the Indians asked was to be allowed to keep their lands. Putnam, however, would not accede to any prospect of an American withdrawal. By the terms of the treaty that the Indians were directed to sign on September 27, they acknowledged American sovereignty and promised to deliver any white prisoners held and to notify the government of any impending attack by the hostiles. In return, they were told that they could keep all the lands "to which they have a just claim."

Putnam then closed the proceedings by ordering that gifts of clothing and some ammunition (for hunting) be distributed. "Beeves, bread and whiskey" were then prepared for a joint feast. At a minimal cost—clothing, several beeves, whiskey, and some trinkets—Putnam alleged that he had concluded "a firm and everlasting peace." "You are now under the protection of the United States," he informed the Wabash tribesmen.[6]

Believing that he had established an important treaty-making precedent, Putnam promptly engaged William Wells for the sum of $300, plus a $200 bonus if the venture was successful, to carry a message to the hostiles in the Miami and Sandusky country. As the Wabash and Illinois-region Indians had concluded a peace, Putnam urged the hostiles, in this message, to "open your ears to the truth." By meeting Putnam at the mouth of the Muskingum River, they too might participate in a similarly beneficial peace.[7]

Wells departed from Vincennes about October 7, taking with him several Eel River Indians as witnesses of the recent treaty. Ironically, it was on precisely the same date that the long-awaited and momentous council of the Indian confederacy was concluded on the banks of the Maumee. Instead of the broadening American influence foreseen by Putnam, a majority of Old Northwest tribes had stated their intention to reclaim their lost lands, and sought the relinquishment of certain United States claims. Thus Wells was unable to alter the inexorable drift toward a final confrontation of the Americans and the Indians.[8] Manifesting the tragic irreversible course of events, he soon took leave of his foster father, Little Turtle, saying: "I now leave your nation for my own people. We have long been friends, we are friends yet, until the sun reaches a certain [designated] height. From that time on we are enemies. Then, if you wish to kill me, you may. If I want to kill you I may."[9]

The pathetic spiral of ruptured lives and abrogated agreements seemed, indeed to reach a new zenith in the spring of 1793. Despite the assurances of Rufus Putnam that the United States "don't want to take away your lands by force—they want to do you justice," the fate of Putnam's Fort Knox treaty served as an appropriate example to the Indians.

Henry Knox had exulted in November, 1792, that Putnam's treaty "will probably detach 800 warriors from the hostile Indians," and thus in 1793 he seemed unconcerned that the treaty remained unconfirmed by the Senate. In fact, congressional action was postponed until the 1793–94 session, following a controversy over the "preemption rights" of the United States to buy the Wabash tribes' land. Ultimately, that question caused the Senate to reject the treaty in 1794 by a vote of twenty-one to four. The senators objected to the treaty's fourth article, in which it was not explicit that only the United States had the power to purchase the Indians' lands. This was, of course, an odd objection to a treaty in which the United States had alleged it did not covet the Indians' domain.[10]

Rufus Putnam, sick with an intermittent fever, languished in Kentucky and at Mariettta for more than two months late in 1792. Ultimately he became so debilitated that he resigned his commission the following February. En route back east in January, 1793, he advised General Wayne of his increasing pessimism: "I am confident that the tribes to whom he [Wells] was sent have not listened to the voice of peace, nor do I believe they ever will until they get a good whipping. . . . I know they are under the influence of the greatest villains in the world [British agents]."[11]

Since political expediency continued to deter any overt military commitment, however, the federal government's declared policy remained little changed through the winter of 1792–93. In fact, in view of practical politics and the military impasse, there eventually would be one more expansive effort at peace—at least so it would be made to appear in the public eye.

It was well understood on the Ohio frontier in 1792 that America's ultimate recourse must be to prosecute the war to a final decision. Lieutenant Colonel James Wilkinson, who arrived at Fort Washington to take command in January, spoke of the "sanguinary disposition of the enemy, and their inveterate animosity." Major John Hamtramck at Vincennes was mortified that the government was attempting to make peace with the Indians "while the ground is yet reeking with the blood of our messengers."[12]

Thus the wilderness army was preoccupied with the predicament that it faced early in 1792. What openly dismayed the military authorities responsible for the security of the frontier was the wretched state of the army there: "To this very moment we are at Fort Washington in the most defenseless state—a single Indian may burn down the works on any night he pleases, not one sentinel [being] posted to give notice of the approach of an enemy," wrote Winthrop Sargent in January, 1792. Wilkinson was equally dismayed by the "greatly inadequate force" of which he assumed the command, stating that the enemy, "if he knew our real situation, would greatly cut across, if not cut off, all communication from post to post."[13]

So precarious were the vital communications links between his vulnerable advanced posts that Wilkinson acted hastily to fashion a more viable system. Noting, from a personal reconnaissance early in February, that the approximately forty-four miles between Forts Hamilton and Jefferson was more than the normal day's march of a pack-horse convoy (which was about 25 miles), the newly appointed brigadier ordered the construction of an interim post. Beginning in mid-March, 1792, a 200-man detachment initiated construction of a structure 120-feet square with four bastions, about twenty-four miles north of Fort Hamilton. Designated Fort St. Clair in honor of the about-to-be-deposed major general, the structure was closed in by pickets within a week.[14]

Compelled by Henry Knox's order to cease all military operations except defensive measures, pending the outcome of the peace initiatives, Wilkinson, beginning in April, was reduced to maintaining a tenuous status quo. Observing that the Indians could easily pen the garrisons up in what they termed their "ground hog holes," a lieutenant of the First regulars anticipated a major disaster during the summer months if the enemy beseiged the forts and the provisions spoiled or the vital wells dried up.[15]

Despite those grim misgivings, the expected enemy onslaught failed to materialize. "Not a single Indian has been discovered since you left us," wrote an incredulous Sargent in a letter to Arthur St. Clair in January, 1792. The diary of a frontier officer confirms the absence of anything more than minor harassment at newly built Fort St. Clair throughout the summer. Garrison duty became so quiet and uneventful that Captain Daniel Bradley was able to cultivate a large garden outside the stockade. The only sizeable incident to mar the summer months—an Indian raid on a detachment of about fifteen men cutting hay near Fort Jefferson on June 25—proved to be only a limited foray.

On June 11 a mixed war party of Shawnees, Delawares, and other tribesmen under the leadership of The Grand Sable had gone forth "to commence our campaign with the seige of Fort Jefferson." It was actually only a small party, numbering about fifty warriors, and they had been content to surprise the hay cutters, capturing all fifteen men, including the sergeant who commanded the detachement. Four dead soldiers were later found amid the stacked hay. The raiders had quickly returned in the direction of the Maumee River following the attack.[16]

Although Rufus Putnam interpreted this incident as an attempt on his life, because he had announced his intention to be at Fort Jefferson about June 25, it proved in reality to have been a rather disorganized, spontaneous raid. British officials reported in July that The Grand Sable's war party subsequently broke up after a squabble over the distribution of the prisoners. A British officer confided that, due to the controversy, ten privates and the sergeant were put to death, while the four survivors were removed to a Chippewa village.[17]

For the Americans there was so little manpower available during 1792 that Wilkinson had only 695 privates on the rolls for the entire six-fort frontier network stretching from Fort Washington to Vincennes. Although the brigadier had long pleaded for strong reinforcements, he received practically none through August. Commenting that his force was insufficient even to secure an adequate supply of hay at Fort Jefferson, Wilkinson became increasingly apprehensive as fall approached.[18]

Several soldiers were killed on September 29 while acting as a cattle guard. This was the first reported killing of a white man by Indians in the Ohio country since an incident involving the capture of a youth, Oliver Spencer, on the Ohio River on July 7.[19] Yet Wilkinson, believing that the enemy was well supplied with clothing and ammunition that they procured from the British traders after their summer hunts, became concerned as November began.[20]

Exactly one year to the day after St. Clair's disastrous battle on the Wabash, Wilkinson wrote that he had just received news of a sizeable enemy force in the vicinity of Fort Hamilton. Three soldiers had been seized by the enemy a few hours before sunset on November 3, within 400 yards of the garrison. When a detachment of thirty men was sent to pursue what was believed to be another small enemy raiding party, the lieutenant in charge quickly returned, saying that he had found signs of too many Indians.

These rather innocuous events marked the advent of the greatest crisis to confront the frontier army in 1792. Wilkinson, suspecting a bold enemy venture in progress against one of the advanced posts, hastened to take command personally of Fort Hamilton. Anticipating that the enemy controlled the road from Fort Washington to the advanced forts, he journeyed through the woods by an indirect route, arriving about daybreak on November 6 at Fort Hamilton.

The savages seemingly had vanished from the vicinity, wrote Wilkinson, yet an uneasy air of expectancy remained. Indeed, within a few hours of his arrival, a bedraggled rifleman and three packhorse drivers stumbled into the stockade and reported an utter disaster.[21]

As the Indian captive Oliver Spencer related in his narrative of his ordeal years later, the youthful prisoner had watched with awe as long lines of Indian warriors dressed in full battle regalia had crossed the Maumee in late October to assume the offensive. There were Shawnees from The Snake's and Blue Jacket's towns, and Miamis from the Auglaize villages. In all, about 200 warriors assembled under the brilliant tactician Little Turtle.

Striking south in the direction of the Ohio settlements, the raiders reached the vicinity of Fort Hamilton on November 3, having bypassed the more advanced Forts Jefferson and St. Clair. From the two prisoners that they took late that afternoon, the Indians learned that a large supply convoy escorted by Kentucky militiamen had gone ahead to Fort Jefferson and was due to return in a few days.

The crafty Little Turtle, sensing a suitable opportunity to surprise an unsuspecting enemy, decided to ambuscade the road between Forts Hamilton and St. Clair. Then, on the evening of November 5, word was received from Indian observers that the Kentuckians were encamped with their empty packhorse convoy near Fort St. Clair. Isolated from the walls of the fort by about 200 yards, and slightly less than 100 men strong, the Kentuckians represented a vulnerable target to the raiders. Particularly lucrative was the prospect of capturing or driving off the more than 100 packhorses that were so vital to the enemy's subsistence operations.

Little Turtle planned a repetition of the successful 1791 attack. By surrounding the camp on three sides and attacking simultaneously about daybreak, another rout might be easily achieved. Before dawn on November 6, the warriors were safely in place, conveniently guided by the location of the sentries' blazing camp fires, which ringed the camp's outer perimeter.[22]

Major John Adair was a likeable, backslapping Kentucky militiaman who had a penchant for getting involved in unfortunate scrapes. On this date he commanded the Kentuckians, most of whom were serving as mounted volunteers. Before daylight on November 6, Adair called in his sentries, "in order that we might mount our horses." Adair later wrote of his astonishment as the Indians moved in close on their heels. It was "a great act of boldness and address," he confided, for by this means they got within the camp perimeter undiscovered.[23]

The first intimation of trouble was a sudden shout and a fusillade of bullets. Almost before the white men could react, the red warriors burst into their midst, grappling with some of the Kentuckians in hand-to-hand fighting. "The enemy came on with a degree of courage that bespoke them warriors, indeed," said Adair, who soon found his men racing past him for the safety of the fort. In the darkness and confusion little resistance was possible, and the Kentucky volunteers ran from camp in utter disorder.[24]

Later, amid the debris of his destroyed campground, Adair assessed the damage. Although the Indians had been in possession of his camp only a short while, the Kentucky major found to his chagrin that "they had stripped it of every article, even my provisions." Among the casualties were six killed, five wounded, and four missing, including a dead lieutenant and an orderly sergeant. The most serious blow of all was the loss of nearly all of the packhorses. From a herd of more than one hundred animals, twenty-six had been killed, ten wounded, and the remainder had been captured or driven off except for twenty-three strays that were later rounded up. Only two dead warriors were found amid the debris—an insignificant loss.[25]

The loss of the men was regrettable, Wilkinson later related, but the virtual annihilation of the packhorses was a devastating blow. "The immediate consequence will be an entire stop to the transport of forage to the advanced posts, as our pack horses are either destroyed or disabled, and the riflemen dismounted," he lamented in a letter to Henry Knox. Recognizing that these horses "were the great object of the enemy," Major Adair concluded that the enemy had gained a "capital" advantage and "the triumph is theirs."

Now in a quandary over the replacement of the packhorses, Wilkinson was compelled to use the few mounted infantry still present at Fort Washington for transportation duties—a reflection of the glaring vulnerability of the frontier army. Chafing under the defensive restrictions imposed by the War Department, Wilkinson could only request an increase in the cavalry, which might be used in a winter retaliatory raid, should such be authorized.[26]

More than three hundred miles away, the man who was entrusted with the responsibility of the American military fortunes agreed wholeheartedly in principle. Anthony Wayne, now involved in raising and training in the East an army capable of eradicating the Indian menace, wrote, "It is a most disagreeable and humiliating position to remain with our hands tied whilst the enemy is at liberty to act upon the offensive." Yet the day was soon coming, he had recently written, when the enemy would feel American superiority in the field."[27]

Thus what the Americans readily understood—but were incapable of then effecting—was what the Indians were capable of accomplishing militarily but lacked the unified perspective to achieve. It was a paradox as strange as its consequences were decisive. Little Turtle, who had handily demonstrated the utter vulnerability of the frontier army, was considered to be a military leader only. His influence was effectively limited purely to martial affairs, which, at this point, involved primarily the hard-core belligerents. In the realm of political policy, which was so vital to a unified and meaningful Indian course of action, the various sachems of the contending factions had obscured the essential requirement for immediate, strong measures.

This was the important consequence of the long-anticipated Grand Confederate Council on the Auglaize, which had convened in October, 1792, to determine a collective Indian policy regarding the American difficulties. Far more significant that any past pitched battle with the encroaching white civilization, the council had signaled the unraveling of the Indian political fabric, rather than a leavening of the native perspective. As absorbing as any modern political contest among spirited, contentious rivals, the Indian Grand Council of 1792 had produced elements of intrigue and suspense as well as an intense drama of contrasting personalities.

22

A Lack of Candor

LATE in August, 1792, British Indian agent Alexander McKee wrote to the newly installed lieutenant governor of Upper Canada, John Graves Simcoe, about the Indians who were gathering for the long-awaited grand council at the junction of the Auglaize and Maumee rivers (a site referred to as the Glaize). McKee reported that "their numbers will be greater this season than heretofore."

It was, indeed, a far-reaching assembly of tribes, beginning with the arrival at the nearby Miami Rapids trading post maintained by McKee of delegates from the eastern regions in mid-July, and continuing through August and into September. There were Sauks and Foxes from the northern regions; the so-called Seven Nations of Canada, who were British-allied dissidents nominally of the Iroquois Confederacy; the more neutral Six Nations tribesmen from the Buffalo Creek region; Senecas of Cornplanter's sect, now aligned with the United States; Creeks and Cherokees from the South; a large agglomeration from the Great Lakes, including Ottawas, Wyandots, Potawatomis, and others; the inveterately hostile Shawnees and Miamis; and even a few Wea and Wabash tribesmen disaffected at the Putnam negotiations.[1]

The wide variety of the Indians' nationalities and allegiances was matched by the divergence of their perspectives on the great policy question at hand. As it was evident that only by establishing a unified position would the Indian confederacy be regarded by their enemies as an imposing force, the council was considered crucial by nearly all.

From the very beginning the general council was plagued with inordinate difficulties. As Hendrick Aupaumut had discovered on his arrival along the Maumee in mid-July, there was "a sore famine" in the region. Many of the tribes had been obliged to spend most of the early summer hunting, despite the summons to council. The Americans had caused further trouble, McKee wrote in his often-repeated explanations of why the council had not begun, because of reports of their active preparations for an offensive at their advanced forts.

The seemingly "daily alarms" concerning an American expedition actually resulted from James Wilkinson's intense efforts to lay in sufficient supplies and otherwise to prepare his posts for any belated Indian offensive. His activities were particularly disruptive because they produced considerable ferment among the more moderate tribes and, ultimately, indignation at being subjected to false war rumors. By late September some of the Ottawas

John Graves Simcoe, the austere British lieutenant governor of upper Canada. Courtesy of William Clements Library, University of Michigan.

had gone home "tired of waiting for the general council." Frequent rancorous outbursts between rival Indian factions were contributing to the deterioration of morale. "You almost eat your own dung this summer for reason of war," scoffed a tribesman who had been berated for advocating peace.[2]

Incessant backbiting and preliminary sparring thus dominated the multitude of fore-councils that were convened between individual nations—an ominous backdrop for the inception of the general council. Further, the political realities were such that control of the general confederacy had rested with the Shawnees since the abdication of Joseph Brant before the Fort Harmar Treaty in 1788. The Shawnees, long regarded by their white adversaries as the most warlike of the Old Northwest tribes, jealously guarded this political leverage. "You suppose you have come to attend a treaty of peace," Simon Girty allegedly warned a newly arrived delegation. "You are mistaken, the tomahawk will be presented to you."[3]

Inspired by the earnest lobbying of the Shawnees, the prevailing mood was one of growing unease with American motives when, in mid-September, several large delegations from the Six Nations belatedly arrived at the council site. Delayed by sickness and a want of prompt transportation, these eastern Indians represented a crucial uncommitted entity in the precarious balance of political power. Having been absent from any general proceedings of the Indian confederacy for four years, the Six Nations chiefs and sachems well reflected their equivocal status.[4]

One of the primary leaders among the Senecas of Buffalo Creek was Red Jacket, the eloquent thirty-four-year-old spokesman for the moderate faction. This glib-tongued chief had increasingly prevailed as a champion of Indian rights in recent councils among the Senecas. In the total perspective, however, he seemed an indecisive orator, and had proved to be influential in the Six Nations' avoidance of an active role in the dispute with the Americans over land encroachment.

Red Jacket's rival among the Senecas, although inferior in rank, was the wily Cornplanter. As an outspoken partisan of the radically pro-American elements, Cornplanter had a more clandestine motive for his attendance at the Glaize. In a confidential arrangement with Cornplanter and his subchief New Arrow, Anthony Wayne had promised an ample monetary "reward" to the two Seneca leaders either for procuring a peace with the hostiles or for providing "an exact account of the tribes and number of Indians with whom we might have to contend."[5]

Further adding to the intrigue among the Iroquois was the absence of Joseph Brant, who remained the preeminent chieftain of the Six Nations. By far the most influential Indian leader of the immediate postwar years, Brant had waited for a summons from Alexander McKee before proceeding westward. Although McKee sent a rather urgent request in mid-September for Brant's immediate presence, the Mohawk leader remained so unwell that his departure was delayed. As the days of September waned, he languished at Niagara, only belatedly beginning his journey westward about October 1.[6]

With so many ambiguities and cross-purposes obscuring the outcome, the bickering and political infighting continued to the very eve of the council. Finally, Alexander McKee and several British observers arrived from the

Miami Rapids on September 27, and the opening session was duly scheduled for September 30.[7]

Like nearly all important Indian state occasions, the Grand Confederate Council of 1792 began with the ceremonial smoking of an ancient calumet. Passed from nation to nation according to seniority, the pipe was emblematic of friendship, said the host, a Shawnee chief. As a prerogative of their leadership, the council had been convened at the Shawnees' village—an important tactical advantage for the war action. Once the preliminary welcoming remarks were concluded, the Shawnees adjourned the gathering until the following day.

When the proceedings resumed on October 2, following a day of rain, the Shawnees were quick to seize the initiative. Messquakenoe, the Shawnee spokesman, chided the Six Nations for their absence of four years, saying that the last general gathering had unanimously agreed, in case of an enemy attack, to defend the Indian country collectively. "But we have never seen you since that time," Messquakenoe admonished.[8]

Red Jacket later attempted to explain the Iroquois conservatism by saying that they merely had been following the advice of their British "father." "We know that the Americans have held out their hands to offer you peace. Don't be too proud spirited and reject it, lest the Great Spirit should be angry with you," he warned.[9]

The mounting tension and clearly defined controversy was rapidly leading to an open rupture when, on October 5, the Shawnees again addressed the council. Talking directly to the Six Nations' delegates, Messquakenoe pointedly accused them of deceit, saying: "We can see your conduct plainly. . . . Whenever you heard [sic] the voice of the United States you immediately take your packs and attend their councils. . . . We see plainly folded under your arm the voice of the United States." Then the Shawnee speaker flung the three strands of wampum that he had been holding in his hand across the fire at the feet of Six Nations' delegates—an insulting gesture.

Red Jacket immediately rose to declare the Iroquois surprise. "You have thrown us on our backs," he said and asked for time to prepare an answer.[10]

On the following day a Seneca messenger came to the principal chiefs and sachems of the confederacy and asked for a private council on behalf of the Six Nations. Speaking for the Buffalo Creek Indians, the Farmer's Brother now related how they indeed had arranged with President Washington, while they had been at Philadelphia the last spring, to act as spokesmen for the Americans and to return the answer of their "Western brethren" to him. Reminding the assembled chiefs that the Americans were the greatest people in the land by virtue of their triumph in the Revolution, he urged the confederated leaders to consider their reply well.[11]

On October 7, the decisive day of the council, matters rapidly progressed to a conclusion. The Shawnees, as spoksmen for the majority, proclaimed that the Six Nations had listened to the "sweet speeches" of the United States and thus had been duped into taking no part in defending the country against American aggression. Messquakenoe then related the mutual "resolution of all the nations." First and foremost, he asserted, the Ohio River must remain as the fixed boundary between red and white people. Furthermore, he said, "We want a restitution of our lands which he [President Washington] holds under false pretenses." As for American peace initiatives, if the United States were sincere in their efforts, he said, "Let them destroy these forts [the advanced posts in Indian territory], and we will meet them next spring at Lower Sandusky [for a council]."[12] Since the Six Nations' representatives were American emissaries to the council, continued Messquakenoe, they were to convey that message to the United States authorities.

Red Jacket, aware that the issue had in effect, been settled, merely acknowledged the determination of the council. He added, "We now join with you, and will put our heads together and endeavor to get all our lands back where the Americans have encroached upon us."[13]

Although the confederacy thus seemed to agree to a common course of action, Red Jacket's statement on behalf of the Six Nations belied the internal ferment that was to lead to further difficulty. As had been mentioned in the preliminary discussions between Henry Knox and the Senecas of Buffalo Creek in mid-1792, and as later had been confirmed by the instructions issued to Hendrick Aupaumut and Rufus Putnam, the federal government had considered a partial withdrawal from the advanced forts to produce a temporary diminution of hostilities. Putnam was told, "upon an ultimate adjustment of differences," he might express his "opinion" that "said reservations [the posts] may be relinquished by the U.S.," with certain exceptions. Aupaumut evidently was assured that as soon as the hostiles complied with the terms of peace by calling in all war parties, the forts on Indian lands would be dismantled.[14]

This idea, of course, had been repeatedly expressed to the western nations by the Iroquois. It was much of the basis for the general confederacy's willingness to convene a council at Lower Sandusky in 1793. Yet, on the Six Nations' return to Buffalo Creek, an inter-Iroquois council was held in mid-November for the purpose of properly preparing a message to the United States as both sides had anticipated. At this meeting the realities of political alignments and special interests became fully manifest. Red Jacket, in the presence of the more moderate British observers and Indian agents from Niagara, as well as Israel Chapin, Jr., who was present on behalf of the United States, presented a much-altered mandate from the Auglaize council. No longer under the close scrutiny of the war faction, Red Jacket portrayed the eminence of the Six Nations as mediators in the dispute, alleging the Shawnees and other hostiles had accepted their "Eldest Brother's" [the Six Nations'] advice by agreeing to meet the United States in council at Sandusky "next spring, or at the time the leaves are fully out."[15]

No mention was made of any terms for this council or of specific boundary demands, only that some land claimed by the confederated tribes on the east bank of the Ohio was to be exchanged for land on the west side. Furthermore, in presenting the summary that was translated into a message to the American officials, a significant statement was attributed to the hostile elements: "We will lay the bloody tomahawk aside until we hear from the President of the United States."[16] The documents thus presented were as remarkable for their omissions as for their lack of candor. Conveyed to the Washington administration was a general attitude of unquestioning compliance on the part of the Indian confederacy, a highly erroneous impression.[17]

While the Cornplanter and others discreetly informed the American authorities that the Shawnees would only agree to terms of peace that involved an Ohio River boundary, Henry Knox utilized the Six Nations' report to initiate active plans for a forthcoming treaty with the Indian confederacy. Writing to the Shawnees, the Miamis, and their allies on December 12, 1792, Knox acknowledged that he had received the confederacy's messages "through our good friends in the Six Nations." "The President of the U.S. embraces your proposal," he added, "and will send commissioners to meet you at the time and place appointed." Promising to furnish a full supply of provisions for the treaty, Knox then related the essential aspect of the bargain: "We shall prevent any of our parties going into Indian country, so that you may with your women and children rest in full security. We desire and shall expect that you call in all your warriors and prevent their going out again. It will be in vain to expect peace while they continue their depredations on the frontier."[18]

On December 7, 1792, Henry Knox wrote to Anthony Wayne of the new perspectives involved in the war. With the prospect of peace through negotiation, the public would not condone offensive military activities at this time. Commissioners would be appointed to treat with the Indians—"The public voice demands it," reasoned Knox. He then added that, if peace proved to be unattainable on the principles of "national character and national justice," it was presumed that public opinon would "support the war in a more vigorous manner." Of particular concern was a resolution then pending before Congress for a reduction in the regular military establishment. Knox, ever the political realist, thus sought to move discreetly in military measures until public opinion was more receptive.[19]

Anthony Wayne, however, was virtually livid with anger over the restraints imposed. Asserting that it was humiliating beyond comprehension "to remain with our hands tied" while the enemy could act with impunity on the offensive, Wayne expressed his disgust at the prospect of protracted negotiations. After learning of the November 6 attack on Major Adair's packhorse convoy, Wayne fairly bristled with indignation: "Be not therefore any longer amused or deceived with ideal hopes of an honorable or lasting peace with a triumphant, insulting, savage enemy. Let every exertion be made to complete the legion, add to the soldier's rations, [and] let us be in a condition to take the field in force in the spring."[20]

Wayne's impatience was matched, however, by the resolve of the president of the United States to proceed with due caution. No offensive operations were authorized.

Indignation over the results of the Grand Glaize Council of 1792 remained high among American military authorities, and their exasperation was shared by some of their opposite numbers among the Indians, but for different reasons. Joseph Brant, hastening to the Glaize in the cause of moderation, had at last arrived on October 8—after the closing of the council. Since the council had decided that the Ohio River must be the boundary between the red and white nations, and that abatement of hostilities depended on removal of the advanced American forts, a raiding party led by Little Turtle already was preparing for a sortie after receipt of their annual supplies from McKee's storehouse. Brant thus was greatly displeased with the result of the late council, according to a British interpreter.

Thereafter the Mohawk chieftain's actions were characterized by a growing intolerence of what he regarded as radical elements, particularly those British Indian agents who aided and encouraged the "hot headed" hostiles.[21]

To the British upper-echelon officers whom the Home Office had charged with the promotion of peace, the Glaize Council of 1792 afforded a dramatic new prospect in what had otherwise been a dismally unproductive year. Frustrated by the utter failure of all efforts through diplomatic channels to arrange for British mediation, Lieutenant Governor Simcoe had concluded in August, 1792, that the British needed to discredit the Washington administration. Noting that Washington and his cabinet officials were "determined enemies of Great Britain," Simcoe had sought to "lessen as much as possible" the president's influence. "There is no person perhaps who thinks less of the talents or integrity of General Washington than I do," he wrote.

Furthermore, Simcoe was greatly concerned that the Indians would conclude a separate peace with the United States, which, he foresaw, might not only force the British to yield their posts but also cause another open conflict with the United States, in which the Indians would be involved as allies of the Americans. It was of the utmost importance, he reasoned, that a neutral barrier state be established, wherein the Indians might continue to be exposed to British influence. This would also ensure the continuation of the valuable fur trade from the midcontinent that was vital to Canada's economy.[22]

Accordingly, Simcoe issued instructions for McKee to utilize every influence that might cause the Indians to insist on British mediation in any peace negotiations with the Americans. It was important that this Indian insistence should appear to be spontaneous, otherwise the guise of British "neutrality" would be violated.[23]

The Auglaize Grand Council thus seemed significant to Simcoe, because the Indians had jointly resolved to include British participation in their forthcoming treaty with the Americans. This had been suggested by the Shawnee speaker Messquakenoe on October 8, and a formal Indian delegation had called on Alexander McKee the following day to request British participation.

Delighted that his covert designs were about to be implemented, and convinced that the United States must now accede to British involvement, Simcoe proceeded to provide for the provisioning of the Indian delegates, so that they would have no doubt who their real benefactors were. Subsequently, when Alexander Hamilton, secretary of the United States Treasury, sought to send an American agent into the territory of Upper Canada to procure a supply of treaty provisions, Simcoe arbitrarily denied Hamilton's request.[24] Simcoe's smug gamesmanship was also evident in February, 1793, when he personally confronted William Hull, the American agent sent by Hamilton to arrange for needed supplies. Hull, a former lieutenant colonel who had considerable Revolutionary War experience, was peremptorily told that he could not proceed with his mission. Simcoe offered the excuse that he was merely following orders and simply lacked the authority, so he stated, to comply with the American request.[25]

As a prime mover in American-British-Indian relationships Simcoe thus was a harbinger of further strained relations with the United States. Because of Dorchester's absence in England and the force of Simcoe's personality, the lieutenant governor of Upper Canada had assumed primary responsibility in the critical unfolding of events. When he was informed by Secretary of State Thomas Jefferson that only several low-level British observers would be allowed at the forthcoming Indian-American council, Simcoe became even more haughty toward the Americans.

Actually, Simcoe had long been active as an adversary of the United States. During the Revolution he had commanded a much-despised Tory regiment, the Queen's Rangers, and had found ample cause to loathe the Americans when he was ambushed, wounded, and captured in October, 1779. Although he was an exceptionally energetic and capable officer, the lieutenant governor was highly prejudiced and opinionated.[26] In 1793 he was burdened by the Home Office commitment to peace, which extended even to the evacuation of the disputed posts if necessary. As a result he saw in the forthcoming Indian-American negotiations an opportunity to recoup a portion of the lost British fortunes in North America. Privately pessimistic about American acceptance of Indian demands, Simcoe nonetheless looked forward to resolution of the claims that were important to Upper Canada, including the retention of Detroit and islands in the Saint Lawrence River.

It was regrettable, Simcoe reasoned, that prompt negotiations with the Americans had not followed the Indian victories of 1790 and 1791.[27]

Enjoined by formal British policy to spend much of his time on the mechanics of attempting a peace, Simcoe all but overlooked in the minutiae of treaty arrangements the more plausible requirements of military assistance and preparedness. This naïve omission on his part was to be greatly significant.

Less than two hundred miles from the Indian frontier that the British sought to protect by mediative bargaining, a powerful American army was gathering in direct contradiction to the British efforts. Although Simcoe had concluded that the expense of maintaining a sizeable military establishment for any length of time must be unacceptable to the United States, a contrary view had long been held by the Washington administration.[28] "In order . . . that the troops shall be prepared for a conflict with the savages . . . , no relaxation [is to] be made in the disciplining of the troops and most especially in making them perfect marksmen," read instructions that were issued in the name of the president. The continuance of the Washington administration's policy to sustain military preparations had been assured by a key vote of the House of Representatives early in 1793. Thereafter Secretary of War Knox anticipated an ultimate triumph of arms: "Adhere therefore to the line in which you have set out," he reassured Anthony Wayne, "and the result must be honor and glory to you and your army."[29]

To John Graves Simcoe the shock was overwhelming when late in May, 1793, he learned that war had broken out in Europe between France and Great Britain. Simultaneously learning of American intentions to establish a fleet upon the Great Lakes to rival the British, Simcoe could now but ponder the double jeopardy from hostile French and American forces. Terming "all the garrison and fortifications of Detroit, Niagara, and Oswego totally inadequate to self defense or general protection," the Canadian lieutenant governor began a drastic internal policy revision. It was, in fact, the renewal of a British preoccupation with local defensive measures to the exclusion of basic Indian interests. Although Simcoe concluded that the Indians were vital "to the safety of this colony," their role was as a potential threat to the enemy rather than an active fighting force. Not wishing to provoke open hostilities with the United States, Simcoe now sought to keep the Americans at bay primarily by bluff. "The most formidable Indian confederacy is in [our] favor, and without striking a blow, may serve to intimidate," he wrote. Citing the "vast advantage" that the Indians might give the British as watchdogs of British territorial integrity until reinforcements could be sent, Simcoe advised, "They have for four years kept the American power in check."[30]

Again, the Indians were being manipulated in their familiar role as instruments of British policy. Since the Canadian strategists sought to delay any direct confrontation with the United States while they made essential defensive preparations, the red nations were to be utilized as controlled buffers, not as independent allies fighting to maintain their own country. While at the operational level British Indian agents continued privately to encourage military activities, it became increasingly evident that the king's administrators were reluctant to risk anything more than verbal bantering on behalf of the tribes—for fear of war.

As yet unsuspecting of any significant contradiction in the British behavior, the Indian confederacy continued to approach the critical negotiations of 1793 with the United States in a state of trust and dependence. "We have a reliance on our [British] father seeing justice done us," they had written. "He never deceives us, and we have always found that we may confidently depend upon him."[31]

At the very time the Indians were awaiting the arrival of the American commissioners that would herald the "removal [of] the causes of complaint," nearly two thousand soldiers of the United States army, under the express orders of Secretary of War Knox, began their journey to the war zone in Ohio. Wrote George Washington on the day following their arrival, "If the sword is to decide [the Indian issue], . . . [it is necessary] that the army of government may be enabled to strike home."[32]

23

"2,500 Commissioners, Properly Appointed"

ANTHONY WAYNE, summoning much of the humility in his nature, had responded to Henry Knox's letter notifying him of his appointment as major general commanding the Army of the United States with fitting rhetoric. "I clearly forsee that it is a command which must inevitably be attended with the most anxious care, fatigue, and difficulty—and from which more may be expected than will be in my power to perform," he wrote in April, 1792.[1]

Little more than sixty days later Wayne truly began to understand how prophetic his remarks had been. Ordered to Pittsburgh to assemble and train an army of conquest, he wrote to Knox on June 15, the day following his arrival, that he had only forty recruits and a "corporal's command" of dragoons in his army. "I really feel awkwardly situated—a general without troops is something similar to a fish out of water," he complained.[2]

Wayne's efforts to fashion an effective military establishment thus began with the most meagre foundation. Amid the budding insurrection of the "whiskey boys"—a disorderly mob of Scotch-Irish farmers who violently protested the levy of an excise tax on distilled spirits—Wayne attempted an uneasy accommodation with the sprawling, half-wild town of Pittsburgh.[3]

Although burdened by a lingering troop deficiency, Wayne saw his army increase from 793 effective rank and file in October, 1792, to about 1,200 in April, 1793. After that, the army was not expected to increase significantly, because of the disparity between civilian wages and army pay. Wayne soon felt confident enough in his hard core of trained regulars, however, to rely on the call-up of mounted militia volunteers to augment his strike force.[4]

The basis for Wayne's cautious optimism was his intensive program of arduous training and strict discipline. Committed to a defensive posture by Knox's orders prohibiting offensive operations against the Indians, Wayne sought to utilize this temporary interlude to maximize his army's preparedness. First and foremost was the matter of discipline. Wayne's orderly book for 1792–93 reads largely as a treatise on harsh punishments. Within five weeks in the fall of 1792 seven deserters were executed. Soldiers found sleeping on duty and evidencing "an intention to desert" were sentenced to receive one hundred lashes. Even officers were held strictly accountable–a veteran captain was cashiered in July, 1792, for being drunk and disorderly. Yet Wayne's methods were both calculating and purgative. Resorting to capital punishment generally only for repeat offenders, Wayne, who

General Anthony Wayne, the American who conquered the Old Northwest Territory. From an engraving of a painting by John Trumbull, courtesy of William Clements Library, University of Michigan.

approved or disapproved all sentences, effectively utilized the "Rules and Articles of War" to cull his army of undesirables.[5]

While the men began quietly to fear Anthony Wayne's harsh discipline, there was even greater controversy about his training methods. Committed to the principle of ingrained response in tactical maneuvers, Wayne practiced his army incessantly in offensive and defensive drills. Sham battles were conducted to instill a sense of realism. These often involved the rifle corps in the role of Indians—"highly painted" and yelling ferociously.

Recognizing the value of an accurate and rapid rate of fire, Wayne had his infantrymen practice repeatedly the motion of loading and firing with "wooden snappers" in the place of flints. Riflemen, armed with the long-barreled Lancaster County (Pennsylvania-Kentucky) rifles, were instructed to practice firing at marks set against trees, so that the lead could be reclaimed. The infantry, armed with Revolutionary War vintage smoothbore muskets, mostly of the United States–surcharged French M1763 or M1777 Charleville pattern, were trained to fire at targets "waist band high." Wayne believed that this maximized the number of enemy struck per shot fired. The combat cartridge issued by his orders was "one ball and three heavy buckshot" instead of the usual "single ball and a very small load of powder." Moreover, Wayne sought to improve the rate of sustained fire by altering the cumbersome firing mechanism of the French flintlocks. By redrilling on an oblique angle and enlarging the touchholes that carried the primer fire to the main charge, Wayne estimated that he could effectually speed the loading process. This would be possible because of the fine-grained powder in the self-contained paper cartridge. All a soldier had to do while in action was to bite off the cartridge and ram it home; the enlarged and angled touchhole ensured a sufficient powder leakage into the priming pan to ignite the charge. Wayne later noted the results of his rather unorthodox methods: "The very men who four or five weeks since, scarcely knew how to load, or draw a trigger, begin now to place a ball in a deadly direction."[6]

To the indigent and uneducated farm boys and urban drifters who constituted much of the army's rank and file, Wayne was very demanding, not only in his training but also in the standard of personal conduct that he required. Pittsburgh, with its rowdy taverns and prostitutes, was exacting a heavy toll in dereliction of duty and venereal diseases. Wayne began to look on the proximity of any sizeable settlement to his encampment as an "ardent poison." Detesting the baneful effect of the dirty, unruly town, Wayne received President Washington's permission to transfer his army from Pittsburgh to a more remote site within the same region. Yet, after he had selected a location twenty-two miles from Pittsburgh and seven and a half miles above Big Beaver Creek, Wayne was delayed by low water for nearly a month before embarking on November 28 for his new campsite.[7]

In deference to the new designation of the United States Army, which was now known as the Legion of the United States (a name that Knox had bestowed), the site was named Legionville. This rather Spartan campground was well suited to Wayne's essential purpose. Although he was compelled to live temporarily in a marquee, while the other officers were provided with cold linen tents, Wayne fairly bubbled with enthusiasm over the new environment.[8]

By December 6 the men were depicted as being "nearly [all] under cover." Thereafter Wayne was relentless and self-driving in his efforts to improve the army. Esprit de corps was particularly emphasized. Distinctively colored trim was ordered for each of the four sublegions (the regiments), and soon the army had a new appearance. White cap bindings and plumes were designated for the first sublegion, red for the second, yellow for the third, and green for the fourth. Battalion-sized flags were procured in the proper colors for each unit, and large legionary standards emblazoned with a life-size silver eagle were proposed. Cleanliness and proper appearance were stressed even to the point of insistance that troops standing guard be "fresh shaved and [their hair] powdered." Twenty lashes were prescribed for carelessly soiling of a uniform, for example, by carrying rations in a coat pocket.[9]

Wayne soon began to perceive a pronounced change in the character of his army, and as 1793 began his confidence in the soldiers' prowess continued to mount. Citing specifically the progress in inculcating order and discipline in the troops, Wayne set exacting standards for officers and men alike in the deadly earnest business of preparing them for active war. Regular patrols were sustained, even in inclement weather, and so rigid were Wayne's demands on his troops that general orders required a pay cut of one-eighth of a dollar for "every cartridge lost, sold, bartered, or damaged" outside of authorized use.[10]

As might be expected, with the approach of warm weather in 1793, Wayne became increasingly restive. He had asked only for time to train and prepare his army, suggesting that "brilliant success" would follow thereafter. Now convinced of the need for prompt and decisive military operations, he was impatient for action and chafed under the restraints imposed by Knox.

Although Wayne's plans to mount "desultory" raids and advance the line of army outposts deeper into Indian country were denied, he received permission in March, 1793, to move his legion to the war zone. By design and by happenstance, it proved to be a most momentous undertaking.[11]

As early as November, 1792, the Washington administration had anticipated that the entire army intended to operate against the Indians would assemble at Fort Washington in the spring of 1793. When Knox authorized such a move in March, 1793, Wayne was of course highly pleased. While he saw no reason to hasten his troops' embarkation before the weather permitted camping in the open, in late April or early May, by April 15 he had nearly everything in readiness.[12]

By late April the last few leaky boats had been repaired. On the thirtieth Wayne embarked his riflemen in the advance craft to provide cover, and the long convoy of keelboats and barges, many fitted with oars, began to drift down the Ohio.[13] As befitted the Legion's commander, Wayne was ensconced in his barge, *The Federal*, which was equipped with a large awning and had twelve oarsmen working the brightly painted oars that were lettered with the barge's name. Thus Wayne bid a not-too-reluctant farewell to western Pennsylvania. Musing that no beneficial consequence would come from catering to the Indians at the upcoming peace treaty, Wayne perhaps reflected on the projectd result of his army's journey into the disputed territory. Earlier that year he had written: "I have a strong propensity to attend the next grand [Indian] council . . . attended with about 2500 Commissioners properly appointed [armed], . . . among whom I do not wish to have a single Quaker."[14]

If not actually moving against the red enemy, Wayne was at least preparing to do so. His attitude reflected the characteristic optimism of the inborn fighter that he was. "I am . . . happy to have it in my power to declare," he wrote on May 9, "that both officers and soldiers have acquired a greater degree of military knowledge in the course of a few months than I ever saw acquired in twice the time by any soldiers during the late war."[15]

By May 5 most of Wayne's troops had safely arrived in the vicinity of Fort Washington, "without a single accident." Greeted by a multitude of citizens and soldiers estimated at eleven hundred persons, who lined the rolling hills about Cincinnati, Wayne and his men were accorded a heros' welcome. Bands blared on shore, as well as from Wayne's boats. A fifteen-cannon salute boomed in their honor. They were feted at an elegant banquet amid the gay flags and bunting that decorated Fort Washington, which was newly painted red. Wayne could but acknowledge the tumultuous welcome, although he soon grew to despise Cincinnati, which he said was "filled with ardent poison [whiskey] and caitiff wretches to dispose of it."[16]

In fact, the major general's mood seemed soon to turn restive. Camped about a mile below Fort Washington on the Ohio, Wayne grumbled about the "wide swamp in our front," which had "no good ground for maneuver or encampment." Derisively he dubbed his location "Hobson's Choice."

In a quandary how best to provide the "heavy and necessary" deposits of provisions at the advanced posts that would be needed in an offensive campaign, Wayne decided on "a provisional arrangement." A detachment of regulars under the veteran Lieutenant Colonel David Strong were to cut a broad road between the advanced forts to facilitate transporting the supplies in heavy ox-drawn carts and wagons. The detachment would also harvest hay on the prairie in the vicinity of Fort Jefferson. Within sixty days Strong had accomplished those tasks, taking great care to cover the troops with improvised breastworks of felled trees at each night's bivouac. He also drove a heard of eighty-two cattle forward to the garrison of Fort Jefferson.[17]

Wayne's preoccupation with logistics and with establishing a viable base of operations had a strategic flaw, however. In fact, the essential consequence of his massive movements down the Ohio and his strenuous activity to improve the Legion's operational capability was materially to delay and compromise the then-maturing peace negotiations.

Prying eyes had followed the progress of Wayne's boats down the Ohio. He himself had reported that "the margin of the Ohio is infested with desultory parties of Indians" all the way back to Pennsylvania. News of the heavy troop movements in the vicinity of Fort Jefferson and of the road-construction details, who advanced six miles beyond that fort, had spread so rapidly that it had reached Niagara by the first week in July. The Indian leaders immediately protested that the "warlike appearance" of the United States Army had all of the marks of treacherous conduct. Wayne's movements therefore occasioned a considerable delay in the forwarding of delegates to meet with the American peace commissioners.[18]

Before descending the Ohio, Wayne had predicted that "the savages . . . expect us to advance to the head of the line, and the accumulation of magazines, so far from having a tendency to prevent a peace, will rather expedite it." He was seriously mistaken.[19] The very movements that were intended to accelerate a decision by force of arms only retarded the political confrontation that was a prerequisite for unleashing a military offensive.

24

A Question of Unanimity

TIMOTHY PICKERING, Benjamin Lincoln, and Beverly Randolph were perhaps three of the more diverse personalities who assumed major roles in the resolution of the Indian difficulties of the post-Revolution era. On the collective efficacy of these three the government placed the enormous burden of arranging an acceptable peace in the spring of 1793. Ironically, however, as commissioners to negotiate with the Indian confederacy, they had not been Washington's preferred choices. Two staunch Federalists, Charles Carroll and Charles Thomson, had declined to serve, despite the president's virtual mandate.[1]

Lincoln and Pickering were both northerners from Massachusetts, but they had widely different backgrounds. Lincoln was an obese former Revolutinary War general; his loose jowls and lame gait accentuated his advancing age of sixty. Nonetheless, he was a competent administrator and an experienced veteran. As the senior ranking official among the commissioners, he was nominally their leader, though his influence was diminished by the force of his companions' personalities.[2]

Timothy Pickering was easily the most learned of the three. A Harvard graduate of 1763, he had been a lawyer, a judge, a soldier, a statesman, and lately, a politician. His recent appointment as postmaster general had been merited largely because of his service during the revolution. Known for his "indefatigable industry and iron determination," Pickering also had a smug, condescending nature. A British observer termed him "a violent, low, philosophic, cunning New Englander."[3]

Least known among the commissioners was the "rakish" Virginian, Beverly Randolph, a born aristocrat. Of an old-line Virginia family, whose decendants were to include Thomas Jefferson, John Marshall, "Light Horse Harry" Lee, and Robert E. Lee, Randolph was the youngest of the three commissioners, being not yet forty. He was also the most outspoken; and not particularly fond of the military. Although he recently had been governor of Virginia, he was regarded with disdain by the British, who did, however, acknowledge him to be "able."[4]

Although Washington considered them to be a select group, "whose situation in life places them clear of every suspicion of a wish to prolong the war," the rather odd threesome were united only by their Federalist affiliation. Foremost in their minds was the fate of the last year's emissaries to the Indians, Colonel Hardin and Major Trueman. Henry Knox was so apprehensive of another bloodbath that he issued special instructions to Anthony

Wayne before the commissioners' departure: "Their lives will depend on an absolute restraining of all hostile or offensive operations, . . . for most indisputably if any incursions into the Indian country should be made . . . the commissioners would be sacrificed." Knox required particular caution of Wayne in forwarding any stores or munitions to the frontier forts or "any considerable accumulation of troops at your advanced posts."[5]

Within sixty days of the issuance of those instructions not only was Wayne involved in the very acts against which Knox had warned him, but also the Indians had discovered that the commissioners had come to treat under false pretenses.

After the forwarding of Knox's initial reply to the Indian confederacy on December 12, 1792, the sachems and chiefs had begun to consider that their original terms for bargaining with the United States had been distorted by the Six Nations' actions as intermediaries. Knox's message, which the Indian confederacy received toward the end of January, 1793, stated that the site of the treaty was to be the Miami Rapids instead of Lower Sandusky, the site that the red nations had designated at the Auglaize council. Knox, moreover, omitted to mention the dismantling of the advanced forts, a prerequisite of formal peace negotiations required by the Fall Council.[6]

In a stinging rebuttal of this apparent American intrigue, the "Western Indians" returned a terse reply, saying that the Americans seemed to be speaking "with a double tongue,"—professing peace on one hand while preparing for war with the other. The Six Nations' demand that the advanced forts be dismantled had been entirely disregarded, and a separate and divisive treaty had been attempted with the Wabash tribes the previous fall.

"Our young men cannot be restrained til they see you taking steps to give up your encroachments on our lands," warned the confederacy. "They are obliged to watch you in their own defense. . . . In the meantime, we shall call in all our war parties and endeavor as much as is in our power to prevent any further hostilities, because we sincerely wish for peace, if upon just and solid terms." The Indians' message further asserted, "we are fully resolved to meet you at no place, but at that place where the council fire is appointed to be by all the nations [Lower Sandusky]."[7]

Knox responded by forwarding only a minimal reply on the last day of February. The mistake in location had been due to misinterpretation, he said; there would be no difficulty in changing the site to Lower Sandusky. There the commissioners would gather on June 1 to hold the conference. Otherwise, nothing was mentioned regarding evacuation of the frontier posts or the general terms that the Indians had proposed. Knox, having been assured by the confederacy of a diminution of hostilities until after the council, obviously saw no reason to make further concessions.[8]

Thus, when the three American commissioners arrived in the vicinity of Niagara between May 16 and 25, what the Indians had understood to be necessary evidence of the United States's sincerity in effecting peace—a partial withdrawal of the frontier garrisons—had become, by formal instructions of the secretary of war, a major concession to be negotiated only in the formal treaty. Furthermore, the commissioners were soon caught up by the machinations of the British, who were determined covertly to manipulate the forthcoming negotiations according to their specific interests.[9]

John Graves Simcoe, acting on behalf of the absent governor in chief, Lord Dorchester, welcomed the American commissioners to Canada by insisting that they stay at his personal residence and share his food. At Simcoe's home near Niagara the commissioners were treated with extreme "politeness and hospitality," said Benjamin Lincoln. Feted at a banquet honoring the king's birthday early in June, they partook of "a splendid ball," which featured mixed dancing from seven to eleven, then supper, of which Lincoln found "everything good and in pretty taste." Simcoe, during the entire duration of the commissioners' stay, seemed the model of a genteel, self-assured nobleman imbued with worldly knowledge and impeccable taste.[10]

The commissioners thus hesitated little in requesting Simcoe's assistance in dispelling the "deep rooted prejudices and unfounded reports" that were said to be circulating among the Indians. In a letter that was presented to Simcoe on June 7 they presumptively requested the presence of several British military officers at the council. Furthermore, they even revealed the terms by which they would agree to settle with the Indians. This trust in Simcoe was fostered, said the commissioners, by a desire to "add to their security from insults and danger" (they trusted the British army more than the Indian department agents).[11]

Just how naïve Lincoln, Pickering, and Randolph were was revealed in the private correspondence of Simcoe. Terming the American commissioners men who "have much of that low craft which distinguishes . . . naturally self opinionated [individuals possessed of] a very trifling education," Simcoe denounced the American intentions as deceitful and said that the peace mission was only ceremonial in nature.[12]

Simcoe's plan, cited in later instructions to his subordinates, was carefully to orchestrate a charade aimed at gathering vital information and disguising Britain's true intentions from a potential adversary. "Show . . . every civility that may be in your power, and manifest upon all occasions . . . kindness and urbanity [to the commissioners]," advised the lieutenant governor of Upper Canada, who meanwhile also instructed his agents to assert their "ascendency" over the Indians by advising them covertly of their "real interests."[13]

Having played into British hands by revealing their bargaining position, the commissioners were most fortunate that Simcoe did not fully reveal the United States's plans to the Indian leaders. The lieutenant governor faced a major dilemma in mid-1793. Less than two weeks before the commissioners' arrival he had learned of the existing war between France and Great Britain. Fearful of an outbreak of warfare in Upper Canada betwen unprepared British troops and the United States (ostensibly acting on behalf of its old ally France), Simcoe avidly promoted an Indian-American peace conference largely as a means of delay. Thus he gained the time to prepare for what he regarded as probable hostilities between the two powers. Simcoe also was awaiting the imminent return to Canada of Lord Dorchester, who would provide more recent Home Office direction.[14] In the meantime, he confided his dilemma in a dispatch to the Home Office, saying he must give no pretext to the United States to begin war, and yet must manage Indian affairs so "as not to loose the affections" of these former allies who were "so essential to the safety of this colony."[15]

Unsuspecting of this widespread British intrigue in manipulating men and events, the American commissioners meanwhile busied themselves with trivial details during their long wait. By the end of June, however, they were reduced to a state of uncertain expectancy. Rumors had been widely circulated that, if the Indians could not make peace, they would commence hostilities by sacrificing the commissioners on the spot. This and other threatening statements, observed Simcoe, had the commissioners apprehensive about their safety, and in late June they decided to go to Detroit "to learn the true state of things."[16]

As the three Americans well realized, the timetable presented in Knox's instructions was of primary importance. The prospect of peace or war was to be determined by August to allow Wayne the opportunity to conduct an offensive during clement weather. Yet it was readily perceived that the treaty would not be concluded by that deadline.

Proceeding to Fort Erie on June 26, 1793, to take passage to Detroit on the British schooner *Dunmore*, the commissioners were detained at Fort Erie by unfavorable winds and still had not sailed by July 5. On that date they were surprised to find a delegation of about fifty Indians aboard the vessel *Chippewa*, which arrived that day. This delegation had proceeded from the preliminary council at the Miami Rapids to meet with the American commissioners about certain controversial matters.[17]

As explained by Joseph Brant in his journal, the Indian precouncil at the Miami Rapids had involved considerable political bickering. Brant, nominally the leader of the Six Nations faction, largely had been shunned by the Shawnees and the other more hostile elements, presumably for his and the Six Nations' absence during the 1791 fighting. Brant, for his part, was resentful of the Shawnee leadership and distrusted the influence of British agents such as Alexander McKee.[18] In this atmosphere of suspicion, which was increased by private meetings among the various factions, the precouncil had received news later in June of the heavy activity by Anthony Wayne's army near Fort Jefferson and the apparent reinforcement of that fort.

Perhaps suspecting that the Americans were professing peace only to mask preparations for an offensive campaign while the red nations were distracted with treaty negotiations, the more hostile Indians, evidently with McKee's concurrence, had decided to send a deputation to the American commissioners. This delegation was to determine why the American troops were actively preparing for war when, by an earlier declaration, the advanced posts in Indian territory were to have been demolished as "preliminaries on which the confederacy consented to meet [the] commissioners." The delegation was also to find out whether the commissioners had full authority to draw a new boundary line in accordance with the Ohio River boundary set by the Treaty of Fort Stanwix in 1768.[19]

With Joseph Brant and various minor Shawnee chiefs on hand, the first preliminary confrontation between the principal Indian and American negotiators occurred in Navy Hall, Simcoe's residence near Niagara, on Sunday morning, July 7.[20] From the beginning it was evident the Americans were to be on the defensive. Joseph Brant, speaking on behalf of the Indian delegation, posed the several key queries. Yet Brant's moderate view of the pending negotiations was very different from that of the Shawnee-Miami-Delaware alliance who presided over the confederacy's affairs. Accordingly, he outlined the two essential issues in a conciliatory manner, first omitting to mention the requisite destruction of the advanced posts and, in the second part of his speech, asking only if the commissioners had the authority to fix any new boundary.

On the following day, July 8, the commissioners presented their answer, asserting that all hostile activity by their army had been temporarily forbidden by the government. In confirmation of this they offered copies of various proclamations by Anthony Wayne and several state governors. Moreover, the commissioners explicitly said that they possessed the authority to make a new boundary line, adding only that where this line should run would be "the great subject of discussion" at the general treaty and that "some concessions must be made on both sides."[21]

When Joseph Brant responded to those statements on the following day, he intimated that the American speech was acceptable and "there is a prospect of our coming together [for a treaty]." In the days immediately following the meetings, the commissioners therefore made preparations to proceed to the Detroit region, as the Indian deputies departed for the Miami Rapids to make their report. Rather optimistically, Benjamin Lincoln addressed a private letter to Henry Knox, speaking of "the present favorable appearance of things." By July 14 the commissioners were safely aboard the *Dunmore* en route to the mouth of the Detroit River, fully expecting to begin the long-awaited treaty within a matter of days.[22]

Although the language of Joseph Brant had deviated only moderately from what the confederacy's leaders had decreed, the subtle difference was to occasion a major confrontation within the confederacy of profound implication. In fact, after his return to the Miami Rapids, Brant became even more deeply mired in controversy. His formal report was greeted with considerable indignation, particularly by the Shawnees. Asserting that he had deviated from the intended ultimatum, the hostile factions berated Brant for "scandalous and shameful" behavior. Buckongahelas of the Delawares even challenged Brant for having assumed leadership of the delegation, saying that the Shawnees were to have spoken.[23]

Brant, who said he had acted as spokesman because of confusion among the delegation about what to say, replied with considerable fervor. "We were not authorized to fix the boundary line," he protested, "but to know from the commissioners if they were empowered to make a boundary." Reminding the confederacy that the land under dispute was "our country" as well, Brant further elucidated a more critical and explosive issue, a matter upon which the outcome of the entire war perhaps rested: "We will not join those few people if they will be so unreasonable as to wish to involve us [Six Nations] in trouble when we have no object to contend for."[24]

Brant's views thus presented the immediate prospect of disunion among the tribes should the more hostile elements insist on a hard line. His latent political influence, as the former acknowledged leader of the confederacy, was well illustrated when the Ottawas, Chippewas, and Potawatomis agreed with Brant and his Six Nations tribesmen and proposed to follow his direction. Faced with the prospect of a ruinous split in Indian solidarity, the various tribes withdrew to confer among themselves in private councils.

Finally, on July 26, matters proceeded rapidly to a determination,[25] when the hostile faction attended a general council meeting with flintlock pistols ominously thrust through their belts. In an impassioned speech the Shawnee chieftain Captain Johnny announced that, as a message must be sent to the commissioners, it had been decided (obviously by the hostile faction) that the Ohio River boundary of the 1768 Fort Stanwix Treaty must be preserved, and that a dispatch to the Americans would go forth with this demand. A new delegation, consisting of representatives from all tribes, was to convey this message. Accordingly, a rather terse statement was prepared for all nations to sign, which read in part: "The deputies we sent to you did not fully explain our meaning. . . . You know very well that the boundary line which was run between the white people and us at the Treaty of Fort Stanwix was the river Ohio. . . . We therefore ask you, are you fully authorized by the United States to continue and firmly fix on the Ohio River as the boundary line between your people and ours?"[26]

Joseph Brant was infuriated by this development. Indignant that the Six Nations had not even been consulted for their opinion before this proclamation, he refused to sign the message.[27] Despite this, on July 29, a delegation estimated at thirty men, headed by the Wyandot chief Sa-wagh-da-wunk, went to meet the American commissioners, they having been suitably instructed about their deportment. Present also were Captain Matthew Elliott, McKee's subordinate, and the war chiefs Buckongahelas and Kakiapalathy. By the evening of the twenty-ninth they had arrived at Bois Blanc Island, opposite Elliott's farm, where the commissioners were lodged.[28]

If the past two weeks had been uneventful for Commissioners Lincoln, Randolph, and Pickering, they had at least been pleasant. After their arrival at the mouth of the Detroit River on July 21 the commissioners had enjoyed the gracious hospitality, the good food, and the pleasant surroundings afforded at Matthew Elliott's house.[29]

Although Simcoe had been "glad to be ridden of the commissioners" at Niagara. the lieutenant governor would not allow them to visit Detroit, which was necessarily a restricted area in view of the potential hostilities between the two powers. Apparently, its defenses were very vulnerable, and Simcoe did not want the commissioners apprised of this.

The weather had been hot and sultry, and the patience of the commissioners was rapidly wearing thin from the oft-repeated warnings of personal harm that would come to them should the treaty fail. It was with considerable relief, therefore, that the Americans observed the arrival of the second Indian delegation on July 29. They were, however, unprepared for the crisis that soon befell them.

On July 30, the Indians with their British escorts and interpreters crossed the river for a meeting. They promptly set the tone of the ensuing negotiations by presenting the confederacy's written ultimatum. Taken aback by the altered circumstances, the commissioners hesitantly delayed their answer until the following day.[30] Then, on July 31, Timothy Pickering belatedly read what amounted to a declaration of United States policy, as represented by Knox's instructions.

The United States regarded the lands north of the Ohio that the various Indian tribes had sold in individual treaties after the Revolutionary War as valid acquisitions. Since those lands had since been resold to, and settled by, whites, it was "impossible to make the river Ohio the boundary," according to the commissioners. Due to "the great expenses" of the settlers in the new country and "the nature of their improvements," the land had become so valuable that it was entirely "impracticable" to remove these people. Thus the commissioners sought confirmation of the cession of lands to the United States by the Fort Harmar Treaty of 1789, plus "a small tract of land at the rapids of the Ohio, claimed by General [George Rogers] Clark."

The Americans earlier had stated to Brant's delegation that "concessions" were necessary on both sides. Thus, for their part, they would agree to negotiate a boundary, if necessary, between the already-sold land tracts and the boundary proclaimed by the Fort Harmar Treaty. Furthermore, they would acknowledge the Indians' right to the remaining soil north of the Ohio. "We only claim particular tracts in it," advised the commissioners, who also claimed that, by "the right of preemption," the United States could be the only future purchaser of lands north of the Ohio.

The "great point" that the United States conceded, then, was that the former American claim "to your whole country southward of the Great Lakes" would be limited to certain regions, and that the earlier post-Revolution treaty commissioners had thus "erroneously" interpreted the Treaty of Peace between Great Britain and the United States.[31]

On the morning of August 1, 1793, a grim and determined delegation of Indians and their British allies returned to Council. The notorious Simon Girty—"who cut a shocking figure," said the missionary John Heckewelder—was present to interpret for the Wyandot speaker So-wagh-da-wunk.

Claiming only that "this side [of the Ohio] is ours," and "you have your houses and people on our land," the Wyandot speaker asserted, "We cannot give up our land." "You may return whence you came and tell [President] Washington," he admonished.[33]

Immediately after that declaration, Matthew Elliott excitedly exclaimed, "No, no, they was not to have said [the last words]," and he appealed to the Shawnee war chief Kakiapalathy to agree there had been a mistake. Following a controversy over Girty's interpretation of the Wyandot's speech, Girty presented a new statement: "Instead of going home, we wish you to remain here for an answer from us. . . . We shall [again] consult our head warriors." The British intrigues to preserve the status quo peace were thus plainly evident.

The commissioners accordingly agreed to wait, provided the confederacy's answer was not excessively delayed.[33]

For the next two weeks the American dignitaries languished at Elliott's farm. The rain fell in torrents, and swarms of mosquitoes tormented the American party, despite remedies such as filling their tents with smoke.[34] Having been denied permission to travel to the Miami Rapids to establish

244

more expeditious communications, the commissioners by August 13 were so exasperated that they forwarded written queries to McKee and the Indian confederacy. Although they were keenly aware of the considerable frustration that was certainly building within the United States government and the army over the delay in forwarding a determination of peace or continued war, the commissioners could but wait impatiently, with taunts of their probable fate ringing in their ears from drunken Indians lingering about Elliott's house.[35]

At the Miami Rapids, meanwhile, the great controversy continued between the moderates led by the Six Nations and the more militant elements headed by the Shawnees, Miamis, and Delawares. Again a crisis had rapidly developed following the return of the second delegation. Joseph Brant, learning from the initial reaction of the Shawnee leadership that no peace treaty was likely, and believing the Six Nations' situation to be "unhealthy" at the Miami Rapids, told his tribesmen to begin packing to go home. On August 7 he refused to smoke the war pipe that was being circulated by the Creeks, pending the outcome of the peace negotiations. Then, two days later, he was "at last" accorded the right to address the assembled general council of nations.[36]

Sensing that the lingering prospects of a peace initiative rested on his personal efforts, Brant presented an effective and dramatic speech. He emphatically reminded the assembled throng that what he proposed—an Ohio River boundary modified by cession of the lands already settled by the whites (a line referred to as the Muskingum boundary)—was exactly the line that the confederacy had proposed two years earlier in discussions with Lord Dorchester. Brant reasoned that such a compromise was in the common interest and "far preferable to an uncertain war."

Although the chiefs of several nations came to him and expressed agreement with his views, Brant had overlooked a vital aspect of Indian affairs— the role of the British advisers. That night at twelve o'clock, Brant said, a "private meeting" was held by Alexander McKee with the confederacy's hierarchy, the Shawnees and their allies. In this meeting McKee strongly urged that the original Ohio boundary be maintained, and argued that the Americans were insisting on keeping too much of the Indians' country. Furthermore, proposed payment was to be in money, which was "useless" to the Indians. Evidently, he was implementing Simcoe's instructions to influence the Indians according to his (McKee's) perspective, and by private means.[37]

Brant, accordingly, was angered when on August 12, the Shawnee speaker Captain Johnny announced that the Ohio River must remain the final boundary. Although ultimately Brant was to protest McKee's involvement, saying "the advice of some whites" was overemphasized, it was evident on the twelfth that a final determination had been made.[39] The Six Nations immediately moved eight miles away, preparatory to returning east. Also, they refused to sign the resounding declaration that was sent to the American commissioners on August 13.[39]

This declaration was in the form of a reply to the commissioners' letter of July 31. Even to this day it endures as a classic statement of Indian rights, and is one of the more lucid and poignant documents of this turbulent era.

Recounting how the various tribes had attended the post-Revolution treaties to make peace, but instead had been intimidated into signing instruments of surrender that ceded vast tracts of Indian country, the confederacy's message disputed the United States' title to those lands. Cited was the long-standing decree by the confederacy that "a few chiefs of two or three nations only could not sell what was commonly owned by all." Repeated warnings against such divide-and-conquer tactics had been ignored by the United States.[40]

As for the prospect of receiving money in payment for the lands, the Indians proclaimed: "Money, to us is of no value . . . , and . . . no consideration whatever can induce us to sell the lands on which we get sustenance for our women and children." Instead, the confederacy suggested a unique way to resolve the issue: "We know that these [white] settlers are poor, or they would never have ventured to live in a country which has been in constant trouble ever since they crossed the Ohio. Divide therefore this large sum of money which you have offered to us among these people, . . . and we are persuaded they would most readily accept it in lieu of the lands you sold to them. If you add also the great sums you must expend in raising and paying armies with a view to force us to yield. . . . our country, you will certainly have more than sufficient for the purpose of repaying these settlers for all their labor and improvements."

Declaring that "we agreed to meet commissioners from the United States for the purpose of restoring peace, provided they consented to acknowledge and confirm our boundry line to be the Ohio," the Indian message concluded, "If you will not consent thereto, our meeting will be altogether unnecessary."[41]

On the afternoon of August 16 the American commissioners were pondering the effect of the several letters that they had dispatched to the Miami Rapids three days earlier when two "wild"-looking Wyandot "runners" arrived. According to John Heckewelder, these Indians merely presented the confederacy's written speech and promptly departed. A short while later a messenger was sent after them, asking the two Wyandots to return to carry the American answer back to the Miami Rapids council.[42]

As Benjamin Lincoln recorded in his journal, the entire business was now abruptly brought to an end. Heckewelder termed the Indian message "impertinent and insolent," and he reported that "the language . . . was such that no person having knowledge of the Indians and their modes of expression would believe it an Indian speech." "We saw quite plainly that the Indians were not allowed to act freely and independently," said Heckewelder, "but under the influence of evil advisers."[43]

In a brief message to the confederacy the American commissioners bluntly announced that, by virtue of the Ohio River ultimatum, "the negotiation is therefore at an end." Then they hastily began to load their belongings aboard the *Dunmore*. On the following morning all of the baggage and the official party were safely on board, and the vessel sailed for Fort Erie.

By August 21 the Americans were ashore at Fort Erie, and on August 23 multiple messengers were dispatched to Anthony Wayne with the coded message previously arranged by Henry Knox. "We did not effect a peace" were the key words announcing the unsuccessful result of the American peace mission. This message gave full authority "for vigorous offensive operation" by the army.[44]

At the Miami Rapids council site the Six Nations had been persuaded to attend one last meeting to conclude any remaining official business. Here, in a brief but forceful speech, Brant addressed the general council almost as an outsider, delivering his long-withheld rebuttal with a measured sarcasm: "Since the council is now over and you are come to a final resolution, we hope success will attend you," decried the impassioned Brant. "At this time it is not in our power to assist you. We must first remove our people from among the Americans."

Brant's announcement reflected the bitter consequences and ineffectiveness of the moderates' quest for peace, which was substantially ended. The breach between the Iroquois and the western tribes had now reached the point of physical rupture. "From the great divisions amongst us," Brant wrote in his explanation to Simcoe, "unanimity by no means prevail[s], without which the Indians, it cannot be expected, will do much."[45]

Brant's and Simcoe's perspectives thus coincided on one crucial point: the need for Indian unanimity. Yet, because many among the Six Nations were exposed geographically, being surrounded on American soil by substantial white settlements, they expressed a great reluctance to endure another ruinous war. Increasingly apparent was an attitude on the part of Brant, as reported by McKee, that both Great Britain and the United States were "actuated by a regard to self interest," and that the Americans, having beaten the British during the late war, were now the "great power on the continent."[46]

Unfortunately, the entire situation had been distorted. By formal instruction of Secretary of War Knox, the American terms could not possibly have been altered to accommodate even the moderate claims of the Six Nations. "You are to understand, explicitly," Knox had written to the commissioners before their original departure, "that the United States cannot relinquish any of the tracts of land which they have already granted [sold]."[47] Thus the debate over the Ohio versus the Muskingum boundary was a moot point. If formal treaty negotiations had begun, that would have been readily apparent. Ironically, however, because there had been no direct political confrontation with the white enemy, the Indian confederacy had suffered the worst possible consequence of any negotiations with the whites—disunion. While Brant and other Six Nations leaders continued doggedly to seek "an honorable peace" based on the Muskingum boundary ultimately they had been prepared for war with the Americans, should such efforts fail; "If that [boundary] could not be obtained we were resolved to join with our western brethren in trying the fortune of war," Brant later wrote.[48]

The loss that the Six Nations represented to the Indian confederacy was evident not only numerically and in the more limited scope of the war but also in the political realm. Lieutenant Governor Simcoe, observing that Brant was regarded as a traitor by the "Western Indians," began to fear a Six Nation–United States alliance. Thereafter, a new distrust of Indian motives seemed to prevail in the minds of the British leaders. Simcoe said that Brant had made "his power to be the subject of just alarm, and that it is necessary by degrees and on just principles that it should be diminished."[49]

If they had any doubts that British intrigue in Indian matters was to be deplored, the Indian confederacy had but to ponder the consequences of their two-year moratorium on major offensive operations due to the false prospect of peace. Whereas their capacity for war had remained static, and perhaps even had diminished because of the alienation of the Six Nations, American military capability had increased enormously. No longer vulnerable on an exposed and overextended frontier, the United States strategy of political delay and military preparation had succeeded even beyond expectation. Instead of being committed in 1791 to the defense of a languishing frontier with depleted troops who were poorly equipped and supplied, the expanded and well-trained United States Army could now operate from strength on an offensive footing.

Yet in late April, 1793, the festive aftermath of the recent council at the Miami Rapids was recorded by Joseph Brant: "When the council was over a war feast was prepared. The Chiefs of the Shawnees [then sang] the war song, encouraging the warriors of all nations to be active in defending their country, saying their father, the English would assist them—and pointed to Colonel McKee."[50]

25

A Test of Initiative

ANTHONY WAYNE spent a rather uneventful first week of September, 1793. A "parade" on the eighth, complete with battle maneuvers and the firing of blank ammunition, had accounted for much of the week's activities.[1] On September 11, however, the innocuous routine of army life at Wayne's Hobson's Choice encampment was abruptly altered when William Wells, the repatriated former Miami warrior, arrived at Fort Jefferson, exhausted after a four-day journey from the Miami Rapids region. Wells had been sent under a white flag by Lieutenant Colonel Hamtramck in July to attempt to attend the grand Indian council as an American "emissary." Actually, he had been a highly paid "confidential agent" whose mission was to gather vital intelligence on Indian activities.

After proceeding to the locale of his former Indian residence, Wells allegedly had attended some of the councils, but he had also relied on information suppled to him by John Kinzie, a silversmith and Indian trader at the Miami Rapids. Learning in early September of the breakdown in peace negotiations and the prospect of a war gathering at the Auglaize villages later that month, Wells had hastened south to Fort Jefferson with this important information. Although news of the failed conference arrived simultaneously by express boat from Pittsburgh on September 11, in the form of the pre-arranged message dispatched by the American commissioners, Wayne relied heavily on Wells's account.[2]

At last vindicated in his hard-line attitude, Wayne immediately issued orders that "the Legion must be in perfect readiness to march at a moment's warning." The forty-eight-year-old army commander anticipated with relish the rapid development of an offensive campaign against the "haughty savages." While the army proceeded to divest itself of all extraneous and heavy baggage, with great anxiety Wayne ordered the procurement of mounted volunteers from Kentucky. Under the venerable Charles Scott, they were to be present at Fort Jefferson by the first of October, which was only two weeks away. To Knox, Wayne confidently wrote, "We might yet compel those haughty savages to sue for peace before the next opening of the leaves."[3]

Yet Wayne was to be bitterly disappointed. Within the span of a few weeks, in fact, he was so distraught that he had to reimplement a defensive strategy. Incredibly, the commanding general suddenly found the frustrations of the past summer returning to haunt him. In rapid succession, the health of his army greatly declined (due to smallpox and influenza), an expected resupply of vital war materiel was delayed in transit by garbled communications, the auxiliary force of Kentuckians arrived drastically under-strength, and the provisions at the head of the line were found to be so inadequate that they belied support of the army.[4]

The crowning blow in Wayne's forlorn effort to mount an offensive was only perceived after the army's arrival at "the head of the line," Fort Jeffer-son—which they reached October 13. Wayne had marched from Hobson's Choice on October 7, averaging about seven miles a day in fine autumn weather. After he arrived at the end of the wide road that he had ordered cut late in May—which had reached a point six miles beyond Fort Jefferson—the major general was compelled to halt when he found that the deposit at Fort Jefferson was not more than one-quarter of what had been previously ordered. Furthermore, the means of transport "was not half equal to the supply of the troops even at Fort Jefferson."

Wayne was livid. Despite the liability of the army's private contractors to supply adequate provisions and the means of their transport, he angrily ordered his quartermaster general to utilize his whole force to supply the army with flour and other rations. Until this matter of logistics was corrected, reasoned Wayne, he would be compelled to remain in place.[5]

Actually Wayne's difficulties with logistics were traceable, in part, to his own earlier actions. Although he had ordered considerable "preparatory arrangements" in May, June, and July, involving the procurement of sixty days' rations for the entire army laid in at Fort Jefferson, by early August he had been forced to countermand those orders. This procurement activity had so alarmed the Indians regarding an imminent offensive that the summer's peace negotiations were seriously jeopardized. Due to Brant's and the other Indians' complaints, Henry Knox on July 20 had unequivocally ordered Wayne to cease and desist in any activity that could be construed as a breach of the temporary truce. Furthermore, Wayne was told to "instantly with-draw" any surplus troops beyond the nominal garrisons at the advanced posts and generally to maintain an inactive posture.[6]

Accordingly, early in August, following receipt of Knox's letter, Wayne had ordered the withdrawal of nearly 200 soldiers deemed in excess at the forward posts and the transfer of "all the wagon teams and pack horses in the quartermaster general's and contractors employ" to his Hobson's Choice camp.[7] In early August, Elliot and Williams, the private contractors for 1793 and 1794, had "just got into [full] operation" by increasing their means of transport to accommodate Wayne's demands. Unfortunately for Wayne, due to the sudden moratorium pending results of the treaty, the contractors had subsequently reduced their large packhorse herd, which was expensive to feed and maintain.[8] Accordingly, the minimal surplus in rations that had been built up during the early summer months was reduced by late August to only a ten days' supply of flour at Fort Jefferson. Also, there was such a scarcity of beef that the garrison was said to be "in a starving condition."[9]

Wayne damned the intrigues of the British for upsetting his plans and preparations. In a mildly abrasive letter to Knox, he complained that "some confidence ought to have been placed in my honor as well as conduct" to allow him discretionary latitude in providing for the army. Wayne could offer little excuse, however, for another serious impairment of his logistic operations that occurred on October 17.[10]

Led by their war chief, Little Otter, a band of Ottawas from the mouth of the Maumee River had journeyed toward the Auglaize villages about October 1. Their arrival there nearly coincided with a report, brought in by Indian scouts, of Wayne's advance. The report was later carried to the British on October 15.

Gathering a war party of about forty warriors, Little Otter proceeded immediately to the vicinity of Fort Jefferson, intent on creating as much havoc as possible in the enemy's midst. On October 14, Little Otter's party confirmed the presence of the entire American army, which had advanced a few miles beyond Fort Jefferson. Then they moved south to operate against the army's vital supply line.[11]

On the morning of October 17, at sunrise, Little Otter's war party lay in ambush at Twenty-nine Mile Creek, seven miles north of Fort St. Clair, on the army road to Fort Jefferson.

The United States Military convoy, in the charge of Lieutenant John Lowry of the Second Sub Legion, had left Fort St. Clair that morning with twenty wagonloads of Indian corn and one of contractor's stores. With the escort of about 90 infantrymen, approximately 120 men were present, enough to provide a false sense of security.

The weather was clear and frosty. Lowry's men apparently were strung out in a random and irregular column. When suddenly fired upon by Little Otter's warriors in the gray of morning, most of the detachment panicked. A survivor later told his captors that of the estimated two dozen men who stood to fight all were killed or captured. The remainder fled at the first fire. Ten prisoners were taken alive, and the ground was later found littered with the corpses of fifteen soldiers, including Lowry and another officer who had fought bravely.

In the booty captured by Little Otter's party were about seventy horses, removed from wagons and driven off, and all the stores and baggage in the convoy. Because of the nature of the shipment—corn—and the Indians' inability to remove the wagons, they were left standing in the road, where a relief detachment from Fort Jefferson recovered the forage nearly intact and brought it in several days later.[12]

Although Wayne dismissed the incident as "a little check to one of our convoys which may probably be exaggerated into something serious," Little Otter's sortie was of much greater significance because it demonstrated to Wayne the utter vulnerability of his extended supply system. The American major general was soon compelled to commit larger quantities of troops to the protection of these vital convoys. Later Wayne admitted that his serious logistic difficulties were largely responsible for his ordering a general encampment at the advanced site, soon named Greeneville in honor of his comrade in the Revolution, Nathaniel Greene.[13]

Wayne's rationale in encamping for the winter "at the head of the line" was either to provoke the enemy into attacking his fortified army, or else to restrict their offensive initiative by the threatening proximity of his troops. "[Our] position will soon compel the enemy to give us battle—or to disperse and abandon Au Glaize," he confidently proclaimed. "In either of those events a post will be established at that place at an early period."[14]

Amazingly, Wayne, an acknowledged proponent of enterprise and audacity, had all but ignored the obvious: his army's extended supply lines not only enhanced the enemy's capacity to wage a successful war of attrition but also afforded the Legion little opportunity to interdict the red raiders. The Indians had greater mobility and familiarity with the wilderness terrain, and as Little Otter had dramatically illustrated with a minimal contingent, Wayne's advanced encampment was most vulnerable logistically. Simply by killing or driving off additional numbers of the already-depleted packhorse herd, the Indians might starve the inadequately provisioned army into mutiny or dispersal.

The crucial war initiative hung in the balance. Although the Indians' capability was undiminished, the question was whether they would perceive their advantage and press an attack.

Wayne, frustrated by his static situation, in fact, already had been tempted into a further indiscretion. Due to the favorable mild weather late in October, he resolved to employ his mounted Kentucky volunteers in a raid against "a small town of Delawares" near the headwaters of the White River. By sending the Kentuckians forth, he hoped to quiet the budding disaffection in their ranks and retain some semblance of offensive operations.[15]

Brigadier General Charles Scott was ordered to march on November 4. Yet nearly half of his 980 men mutinied on receipt of these orders, most fleeing south to Kentucky in outright desertion. On the morning of the fifth only 488 mounted volunteers remained, and a disappointed Scott glumly reported to Wayne that he doubted that he could accomplish much.

Scott's prophecy proved to be entirely accurate. After little more than a meaningless journey through the woods Scott's men recrossed the Ohio at Fort Washington on November 14 and went home without so much as killing a single Indian.[16]

Wayne's army, minus his auxiliary force, was now reduced to the understrength regular establishment, which was soon even more widely dispersed in attempting to protect vital communications. At the beginning of the forward move on October 5 the Legion had numbered about 2,600 effectives. Yet the ravages of disease and expiring terms of service by mid-November seriously depleted the ranks. Damning the imposed reliance on auxiliaries, such as had recently failed him in the hour of need, Wayne fumed at the minimal force to which his army of conquest was now reduced. "Let the Legion be completed [to full strength]," he pleaded.[17]

While the army languished at its Greeneville encampment, morale sagged to a low ebb. "I am sick of everything and almost everybody around me," wrote a disgruntled army major. Rations were reduced to a minimal level and became the source of constant complaints and desertions. Clothing was so scarce that Wayne acknowledged "the greater part of the troops are nearly naked." Bickering between officers, especially of junior grades, was so frequent that an observer reported that fifteen duels had been fought within the Legion over the span of a single year. "There was the most quarreling, jargon, and confusion throughout the whole Legion that I ever knew in any army," wrote a veteran of the Revolution.[18]

Wayne, ill-tempered and afflicted with painful attacks of gout, seemed increasingly unpredictable and capricious. On one occasion he arbitrarily confirmed the death penalty imposed on two soldiers found sleeping while on sentry duty, after having just spared the life of a private who allegedly had led a retreat in the face of an enemy patrol.[19]

Soon reports of the major general's "despotic" behavior, "feeble" judgment, "irascible" temper, and "indecent and abusive" language were leaked to newspapers by a growing anti-Wayne faction. The commander was said to be vindictive to the point of deliberately purging his suspected detractors from the Legion on trumped-up charges.[20]

Admittedly, Wayne was foundering in his attempt to maintain a limited offensive status. "I am at a loss to determine what the savages are about, and where they are," he admitted to Knox in mid-November.[21]

To complicate the already-difficult situation, three enlisted men, two of them former deserters, defected to the enemy on the night of November 12, 1793. The accurate and significant intelligence that they willfully supplied was of compelling interest to the Indians and the British. John Watkins, spokesman for the deserters, testified that Wayne's army had been reduced to less than 2,500 men since the Kentucky militiamen had gone home. The troops were building winter quarters, and the cavalry, except for an escort of about fifty men, had been sent to Kentucky, he reported. Most significant, however, was Watkins's estimate that at the time of his departure there were "not more than 18 or 20 days" provisions on hand for the army. "The loss of their horses, taken by the Indians, and by death, has occasioned the scarcity and delayed the movements of the army," Watkins continued, adding that "it was owing to the smallness of the ration" that the three men had deserted.[22]

Accurate information about Wayne's plight thus was put directly in Indian hands. The certain knowledge that crucial convoys must immediately operate over the tenuous seventy-mile route, to supply the depleted and discouraged Legion, afforded the natives an obvious opportunity for a major triumph.

Wayne was compelled to order a heavily escorted convoy of unladen packhorses back to Fort Washington on November 13 to bring up crucial supplies and provisions. Every "public"-owned horse in the camp, including those in the possession of officers, was to be delivered to the quartermaster. The importance of this convoy was made more apparent by the assignment of Bridgadier General James Wilkinson to its command. Wilkinson was to take with him nearly 500 infantrymen as escorts—eleven companies in all—and most of the few remaining cavalrymen.[23]

Further compounding this admittedly "arduous and dangerous business," the weather had turned intensely cold and stormy. Wilkinson, en route, sent back word in late November of his "great embarrassment from crazy teams and bad roads." The snow was falling heavily, and bitter cold weather plagued his efforts at speed. At Greeneville a concerned officer recorded in his journal how they expected daily to hear that Wilkinson had been attacked by Indians.[24]

In late October, Alexander McKee had been so apprehensive of an American advance to his Miami Rapids storehouse that he had abandoned that site and had withdrawn to the mouth of the Maumee River for safety. By November 2, however, McKee had returned to the Miami Rapids, where he found that no news of an American advance had been received.[25]

Throughout October continual warnings of the American army's imminent approach had poured in from Indian scouts. Frequent messages urging the lake-region tribes immediately to assemble and oppose the American advance had simultaneously gone forth into the northern country. By the first week in November, Potawatomis, Ottawas, and Chippewas had passed McKee's storehouse, going forward to defend the Auglaize villages. Urgently requested gunpowder and lead shot, forwarded to McKee from Detroit late in October, was received and distributed to these war parties. In fact, so many supplies had gone forth to the Indians from Detroit in a new large boat built for the British Indian Department that a military storekeeper had christened the boat *Indian Feeder* (though it was soon renamed *The Shawanese*.)[26]

On November 7, McKee learned that the Americans were six miles beyond Fort Jefferson, where they had "encamped and entrenched." A few weeks later he had certain intelligence of the United States Army's dire want of provisions. Here obviously was the Indians' great opportunity.[27]

Yet, confronted by conflicting accounts of the Americans' strength and situation, the Indians' resolution had waned. Large bodies of warriors had "scattered and gone hunting farther off than they ever used to," McKee wrote. His journal entry for November 14, 1793, adequately reflected the decisive turn of events: "The Potawatomis have all returned home from a belief that the Americans do not intend to come on this winter, so that the numbers who are left to oppose this army are small indeed."[28]

Scattered in small parties over a vast country, their villages exposed to raids from a nearby enemy, and faced with the imminent close of river navigation for the year, the Indians of the Auglaize region could only ponder a familiar, gnawing question: Had they secured enough provisions of their own to last through the winter?

James Wilkinson's return to the Greeneville encampment on December 2 was heralded by considerable excitement. Despite the adverse weather his convoy had come through safely. The only Indian contact had occurred when two furloughed officers, travelling in advance of the main column, were fired on by a small war party. Yet, because of the long journey of nineteen days, the horses had consumed so much of the bulk forage that it was immediately necessary to start another convoy for Fort Washington. Since the road was uncontested by Indians, Wayne expressed little concern about this second convoy's safety. Indeed, 800 head of cattle and about 800 packhorses loaded with clothing, salt, flour, and corn arrived intact at Greeneville on December 22. The escort had not seen a single Indian.[29]

Wayne, relieved of his pressing logistics problems, by now had his army comfortably ensconced in winter quarters. Their camps had six fourteen-foot huts to a company and were complete with bakehouses and ovens. Moreover, the whole encampment was enclosed by an enormous stockade.[30]

Confronted by adversity of a serious and limiting nature, Wayne had persevered in his resolve to maintain an offensive footing. It was his conviction that he who seizes the initiative at a time of relative inertia has the greatest prospect of success. Such an adversary, unintimidated by adversity, augured ill for the Indian confederacy.

In fact, on the day following the receipt of the crucial December 22 convoy of provisions, Wayne initiated a bold "maneuver" that was designed to pave the way for a spring offensive. During the past few months he had resolved to occupy and fortify the site of St. Clair's defeat in 1791, which was about twenty-three miles from the Greeneville encampment. Occupying the old battlefield represented a political expediency, an opportunity perhaps to alter the complexion of the war by seizing the very ground where the Indians had shown their prowess. Furthermore, the movement would establish a forward base to be utilized in an early spring advance against the Indians.[31]

On December 23, Wayne, with eight companies of infantry and a detachment of artillerymen, began a rapid march overland toward the site of the bloody former defeat. Their arrival on Christmas Day, 1793, marked the beginning of a new phase in the Indian War begun in 1790—that of strategic momentum.

Wayne, who had been sick during much of the past month, had declined to partake of a lavish Christmas dinner offered by the Wilkinsons at Fort Jefferson. Instead, in the company of his soldiers, he pitched his tent that night on the cold, skeleton-strewn ground and endured the rigors of the season.

All about the awed and benumbed soldiers lay the debris of the disaster, including a variety of abandoned army muskets—most of which were broken off at the breech by the Indians, their barrels bent double, and the locks stripped from the stock. So many bones littered the site—many still held together by the sinews, although the flesh had completely rotted away—that one observer wrote that they had to scrape these grisly remains together in a pile to have room to place their tents. Here, under the same sprawling oak tree where he had left him in 1791, Captain Edward Butler found the remains of his brother Richard, identified by a broken and mended thigh bone, an injury that Richard had sustained at an earlier age.

On the following morning all the remains, including an estimated four to six hundred skull bones, were "piously" interred by a detachment. Meanwhile, other soldiers began constructing the fortification ordered by Wayne.[32]

Formed of sturdy timbers, many of which bore the scars of battle from November, 1791, this small four-blockhouse structure was soon enclosed by a fifteen-foot stockade, and the ground for a thousand feet around the fort was cleared of large trees to provide a clear field of fire. Wayne was so pleased by the construction that he termed the single-story fort "impervious to savage force." Apparently, he was referring to such refinements as doors and shutters that were proof against musket balls and multiple embrasures for artillery.[33]

Most significantly, Wayne sought to utilize a unique defense that was already present on the ground. In October 1792, William May, the spy who had been sent in the guise of deserter to discover the fate of Alexander Trueman during April, 1792, had returned from Canada with substantial information on enemy activities. While a captive of the Indians, May had passed through St. Clair's 1791 field of battle, where, he had been told, the cannon taken during that fight had been buried nearby. Unable to move the eight heavy guns through the wilderness, the red warriors had disassembled the gun tubes and hidden them nearby. The field guns, one a six-pounder that May had been allowed to examine personally, lay in an adjacent creek. Three others, "given to Simon Girty by the Wyandots," were buried under a hollow tree across the Wabash, "just at the rising of the hill," May said.

Since the creek and ground had been heavily frozen during Wilkinson's reconnaissance of the site in February, 1792, the guns had remained undisturbed. Now, in December, 1793, May's presence and the favorable weather permitted the rapid location and recovery of three of the eight cannon. Cleaned and remounted by Wayne's Legionnaires, the guns served to fire a nine-volley salute upon the activation of the new outpost, which was named Fort Recovery by Wayne. Then, on December 28, the detachment returned to Greeneville, without having seen a single Indian. One company of riflemen with a company of artillerists were left behind to garrison the fort. On New Year's Day, 1794, Wayne celebrated his newest adventure with a munificent banquet at Fort Jefferson that included such delicacies as roast mutton, plum pudding, and ice cream.[34]

The advent of the new year 1794, according to Anthony Wayne, represented a most fortuitous occasion. To the bold general a "present, golden favorable opportunity" existed, whereby the Legion might easily advance "while the wide deep swamps are strongly frozen over" and strike the enemy with great effect. Yet on January 11 a lone Delaware warrior, accompanied by the British Indian trader Robert Wilson, arrived at Greeneville bearing aloft a white flag. This Indian, a messenger, promptly explained that he had been sent to learn if the Americans were "yet willing to treat." The Ottawas and Delawares of this band, said the warrior, were tired of the war and wanted to make peace.[35]

Wayne, although genuinely suspicious of a possible Indian stratagem, was taken aback by this "extraordinary embassy." Believing "[it] is in consequence of our sudden and unexpected possession of General St. Clair's field of battle," he decided to offer the Indians an opportunity to bury the war hatchet "so deep that it can never again be found." Accordingly, on January 14 he decreed that "the Indians must give adequate proof of their peaceful intent within thirty days." Specifically, he demanded that they deliver "every American or white prisoner now in your possession to the officer commanding at Fort Recovery." Thereafter a peace treaty might be arranged.[36]

After dispatching the Indian messenger back to his village on Janaury 14, Wayne informed Knox that he could not in good conscience "take new ground until after the expiration of the thirty days."[37]

To the multitude of dispirited and now starving Indians of the Auglaize region the winter of 1793–94 had brought incalculable hardship. Because of the "continual alarms" of the previous fall the annual distribution of British "presents" had been minimal, and an unusually mild December had worked against the Indian trappers. "[The Indians] by the failure of their usual hunts have almost been in a starving condition," wrote a British official in mid-January, 1794. Indeed, because of the lingering despair of the Indians, virtually all of the Detroit-based British Indian Department officers remained in "the Miamis Country" during the midwinter.[38]

Although the mid-January Delaware peace offer was viewed with much concern by the British Indian agents, it was quickly learned that only a small portion of the Delawares had resolved to act independently. The chiefs of the Shawnees, in particular, would have little to do with any talk of capitulation, and the matter was thus allowed quietly to terminate.[39]

Since the Indians were plagued with inordinate difficulties in obtaining subsistence, their plans to waylay troops and convoys passing between the forts had not been implemented. During midwinter 1793–94 several British agents reported that the disarray and frustration among the Indians seemed to be at a new height. Indeed, they surmised that the Americans would have little difficulty in occupying the Miami country almost at will, perhaps even taking Detroit.[40]

Anthony Wayne, writing to Henry Knox in March, 1794, confided, "We have neither heard from or seen an enemy" since mid-January. Since this was evidence that the Indians were not seriously intent on peace, Wayne considered that the "true object" of the Delaware flag of truce had been "to gain time and to reconnoiter." "There is something, however, rather mysterious in the present conduct of the savages . . . —they have not committed any murder or depredations since that period," Wayne mused.[41]

Believing strong action was now necessary, the American major general announced, "I am determined to establish a strong post on the banks of the Auglaize [which] will most certainly bring the business to a speedy issue." The proximity of this post to the Indian villages would compel the enemy to fight or abandon their country, and he foresaw that the former event would be most likely.[42]

To facilitate this advanced fortification, Wayne planned to utilize water transportation. Thus he only awaited favorable weather to continue in his application of relentless, if gradual, pressure on what he considered to be an arrogant enemy.[43]

In a letter to Knox Wayne exulted, "I shall [soon] bring those haughty savages to a speedy explanation." His remark was as revealing as it was befitting of the increasingly confident commander of the suddenly imposing United States Legion.[44]

26

Facts Are Stubborn Things

SIR Guy Carleton, Lord Dorchester, was a man of less than imposing physical stature. Although tall, the aging Canadian governor-general was thin and austere in appearance. In 1794 he was nearly seventy and suffered from various infirmities. Yet there burned within the soul of this Irish-born veteran soldier a dogged combativeness that caused one critic to assess him as "probably the ablest British general in America."[1]

Less flamboyant and more orthodox in style that Anthony Wayne, Dorchester, nonetheless, was a capable administrator, and he was convinced that the weakness of Canada's military establishment was all too apparent. "Four thousand men should be sent to enable Canada to make a tolerable defense in case the Americans should attack," he wrote shortly before his return from England in August, 1793.[2] While he believed "all measures hostile to the [United] States [to be] highly inexpedient" because of his colony's unfavorable strategic situation, when Dorchester returned to Canada in late September, he was met by a crisis of burgeoning proportions. Indeed, after the failure of the Miami Rapids Indian council to reach a peaceful accord with the Americans, Dorchester became increasingly apprehensive of widespread war.[3]

The border difficulties with New York, Pennsylvania, and Vermont had intensified due to several ugly incidents, of which not the least was the threatened occupation of Presque Isle on Lake Erie (modern-day Erie, Pennsylvania) by the Pennsylvania militia. This caused Dorchester to order immediate preparations to place the Canadian defenses on a limited war footing.[4]

Particularly obnoxious to Dorchester was the "impudence" of the Americans. "They now impudently tell the commandant [at Lake Champlain] that his jurisdiction extends no further than his guns," he fumed. Being further angered by "Mr. Wayne's intention to close us up at Detroit," he proceeded like a man who was bristling with indignation.[5]

On February 10, 1794, Dorchester greeted a Six Nations delegation, who were sent to learn of his views on British Indian policy (following his recent journey to England), with a spontaneous and emotional "speech." "From the manner in which the people of the [United] States push on, and act, and talk on this side, and from what I learn of their conduct towards the sea, I shall not be surprised if we are at war with them in the course of the present year," he proclaimed. "We have acted in the most peaceable manner, and . . . with patience, but I believe our patience is almost exhausted."[6]

Sir Guy Carleton (Lord Dorchester), the able but frustrated British governor general. Courtesy of William Clements Library, University of Michigan.

This was possibly the most outspoken British colonial declaration of the postwar years. Soon being widely publicized it created an immediate furor. Indeed, to the very people Dorchester had sought to avoid provoking upon his return from England the speech was inflammatory in the extreme. It came as an added contradiction to several British orders-in-council dating back to June and November 1793, which had severely restricted United States shipping and commerce. (The orders had ruled that all ships of neutrals during the existing war with France were liable to capture if found carrying enemy-owned goods, and that the lucrative West Indian trade would be denied Americans by virtue of the "rule of 1756," which stated that a trade closed in time of peace could not be opened in a time of war.) Dorchester's statements threw the American people "into a flame," confided George Washington. "The aggressions of Britain have increased to a height to silence the voice of her friends, or nearly so," raged James Monroe. Thomas Jefferson spoke of the "kicks and cuffs Great Britain has been giving us."[7]

Within a few months measures were adopted in Congress placing a temporary embargo on all ships in United States ports to prevent them from proceeding to foreign destinations, providing for fortification of the principal seaports, and raising sufficient artillerymen to man those defenses. Other measures for expanding the regular army and prohibiting the importation of British goods were narrowly defeated.[8]

Yet Washington remained level-headed in the storm of indignation that followed Dorchester's remarks. Considering that the attitude of the British ministry might have mellowed since their original instructions to the Canadian governor-general, Washington proposed a special envoy to resolve all difficulties "in a temperate way by fair and firm negotiation." On April 6 the name of John Jay, chief justice of the United States, was sent to the Senate for confirmation as this envoy. Departing for England in May, 1794, Jay proceeded with a reputation for "good sense and judgment," though he was also a man of outspoken manner and excessive vanity. "If he succeeds, well," wrote Washington at the time. "If he does not, why, knowing the worst, we must take measures accordingly."[9]

To those people most directly affected by the long crisis, the Indians, Dorchester's dramatic speech represented the most cherished of gifts— renewed hope.

On learning of Dorchester's comments, Joseph Brant prophesied, "Matters will take an immediate change to the westward, as it will undoubtedly give those nations high spirits and enable them . . . to check General Wayne if he advances any further." Men such as the veteran Indian agent Alexander McKee were ecstatic in their reports of the effect of the governor-general's remarks. "The face of the Indian affairs in this country, I have the greatest satisfaction to inform you, seems considerably altered for the better," wrote McKee in early May. "His Excellency Lord Dorchester's Speech . . . induce[s] me to believe that a very extensive union of the Indian nations will be the immediate consequence."[10]

Although the red nations had endured a particularly bitter and impoverished winter, the spring of 1794 had brought a radical change that foreshadowed the creation of an imposing and effective native military force.

Even more ultimately meaningful were the British actions that implemented the new war-preparedness policy. Infusing substance into his remarks of February 10, Dorchester, a week later, forwarded instructions to Lieutenant Governor Simcoe providing for Detroit's security. "Self-defense" requires that "we should occupy nearly the same posts on the Miami [Maumee] River which we demolished after the peace [of 1783]," wrote Dorchester. "You will therefore order such [regular British military] force from Detroit to the Miamis River, with the artillery requisite for that service."[11] Simcoe was allowed to use his discretion in finding "the most advantageous position" for a reconstructed fortification. He was also empowered to arm all ships and vessels in the govenment service.

Since it had long been the practice to defend Detroit at a forward site chosen for its tactical advantages, Dorchester's mandate reflected the perspective and former advice of Alexander McKee, who in June, 1791, had advised his superior, Sir John Johnston, as follows:

In case of the approach of an army the safety of the King's post of Detroit does require that troops should occupy a distant station, and without such aid the post and country will be in immediate danger of falling by surprise. The station . . . I conceive to be the most proper and advantageous is the Foot of the Miami Rapids or its vicinity. The number of troops to be posted there ought not to be less than 100 regulars and 50 militia, in a small work of sod or pickets. In time of danger during the late war posts were found expedient both at this place and the Miami Towns, and should never have been evacuated as long as Detroit was an object of preserving, for in respect thereof these places are the key to it."[12]

McKee's ideas thus were the basis of the govenor-general's orders to Lieutenant Governor Simcoe in 1794.

Before proceeding to Detroit late in March, an uncertain Simcoe confided: "There appears to me to be little doubt but that the possession of these posts will be construed into hostility [by the United States]. Whether such shall immediately take effect may depend upon the temper of General Wayne, and his force.[13]

Accordingly, Simcoe was particularly active in the execution of his orders, considering it "of great moment" that the fort be erected before Wayne's army should approach. By April 10 the lieutenant governor was on the site at the Miami Rapids, directing the physical layout of the fort, which was located on the west bank of the Maumee River. This site was readily accessible to reinforcement by river from the north, and yet it controlled the approaches from the south strategically.[14]

One hundred and twenty regulars of the Twenty-fourth Regiment, together with a detachment of the Royal Artillery, were ordered forth from Detroit on April 18 to serve as a garrison. Eight cannon, including four nine- and four six-pounders, were designated for the fort upon its completion.

After his departure from the area on April 18, Simcoe wrote to Dorchester about the Miami fort's establishment, saying that, if Wayne left Fort Miamis in his rear and advanced against Detroit, he would expose his communications for sixty miles or more. For that reason Simcoe had directed that the fort's cannon were to "be of larger caliber than what Mr. Wayne can bring against it."[15]

Constructed under the direction of Lieutenant Robert Pilkington of the Royal Engineers, Fort Miamis gradually assumed shape, despite a lack of intrenching tools and workmen. Throughout June the "gunboats" *Brazen* and *Spitfire* made repeated trips from Detroit with provisions and materials. In early July, Pilkington reported that the fort consisted of an elevated parapet of earth, completely fraised and surrounded by a ditch, with logs twelve inches thick forming part of the rampart. By late July, Colonel Richard G. England at Detroit had routinely reported to Simcoe that all the designated cannon had been forwarded and at least four guns were already mounted.

Simcoe's orders also had provided for the activation of supporting establishments: a log stockade on Turtle Island in Maumee Bay, a post at the Raisin River, and a "corporal's guard" at Roche de Bout, which was south of Fort Miamis on the Maumee River. All of those projects had been implemented by July.[16] In early August, Simcoe, who had begun the project about ninety days earlier, boldly announced in a letter to the Home Office in London, "The fort at the Miamis is in a complete state of defense."[17]

To the astonished American officials, who learned of it in mid-May, the construction of Fort Miamis was a premeditated act of aggression. Dorchester's speech only "forbodes hostility," protested the newly installed American Secretary of State, Edmund Randolph, in a scorching letter to the British ambassador, George Hammond, while "the intelligence which has been received this morning [of the building of Fort Miamis] is . . . hostility itself." "This possession of our acknowledged territory has no pretext of statu[s] quo on its side; it has no pretext at all," fumed Randolph. "It is an act . . . calculated to support an enemy whom we are seeking to bring to peace. . . . Our honor and safety require that an invasion shall be expelled."[18]

Anthony Wayne, who learned of Simcoe's activities about the same time, was vehement in his anger: "Would to God that early and proper means had been adopted by Congress for the completion of the Legion," wrote the American commander on May 30. "I would not at this late hour have to call for militia auxiliaries from Kentucky, who may not have a relish to meet this hydra now preparing to attack us" (the heterogeneous army composed of British regular troops, the militia of Detroit, and all the hostile Indians northwest of the Ohio). Wayne reflected that he was "placed in a very delicate and disagreeable situation; the very quarter which I wish to strike at—ie. the center of the hostile tribes—the British are now in possession of."[19]

As if Wayne's intensifying military problems were not enough, he was burdened by strategic difficulties that threatened to alter the entire complexion of the war. At this inopportune time the diplomatic offensive, which was supposed to prevent the Six Nations from actively joining the hostile tribes, suddenly and dramatically dwindled to the point of outright failure.

In October, 1793, the Six Nations under Brant's leadership had petitioned the American government about the acceptability of the Muskingum modification of the Ohio River boundary. (Subsequently, this moderate Indian element had been alienated in a series of councils at Buffalo Creek with American negotiators.)[20]

262

Joseph Brant was so indignant over the "fraudulent conduct towards us," by individuals who had purchased large parcels of land from a few Indians, that he expressed unwillingness to engage in any further carefully managed treaties promoting American objectives. "Our patience is now exhausted," he proclaimed, and therefore the Six Nations would make no further efforts to bring about peace.[21]

Blaming this supposed change in attitude largely on Dorchester's "inflammatory speech" of February 10, the American agent, Israel Chapin, soon reflected that the entire New York frontier "was very much alarmed at the present appearance of war" involving the Six Nations as British allies. "Destitute of arms and ammunition, the scattered inhabitants of this remote wilderness would fall an easy prey to their savage neighbors," he said. Chapin could only recommend that the United States give the Indians more presents as a means of keeping the Six Nations peaceful.[22]

Already Brant and other leaders were secretly directing a concentration of the Six Nations tribes with the intention of improving their operational capability. The disunion fostered at the 1793 Miami Rapids Grand Council seemed to be on the verge of resolution as the Six Nations later in the spring of 1794 appeared at last to be aligning themselves with the interests of the general confederacy. The dreaded combination which filled the American populace with the greatest fear seemed about to be realized, auguring perhaps an expanding international war.

Presque Isle on the southern shore of Lake Erie was a site long recognized for its strategic advantage. Both British and American interests had coveted an establishment at this important harbor. Located on land ceded by the Treaty of Peace in 1783 to the United States, British officials warily anticipated the occupation of the site by American military units, though ostensibly it was in Indian country. Accordingly, any occupation of the shoreline along the lake was to be regarded as a serious threat to the safety of Canada.[23] Thus, there was an immediate furor in May, 1794, when an armed detachment of Pennsylvania militia advanced to occupy Le Boeuf (present-day Waterford, Pennsylvania), which was within twenty miles of Presque Isle. Angry and aroused to the point of a hostile commitment, impassioned Six Nation chiefs, including the American-aligned Cornplanter, threatened to fight to defend their lands.[24]

As the British well understood, the Six Nations were on the brink of going to war against the Americans. To provide for Canada's "self defense and proper precaution," the British promptly intensified their efforts to encourage and supply the Six Nations. Joseph Brant, who talked of "an expedition against those Yankees," was provided with "a hundred weight of powder, and ball in proportion." Cornplanter was promised a British pension. Other presents were allocated for lesser leaders.[25]

Yet there was substantial duplicity in these arrangements. This calculating British involvement in the Six Nations' affairs was structured to be in the best interest of the Canadian colonial government, nor of the general Indian confederacy. Although the native peoples were primarily concerned with the threat of imminent invasion by the American army under Anthony Wayne, the Six Nations' attention was directed instead to the Presque Isle situation because of the expressed purpose of the British officials, which was Canada's defense.

Simcoe, writing to the Home Office in November, 1793, offered the opinion that it would be of greater advantage to the British if the Six Nations prevented the Americans from garrisoning Presque Isle than if they openly assisted the hostile western tribes. In fact, Simcoe's concept of "protecting" Canada involved the active use of the Six Nations as auxiliaries in an offensive campaign on the Genesee River and in other eastern regions in the event of war with the United States. For that reason the subordinate British Indian agents were instructed to concentrate the Six Nations for effective operation in the eastern regions. Subsequently, after an American defeat in the West, British strategists readily acknowledged "that a very few weeks would suffice to drive back the post of Le Boeuf, [and] to force the inhabitants of the Genesee to abandon that country."[26] All but ignored in 1794, however, was the possibility of an overwhelming combination to defeat the primary American army of conquest.

British intrigue notwithstanding, early in the summer of 1794 it appeared more evident with each successive day that an expanding war involving the Six Nations as belligerents must soon occur. Dorchester, again anticipating the probable war with the United States, issued a formal warning to the Americans encompassing both the eastern and western reaches of British sovereignty. "Taking possession of any part of the Indian Territory, either for the purpose of war or sovereignty," he proclaimed, would be held as a "direct violation of His Britannic Majesty's rights."[27]

Anthony Wayne had planned to advance with the Legion so as to progressively occupy the enemy's domain. By late in the spring of 1794, however, the considerable optimism and growing confidence that he had expressed only a few months earlier had already been dissipated by a rash of untoward incidents. Wayne was distraught, for example, over the "continued and criminal default upon the part of the contractors" that had kept his army inactive through the initial months of fair weather.

Principal among the multitude of resulting problems was the familiar insufficiency of logistical support. This difficulty was so completely out of hand that Wayne was forced belatedly to take drastic action just to keep his army from starving. Since the fall of 1793, he had required Williams and Elliot, the civilian contractors responsible for provisioning the army, to lay in the equivalent of 270,000 surplus rations, beyond the daily usage of 4,125 units. This was to provide for an early spring offensive. Yet Elliot and Williams, operating from Fort Washington, treated the matter with contempt, said James O'Hara, Wayne's quartermaster.[28] Following further losses from the already-meagre packhorse herd throughout the spring, the supply of rations at the forward posts continued to dwindle.

Wayne was compelled to retard his plans for an offensive from April 15 to May 1 and then to May 15, and thereafter the offensive was postponed indefinitely. Elliot and Williams had only 153 packhorses in service during April, Wayne complained, and by mid-May they still utilized only 252, far short of the 600-horse herd (plus a 250-horse reserve) that Wayne had demanded in March.[29] Livid with anger, Wayne advised Elliot and Williams, "I will be no longer imposed upon or trifled with, nor shall the army be starved to death." He promptly ordered Major William McMahon to march to the rear and virtually seize "all and every" packhorse that he found. McMahon then was immediately to return to Greeneville with flour and all of the cattle available.[30]

On May 1 the Legion was down to only eight days' issue of meat and a nineteen-day supply of flour. Wayne angrily asserted to the contractors that they had "deceived both yourselves and me." "Facts are stubborn things," he continued. Observing that on May 12 the garrison at Fort Recovery had been reduced to a single day's supply of all provisions, Wayne decreed that Elliot and Williams would no longer "direct the movements of this army."[31]

Accordingly, since the Legion's transport did not have one-half of the means necessary, the quartermaster's department was directed to obtain the needed horses and cattle and charge the contractors for all expenses involved. Thereafter, Wayne noted with some bitterness, he was directly involved in the provisioning of the army, regularly utilizing the animals of the quartermaster's department to transport provisions, "to the extreme injury of that department."

"Avaricious individuals will always consult their own private interests in preference to that of the public," complained Wayne. "They will not part with so great a sum of money at any one time as will be necessary to purchase a large quantity of provision in advance, . . . because that is the most expensive part of the business. Thus will the public service always suffer . . . so long as supplies depend on a contract with private individuals in time of war."[32]

Gradually, by continual prodding and the ardent exertions of the quartermaster's staff, Wayne was able to improve his supply of provisions, until in June he could anticipate the arrival of several large lots, including "250 excellent, fat cattle" on the hoof, with the prospect of 800 more. With the arrival in mid-June of additional supplies, including quartermaster's supplies from the East, Wayne was able to turn to other pressing matters.[33]

The commanding general had recognized early in March that the enlistments of many men in the First and the Second Sub Legion would expire by mid-May, and he estimated that his effective force then would not exceed two thousand men. Accordingly, he prepared tentative plans to call out one thousand mounted volunteers from Kentucky to rendezvous at Georgetown on June 20 and march immediately thereafter for Greeneville.[34]

The news of the British occupation and fortification of the Miami Rapids, however, caused Wayne to seek an accelerated advance, lest the enemy regain the initiative. Learning that the War Department had belatedly authorized two thousand Kentucky volunteers as auxiliaries for the forthcoming campaign, the general insisted that all of them be present at Greeneville by July. Yet, due to delays in organizing and recruiting these volunteers, the Kentucky Board of War failed to meet until mid-June, and they then appointed July 10 and 14 for the rendezvous at two locations in Kentucky. Charles Scott, their designated commander, could only proffer a half-hearted excuse for this, saying that in the last year "much haste made least speed," and that the best recruits would not join the ranks until their harvest was in.[35]

265

Wayne, increasingly peevish and ill-tempered, was thus compelled to remain inactive throughout June, until the Kentuckians might come forth.[36]

Adding to the burden of the tedious delay was the demoralizing presence of what Wayne called "certain ambitious, factious, restless characters" in the army.[37] Foremost among them, although it was not then known to the commanding general, was James Wilkinson. Wilkinson was the leader of an insidious faction of malcontents who sought to depose Wayne as commander of the Legion. He had long coveted Wayne's position, and although he carefully maintained the appearance of proper subordination and respect, he had surreptitiously, from the first arrival of Wayne in the war zone, conspired against his commander.

Wilkinson had already become entangled in an illicit intrigue with the Spanish governor of Louisiana. Then he had become so despondent, when Wayne assumed absolute control of the Legion in 1793, that he considered resigning. Sick with influenza and bilious colic in the summer and fall of 1793, Wilkinson had been made even more miserable by what he regarded as the pointed neglect of Wayne. "My General treats me with great civility and with much professed friendship," wrote the embittered Wilkinson to a close friend, "yet I am 0 [zero], for he conceals his intentions from me, never asks my opinion, and when sense of duty forces me to give it, he acts against it."[38]

Terming Wayne a "blockhead," Wilkinson had taken particular exception to Wayne's original reluctance to use mounted volunteers from Kentucky as anything other than auxiliaries. Wilkinson had long sought their use as a primary striking force while the Legion was incapacitated by weather or logistics. "The volunteers may go to damnation and stay at home for all we care, we can do better without them," said Wilkinson in mockery of his commander's attitude.[39]

Matters continued to deteriorate, from Wilkinson's perspective, through the late spring of 1794. Fearful of being shunted aside during active campaigning by Major General Charles Scott of Kentucky, who was his political enemy, Wilkinson ranted that, "though a fool, a scoundrel, and a poltroon," Scott was slated to succeed to the command of the army if Wayne became incapacitated. Further upset by the alleged insinuation by Wayne that Wilkinson had not adequately expedited the procurement of the provisions for mounting an offensive at the head of the line, the outraged brigadier general wrote several private letters to his professed "friend," Henry Knox, in May, 1794, accusing Wayne of high crimes.

Knox, while somewhat shocked by the "coolness" between Wayne and Wilkinson, cautioned the hotheaded brigadier that, before any action could be taken, charges must be made public and "supported by well authenticated evidence."[40]

Wayne, for his part, remained outwardly oblivious of Wilkinson's deceit. Having highly commended Wilkinson in May, 1793, for "his attention to the discipline of his troops," Wayne also commented favorably on his brigadier's conduct in other official correspondence. Thus, while Wilkinson fretted to his friends about the state of the army, saying "we have little to hope [for] and everything to fear," he simultaneously attempted to gain Wayne's full confidence by pledging his fidelity. "Ever anxious for action and ready for duty, you have only to order, and the execution will follow with promptitude and energy," he advised Wayne at the very time when his accusations against the major general were being forwarded to Knox.[41]

Emboldened by the receipt of $4,000 in Spanish gold during 1792 (sent by Louisiana Governor Francisco Louis Hector, Baron de Carondelet, at New Orleans), Wilkinson intensified his efforts to secure additional secret service grants. Preying on Spanish vulnerability in the war that France had declared against Spain in March, 1793, Wilkinson asked for money to further his efforts on Spain's behalf. His personal pension, he suggested, should be raised from $2,000 to $4,000 annually, and perhaps $6,000 to $10,000 more might be included for bribes to influential persons. Wilkinson even reported to Carondelet that about sixteen of his subordinate officers were anxious to enter the service of Spain, and that he, Wilkinson, had lately spent $8,640 in breaking up a proposed expedition by George Rogers Clark and French-paid mercenaries against New Orleans. To cover those and other "expenses," Wilkinson dispatched two confidential agents to Carondelet in June, 1794, asking that the $12,000 that the agents were to procure be shipped separately for security in transit.

Carondelet, eager to induce the Kentuckians to separate from the United States and seek a Spanish alliance, was so gullible that he ultimately agreed to Wilkinson's scheme. In August he sent the first of Wilkinson's agents north with $6,000 in specie, packed in three small barrels. A second shipment went by sea later that month. Of the $12,334 total, $4,000 was to be credited to Wilkinson's expanded "pension."

In an undated letter to Carondelet of that period, Wilkinson wrote: "Do not believe me avaricious, as the sensation never found a place in my bosom. Constant in my attachments, ardent in my affections, and an enthusiast in the cause I espoused, my character is the reverse."[42]

Such were the elements of the major sub-rosa scandal spawned by "that worst of all bad men," as Wilkinson later came to be called. Yet Wilkinson in June, 1794, was counted on for a substantial contribution to the Legion's preparedness. "Every moment is now precious," Wayne advised him on June 8, and the commander relied on Wilkinson for advice and cordial assistance, especially in getting forward ample provisions.[43]

Just how offensive Wilkinson's conduct had become, is suggested by evidence that for months Wilkinson had maintained a secret correspondence with "Robin" Elliot, advising that contractor on what, when, and how to supply the army![44]

While another difficult circumstance seemed to thwart the progress of the Legion at every turn, Wayne was suddenly confronted, beginning in the late spring, by increasing enemy raids directed against his admittedly vulnerable line of communications.

As early as March 5 wagons en route to the forward posts had been attacked with serious losses, often at the hand of only small war parties. As the raids increased in intensity through late April and into May, Wayne had to expand his escorts and allocate more time and money for the safe transport of vital provisions.[45] Recognizing his army's obvious vulnerability, he cast about for a more effective and reliable means of supply, including water routes, yet the increasingly frustrated general was ultimately compelled to rely on the heavily escorted overland transports.

By late spring the critical delay in the timing of the army's offensive was becoming more evident with each passing day. Clearly worried that the enemy would attack in force before he could inhibit the Indians' offensive capability, Wayne sought to parry all forthcoming blows by acquiring advance information of any impending attack. To accomplish this, he relied heavily on a small but determined group of special forces, his military scouts and spies.

Headed by the invaluable William Wells (who had had the pay and the honorary rank of captain in the Legion since September 14, 1793), a select detachment of scouts was kept constantly on patrol in the vicinity of the enemy villages. Their mission almost invariably was to capture a prisoner from whom information might be obtained.[46] Aided by Samuel Dold, a sergeant from Virginia and an expert woodsman, Wells, dressed in the garb of an Indian, had conducted several particularly productive patrols throughout the spring and early summer. On March 13 a reconnaissance to the vicinity of the French Store and Girty's Town had resulted in the capture of an important prisoner. In one of the more ironic incidents of the war, Wells and several companions had discovered three Indians camped in an open woods and had resolved to capture at least one. After sneaking undiscovered within close proximity of the camp, the scouts had decided to shoot the two enemy on either side and rush the warrior in the middle. At the crack of the scouts' rifles, both Indians fell, and a dash was made by a third scout, Robert McClelland, for the lone survivor. After a brief footrace McClelland had cornered the Indian in a creek bottom, where he was forced to surrender. When the muck was washed from the captive's face, it was discovered that he was a white man. Soon Henry Miller, another of Wells's men, recognized the prisoner as his brother Christopher, taken captive by the Shawnees ten years earlier at about age twelve. Since Christopher still spoke English "tolerably well," the captive not only became the source of much information on Indian attitudes and plans, but also was soon persuaded by Henry to join Wells as one of Wayne's scouts. Christopher Miller, and the "mysterious providence" that had placed him in the middle when he and his two companions were attacked, were the talk of the army. "Had he been standing on the right or left," wryly noted a veteran frontiersman, he would inevitably have been killed."[47]

With increasing intensity and effectiveness, Wells, Dold, and others roamed the wilderness looking for prisoners. An expanded reconnaissance about June 1 under Captain Alexander Gibson, commander at Fort Recovery, resulted in the capture of two Potawatomi warriors returning from a hunting foray to the west. These captives confirmed the presence of Simcoe and four hundred British troops at the Miami Rapids, plus two pieces of artillery in the newly erected fort. "All the speeches that we have received from him [British Lieutenant Governor Simcoe] were as red as blood," they declared. "All the wampum and feathers were painted red, the war pipes and hatchets were red, and even the tobacco was painted red."[48]

A few weeks later, newly promoted Ensign Samuel Dold captured two Shawnees during a scout to the Maumee region above Grand Glaize. Although the Shawnees had been absent, hunting towards the Wabash, since March, they had met several parties in the woods en route to the concentration of all nations at the Auglaize Villages. A great council was gathering there, they related, and since the British had told the Indians that they would come forth to help them fight against the Americans, there had been renewed optimism in the red nations. Blue Jacket had gone forth to bring the northern-region Indians to the war council, and it seemed certain that the course of the war would evolve around British participation.[49]

This raw intelligence convinced Wayne that the Indians were collecting in force along the Maumee and Auglaize rivers "under the protection of the British preparatory to [an] offensive operation." Privately he believed that Simcoe and the British would not dare to attack the Legion without the official sanction of the Home Office, and that such approval was unlikely. Instead Wayne envisioned the British establishing an asylum area for the Indians and abetting them in their selective strikes against American targets of opportunity.[50]

Accordingly, Wayne expedited the preparations for his own offensive, even as he pondered the increasing signs that the enemy would attack before he could possibly advance. On June 29 he stated, "The war has assumed so new and so serious a complexion," that he would not allow any decrease in personnel or even resignations at that time. His only option, it seemed, was the "endeavor to draw the attention of the enemy from our escort in the rear" by threatening their own safety.[51]

The way to accomplish that diversion, so that all vital supplies and reinforcements might be forwarded to the head of the line with safety, he foresaw, was to raid isolated enemy villages with chosen detachments. Important in that context was the presence of about one hundred friendly Chickasaw and Choctaw Indians from the Tennessee country, who had been expressly sent by the famed frontiersman James Robertson for active service with Wayne's army. Long the inveterate foes of the "northern Indians," these southern Indians came forth "resolved to have hair (as they call it)," said Robertson.[52]

Joined by Robertson with a contingent of Choctaws in late June, these Indians were dipatched by Wayne about June 26 in three separate parties, under orders to gain intelligence. Identified by yellow ribbons tied to the tuft of hair at the crown of their heads, two war parties of Chickasaws went toward Grand Glaize and the White River, while a third party, composed of about forty-five Choctaws and ten of Wayne's best scouts, searched in the direction of the Saint Marys, near Girty's Town.

By June 28 the latter party was back at Greeneville, having been driven in by a "vastly superior" number of hostile Indians. One friendly Indian, said to be The Mountain Leader, a Chickasaw chief, was killed in the skirmish. Grim warnings were reported of a large concentration of hostiles en route south, accompanied by a great number of white men.[53]

Wayne, immediately concerned, noted that he was in the process of forwarding a large escort under Major McMahon with 360 packhorses laden with flour for Fort Recovery. Fearing that the enemy might intercept Mc-Mahon's party and surround the fort, Wayne immediately began formulating contingency plans to relieve the garrison. Regretfully, he concluded that this might lead to a general action before the Kentuckians arrived to help.[54]

Wayne's grasp of the enemy's plans was entirely correct. Yet even this sagacious appraisal of the enemy's movements underestimated the grave threat that was at hand. As the British commandant at Detroit, Colonel England, perceptively noted, the concentration of Indians now advancing against Wayne's Legion amounted to 1,600 warriors, "a more formidable force, considerably, than ever collected since the contest commenced."[55]

In response to the continual alarms about the American army advancing, urgent requests had been forwarded by the Auglaize tribes, particularly, to the lake-region Indians, asking for immediate assistance. Reports that Wayne would soon send his light cavalry out to cut down the growing corn in the Indian villages, and that he would establish a fort at Auglaize before advancing against Detroit, were predicated on the testimony of an Irish deserter, William Sullivan, who had fled Greeneville in late May. A thousand-dollar reward was offered for the scalp of Simon Girty, said Sullivan, and the company of spies led by William Wells were paid a dollar a day, plus forty dollars for each Indian scalp.[56]

As a result of such messages Indian warriors had hastened forth, from the Detroit region prepared for war, and from as far away as Michilimackinac. By June 10 sixty Ottawas, twenty-five Chippewas, and another war party of twenty-one Indians under Grand Sable were en route from northern Michigan. Five hundred Indians from the lake region were present at Detroit about June 1. All were directed to the Maumee gathering by the British commandant there.[57] Within weeks a British officer reported in excess of 1,700 Indians along the Maumee, with more arriving daily.

Emboldened and strengthened by arms and munitions from McKee's storehouse, the Indians soon became insistent, reminding the British that they had promised to go along and fight in the forthcoming action. "A few days will now decide either for or against us," they asserted, and they called on the British to "rise" and lead the nations forth.[58]

On June 16, after a large contingent of Ottawas and Wyandots had just arrived, a council of war was called to formulate a plan of action. It was agreed, said McKee, that the Indian army would operate against Wayne's vulnerable convoys, while keeping their attacks distant from the forts. Thus they might entrap any relief column that was sent against them.

When a resolution was passed in the council that all whites present with the army must serve in the fighting ranks, Matthew Elliott, McKee's subordinate, and others, including a regular British officer and several traders of the region, were required to don Indian dress so that there would be no mistake about their identity in the midst of the action.[59]

Departing from their council site at the Glaize on June 19 and 20, the Indian column split into several segments. One sizeable group, the Delawares under Buckongahelas, remained behind to guard against a sudden American strike against the Indian villages, which were deserted of nearly all but women, children, and old men.[60]

Because of the enormous logistical burden, the Indian columns went forth relatively dispersed. Often they traveled in as many as twelve open files, with ten rods between each file. By one or two o'clock in the afternoon a halt was ordered so that the hunters might drive the surrounding countryside for game, this being the only means of keeping the army supplied. An observer reported that as many as two hundred deer and several hundred turkeys were taken in a single day. These necessary hunts slowed the Indian army's progress, however, so that only sixty-six miles were traversed in three days.

Finally, the general rendezvous for the dispersed columns was reached, a site called Old Fallen Timber in the vicinity of Lake Saint Marys (Grand Lake). After a three-day wait there, it was learned that the Delawares under Buckongahelas had not yet departed from the Glaize. The Indian army then moved on, numbering 1,159 fighting men.[61]

Marching south-southwest in the direction of Greeneville, the Indian column halted on June 27 an estimated ninety miles from the Auglaize villages. Also on that day a flank scouting party encountered the American scouts with the Choctaw and Chickasaw warriors dispatched by Wayne. At this point the course of the war quickly changed.

Following this brief skirmish the Mackinac-region Indians, in particular, insisted that the column should attack the closest American installation, thus "taking the lead," said one observer, in directing the movements of the Indian army. Although Blue Jacket was present in command of the Shawnees, the change in direction was approved, probably because of the sheer political strength of the lake-region tribes and the northern Indians, who together comprised more than half of the total army. Thus the Indian force became committed to a revised plan that was predicated on reducing one American fort after another by direct assault.[62]

Only about fifteen miles away was the most advanced American outpost, Fort Recovery—a new fortification of uncertain strength. Also, Indian scouts soon observed a large convoy of packhorses laden with supplies headed for that site. Being presented with an obvious target of opportunity, the Indian force prepared for action.

Advanced pickets were posted on the trail leading toward the enemy. All horses were tied up, and their bells stopped. Arms were checked to see that they were in proper order. After the arrival of forty Wyandots on June 29, the army was ready for the fray.[63]

As the Delawares, Shawnees, and Miamis had ardently proclaimed in May, the Indian nations were determined to drive the Americans out of their country. This prospect was greatly relished by the British. The commandant of Detroit, in particular, fairly bristled with expectation. "I think it is natural to expect something interesting shortly," Simcoe wrote on June 25.[64] Like his quasi-adversary, Wayne, the British officer was entirely correct, but he too seriously underestimated the consequences of what was to follow.

27

The Fortuitous Events of War

FORT RECOVERY, twenty-three miles north-northwest of Greeneville, stood as the very symbol of American military prowess early in the summer of 1794. Anthony Wayne had warned that the fort must be maintained at every expense of blood, when he had departed the site after establishing it in late December, 1793.[1] Commanded by a highly regarded Virginian, Captain Alexander Gibson, the fort recently had been expanded and improved by its energetic commandant.

Beginning in February, Gibson had cleared the ground of small growth and fallen timber for a distance of 200 to 250 yards around the garrison, providing a clear field of fire. In March he had raised to two stories and completed the four blockhouses at each corner of the stockade. By May 1, Gibson had the construction and physical refinements so well in hand that he was practicing his men in musketry, despite a shortage of powder.[2]

With the advent of warm weather many of the garrison became so assured that they participated in a favorite pastime at Fort Recovery—searching for the hidden cannon and equipment buried by the victorious Indian army after the battle of November 4, 1791. Of the eight cannon captured on that occasion, Wayne had as yet recovered only three, despite detailed descriptions of other hiding places by prisoners and former Indian captives.[3]

Amazingly, for months the garrison virtually had been treading over two of the missing guns, a brass three-pounder cannon and iron four-pounder howitzer, which were discovered about May 11 between the barracks "and the rear redoubt near the east angle of the square." As a rather red-faced Alexander Gibson explained, the three-pounder had been buried under an insignificant log that had almost rotted away, while the howitzer was only five yards away under a log so small that it had never been suspected as a cover.[4]

On June 24, only a week before the impending crisis, two Potawatomi warriors, whom Ensign Samuel Dold had captured during the first week in June, supplied information leading to the recovery of a valuable six-pounder gun tube. This piece had been described by one of the captives, Christopher Miller, in mid-March as hidden beneath an old tree about 200 yards across a little creek. Gibson dutifully reported, after the gun's recovery, that Miller's earlier description had been correct except that the location was wrong: the cannon was found to the northeast, nearly one-half mile from the garrison.[5]

With the receipt of additional gunpowder in mid-March to supplement the single keg of cannon powder that he had on hand in late February, Gibson was able to incorporate the recovered guns into the defenses of the fort. Manned by a total garrison of about two hundred men, Fort Recovery now represented a formidable wilderness outpost.[6]

Only the want of adequate provisions prevented Gibson from enjoying the complete security that he ardently sought. Reduced to a single day's issue of provisions of all kinds on May 12, the garrison of Fort Recovery sustained a hand-to-mouth existence. Some cattle driven through the wilderness by Lieutenant Samuel Drake in mid-June afforded temporary relief, but it was the depleted state of all provisions that necessitated Major McMahon's heavily escorted supply mission from Greeneville to Fort Recovery on June 29. Fully cognizant of Wayne's intention to utilize Fort Recovery as a forward base in launching his midsummer offensive, Gibson had set about preparing for the receipt of further large quantities of provisions.

McMahon, with 360 packhorses laden with 1,200 kegs of flour, had been ordered to march at reveille on June 29 for Fort Recovery. His escort, fifty dragoons and ninety riflemen, were to carry two days' provisions and twenty-four rounds of ammunition per man. Since the war party of Chickasaws and Choctaws sent toward Girty's Town had returned that day warning of a large enemy column moving south, Wayne had cautioned McMahon to be particularly on his guard. "If attacked you must charge and cut your way through the enemy," he warned.[7]

On the evening of June 29, Major McMahon's long convoy arrived at their destination. Since the restricted area of the outpost would not allow comfortable billeting of the escort, an overnight camp was established about a hundred yards away.

Early the following morning, June 30, a lone, friendly Chickasaw warrior, Jimmy Underwood, wandered into the garrison, "much agitated and fatigued." Underwood had been with a scouting party of his tribesmen in the vicinity of the Wabash. Unable to speak English, he conveyed an excited if unintelligible narrative. "All we could get from him," Alexander Gibson later wrote, "was that he had seen a great many tracks, and heard some firing." No particular significance was given to his report, and the normal routine of the army outpost continued.[8]

Unfortunately for the American army, Underwood had most significant intelligence to convey. In company with others of his tribe he had picked up the unmistakable trail of the heavy Indian columns moving south. Before they had been scattered, the Chickasaws had followed these trails and had discovered a large concentration of hostiles moving toward Fort Recovery. Armed white men were among the Indians, they observed, and all were dressed for combat.

Indeed, at the very time when Underwood passed through to the fort, the Indian army was stealthily moving toward Fort Recovery from the east, intending to lay a deadly trap for the returning packhorse convoy and their escorts.[9]

At 7:00 A.M. on June 30 the breakfast call for the officers summoned those of the escort infantry and dragoons into the garrison. While the enlisted dra-

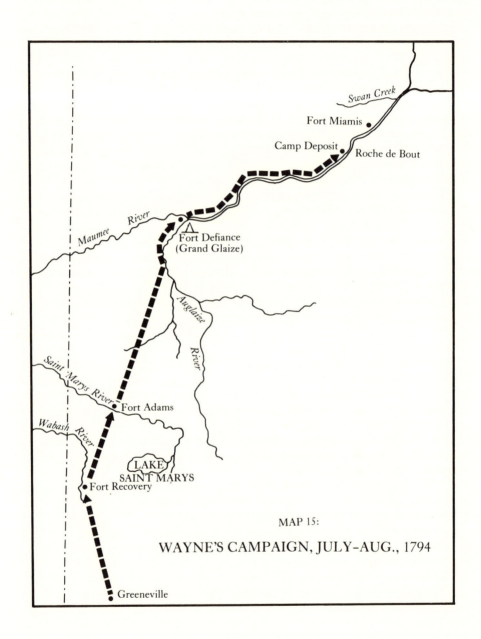

Swan Creek

Fort Miamis

Camp Deposit

Roche de Bout

Maumee River

Fort Defiance
(Grand Glaize)

Auglaize River

Saint Marys River

Fort Adams

Wabash River

LAKE SAINT MARYS

Fort Recovery

MAP 15:

WAYNE'S CAMPAIGN, JULY-AUG., 1794

Greeneville

274

goons prepared their mounts for the return journey to Greeneville, Major McMahon and others dined on the simple fare of army provisions.

Shortly after reveille that morning, Captain Gibson had sent four men to scout the Greeneville road for signs of the enemy. As he had received no adverse report, at about 7:00 A.M. he had allowed the packhorse drivers to move their large herd forward along the road to graze on the lush woodland grass.[10]

The gradually moving animals had moved about a half mile along the road when, suddenly, random firing broke out, followed by a few yells. Believing that a small war party had attacked the foremost packhorse drivers and might disperse a part of the valuable herd, Major McMahon dashed bareheaded from the fort to mount the dragoons and give chase. Led by the frantic major, Captain James Taylor and his detachment of fifty dragoons swiftly galloped toward the sound of gunfire. In their rear Captain Asa Hartshorne and his ninety riflemen followed as rapidly as possible.[11]

McMahon and Hartshorne were doomed men. In fact, of the more than one hundred soldiers who hastened south into the woods, nearly a third were to become casualties.

As a British officer accompanying the Indians observed, the massive column of warriors, intending to ambush the road, had suddenly discovered the vanguard of the packhorse herd and attacked. Three drivers were taken captive, two were killed, and another wounded. The frightened packhorses were quickly scattered. Then the American cavalry had dashed into this mounting confusion and disorder. An eyewitness said that they rode directly into the serried Indian ranks with sabers flashing, but went down in an instant.

Major McMahon, a conspicuous six feet six inches tall, was among the first to fall. Struck by a bullet that entered his temple and exited at the rear of his skull, he died instantly. Captain Taylor was also shot and seriously wounded, just before the badly mauled dragoons fled through the ranks of Captain Hartshorne's onrushing riflemen.[12]

Hartshorne's detachment had advanced only a few hundred yards into the woods when it was struck by the full force of the horde of Indians pursuing the dragoons. Immediately overwhelmed in front and on both flanks, the command broke up into fragments. Hartshorne was shot in the thigh, Lieutenant Robert Craig was killed, and the wildly yelling Indians pursued the fleeing Americans so closely that it seemed that all would be killed or captured.

Only about fifteen minutes had elapsed from the first fire, but Captain Gibson sent forward every man who could be spared from his garrison to support McMahon's troops. Led by Lieutenant Samuel Drake and Ensign Dold, this second infantry detachment rushed forward toward the fringe of the woods, which was several hundred yards from the fort. Suddenly they met the remnant of McMahon's regulars and the victorious savages, "much [inter] mixed."

After discharging a hasty volley, Drake's command also broke for the safety of Fort Recovery. Soon only the scattered survivors among the dragoons remained beyond the stockade walls. Finally, driven toward the blockhouse on the south side, they came under such a heavy fire, from

Indians who were lurking behind stumps and logs in that sector, that the few surviving troopers had to dash for shelter inside the fort. Quickly thereafter the abandoned horses cowering near the walls were shot down, noted Alexander Gibson, and the entire cattle herd, about thirty head, driven off.[13]

Surrounded on all sides by an overwhelming enemy force, and having sustained a loss of approximately forty casualties, Gibson pondered his uncertain fate. Rifle powder was in such short supply that instructions had to be passed to the men to fire only at sure targets. Devoid of adequate hospital supplies and low on fixed ammunition for his cannon, Gibson felt ill prepared to sustain a siege.[14]

What next occurred, wrote an informed British Indian agent, was, simply, an inexplicable and foolhardy action on the part of the Indians. Indeed, it later came to be recognized as a turning point in the war. Only three Indians had been killed in the initial fighting, and the red warriors were much "animated" by their success.

Suddenly, a segment of the warriors dashed toward the fort in an impetuous attempt to storm the walls. Gibson's well-practiced infantrymen fired from their loopholes at the oncoming Indians, having a clear zone of fire because of Gibson's earlier efforts. Although the Indians dodged from stump to stump and hid behind logs and what cover remained, they sustained frequent losses. Marksmen such as Samuel Dold were credited with bringing down several warriors. Added to the volume of small arms fire coming from the fort were demoralizing blasts of cannon fire. In fact, Gibson soon began firing his six-pounders, and at least one Indian was partially decapitated by a solid shot.[15]

For about four hours the Indians remained in close proximity, firing at anyone who exposed his person. Yet little further damage was sustained on either side. When a lengthy lull took place that afternoon, three soldiers dashed from the gate and scalped a dead warrior whose body was within seventy yards of the fort. Later the Indians returned to the fray, and the yelling and firing continued even after nightfall.[16]

It was of particular interest to Gibson that during the afternoon's fighting a number of Indians had been seen turning over old logs as if in search of the buried cannon. As Anthony Wayne later surmised, the enemy planned to use these old hidden guns in reducing the fort. "Fortunately," he noted, "they served in its defense."

As was discovered much later, the Indians did unearth at least one of the two remaining unrecovered guns, but they were unable to utilize it for want of adequate gunpowder. "Had we two barrels of powder," lamented a British officer present, "Fort Recovery would have been in our possession with the help of St. Clair's cannon."[17]

Late that night the Indians were observed searching the field by torchlight to bring off their dead and wounded. A knowledgeable British eyewitness estimated the Indian dead at seventeen, which, with as many wounded, represented a considerable loss. It was an added insult that, despite the intense darkness and lingering fog, the fort's riflemen were able to prevent the removal of many of the bodies.

At daylight on July 1 the sniping from concealed Indian marksmen continued, but, when Gibson threw several shells in their direction, the firing ceased. One act of Indian courage seems to personify the futile drama of this final act. Unwilling to leave any wounded to be brutalized by the whites, several Indians dashed to within sixty yards of the forbidding stockade to bring away a supposedly wounded comrade. Amid a hail of musketry the warriors reached their tribesman and carried him off. One of the Indians present, Jonathan Alder, said that, when they picked the warrior up, his shirt flew open, revealing an ugly bullet wound in the stomach. "It was green all around the bullet hole," said Alder, "and I concluded that we were risking our lives for a dead man."[19]

At eight o'clock on July 1, reported Captain Gibson, an army scouting party scurried into the woods to locate the Indians. They observed long columns of warriors crossing the creek above and below Fort Recovery, evidently heading north. Two hours later Gibson led a strong detachment from the fort onto the battlefield, from which the enemy had vanished. The soldiers cautiously searched for dead enemy about the fort, and six scalps were taken. Some ounce balls were found inbedded in the stockade wall, which Wayne later asserted were proof of the British involvement (the standard "Brown Bess" service arm of the English troops fired such a ball).[20]

Thus ended the "unlucky" attack on Fort Recovery, as a British leader later called it. His comment was comparatively mild in relation to those of others who had been present. One unidentified British observer recorded in his diary his extreme disgust, saying "I am sorry to say that for want of good conduct this affair is far from being so complete as might be expected." British agent Alexander McKee, whose son Thomas was present and allegedly had killed an American officer, was particularly bitter in his assessment. The Indians "kept up a useless attack upon the fort," he said, adding that lasting damage would likely result from their impetuosity in altering their original plans, which had been to operate only against convoys at a distance from the forts. By nearly all accounts, the brief victory over McMahon's soldiers was inconsequential, and the results of what had been conceived as a major offensive were meagre. "Such a disappointment never was met with," wrote a British adviser present in the action. "I must observe with grief that the Indians never had it in their power to do more—and have done so little."[21]

Allegedly, 109 of the warriors had gone into the action without firearms, and the great deficiency of ammunition and a general want of provisions had caused the Indians to retreat rather than sustain the siege of Fort Recovery. As the American scouts soon discovered in tracking the retreating Indian columns, the red enemy had been so destitute of food that they ate several of the captured packhorses. Their morale and the conditions within their disconsolate ranks became so dismal that a major segment, the Great Lakes-region tribes, subsequently broke away from the main column and started home. This in turn caused the entire army to break up on July 2, as an appalled British adviser reported.[22]

Soon the disarray in the Indian ranks was such that the Ottawas and the Chippewas, who had constituted the largest portion of the Indian column marching against Fort Recovery became disaffected. Nearly 800 warriors of the original 1,500 present were said to be from those two tribes, and they had suffered the greatest casualties. Once the straggling columns had returned to their Grand Glaize villages, bitter accusations and countercharges regarding the role of the lake-region Indians greatly divided the general alliance. Claiming that the Mackinac and Saginaw-region Indians had committed depredations on various tribal villages while en route to join the army, including raping their women, the Shawnees, in particular, blamed the confederacy's lack of success on the untoward influence of the northern tribes. For their part, the Ottawas and Chippewas accused the Shawnees of firing on their rear while they were in the act of attacking the fort. The intensity and extent of such bickering soon produced a steady stream of northward-bound Indians, which was reported in Detroit during the first two weeks in July. Moreover, reports of an outbreak of smallpox in the Illinois country spread fear and consternation among the northern tribesmen, undoubtedly hastening their departure.[23]

Thus for the Shawnee, Delaware, and Miami tribes the worst possible circumstances had occurred. Much concerned over their dire military situation, some of the leaders of those tribes reportedly considered abandoning the Auglaize country. The perceptive leader of the Miamis, Little Turtle, however, went directly to the commandant of Detroit to question that officer on the extent of British assistance. Little Turtle, in fact, was emphatic: the confederacy did not wish to continue the war on the present terms, he said. Specifically, he wanted twenty British regulars and two pieces of cannon to assist in any future attack on Fort Recovery. Yet Colonel England merely attempted to appease the Miami chieftain with noncommital talk of British aid.[24]

The underlying consequence of the attack on Fort Recovery in Indian politics was the emergence of greater controversy over their overall leadership. Since the Miamis were among the weakest numerically of the three primary Auglaize-region tribes, an increasingly vociferous Shawnee hierarchy began to dominate the general policy making. The frequent war councils in mid- and late July were led by the bellicose Blue Jacket and Captain Johnny, the principal Shawnee warriors, aided and abetted by British Indian agent Alexander McKee. Little Turtle, whom a senior British officer called "the most decent, modest, sensible Indian I ever conversed with, was increasingly shunted into the background because of his more moderate views, even though he was one of the ablest Indian tacticians.[25]

Informed of Wayne's plans to begin an offensive "about the beginning of next month," Alexander McKee wrote in July to the secretary of Indian Affairs that "there is an absolute necessity of sending provisions and ammunition" to the Indians for the defense of their country. Implicit in this and the various other messages of alarm, moreover, was the direct involvement of British regular troops and garrisons against any American thrust into the lower Maumee River region. The commandants of the most advanced British outposts repeatedly pleaded for specific orders concerning the proper action to take upon the approach of Wayne's soldiers. As they increasingly understood, the imminence of a direct confrontation with the American army was a matter of the utmost consequence to the British. In fact, the entire fortunes of the Indians and the British in mid-America seemed to turn on the forthcoming confrontation. In a review of the Indians' situation Little Turtle warned Colonel England at Detroit that, "If not assisted by the English, they would be obliged to desist in their plan of attempting to stop the progress of the American army."[26]

Anthony Wayne, aware of the great strategic importance of the June 30 fight, was quick to laud the garrison of Fort Recovery for their gallant defense. Noting that the enemy had retreated "with loss and disgrace from that very field where they had upon a former occasion been proudly victorious," Wayne issued one gill of whiskey to every soldier on July 4 in fitting celebration of the victory and the national holiday. That evening the celebration perhaps was carried a little too far when one of the "sky rockets" set off by a lieutenant landed on the Greeneville garrison's ordnance laboratory, setting afire several boxes of artillery shells.[27]

Notwithstanding the injured pride of several of his officers, Wayne remained undeterred in his exuberance. To his long-time friend Sharp Delany in Philadelphia, Wayne wrote that he was "only waiting the arrival of the mounted volunteers from Kentucky in order to have an interview with those hardy sons of the wilderness in their own towns." "[There] we may probably meet with Mr. Simcoe at the head of the British troops and militia of Detroit," he continued, "between whom and the savages it may be difficult to discriminate in the hour of action."[28]

Expressing a general confidence in the Legion, Wayne wrote to Knox in July that his plans had matured to the point of execution. His offensive was to be deceptively simple: By seizing the main village sites and forcing the Indians to defend their plantings (or face the prospect of starvation during the coming winter), Wayne foresaw that the issue would be joined. Thus he wrote to Knox in rather specific terms on July 16, "Our movements will be rapid until we gain it"—the objective of Grand Glaize or Roche de Bout. Should the British venture forth to assist the Indians, Wayne anticipated an opportunity for the mounted volunteers to operate at their rear, interdicting supplies and threatening vital lines of communication and retreat.[29]

Based on notice from Brigadier General Charles Scott in mid-July that 760 Kentucky volunteers were en route and the balance would soon follow, Wayne ordered the immediate preparation of tents and camp equipment so that the army would be ready for a forward move "at a moment's warning."

After the arrival of a large portion of the Kentuckians on July 25, Wayne looked at his army with great confidence. It was with a flourish that the Legion was put in motion on July 28, 1794. To the drum roll of "general quarters" the army was ordered to rise and to begin marching at the sound of a signal cannon shot from the Greeneville redoubt. Provided with five days' rations of bread, two rations of beef and whiskey, and twenty-four rounds of ammunition per man, the column began the long trek north at 8:00 A.M. in intensely hot weather. In dispatching a final brief note to the administration on the commencement of his campaign, a rather pensive Wayne reflected on the events to come and added in anticipation, "the issue may probably be tried in the course of a few days."[30]

279

Determined to avoid the laxity in discipline and indiscretions in vigilance that had ruined his predecessors, the general implemented a generally conservative system of advance. The route that he chose was the most practical way to the Grand Glaize rather than the shortest. In fact, the army utilized the same route that the main Indian columns had traveled as they advanced from Auglaize to attack Fort Recovery, for the path had been well scouted by his spies.[31]

To guard against the favorite Indian stratagem of surprise, Wayne required the construction of breastworks at each night's bivouac. Further caution was manifest in the calling of the army to arms at reveille, one hour before daylight each morning. Regular battle lines were then formed and maintained until it was light enough to call the rolls. As was soon apparent to all, the Legion marched through the wilderness as a mobilized armed camp, presenting little opportunity to an enterprising enemy.[32]

While Wayne insisted that the usual ten- to twelve-mile distances covered in one day were minimal, by such rapid marches he hoped to seize the strategic enemy villages before effective opposition could be mounted.[33]

As was well known to the soldiers of Wayne's legion there were considerable hardships involved in the campaign, though too few of the soldiers fully understood the grim determination of their commander to persevere under all conditions. The mosquitoes were intensely bothersome, and "larger than I ever saw," a lieutenant recorded. The muddy creek water was so vile that "nothing but excessive thirst would induce us to drink [it]," he added. Another officer was dismayed by the wretched terrain. The numerous creeks were quagmires of bottomless mud or jungles of swamp grass, and the men soon became so fatigued that it was difficult to keep some of them from falling out of line. Wayne, nonetheless, insisted on maximum individual effort and dogged perseverance. "It was in vain to speak to the commander . . . as he will hear no man's opinion," a riled staff officer recorded, indignant over Wayne's demand for urgency.

Wayne's restlessness in pesonally riding forward with only a small escort to and beyond the details who were hacking a road through the wildernes was generally misconstrued as wanton carelessness. "This is highly imprudent," wrote an officer, "but he will receive no advice." Wayne, it seems, could not be dissuaded in his resolve, nor would he compromise regarding the efforts that had to be made. It was, said a doubting critic, as though he had "to be first everywhere"—as if his honor was in question.[34]

From Wayne's point of view, the campaign was indeed a responsibility requiring the deepest personal commitment. Writing to his son Isaac shortly before the march began, the general had reflected on the task and the awful responsibilities that were his: "The most numerous body of savages that were ever assembled . . . in America are now collected . . . in our front. . . . From every information Governor Simcoe has solemnly promised to join the Indians with a large body of British troops and the militia of Detroit to cooperate against the Legion. It is therefore more than probable that we shall soon have an interview with this hydra . . . , and as the fortuitous events of war are very uncertain, I feel it my duty to prepare for the worst."[35]

Accordingly, Wayne had advised his son that he had prepared his will—a document in which he candidly admitted the "certainty of death and the possibility that the event is not far distant." Further to emphasize his commitment, Wayne had told Isaac that, if he was doomed to fall, his conduct would be "such as never to cause a blush upon the face of my children." Fully prepared to make the ultimate sacrifice, Wayne soon was to realize how prophetic his innermost thoughts had been, although the manner of his encounter with death would be totally unexpected.[36]

The army had traversed about twelve miles on July 29, passing Fort Recovery to the echo of a fifteen-gun salute. On the thirtieth the Legion crawled through deep marshes and crossed numerous watercourses, often having to cut their way through the thickest wilderness. After an entire day's delay, while a bridge was constructed over Beaver Creek (said to be about seventy yards wide), the army again advanced on August 1. Then twelve and a quarter miles were marched, the last two through "the largest and most beautiful prairie I ever beheld," according to Lieutenant John Bowyer. A "luxuriantly fertile" open plain, set off by small groves of trees, afforded a view of the entire Legion as the long column wound through the meadowland. Wayne sat on his horse watching the enthralling sight.[37]

Having reached the banks of the Saint Marys River, which was described as a "slow, turbid stream" about fifty yards wide, the army halted on the evening of August 1 prepared for a lengthy bivouac. Wayne had decided to build a small fortification here to protect his line of communications. While the work progressed, with undue slowness according to Wayne, many of the nondetailed men bathed in the muddy waters of the stream or organized fishing parties. By sewing the blankets of eight or more soldiers together and using this as a seine, the fishermen dragged the river for twenty or thirty yards, moving upstream. Their catch was often eight to ten pike or pickerel of excellent size, said an observer. Thus they kept the army well supplied with fish.[38]

On through August 2 and into August 3 the labor details worked with "spirit." Yet the two blockhouses remained uncompleted, and Wayne requested that even the officers help out by assisting in the construction. At three o'clock that afternoon Wayne had retired to his marquee to rest from the intense heat. Suddenly, at that hour, a large beech tree crashed squarely down upon his tent, flattening the structure and even crushing the neighboring tent of his aide de camp, Captain Henry De Butts. Passersby immediately rushed to the scene and dragged Wayne from the debris. "His pulse was gone," said an officer, "but by the application of a few volatile drops [whiskey] he was soon restored." The huge trunk had smashed down only inches from where Wayne lay, reported an unnamed journalist, and the bed of Captain De Butts was "crushed to pieces." "The escape of each was miraculous," he added. Even Wayne regarded his escape as incredible, confiding that only "an old stump" adjacent to his tent had deflected the falling tree and had prevented it from "crushing me to atoms."[39]

Wayne proved to be more scared than injured, related another observer, and although he had received a heavy blow on his left leg and ankle, he was able to ride at a slow pace. Months later Wayne considered the incident as "probably premeditated," inferring that several of the Wilkinson faction had deliberately planned to murder him. Because of Wilkinson's malevolent nature, his clandestine activities, and the burning resentment that he secretly expressed toward Wayne, there is some evidence to support that conclusion. At the time, however, Wayne probably regarded the affair as an accident. No further inquiry about it was made, which is puzzling, since the weather was "very hot and dry," hardly of the kind to produce a natural collapse of heavy timber.[40]

During the evening of August 3, Brigadier General Thomas Barbee and the Second Division of Kentucky volunteers arrived with a large supply of provisions. Wayne was now determined to move on, despite the vulnerable state of the uncompleted fortification, which was later named Fort Adams after Vice-President John Adams. A lieutenant and about forty invalids were left behind as a garrison, and at 5:30 A.M. on August 4 the Legion again marched forth into the thick, but dried-up, swamps.[41] Already water was so scarce that, to obtain drinking water, holes had to be dug "in boggy places," which produced a vile-tasting, murky liquid.

After traveling three days over a distance of about thirty miles, the parched Legion encamped on the banks of what was called Upper Delaware Creek, a tributary of the Auglaize River. Soon the advanced scouts, headed by William Wells, discovered the camp of an Indian war party nearby, and they urged that a mounted detachment venture forth. Wayne, however, denied permission for the foray.[42]

Wayne's grasp of tactical practicality was evident in this decision, as it was quite apparent that he did not want to repeat the mistakes of his predecessors in detaching large segments of the army toward an uncertain fate. Although a variety of officers grumbled about the wasted opportunity of "driv[ing] the enemy into the Lakes," Wayne remained steadfast in his resolve to commit the Legion only as a unit. The intense bitterness of Wilkinson, who had urged the raid, was such that he regarded the decision as a particular "insult." To Wilkinson, Wayne was a "despotic, vain glorious, ignorant general," and he took privately to calling him "Mars" and the "the Old Horse." Wilkinson's subordinates, particularly in the First and the Third Sub Legion, had long been exposed to this insidious bile, and a growing distrust of Wayne's capacity began to manifest itself in the officer corps.[43]

Aware that many Indian villages were now within easy striking distance, Wayne contemplated how best to achieve a progressive, permanent occupation of the enemy domain which would deny the hostile red nations possession of their vital cultivated fields. A reconnaissance to and beyond Delaware Town, which had been abandoned the previous fall according to the scouts' estimation, had suggested the presence of abundant Indian crops. One young officer of the Third Sub Legion eagerly wrote in his journal that he expected to eat green corn tomorrow.[44]

On August 7, about noon, Wayne learned that the enemy had recently evacuated their extensive villages near the confluence of the Auglaize and Maumee rivers, which was only about twelve miles away. With a small detachment Wayne galloped four miles ahead to the first of these newly abandoned villages, where he observed a vast panoply of cultivated fields. Corn, melons, beans, and "vegetables of almost every description" abounded. After his return to the army that evening an exuberant Wayne decide to establish a fort in the midst of this cultivated region. He was particularly satisfied that the enemy had abandoned their vital crops without a fight. This and the absence of any signs of organized resistance convinced him that the enemy was badly disorganized and unable to contest his advance.[45]

Acting now with increased boldness, Wayne resumed his march at six o'clock the following morning, despite a driving rainstorm that lasted until noon. Beginning with the village observed by Wayne, his soldiers soon witnessed a breathtakingly beautiful scene. Stretching for about six miles along the Auglaize River, to its confluence with the Maumee, lay "extensive corn fields, beautifully green and flourishing." Both sides of the river were under cultivation and presented a most luxuriant appearance "as far as the eye can see," an officer said.[46]

Amazed at the quantity and variety of vegetables and other produce that they found, Wayne's soldiers could but marvel at the spectacular scenery, particularly at the confluence of the Auglaize and the Maumee, which they reached at 10:30 A.M. This location was known generally as Grand Glaize. Anthony Wayne termed it "the grand emporium of the hostile Indians of the West," and it was reported that even the noted Shawnee war chief Blue Jacket had lived there. A smoldering remnant of "two or three trading houses," burnt by the retreating populace, confirmed that the enemy had made a hasty flight.[47]

Wayne immediately issued congratulatory orders and directed one gill of whiskey be issued to each soldier in recognition of their apparent triumph. After encamping the main column on the southwest section of land at the rivers' confluence, he ordered the erection of a four-blockhouse fortification at that point. The fort was to be of formidable construction, utilizing heavy log pickets fifteen feet long and at least twelve inches in diameter. Work was soon begun by fatigue details and continued for more than four days.[48] Meanwhile, Wayne and the rest of the army languished at Grand Glaize under mostly cloudy and damp weather.

Thus far the absence of Indian resistance had been the marvel of the entire army. Despite frequent false alarms the Legion had discovered only a few Indian scouts reconnoitering the army at a distance. Wayne, in fact, was so anxious for information on the missing enemy that he offered a $100 reward to his spies for the capture of an Indian warrior. On August 10, the general dispatched William Wells, Robert McClelland, and four other spies toward Roche de Bout, to take a prisoner if that was at all possible.[49]

Wells's foray, which soon became one of the more recounted incidents of the campaign, provided the first indication of the Indians' designs in nearly three weeks. Wells was recognized as the principal scout of Wayne's army, and he and his men were well mounted, and dressed in Indian fashion, to conceal their identity. On the afternoon of August 11 the spy party encountered and captured a Shawnee warrior and his squaw between Roche de Bout and the Miami Rapids. In returning toward Grand Glaize that evening, Wells discovered a small Delaware hunting camp, at which an estimated seven or eight warriors were present. After first bypassing this site, the scouts agreed to leave their prisoner with two guards and return to the Indian bivouac. Brazenly riding into camp with their rifles across their saddle pommels, Wells and his three scouts engaged the Delawares in conversation. The Indians' suspicions were aroused, however. Wells, in fact, was well known among the hostile tribes. According to a contemporary account, the Indians, numbering about fifteen, suddenly seized their guns and fired among the scouts. McClelland took a wound in the shoulder, the ball entering below the blade and exiting at the top of his shoulder. Wells, who had snapped his firelock three times at one warrior only to have the weapon misfire, was struck in the wrist as he dashed for safety, suffering a wound that shattered several bones and caused him to drop his rifle. In a brief melee, one Delaware woman was killed before the scouts escaped. Traveling as rapidly as possible on horseback, the scattered spies returned to their comrades, who were waiting with the prisoners. All immediately departed for Wayne's encampment.

On August 12, a militia scouting patrol encountered Wells's party painfully making their way south. Word was sent back to the Grand Glaize encampment, and a detachment of dragoons with a surgeon was quickly sent forward to assist the spies.[50]

The Shawnee prisoner, whom the Americans interrogated in Wayne's presence later that day, provided much useful information. According to the captive, about 700 hostile Indians were gathered in the vicinity of Alexander McKee's storehouse. Another 500 to 600 Wyandots and Ottawas were expected to soon join forces with them, while the British, at nearby Fort Miamis, were said to be preparing to fight alongside their red allies. The Indians intended to fight the Americans at the Foot of the Miami Rapids, the Shawnee reported, observing that a deserter from Wayne's Legion had informed them of the army's destination. Some of the Indians seem equivocating, he added, and many contemplated moving off at a distance to see if the British would, as promised, fight the Americans.[51]

To Wayne and his officers this revelation was both encouraging and alarming. Of great concern was the news that the army defector had imparted detailed intelligence to the red enemy. On the morning of August 1, Robert Newman, acting quartermaster, had disappeared from the vicinity of the Saint Marys, allegedly taken by an Indian scouting party. Newman had served with Simon Kenton's Kentucky scouts and spies during the 1793 campaign, and he was regarded as an informed individual.[52]

Although greatly angered that the enemy had apparently been well informed by Newman of the strength and operational details of his army, Wayne was encouraged to learn from the Shawnee prisoner that the Indians were very short on provisions. The corn promised by the British had not yet arrived, he said.

In essence, the prisoner's information only corroborated Wayne's own estimation that the Indian tribes were in great disarray and might be persuaded to abandon the British, whom Wayne increasingly regarded as the true enemy.[53]

Since the American army was firmly in possession of the Indians' vital heartland villages, as early as August 11, Wayne had considered sending an offer to conclude a peace with the hostiles. On August 13 he composed a lengthy message stating that he would receive Indian deputies in order to settle the "preliminaries" of a "lasting peace." The American major general further proclaimed that, since he was now in possession of their villages, only prompt action to conclude a peace would restore their country to them and save their "helpless women and children" from famine during the approaching winter."[54]

Then, in a key element of the message, Wayne announced: "Brothers, be no longer deceived or led astray by the false promises and language of the bad white men at the foot of the rapids; they have neither the power nor inclination to protect you." This admonition was well calculated to intensify the Indians' doubts about the extent of British cooperation in any armed confrontation. Wayne also raised a vital question: Which white society was now dominant in the Northwest territory? If the British no longer had "the power" to protect their vulnerable Indian allies, as Wayne suggested, the fate of the red men would lie with the American people rather than the British Canadians. Subtly yet significantly, Wayne thus refocused attention on the role of the British and the subsequent plight of the red man, should their benefactors fail them.[55]

To emphasize this sincerity, Wayne dispatched the bilingual Christopher Miller to the hostiles, along with the Shawnee warrior taken on the eleventh by William Wells. These emissaries were to represent the "kindness" that Wayne had shown to Indian prisoners. Should any harm befall Miller, warned Wayne, five warriors and two squaws held prisoner at Greeneville would be put to death. Otherwise, Miller was to return to the army on or before August 16, three days hence.[56]

Meanwhile, by the middle of the month, the new stockade (aptly named Fort Defiance) was generally completed, and Wayne prepared to resume his march northward.

On Friday, August 15, beginning at 6:00 A.M., the Legion of the United States resumed their offensive by crossing the Maumee to the northern shore and striking ahead "with cheerfulness and life." The rhythmic drumming of the musicians provided a jaunty air, and the clear and cool weather seemed invigorating. On the southern bank the Kentucky mounted volunteers marched forth, accompanied by the cavalry and light infantry of Wilkinson's right wing.

"We are in high spirits," recorded an expectant officer, who realized that though the flour ration had been reduced by half, the abundance of abandoned enemy produce ensured a more-than-adequate food supply. Even the resentful Brigadier James Wilkinson saw the offensive as an opportunity to win important new laurels, and he looked forward to the reduction of the nearby British fort. As for Anthony Wayne, who remained so ill with the gout that day that he had to be lifted onto his horse, he was "sanguine" that a dictated peace would follow the return of Christopher Miller with an Indian deputation.[57]

Behind the long columns of the Legion marching northeast that day swirled the rising, acrid smoke of a devastated countryside. The beautiful and cultivated landscape of a few days past was now a virtual wasteland. Everywhere the army had remained and foraged, the plantings were a despoiled shambles. Broken cornstalks, ripped-up vines, and mashed pumpkins and vegetables lay scattered in profusion. Cattle and horses had been turned loose in the gardens and fields, intensifying the destruction. Remaining cabins and unappropriated personal property had been burned.[58] Said James Wilkinson, in smug justification of the retribution that he had long urged against the red nations: "Their insolence will not keep pace with our clemency until they are taught to feel our power—substantially and permanently."

Anthony Wayne, increasingly confident, reported that from the spirit and ardor of the troops he anticipated ready success. "Should war be their [the Indians'] choice," he advised Henry Knox in a brief dispatch from Grand Glaize, " . . . blood [will] be upon their own heads."[59]

28

Season of the Blacksnake

HE was "the greatest of all the Miamis, if not the greatest Indian that ever lived," wrote the noted modern historian Otho Winger. "Perhaps there is not left on this continent one of his color so distinguished in council and in war," read a tribute by his enemies.[1] Little Turtle, war chief of the Miamis and the mastermind of Harmar's and St. Clair's defeats in 1790 and 1791, stood on the threshold of enduring fame in the midsummer of 1794. His record as one of the greatest Indian soldiers was unblemished by a major defeat. While he was also revered for his great modesty, decorum, and intelligence, Me-she-kin-no-quah, as his tribesmen called him, represented the very essence of Indian military prowess.[2]

Yet at the approach of Wayne's army in August, 1794, Little Turtle became a spokesman for peace.

This dramatic decision required not only the courage of strong convictions but also exceptional perception and wisdom. Although the reasons for his decision have long been obscured by conflicting accounts and uncertain references, fortunately, the essential truth remains.

In 1794, Little Turtle was in his prime as an experienced, battlewise leader. Being then about forty-two and of a stern, forbidding appearance, the six-foot Miami tribesman had risen from obscurity to become the exalted principal warrior of his nation. Although he was the son of Aquenackque, a tribal chief, his mother was Mohican. Little Turtle thus was denied a chief's status that might have been his birthright. Yet, because of his prowess in battle and his remarkable courage and acumen, Little Turtle's name became increasingly familiar to British Indian agents as that of an important post-Revolution leader.[3]

After his unsuccessful visit to Detroit in late July, 1794, to solicit direct British involvement in the war, Little Turtle evidently became convinced that the war ultimately would be lost by the Indians. Considering the great disparity between the Indian and white numbers, and because of the ineffectiveness of the confederacy's recent joint offensive operations, he despaired of military success against Wayne's army. Indeed, the recent Indian evacuation of the Grand Glaize villages suggested their dire future prospects.

As early as mid-July the Indians had warning of Wayne's imminent advance. Yet there was considerable confusion about the proper action to take. Although several small war parties were near the American forts late in July, the first concrete information about the general advance came from the deserter Robert Newman on August 1. Newman, whose tailored dress set him apart from the common soldier, was regarded with suspicion by the British authorities. Yet the detailed information that he conveyed proved to be generally accurate. Newman said that Wayne with 3,300 men had advanced twenty-one miles from Fort Recovery and that he was preparing to establish a chain of posts leading to the Grand Glaize and beyond. Further, Wayne's objective was reported to be the reduction of the British fort at the Miami Rapids. This vital information was soon confirmed and conveyed to the Indian leaders at the Glaize.[4]

The news of Wayne's approach, coupled with fear that the mounted volunteers would be raiding ahead of the army, kept the Indians defensively oriented. Some, probably including Little Turtle, were skeptical that the British would participate in any actual fighting. Accordingly, they urged that the Indians withdraw beyond Fort Miamis in order to implicate the British directly in a military confrontation with the Americans. Yet the tribes' primary impetus for abandoning the vital Auglaize villages was, simply and undeniably, that they were confused and did not have sufficient strength to oppose Wayne's militia-augmented Legion.[5]

The Shawnee prisoner taken by William Wells on August 11 reported that six hundred warriors were present at Grand Glaize to oppose Wayne's advance. An Ottawa chief many years later vividly remembered the bewildered consternation around the Glaize as the tribes prepared to evacuate the region. In haste, the red people fled from the fertile bottomlands in canoes, by travois, and on foot, leaving behind everything that they could not carry. "Old women, burdened with immense packs strapped to their shoulders, followed their retreating families with all the haste their aged limbs would permit," sadly remembered the Ottawa chief. All were fleeing from Wayne's dreaded Long Knives, and the atmosphere was one of near panic.[6]

From the beginning the trek north beyond the land of plenty became an ordeal of want and misery. The ultimate relocation point near the Fort Miamis (the site known as the Miami Rapids) soon became so overcrowded with starving refugees that the already overworked British Indian Department faced a logistics crisis.

Alexander McKee was so distraught because of this "unexpected retreat" that he considered the entire Auglaize country as now "perfectly open" to the Americans. The enormous demand for food far outstripped the British agent's supplies. While he sent an express to Detroit to hasten a vessel with provisions,[7] the immediate, harrowing dilemma remained: the necessity of halting Wayne's offensive.

For the past several weeks Indian runners had been sent throughout the Old Northwest seeking reinforcements from all regions. Messengers with red-painted tobacco had gone to the Wyandots and other lake-region tribes, calling all of the warriors to arms. A determined attempt had been made to reconcile the Maumee and lake-region Indians after the Fort Recovery incident. The Shawnees even had sent white prisoners to the Ottawas as presents. As a result of these efforts more than 600 Ottawas and Wyandots were allegedly recruited, particularly through the influence of Egushawa, one of the more warlike of Ottawa chiefs. On August 13, Alexander McKee favorably reported that 1,000 Indians were present at the Miami Rapids, and that more were en route.[8]

The Indians' morale soon soared, and was further enhanced by the prospect of the Bitish militia from Detroit joining with the Indian army. Perhaps, as McKee suggested, even regular troops would participate. Meanwhile, the scouts, who were kept constantly out to observe Wayne's columns, reported the American troops' halt at Grand Glaize from August 9 to 15. This delay of a full week provided an important respite, allowing the British and the Indians to reorganize their forces.[9]

Particularly encouraging at this time was the arrival of Major William Campbell of the Twenty-fourth Regiment, who landed at Fort Miamis in the schooner *Chippewa* on August 10. Campbell, Fort Miamis's designated commander, had returned to the fort from a trip to Detroit with a squad of artillerists, a detachment of Queen's Rangers for Turtle Island, and two "strong" infantry companies of the Twenty-fourth Regiment. Also on board the *Chippewa* were a fresh supply of ammunition, one hundred barrels of provisions for the Indians, and two small howitzers mounted on mobile "grasshopper carriages." As improvements of the defenses of Fort Miamis continued at an accelerated pace, the Indians were duly heartened.[10]

Various agents of the British Indian Department, of course, were increasingly aggressive in urging the Indians to defend their country. Yet the senior officer present, Alexander McKee, was particularly influential. Known as "the White Elk" to his Indian charges, McKee was acting on the premise that the red nations were essential to Britain's defense of the region. His persuasive techniques, including inflammatory speeches and the outpouring of war materiel, served to embolden the Indians militarily. "I shall endeavor to keep the Indians together," he reported to the commandant at Detroit on August 10, "and hope . . . to make arrangements for their cooperation with us to defeat any attempts that may be meditated against Fort Miamis or Detroit." Anthony Wayne later was so angered by accounts of McKee's efforts that he accused McKee of being the "principal stimulator" of the entire Indian conflict.[11]

Diametrically opposed to the inveigling of McKee was Little Turtle, who perceived what was historically obvious—that the British commitment would fall far short of the massive intervention required. Accordingly, when Wayne's emissary, Christopher Miller, rode into the bustling Anglo-Indian war camp on August 14, there was an immediate furor among the Indians. In fact, Wayne's peace message soon created an open split in the Indian ranks. Perhaps mindful of Little Turtle's skepticism about direct British military involvement and of his concern that the American soldiers were too numerous for the Indians alone to overcome, others of the moderate faction supported a negotiated settlement with Wayne. Such an attempt was not only contrary to the advice of McKee, Elliot, Girty, and other British agents, but also in contrast to the rampant war spirit of the other Indians. In this manner the stage was set for a decisive grand council that took place on the night of August 14.

An aged Ottawa chief later recalled how the great meeting began under the large "council elm" near the Miami Rapids. First to speak, after the traditional calumet of tobacco had been passed, was Little Turtle, the gifted war chief. Recounting the numerous ordeals of the Indian people throughout

James Wilkinson, the treacherous frontier general and Spanish agent number 13. Courtesy of William Clements Library, University of Michigan.

the current war, he related: "The trail has been long and bloody; it has no end. The pale faces come from where the sun rises, and they are many. They are like the leaves of the trees. When the frost comes they fall and are blown away. But when the sunshine comes again they come back more plentiful than ever before." Stating that the Manitou (Great Spirit) would hide his face in a cloud if his red children refused to listen to the voice of peace, Little Turtle proposed that a delegation talk with the great white chief Wayne.

Silence greeted the conclusion of Little Turtle's speech—strong evidence of its unpopularity. [12]

Although considerable controversy exists over the identity of the principal spokesman for the war faction, the substance of his reply has been preserved. Traditional accounts credit Blue Jacket of the Shawnees with the rebuttal speech, though contemporary evidence suggests that Egushawa of the Ottawas may have delivered it. Egushawa had served as the confederacy's spokesman throughout 1794, and his band were among the most inveterate of the hostile elements. [13]

In deliberately measured rhetoric the militant Indian leader delivered a terse, harsh invective belittling Little Turtle's intention to "smoke in the lodges of the Long Knives, our enemies." "[Wayne], the great war chief, will walk in a bloody path," urged the aroused chieftain. "Will the braves of his red children fight? Will they defend the council fires and graves of their fathers?" A participant remembered that a rousing war cry greeted the conclusion of the speech, "and the words 'How, How,' signifying assent went up from some five hundred throats." Other spokesmen for the Ottawas, Potawatomis, and Shawnees followed with ringing endorsements of war. Only a single Ottawa leader, the youthful chief Kin-jo-i-no, allegedly dissented from the militant view. [14]

"The Indians had been so successful against St. Clair that they were very sanguine of success," explained a subsequently repatriated white savage. "They talked as though it would be an easy victory." Wayne's army was said to be rich in everything that the Indians desired—horses, blankets, clothing, guns, and ammunition. Too, the British were close at hand, ostensibly preparing to assist their "red children." [15]

Little Turtle, forlorn and perhaps bitter over the implication that he had lost his courage, again rose to address the throng: "I have heard the words of the great chiefs of the Ottawas, Potawatomis and Shawnees. . . . They are young men and their arms are strong. . . . The chief of the Miamis is old. . . . He is waiting for the Great Spirit to say come." Then, after passing the command of the assembled warriors to other hands, he proclaimed, "The chief of the Miamis will follow." [16]

In order to deceive the Americans of their intentions, the Indians agreed to send a conciliatory answer to Wayne via Miller. In an unsigned "speech," allegedly written by White Eyes, war chief of the Delawares (who had sided with the United States during the Revolution), the Indians told Wayne not to be in "too great a hurry." The assembled Indian tribes had been "on their feet to meet you [in battle]," read the message, but in ten days time they would gather representatives from all of the confederated nations and come forth with a flag. Meanwhile, Wayne was to "sit down still where you are, and not build forts in our village[s]." [17] On August 15, Miller returned with that message to Wayne's Legion, while war preparations continued in earnest at the Miami Rapids.

Before Miller had departed, Alexander McKee had overheard the American messenger talking with the Indians about the campaign that was in progress. The real objective was the British, according to Miller, who probably was merely hedging about his own involvement in a war against his former comrades to ensure his personal safety. Nonetheless, McKee had Miller execute a signed affidavit that Wayne's efforts were "not to be directed against them [Indians], but to drive away the English from the country."[18] The affidavit represented further justification for overt British action on behalf of the Indians. Indeed, the prospect of a direct military confrontation was of primary concern to the British.

Lieutenant Governor Simcoe had issued his official instructions in mid-July, with revisions in early August. His basic premise was that British actions were to be predicated on self-defense. In July he had professed that "the universal aggressions of the United States" warranted defensive precautions. This was especially true, Simcoe said, because a large foreign army menacing the Canadian frontier would interfere, if only inadvertently, with the commercially valuable fur trade, in which both the British and the Indians were entitled to participate. Accordingly, the "reoccupation" of Fort Miamis was merely a defense that the British were entitled to establish. Simcoe also decreed that his agents should continue to furnish "all supplies" reasonably required by the Indians, including munitions, but that they should be circumspect in their behavior and not provoke an American attack. The lieutenant governor considered war with the United States a certainty and that Wayne would attack Fort Miamis if given the opportunity.[19]

In mid-August, having received news of Wayne's offensive thrust, Simcoe reported that the Indians must remain at the front line of defense. Yet, in all practicality, he considered that they could not adequately defend their country without British assistance. Beyond drafting operational war plans that called for the reduction of Forts Recovery and Greeneville, should war break out, he further counseled his subordinates on the premise of "repel-[ing] force by force."

In essence, Simcoe's instructions not only provided great latitude for individual interpretation but also indirectly encouraged a warlike British posture. While he was not intentionally seeking war with the United States, Simcoe suggested that the "inevitability" of that conflict warranted overt preparations.

Although the lieutenant governor despaired of stopping Wayne short of Detroit, on August 18 he nonetheless prepared to hasten from Niagara to Detroit "with all the force I can muster."[20] In light of the powder keg that existed at the Miami Rapids, all of the circumstances necessary for the outbreak of an international war were present. The outcome now seemed to depend in a large measure on the individuals in positions of responsibility— particularly on their personalities and the extent of their forebearance.

The first British commander to endure the building pressure of the war was Lieutenant Colonel Richard G. England, commandant of Detroit. England was an experienced and able Irishman of such prodigious size that the Prince of Wales allegedly had joked about his name, saying that he should be renamed Great Britain. As it turned out, England had an ample measure of composure to match his large frame.[21]

On August 5 a delegation of Wyandots, headed by Tarhe ("the Crane"), had returned to Lieutenant Colonel England the war hatchet that the British had placed in inactivity at the end of the Revolution. Of great symbolic significance, this tomahawk was presented to the British in a formal ceremony. In essence, the British were being asked to fight as allies as they had promised to do on the former occasion, should danger threaten.[22]

Lieutenant Colonel England, on the following day, answered the Wyandots in much the same manner as he had Little Turtle's request for direct involvement. First reminding the Indians that the British had sent soldiers to the Miami Rapids to offer protection, he said that he could not march to war without his superior's orders. Lieutenant Colonel England then recommended to the delegation that they return to the Maumee region and listen to the advice of McKee, their agent.[23]

Simcoe, who was soon advised by express of the return of the war hatchet, was greatly concerned. He foresaw the need for further British encouragement, short of war, lest the Indians cease to defend their country. In this context he dispatched Captain Joseph Bunbury of the Fifth Regulars to occupy and fortify Turtle Island at the mouth of the Maumee. Bunbury was to take with him a portion of the Queen's Rangers and several cannon to use as needed so as to effectively "block up the bay." On August 17 this strong detachment sailed for the mouth of the Maumee, where it was anticipated that Bunbury could reinforce Fort Miamis if necessary.[24]

For Lieutenant Colonel England at Detroit the continuing necessity for crucial decisions in the absence of higher authority reached a new height on August 12. Having sent Major William Campbell and several companies of the Twenty-fourth Regiment to Fort Miamis on August 9 because of the "critical situation" along the Maumee, England realized that the fort lacked sufficient workmen to complete its defenses before Wayne's approach. In consultation with James Baby, the Kent County militia commander, he therefore called up one hundred unarmed Canadian militia, who would proceed to Fort Miamis and serve as workmen for about two weeks. A detachment of fifty militia volunteers from the Lake Erie region, fully armed, were also allowed to go along, to be used as the commandant might decree.[25]

After these troops had sailed on August 12, England, the following week, placed all of the nearby militia units on alert and prepared to concentrate them as a reserve at Detroit. By August 14 the Canadian militia had arrived at Fort Miamis, where their "very very odd but very gallant" commander, Lieutenant Colonel William Caldwell, made immediate preparations to support the Indian army—in a combat role if necessary.

With the reported advance of Wayne's Legion on August 17 to Roche de Bout, the expanded concentration of Indians and British auxiliaries girded for combat. Said a senior Canadian militia official about that time, "I am as confident as ever they [the Indians] will conquer their enemy."[26]

It now seems deeply ironic, but explicit Home Office instructions were then en route to the British officials in Canada to prepare to evacuate the disputed posts and to maintain the peaceful status quo. Because of the probability of an amicable settlement of the existing disputes between England and the United States, Henry Dundas had written to Lieutenant Governor Simcoe on July 4 that a "pacific line of conduct" was to be followed. In fact, "the immediate protection" of the post of Detroit was the only matter to be regarded—thus by implication Fort Miamis was to be excluded. Moreover, the ceded posts were to be looked on as "temporary objects"; the final arrangements "in all probability leading to their evacuation."[27]

This stunning declaration of revised British policy was largely the work of the "envoy extraordinary" whom George Washington had dispatched to London in May, 1794. Chief Justice John Jay, contrary to his expectations, had found the British government peacefully inclined. His prolonged negotiations with the highest officials seemed to defuse much of the animosity and uncertainty that had previously existed. Jay's assurance that Wayne had no orders that would authorize him to attack any pre-1784 British post on ceded land seemed to be a primary consideration.[28]

The Duke of Portland thus wrote to Dorchester in mid-July stating that the "status quo" should govern all future conduct until the negotiations were concluded; that all hostile measures should cease, and captured property and prisoners, if any, should be restored.

Although London's instructions were issued far too late to be received by Canadian officials prior to mid-August, they were designed to end any threat of an unpopular war with the United States. Unfortunately, however, the impetus for war or peace rested not at the diplomatic level in the sweltering summer of 1794 but at a remote, advanced outpost on the Maumee, where overt actions were to mandate the course of history.[29]

The road through the ravines was exceedingly bad, almost impassable for wagons—wrote an officer of the Legion's march on August 16. Moreover, the weather was so oppressively hot that Wayne had to order frequent halts. About twelve o'clock another lengthy delay had occurred, but just as the army was again preparing to march, Christopher Miller rode in.[30]

Miller, beyond delivering the written message that had been entrusted to him, conveyed an impression of general Indian alarm; that fighting was their "decided intention." Accordingly, the Indian message was generally interpreted to be a challenge.[31] Proceeding several miles farther, the army encamped along the northern riverbank early in the afternoon, after again constructing the usual temporary breastworks of fallen timber. Wayne, who was said to be not well enough to stand unsupported or to mount his horse without help, continued to be unrelenting in his insistence that the army push ahead as rapidly as possible. About fourteen miles were traveled on August 17, bringing the army to the head of the Maumee Rapids, which was only an estimated eighteen miles from the enemy.[32]

The trek that began at 7:00 A.M. on August 18, wrote a soldier in great wonderment, proved, surprisingly, to be romantically beautiful. The broad Maumee River spread in a wide corridor with sparkling falls every mile or two, and from the high riverbanks the inviting scene reflected all the intense grandeur of the unspoiled midcontinent. Along the route stood several abandoned traders' houses replete with account books, silversmiths' tools, and "delightful gardens" filled with produce. Orchards of peach, apple, and plum trees graced the scene and provided ample fruit for the refreshment of the troops.[33]

At Roche de Bout, the site of that evening's halt, the view was breathtaking. "We behold one of the most beautiful landscapes ever painted," wrote Lieutenant William Clark. Here a small island dotted with dark clusters of cedar and craggy rocks jutted from the majestic river's surface. The expansive Maumee looked to one Kentuckian like "a flooded meadow" with rugged protruding rocks extending for miles upriver. These were the famed Wolf Rapids of Indian lore.[34]

This elegant natural setting was, however, hardly appealing to Wayne, who had recently termed it an asylum from which the red enemy carried on a deadly warfare. In fact, on the evening of August 18, Wayne was fuming with indignation. On that afternoon his detachment of regular spies, commanded by Captain Ephraim Kibby, had suffered a crippling ambush. Already weakened by the loss of Wells and McClelland, Kibby's force had consisted of no more than fifteen woodsmen. Riding some miles in advance of the army's vanguard, these scouts had been waylaid by a superior Indian force and quickly scattered. In the tumult and confusion of the retreat William May, who had served as General Wilkinson's spy among the Indians in 1792, was captured after his horse "failed."[35]

To Wayne this attack was most serious because it was hard evidence of the enemy's willingness to fight—the first such indication in many days. Accordingly, Wayne directed the construction of a temporary "place of deposit" for heavy baggage, so that the Legion might advance more rapidly and in better fighting order. A garrison of about one hundred regulars was detached to remain at this site, and Wayne devoted the entire day of August 19 to the construction of this Camp Deposit.[36]

While the army labored in generally clear weather on August 19, felling large timbers for their temporary fort, Major William Price's batallion of Kentucky mounted spies rode forward to scout the countryside. Dispersed along a broad front to prevent surprise, a cautiously advancing segment, under the major's personal observation, suddenly discovered a concealed line of Indians lurking in their immediate front. Quickly falling back without becoming engaged, Price's batallion hastily withdrew to camp. About 11:00 A.M., Major Price reported to Wayne that he had passed to within an estimated two miles of the British fort and had seen at one point the trampled grass and numerous trails where a strong Indian force had recently formed in line to receive the American army. It was his decided opinion, said Price, that the Indians would fight tomorrow morning at that very spot.[37]

Wayne immediately prepared his army for battle. Although one side of the deposit structure remained unfinished, he ordered that the Legion sleep on their arms and prepare to advance at 5:00 A.M. on the following morning.[38]

To the aroused soldiers of the American Legion it was quite apparent that the long-expected crisis was at hand. In the daily journal of one young army lieutenant the prospects for the morrow were recorded with almost casual assuredness: "The troops are in such high spirits that we will make an easy victory," he claimed. Another soldier considered the task ahead and reflected on the consequences: "Tomorrow will in all probability produce a victory or a defeat—the latter we fear not, the former we flatter ourselves we are assured of. . . . Be this as it may, resolved we are of victory or death."[39]

A captured Shawnee warrior related in mid-August that the deserter Robert Newman had provided a great quantity of tactical information in his debriefing by the Indians. Newman not only had told the Indians how to distinguish between the dress of officers and enlisted men in battle but also had advised them to attack Wayne's army on the march, where they were most vulnerable.[40]

Wayne's manner of advance had long since been analyzed by the Indian commanders, particularly his custom of marching only until early in the afternoon of each day and constructing a fortified camp to protect his bivouac at night. The Legion's security was so intact, related a Shawnee warrior, that it was next to impossible to steal even so much as a horse from his camp. The great trees felled each night to "fence in" his soldiers not only prevented access but also screened his troops and equipment from view. Wayne's system of limiting the opportunities for attack by an enterprising enemy had already earned him the rather reverent sobriquet "Blacksnake." He obviously possessed all of the art and cunning of that reptile, the Indians said.[41]

Because it was impractical to attack the American army in their camp, the Indians were determined to await Wayne's approach and engage him in battle on favorable terrain that was well adapted for the favorite Indian stratagem of ambush.

Another important source of up-to-date information was William May, the American scout whom the Indians had captured on the afternoon of August 18. A former captive, whose life had been spared through the influence of Simon Girty in 1792, May must have quickly realized his desperate predicament. He had long been associated with the turncoat William Wells as a key American spy, and he was immediately recognized and closely interrogated by the Indians. The generally accurate information that May provided revealed that Wayne intended to advance and attack the Indians on August 19, unless it was determined to build a fort for deposit of baggage, in which case he would proceed on the twentieth.[42]

Having been gleaned of this vital intelligence, May was informed of his impending fate. "Tomorrow we take you to that tree," warned a red warrior, who pointed to a large burr oak at the edge of the clearing near the British fort. "We will tie you up and make a mark on your breast. We will [see] what Indian can shoot nearest [to] it."

Alexander McKee, charged with direct management of Indian affairs in the best interest of the British government, now urged the Indian force to march to the intended battlefield and exert themselves in battle. Even many of the dissident faction in favor of peace were induced to go along.

Early on the morning of the nineteenth the unfortunate scout William May was dragged to the designated tree and summarily executed. His body was riddled with "at least fifty bullets," a former Kentucky scout later related. Then the Indian column quickly passed forth into the woods.[43]

Blue Jacket of the Shawnees was apparently the overall commander of the Indian force (he was a special object of McKee's politicking with that tribe). Under his leadership an estimated thirteen hundred red warriors and a detachment of white auxiliaries dressed as Indians prepared to lie in ambush.[44]

Blue Jacket, the bitter rival of Little Turtle, had once again emerged as the principal war leader of the Shawnees, following his role as commander of that nation's warriors at St. Clair's defeat. Boasting of a British commission as a "war chief" dating from 1784, Blue Jacket's fondness for fancy dress and strong drink had long been noted.[45] Since the chief was nearly six feet in height, with large, piercing eyes, one observer thought him a "brave masculine figure of a man." Nonetheless, though Blue Jacket was an able and courageous warrior, he lacked the sagacity and tactical wisdom of the brilliant Little Turtle. Moreover, his superior mien, haughty spirit, and inveterate hostility to his white enemies did little to further his reputation with the British military authorities. In 1793, Lieutenant Colonel England at Detroit had regarded him as much of a drunken boor, writing that he had "not the highest opinion of either his zeal or abilities."[46]

Seemingly, Blue Jacket was, like Little Turtle, at the pinnacle of his reputation in 1794. To McKee, more than ever the behind-the-scenes mastermind of Indian affairs, Blue Jacket was just the sort of impetuous if not too brilliant, military leader that the British required in the existing crisis. Urging by every means in his power that the Indians strike Wayne's troops before they penetrated to the British fort, McKee hoped to avoid the investment of that post by a decisive victory.

As had been outlined by Lieutenant Governor Simcoe during his visit in April to the region, it was anticipated that Wayne's approach to Fort Miamis would be along the Maumee. Accordingly, plans had been made to waylay the American column about five miles southwest of Fort Miamis within the dense thicket of fallen timber and undergrowth known as Presque Isle.[46] Here the timber had been devastated by a tornado or heavy windstorm some years earlier, producing a tangled thicket about a mile long and from forty to eighty rods wide. Within this area, amid a second growth of heavy brush and saplings, downed oak timber formed natural abatis so thick that they were nearly impervious in places. According to one Indian participant, these conditions were intensified by cutting the young saplings off to about breast height so that they formed an additional barrier.[47]

Last but not least, the Indians had prepared for the coming battle by fasting, in order that a warrior shot in the stomach might survive without danger from digesting food. Since warriors were accustomed to occasional periods of abstinence, such a traditional fast was not particularly debilitating, even when the general advance of Wayne's army failed to occur on the nineteenth. Only the brief appearance of the Kentucky mounted infantry under Major Price had disturbed the Indians' uneventful wait.

Since the Indians also had been in line of battle on August 18, the morning of the twentieth marked the third successive day without food for many of the warriors. Nonetheless, they remained in position, expecting Wayne's approach with the coming of daylight.[48] Arranged in a long line running obliquely from the Maumee to the northwest for nearly three-quarters of a mile, the Indian army anticipated an effective ambush. Their flanks were thus extended to prevent envelopment by the American cavalry. Posted in the middle of their formation were the Ottawas and lake-region tribesmen, who were among the most numerous of the tribal groups present.[49]

Led by Little Otter and Egushawa, two of the more outspoken of the war leaders, the strategically placed Ottawas and lake-region Indians were certain to play a key role in the coming action. Nearby, about seventy Canadian militia, painted and dressed like Indians, stood to arms under their commander, Lieutenant Colonel William Caldwell. Even Alexander McKee and his assistants, Matthew Elliott and Simon Girty, were prepared to take the field as observers.[50] To the rear a strong British fort served as added security, and tangible evidence of the King's promised protection.

All but forgotten in the rush of events were the dire predictions of Little Turtle, and also Wayne's warnings that the British had "neither the power nor inclination" to protect their red allies. For now the impending contest of arms was paramount in the warriors' minds, especially since such encounters had, since the beginning of the war, demonstrated the military superiority of the Indian peoples.[51]

29

"Our Moccasins Trickled Blood"

THE morning of August 20, 1794, dawned damp and rainy. "A shower of rain prevented our move at the hour appointed [5:00 A.M.]," wrote Lieutenant William Clark. Yet two hours later the Legion was in motion under clearing skies that foreboded another sultry and oppressively humid day in the Maumee valley.

The soldiers traveled light that morning, carrying only a blanket and two days' provisions in addition to their arms and accouterments. Marching in close order, the Legion again traversed innumerable steep ravines and thick woods, and at 8:45 A.M., by one officer's reckoning, had covered about four and one half miles.[1]

Holding the post of honor as the forwardmost elements of the entire Legion that morning were two privates, Sherman Moore and William Steele, of Major William Price's Kentucky militia. Next seventy-four regulars of the Fourth Sub Legion, under Captain John Cook, were deployed as a reserve about four hundred yards behind Price's battalion. In the rear of Cook's two companies the main elements of Wayne's army sprawled through the wilderness in extended columns. There were two wings, consisting of the Second and Fourth Sub Legions, under Lieutenant Colonel John F. Hamtramck, and on Hamtramck's right, Brigadier General James Wilkinson commanding the Third and First Sub Legions. In all, the regulars numbered about eight hundred troops, and they were reported to be in fine spirits due to the anticipation of a fight.[2]

By Wayne's express orders, the columns that day advanced two deep and in a more compacted manner than usual, with the detachments of dragoons and artillery in the center. Wayne, it seems, was intent on distributing his strength evenly, so that the army might defend itself along any perimeter if necessary. Much depends upon the first dispositions in an encounter, admonished the commander in his battle orders; every effort had to be made to turn the Indians' flank. In fact, the red enemy were to be regarded as formidable only when pursuing their opponents, not when being driven back. This test of initiative, Wayne reminded his troops, was critical, and should any soldiers give way without being ordered to withdraw, the fire of the artillery and supporting infantry would be directed at them.[3]

Moore and Steele were observed carefully working their advanced points ahead of Price's battalion. The gound being traversed was "a close thick wood," covered with old fallen timber. High grass and considerable brush obscured even the sparse openings, limiting visibility to less than twenty yards in spots.

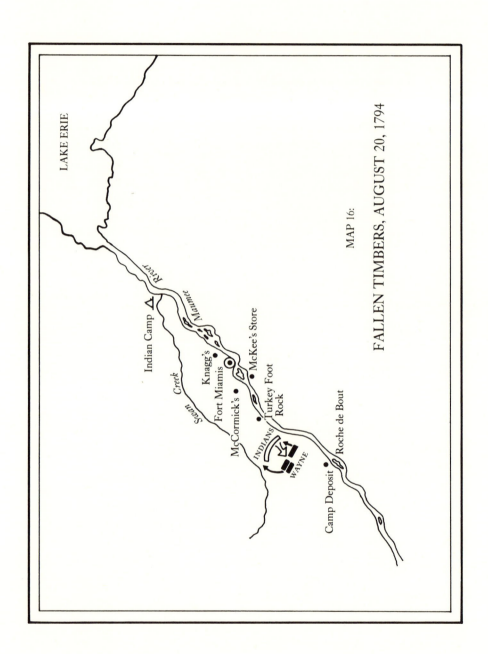

LAKE ERIE

Maumee *River*

Swan *Creek*

Indian Camp

Knagg's

Fort Miamis

McKee's Store

Turkey Foot
Rock

McCormick's

INDIANS

WAYNE

Roche de Bout

Camp Deposit

MAP 16:

FALLEN TIMBERS, AUGUST 20, 1794

For horsemen the terrain proved to be exceedingly difficult, and their progress was much slowed. The two Kentuckians had passed only about one hundred yards into the downed timber when the roar of rifle fire erupted about them.[4]

Caught in an ambush, Moore and Steele were downed by those first shots, paying with their lives for their voluntary duty. Yet before Price's nearby line could turn back, a rolling volley had felled many men and horses. Inclining to the left, these Kentuckians came under fire at almost point-blank range from another concealed line. The "tremendous roar" in their faces confused and scattered the 150-man battalion within moments, said Lieutenant William Sudduth. His half-crazed horse had been shot through the body, and it began rearing and plunging so that it was unmanageable. With a horde of screaming Indians charging toward him, Sudduth rammed his spurs into the animal's flank. The blood gushed from his horse's wounds—particularly his mouth and nose, related Sudduth—but the animal sprang forward and ran for about a hundred and fifty yards before collapsing. Desperately Sudduth leaped from the saddle and dashed for safety. "The [tree] bark flew into our faces," he said, but nearly all of his company escaped, only five men being lost. One man, John O'Brien, in attempting to flee had been shot in the small of the back, the ball passing through his intestines and lodging in his penis. Miraculously, O'Brien made it to safety despite the intense pain.[5]

In Captain John Cook's sector the fusillade immediately ahead had served as an entirely too brief warning. Cook's "front guard," in fact, delivered their first volley at Price's retreating Kentuckians. They were fleeing without so much as even returning the enemy's fire, Cook concluded. Remembering Wayne's standing orders, he directed his two companies to shoot them down. This halted the panicky militiamen for about a minute, before they again broke away to the right, wrote Cook.[6]

Immediately in their rear loomed the pursuing Indians. Yet due to the chaos on the right in Cook's line, where the Kentuckians were streaming past, Cook's soldiers fell into disorder. "My men began to flee their post," admitted Cook, and it required his full exertion to rally "thirteen or fourteen" of the thirty-seven men of his own company.[7]

By now the Indians were close enough in front to deliver heavy fire on Cook's second company. The infantrymen nervously stood in line and returned three "well-directed" volleys before the pressure became too great. Ordering the remnant to withdraw while fighting, Cook stumbled toward the rear with his men, soon losing all control as the red warriors broke in among the ranks in hand-to-hand fighting. From then on it was every man for himself, wrote Cook.[8]

The drizzling rain that fell just before daylight had materially altered the complexion of the day for the entire Indian army, an Ottawa chief later remembered. The wet and dreary weather seemed to preclude the prospect of an American advance that morning, and accordingly, many of the fasting Indians resolved to go to the rear for provisions, this being their third morning without food. Some evidently had returned to the vicinity of Fort Miamis when the sound of gunfire suddenly issued from the southwest. While a few hurried back toward the Presque Isle ambush site, many apparently "hung back," not knowing if a battle was imminent or merely some desultory skirmishing.[9]

As was expected, the route of the American column that morning had generally coincided with the Indians' calculations. The center of the Indian line had been approached as anticipated, and the trap had been sprung in an effective manner. Yet the warriors positioned in this central sector were the Ottawas and the Potawatomis, the very same tribes who had initiated the abortive Fort Recovery assault. Led by their impetuous war chiefs Little Otter and Egushawa, these combatants were noted for their ardor, but in the past they had been heavily criticized for their lack of tactical perspective.[10]

This morning their actions were again to thrust them in the center of heated controversy. In an impulsive manner, the Ottawas and others suddenly rose from behind their ambuscades and pursued the vanguard of Wayne's Legion beyond the downed timber. Their "shrill hallow" filled the woods, remembered a retreating Kentuckian. Brandishing tomahawks and scalping knives, they ran on, chasing the routed soldiers with bold assuredness for about a quarter mile—into relatively open timber.[11] To the suddenly committed Legionnaires of Wayne's main column the confusion of those first few moments nearly became a prelude to disaster. The remnants of the mounted militia and Captain Cook's front guard streamed toward the extreme right flank of Colonel Hamtramck's left wing, which was just then forming. These wildly retreating men broke through the ranks of Captain Howell Lewis's company, observed a nearby lieutenant, and caused many of Lewis's men to fall back in confusion. Lewis, in fact, was compelled to withdraw his entire company without so much as firing a shot. They angled diagonally toward the right for about forty yards, where they fell in with some of Wilkinson's right wing. Here they formed a new line, under a "feeble, scattered fire" from the Indians.[12]

Abruptly, the red warriors had halted at a distance of about sixty to one hundred yards to probe this new line, which was drawn up in an extended order. Wayne, on hearing the firing ahead, had shouted "prepare to receive the enemy in front in two lines." Yet in the bustle of activity his command had not been heard by all. Hamtramck rushed his men into line in the prescribed two ranks, but Wilkinson's men formed in one extended line covering nearly all of the 800-yard front for which his right wing was responsible.[13]

Immediately, firing began on Wilkinson's left, committing the Third Sub Legion before the entire line was in position. As several officers now realized, a concentrated Indian attack at any one point would certainly break through and create "great havoc," perhaps even routing the army. "Everything is in confusion," blurted out a dragoon officer caught up in the disorder of attempting to straighten out the line on Wilkinson's left. No attempt had been made to form a defensive square, and the Fourth Sub Legion, deployed across Hamtramck's front, was so compacted that they invited a flank attack.[14]

Yet this crisis passed without a challenge from the serried line of red warriors, and for a valid reason. As an Indian observer later admitted, only about 400 to 600 warriors were present in this sector, some of whom were armed merely with tomahawks. Since only a portion of the estimated 800 Indians who had been in line at the commencement of the fighting had spontaneously sortied under Little Otter and Egushawa, the entire Indian defensive alignment was severely disrupted. The Ottawas and other forward elements were entirely out of position, confronting the full American battle line in open timber and high grass. Meanwhile, the scattered remnant of the hostiles lingered in their chosen downed-timber ambush site, effectively out of the action. Morever, the more organized components, the Canadian militia under Lieutenant Colonel Caldwell, were posted on the extreme right flank of the prolonged three-quarter-mile original line and thus were of little use. As a further complication, there had been no purpose or direction to the attack, which consisted merely of headlong rushes led by the two Ottawa war chiefs. Blue Jacket, in fact, may have been entirely removed from the immediate scene of fighting; his Shawnees were later said to have been largely unengaged. Certainly, there was no brilliant execution of an effective tactical plan, such as the deposed Little Turtle had formerly achieved. Out-numbered and confronted by an extended American battle line, Egushawa and Little Otter could only maintain a tentative and ineffective defensive alignment.[15]

At this point the burden of the incoming fire was falling on Hamtramck's right and Wilkinson's left, noted a perceptive officer. Yet this Indian musketry was so light that several officers were already begging their senior commanders for permission to charge. Wilkinson, who said he had received no orders to do so, demurred.[16]

Behind Hamtramck's double line Wayne now moved with restless energy. Because of the location of the enemy's fire, he was concerned that they were endeavoring to turn his left flank. Lieutenant William Henry Harrison, Wayne's aide de camp, fearing his general might become too absorbed in the battle action to issue the necessary field orders, excitedly asked what to do. "Charge the damned rascals with the bayonet!" Wayne replied. Immediately Hamtramck's soldiers were told to charge and root out the enemy with fixed bayonets. When they were close upon the fleeing savages, urged Wayne, they should fire into their backs, while continuing to charge so as to prevent the Indians from reloading.[17]

Captain Robert Mis Campbell, with drawn saber, was the first to respond, sending his small command of dragoons forward through the left of Wilkinson's line in such a rush that they apparently threw some of the infantrymen into disorder.

Yet Campbell's charge was premature. Brigadier General Wilkinson saw that the small troop was heading to almost certain destruction, rushing toward a concealed enemy across about eighty yards of mostly open ground. In an effort to support Campbell, he ordered his whole line forward, on his own responsibility. Because of the tall grass in front, however, Wilkinson's riflemen were unable to make rapid headway, and Campbell's dragoons broke in among the Indians with sabers flashing, entirely unsupported. Campbell was instantly shot and killed, and nearly a dozen of his dragoons were felled in the brief melee. Yet when Wilkinson's entire line was seen to be approaching, the outnumbered Indians got up and ran, barely bothering to return the heavy fire directed at their backs.[18]

Charging forward with fixed bayonets, Wilkinson's Third and First Sub Legions breathlessly pursued the Indians along the high ridge bordering the Maumee, scarcely receiving a shot in return. "The fire was truly so light and the resistance so feeble," wrote one of Wilkinson's officers, "that we began to apprehend a deception." Fearing that the Indians were merely baiting the army, Wilkinson rode to the rear to look for Wayne—to ask if they might use greater caution in advancing.[19]

In Wayne's immediate front, Hamtramck's two sublegions had belatedly rushed forward with trailed muskets, similarly routing the thin red line of enemy warriors with ease. Only fifteen minutes had elapsed from the first fire on the main army—reported one of Hamtramck's lieutenants—and yet, once they were in the heavy underbrush, the Legion abruptly met face to face with the Wyandots and Canadian militia. Since the extended hostile line ran at an angle beyond Hamtramck's flank, it appeared to many that the Indians were attempting to outflank the American line.[20]

This proved to be only of momentary concern, wrote a participant. Rushing straight ahead, Wayne's soldiers endured a "most heavy fire" from the nearly sixty Canadians on the left. Yet they pressed on, routing the scattered Wyandots and Delawares. On the left of the Fourth Sub Legion, Todd's dismounted brigade of Kentucky militia moved through the swampy, timber-strewn terrain to fall briefly on the Canadians' flank. They promptly sent the entire mixed line of Indians and British militia reeling northeast in disorder.

Several prominent Canadians fell in the fighting there, including Captain Daniel McKillop, who formerly had been a sergeant in Butler's Rangers during the Revolution; and Charles Smith, clerk of the court of Detroit. The accurate fire of Captain Alexander Gibson's battalion of riflemen accounted for the majority of the enemy casualties, according to a lieutenant of the Fourth Sub Legion. Quickly, the combined American troops rushed on with fixed bayonets.

"We were driven by the sharp end of the guns of the Long Knives," remembered an Indian participant. Since the Indians' original tactical formation was now scattered and in disarray, they were unable to form an effective line in the fallen timber.[21]

The pursuit continued for about a mile as it seemed to several participants; or for nearly two miles, according to others. Although scattered and random firing continued throughout the underbrush, Wayne's soldiers soon became so fatigued that considerable dispersion and irregularity disrupted their battlelines. Captain Mahlon Ford of the artillery, laboring to get his howitzers forward in the rough terrain, even allowed his sweating men to remove their uniform coats. For this he later endured Wayne's ire—such being a breach of discipline, according to Wayne.[22]

On the right, Wilkinson's wing had resumed their attack after a momentary pause. Wilkinson, puzzled by and almost contempuous of the enemy's light resistance, termed the affair "no fight" at the time and hastened on, though he was wary of another ambuscade. Although his troops were impeded by several "deep and steep ravines" that cut through the high ground adjacent to the Maumee, they soon chased the hostiles back to "the end of the hill," near the Indian trader McCormick's house. Here the high ground briefly terminated before resuming, across a wide ravine, as a long ridge running northeast toward Fort Miamis.[23]

Atop a large rock, according to Indian lore, stood the Ottawa war chief Turkey Foot exhorting his warriors to make a stand. "Suddenly, his voice ceased," remembered a subchief who had been present, "and he slid from the rock, shot through the breast with a rifle ball." Actually, Little Otter and Egushawa, the principal Ottawa war chiefs, captained the fighting at this point, though both had been seriously wounded. Egushawa, the senior chief present, had been shot in the eye, and Little Otter had taken such a severe wound that he had to be carried from the field, supposedly mortally injured.[24] Alexander McKee later reported forlornly that the loss of their principal leaders caused the Indians to fear that their losses were much greater than they actually were. Thus they ran from the field utterly demoralized.

An unidentified American staff officer later recorded in his journal that the terrain at this point was moderately open. Eagerly, the dragoons swept ahead, quickly cutting the scattered fugitive Indians down. One of Wilkinson's mounted aides, Lieutenant Bartholomew Schaumburgh, raced into a thicket and drove a frightened warrior out in the direction of the onrushing First Sub Legion. As an officer elatedly observed, the Indian was literally driven onto the bayonets of Wayne's advancing troops.[25]

"We could not stand against the sharp end of their guns," related a routed Indian leader, "and we ran to the river, swamps, thickets, and to the islands in the river, covered with corn. Our moccasins trickled blood in the sand, and the water was red in the river. Many of our braves were killed in the river by rifle [fire]."[26]

The Indians were terrified of the infantry's bayonets, and were particularly afraid of the dragoons, related one of the Indians' prisoners following his release. Dejectedly, they streamed in broken remnants toward the British fort.

McKee, observing the action from a distance with Matthew Elliot and Simon Girty, attempted to rally the remnants, but they passed on in broken clusters until they reached Fort Miamis.

Only the rearguard action of the Canadian militia and the Wyandots, who stood off the charge of Wayne's pursuing dragoons, saved the Indians from further embarrassment. Little Otter, grievously wounded, was unceremoniously thrown across the back of a white horse and carried from the battlefield, only narrowly escaping capture. Beaten, disconsolate, and virtually panic-stricken at the thought of further pursuit, the badly disorganized Indian army converged on Fort Miamis, seeking its protection.[27]

It had been a rather odd kind of day, wrote Major William Campbell, commandant of Fort Miamis, during the afternoon of August 20. That morning his working parties had gone out to continue clearing a perimeter zone of fire, when musketry had sounded in the distant woods. As its intensity increased, and the firing came closer, the Canadian workmen became frightened and withdrew to the fort. Campbell, by 11:00 A.M., had discovered clusters of Indians streaming out of the woods and moving towards the fort in disarray. Fully alarmed, Campbell now ordered the garrison under arms; the gaps in the abatis were filled, and the chevaux de frise emplaced. "Not knowing at what moment we might be attacked," Major Campbell felt impelled to cut off all communications from outside the fort.[28]

To the astounded, confused Indian force, their enormous defeat of the morning perhaps seemed less of an outrage than this, the sudden withdrawal of the fort's promised protection. Buckongehelas of the Delawares felt blatantly insulted. Even Joseph Brant later chided the English for leaving the Indians "in the lurch." Fort Miamis was built in Indian country "under pretense of giving refuge in case of necessity," wrote the angered Brant, "but when that time came the gates were shut against them as enemies."[29]

Deceived, frightened, and badly disorganized, the Indian army was unable to regroup. Gradually the warriors scattered in confusion from an area that was immediately behind the fort, despite McKee's arduous efforts to rally them. At the nearby house of a trader, named Knaggs, about a mile north of Fort Miamis, a similar brief halt resulted only in a further flight approximately to the vicinity of Swan Creek, where the families of the hostiles were encamped. Here McKee "exerted all his powers to make them stand, but in vain," wrote an eyewitness of the confused scene. "They absolutely refused to fight again."[30]

The panic among the returning warriors and their families was so great, wrote a British official, that the appearance of fifty Americans would have totally routed them. "We were no longer strong like braves and warriors, but like women weak and afraid," admitted an Indian participant many years later. Recalling Little Turtle's prophecy about how the Great Spirit would hide his face in a cloud, should his red children not talk of peace with the great chief Wayne, he added that the morning had begun dark and gloomy—an evil omen. "The Great Spirit was in the clouds, weeping over the folly of his red children," he confided, " . . . and many of our young men knew the Great Spirit was angry, and would not help them."[31]

When recall was sounded about 11:05 A.M., many of the American officers regarded the affair thus far as a farce. Brigadier General Wilkinson regarded what came to be known as the Battle of Fallen Timbers as a mere skirmish. It was noted that the entire action had lasted only an hour and ten minutes from start to finish. "This affair . . . does not deserve the name of a battle," wrote an unimpressed officer. Yet when the casualties were counted, it was discovered that the Legion's losses amounted to 133, including 33 dead, 31 of whom were regulars. Only two officers had been killed, and seven were wounded—an insignificant, if lamented, loss.[32]

Due to the intense heat and the fatigue of the men, the disorderly pursuit had been abruptly suspended, and an issue of one-half gill of whiskey per man was made to the army. Only Lieutenants Leonard Covington and John Webb had attempted to harry the enemy's rear with their small detachments of dragoons, but they were largely ineffective, because the dragoons had been "fritter[ed] up" into small detachments, said an officer.[33]

Wayne, meanwhile, had the ground in front reconnoitered for the entire distance to the British fort. At length, after a delay of about four hours, the Legion methodically advanced to within a mile and a quarter of Fort Miamis, where they encamped for the evening.[34]

Here, said Brigadier General Wilkinson, was an imposingly beautiful sight. The Maumee River meandered in various directions through a natural meadow, which was well cultivated, and through a plain bounded by lofty stands of timber. In the midst of this impressive scene stood a defiant Fort Miamis, with the British flag flying. "We could discern the officers and soldiers walking around the garrison," wrote Captain John Cook of the Fourth Sub Legion. Always in view was the familiar scarlet and white Union Jack, reminiscent of another era and another war. "Mad" Anthony Wayne, riding along with his troops toward the enemy fort that afternoon, had jubilantly reminded them that, wherever he went, "he always flogged Indians and British."[35]

"We beat our drums, [and] blowed our trumpets," wrote a senior American officer of the Legion's arrival in front of Fort Miamis on the afternoon of August 20. Indeed, British Major William Campbell had watched their approach with great concern, believing "our situation will not long admit of silence between general Wayne and me." Swarms of cavalry were observed, feeding their horses "upon Colonel McKee's island," wrote Campbell; and while he confided, "I still do not expect him [Wayne] to storm our works," he prepared to act "in every respect in the safety of [this] post as if I did." "[If] he shows himself in any force near to us, and if he does not speak, I shall feel it my duty to do so," warned the anxious British commandant. Adding that "you may rest assured that we shall not sleep very soundly tonight," Campbell closed his dispatch to Detroit with a plaintive reminder that only 160 men rank and file, together with twenty-four Canadians, garrisoned Fort Miamis. "Would to God the Governor himself were here," he asserted. "Whatever happens I shall do for the best. No one can do more."[36]

That night an American deserter, James Johnson, crept through the defenses and provided additional valuable information. It was uncertain whether the Legion would attack Fort Miamis, he related. Different opinions were being expressed about this, especially since the Legion had only twenty small howitzers with it, said Johnson. Still, he described the army as generally healthy and well supplied, but only on half allowances of flour.[37]

Campbell awakened on the morning of August 21 to find "hundreds of the American cavalry . . . constantly skirting the woods all around us." American officers were observed peering through their spyglasses from the point of the nearby island. By midmorning Campbell had had enough. The entire American army had taken posts on the heights, "almost within reach of the guns of this fort," without "any explanation," he said. Campbell belatedly decided to send a flag to Wayne, inquiring, "In what light am I to view your making such near approaches to this garrison?"[38]

The captain who carried the message to the Americans at 11:00 A.M. was

307

sent back by their outposts, who feared for the British officer's safety, Major Campbell related. The major had to wait until 4:00 P.M. for Wayne's answer.

"Without questioning the authority or the propriety, sir, of your interrogatory," Wayne finally responded, "I think . . . that were you entitled to an answer, the most full and satisfactory one was announced to you from the muzzles of my small arms yesterday morning in the action against the horde of savages in the vicinity of your post." Wayne further observed that, had this action continued to within range of the British guns of Fort Miamis, they "would not have much impeded" his victorious army, as no such post was present at the beginning of the current Indian war, and the surrounding country was far within the acknowledged jurisdiction of the United States.[39]

According to Campbell, this "vain production" still left him with "a cautious part to act." Yet, "if any of his troops wantonly insults this post, it shall not be with impunity," he warned. Suspecting that Wayne's belligerent maneuvering "was more of the gasconade than the gentlemen," Campbell anxiously looked for the arrival of expected reinforcements from Detroit. Nonetheless, he remained generally in a quandary about what to do.[40]

Anthony Wayne, wrote James Wilkinson, had considered Fort Miamis too strong to take by assault, and in view of the current scarcity of provisions it was considered impractical to take it by regular siege or entrenched approaches. Furthermore, it was said that no more than ten days' provisions remained, despite the availability of corn and other produce. The only artillery on hand were about twenty "pop gun howitzers," as Wilkinson termed them, and Wayne forlornly resigned himself to withdrawing to Camp Deposit during the afternoon of the twenty-first.[41]

Yet Campbell's "interrogatory" seemed to change everything. Wayne, indignant over Campbell's implied challenge, became determined to remain upon the ground, and he ordered two days' rations brought forward from Camp Deposit. That evening he even proposed reducing Fort Miamis by storm or surprise, provided that a practical means to do so was found. Wayne thus planned a close personal reconnaissance of Fort Miamis for the following morning. Based on intelligence provided by Antoine Lasselle, a French trader who had been found in Indian garb hiding near the riverbank after the fight on the twentieth, the fort's garrison was estimated to be only about 250, of whom 50 were sick.[42]

This information was further corroborated by John Bevan, a drummer of the Twenty-fourth British Regiment, who deserted to the Americans during the morning of the twenty-first. Bevan described the cannon mounted in Fort Miamis in detail, and he declared that the Indians were regularly supplied with provisions drawn from the garrison's magazine.

Wayne therefore reasoned that further action was desirable to convince the savages that the British had neither the power nor the inclination to protect them. With that purpose in mind, he ordered the destruction of all valuable property in the vicinity on the twenty-second, including McKee's and other traders' storehouses. Moreover, Wayne planned that his personal reconnaissance on that morning would come so close to the British garrison as to be insulting.[43]

The morning of Friday, August 22, 1794, dawned cool and overcast. Wayne, at 9:00 A.M., gathered four companies of light infantry and four troops of dragoons, and advanced to carry out his personal reconnaissance. After posting these troops in a perimeter around the garrison about 100 yards distant (on the edge of the thick woods), Wayne, alone, rode toward the British fort. Campbell, amazed and awkwardly circumstanced, watched the American general ride forth in bold defiance. The fort's garrison stood at their posts, and the loaded cannon were trained in the direction of the Americans.

Wayne kept coming—to within easy pistol shot of the walls. Slowly and deliberately he continued riding around the perimeter. According to one account, he hurled insults and cursed the British soldiers standing on duty within the walls. One British officer allegedly wanted to shoot "the bravo" with his pistol.[44]

Campbell, choking down his anger at this "extreme insolence," refused to permit it. He later reported, "My situation was a very delicate one," and if an error was to be made in forebearance, it would be "on the safe side." Therefore, as Wayne closely reconnoitered the fort, Campbell prepared another note, warning the American commander that he had endured these "insults" to the British flag thus far because he wished to prevent "that dreadful decision" of actual warfare. Yet, if Wayne did not cease and desist from his "threatening" approaches, Campbell said he would, from duty and honor, fire on him.[45]

Before this note could be prepared and delivered, Wayne had returned to his waiting line of troops, and due to the threat of rain he soon retired to his headquarters marquee. Observing that the British fort was a "regular, strong work," with walls twenty feet high from the bottom of the deep, and a wide ditch in front, Wayne clearly understood that it could not be carried but "with great loss of blood" by direct assault. Lacking the necessary provisions and artillery for entrenched approaches, he again resigned himself to withdrawing the Legion to his regular chain of forts.[46]

Yet Campbell's terse message provoked further resentment. Wayne immediately sent a heated reply, saying that the hostile presence of the British in American territory was an act of "the highest aggression." Accordingly, he demanded in the name of the president the withdrawal of the garrison forthwith to Detroit, saying safe passage would be permitted for that purpose.

Moreover, Wayne hastened to carry out his previous orders to destroy "everything within view of the fort, and even under the muzzles of [its] guns." Squadrons of cavalry thereafter roamed the countryside, burning Indian huts, McKee's storehouse, and even the stacked hay collected on McKee's island. "For spite," recorded an American lieutenant in his journal, "[we have] burned all the Indian huts . . . and put the finishing stroke to the destruction of the cornfields, gardens, hay stacks, etc."

Soon an enormous pall of smoke hung against the dark storm clouds that were gathering in the distance.[47]

For his part, Major Campbell, the more he thought about the morning's incidents, the angrier he became. With the arrival of Wayne's insulting demand for the fort's surrender, added to the burning of everything valuable within view, Campbell became highly incensed. Immediately dispatching a reply to Wayne, he asserted that he would not abandon his post at the summons of any power until he had received such orders from his superiors. Reiterating his earlier warning, Major Campbell declared that any individual or unit of Wayne's army approaching Fort Miamis must expect to suffer the consequences.[48]

Soon thereafter a squadron of United States dragoons, evidently riding close to the British fort to destroy Indian and British property, came within range of the garrison's nine-pounders. Campbell ordered a cannon trained on this troop and the priming ball lighted. "They prudently withdrew," wrote a British offical, "but had . . . they remained, the shot would have been fired, and would have been the signal for war." "Once begun," he later added, "I see no measures from the nature of the means . . . of saying 'stop' with any degree of effect."[49]

Thus a war that might have resulted from Wayne and Campbell's abstract interpretations of duty and honor was averted by the narrowest of margins. Campbell had been right. Wayne, despite his bluff, had no intention of initiating an international war by firing the first shot. While Campbell's garrison stood to arms at their posts that night, even sleeping beside their loaded cannon, Wayne's Legion was preparing to withdraw.[50]

Before they left, on the morning of August 23, by Wayne's order the army was drawn up within sight of the garrison, and a "funeral ceremony" was performed for the Legion's dead, including a solemn dirge and a sixteen-gun salute from the small howitzers. Despite the accidental burning of three artillerists by a premature explosion, the ceremony was completed. Then the army about-faced and marched away before noon.[51]

After sweeping the battlefield to recover any remaining property and count the enemy dead, Wayne's Legion returned to Camp Deposit that evening. Soon resuming their march southwest, in weather that was often rainy and gloomy, they traversed nearly fifty miles in five days, arriving at Fort Defiance on August 27. Since the army was severely lacking in provisions, nearly a dozen more deserters had fled the Legion during the rather disorderly march south.[52]

In fact, so impoverished of supplies were Wayne's soldiers that by August 29 a serious crisis was developing. The army on that date was reduced to 12,000 pounds of flour and eight days' supply of beef. "The corn and vegetables which have hitherto supplied the deficiency," wrote a disgruntled officer, "are failing, and will soon be exhausted."[53]

Wilkinson, ever the malcontent, grumbled that, should the resupply convoy under Brigadier General Robert Todd be halted by bad weather or cut up by the enemy, "this army must dissipate and find their way to Greeneville . . . at the expense of all property, public and private." If the Indians prosecuted the war, Wilkinson surmised, they would "send us back to Greeneville before December." "On what precarious grounds does the issue of the campaign depend," wrote another officer. "Fortune, the blind goddess, favors us—Heaven grant a continuance—for in her smiles consists our main dependence." If five hundred Indians had then attacked, it was be-

310

lieved the consequences would be fatal to the army. All that the enemy lacked in this regard, said one of Wilkinson's cronies, was "either firmness, enterprise, or judgment."

Major William Campbell had observed the departure of Wayne's army with great relief. Based on information supplied by several of the American deserters, he learned that Wayne was very short of provisions and, lacking heavy artillery, had given up all idea of storming the fort because of the great loss in life that it would have required. Immediately dispatching this intelligence to McKee at nearby Point Aux Chênes, Campbell anticipated that his news might be of "great consequence" in stimulating the Indians to counterattack. On the following day he reported to Detroit that "great numbers" of mounted Indians were going in pursuit of Wayne. McKee, for his part, reported the desecration of the Indian corpses left on the Maumee, where stakes allegedly had been driven through the remains. This "call[ed] for more than human vengeance," declared McKee, who urged the Indians forth.[55]

It was not to be. The pitifully few hostiles who actually followed Wayne's retreat were so disorganized and careless that they became victims themselves rather than predators. On August 24 several American stragglers allegedly were taken by Indians hovering about the Legion's rear. Intending to bait these bothersome hostiles, Major William Price's Kentucky scouts ambuscaded the army's camp after the main column's departure on August 25. A mounted party of eight Indians rode in during the early morning, and promptly suffered a loss of one killed and two wounded.[56]

Thereafter harassment of the Legion was virtually nonexistent. Only a "howling like wolves" and a "crying like owls" betrayed a few Indians' presence at night. Even the detractors of Wayne's "puny victory" of August 20 were compelled to comment on the enemy's silence and invisibility. Wilkinson, in fact, had to admit that the Indians were so quiet that "we know nothing about them"—not where they were or what they would do.[57]

Wayne, realizing that the Indians must now be completely sustained by the British because of the enormous destruction of their cornfields and villages, began to ponder the end of the war. Assured as he was that the enemy had been "taught to dread" the bayonets of his Legion, the general could reflect happily on the consequences of his campaign, while enjoying full latitude of maneuver and a significant absence of enemy activity.[58]

Whatever the end result might be, Wayne wrote, it was self-evident that his "brilliant success" during the recent campaign must prove beneficial, and that the Indians' prospects "must naturally be gloomy and unpleasant."[59]

311

30

The Essence of Despair

THE Indians on this occasion [the Battle of Fallen Timbers] have forfeited every pretention to a warlike or gallant character," wrote a disgusted senior British military commander. "They behaved excessive ill in the action at the falls, and afterwards fled in every direction. [Later] their panic was so great that the appearance of fifty Americans would have totally routed them." Only about forty Indians, ten of whom were chiefs, had been lost in the action, yet, said Lieutenant Colonel England, it was increasingly evident that the confederated tribes no longer could be relied on for the primary defense of the Detroit region.[1]

Another British commander estimated that only the unexplained and rather mystifying withdrawal of Wayne's Legion had spared the Indians from complete disaster. Also, the sullen Alexander McKee reported, the Indians' camp at Swan Creek was seething with resentment. Their cornfields and villages had been completely destroyed, and with winter rapidly approaching, the question of their survival loomed like a dreaded specter. McKee now worked diligently to prevent the various nations from abandoning the region for Spanish-controlled territory, openly offering the prospect of expanded issues of provisions to entice the tribes to remain under British control.[2]

Exasperated, Lieutenant Colonel England stated that an estimated 1,300 barrels of flour and as many of pork would be required to supply the 2,556 Indian men, women, and children at Swan Creek for six months. Three thousand daily rations were being issued by McKee's agent, and only a meager quantity, 94 barrels of pork and 20 barrels of flour, were available in mid-September at Swan Creek.[3]

Alexander McKee soon was compelled to encourage the chiefs to send their young men out to hunt to supplement the handouts. Yet the powder issued for this purpose proved to be damaged. Then the arrival of a trader's pirogue with eight or ten kegs of rum precipitated a prolonged debauch. One of McKee's agents, Thomas Smith, soon reported: "Unless some method may be fallen upon to stop the rum, it will be out of the power of [a white] man to remain at this place. I need not tell you how unreasonable drunken Indians are."[4]

Into this riled cauldron of adversity and malcontent journeyed Lieutenant Governor Simcoe on September 27. Simcoe had been determined to come out and restore the Indians "to their wanted resolution" in late August. The Indians thickly lined the banks of the Maumee at his approach, an accompanying officer observed. Greeted by a spontaneous salute of rifle fire,

Simcoe nonetheless found conditions in the region disheartening. Fort Miamis's garrison was in a "most melancholy" situation, he said, being prey to despondency and sickness. Complaints from the Chippewas over the beating of a warrior by a Canadian rankled Simcoe, and he was pressed on all sides for information about future British plans.[5]

After touring the battlefield and visiting the garrison, Simcoe promised to give his counsel at a grand meeting to be held at the Huron Village, alias Brownstown, near the mouth of the Detroit River. Simcoe's reason for convening the council at that site which was also known to the Indians as Big Rock, was based on the arrival of Captain Joseph Brant with ninety-seven Mohawks from the Niagara region.[6]

Brant, however, was found to be in a particularly foul mood. He belatedly had come from the Niagara region with the direct encouragement of Simcoe, for military purposes. The Presque Isle crisis had temporarily abated in August because President Washington had instructed the Pennsylvania authorities not to proceed with occupation at least until the completion of Wayne's campaign. Brant therefore had determined to join the western Indians with every man he could muster, because, he said, "our fate depends upon the repulse of Wayne."[7] His belated arrival was nearly a month too late to assist the hostiles militarily. Brant complained that no timely notice had been sent to him of Wayne's approach, and at first, he seemed confused and uncertain of what policy to pursue.

Then, because of the disorganization and vacuum in leadership in the aftermath of the Indians' defeat at Fallen Timbers, Brant perceived an opportunity to reassume a dominant role in the confederacy's affairs.

With political acumen Brant promptly utilized the "mediation" of the British and assumed the role of principal spokesman of all the nations, despite marked coolness on the part of the Shawnees, Delawares, and Miamis for his absence during the recent fighting. In a stormy session from October 11 to October 14 at Brownstown, Brant and a Wyandot leader demanded a specific British commitment for attacking a United States frontier post.[8]

Simcoe, hard pressed to appease the Indians and yet not exceed the bounds of discretion, could only weakly assure the red nations that their father, the king, would "uniformly fulfill all his engagements with you," including protecting and defending them from "all his [the king's] enemies." As a token of appeasement Simcoe hastily issued orders that, upon the approach of any armed American troops to Fort Miamis, the commander was to consider this an aggression and to fire on them. Further, "every indulgence" and "the kindest attention" was to be shown to "these gallant [Indian] people."[9]

Far short of a meaningful commitment, Simcoe's rhetoric merely reiterated the equivocating British policy of self-interest. Brant was bitterly disappointed, saying "we are now low spirited by waiting so long [for British help], and we are nearly at the end of our expectations." After demanding that Simcoe petition Dorchester to find out if any direct military assistance would be forthcoming, Brant angrily closed the council, urging the Indians to reassemble the following spring at the same site and to avoid any "separate or partial treaties with the Americans." Brant, wrote a British observer, foresaw that the entire country was "on the brink of being lost and forsaken." Thereafter the entire council broke up in uncertainty and dismay, and the various nations scattered to their respective villages. Yet soon there was to be further distressing news.[10]

While returning to the Niagara region in mid-October, Brant learned that in his absence the federal authorities had convened another Six Nations treaty to deal with the sticky Presque Isle problem. This council at Canandaigua, New York, had been instigated by President Washington's instructions in July, as a stratagem to keep the Six Nations from joining the hostiles until Wayne's campaign was completed. It was also promoted for the purpose of approving an American settlement at Presque Isle.

Duped by misleading information that Brant had approved of the proceedings, the Buffalo Creek Senecas and others of the Six Nations had proceeded to Canandaigua in mid-October, 1794.[11] Once there, they were reduced to accepting the American terms and yielding the disputed lands, as a result of the recently altered military and political situation. The Six Nations delegation headed by Cornplanter obligingly placed their signatures on the document and returned to their villages, only to receive the bitter criticism of the British and the more conservative Six Nations tribesmen who had been absent.

Brant, having just striven for unity and dedication of purpose at Brownstown, thus returned to witness the virtual destruction of his most coveted plans, long before they could be implemented. Recrimination, accusations, and distrust thereafter were to characterize internal Six Nations politics, and in light of the serious blow to the prospect of British intervention as a result of the Battle of Fallen Timbers, the Canandaigua agreement became the coup de grace to Indian hopes in the East.[12]

Lieutenant Governor Simcoe had been en route from the Brownstown Council to Niagara when, on October 17, he received the Home Office dispatches of midsummer, 1794. Advised by Secretary of State Dundas and his successor, the Duke of Portland, that peace and the status quo were to be paramount in colonial policy as a result of Jay's negotiations—and that the posts ceded in 1783 would probably be evacuated—the astounded Simcoe immediately altered his perspective. In a letter to the British minister in Philadelphia, Simcoe asserted that he had acted in "strict adherence" to his superiors' orders and consequently had maintained an "impartiality" between the United States and the Indians. "I have ever shown the utmost inclination to cultivate the most perfect harmony between his Majesty's subjects and those of the United States," he declared. Then, in a letter to the Duke of Portland, he discreetly confided that the biggest problem with evacuating the posts would be the further alienation of the Indians. Plaintively asking what could be done under the existing circumstances, Simcoe finally began to show the despair that he felt.[13]

The more he pondered "the very serious hazards" involved in the Indian situation, the more Simcoe realized that matters were already beyond his control. Communications from Great Britain, never swift under ordinary circumstances, were even more protracted in the crucial aftermath of the summer of 1794. First, the August packet from England was captured on the high seas by the French, causing crucial communiqués to be lost. Even more damaging was the similar loss of the Tankerville packet carrying the November and December mails from England, which announced the signing of Jay's Treaty and the adjustment of "all matters in dispute" between Great Britain and the United States.[14]

This void in Home Office instructions caused enormous embarrassment throughout the British colonial establishment, and as late as April, 1795, the British minister was acting upon dispatches more than six months old. To add to the dilemma, American newspapers were filled with explicit information on British withdrawal from the ceded posts, devastating British morale in Canada.[15]

Simcoe was politically uncomfortable because of the burgeoning criticism of his superior, Lord Dorchester, and he began casting aspersions on his commander in letters to the Home Office, ostensibly explaining his own conduct as "in obedience to the orders of Dorchester." The budding feud over the proper policy to pursue soon intensified. Moreover, fears that the Indian nations might even consummate a military alliance with the United States, involving actual warfare against Canada, deepened Simcoe's gloom.[16]

The British colonial government was so racked by internal discord, Indian difficulties, and a glaring void in Home Office communications early in 1795 that Dorchester admitted that his administration was "greatly disorganized." He finally became so distressed that he asked to be relieved, after roundly denouncing the pacifist policy that he was instructed to carry out. Pressed by Simcoe and the Indians for specific instructions and guidance, he could but attempt to "temporize" until "the arrival of my successor."[17]

Those of Dorchester's officers who were charged with Indian management were also insecure, discomfited, and sadly disorganized. They speculated that the Indians, "who have long fought for us and bled fairly for us," would be "left to shift for themselves" as a result of Jay's negotiations, which were then proceeding in Europe.[18] Indeed, the greatest fears of the Canadian officials were soon confirmed by publication of Jay's Treaty in the American newspapers—which, to the intense embarrassment of the colonial government, still served as their primary source of information. By the terms of the treaty the British were to evacuate all posts on American soil in June, 1796. This "disgrace," Simcoe said, would have the appearance of having been "extorted by armed America," recalling all of the "loss of honor" associated with the Revolution. Besides the prospect of anarchy in British settlements on ceded land, this "dreadful report" was certain to create havoc for the fur traders and affect their allegiance to the crown. To the Indians it could be but the final proof of Wayne's assertion that the British were no longer the dominant force, and thus were incapable of further protecting them. Simcoe so feared these consequences he conspired to temporarily keep this information from the Indians.[19]

The great emergency portrayed by Simcoe in the spring of 1795 was, in fact, to lead to the termination of the five-year-old Indian war—to the complete frustration of all of the British objectives as military abettors of the Indians. As

Alexander McKee and his subordinates had long predicted this inevitable consequence of British inaction and equivocation, which was a disaster of the greatest magnitude to the Indian Department.

Almost from the termination of the Brownstown conference in mid-October, 1794, there had been recurring talk of Indian peace initiatives. Foremost among the exponents of peace were a dissident group of Wyandots at Sandusky, including a faction that had lost several chiefs at Fallen Timbers. In late September the half-blood Indian agent for the Sandusky Wyandots, Isaac Williams, Jr., had written to Anthony Wayne to obtain the American terms of peace. Four warriors conveyed Williams's message to Wayne's camp at Greeneville in October, and Wayne responded to it during the first week in November. Asserting that Williams would be "liberally rewarded" for his fidelity and troubles, Wayne wrote that the basis for peace must rest on the Fort Harmar Treaty that Arthur St. Clair had concluded with the pacifist factions in 1789.[20]

Further augmenting this peace offensive was another rather unorthodox attempt with commercial overtones. Antoine Lasselle, who had been taken prisoner on the field immediately after the Battle of Fallen Timbers, had proved to be a rather enterprising character. A French trader of long standing along the Maumee River, Lasselle had narrowly extricated himself from an army court-martial that had convicted him as a spy and sentenced him to be hanged. His brother François had turned up at Wayne's headquarters in mid-October with three American prisoners whom he sought to exchange for Antoine, and he had word that even the intractable Blue Jacket of the Shawnees was inquiring about peace. On the advice of his scout William Wells, who had long known Lasselle and attested to his good character, Wayne allowed Antoine to return to Detroit to attempt to persuade the hostiles to come forth in peace.[21]

Immediately, Antoine Lasselle returned to Detroit, bringing, in the aftermath of the failed Brownstown council, word that Wayne desired to make peace, and that only the British were the cause of all of the lingering difficulties. Thereafter Lasselle and his family and relatives began ardently to recruit red delegates for the peace negotiations. Within two weeks they had covertly organized a return expedition to Fort Wayne (the former Miami Villages), and they set off from Detroit about November 15. Lasselle's party ultimately included sizeable elements from the Chippewas, Ottawas, Potawatomis, and Sauks, all which arrived for a conference with Wayne on January 19.[22]

As Lasselle admitted in a letter to his nephew, the root of the matter in his dealings with the Americans was the prospect of a financial bonanza for him as an exclusive trader among the Indians in United States territory. Seeking to snare even bigger game, Antoine then told his nephew Jacques that Blue Jacket of the Shawnees must be persuaded to come forth; that would certainly ensure the trading monopoly that they were endeavoring to establish.[23]

Ironically, Blue Jacket and about fifty warriors had already departed from Swan Creek on January 24, long before the arrival of Antoine's letter. The fearsome Shawnee war chief had managed to evade Alexander McKee's return to the area by two days, saying he was only going to Wayne to exchange

316

some prisoners. McKee, who had hastened to Swan Creek from Detroit upon hearing the rampant peace rumors, dejectedly wrote that "there is little doubt of his [Blue Jacket's] intention to change sides."[24]

From an Indian perspective, the long Euro-American conflict for control of the mid-American continent had been adequately resolved by conquest. Not only was the United States dominant in the region militarily, but also, as of late, it was politically assertive. Wayne had intentionally forwarded to the hostiles, via the Sandusky Wyandots, Dorchester's letter to him of October 6, 1794, announcing a status-quo diplomacy pending negotiation of a peace treaty in Europe. Dorchester's letter seemed openly to assent to these means and promised the Canadian governor general's ready cooperation with the United States.[25]

In contrast to the harsh invective of British agents, such as McKee, Dorchester's letter further delineated the cross-purposes and evasive rhetoric of British diplomats. Coupled with the inadequacy of provisions at Swan Creek during early in the winter of 1795, a growing incentive to negotiate with the Americans permeated nearly every tribe. Due to the emotional intensity of the issue, nations, bands, and even families were frequently split apart over the proper policy to pursue. Yet a Detroit-based observer wrote that the local Indians were "sneaking off to General Wayne every day."[26] The British lack of control became more obvious, moreover, once the tribesmen who had gone to Wayne in January and February returned and reported good treatment at the hands of the Americans.

At Greeneville the first visiting chiefs and delegates had been feted by Wayne and treated to gifts of clothing for themselves and their wives. It was but the inception of the calculating diplomacy of Wayne, who envisioned the establishment of United States interests in control of the commerce of the region. Believing that the British would continue to supply arms and munitions to the Indians in exchange for furs, in order to perpetuate the Indians' dependence on Canadian-based traders, the American general discreetly planned for the establishment of American-based trading houses to counter that threat.

Believing that the Indians were unlikely to remove to Canada, Wayne foresaw that the tribes would gravitate to United States allegiance. All that was required was to hold a reasonable but firm posture and to cater to the Indians' considerable vanity, for "their eyes and ears are no longer closed," Wayne observed. He later explained this rationale with considerable levity: "The Legion are excellent oculists and aurists, and . . . the bayonet is the most proper instrument for removing the film from the eyes—and for opening the ears of the savages. . . . Its glitter instantly dispelled the darkness, and let in the light."[27]

Wayne's relative confidence was predicated on knowledge that his prowess was already legend among the Indian people. A group of Potawatomis arriving at Fort Wayne early in 1795 expressed their great desire to see "The Wind," as they called Wayne after his victory of August 20—like a hurricane he had driven or knocked down everything before him.[28]

Wayne thus was well able to combine his most essential demands with the modicum of benevolence in victory that he calculated would secure the desired results. Fully subscribing to a premise of Hamtramck's that "flies are not to be caught with gall or bitter, particularly after having experienced for sixteen years the dulcet deceptions of the British," Wayne ordered from the East a variety of "trinkets," including blank commissions to be made out to the head chiefs. "Great [Indian] kings, or chiefs, like children, esteem those trifles as objects of great price or value," he explained. "They cost nothing, and they will have a good effect."[29]

At the inception of the first of several preliminary councils on January 19, 1795, it was quite evident the Indians sincerely contemplated peace, for some of the inveterately hostile Miamis had brought in American prisoners to be exchanged for a squaw. Wayne, responding in kind, directed that all of the Indian prisoners were to have their chains removed, and he would deliver them up at the time of the general treaty, which he announced would be held June 15 at Greeneville.[30]

Although some Indian delegates objected, preferring Fort Wayne as the site, Wayne reasoned that the sufficiency of troops for adequate protection and the need to minimize expenses mandated a Greeneville location.

Thereafter, with solemn ceremony, the assembled sachems and chiefs of the Chippewas, Ottawas, Potawatomis, Sauks, and Miamis placed their marks alongside Wayne's signature, concluding the preliminary articles of peace. By agreement all hostilities were to cease forthwith, and any knowledge of pending hostile action by other nations was to be communicated to the nearest United States officials immediately.

Looking back at this elaborate ceremony several days later, Wayne said the Indians were "no more to be trusted than an adder fanged." Yet to secure their cooperation was to deny the British, who remained as the United States's major competitor on the continent, the role of dominant power in North America's heartland.

No longer a major military threat in the region, the divided and impoverished Indians at this point represented more of a ready means to an end than a liability. Wayne increasingly began to covet their favor, without compromising the ultimate objective of the war—acquisition of their lands.[31]

When the famous Blue Jacket arrived at Fort Defiance with a delegation of Shawnees and Delawares on January 29, Wayne was overjoyed at the prospect of a general peace. Blue Jacket's subsequent arrival at Greeneville on February 7 resulted in the enactment of another preliminary treaty, which prompted the Shawnee chief to declare that at last the Indian nations had recognized the "true character" of the British. Even when Anthony Wayne explained that the Fort Harmar Treaty of 1789 would serve as the basis for the general treaty during mid-June, no objection was raised. Of more than casual significance was the $300 yearly subsidy later granted to Blue Jacket, which represented an astute if devious bribe.[32]

Wayne, encouraged by the prospect of a larger than anticipated treaty, soon began to maneuver to amplify its beneficial effect. Thus Antoine Lasselle and other French traders were encouraged and even subsidized, based upon Colonel Hamtramck's suggestions. "All the French traders, who were so many machines to the British agents, can be bought," Hamtramck wrote. Wayne contrived to increase the amount of treaty goods, even sending his quartermaster general, James O'Hara, to Pittsburgh to expedite the procurement of additional Indian presents.[33]

It was encouraging that various formerly hostile parties were observed coming forward in a continual stream to Wayne's outposts. Besides Blue Jacket's visit during February, Isaac Williams, Jr., came on behalf of the Sandusky Wyandots later in the same month. Then the Great Lakes tribes sent emissaries, including several principal Potawatomi chiefs, who met in council and signed in March the same preliminary agreement that Blue Jacket had signed. Even the Delawares at Swan Creek, led by the pro-American chief George White Eyes, sent peace overtures.

Wayne, of course, was greatly pleased with this "cheerful and ready compliance" with American objectives. To his commandant at nearby Fort Defiance, he even suggested the issuing of minimal provisions to the Delawares in order to help them relocate at their old Grand Glaize villages. What Wayne was thus enabled to achieve, by positive influence on the Indians, was precisely what Alexander McKee foresaw as a bane to the reestablishment of British influence—widening Indian distrust of their former benefactors. According to Blue Jacket and Grand Glaize King, a Delaware chief, the Indians had lost all confidence in the British since the Fallen Timbers fight, "because they remained idle spectators, and saw their [Indian allies'] best and bravest chiefs and warriors slaughtered . . . under the muzzles of their great guns, without attempting to assist them." The king's soldiers were not only liars, they asserted, "but also cowards."[34]

Adding to the inefficacy of the Canadian civil and military establishment, the operational capability of the British Indian Department had been much impaired in the spring of 1795. Alexander McKee, promoted to deputy superintendent general of Indian affairs, became incapacitated by rheumatic fever.

The British garrison at Fort Miamis, ravaged by fever and restricted in all expenses because of its impending evacuation, was unable even to halt an illicit trade between the Indians of the interior and the local traders.[35]

Of further worry to the Canadian administration were reports that French traders, in defiance of British authority, were rife throughout the frontier. Added to their concern that the tribes would soon press impossible demands for provisions and merchandise was the certain knowledge that all of the British attempts to perpetuate the Indian war had failed.[36]

Wayne, who had withdrawn from Fort Defiance in mid-September, 1794, had constructed a large fort at the Miami Villages en route to his winter camp at Greeneville. Named by Colonel Hamtramck in honor of the commanding general, Fort Wayne was garrisoned by about three hundred men. Of considerable significance, it represented another effective means of controlling the Indian trade along the important navigable interior waterways.[37]

Already discouraged by their defeat on August 20, from which Wayne had withdrawn unopposed, the handful of Indians who remained hostile were again unable to accomplish much. One war party of four Mackinac Indians had ambuscaded the road between Greeneville and Fort Recovery in late September, killing three soldiers and capturing one man and a woman.

Another small raiding party, said to be only two Indians, had waylaid the road near Fort Hamilton on October 6, killing Robert Elliot, the contractor, who was carelessly riding a few miles in front of a packhorse convoy. Otherwise, the Indians had remained so quiet that Wayne was able to conclude that he had indeed divided and distracted the hostiles' councils to the point of achieving a general peace.[38]

Concerned only with the ever-present logistical problem, Wayne approached the spring with heightened optimism. Bolstered by news that the regular military establishment would be continued, and that Congress had increased the pay of his soldiers, while doubling the bounty of recruits, Wayne exuded enthusiasm to those about him. In mid-1795 he wrote in gleeful contemplation of the forthcoming capitulation: "I believe it will not be in the power of all the British emissaries to prevent our treaty from taking place at about the time proposed."[39]

It had been announced that the Canadian governor general, Lord Dorchester, was personally to attend the British-sponsored Brownstown council in May or June, 1795, to "support the hostile Indians in all their distresses." As had been proclaimed by Joseph Brant in the fall of 1794, this late-spring conference would conclusively determine the extent of British involvement and the course of Indian affairs for years to come.[40]

Joseph Brant and his Mohawk delegation prepared to depart about June from their Grand River villages. Yet at the time Dorchester, Simcoe, McKee, and most of the other Canadian administrators involved were either sick or contemplating resignation amid the chaos caused by the pacifist directives from the Home Office.

Simcoe was particularly in feeble health, which prevented him from journeying to Detroit. In fact, his despair that Britain was about to abandon control of the Old Northwest caused him to cease further efforts to appease the Indians who resided north of the new international boundary line. Dorchester, being as chagrined as Simcoe about the adverse turn of events, bitterly contemplated his replacement in the face of the Home Office's censure of his conduct. He too remained in a protracted limbo of inactivity. Most damaging of all, however, was the absence of Alexander McKee, who sailed east for Lower Canada about June 1. Brant, who arrived at Detroit on the sixteenth, was astonished to find the western Indians "entirely left to themselves." He asked, How could McKee be allowed to leave, with no one in authority to advise and direct the Indian nations in this intensely critical situation? Three weeks later Brant himself returned home, thoroughly disgusted over the failure to convene a meeting. He related angrily that the few Indians present at Brownstown had been greatly confused among themselves. They had been made "continually drunk," he said, by the expressed design of "land jobbers," who were buying lands in exchange for rum, fully expectant that Wayne would confirm their titles upon the American occupation. Most of the various nations' representatives had already departed for Wayne's Greeneville treaty, and the few sober individuals remaining were preparing to do so, when Brant, in disgust, had given up and returned home.[41]

320

Thus, instead of reorganizing and invigorating the red cause, the Brownstown fiasco only complicated the already absurd situation. The Six Nations were so destitute of resources that they soon attempted to sell a small section of their lands on the Grand River. Although they were stopped in this attempt by Governor Simcoe during a separate council at Fort Erie in August, Brant made such an issue of this matter that it became the object of a heated personal controversy between him and the British administration.[42]

To add to Brant's difficulties, his son Isaac shot and murdered a white man near their Grand River settlement, initiating another crisis. Indicted by a white grand jury at Niagara, young Brant was defiantly protected by various Six Nations tribesmen. Indeed, an ugly confrontation was avoided only by a further tragedy. While at Grand River in November, Isaac Brant in a drunken frenzy cursed his father "in the most shameful manner," initiating a scuffle. Isaac, swinging wildly with a knife, wounded his father in the hand. Joseph then plunged his dirk into his son's head, mortally wounding him.[43]

Violence, so long a fact of life on the frontier, thus seemed doggedly to linger pursuing those most distressed by the enormous upheaval then in progress. Even those who were comparatively removed from the squalid, commonplace misery were broken by the ordeal in the Northwest. George Hammond, the king's minister plenipotentiary to the United States, was relieved from his assignment for the sake of conciliation, at John Jay's suggestion. John Graves Simcoe, his wife "a walking skeleton" due to poor health, again became so sick with a "slow fever" that he requested a leave of absence to return to England. In nearly all aspects, the prospect of a Canadian empire in the Old Northwest was collapsing in ruin, and the administration could but submit to the inevitable.[44] The ultimate prospect of unconditional surrender by now had become self-evident to the Indians. Accordingly, most of the nations looked forward to a general accommodation with Wayne, even at the cost of their long-standing British subsidies.

In the face of the certainty of American occupation only the subordinate British Indian agents made last-ditch efforts to interfere. One contingent of treaty-bound Indians reported that Matthew Elliott had told them that they would be poisoned at Greeneville. Moreover, a group of half-starved natives complained that the British agents had refused to issue provisions to those who were going to visit the Americans. According to one appalled observer, the pending British withdrawal and the protracted bickering among the various Indian militants and moderates, complicated by the intrigues of the king's Indian agents, caused Detroit to degenerate into a virtual "hell hole."[45]

As reported by a disaffected Chippewa chieftain, who spoke of his great anticipation of partaking of the bounty and protection of the Indians' new "elder brothers," the United States, the realignment of power in the Old Northwest would rectify past injustice by the British "bad birds." "[These bad birds] have frequently . . . been singing in our ears bad songs, but we were deaf to their notes and drove them from among us," the chief proudly announced to a man who listened with rather bemused interest, Anthony Wayne.[46]

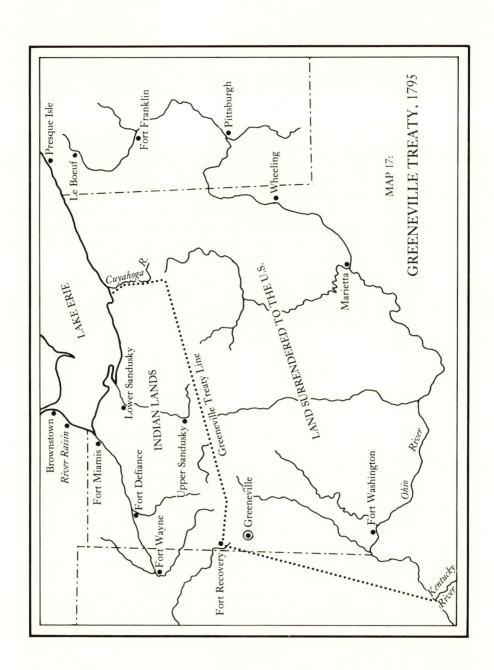

LAKE ERIE

Presque Isle

Le Boeuf

Fort Franklin

Pittsburgh

Wheeling

Cuyahoga R.

Lower Sandusky

INDIAN LANDS

Upper Sandusky

Greeneville Treaty Line

Marietta

LAND SURRENDERED TO THE U.S.

Brownstown

River Raisin

Fort Miamis

Fort Defiance

Fort Wayne

Fort Recovery

Greeneville

Fort Washington

Ohio River

Kentucky River

MAP 17:

GREENEVILLE TREATY, 1795

322

31

"We Will Make A New World"

IF the long, harsh war had demonstrated a disparity in the participants' vital resources and military efficacy, it had likewise manifested the different stakes involved. Particularly revealing was the plight of the vanquished. The British colonial establishment was seriously frustrated in its pursuit of a North American empire, yet Canada remained as a sovereign entity. Its territorial integrity was assured though its power base was reduced. Loss of the rich natural resources of the Old Northwest essentially represented more an economic threat than a threat to Canada's survival.

To the exhausted Indian civilization of the midwestern United States the lost war was perceived initially as a crisis resolved. Rather than the ruinous cataclysm predicted by the more radical elements, the American victory appeared in midsummer 1795 to dissipate much of the internal discord plaguing Indian affairs. The sovereign power that had established control over their vast territory represented essentially a new "elder brother" to the red peoples. "Our hearts and minds are changed, and we now consider ourselves your friends and brothers," announced Blue Jacket in February, 1795. Much as a conditioned response, the Indian nations proceeded as if the United States had replaced the British as their allies and benefactors, by virtue of "the fate of war."[1]

As they were independent peoples with a primitive wilderness life-style, there were historic precedents for the Indians' practical allegiance to the most dominant neighboring white society. Since the Americans' ascendency had resulted from their overwhelming numbers and advanced technology, there really was no alternative for the Indians but to accept their altered status.

Accordingly, the Indian leaders were generally venturous in acknowledging their subservience, in order that an effective foundation might be established for future mutually beneficial relations. "You have made the path safe, wide, and clear; we can now come to you without fear," professed a Michilimackinac chief at a preliminary council. "We shall settle all matters to the satisfaction of all parties," expectantly wrote a war chief of the Wyandots, who promised to bury the war hatchet so deep that none in the future could find it. One Chippewa chieftain even asserted that they would soon agree upon a peace with the United States "that would last forever."[2]

Yet the Indians had deluded themselves. Their situation was not one of altered patronage; they were now conquered, despised enemies. Throughout the era of French and British supremacy a direct economic liaison had been cultivated and exploited between Indians and whites for the essential purposes of commerical gain and military assistance. Now the people of the United States were more concerned with exploiting the land than the native peoples who occupied it. The land, to be settled and commercially developed, was perceived as the significant asset.

Instead of having a meaningful status as the means of procuring valuable fur pelts, the Indians were soon to find themselves in the role of unwanted squatters—obstacles to civilized progress. The complex differences between the colonial and American governments and their objectives were then little understood by the red nations. Moreover, as conquered people the Indians had very little basis for equitable redress of grievances. The popular will of the American nation had been prejudiced against them by decades of bitter warfare.

If the consequences of the war had been largely obscure at its beginning, they were to be only too apparent after a further, protracted ordeal. Tragically, the decisive defeat produced the most dreaded of alternatives: assimilation with the alien white society or annihilation because of the impact of that society.

While the British, as accessories in the war, had suffered considerable disappointment, the native residents were compelled to yield the very land that gave vital meaning to their lives.

Despite these dismal future prospects, at the inception of peace in 1795 it was politically expedient for the United States to implement the all-consuming changes in land utilization by progressive settlement and development, with a minimum of racial friction. Because the lands remained to be divided and occupied, and the Indian tribes dwelled and hunted within this domain, a measure of circumspection was due. In June, 1795, Secretary of War Thomas Pickering delineated this consolidation-of-gains policy when he told Wayne that peace was essential to facilitate the settlement of the enormous tract of land that the United States would claim from the Indians. Accordingly, the extent to which compromise and restraint would facilitate the victors' objectives provided much of the initial suspense in the treaty negotiations. Tragically, this duplicity raised false hopes of an equitable accommodation among the native peoples.

"The poor devils were almost starving to death before they got here," wrote the commandant of Fort Defiance, Major Thomas Hunt, to Wayne in May, 1795. Colonel Hamtramck dispatched a nearly identical report from Fort Wayne, observing that, until the Indians' crops were planted and harvested, they would starve unless supported by the army.[3]

The advance contingents of tribes and bands that appeared before June 15, the date announced for the general peace treaty, thus raised a fundamental issue—the extent to which the United States military was prepared to subsidize their late enemies. Recognizing the considerable stakes involved, Wayne favored an attitude of cautious appeasement. "I have a difficult and delicate part to act," he told the secretary of war in March, 1795. Accordingly, Wayne directed his subordinates to indulge in the measures necessary to facilitate a treaty. Short of stripping the outer forts of provisions for their own use, his various commanders were instructed to issue the Indians corn, meat, and other foodstuffs from army stores.[4]

Wayne's benevolence was based on practical considerations, however, for his own instructions were above all to conclude a viable peace. Moreover, when several minor incidents were perpetrated by a few Indian banditti in June, Wayne, ever the vigilant soldier, warned that, "unless the culprits are discovered and punished they [the Indians] cannot expect to draw subsistence."[5]

Timothy Pickering's experience as a veteran negotiator in treaties with the Six Nations led him as secretary of war to urge upon Wayne what was tantamount to an exercise in practical psychology during the forthcoming treaty. Despite his firm declaration that "peace and not increase of territory has been the object of this expensive war," Pickering's attitude was revealed by the specific terms on which he instructed Wayne to insist. Stating that the "altered circumstances" occasioned by Wayne's victory justified "a demand of some indemnification for the blood and treasure expended," Pickering announced that the former proposed boundary line should now be modified to give more territory to the United States. "The final cession and relinquishment by the Indians of the entire body of land lying eastward and southward of the general boundary . . . from the mouth of the Cuyahoga to the mouth of the Great Miami . . . are to be an indispensable condition of peace," he wrote. Moreover, Wayne was to insist on various reservations of land and a corridor within the country retained by the Indians as a "means of useful intercourse which will cement that [professed] friendship." Actually, these military reservations were "to connect the settlements of the people of the United States by rendering a passage . . . more practicable and convenient," and to establish a base from which American fur traders would monopolize the region's commerce.[6] Wayne was also instructed that the Indians might be permitted to negotiate as one entity at Greeneville, notwithstanding the former separate-treaties concept. The reason, Pickering said, was that this would facilitate the treaty and "save much time and trouble." As further proof of the triumph about to be realized, Pickering boldly announced, "The State of Pennsylvania will this spring survey the plat of a town at Presque Isle."[7]

In consideration of the yielding of their lands, and in order "to gratify the usual expectation of Indians" for treaty goods, $25,000 was appropriated for Wayne's Greeneville negotiations. Yet the goods purchased consisted of various commodities, including thousands of calico shirts; reams of colored cloth; dozens of axes, tomahawks, cutting knives, butcher's knives, bales of brass wire, hats, blankets, shoes, brass kettles, silver armbands and nose bobs; wampum; looking glasses; boxes of ribbons; ivory, iron, and horn combs; and even brass thimbles. These "trinkets" were the end result of Pickering's proclaimed intention to furnish the red men with "their real wants, rather than to soothe and foster their childish passion for baubles."

Included with these goods, yet deducted from the total compensation offered, were numerous casks of wine and liquor, to be issued in the manner of a persuasive influence. Finally, an annual gratuity amounting to no more than $10,000 would be delivered annually to the confederacy, payable in the form of merchandise.[8]

Characteristically, the rationale involved in this frivolous outlay was perhaps even more devious than the terms that were about to be imposed. Pickering said that the goods would be delivered only if a successful treaty were held. Further, the substantial cost of transporting them would be deducted in figuring the merchandise appropriation. He reasoned that the annual bounty was specifically calculated to keep the Indians dependent upon the goods—"making it in their interest to be our friends," he said. Then a crowning touch was added during June, 1795, when Pickering arbitrarily declared that, due to cost, the original quantity of treaty goods would be "purposely lessened." "The blood and treasure . . . expended authorized a purchase at a lower price," he sheepishly wrote in an explanatory note to Wayne.[9]

If any uncertainty about American procedures remained, Wayne was further burdened with the explicit instructions of President Washington to be on guard against Indian treachery. Accordingly, though convinced "there is no occasion for it," Wayne warned his commanders to be alert against an Indian attack. "They will not find us like unto the foolish virgins—without oil," responded Lieutenant Samuel Drake at Fort Recovery, who confidently noted the good condition of his men and the fine order of their equipment.[10]

At Fort Wayne the preliminary indications of a successful peace treaty had been highlighted by the attachment of Blue Jacket to the American cause. As early as the first week in May, Colonel Hamtramck had proclaimed the "firm" friendship of the famous Shawnee chieftain. Blue Jacket had made several trips to and from the American posts during the late spring, and he seemed to be an ardent spokesman for peace and alignment with the United States at the forthcoming treaty. According to the negro servant of British agent Alexander McKee, who had deserted to the Americans in June, Thomas McKee had threatened to kill Blue Jacket for urging the Shawnees to go to the United States treaty. On learning of his defection McKee even threw a pair of gold epaulets that were being made for the Shawnee leader into a fire.[11]

Beginning early in June, chiefs and warriors of the Chippewas, Ottawas, and Potawatomis arrived in small contingents at the prepared council site at Greeneville. Yet by June 15, the day designated for beginning the sessions, only a few more Delawares and Eel River tribesmen had arrived. Accordingly, Wayne gathered the red delegates together at the specially constructed log council house to explain that he would "cover up" the council fire until "the remainder of the tribes arrived."[12]

Wayne, who perceived that some of the tribes would be slow in gathering, looked for the arrival of the more hostile nations, particularly the Shawnees. Buckongahelas and his party of Delawares came in on June 21, Little Turtle and Le Gris of the Miamis arrived on the twenty-third, and finally Egushawa of the Ottawas was present on July 4. Yet many of the Shawnees, including Blue Jacket, remained absent. Although Colonel Hamtramck advised Wayne that Blue Jacket made three separate journeys to bring forth his tribesmen, Wayne remained concerned about British tampering.[13]

Finally, with about a thousand Indians present at Greeneville, Wayne on July 9 allowed the Indians to fix the date for the opening of the council, well realizing that he could delay no longer. When a sizeable party of Wyandots arrived on July 12, a new commencement date, July 15, was agreed upon. Still, there were only a few Shawnees present, noted a concerned Anthony Wayne.[14]

Mindful of Secretary Pickering's instructions to conduct the proceedings with "mildness and friendly manner," Wayne had given up his exterior redoubts to the Indians for their comfort and convenience. Yet, like most of the other seemingly innocuous maneuvering, even this simple expediency was of strategic intent. "The guns of our bastions . . . look directly into them—so that they [the redoubts] will be very harmless covers should the Indians [attempt to attack]," wrote Wayne sternly.[15]

"Younger brothers, . . . I take you all by the hand," began General Wayne in his opening remarks. "Rest assured of a sincere welcome . . . from your friend and brother, Anthony Wayne." Such proclamations of friendship reflected the measured rhetoric of Wayne's formal statement on Wednesday, July 15, 1795—a "fair and pleasant" day, he declared, for the "good work" at hand.

Yet Wayne's more pointed comments touched at the very basis of the treaty. Soon he described the terms that the United States would impose as being predicated on the Fort Harmar Treaty of 1789. "That treaty appeared to be founded upon principles of equity and justice, and to be perfectly sastisfactory to all parties at that time," related a now somber Wayne. Accordingly he offered the assembled Indians "two or three days" to consider the terms and prepare an answer.[16]

When the general council resumed on Saturday, June 18, Little Turtle, as the initial spokesman, questioned Wayne's reasoning. The Fort Harmar Treaty had involved primarily the pacifist Seneca factions, he observed. Not only was he unfamiliar with the substance of that treaty, he had no direct knowledge that it was acceptable to all of the Indian nations.[17]

Thus Little Turtle again became the champion of Indian rights. Although he had chosen an unpopular role a year earlier in urging the tribes to negotiate with Wayne rather than fight, the Miami chieftain now questioned the United States' claims. Regarded by an American officer at Fort Defiance as a modest, manly chief, who never became intoxicated, Little Turtle impressed neary everyone with his keen intelligence. Indeed, the Miami chief's perception of Wayne's motives was truly remarkable, and the American commander suddenly found himself on the defensive.

"These lands were disposed of without our knowledge or consent," proclaimed Little Turtle, in reference to the Fort Harmar Treaty that his tribe had boycotted. Furthermore, he asserted that his forefathers had always charged the Miami chieftains not to sell or part with their country. In view of this ancient tradition, asked Little Turtle, how was it possible that British or other unconcerned Indian tribes could give up what was not theirs.[18]

Before Wayne was committed to answer, the council was ajdourned at his discretion. On Thursday, July 23, the first to speak was Wayne's paid and covertly recruited ally, Blue Jacket, who had only recently arrived with thirteen Shawnee warriors. Blue Jacket was effusive in his support of the pacifist Wyandots, as were the subsequent statements of other chieftains. "When I view my situation I consider myself as an object of compassion," declared a Chippewa chief to Wayne. Citing that it was the British "who urged us to bad deeds and reduced us to our present state of misery," the Chippewa sage asked the United States to have pity: "We will assist you to the utmost of our power to do what is right . . . , we will make a new world." Furthermore, they would not contest the land appropriations. "For why should I?" said Mashipinashiwish of the Chippewas. "You have told us we might hunt upon your lands [and] . . . we will for the future live and hunt in peace and happiness."[19]

Thereafter, Wayne reasserted his calculated strategy. According to his reasoning, the United States had twice paid the Indians for the lands it was now claiming. Both at the Fort McIntosh and the Fort Harmar treaty adequate restitution had been made. "Such is the justice and liberality of the United States," Wayne announced, "that they will now, a third time, make compensation for them."

In response to Little Turtle's remarks, Wayne disputed the Miami claim to such a large section of land, pointing out that at least six other tribes claimed portions of the same country. Moreover, remnants of British and French forts in the region suggested that Little Turtle's forefathers had sold some of their country to these white nations. "[Little Turtle's charge] comes with a bad grace, indeed," declared Wayne, and he flatly asserted: "I will now inform you who it was that gave us these lands, . . . It was your fathers, the British." Wayne then produced a copy of the 1783 peace treaty and Jay's recently completed treaty, which were read to substantiate his assertion that the "Americans [had] proved too powerful for the British."[20]

In closing, Wayne declared that the United States might thus have claimed all of the Indian lands, but being benevolent people, the Americans "never intended to take advantage of you," and "wish you to enjoy your just rights . . . and promote your happiness." Accordingly, the United States had only claimed a little more land than had been designated at the Fort Harmar Treaty.

With a diplomatic flair, Wayne then terminated the proceedings by declaring a double allowance of liquor for the evening.[21]

Little Turtle was outraged. Following a further elaboration on June 27 by Wayne, outlining the specific territory that the United States required, the ten-article treaty was delivered to the Indians to sign. Tarhe of the Wyandots and others quickly acted in support of Wayne's demands. The Wyandot chieftain proclaimed, "We are persuaded you have acted with great equity and moderation in dividing the country . . . , We are highly pleased with your humanity towards us."[12]

By the time Little Turtle rose to address the assembled throng on July 29 a variety of speakers had assented to the American terms.

Angry, and yet dignified, in his rebuttal speech, Little Turtle told Wayne that the Americans were usurping the best part of the Indians' lands. "You take too much of [our] lands away," he said, stating that the Indian hunters would be confined to a restricted area. By proposing a boundary that would extend no farther north than Fort Recovery, Little Turtle attempted to achieve a compromise. Then, denying that the British or the French had possessed the Indians' land by purchase (stating that their gratuitous occupation had been by mutual agreement), the principal Miami spokesman further chided Wayne for demanding hostages in his treaty terms. "I expect to [live among] you every day when you settle on your reservations," he intoned, "and it will be impossible for me or my people to withhold from you a single [white] prisoner."[23]

Wayne, in decisive language, quickly crushed any prospect of further negotiations. Having listened to the complete acquiescence of the other chieftains, he used the submission of those tribes as leverage. According to Wayne, their support represented a mandate to proceed, and he proclaimed, "I am pleased to hear you say with one voice . . . that I have done the greatest justice to you in dividing the lands." For that reason, he said, he would reward the Wyandots of Sandusky by soon building a fort to serve as protection "against the common enemy."

As for the Miamis and Little Turtle, they were singled out as being contrary to the will of the other nations. Little Turtle's boundary "would be very crooked" and "productive of unpleasant mistakes and differences." The annual annuity of $8,000 would compensate the Indians for any loss of game and fur trade. Wayne continued by appealing to all of the nations present to say "whether the United States [was thus] acting the part of a tender father, . . . [by] providing for them . . . forever."[24] Then, in rapid succession, he proposed a conclusion to the "negotiation" and called for a voice vote on the acceptance of the ten articles.

One by one, the name of each nation was called, and even the Miamis, polled near the end of the list, added their affirmation to what was a unanimous declaration. While the treaty was recorded on parchment, a matter requiring several days, Wayne decreed, "we will eat, drink, and rejoice."[25]

Adding luster to the accomplished fact was the arrival on July 31 of eighty-eight Shawnees under Red Pole, who had been at Swan Creek. Red Pole proved to be a staunch supporter of Wayne, and even offered to proceed to the Scioto River and bring in a lawless band of Shawnees who had refused to come to the treaty.[26]

When the formal documents were presented for signature on August 3, the signing proceeded as planned with the Indians placing their mark as directed by the interpreters. Instead of the authorized $10,000 annuity, Wayne pledged $9,500, which seemed more liberal than the $8,000 formerly discussed. Also, the value of the commodities to be delivered was set at $20,000, down from the $25,000 first fixed by Pickering, but that was not known to the Indians. Conspicuous by its absence was the name of Little Turtle. Richardville, a village chief, signed for the Miamis.[27]

Proclaiming the treaty "a sacred pledge of the establishment of our future friendship," Wayne at last announced what had long been utilized as bargaining leverage during the council, the forthcoming apportionment of goods.

Thereafter, Tarhe on behalf of the confederacy arose and decreed that the United States would henceforth be the Indians' father. "The Great Spirit has crowned them with success in all their undertakings," said Tarhe. Taking Wayne by the hand, he offered his pledge of "our sincerity and of our happiness in becoming your children . . . . Be strong, now and take care of all your little ones."

Indeed, within the following several days Wayne was besieged with requests from his newly acquired "children." Licenses for favorite traders, horses for the use of chiefs, and liquor were among the favors asked.[28]

Wayne, who was seemingly pleased by the testimonials of the various nations, decided to release the ten hostages that he had demanded. He offically closed the council after advising the Indians that their future welfare depended upon the "faithful and strict observance" of the treaty. Expressing his wish that the Indians would "open your eyes to your true happiness" and cultivate the earth, he bid the assembled nations "an affectionate farewell" on August 10.[29]

As the 1,130 Indians present slowly dispersed to their various villages during mid-August, there remained the lingering euphoria of a new-found alliance. Buckongahelas, the Delaware war chief, promised to be as true a friend to the United States "as I have heretofore been an active enemy." A Chippewa chief acknowledged his gratitude and "perfect satisfaction," saying his people would rejoice "in having acquired a new, and so good a father."[30]

Even the reluctant Little Turtle reached a practical accommodation with Wayne. At a private council held August 12, Little Turtle promised to give his allegiance to the United States and to observe the terms of the treaty, citing his plans to live in the vicinity of Fort Wayne as a mark of this sincerity.

Wayne had prevailed upon the Miami chieftain only by saying that he alone had not entered into the accord, and that thus Little Turtle stood in opposition to the will of the majority. Little Turtle's name was then entered upon the Treaty of Greeneville. Being the last to sign, he said that he would be the last to break it, although his heart did not approve of the treaty terms. Furthermore, it was his duty, recorded the proud Miami chieftain, to speak with candor and dignity, and he hoped the United States would not therefore treat him disdainfully.[31]

Wayne's attitude on the closing of the treaty was much as if a protracted ordeal had suddenly been terminated by sheer will power. Yet his lengthy letter to Pickering on August 9 contained only one modest paragraph on the successful conclusion of the most important Indian treaty in the nation's history. The terms had been "unanimously and voluntarily agreed to," asserted Wayne, who added that all the sachems and war chiefs had "cheerfully signed" the document.[32]

With the departure of many of the tribes and bands from Greeneville, Wayne's problems were largely transferred to the commanders of the outer posts. Several tribes were furnished with wagons to carry away their merchandise, and Egushawa's band was loaned a boat to float their goods to Fort Defiance. Typical of other special favors were Wayne's instructions to Colonel Hamtramck to build Blue Jacket "a decent house" based on the Shawnee leader's requisition.[33]

Perhaps the most affecting of all the varied and incongruous scenes at Greeneville and the frontier posts following the Treaty of Greeneville were the prisoner exchanges. Since early 1795 a steady influx of white captives had continued—positive evidence of the Indians' sincerity for peace. Many of the prisoners had been treated extremely well, and were so integrated into Indian life that they only came forth when forced to do so by their particular tribes. When an adopted Wyandot white girl refused to be exchanged, preferring to live with the Indians, Wayne's aide refused to permit it, saying that her race did not allow her to make a free choice. The Wyandots were duly required to deliver the girl to American custody.

Although most of the prisoners were promptly received by relatives, one woman, the wife of a corporal who had escaped from the battlefield of St. Clair's defeat, remained at Fort Defiance for several weeks before the corporal could come to her. By that time, recorded a bemused officer, the woman had taken up with a sergeant, who kept her in his quarters. When the corporal belatedly arrived, instead of a nasty scene the husband praised the sergeant for his attention to her. "Where women are scarce," observed the officer, "the men must not be dainty."[34]

Amid the general celebration occasioned by the signing of the treaty, at the outermost posts considerable revelry occurred between red and white. Dances with the "tawney ladies" were a favorite activity, and a large feast at Fort Defiance on August 20 included extra issues of whiskey and a supper of roasted pig and fried chicken from stock provided by "poultry the Indians left at this place in their precipitate flight last summer." This occasion was highlighted by a fifteen-cannon salute at twelve noon—it was the anniversary of the American triumph at Fallen Timbers.[35]

Major Thomas Hunt, reflecting the exultation of victory, wrote, "It's my hearty wish that all our enemies may [thus] be brought to a sense of their duty." Indeed, the altered mood of post-treaty accommodation was already manifest. The vanquished tribesmen were now regarded largely as objects of opportunity. Provisions issued to the Indians at Fort Wayne had recently been cut to less than one ration per person, due to "the number of small children" included. Then the returning Shawnee delegation under Red Pole found eager Indian traders waiting at Fort Defiance. The more than twenty horseloads of treaty goods possessed by Red Pole's band were nearly all in the hands of one Felix by the following day, bartered for rum.[36]

Through all of the ensuing travesty, the sorrow of one man lingers in vivid perspective. On the day folllowing the signing of the general treaty, the wife of Little Turtle had died in camp at Greeneville. The bitter irony of American soldiers carrying the corpse to the grave, where it was buried to the accompaniment of "military music" and a three-gun salute, perhaps augured the fate of the Indian peoples.

To a duly impressed American officer, the memory of Little Turtle slowly walking over the ground near Fort Defiance reflected the great burden of his people. After looking over the gardens that the soldiers of the garrison had planted, the chief appeared melancholy, and the young American officer observed that Little Turtle was deeply affected. This land had once been his own property, he uttered softly, and his gaze wandered off to the distant forest that was wilderness no more.[37]

331

32

Epilogue
"All My Sorrows"

ON Monday, July 11, 1796, the schooners *Weazell* and *Swan*, chartered from several local merchants, approached the river landing below Fort Lernoult. Aboard were sixty-five soldiers under Captain Moses Porter, United States Army. On Porter's approach the British flag was lowered and the garrison of Fort Lernoult marched out. It was about noon, wrote an American staff officer, when the United States flag was quietly raised over the works. Detroit, the symbolic key post of the Old Northwest, was at last in the possession of the United States.[1]

To Anthony Wayne, who had once feared British duplicity in yielding the ceded posts, the uneventful occupation was the fruition of an American vision. "[It is] an event that must naturally afford the highest pleasure and satisfaction," he jubilantly wrote, " . . . and I trust [it] will produce a conviction to the world that [this result was] secured by that unshaken fortitude, patriotism and virtue [of President Washington's policy]." When Wayne arrived at Detroit on August 13, he found the fortification and town intact, "without any injury or damage other than what time has made." The British had surrendered the forts at Detroit, Niagara, Oswego, and along the Maumee "in the most polite, friendly and accommodating manner," said Wayne. Moreover, the Canadian administration authorized the loan of fifty barrels of pork to the United States Army so that Fort Michilimackinac might be occupied.[2]

Feted at private dinners by Detroit's prominent citizens, Wayne found the community populated by "wealthy and well informed merchants and gentlemen, and fashionable and well-bred women." In all, the ebullient American commander was delighted with the Fort and its beautiful situation, even expressing his amazement at the many large sailing vessels plying the river.[3]

Despite several lingering domestic political difficulties, such as the threatened reduction of the American army after the reestablishment of peace, Wayne had reached a new pinnacle of importance and popularity. The new secretary of war, James McHenry, preoccupied with "measures of economy," had proposed several austere cutbacks. For example, the Legion was to be withdrawn and stationed along the Ohio River. Wayne fought these measures ardently and successfully. He also continued to rant against "the worst of all bad men, to whom I feel myself as much superior in every virtue as Heaven is to Hell," James Wilkinson.[4]

In January, 1795, Wilkinson's treachery had been revealed in a formal notice by Henry Knox, which included copies of derogatory letters privately conveyed by the conspiring brigadier to Philadelphia. Wayne, who had long suspected upper-echelon betrayal, was so enraged by Wilkinson's "vile insidious" treachery that he now considered the fallen-tree incident during the Fallen Timbers campaign as "probably premeditated." Inwardly burning with resentment and indignation, Wayne quietly gathered evidence on the "criminal" activities of Wilkinson, apparently planning the court-martial, the cashiering, and perhaps the execution for treason of his archenemy.

The returning deserter Robert Newman, to save his own life, conveyed to Wayne certain information implicating Wilkinson in treasonous correspondence with the British. Beyond this initial testimony, there were tantalizingly damning fragments of evidence linking Wilkinson to a Spanish pension and a conspiracy to separate the Union. Yet Wayne was unable to obtain positive proof that would stand up in a court of law. While biding his time, he planned a tour of inspection to Presque Isle, journeying there on the sloop *Detroit* in mid-November, 1796. There on December 15, following an acute attack of the gout and an intestinal disorder, Wayne died, just as a physician summoned from Pittsburgh arrived. He was not yet fifty-two years of age. In one of his last letters to the secretary of war, he had proclaimed further knowledge of his disloyal subordinate's treachery.[5]

James Wilkinson, newly installed as the commander of the United States Army and still serving as Spanish secret agent number thirteen, was destined for a checkered career that at one point involved praise from President Thomas Jefferson and $11,000 in "expenses" for the betrayal of Aaron Burr, the same matter for which he requested $122,000 (which he failed to collect) from his Spanish employers. Playing both sides for his personal financial gain, the double-dealing Wilkinson once wrote that his clandestine activities were predicated on the regard "which I feel for the prosperity of the two powers, which I love equally."[6]

While the highly intelligent Wilkinson was wholly self-serving and devoid of scruples, he adroitly shifted political ties and friendships according to circumstances. Thus he managed to keep one step ahead of his detractors. Amazingly, he somehow escaped condemnation during a total of three major inquests or courts-martials between 1808 and 1815, blatantly asserting his innocence while he was guilty of the very illegalities that he disclaimed.

Twice commander of the United States Army as a brigadier, Wilkinson was promoted to major general in 1813 and died in 1825 just short of his sixty-ninth birthday. Although damned by Andrew Jackson as "a double traitor," the extent of Wilkinson's treachery was not revealed until the Spanish archives were made available to American scholars in the twentieth century. Fittingly buried in an unidentified common grave in Mexcio City, he is remembered according to one modern historian, "as perhaps America's most disreputable soldier, Benedict Arnold not excepted."[7]

It was an ironic twist that the careers of those who had most ardently opposed Wayne and Wilkinson during the crisis in the Old Northwest were significantly plagued by ill health and misfortune. Both Lord Dorchester and John G. Simcoe were recalled or reassigned by the Home Office in 1796. Dorchester survived a major shipwreck on Quebec's Anticosti Island during his voyage home. Simcoe, although appointed overall commander in India during 1806, died after taking sick on his journey to that post. Alexander McKee, whom Anthony Wayne had referred to as the "principal stimulator of the war," suddenly died on January 14, 1799, of a high fever. His son Thomas attempted to superintend the Indians at Amherstburg (Fort Malden), south of Detroit, but was replaced in 1808 for drunkenness and inefficiency. Simon Girty, half blind and prone to drunken stupors, was regarded "incapable of anything." The memory of his defiance of the United States occupation of Detroit in 1796, when Girty allegedly swam his horse across the river shouting invectives and gesturing with his fist, was but a shadow in 1813. Then the aged Girty was compelled to flee his farm in the face of an American invasion and was unable to return until the War of 1812 ended.[8]

The British-allied Indian leaders also endured hardships. Joseph Brant, disillusioned with the rival Six Nations factions led by Red Jacket and Cornplanter, and plagued by the intrigues of McKee's replacement, William Claus, at one point seriously considered moving under the protection of the United States. Following the death of his son Isaac by his own hand, Brant was periodically burdened by debilitating sickness in his family, as well as the recurring political intrigues among the Iroquois tribes. After a lengthy illness Brant died at age sixty-four at his spacious Lake Ontario residence on November 24, 1807. His unyielding spirit was evident to the end.

Despite his former New Lebanon, Connecticut, education, the Mohawk chieftain had once written to an unidentified correspondent a sarcastic reflection on the white men's way of life, citing the American penal system as an example of the "dreadful contrast" between the native and white societies. Brant wrote that protracted incarceration of wrongdoers was beyond the natives' conception. "Perhaps it is [best]," he said,

that incorrigible offenders should sometimes be cut off [from society]. Let it be done in a way that is not degrading to human nature. . . . Liberty to a rational creature, as much exceeds property as the light of the sun does that of the most twinkling star. But you put them on a level—to the everlasting disgrace of civilization. I seriously declare I had rather die by the most severe tortures ever inflicted on this continent, than languish in one of your prisons for a single year. . . . Does then the religion of Him whom you call your Saviour inspire this spirit and lead to such practices? Surely no. It is recorded of Him a bruised reed he never broke. Cease then to call yourselves Christians, lest you publish to the world your hypocrisy. Cease, too, to call other nations savage, when you are tenfold more the children of cruelty than they.[9]

Brant's outrage foreshadowed the profound sadness of the century to come, during which the Indian peoples struggled to adopt to the alien white civilization.

Little Turtle, whom even his former enemies acknowledged to be "a remarkable man," perhaps best reflected the somber dignity of the lost cause. Residing near Fort Wayne, he remained loyal to the United States, despite the provocations of the years before the War of 1812, and worked tirelessly in the cause of temperance among his people. During a visit to Philadelphia in 1797, the Miami chief expounded on the unhappy plight of the red race. "Here I am deaf and dumb," he perceptively noted in speaking of the inability of his people to adopt to urban life. "When I walk through the streets I see every person in his shop employed about something. One makes shoes, another hats, a third sells cloth, and everyone lives by his labor. I say to myself, which of all these things can you do? Not one. I can make a bow or an arrow, catch fish, kill game, and go to war, but none of these is of any use here. . . . I should be a piece of furniture, useless to my nation, useless to the whites, and useless to myself."[10]

Inevitably, the future required adaptation and a new kind of education from succeeding generations of Indians. Yet assimilation under adverse circumstances was to be a tediously painful process. One historian of the period wrote that the Indian civilization was like a rock, which cannot be changed in form without its destruction. This immutability was to be fully evident after the advent of widespread development and settlement in the Old Northwest lands. Little Turtle was one of the Indian leaders who foresaw the tragic consequences of the many nuances associated with the American lifestyle. Particularly distressing was the Indians' affinity for, and inability to tolerate, strong liquor. He had warned, in vain, that it would perhaps be better to be at war with the white people than submit to the degradation of alcoholism: "This liquor that they introduce into our country is more to be feared than the gun and tomahawk," he said around the turn of the eighteenth century. "More of us have died since the Treaty of Greeneville than we lost by the years of war before, and it is all owing to the introduction of liquor among us."[11]

Granted a yearly annuity, which was all too frequently misspent, his Miami tribesmen continued to degenerate, so that by 1814 William Henry Harrison reflected that they were "merely a poor drunken set, diminishing every year." An estimated five hundred deaths occurred among the Miami tribe alone from drink-related murders and accidents between 1813 and 1830. Devastated by smallpox and other diseases of European origin, the Miamis, once one of the largest and most powerful tribes of North America, had dwindled to a mere three hundred to five hundred souls by the early 1900s.[12]

Throughout his life Little Turtle refused to compromise his dignity, and while younger, more radical leaders, such as Tecumseh, urged open defiance of the Americans, he advocated accommodation with the white civilization that he knew the Indians could not withstand. It was characteristic of the aged Miami chieftain that, shortly before hostilities began in 1812, he wrote to Indiana Territorial Governor William Henry Harrison professing his strong commitment to peace.[13]

Only a few months later Little Turtle was dead. Afflicted with the gout, he had pitched his camp on the property of William Wells, who since 1795 had been his son-in-law. There he died on July 14, 1812, following treatment by an army surgeon. Although he was buried with appropriate honors in an old orchard on the Saint Joseph River, even a century later his body was not to escape desecration by white men.[14]

In July, 1911, two brothers, while excavating a cellar for their house near Fort Wayne, uncovered Little Turtle's remains. Appropriated by the laborers were many of the chief's prized belongings, including a pistol presented by Kosciusko and his sword, a gift of President Washington in 1797. Eternal peace obviously did not extend to Indian grave sites.[15]

Of Little Turtle's contemporaries there were few who found enduring happiness. Blue Jacket, regarded with enmity by Little Turtle for his political liaison with the Americans, failed to survive long in the limelight. A heavy drinker, the once inveterate Shawnee war chief had become so disenfranchised by August, 1800, that he conveyed intelligence to the British on confidential American plans at the risk of his yearly pension. Although his name appeared on the Treaty of Fort Industry, Ohio, in 1804, there are few references to Blue Jacket in the histories of the succeeding years, and his own obscurity was accentuated by the rise to prominence of his two sons.[16]

To the others time brought varying fortunes and controversy. Buckongahelas, the Delaware, died in 1804 amid rumors that he was poisoned by a rival. Tarhe (The Crane) perhaps personified the American interpretation of a "good Indian." First to sign at Greeneville, he remained dedicated to a United States alliance despite alienation by many of his Wyandot tribesmen. In 1813, during the unpropitious War of 1812, Tarhe, who was then about seventy, led a contingent of Indian scouts under William Henry Harrison into Canada to confront his former allies and tribesmen.[17]

It was during that conflict that another contemporary, William Wells, was slain while attempting to rescue the garrison of Fort Dearborn (Chicago) in August, 1812. The War of 1812, in fact, witnessed the last great Indian insurrection east of the Mississippi River. The insurrection was as anticlimactic as it was futile.[18]

Yet one of the most gifted of the Indian leaders was spectacularly influential during the bloody and much publicized conflict. This man was Tecumseh, whom William Henry Harrison described as "one of those uncommon geniuses which spring up occasionally to produce revolutions and overturn the established order of things. If it were not for the vicinity of the United States, he would, perhaps be the founder of an empire that would rival in glory Mexico or Peru. No difficulties deter him."[19]

Regarded as one of the greatest soldiers of his race, Tecumseh was to throw the entire Old Northwest into alarm. A brilliant orator, he conceived of a grand uprising of all Indian people to throw the whites back into the great waters whose "accursed waves brought them to our shores." "The annihilation of our race is at hand unless we unite in one common cause against the common foe," he told the southern tribes during a six-month journey that he made to unite all of the red nations. More numerous than their northern brethren, the Creeks and Choctaws were perceived as a crucial, largely untapped source of warriors to supplant the divided and irresolute Iroquois. Tecumseh's mother was a Creek, and she, in fact, had inspired him with his burning desire for vengeance against the whites. Aided by his brother Tenskwatawa (The Prophet), Tecumseh had forged an alliance of various tribes at Prophet's Town in the upper Wabash country, and he proposed a coordinated date for a simultaneous Indian uprising in the North and South. "War now, war forever!" was his rallying cry. "Our country must give no rest to a white man's bones."[20]

Yet Tecumseh was an anachronism. His efforts to achieve a widespread Indian alliance lacked a common perspective. The southern tribes, with the exception of some Muskogees and Seminoles, remained unconvinced. The whites were too many and too well equipped, "far beyond that of all our race combined," reasoned a Choctaw chief. Moreover, in Tecumseh's absence William Henry Harrison had led a "voluntary" expedition against Prophet's Town and had inflicted a stunning defeat on the Indians at the Battle of Tippecanoe. Tecumseh, in tears, returned to swear "once more eternal hatred—the hatred of an avenger." Yet matters were already beyond the great Shawnee leader's control. Despite some initial successes in the War of 1812, the hope of reconquering the already-lost mid-continent was in vain. Forced into a war that neither side wanted (with the exception of western and southern Americans, known as War Hawks), the British groped desperately to defend Canada with insufficient troops and uncertain leadership. Following the loss of the highly competent British Major General Isaac Brock, the plight of the Indians' allies became so ludicrous that Tecumseh observed, "We must compare your conduct to a fat animal that carries its tail on its back, but when frightened, drops it between its legs and runs."[21]

At the Battle of the Thames, October 5, 1813, Tecumseh, fighting ferociously following the retreat and surrender of British regulars under the blundering Major General Henry A. Procter, was killed and buried in an unknown grave. In conjunction with Isaac Brock, he may well have preserved the present boundaries of Canada from American encroachment by his earlier victories. Yet even the more vigorous exponents of Tecumseh have admitted that alone, without the protection of the British, the Indians could not have maintained an independent state. "He and his race were centuries behind their opponents [in military efficacy]," concluded a recent biographer, Glenn Tucker, and Tecumseh's "vision of glory" had long been reduced to a mere illusion.[22]

The future, as Tecumseh had predicted regarding an unsuccessful outcome of the War of 1812, brought only the relentless agony of persecution by the Long Knives. "We see this plainly," Tecumseh had warned. "It will not be many years before our last place of abode and our last hunting ground will be taken from us, and the remnants of the different tribes between the Mississippi, the [Great] Lakes, and the Ohio River will all be driven toward the setting sun."[23]

Tecumseh's observations were founded on the already dire history of the post–Greeneville Treaty years. No sooner had the treaty been published than the quest for land began. "Land jobbers," as Anthony Wayne termed them, descended on the Indians, exacting title to their land in exchange for liquor and other merchandise. So persistent were these attempts that James Wilkinson had to issue a proclamation in May, 1796, invalidating such transactions. United States Army personnel were busy purchasing ceded lands for friends and investors in the East, and the survey of the Lake Superior region for valuable minerals was initiated as early as several weeks after the Greeneville treaty.

A veritable flood tide of farmers, land speculators, adventurers, and would-be entrepreneurs swiftly occupied the Ohio lands, producing enormous profiteering. The Indiana Territory was split from Ohio in 1800, and the heavy influx of settlers at that time forboded further pressure for the remaining Indian lands. Just as Secretary of War Pickering had predicted in 1795, once control was secured of the relinquished country, further inroads could be made with minimal difficulty. Suggestive of subsequent American tactics were the methods used by American commissioners at the Treaty of Fort Wayne in the fall of 1809, where liberal issues of whiskey enabled certain whites to obtain 3 million acres of prime Wabash and White River lands at a cost of $10,550. Since the prevailing government selling price was $2 per acre, a tidy profit of nearly $6 million was thus secured. In fact, from the estimated 190 million acres of land obtained from the Indians before 1820 a net yield of $213 million was realized. This profit was an important means of repaying the national debt.[24]

As was to be expected, the victimized tribes' protests brought them little practical relief. Because of the insatiable American desire for Indian lands, from 1803 to 1818 six separate treaties involving the Miami Indians occurred. The Indians were frustrated by delays and irregularities in the issuing of their annual annuities, and their inability to withstand pressures from the treaty makers was readily apparent to all.[25]

Unfortunately for the tribes, the extent of their embarrassment did not end with practical matters. The personal degradation long prevalent on the frontier seemed to reach new heights with the increasing proximity of white settlements. Indians were compelled to beg for scraps of food at Fort Wayne during the winter of 1795–96.[26]

Moreover, increasing the Indians' personal indebtedness became a strategic technique of the white land grabbers. By encouraging profiteering at the government-controlled trading houses, President Thomas Jefferson reasoned that, when the most influential Indians had incurred debts beyond what they could pay, "they became willing to lop them off by a cession of lands." The ultimate solution, endorsed by Jefferson, involved further humbling of the red race. "You will mix with us by marriage," he assuredly told a delegation of Delawares. "Instead then . . . of the gloomy prospect . . . of your total disappearance from the face of the Earth, which is true if you continue to hunt the deer and buffalo and go to war, you see what a brilliant aspect is offered to your future history if you . . . adopt the culture of the earth and raise domestic animals."[27]

To confine the freedom-loving and traditionally mobile Indians to a minimal parcel of ground in a dreary pursuit of agriculture was tantamount to slavery. "It was unthinkable that a tribe should be surrounded by fenced land and tied to a flock of chickens," wrote a keen modern observer of the Indians' passion for personal freedom.[28]

Predictably, the desecration of Indian life continued unabated. Women were never plentiful on the post-Revolutionary War frontier, and the native women experienced some of the deepest emotional scars. Typical of the often cruel desecration of Indian women was an unsavory incident at Fort Defiance in 1795, where a drunken trader, demanding a squaw for his use, recruited an interpreter to procure the woman. When the interpreter returned, he presented a squaw "blind of an eye and who, besides many deformities, was upwards of sixty." Yet the inebriated trader took her to his bed "as if she had been the greatest belle on Earth." In the morning the mortified trader discovered his mistake and shoved the Indian woman from his bed as if she were so much rubbish.[29]

Another Indian girl, the mistress of an American officer, delivered a child in December, 1795. The father, however, denied his reponsibility on account of the time, saying it was not possible for a child to be born in less than nine months, and only eight had passed since his first liaison with her.[30]

The wanton sexual abuse of Indian women led to a profusion of mixed-bloods and the spread of the dreaded venereal diseases that were rampant through the tribes. So pitiful was the plight of the once-powerful Piankashaw and Wea nations, ravaged by disease, drunkenness, and abject poverty—all produced by prolonged exposure to white culture—that Governor Harrison termed them "the most depraved wretches on Earth."[31]

Tragically, the ultimate humiliation of the eastern tribes was reserved for those who survived the early years of submission. By 1830, Americans would no longer tolerate the close proximity of the red nations in mid-America. Indian removal acts, designed to separate the tribes from their remaining parcels of lands and send them west of the Mississippi, provided another chapter of the tragic saga. From the Algonquian tribes of the North to the Seminoles and Cherokees in the South, the terror and trauma of lives mercilessly uprooted, of demoralizing graft and special favoritism, of indescribable hardship and suffering, blended into the common ordeals exemplified by the Cherokee Trail of Tears.

From 1830 to 1850 this great upheaval continued. The Miamis, already reduced from a domain consisting of many thousands of acres to ten square miles of tribal lands in Indiana, during the 1840's were deported to Kansas. Many warriors had to be forcibly removed after being hunted down in the swamps and captured like wild animals by the army. Shuttled west in canalboats without adequate food, clothing, or equipment, nearly a third died before the anniversary of their removal.

The appalled wife of the Indian agent who accompanied the Miamis on their long march west recalled how during the first winter in Kansas many Indians wandered about barefooted, begging their way, and enduring insults as they asked for a crust of bread at remote homesteads. Distraught fathers and mothers, unable to care for their children, were seen to give them up for tribal adoption and wander away into the swirling snow never again to be seen alive.[32]

This tragedy, while later regarded as "one of the most pitiable incidents of American History," was compounded in the late 1860's by further removals to the Indian Territory, which is now Oklahoma. Only in 1871, when the tribes were denied status and recognition as independent entities in governmental transactions, was the stage set for the final act of nineteenth-century white persecution. In 1887 the Dawes Act was passed dividing tribal lands into minimal individual parcels that were allotted to each Indian as personal property. It almost achieved the complete demise of the Indian tribes. By the terms of this devious legislation, homesteading whites claimed about 90 million "surplus" acres of Indian lands.[33]

The expansionists of the 1840's had called it Manifest Destiny. Others had termed it the course of empire. Yet the language of the white triumph was relatively unimportant. What had occurred was simply and undeniably the conquest of the continent at the expense of all rivals. It mattered not that the native civilizations had virtually been exterminated or forced to assimilate with the dominant society. By both divine and natural law, reasoned the white majority, the ascendancy of an advanced society, as characterized by the United States, was for the benefit of all mankind. The blessings of "liberty, civilization, and religion" were not to be withheld at the whim of a pitiful few, concluded Andrew Jackson. Convinced of the moral, political, and economic superiority of the United States, American statesmen endeavored to achieve their mandate by impressing "less fortunate people" with the professed benefits of "freedom" and "democracy"[34]

Widely publicized in this century have been the Indian wars in the American West between 1862 and 1890. Yet these sordid affairs were to prove anticlimactic. As surely as the fate of the red men was sealed by the loss of mid-America in 1795, the hope of sustained resistance west of the Mississippi River by the few remaining unconquered tribes was truly forlorn.

Today it seems regrettable that the earlier, perhaps central crisis in Indian history has so long suffered relative obscurity. Indeed, because the ramifications of history impinge on subsequent generations, the world may do well to remember the wisdom of a vanquished Indian chieftain who at the Treaty of Greeneville cautioned his conquerer, "My friend, I am old, but I shall never die. I shall live in my children, and my children's children." Long after succeeding generations have passed into eternity, the Indians' legacy remains, well fulfilling a prophesy that physical persecution is inevitably momentary, while the free spirit of man endures forever.

Notes

Chapter 1. River of Many White Caps

1. Hulbert, *The Ohio River*, pp. 2, 3, 16, 92–98.
2. Flexner, *George Washington and the New Nation*, pp. 295–98.
3. Havinghurst, *River to the West*, p. 18; Hulbert, *The Ohio River*, p. 3.
4. Hulbert, *The Ohio River*, pp. 4, 6, 158, 260.
5. Ibid., p. 250.
6. Ibid., pp. 69, 158.
7. Carman and Syrett, *A History of the American People*, 2:201.
8. Van Every, *Ark of Empire: The American Frontier, 1784–1803*, p. 7.
9. Hulbert, *The Ohio River*, p. 158.
10. Carman, *History of the American People*, 1:670; Van Every, *Ark of Empire*, pp. 159, 229.
11. Stone, *Life of Joseph Brant*, 2:238; Downes, *The Conquest*, p. 57.
12. Keek and Sanders, eds., *Literature of the North American Indian*, p. 226.
13. O'Callaghan, ed., *Documents Relative to the Colonial History of the State of New York*, 8:125–30; Downes, *Council Fires*, p. 283.
14. Keek and Sanders, *Literature of the North American Indian*, pp. 249, 271.
15. Downes, *Council Fires*, p. 300.
16. Burton, ed., *Michigan Pioneer and Historical Collections* 25:692; Keek and Sanders, *Literature of the North American Indian*, p. 274.
17. Keek and Sanders, *Literature of the North American Indian*, p. 274.

Chapter 2. Seeds of War

1. Smith, *An Account of the Remarkable Occurrences in the Life and Travels of Colonel James Smith During His Captivity with the Indians, in the Years 1755–1759*, p. 139; Deetz, Fisher, and Owens, eds., *The North American Indians*, p. 625.
2. Keek and Sanders, *Literature of the North American Indian*, p. 274.
3. Deetz, *The North American Indians*, p. 635.
4. Heard, *White into Red*, pp. 11, 12.
5. Galloway, *Old Chillicothe, Shawnee, and Pioneer History*, p. 178; Smith, *Smith's Captivity*, pp. 140, 149.
6. Heard, *White into Red*, pp. 12, 27; Keek and Sanders, *Literature of the North American Indians*, p. 272.
7. Smith, *Smith's Captivity*, pp. 144–46; Craig, *The Olden Time*, 1:278.
8. Smith, *Smith's Captivity*, p. 146; Tucker, *Tecumseh*, p. 99.
9. Heard, *White into Red*, pp. 27, 101.
10. Ibid., p. 27.
11. *Pennsylvania Archives*, 2d ser., 7:405.
12. Craig, *The Olden Time*, 1:124.

341

13. Drake, *Book of the Indians*, p. 46; Burton, *Michigan Pioneer*, 25:692.

14. Deetz, *The North American Indians*, pp. 632, 633.

Chapter 3. The Lion in Winter

1. United States, *American State Papers*, vol. 1, *Indian Affairs*, p. 179; St. Clair, *St. Clair Papers*, 2:197.

2. Carman and Syrett, *A History of the American People*, 1:168; Russell, *The British Regime in Michigan and the Old Northwest*, pp. 222, 227–29; Bemis, *Diplomatic History of the United States*, pp. 59–60; Downes, *Council Fires*, p. 277; Guthman, *March to Massacre*, preface.

3. Burton, *Michigan Pioneer*, 20:108, 118, 221, 243, 681.

4. Ibid., 20:128.

5. Downes, *Council Fires*, pp. 280–81; Burton, *Michigan Pioneer*, 20:226, 269.

6. Ibid., 10:663, 20:279.

7. Ibid., 20:165–68, 269; Carman, *A History of the American People*, p. 197; Downes, *The Conquest*, p. 31.

8. Downes, *Council Fires*, pp. 280–81; Burton, *Michigan Pioneer*, 20:139.

9. Downes, *Council Fires*, pp. 276–78.

10. Burton, *Michigan Pioneer*, 10:351–53.

11. Graymont, *The Iroquois*, pp. 122–27; Burton, *Michigan Pioneer*, 10:339, 399, 434, 444, 484, 632, 663, 20:285.

12. Burton, *Michigan Pioneer*, 10:352, 434, 453, 462, 476, 580.

13. Ibid., 10:416.

14. Ibid., 10:434.

15. Ibid., 10:352, 357.

16. Tucker, *Tecumseh*, p. 74; Burton, *Michigan Pioneer*, 11:384, 14:273, 486.

17. Burton, *Michigan Pioneeer*, 1:400, 577, 20:170.

18. Ibid., 10:408, 416, 11:336, 16:18, 20:128.

19. Ibid., 10:536–37, 663, 11:371, 20:163.

20. Ibid., 11:326, 336, 370, 374, 20:123.

21. Ibid., 10:663, 11:327, 332, 371, 374.

22. Burton, *Michigan Pioneer*, 10:121, 20:118–19.

23. Ibid., 10:663, 20:121–23.

24. Ibid., 10:298; Horsman, *Matthew Elliott*, pp. 8–11.

25. Downes, *Council Fires*, p. 186; Graymont, *The Iroquois*, pp. 120–27.

26. Downes, *Council Fires*, pp. 186, 250; Burton, *Michigan Pioneer*, 11:380.

27. Burton, *Michigan Pioneer*, 20:131–32.

28. Ibid., 20:128, 137, 147, 157, 174–75; Downes, *Council Fires*, pp. 282–83.

29. Burton, *Michigan Pioneer*, 20:163–64, 171–82; Stone, *Life of Joseph Brant*, 2:238–39.

30. Ibid., 20:175; Downes, *The Conquest*, p. 32.

31. Burton, *Michigan Pioneer*, 20:177.

32. Ibid., 20:175–81.

33. Ibid., 20:182–83.

34. Ibid., 20:154.

35. Ibid., 11:385.

36. Ibid., 11:355.

37. Ibid., 20:139.

Chapter 4. Nothing but the Soil They Live On

1. Craig, *The Olden Time*, 1:406.

2. Downes, *Council Fires*, p. 289; Boatner, *Encyclopedia of the American Revolution*, p. 110.

3. Craig, *The Olden Time*, 2:416; Downes, *Council Fires*, p. 288; Graymont, *The Iroquois*, p. 73.

4. Craig, *The Olden Time*, 2:406–15.

5. Stone, *Life of Joseph Brant*, 2:245.

6. Downes, *Council Fires*, p. 287; Stone, *Life of Joseph Brant*, 2:246.

7. Craig, *The Olden Time*, 2:414.

8. Ibid., 2:343; Downes, *Council Fires*, p. 290.

9. Ibid., 2:418.

10. Ibid., 2:421–23; Downes, *Council Fires*, pp. 184, 291.

11. Craig, *The Olden Time*, 2:424.

12. Ibid., 2:425.

13. Washington, *George Washington's Writings*, ed. Fitzpatrick, 8:480–84; Craig, *The Olden Time*, 2:404; Charles J. Kappler, ed., *Indian Treaties*, pp. 5, 6, 17.

14. Craig, *The Olden Time*, 2:424–26; Kappler, *Indian Treaties*, pp. 5, 6.

15. Craig, *The Olden Time*, 2:427.

16. Kappler, *Indian Treaties*, pp. 5, 6.

17. Downes, *Council Fires*, p. 292; *Pennsylvania Archives*, 1st ser., 11:508–509.

18. Burton, *Michigan Pioneer*, 24:320; Graymont, *The Iroquois*, pp. 283–84.

19. Burton, *Michigan Pioneer*, 10:359, 11:483, 20:283–84; Stone, *Life of Joseph Brant*, 1:238.

20. Downes, *Council Fires*, p. 292.

21. Craig, *The Olden Time*, 2:290, 296, 342–43; Burton, *Michigan Pioneer*, 11:468; Stone, *Life of Joseph Brant*, 2:245–48.

22. Craig, *The Olden Time*, 2:301, 342–43; Downes, *Council Fires*, pp. 305–306; Burton, *Michigan Pioneer*, 11:457–58.

23. *Writings of George Washington*, ed. Sparks, 8:477–81; Downes, *Council Fires*, p. 284; Ford, *Journals of the Continental Congress*, 25:682–83.

24. *Writings of George Washington*, ed. Sparks, 8:480, 484.

25. Ford, *Journals of the Continental Congress*, 25:680; Downes, *Council Fires*, p. 284.

26. Ford, *Journals of the Continental Congress*, 25:685–86.

27. Ibid., 25:682–88.

28. Downes, *Council Fires*, p. 289; Ford, *Journals of the Continental Congress*, 25:687.

29. *Pennsylvania Archives*, 1st ser., 11:510; Boatner, *Encyclopedia of the American Revolution*, p. 382; Craig, *The Olden Time*, 2:343; Downes, *Council Fires*, p. 293.

30. Craig, *The Olden Time*, 2:340–43; Downes, *Council Fires on the Upper Ohio*, pp. 293–94.

31. Downes, *Council Fires*, p. 294; Kappler, *Indian Treaties*, pp. 7–8; Craig, *The Olden Time*, 2:341–43.

32. Russell, *British Regime in Michigan and the Old Northwest*, p. 228; *The Writings of George Washington*, ed. Ford, 10:425, 447; Carter, ed., *The Territorial Papers of the United States*, vol. 2, *The Territory Northwest of the River Ohio, 1787–1803*, pp. 12–18.

33. Craig, *The Olden Time*, 2:456.

34. Downes, *Council Fires*, p. 295; Burton, *Michigan Pioneeer*, 24:21.

35. Burton, *Michigan Pioneer*, 24:24–25.

36. Craig, *The Olden Time*, 2:483–504.

37. Ibid., 2:512–17, 531.

38. Ibid., 2:488, 512.

39. Ibid., 2:513–25.

40. Ibid., 2:522–23.

41. Ibid., 2:523–24; Ebenezer Denny, "A Military Journal Kept by Major E. Denny 1781 to 1795," p. 277.

42. Craig, *The Olden Time*, 2:518, 524.

43. Ibid., 2:529; Kappler, *Indian Treaties*, p. 11.

44. Craig, *The Olden Time*, 2:529, 531; Kappler, *Indian Treaties*, p.11.

1. Palmer, ed., *Calendar of Virginia State Papers*, 4:160.
2. Ibid.
3. Ibid., 4:156–60.
4. Denny, *A Military Journal*, p. 293.
5. Palmer, *Virginia State Papers*, 4:119.
6. Ibid., 4:159–60.
7. Ibid., 4:122; Helderman, "Northwest Expedition," p. 326.
8. Palmer, *Virginia State Papers*, 4:157; Denny, *A Military Journal*, p. 293.
9. Palmer, *Virginia State Papers*, 4:157, 166; Helderman, "The Northwest Expedition," p. 326.
10. Palmer, *Virginia State Papers*, 4:157, 166.
11. Ibid., 4:122.
12. Ibid., 4:122; Young, *Little Turtle*, p. 31.
13. *Writings of George Washington*, ed. Ford, 12:11; Burton, *Michigan Pioneer*, 20:60, 24:30.
14. Drake, *Book of the Indians*, pp. 55–57; Young, *Little Turtle*, p. 136; Helderman, "Northwest Expedition," p. 324.
15. Helderman, "Northwest Expedition," p. 326; Bradley, *Lord Dorchester*, pp. 282–85; Palmer, *Virginia State Papers*, 4:188, 192, 238, 258–60.
16. Helderman, "Northwest Expedition," pp. 166, 192, 327; *St. Clair Papers*, 2:19.
17. Helderman, "Northwest Expedition," p. 327.
18. Palmer, *Virginia State Papers*, 4:166, 204, 205.
19. Ibid., 4:166.
20. Ibid., 4:192.
21. *The St. Clair Papers*, 2:16, 17; Denny, *A Military Journal*, p. 291.
22. Helderman, "Northwest Expedition," p. 324.
23. Palmer, *Virginia State Papers*, 4:187; Helderman, "Northwest Expedition," pp. 321–27.
24. Helderman, "Northwest Expedition," p. 322, 327; Bodley, *George Rogers Clark*, p. 288; Smith, *History of Kentucky*, p. 268.
25. Bodley, *George Rogers Clark*, p. 289–90; Burton, *Michigan Pioneer*, 24:33, 38; Young, *Little Turtle*, p. 25; Smith, *History of Kentucky*, p. 268; *St. Clair Papers*, 2:19; Helderman, "Northwest Expedition," pp. 327–28; Palmer, *Virginia State Papers*, 4:189, 202.
26. *St. Clair Papers*, 2:19; Palmer, *Virginia State Papers*, 4:204.
27. 1 W 249, Lyman C. Draper Manuscript Collection, Wisconsin Historical Society, Madison.
28. 12 S 136, 9 BB 60, Draper Manuscripts.
29. Burton, *Michigan Pioneer*, 24:35–37; Denny, *A Military Journal*, p. 297.
30. Burton, *Michigan Pioneer*, 24:24–36; *St. Clair Papers*, 2:17, 19; Denny, *A Military Journal*, pp. 285, 291.
31. 8 BB 36, Draper Manuscripts; Burton, *Michigan Pioneer*, 24:34, 37; Howe, *Historical Collections of Ohio*, p. 299; Eckert, *Frontiersmen*, p. 298.
32. Denny, *A Military Journal*, p. 297; Craig, *The Olden Time*, 2:530–31; 12 CC 79–99, Draper Manuscripts; *St. Clair Papers*, 2:17, 19; Burton, *Michigan Pioneer*, 24:35; Palmer, *Virginia State Papers*, 2:19.
33. Howe, *Historical Collections of Ohio*, p. 299–300; 12 S 136, 139, Draper Manuscripts.
34. Howe, *Historical Collections of Ohio*, p. 300.
35. 8 BB 37, 9 BB 562, Draper Manuscripts.
36. Howe, *Historical Collections of Ohio*, p. 299–300.
37. 13 S 135, 9 BB 574, Draper Manuscripts; Smith, *History of Kentucky*, p. 269.
38. Howe, *Historical Collections of Ohio*, p. 300; Burton, *Michigan Pioneer*, 24:34–36.

39. Smith, *History of Kentucky*, pp. 209–15; Eckert, *Frontiersmen*, pp. 264, 300; Howe, *Historical Collections of Ohio*, p. 300; 12 S 134, Draper Manuscripts.

40. Howe, *Historical Collections of Ohio*, p. 300; 12 S 134, Draper Manuscripts.

41. Howe, *Historical Collections of Ohio*, p. 300; Palmer, *Virginia State Papers*, 4:258–60; 8 BB 36, Draper Manuscripts.

42. Howe, *Historical Collections of Ohio*, pp. 300–301.

43. Burton, *Michigan Pioneer*, 24:26–37; 23 U 38, 5 BB 107, Draper Manuscripts.

44. 8 BB 36, 1 W 264, Draper Manuscripts.

45. 9 BB 572, 608, 1 W 264, 8 BB 575, Draper Manuscripts.

46. 1 W 264 Draper Manuscripts; Palmer, *Virginia State Papers*, 4:182, 204; *St. Clair Papers*, 2:19.

47. Palmer, *Virginia State Papers*, 4:191, 192, 237; 1 W 267, Draper Manuscripts.

48. Howe, *Historical Collections of Ohio*, p. 302; Denny, *A Military Journal*, p. 309.

49. Horsman, *Matthew Elliott*, p. 56; Downes, *Council Fires*, p. 298.

50. Downes, *Council Fires*, p. 300; Burton, *Michigan Pioneer*, 11:467.

51. Denny, *A Military Journal*, p. 280; Downes, *Council Fires*, pp. 301–303.

52. Burton, *Michigan Pioneer*, 11:467–69.

53. Ibid., 11:470; Stone, *Life of Joseph Brant*, 2:252–56.

54. Burton, *Michigan Pioneer*, 11:470–72.

55. Q27-1-44, 45, Canadian Colonial Office Records; Stone, *Life of Joseph Brant*, 2:267–68.

56. Stone, *Life of Joseph Brant*, 2:268, 271.

57. Ibid., 2:271.

58. Carter, *U.S. Territorial Papers*, 2:25, 40 n.

59. Palmer, *Virginia State Papers*, 4:192, 212, 258–60.

Chapter 6. By Act of Congress

1. Carter, *U.S. Territorial Papers*, 2:26–35.

2. Helderman, "Northwest Expedition," pp. 86–87, 318, 321.

3. Carter, *U.S. Territorial Papers*, 2:27, 28.

4. Ibid., 2:24–29; Barrett, *Evolution of the Ordinance of 1787*, pp. 46–47.

5. Carter, *U.S. Territorial Papers*, 2:31; Palmer, *Virginia State Papers*, 4:284, 312, 317.

6. Carter, *U.S. Territorial Papers*, 2:32–33.

7. *St. Clair Papers*, 2:125; Carman and Syrett, *History of the American People*, 1:201.

8. Palmer, *Virginia State Papers*, 4:281, 294; *St. Clair Papers*, 2:123, 124; Carter, *U.S. Territorial Papers*, 2:40.

9. *St. Clair Papers*, 1:131 n, 125, 126; Carter, *U.S. Territorial Papers*, 2:39–50; Barrett, *Evolution of the Ordinance of 1787*, pp. 68–72.

10. *St. Clair Papers*, 1:126; Bond, *Civilization of the Old Northwest*, p. 279.

11. *St. Clair Papers*, 1:125; Palmer, *Virginia State Papers*, 4:288, 295, 300, 312, 317; Carter, *U.S. Territorial Papers*, 2:6–9.

12. *St. Clair Papers*, 1:125–29n.

13. Carter, *U.S. Territorial Papers*, 2:52n, 55, 62, 84n; *St. Clair Papers*, 1:130.

14. *St. Clair Papers*, 1:130.

15. Ibid., 1:128; Carter, *U.S. Territorial Papers*, 2:52, 54, 61, 63; *St. Clair Papers*, 1:129.

16. *St. Clair Papers*, 1:130.

17. Carter, *U.S. Territorial Papers*, 2:3, 12, 80.

18. Carmen and Syrett, *History of the American People*, 1:195; Bond, *Civilization of the Old Northwest*, pp. 279–80; Carter, *U.S. Territorial Papers*, 2:87.

19. *St. Clair Papers*, 1:130; Howe, *Historical Collections of Ohio*, p. 576; Carman and Syrett, *History of the American People*, 1:196.

20. Bond, *Civilization of the Old Northwest*, pp. 279, 281.

21. Ibid., p. 280; Howe, *Historical Collections of Ohio*, p. 236.

22. Carter, *U.S. Territorial Papers*, 2:51, 89.

23. Horsman, *Expansion and American Indian Policy*, pp. 36–43; Ford, *Journals of the Continental Congress*, 33:447–81.

24. Horsman, *Expansion and Indian Policy*, pp. 37, 86, 95, 97; Ford, *Journals of the Continental Congress*, 32:334–43.

25. *St. Clair Papers*, 2:36, 37.

26. Ibid., 2:37; Carter, *U.S. Territorial Papers*, 2:77, 78.

27. Carter, *U.S. Territorial Papers*, 2:31, 77, 103.

Chapter 7. The Course of Empire

1. Palmer, *Virginia State Papers*, 1:783–87.

2. Butler, *Butler Family in America*, p. 155; 5 BB 118, Draper Manuscripts; Douglas, "Major General Arthur St. Clair," p. 458.

3. Boatner, *Encyclopedia of the American Revolution*, p. 110; Johnston, ed., *Dictionary of American Biography*, 2:604.

4. Stone, *Life of Joseph Brant*, 2:282–83.

5. Carter, *U.S. Territorial Papers*, 2:33, 78, 89–91.

6. Stone, *Life of Joseph Brant*, 2:273–74.

7. Burton, *Michigan Pioneer*, 11:468–69, 494; Craig, *The Olden Time*, 2:445.

8. Butterfield, ed., *Washington-Irvine Correspondence*, pp. 109, 148, 193, 231–33, 244, 320, 339, 410, 411 n., 412.

9. Burton, *Michigan Pioneer*, 20:174–83; Butterfield, *Washington-Irvine Correspondence*, p. 339; *St. Clair Papers*, 2:16.

10. Butterfield, *Washington-Irvine Correspondence*, pp. 196, 199.

11. *Writings of George Washington*, ed. Sparks, 8:477, 480–83; *Writings of George Washington*, ed. Ford, 10: 446–47.

12. Butterfield, *Washington-Irvine Correspondence*, p. 196 n.

13. *St. Clair Papers*, 2:3n.

14. Ibid., 2:3, 4.

15. Ibid., 2:12; Jacobs, *Beginnings of the U.S. Army*, p. 26.

16. *St. Clair Papers*, 2:12–14.

17. Ibid., 2:22.

18. Ibid., 2:20; Carter, *U.S. Territorial Papers*, 2:26.

19. *St. Clair Papers*, 2:37; Kappler, *Indian Treaties*, p. 10; Burton, *Michigan Pioneer*, 25:691.

20. Howe, ed., *Historical Collections of Ohio*, pp. 377, 456; *St. Clair Papers*, 2:16.

21. *St. Clair Papers*, 2:36, 37, 42.

Chapter 8. They Must and Will Have Our Country

1. Withers, *Chronicles of Border Warfare*, p. 389n; Howe, *Historical Collections of Ohio*, p. 510; Boatner, *Encyclopedia of the American Revolution*, pp. 904–905; Denny, *A Military Journal*, pp. 317, 323; *St. Clair Papers*, 1:148.

2. Denny, *A Military Journal*, pp. 323, 325, 440, 430.

3. Ibid., p. 323; Howe, *Historical Collections of Ohio*, pp. 507–508; Withers, *Border Warfare*, 389n.

4. Denny, *A Military Journal*, p. 323.

5. *St. Clair Papers*, 1:150; Howe, *Historical Collections of Ohio*, p. 510.

6. Withers, *Border Warfare*, p. 390; Carter, *U.S. Territorial Papers*, 2:70–71; *St. Clair Papers*, 1:135, 2:130, 162n; Howe, *Historical Collections of Ohio*, p. 206–207.

7. Stone, *Life of Joseph Brant*, 2:285; 1 W 249, 11 F 61–62, Draper Manuscripts.

8. Downes, *Frontier Ohio*, p. 7; Downes, *Council Fires*, pp. 302–303; *Pennsylvania Archives*, 1st ser., 11:562; Stone, *Life of Joseph Brant*, 2:275; Guthman, *March to Massacre*, pp. 58–59.

9. Stone, *Life of Joseph Brant*, 2:276.

10. Ibid., 2:276–78; Palmer, *Virginia State Papers*, 4:438.

11. Stone, *Life of Joseph Brant*, 2:278.

12. *St. Clair Papers*, 2:95.

13. *St. Clair Papers*, 1:138, 2:40–43, 51–53; 23 U 57, Draper Manuscripts.

14. *St. Clair Papers*, 2:41–45 n.

15. Ibid., 2:45 n.; 1 W 429–34, Lyman C. Draper Manuscript Collection, Wisconsin Historical Society, Madison.

16. 1 W 429–34, Draper Manuscripts.

17. 1 W 465, Draper Manuscripts.

18. 1 W 429–34, Draper Manuscripts; *St. Clair Papers*, 2:50–53; Carter, *U.S. Territorial Papers*, 2:127–28.

19. Carter, *U.S. Territorial Papers*, 2:128.

20. Ibid., 2:118, 130.

21. Ibid., 2:131.

22. Denny, *A Military Journal*, p. 326; 1 W 431, Draper Manuscripts; *St. Clair Papers*, 2:63.

23. *St. Clair Papers*, 2:81–82.

24. 1 W 464–65, Draper Manuscripts; *St. Clair Papers*, 2:60, 61, 88.

25. *St. Clair Papers*, 2:95–97; 1 W 451–69, 488–89, Draper Manuscripts; Denny, *A Military Journal*, pp. 328–30.

26. Denny, *A Military Journal*, p. 436.

27. 1 W 481, 23 U 66, Draper Manuscripts; *St. Clair Papers*, 2:98.

28. 23 U 66–68, Draper Manuscripts.

29. *St. Clair Papers*, 2:97, 99.

30. 23 U 66, Draper Manuscripts; *St. Clair Papers*, 2:50–51.

31. 1 W 481, 23 U 66–67, Draper Manuscripts.

32. 23 U 68–69, Draper Manuscripts.

33. *St. Clair Papers*, 2:97; 23 U 70–73, Draper Manuscripts.

34. 23 U 70–74, 93, Draper Manuscripts.

35. 23 U 74, Draper Manuscripts.

36. *St. Clair Papers*, 2:93, 97, 102; Carter, *U.S. Territorial Papers*, 2:168.

37. 3 U 624, 23 U 74, 93, Draper Manuscripts.

38. 23 U 66, 85, 130, 172–79, Draper Manuscripts; *St. Clair Papers*, 2:102.

39. 23 U 172–79, Draper Manuscripts.

40. *St. Clair Papers*, 2:103.

41. Ibid., 2:100–101.

42. 1 W 486, Draper Manuscripts.

Chapter 9. This Is the Road to Hell

1. Edgar, *Ten Years of Upper Canada*, p. 342.

2. Ibid., p. 343.

3. Ibid., pp. 344–45.

4. Ibid., pp. 349–50.

5. Ibid., pp. 352–71.

6. Johnston, *Narratives of Captivities*, pp. 7, 25, 29–30.

7. Ibid., pp. 34–35.

8. Ibid., pp. 36–40.

9. Ibid., pp. 42–48.

10. Ibid., pp. 44, 50, 104, 118–21.

11. Boatner, ed., *Encyclopedia of the American Revolution*, p. 434; Horsman, *Matthew Elliott*, p. 86; 1 W 409, Draper Manuscripts.

12. 2 W 51–52, Draper Manuscripts; *St. Clair Papers*, 2:20, 38, 45 n.

13. 13 CC 1, 8 BB 69, Draper Manuscripts.

14. 18 CC 18, Draper Manuscripts.

15. 12 CC 229, 14 CC 192, Draper Manuscripts.

16. Denny, *A Military Journal*, p. 435; *St. Clair Papers*, 2:49–87.

17. *St. Clair Papers*, 2:102, 106.

18. 1 W 336, 350, 2 W 2, Draper Manuscripts; Downes, *Frontier Ohio*, p. 10.

19. Denny, *A Military Journal*, pp. 12–13; 3 U 623, 23 U 75–139, Draper Manuscripts; *St. Clair Papers*, 2:111–12; *Pennsylvania Archives*, 1st ser., 11:405, 2d ser., 4:758; Graymont, *The Iroquois*, p. 290.

20. Denny, *A Military Journal*, p. 334; *St. Clair Papers*, 2:113.

21. 23 U 141, Draper Manuscripts; *St. Clair Papers*, 2:108.

22. Denny, *A Military Journal*, p. 334.

23. U.S., *American State Papers: Indian Affairs*, 1:57; *St. Clair Papers*, 2:109–13; 2 W 3–10, Draper Manuscripts; Stone, *Life of Brant*, 2:281 n.

24. 23 U 172–74, Draper Manuscripts.

25. Burton, *Michigan Pioneer*, 12:10.

26. 2 W 25, 39, 49–52; 23 U 173–76, Draper Manuscripts; Palmer, *Virginia State Papers*, 5:7–9.

27. 2 W 56, 60, Draper Manuscripts.

28. 26 CC 78, Draper Manuscripts; Howe, *Historical Collections of Ohio*, pp. 160–61; Eckert, *Frontiersman*, pp. 251–52, 330.

29. 26 CC 78, Draper Manuscripts.

30. Archibald Loudon, *Outrages Committed by the Indians*, p. 188.

31. Howe, *Historical Collections of Ohio*, p. 253.

32. Ibid., p. 240; 2 W 70–74, 89, 93, Draper Manuscripts.

33. 2 W 69–89, 115, Draper Manuscripts.

34. Palmer, *Virginia State Papers*, 4:631.

35. Ibid., 5:7–9, 32.

36. *American State Papers: Indian Affairs*, 1:13.

Chapter 10. An Eagle Untethered

1. *St. Clair Papers*, 1:158; *Writings of George Washington*, ed. Sparks, 11:488; Van Every, "Washington's Calculated Risk," *American Heritage* 9, no. 4 (June 1958): 57.

2. Guthman, *March to Massacre*, pp. 4, 174–75.

3. Ibid., pp. 2–5, 21–23.

4. Jacobs, *Beginnings of the U.S. Army*, p. 41.

5. Ibid., p. 43.

6. U.S., *American State Papers: Indian Affairs*, 1:57, 58; Van Every, "Washington's Calculated Risk," pp. 57–61.

7. *St. Clair Papers*, 2:149.

8. Van Every, "Washington's Calculated Risk," pp. 57–61.

9. *St. Clair Papers*, 2:147–48; *Writings of George Washington*, ed. Ford, 12:2; 2 W 68, 117, Draper Manuscripts.

10. Craig, *The Olden Time*, 1:481, 2:343; St. Clair to Harmar, 2 May 1790, Josiah Harmar Papers, William L. Clements Library, Ann Arbor, Michigan; Guthman, *March to Massacre*, p. 15; 2 W 33, Draper Manuscripts.

11. Guthman, *March to Massacre*, p. 15.

12. Denny, *A Military Journal*, p. 285; Jacobs, *Beginnings of the U.S. Army*, p. 33.

13. Denny, *A Military Journal*, p. 324; Guthman, *March to Massacre*, pp. 5 n, 145–46, 174–75; Jacobs, *Beginnings of the U.S. Army*, pp. 50–51.

14. 2 W 43, Draper Manuscripts; *American State Papers: Indian Affairs*, 12:14.

15. *American State Papers: Indian Affairs*, 1:58.

16. Ibid., p. 57; *St. Clair Papers*, 2:125–27.

17. *St. Clair Papers*, 2:125–27.

18. Ibid., 1:162–63, 2:155 n.; *American State Papers: Indian Affairs*, 1:58.

19. St. Clair to Harmar, 26 January 1790, Harmar Papers.

20. *St. Clair Papers*, 2:130, 132, 139.

21. Ibid., 2:135–36, 155–59; 2 W 182, Draper Manuscripts; *American State Papers: Indian Affairs*, 2:291n.; Hamtramck to Harmar, 17 March 1790, Harmar Papers.

22. 2 W 244, Draper Manuscripts; Hamtramck to Harmar, 16 May 1790, Harmar Papers.

23. *American State Papers: Indian Affairs*, 1:87, 92; *St. Clair Papers*, 2:137; Carter, *U.S. Territorial Papers*, 2:283–84; Josiah Harmar Diary, 11 July 1790, Harmar Papers.

24. Carter, U.S. Territorial Papers, 2:284; *American State Papers: Indian Affairs*, 1:92; Harmar Diary, 15 July 1790, Harmar Papers.

25. 2 W 193–95, Draper Manuscripts; Josiah Harmar Letter Book A, 9 June 1790, and Harmar Diary, 15 to 28 April 1790, Harmar Papers; *American State Papers: Indian Affairs*, 1:91.

26. Harmar Letter Book A, 9 June 1790, and Harmar Diary, 28 April 1790, Harmar Papers; Denny, *A Military Journal*, p. 138; *American State Papers: Indian Affairs*, 1:91.

27. Harmar Letter Book G, 8 and 9 June 1790, Harmar Papers.

28. *St. Clair Papers*, 2:125–27; *American State Papers, Indian Affairs*, 1:95.

29. *American State Papers: Indian Affairs*, 1:92, 95; Harmar Letter Book H, Harmar to Hamtramck, 15 July 1790, Harmar Papers.

30. *American State Papers, Indian Affairs*, 1:58.

31. Ibid., 1:84–90.

32. Ibid., 1:91, 97; *St. Clair Papers*, 2:146; *American State Papers: Indian Affairs*, 1:97.

33. *St. Clair Papers*, 2:147; *Writings of George Washington*, ed. Ford, 12:1–3.

34. Letter Book G, Harmar to Hamtramck, 13 January 1790, 20 February 1790, Harmar Papers; 2 W 117, Draper Manuscripts.

35. 2 W 98, 192, Draper Manuscripts; John P. Wyllys to James Watson, 25 August 1790, Wyllys Papers, Connecticut Historical Society, Hartford.

36. *St. Clair Papers*, 2:167 n., 184–85; Melcher to Hamtramck, 28 July 1790, Harmar Papers.

37. *St. Clair Papers*, 2:151, 184, 187; Letter Book G, Harmar to Ward, 14 September 1790, Harmar Papers.

38. 2 W 298, Draper Manuscripts.

39. 2 W 295, Draper Manuscripts.

Chapter 11. Forth into the Wilderness

1. Peckham, "Josiah Harmar and His Indian Expedition," pp. 288 ff.; Huber, General Josiah Harmar's Command: Military Policy in the Old Northwest, 1784–1791, Ph.D. diss., University of Michigan, 1964, pp. 13ff.; Boatner, ed., *Encyclopedia of the American Revolution*, p. 491; Guthman, *March to Massacre*, p. 5.

2. Huber, "Harmar's Command," pp. 25, 97–99; Guthman, *March to Massacre*, p. 61; 2 W 195, Draper Manuscripts.

3. Guthman, *March to Massacre*, pp. 9, 11.

4. Letter Book G, Harmar to Knox, 14 January 1790, Harmar Papers; *St. Clair Papers*, 2:123, 130; 2 W 66, Draper Manuscripts.

5. Letter Book G, Harmar to Hamtramck, 20 February 1790, Harmar Papers.

6. Letter Book 13, Jeffers to Harmar, 1 January 1790, Harmar Papers; *St. Clair Papers*, 2:39, 133.

7. Letter Book 13, Harmar to Elliott, 15 July 1790, Harmar Papers; *American State Papers: Indian Affairs*, 2:92–93; *St. Clair Papers*, 2:160–61.

8. Letter Book H, Harmar to Wyllys, 15 August 1790, Harmar Papers; Guthman, *March to Massacre*, pp. 91–92; 2 W 314, 328, Draper Manuscripts.

9. 2 W 312–13, Draper Manuscripts.

10. 2 W 309, Draper Manuscripts; *American State Papers: Indian Affairs*, 1:98–99.

11. Carter, *U.S. Territorial Papers*, 2:299; *St. Clair Papers*, 2:162–63.

12. Palmer, *Virginia State Papers*, 5:193–94; Guthman, *March to Massacre*, p. 104; *American State Papers: Indian Affairs*, 1:92, 95, 99; 2 W 327, Draper Manuscripts; Wyllys to Watson, 25 August 1790, Wyllys Papers.

13. Beatty, "Diary of Major Erkuries Beatty," p. 437; Denny, *A Military Journal*, p. 306.

14. Denny, *A Military Journal*, p. 437; 2 W 85, Draper Manuscripts; Harmar to Mifflin, 4 September 1790, Letter Book H, Harmar Papers.

15. 3 MM 15, Draper Manuscripts; Harmar to Elliott 15 August 1790, Harmar to McDowell, 12 August 1790, Harmar to Henry Lee, 3 August 1790, Letter Book H, Harmar Papers.

16. 2 W 328, Draper Manuscripts; Denny, *A Military Journal*, p. 140.

17. *American State Papers: Military Affairs*, 1:20.

18. Ibid., 1:24; 2 W 335, Draper Manuscripts.

19. *American State Papers: Indian Affairs*, 1:96, and *Military Affairs*, 1:20, 21, 34; 2 W 323, Draper Manuscripts; Harmar to Elliott 29 September 1790, Harmar to Wyllys, 15 August 1790, Letter Book H, Harmar Papers.

20. *American State Papers: Military Affairs*, 1:20–24, and *Indian Affairs*, 1:95; 2 W 325 Draper Manuscripts.

21. *American State Papers: Military Affairs*, 1:20–24; 2 W 314, Draper Manuscripts.

22. *American State Papers: Indian Affairs*, 1:99.

23. *St. Clair Papers*, 2:163, 185.

24. Ibid., 2:185–87, 194; Carter, *U.S. Territorial Papers*, 2:308.

25. *St. Clair Papers*, 2:186 n.

26. *American State Papers: Indian Affairs*, 1:96, and *Military Affairs*, 1:21; 2 W 329, Draper Manuscripts.

27. 2 W 324, 330, Draper Manuscripts.

28. St. Clair to Harmar, 1 October 1790, Harmar Papers.

29. Ibid.

30. Denny, *A Military Journal*, p. 145; 2 W 336, Draper Manuscripts; *American State Papers: Indian Affairs*, 1:96.

31. *American State Papers: Military Affairs*, 1:21, 24, 29, 31.

32. 2 W 238, 337, Draper Manuscripts.

33. 2 W 338, 4 JJ 5, Draper Manuscripts.

34. Denny, *A Military Journal*, p. 143.

35. Ibid. p. 143; 2 W 338, 4 JJ 5, Draper Manuscripts; *American State Papers: Military Affairs*, 1:34; Irvin, "Harmar's Campaign," *Ohio Archaeological and Historical Quarterly* 19:393–94; Meek, "General Harmar's Expedition," p. 82.

36. *American State Papers: Military Affairs*, 1:21–28.

37. Ibid., 1:24, 25, 34.

38. Ibid., 1:21, 25; 2 W 339, Draper Manuscripts; Meek, "General Harmar's Expedition," p. 83.

39. 2 W 285, 304, 315, 361, Draper Manuscripts.

40. 2 W 285, 296, Draper Manuscripts; Gale Thornbrough, *Outpost on the Wabash*, pp. 254–56.

41. 2 W 361, Draper Manuscripts.

42. 2 W 315, 361, Draper Manuscripts.

43. 2 W 369, 379, Draper Manuscripts; Thornbrough, *Outpost on the Wabash*, p. 265.

44. Hildreth, *Pioneer History*, p. 269; Q 49–107, Q Series, Colonial Office Records, Public Archives of Canada.

45. Q 45-2-504, Q 49-107, Colonial Office Records, Public Archives of Canada.
46. Q 27-1-44, W 46-2-523, Q 49-109, Q 49-116, Colonial Office Records.
47. 2 W 339, Draper Manuscripts.
48. Q 50-1-28, 30, 43–58, Colonial Office Records.

Chapter 12. They Fought and Died Hard

1. Young, *Little Turtle*, p. 31; Horsman, *Matthew Elliott*, p. 60; Q 49-116, Colonial Office Records.

2. 2 W 36, 44, 192, 285, 293, Draper Manuscripts; Carter, *U.S. Territorial Papers*, 2:301; *St. Clair Papers*, 2:181–83.

3. 2 W 192, Draper Manuscripts.

4. St. Clair to Harmar, 1 October 1790, Harmar Papers.

5. Quaife, "Fort Wayne in 1790 (Journal of Henry Hay)," pp. 300, 307, 316, 334.

6. Ibid., p. 313.

7. Ibid., pp. 313–15, 334.

8. *American State Papers: Indian Affairs*, 1:104; Denny, *A Military Journal*, p. 145.

9. 2 W 330, Draper Manuscripts; Q 46-2-530, Q 49-116, Q 50-1-31, Colonial Office Records.

10. Q 49-111, Colonial Office Records.

11. Q 50-1-28, 37, ibid.

12. Q 50-1-27–30, 111, ibid.

13. Q 50-1-30, Ibid.; 2 W 339, Draper Manuscripts.

14. *American State Papers: Military Affairs*, 1:25, 26; Denny, *A Military Journal*, pp. 144–45; John Pratt to Samuel Wyllys, 4 November 1790; Wyllys Papers, Connecticut Historical Society, Hartford, Conn.; J. Backus to _____, Woodbridge Papers, Detroit Public Library; Meek, "Harmar's Expedition," p. 38.

15. *American State Papers: Military Affairs*, 1:26; 4 U 5–7, 4 JJ 6, Draper Manuscripts.

16. *American State Papers: Military Affairs*, 1:26.

17. Ibid., 1:25, *American State Papers: Indian Affairs*, 1:105; 2 W 339, Draper Manuscripts.

18. Denny, *A Military Journal*, p. 144; 2 W 339, Draper Manuscripts; Meek, "Harmar's Expedition," p. 83; *American State Papers: Indian Affairs*, 1:105, *Military Affairs*, 1:26.

19. *American State Papers: Military Affairs*, 1:26; 4 JJ 5, 8, Draper Manuscripts.

20. *American State Papers, Military Affairs*, 1:21, 27, 34; *Indian Affairs*, 1:104.

21. *American State Papers: Military Affairs*, 1:34; 2 W 340, 4 JJ 5, Draper Manuscripts.

22. *American State Papers: Military Affairs*, 1:34.

23. Ibid.

24. *American State Papers: Military Affairs*, 1:22–28; *Indian Affairs*, 1:105; Irvin, "Harmar's Campaign," p. 394.

25. 4 JJ 5, Draper Manuscripts; *American State Papers: Military Affairs*, 1:26, 27, 34; Irvin, "Harmar's Campaign," p. 394; report of Ebenzer Denny, 1 January 1791, St. Clair Papers, Ohio Historical Society, Columbus.

26. Denny, *A Military Journal*, p. 145–46; *American State Papers: Military Affairs*, 1:21–28.

27. Denny, *A Military Journal*, p. 145; *American State Papers: Military Affairs*, 1:27.

28. J. Backus to _____, 24 November 1790, Woodbridge Papers; Meek, "Harmar's Expedition," p. 83; Irvin, "Harmar's Campaign," p. 394.

29. Irvin, "Harmar's Campaign," p. 395; *American State Papers: Military Affairs*, 1:27.

30. *American State Papers: Military Affairs*, 1:27; 4 U 5–17, Draper Manuscripts; Irvin, "Harmar's Campaign," p. 395.

31. Otho Winger, "The Indians Who Opposed Harmar," pp. 55–59; *American State Papers: Military Affairs*, 1:21, 27; Q 50-1-33, 37, Colonial Office Records.

32. Irvin, "Harmar's Campaign," p. 395; *American State Papers: Military Affairs*, 1:23; Meek, "Harmar's Expedition," p. 83; Denny's Report, 1 January 1791, St. Clair Papers, National Archives; Denny, *A Military Journal*, p. 146.

33. *American State Papers: Military Affairs*, 1:27; Irvin, "Harmar's Campaign," p. 395.

34. Meek, "Harmar's Expedition," p. 84; *American State Papers: Military Affairs*, 1:23–27; J. Backus to _____, 24 November 1790, Woodbridge Papers.

35. Irvin, "Harmar's Campaign," p. 395.

36. 4 U 5–17, Draper Manuscripts.

37. 4 U 5–17, 4 JJ 8, Draper Manuscripts; Irvin, "Harmar's Campaign," p. 395; *American State Papers: Military Affairs*, 1:22, 29.

38. *American State Papers: Military Affairs*, 1:22–35; 2 W 341, Draper Manuscripts; Meek, "Harmar's Expedition, p. 83.

39. Meek, "Harmar's Expedition," p. 83; *American State Papers: Military Affairs*, 1:27.

40. *American State Papers: Indian Affairs*, 1:105.

41. *American State Papers: Military Affairs*, 1:22, 26, 35; Denny, *A Military Journal*, p. 146.

42. *American State Papers: Military Affairs*, 1:35; *Indian Affairs* 1:105.

43. *American State Papers: Indian Affairs*, 1:104, 105; *Military Affairs*, 1:25; Denny, *A Military Journal*, p. 147. Winger, "Indians Who Opposed Harmar," pp. 55–57.

44. Denny, *A Military Journal*, p. 147; 11 CC 61, Draper Manuscripts.

45. *American State Papers: Indian Affairs*, 1:105.

46. *American State Papers: Military Affairs*, 1:25; Denny, *A Military Journal*, p. 144; Q 50-1-37, Colonial Office Records.

47. *American State Papers: Military Affairs*, 1:35; 4 U 5–17, 3 MM 20, 4 JJ 10, Draper Manuscripts.

48. *American State Papers: Military Affairs*, 1:21–29; 2 W 342, Draper Manuscripts.

49. *American State Papers: Military Affairs*, 1:28, 35.

50. Ibid.

51. Ibid., 1:25, 28, 35.

52. Q 50-1-33 to 43, Colonial Office Records; Wallace A. Brice, *History of Fort Wayne*, p. 315 n.; Lossing, *Pictorial Field Book of the War of 1812*, p. 44.

53. Q 50-1-35, 39, 58, Colonial Office Records.

54. 4 JJ 11, 12, Draper Manuscripts; Huber, "General Harmar's Command," p. 110; *American State Papers: Military Affairs*, 1:23, 28.

55. Pratt to S. Wyllys, 4 November 1790, J. Wyllys to James Watson, 25 August 1790, Wyllys Papers.

56. Quaife, *Fort Wayne in 1790*, p. 313, 347; 4 U 18, 2 W 342, Draper Manuscripts; Meek, "Harmar's Expedition," p. 83; Brice, *A History of Ft. Wayne*, pp. 128–129n.

57. Brice, *A History of Fort Wayne*, pp. 128 n, 129 n, 315 n.

58. 4 U 18, Draper Manuscripts; Guthman, *March to Massacre*, p. 193; Elmore Barce, *The Land of the Miamis*, p. 44.

59. 4 JJ 11–12, 4 U 99, Draper Manuscripts; *American State Papers: Military Affairs*, 1:28.

60. 4 JJ 12, Draper Manuscripts; Denny, *A Military Journal*, p. 147; *American State Papers: Military Affairs*, 1:28; Quaiffe, *Fort Wayne in 1790*, p. 327.

61. Denny's Report, 1 January 1791, St. Clair Papers; Lossing, *Field Book of the War of 1812*, pp. 43–45; *American State Papers: Military Affairs*, 1:28. Q 50-1-1 35, Colonial Office Records; 4 JJ 13, Draper Manuscripts; Pratt to S. Wyllys, 4 November 1790, Woodbridge Papers.

62. Pratt to S. Wyllys, 4 November 1790, Wyllys Papers; Backus to _____, 24 November 1790, Woodbridge Papers; Q 50-1-39, Colonial Office Records; 4 JJ 13 Draper Manuscripts.

63. 3 MM 20, Draper Manuscripts; Denny, *A Military Journal*, p. 148; *American State Papers: Military Affairs*, 1:25, 28.

64. Denny, *A Military Journal*, p. 148; 3 MM 20, Draper Manuscripts.

65. 4 U 5–17, Draper Manuscripts.

66. 4 U 11–12, Draper Manuscripts.

67. 4 U 5–17, 99, Draper Manuscripts.

68. Denny, *A Military Journal*, p. 148; *St. Clair Papers*, ed. W. H. Smith, 2:188.

69. *American State Papers: Indian Affairs*, 1:106; *Military Affairs*, 1:28; Denny's Report, 1 January 1791, St. Clair Papers.

70. 4 U 12, 14 U 173–75, Draper Manuscripts.

71. Denny, *A Military Journal*, p. 148; *American State Papers: Military Affaris*, 1:25, 26, 35.

72. 2 W 342, Draper Manuscripts; Denny, *A Military Journal*, p. 148; *American State Papers: Military Affairs*, 1:35.

73. *American State Papers: Military Affairs*, 1:20–29; Denny, *A Military Journal*, p. 148.

74. 2 W 342, Draper Manuscripts; Denny, *A Military Journal*, p. 149.

75. *American State Papers: Military Affairs*, 1:23; *Indian Affairs*, 1:106.

76. Brice, *History of Fort Wayne*, pp. 128n, 129n; 3 MM 20, Draper Manuscripts.

Chapter 13. The Miami Moon

1. 2 W 342, Draper Manuscript; Q 50-1-35 to 39, Colonial Office Records; St. Clair to Harmar, 1 October 1790, Harmar Papers.

2. Q 50-1-36, 40, Colonial Office Records.

3. Q 50-1-40 to 43, ibid.

4. Harmar meteorological records, 22 October 1790, Harmar Papers; von Oppolzer, *Canon of Eclipses*, p. 371; Q 50-1-35, 43, 44, Colonial Office Records.

5. *American State Papers: Military Affairs*, 1:25.

6. *American State Papers: Military Affairs*, 1:35; *Indian Affairs*, 1:106; 2 W 342, Draper Manuscripts.

7. Denny, *A Military Journal*, p. 149; 4 JJ 8, 17, and 2 W 342, Draper Manuscripts.

8. 2 W 342, Draper Manuscripts; *Correspondence of John Cleves Symmes*, pp. 132–38; *American State Papers: Military Affairs*, 1:21.

9. Denny, *A Military Journal*, p. 150; *American State Papers: Military Affairs*, 1:21–29, 35; *Indian Affairs*, 1:106.

10. Denny, *A Military Journal*, pp. 150–51.

11. 3 JJ 491; 4 U 12; 2 W 403–404, Draper Manuscripts; Wilkinson to Harmar, 24 November 1790, Harmar Papers; Palmer, *Virginia State Papers*, 5:222.

12. 4 JJ 11, Draper Manuscripts; W. H. Smith, *St. Clair Papers*, 2:188.

13. W. H. Smith, *St. Clair Papers*, 2:190; Palmer, *Virginia State Papers*, 5:222; *American State Papers: Indian Affairs*, 1:104; Wilkinson to Harmar, 24 November 1790, Harmar Papers.

14. J. Backus to _____, 24 November 1790, Woodbridge Papers.

15. *Correspondence of John Cleves Symmes*, pp. 132–38.

16. 2 W 342, 348, 355, Draper Manuscripts.

17. 2 W 326, 394–401, Draper Manuscripts.

18. *Writings of George Washington*, ed. Ford, 11:506–507.

19. 2 W 345–55, 401, Draper Manuscripts; *St. Clair Papers*, 2:193–97, 201; Beatty to Harmar, 9 March 1791, Harmar Papers.

20. 2 W 407, Draper Manuscripts; Beatty to Harmar, 9 March 1791, Harmar Papers; *St. Clair Papers*, 2:257; Denny, *A Military Journal*, p. 152.

21. 2 W 417 to 421, Draper Manuscripts; Wilkinson to Harmar, 20 June 1791, Harmar Papers; *St. Clair Papers*, 2:251.

22. Armstrong to Harmar, 9 March 1791; Beatty to Harmar, 9 March 1791, Harmar to Howell, 5 January 1791, Harmar Papers.

23. Harmar to Howell, 5 January 1791, Harmar Papers; *St. Clair Papers*, 2:262.

24. Q 50-1-41–46, Colonial Office Records.

25. Q 50-1-48–49, Colonial Office Records.

26. Q 42-144 to 146; Q 49-173; Q 50-1-66, 95, 96, Colonial Office Records.

27. Q 50-1-66, Colonial Office Records.

28. Q 27-1-44–47, Colonial Office Records.

29. Burton, *Michigan Pioneer*, 24:260; Q 49-173, Colonial Office Records.

30. Burton, *Michigan Pioneer*, 24:171, 172, 260.

31. Q 50-1-21, Colonial Office Records.

32. Q 50-1-16, 17, Colonial Office Records; Burton, *Michigan Pioneer*, 24:144, 171.

33. Q 52-206, Colonial Office Records.

34. Q 27-1-44, Q 50-1-48, Q 52-206 to 209, ibid.

35. Q 50-1-33, Colonial Office Records; Horsman, *Matthew Elliott*, pp. 4, 19, 79, 91; Consul Willshire Butterfield, *History of the Girtys*, p. 249; Huber, *Harmar's Command*, pp. 64–65.

36. Butterfield, *History of the Girtys*, pp. 41, 54, 95, 210, 336.

37. Q 50-1-39 to 56, Colonial Office Records.

38. Q 50-1-46–47, Colonial Office Records.

39. Butterfield, *History of the Girtys*, p. 251; 2 W 383, Draper Manuscripts; Harmar to Hamtramck, 15 January 1791, Harmar Papers.

40. 2 W 386, Draper Manuscripts; meteorological tables, January 1791, Harmar Papers; Stephen Decater Cone, "Indian Attack on Fort Dunlap," pp. 64–66.

41. Frances B. Heitman, *Historical Register and Dictionary of the United States Army . . . September 29, 1789 to March 2, 1903*, 1:601; 2 W 385–86, Draper Manuscripts; Harmar to Symmes, 21 January 1791, Harmar Papers; Cone, "Attack on Fort Dunlap," pp. 66–68.

42. Meteorological tables, January 1791, Harmar Papers; Cone, "Attack on Fort Dunlap," pp. 67–68; 2 W 386, Draper Manuscripts.

43. 2 W. 386, Draper Manuscripts; Cone, "Attack on Fort Dunlap," pp. 67–68; Butterfield, *History of the Girtys*, p. 253.

44. Cone, "Attack on Fort Dunlap," pp. 68; 2 W 386, Draper Manuscripts.

45. 2 W 386–88, Draper Manuscripts; Butterfield, *History of the Girtys*, p. 254.

46. Hildreth, *Pioneer History*, pp. 429–39.

47. Ibid.

48. Ibid.

49. *American State Papers: Indian Affairs*, 1:122; Hildreth, *Pioneer History*, p. 433; C 24, Draper Manuscripts.

50. *American State Papers: Indian Affairs*, 1:122; 2 W 393–94, C 24, Draper Manuscripts.

51. Cone, "Attack on Fort Dunlap," p. 68; Hildreth, *Pioneer History*, p. 437; *American State Papers: Indian Affairs*, 1:121.

Chapter 14. The Town Destroyers

1. *Writings of George Washington*, ed. Ford, 12:2.

2. Ibid., 12:20n.

3. *Writings of George Washington*, ed. Sparks, 10:153; *American State Papers; Indian Affairs*, 1:112–12.

4. *American State Papers: Indian Affairs*, 1:112–13, 118.

5. Beatty to Harmar, 9 March 1791, Harmar Papers.

6. *American State Papers: Indian Affairs*, 1:113, 129, 172; *Writings of George Washington*, ed. Sparks, 10:115–56.

7. *Writings of George Washington*, ed. Sparks, 10:153–56n; *American State Papers, Indian Affairs*, 1:139.

8. *Pennsylvania Archives*, 1st ser., 11:733; *American State Papers: Indian Affairs*, 139–42, 151–52.

9. *American State Papers: Indian Affairs*, 1:146–50.

10. Ibid., 1:146.

11. Ibid., 1:146, 161.

12. *American State Papers: Indian Affairs*, 1:152, 174; *St. Clair Papers*, 2:201–205.

13. *American State Papers: Indian Affairs*, 1:153, 155–57, 163; *Writings of George Washington*, ed. Ford, 12:8.

14. *American State Papers: Indian Affairs*, 1:159, 163.

15. Ibid., 1:157–64; Burton, *Michigan Pioneer*, 24:232–34.

16. *American State Papers: Indian Affairs*, 1:139, 158; Burton, *Michigan Pioneer*, 24:237–39.

17. *American State Papers: Indian Affairs*, 1:129, 171; 12 CC 248, 13 CC 19, 217, 3 JJ 513, Draper Manuscripts; Arthur St. Clair Diary, March–April 1791, Winthrop Sargent Papers, Detroit Public Library; Burton, *Michigan Pioneer*, 24:221; Kenton, *Simon Kenton, His Life and Period*, pp. 202, 202n; Thornbrough, *Outpost on the Wabash, 1787–1791*, p. 278.

18. 12 CC 248, 3 JJ 505, 4 JJ 175, Draper Manuscripts; Burton, *Michigan Pioneer*, 24:222.

19. 8 BB 91–92, 4 JJ 175, Draper Manuscripts; Burton, *Michigan Pioneer*, 24:222.

20. Burton, *Michigan Pioneer*, 24:106, 222; Kenton, *Simon Kenton*, pp. 44–45.

21. 6 BB 93, 8 BB 92, 11 CC 65, 13 CC 217, 4 JJ 175, Draper Manuscripts.

22. 8 BB 92, 11 CC 65, 4 JJ 175, Draper Manuscripts.

23. 8 BB 94–98, 13 CC 154, Draper Manuscripts; Kenton, *Simon Kenton*, pp. 203–207.

24. 4 JJ 170, Draper Manuscripts; *St. Clair Papers*, 2:212–14; "Diary of Major Erkuries Beatty, Paymaster in the Western Army, May 15, 1786 to June 5, 1787," *Magazine of American History*, p. 435.

25. 4 JJ 171, Draper Manuscripts.

26. *St. Clair Papers*, 2:203, 212–13; *American State Papers: Indian Affairs*, 1:174; *Military Affairs*, 1:36.

27. *St. Clair Papers*, 2:207, 212–14.

28. *American State Papers: Indian Affairs*, 1:131.

29. Burton, *Michigan Pioneer*, 24:201, 213, 223, 262.

30. Ibid., 24:223, 246–47, 262.

31. Ibid., 24:247–51.

32. Ibid., 24:129, 132–33, 251, 261.

33. Ibid., 24:261; *American State Papers: Indian Affairs*, 1:131; Craig, *Ouiatanon, A Study in Indiana History*, pp. 318–48.

34. *American State Papers; Indian Affairs*, 1:131, 133.

35. Ibid., 1:131–32; Burton, *Michigan Pioneer*, 24:273.

36. *American State Papers: Indian Affairs*, 1:113; Craig, *Ouiatanon*, pp. 318–48.

37. Burton, *Michigan Pioneer*, 24:261; *American State Papers: Indian Affairs*, 1:132–33.

38. Burton, *Michigan Pioneer*, 24:251, 261, 273–74.

39. Ibid., 24:251, 262, 270.

40. Ibid., 24:173, 262, 263.

41. Ibid., 24:263, 274, 280, 300.

42. Ibid., 24:270, 280; 11 F 62, Draper Manuscripts.

43. *St. Clair Papers*, 2:222–23.

44. 4 U 118, 2 W 413–14, Draper Manuscripts; Burton, *Michigan Pioneer*, 24:330–31; Arthur St. Clair, *A Narrative of the Campaign Against the Indians under the Command of Major General St. Clair*, p. 128; Keek, *Literature of the North American Indian*, p. 249.

Chapter 15. A Disaster in the Making

1. *American State Papers: Military Affairs*, 1:59; *Writings of George Washington*, ed. Ford, 12:22; *St. Clair Papers*, 2:283; Callahan, *Henry Knox, General Washington's General*, p. 320.

2. St. Clair, *A Narrative of the Campaign*, p. 36; *Writings of George Washington*, ed. Ford, 12:22; *American State Papers: Indian Affairs*, 1:171–72.

3. *American State Papers: Indian Affairs*, 1:112, 113, 171, 173.

4. *American State Papers: Indian Affairs*, 1:172.

5. Ibid., 1:147, 148; Burton, *Michigan Pioneer*, 24:216, 240, 248; St. Clair, *Narrative of the Campaign*, p. 39.

6. *American State Papers: Indian Affairs*, 1:172–74, *Military Affairs*, 1:36; *St. Clair Papers*, 2:212–13.

7. Harmar to Hamtramck, 15 January 1791, Howell to Harmar, 22 April 1791, Beatty to Harmar, 9 March 1791, Harmar Papers; Doughty to Knox, 8 March 1791, Knox Papers, Massachusetts Historical Society; *American State Papers: Indian Affairs*, 1:113.

8. *American State Papers: Military Affairs*, 1:36.

9. Howell to Harmar, 22 April 1791, Harmar to Clarksville, 26 January 1791, Harmar Papers.

10. *American State Papers: Indian Affairs*, 1:189; *Military Affairs*, 1:36; *St. Clair Papers*, 2:262.

11. *American State Papers: Indian Affairs*, 1:113, 140, 176–90.

12. Ibid., 1:117–79; *St. Clair Papers*, 2:231, 233, 241, 243; Burton, *Michigan Pioneer*, 24:328; St. Clair to Knox, 24 August 1791, 4 September 1791, Knox Papers.

13. *St. Clair Papers*, 2:251–52; *American State Papers: Indian Affairs*, 1:171, 176–82.

14. *St. Clair Papers*, 2:240, 242; Burton, *Michigan Pioneer*, 24: 180, 201; *American State Papers: Indian Affairs*, 1:185.

15. *American State Papers: Military Affairs*, 1:36; *Indian Affairs*, 1:175, 184.

16. St. Clair, *Narrative of the Campaign*, p. 201; Butler to Knox, 7 June 1791, Butler Papers; Burton, *Michigan Pioneer*, 24:276, 281; *American State Papers: Indian Affairs*, 1:186–89.

17. Boatner, *Encyclopedia of the American Revolution*, p. 339; *American State Papers: Military Affairs*, 1:36, 42; Knox to Walker, 5 March 1791; Knox/Duer document, 28 April 1791, Jackson document, 2 June 1791, Benny/Rogers doc., 14 May 1791, Duer to Knox, 27 August 1791; Knox to Duer, 8 June 1791, Knox Papers.

18. Callahan, *Henry Knox*, p. 341.

19. *American State Papers: Military Affairs*, 1:36; *Indian Affairs*, 1:188; Knox to Duer, 26 June 1791, 2 July 1791, Knox Papers.

20. *American State Papers: Indian Affairs* 1:118–91; *St. Clair Papers*, 2:244; Knox to Duer, 26 June 1791, Knox Papers.

21. Callahan, *Henry Knox*, p. 266; Heitman, *Dictionary of the U.S. Army*, 1:533; Jackson to Knox, October 1791, Knox Papers; St. Clair, *A Narrative of the Campaign*, pp. 201, 206; Guthman, *March to Massacre*, p. 207n; *American State Papers: Indian Affairs*, 1:175–95; Burton, *Michigan Pioneer*, 24:264–68.

22. *American State Papers: Indian Affairs*, 1:117–95; *Military Affairs*, 1:36–38; St. Clair, *A Narrative of the Campaign*, p. 228; Denny, *A Military Journal*, p. 152; *St. Clair Papers*, 2:240–41; St. Clair to Knox, 8 August 1791, Knox Papers.

23. *American State Papers: Indian Affairs*, 1:179–95.

24. *Journal of Captain Daniel Bradley*, p. 8; "Adjutant Crawford's Orderly Book," William D. Wilkins Papers, Detroit Public Library, p. 7; *American State Papers: Military Affairs*, 1:43; Winthrop Sargent, "Winthrop Sargent's Diary While with General Arthur St. Clair's Expedition Against the Indians," *Ohio Archaeological and Historical Quarterly*, 33:241; St. Clair, *A Narrative of the Campaign*, p. 31.

25. *American State Papers: Indian Affairs*, 1:184; *Military Affairs*, 1:37, 38; St. Clair to Knox, 8 August 1791, 4 September 1791, 16 September 1791; St. Clair to Wilkinson, 28 August 1791, Knox Papers; *St. Clair Papers*, 2:210, 246, 251.

26. St. Clair to Knox, 4 September 1791, 15 September 1791, Knox Papers; Harmar's Meteorological Tables, 9 September, 1791, Harmar Papers; *St. Clair Papers*, 2:249; St. Clair, *A Narrative of the Campaign*, pp. 56–57.

27. Harmar's Meteorological Tables, 14 August 1791, Harmar Papers; St. Clair to Knox, 19 July 1791, 8 August 1791, Knox Papers; *St. Clair Papers*, 2:239–40; *American State Papers: Military Affairs*, 1:37; Sargent, "Sargent's Diary," p. 240.

28. *St. Clair Papers*, 2:239; Sargent, "Sargent's Diary," p. 240; St. Clair to Knox, 15 September 1791, Knox Papers.

29. Sargent, "Sargent's Diary," p. 239; St. Clair to Knox, 4 September 1791, 23 September 1791, Knox Papers; *St. Clair Papers*, 2:241.

30. *American State Papers: Military Affairs*, 1:20–36; Denny, *A Military Journal*, pp. 152–53; Harmar's Meteorological Tables, 27 September 1791, Harmar Papers.

31. Denny, *A Military Journal*, pp. 153–56.

32. *St. Clair Papers*, 2:252.

33. Harmar's Meteoroglical Tables, 10 August 1791, Harmar Papers; 4 U 121, Draper Manuscripts; St. Clair to Knox, 15 September 1791, Knox Papers.

Chapter 16. March into Oblivion

1. Boatner, *Encyclopedia of the American Revolution*, pp. 1205–1207; *St. Clair Papers*, pp. 12–13; *Writings of George Washington*, ed. Ford, 12:309.

2. James Ripley Jacobs, *Tarnished Warrior: Major General James Wilkinson*, pp. 104–105.

3. *American State Papers: Indian Affairs*, 1:132; *St. Clair Papers*, 2:223.

4. *St. Clair Papers*, 2:223, 227; *American State Papers: Indian Affairs*, 1:132–34.

5. *American State Papers: Indian Affairs*, 1:134; Harmar's Meteorological Tables, August 1791, Harmar Papers.

6. *American State Papers: Indian Affairs*, 1:135; St. Clair to Knox, 4 September 1791, Knox Papers.

7. *American State Papers: Indian Affairs*, 1:135, 182, 184.

8. Ibid., 1:134, 235; Burton, *Michigan Pioneer*, 20:310–11, 24:274–97; Pickering to Butler, 19 July 1791, Richard Butler Papers, Detroit Public Library; *Diary of David Zeisberger*, 2:198–217.

9. Burton, *Michigan Pioneer*, 24:310, 331: Q 54-2-617, Colonial Office Records; *Diary of David Zeisberger*, 2:205, 206, 214–16.

10. *Diary of David Zeisberger*, 2:214; Burton, *Michigan Pioneer*, 24:280.

11. *Diary of David Zeisberger*, 2:220; Burton, *Michigan Pioneer*, 24:280–81, 286, 300, 330.

12. Burton, *Michigan Pioneer*, 24:319.

13. Ibid., 24:281, 310–11, 318, 320.

14. Ibid., 24:300–312; Bradley, *Lord Dorchester*, p. 269.

15. *Diary of David Zeisberger*, 2:201, 216, 222; Burton, *Michigan Pioneer*, 24:330.

16. *Diary of David Zeisberger*, 2:205, 218; Burton, *Michigan Pioneer*, 24:300.

17. St. Clair to Knox, 15 September 1791, Knox Papers; *St. Clair Papers*, 2:233; General St. Clair's First Communication of Inquiry, Records Relative to the Expeditions of Generals St. Clair and Wayne Against the Indians, RG 94, National Archives, p. 6.

18. Harmar's Meteorological Tables, September, October, 1791, Harmar Papers; *Journal of Captain Bradley*, 17 September to 3 October, 1791; Adjutant Crawford's Orderly Book, 20, 28 September, 4 October 1791, Detroit Public Library.

19. General St. Clair's First Communication, p. 12; *St. Clair Papers*, 2:240–52; St. Clair to Knox, 15 September 1791; Wilson, *Fort Jefferson*, p. 7.

20. Harmar's Journal, 18, 20 September 1791, Harmar Papers; *St. Clair Papers*, 2:240–41; St. Clair to Knox, 4, 23, 25 September 1791, Knox Papers; Sargent, "Sargent's Diary," pp. 241–43; General St. Clair's First Communication, p. 13; 4 U 120–24, Draper Manuscripts; Adjutant Crawford's Orderly Book 27, 29 September, 3, 4 October 1791.

21. *St. Clair Papers*, 2:245, 252; General St. Clair's First Communication, pp. 12–13; St. Clair, *A Narrative of the Campaign*, pp. 196–97, 212.

22. *St. Clair Papers*, 2:245, 253; 2 W 402, Draper Manuscripts; St. Clair, *A Narrative of the Campaign*, p. 212; Sargent, "Sargent's Diary," pp. 246–47.

23. *St. Clair Papers*, 2:245; Adjutant Crawford's Orderly Book, 2, 4 October 1791.

24. Butler, *The Butler Family in America*, p. 155; 4 U 125, Draper Manuscripts; Adjutant Crawford's Orderly Book, 30 September, 3 October 1791; S. P. Hildreth, ed., *The American Pioneer*, 2:135; St. Clair, *A Narrative of the Campaign*, p. 207.

25. Sargent, "Sargent's Diary," pp. 211, 242–43; 4 U 125, Draper Manuscripts; Adjutant Crawford's Orderly Book, 4 October 1791.

26. *St. Clair Papers*, 2:245, 253; St. Clair to Knox, 10 October 1791, Knox Papers; General St. Clair's First Communication, pp. 27, 36.

27. Adjutant Crawford's Orderly Book, 17 October 1791; General St. Clair's First Communication, pp. 33, 34; St. Clair, *A Narrative of the Campaign*, pp. 34, 51.

28. General St. Clair's First Communication, pp. 29–31; St. Clair, *A Narrative of the Campaign*, pp. 223, 227; Sargent, "Sargent's Diary," p. 231; Burton, *Michigan Pioneer*, 24:291.

29. *St. Clair Papers*, 2:246–47, 253.

30. *St. Clair Papers*, 2:246–47, 253; St. Clair to Knox, 10, 21 October 1791, Knox Papers.

31. General St. Clair's First Communication, pp. 39–40; St. Clair to Knox, 24 August 1791, Knox Papers.

32. St. Clair to Knox, 8 August 1791, Knox Papers; *St. Clair Papers*, 2:254; St. Clair, *A Narrative of the Campaign*, p. 200; Hildreth, *American Pioneer*, 2:136.

33. Sargent, "Sargent's Diary," p. 246; 4 U 130, Draper Manuscripts.

34. *Journal of Captain Bradley*, 11–18 October 1791; Wilson, *Fort Jefferson*, pp. 5, 11, 12; *St. Clair Papers*, 2:253; 4 U 126, Draper Manuscripts; Sargent, "Sargent's Diary," p. 245; St. Clair, *A Narrative of the Campaign*, p. 209.

35. Sargent, "Sargent's Diary," pp. 245–46; St. Clair to Knox, 10, 21 October 1791, Knox Papers; St. Clair, *A Narrative of the Campaign*, pp. 199–207; 4 U 121, 130, Draper Manuscripts; *American State Papers: Indian Affairs*, 1:188; *Journal of Captain Bradley*, 19 October 1791.

36. *American State Papers: Military Affairs*, 1:38; St. Clair, *A Narrative of the Campaign*, pp. 201–207, 219; 4 U 130, Draper Manuscripts; Sargent, "Sargent's Diary," pp. 246–47.

37. St. Clair to Knox, 21 October 1791, Knox Papers; Sargent, "Sargent's Diary," p. 246; *St. Clair Papers*, 2:254; *Journal of Captain Bradley*, 19 October 1791; M. McDonough to McDonough, 10 November 1791, Clements Library, Ann Arbor, Michigan; Adjutant Crawford's Orderly Book, 8 October 1791; Hildreth, *American Pioneer*, p. 137.

38. St. Clair to Knox, 17 October 1791, Knox Papers; *St. Clair Papers*, 2:254.

39. Sargent, "Sargent's Diary," pp. 247–48; *St. Clair Papers*, 2:252–54; Q 58-1-54, Colonial Office Records; Burton, *Michigan Pioneer*, 24:328–29; 4 U 130, Draper Manuscripts.

40. Sargent, "Sargent's Diary," pp. 246–48; General St. Clair's First Communication, pp. 17, 36; Adjutant Crawford's Orderly Book, 19, 22, 23 October 1791; Burton, *Michigan Pioneer*, 24:420; *St. Clair Papers*, 2:249.

41. *St. Clair Papers*, 2:254; Sargent, "Sargent's Diary," p. 247.

42. General St. Clair's First Communication, pp. 15, 16, 28; Sargent, "Sargent's Diary," p. 247.

43. *St. Clair Papers*, 2:255; St. Clair to Knox, 21 October, 1791, Knox Papers.

44. Sargent, "Sargent's Diary," p. 247; *St. Clair Papers*, 2:249; Adjutant Crawford's Orderly Book, 22 October 1791; McDonough to McDonough, 10 November 1791, Clements Library.

45. *St. Clair Papers*, 2:249–57; Sargent, "Sargent's Diary," p. 249.

46. Sargent, "Sargent's Diary," pp. 249–50; *St. Clair Papers*, 2:250–56; Adjutant Crawford's Orderly Book, 27 to 29 October 1791.

47. *St. Clair Papers*, 2:250, 256; *Journal of Captain Bradley*, 28 October 1791.

48. *St. Clair Papers*, 2:250–57; Sargent, "Sargent's Diary," pp. 250–51.

49. *St. Clair Papers*, 2:257; Sargent, "Sargent's Diary," p. 251.

50. General St. Clair's First Communication, p. 23; *St. Clair Papers*, 2:251; St. Clair, *A Narrative of the Campaign*, p. 39.

51. *St. Clair Papers*, 2:251, 257; Sargent, "Sargent's Diary," p. 251.

52. *St. Clair Papers*, 2:25, 257; St. Clair, *A Narrative of the Campaign*, p. 223; Burton, *Michigan Pioneer*, 24:331; Sargent, "Sargent's Diary," p. 251; Hildreth, *American Pioneer*, 2:137; McDonough to McDonough, 10 November 1791, Clements Library; Adjutant Crawford's Orderly Book, 28 October 1791; St. Clair to Knox, 21 October 1791, Knox Papers.

53. General St. Clair's First Communication, pp. 17, 34, 35; St. Clair to Knox, 4 September 1791, Knox Papers.

54. Sargent, "Sargent's Diary," pp. 241–53; *St. Clair Papers*, 2:250–58; St. Clair to Knox, 21 October 1791, Knox Papers; Adjutant Crawford's Orderly Book, 29 October 1791.

55. 4 U 123, Draper Manuscripts; Burton, *Michigan Pioneer*, 24:334; *St. Clair Papers*, 2:258; Sargent, "Sargent's Diary," p. 253; St. Clair to Knox, 21 October 1791, Knox Papers.

56. Burton, *Michigan Pioneer*, 24:329.

57. Sargent, "Sargent's Diary," p. 251; *St. Clair Papers*, 2:251, 257; Burton, *Michigan Pioneer*, 24:331; St. Clair to Knox, 21 October 1791, Knox Papers.

58. Sargent, "Sargent's Diary," p. 252; *St. Clair Papers*, 2:258.

59. Burton, *Michigan Pioneer*, 24:332.

60. Ibid., 24:331–33; Sargent, "Sargent's Diary," p. 252; *St. Clair Papers*, 2:258.

Chapter 17. **A Mouthful of Earth**

1. Sargent, "Sargent's Diary," p. 253; Wilson, "St. Clair's Defeat," p. 378; *St. Clair Papers*, 2:258.

2. *St. Clair Papers*, 2:257, Sargent, "Sargent's Diary," p. 252.

3. *St. Clair Papers*, 2:258; roll 6, nos. 446, 452, St. Clair Collection, Ohio Historical Society, Columbus, Ohio.

4. 4 JJ 217 Draper Manuscripts; *St. Clair Papers*, 2:263; Sargent, "Sargent's Diary," pp. 252, 256, 259.

5. Sargent, "Sargent's Diary," p. 252; Adjutant Crawford's Orderly Book, 25 October 1791.

6. *St. Clair Papers*, 2:258–71; Sargent, "Sargent's Diary," pp. 256–57; St. Clair, *A Narrative of the Campaign*, pp. 225–26; Darke to Knox, 9 November 1791, Knox Papers.

7. Butler, *The Butler Family*, pp. 281–96; St. Clair, *A Narrative of the Campaign*, p. 214; Sargent, "Sargent's Diary," pp. 257, 267.

8. Burton, *Michigan Pioneer*, 24:276; St. Clair to Butler, 6 July 1791, Burton Collection, Detroit Public Library; St. Clair, *A Narrative of the Campaign*, pp. 214–20.

9. St. Clair, *A Narrative of the Campaign*, pp. 216–20.

10. Ibid.

11. Ibid.; Butler, *Butler Family*, p. 157.

12. St. Clair, *A Narrative of the Campaign*, p. 218, 244.

13. Roll 6, no. 441, St. Clair Collection; St. Clair to Knox, 10 October 1791, Knox Papers; Sargent, "Sargent's Diary," pp. 252–53, 258.

14. Young, *Little Turtle*, p. 125, 141, 142; *Minutes of Debates in Council on the Banks of the Ottawa River, November, 1791*, p. 6.

15. Q 58-178, Colonial Office Records; Sargent, "Sargent's Diary," p. 271; Burton, *Michigan Pioneer*, 24:358.

16. Burton, *Michigan Pioneer*, 24:329–30, 336, 358; Butterfield, *History of the Girtys*, p. 263; *American State Papers: Indian Affairs*, 1:243; Milo M. Quaife, ed., *The Captivity of O. M. Spencer*, pp. 92–93; 4 U 166, Draper Manuscripts; Howe, *Historical Collections of Ohio*, 2:231.

17. Burton, *Michigan Pioneer*, 24:329–30.

18. Quaife, *Captivity of Spencer*, p. 23; McDonough to McDonough, 10 November 1791, Clements Library; Sargent, "Sargent's Diary," p. 258; roll 6, no. 453, St. Clair Collection, Ohio Historical Society.

19. 4 U 142–46, Draper Manuscripts; Wilson, "St. Clair's Defeat," p. 379.

20. Howe, *Historical Collections of Ohio*, 2:229.

21. St. Clair, *A Narrative of the Campaign*, pp. 211–12; Sargent, "Sargent's Diary" p. 258; 4 U 142–44, Draper Manuscripts.

22. 4 U 142–44, Draper Manuscripts.

23. St. Clair, *A Narrative of the Campaign*, p. 220; Sargent, "Sargent's Diary," pp. 257–58; McDonough to McDonough, 10 November 1791, Clements Library; *Columbian Centinal*, 28 December 1791, Burton Collection, Detroit Public Library.

24. Howe, *Historical Collections of Ohio*, 2:227; Sargent, "Sargent's Diary," pp. 258–59; *Columbian Centinal*, 7 January 1792, and McDonough to McDonough, 10 November 1791, Burton Collection.

25. Sargent, "Sargent's Diary," p. 259.

26. 4 JJ 216, Draper Manuscripts; *St. Clair Papers*, 2:259; Sargent, "Sargent's Diary," pp. 259–60; Wilson, "St. Clair's Defeat," p. 379; *Remarkable Adventures of Jackson Johonnot*, p. 16; Hildreth, *American Pioneer*, 2:150; roll 6, no. 479, St. Clair Collection, Ohio Historical Society.

27. Sargent, "Sargent's Diary," pp. 259–60; St. Clair, *A Narrative of the Campaign*, pp. 181–82, 221; Burton, *Michigan Pioneer*, 17:606; Quaife, *Captivity of O. M. Spencer*, p. 24; Hildreth, *American Pioneer*, 2:150; *St. Clair Papers*, 2:259.

28. Wilson, "St. Clair's Defeat," p. 380; 4 U 142–44, Draper Manuscripts.

29. Sargent, "Sargent's Diary, pp. 259, 261; McDonough to McDonough, 10 November 1791, Clements Library; St. Clair, *A Narrative of the Campaign*, p. 222; *American State Papers: Indian Affairs*, 1:157.

30. *St. Clair Papers*, 1:176–77n; St. Clair, *A Narrative of the Campaign*, pp. 2, 48.

31. Sargent, "Sargent's Diary," p. 260; 4 JJ 223, Draper Manuscripts; *Columbian Centinel*, 7 January 1792, Burton Collection; *St. Clair Papers*, 1:176n; General St. Clair's First Communication, p. 49.

32. St. Clair, *A Narrative of the Campaign*, p. 22; Sargent, "Sargent's Diary," p. 260.

33. St. Clair, *A Narrative of the Campaign*, p. 210; Howe, *Historical Collections of Ohio*, 2:144.

34. *American State Papers: Indian Affairs*, 1:172; Adjutant Crawford's Orderly Book, 24 October 1791.

35. *American State Papers: Indian Affairs* 1:137; Darke to Washington, 9 November 1791, Knox Papers; St. Clair, *A Narrative of the Campaign*, p. 222; *St. Clair Papers*, 1:176n.

36. McDonough to McDonough, 10 November 1791, Clements Library; Darke to Washington, 9 November 1791, Knox Papers; Howe, *Historical Collections of Ohio*, 2:227; roll 6, nos. 444, 460, St. Clair Collection, Ohio Historical Society; Sargent, "Sargent's Diary," p. 266; 4 JJ 231, Draper Manuscripts.

37. Darke to Washington, 9 November 1791, Knox Papers; Martha Rohr, *Historical Sketch of Fort Recovery*, p. 28; roll 6, no. 444, St. Clair Collection; *American State Papers: Indian Affairs*, 1:137.

38. Burton, *Michigan Pioneer*, 24:358; Howe, *Historical Collections of Ohio*, 2:227; Hildreth, *American Pioneer*, p. 151; roll 6, no. 460, St. Clair Collection, Ohio Historical Society.

39. Metcalfe, *Life of Colonel James Smith*, p. 204; Craig, *The Olden Time*, 1:124.

40. Darke to Washington, 9 November 1791, Knox Papers; *St. Clair Papers*, 2:259; Hildreth, *American Pioneer*, p. 151.

41. 4 U 143, Draper Manuscripts; *Columbian Centinel*, 28 December 1791, 7 January 1792, Burton Collection.

42. Darke to Washington, 9 November 1791, Knox Papers; McDonough to McDonough, 10 November 1791, Clements Library; Sargent, "Sargent's Diary," p. 269.

43. 4 JJ 231, Draper Manuscripts; Howe, *Historical Collections of Ohio*, 2:227.

44. *St. Clair Papers*, 2:259; Howe, *Historical Collections of Ohio*, 2:227.

45. St. Clair, *A Narrative of the Campaign*, p. 225; *Columbian Centinel*, 28 December 1791, 28 January 1792, Burton Collection; Darke to Washington, 9 November 1791, Knox Papers; Howe, *Historical Collections of Ohio*, 2:227; Sargent, "Sargent's Diary," p. 266.

46. Sargent, "Sargent's Diary," p. 285; 4 U 143, Draper Manuscripts.

47. Darke to Washington, 9 November 1791, Knox Papers; Sargent, "Sargent's Diary," p. 261.

48. Sargent, "Sargent's Diary," pp. 255, 259–61; *St. Clair Papers*, 2:259; St. Clair, *A Narrative of the Campaign*, p. 196; Darke to Washington, 9 November 1791, Knox Papers; 4 JJ 223, Draper Manuscripts.

49. Sargent, "Sargent's Diary," p. 259, 268; Darke to Washington, 9 November 1791, Knox Papers; Howe, *Historical Collections of Ohio*, 2:144; *Columbian Centinel*, 7 January 1792, Burton Collection; *American State Papers: Indian Affairs*, 1:137; Butler, *Butler Family*, p. 203.

50. 4 JJ 223, Draper Manuscripts; Butler, *Butler Family*, p. 203; Wilson, "St. Clair's Defeat," p. 379; Sargent, "Sargent's Diary," p. 260: *American State Papers: Indian Affairs*, 1:137; *St. Clair Papers*, 2:259.

51. *St. Clair Papers*, 2:259; *Columbian Centinel*, 7 January 1792, Burton Collection; Butler, *Butler Family*, p. 203; 4 U 143, Draper Manuscripts.

52. St. Clair, *A Narrative of the Campaign*, p. 224; *Remarkable Adventures of Jackson Johonnot*, p. 6.

53. Butler, *Butler Family*, p. 157; Sargent, "Sargent's Diary," p. 265; St. Clair, *A Narrative of the Campaign*, pp. 220–21.

54. Butler, *Butler Family*, p. 157, 162, 282; *Columbian Centinel*, 7 January 1792, Burton Collection; 4 JJ 102, Draper Manuscripts.

55. Howe, *Historical Collections of Ohio*, pp. 226–28; St. Clair Papers, 2:259–60; Sargent, "Sargent's Diary," p. 269; 4 U 142, Draper Manuscripts; Hildreth, *American Pioneer*, 2:150–51.

56. Darke to Washington, 9 November 1791, Knox Papers; Sargent, "Sargent's Diary," p. 268; Hildreth, *American Pioneer*, 2:152.

57. Darke to Washington, 9 November 1791, Knox Papers; Sargent, "Sargent's Diary," p. 261; *St. Clair Papers*, 2:250.

58. *St. Clair Papers*, 2:265; *Columbian Centinel*, 7 January 1792, Burton Collection; 4 U 142, Draper Manuscripts.

59. *Columbian Centinel*, 7 January, 1792, Burton Collection; Howe, *Historical Collections of Ohio*, p. 227.

60. *Columbian Centinel*, 7 January 1792, Burton Collection; Sargent, "Sargent's Diary," p. 261; *St. Clair Papers*, 2:260; 4 U 142, 143, Draper Manuscripts; General St. Clair's First Communication, p. 54.

61. Darke to Washington, 9 November 1791, Knox Papers; *American State Papers: Indian Affairs*, 1:138; Sargent, "Sargent's Diary," p. 261; Wilson, "St. Clair's Defeat," p. 379.

62. Wilson, "St. Clair's Defeat," p. 379.

63. *St. Clair Papers*, 2:260; Sargent, "Sargent's Diary," p. 261; McDonough to McDonough, 10 November 1791, Clements Library; Hildreth, *American Pioneer*, 2:151.

64. *Columbian Centinel*, 7 January 1792, Burton Collection; Hildreth, *American Pioneer*, 2:151.

65. *St. Clair Papers*, 1:176n, 2:260; St. Clair, *A Narrative of the Campaign*, pp. 49, 51; General St. Clair's First Communication, p. 48.

66. Hildreth, *American Pioneer*, 2:151; Sargent, "Sargent's Diary," pp. 261–62; *St. Clair Papers*, 2:260.

67. Craig, *Olden Time*, 2:522; Butler, *Butler Family*, pp. 157, 282; Quaife, *Captivity of O. M. Spencer*, p. 25.

68. Butler, *Butler Family*, pp. 161–62; Craig, *Olden Time*, 2:523–24.

69. Sargent, "Sargent's Diary," p. 271; James H. Perkins, *Annals of the West*, p. 377.

70. Quaife, *Captivity of O. M. Spencer*, p. 27; Q 58-223, Colonial Office Records; 4 JJ 215, Draper Manuscripts; Sargent, "Sargent's Diary," p. 265; Burton, *Michigan Pioneer*, 24:328, 358; *American State Papers: Indian Affairs*, 1:243.

71. Burton, *Michigan Pioneer*, 24:336, 358, 365, 373; Sargent, "Sargent's Diary," p. 265; Quaife, *Captivity of O. M. Spencer*, pp. 27, 28, 92; 4 U 166, Draper Manuscripts.

72. *American State Papers: Indian Affairs*, 1:137; *St. Clair Papers*, 2:260–61; Sargent, "Sargent's Diary," p. 262.

73. St. Clair, *A Narrative of the Campaign*, p. 211; *Columbian Centinel*, 7 January, 1792, Burton Collection.

74. Howe, *Historical Collections of Ohio*, p. 227.

75. Ibid., p. 230.

76. Ibid., p. 230; Sargent, "Sargent's Diary," pp. 261, 266–67; *American State Papers: Indian Affairs*, 1:137.

77. Howe, *Historical Collections of Ohio*, 2:228; Lossing, *Pictorial Field Book*, p. 48n; Hildreth, *American Pioneer*, 2:152; Sargent, "Sargent's Diary," p. 269.

78. *Columbian Centinel*, 11 January 1792, Burton Collection; 4 U 100–130, Draper Manuscripts.

79. *St. Clair Papers*, 2:260, 261; *Columbian Centinel*, 7 January, 1792, Burton Collection; *American State Papers: Indian Affairs*, 1:138.

80. Hildreth, *American Pioneer*, 2:137; *St. Clair Papers*, 2:261.

81. Sargent, "Sargent's Diary," pp. 259–60; Hildreth, *American Pioneer*, 2:153; Howe, *Historical Collections of Ohio*, 2:228; McDonough to McDonough, 10 November, 1791, Clements Library; Darke to Washington, 9 November 1791, Knox Papers; St. Clair, *A Narrative of the Campaign*, p. 58; Butler, *Butler Family*, pp. 160, 282.

82. Burton, *Michigan Pioneer*, 24:336; Quaife, *Captivity of O. M. Spencer*, pp. 27–28; *Minutes of Debates in Council on the Ottawa River*, November, 1791, p. 6.

83. Quaife, *Captivity of O. M. Spencer*, pp. 27–28; Howe, *Historical Collections of Ohio*, 2:229; Q 57–178, Colonial Office Records.

84. Lossing, *Pictorial Field Book*, p. 48n; Drake, *Book of the Indians of North America*, p. 54; *Minutes of Debate in Council*, p. 19.

Chapter 18. **This Moment May Never Return**

1. McDonough to McDonough, 10 November 1791, Clements Library; Sargent, "Sargent's Diary," p. 253.

2. Sargent, "Sargent's Diary," p. 253; *American State Papers: Indian Affairs*, 1:137–38; Wilson, *Journal of Captain Bradley*, 4 November 1791; Hildreth, *American Pioneer*, 2:151.

3. Darke to Washington, 9 November 1791, Knox Papers; Sargent, "Sargent's Diary," p. 262; *St. Clair Papers*, 2:261–66.

4. Darke to Washington, 9 November 1791, Knox Papers; *St. Clair Papers*, 2:261; Hildreth, *American Pioneer*, 2:138; Sargent, "Sargent's Diary," p. 262.

5. Darke to Washington, 9 November 1791, Knox Papers.

6. Ibid.; *St. Clair Papers*, 2:266; Sargent, "Sargent's Diary," pp. 245, 253, 256; Wilson, *Journal of Captain Bradley*, 24 November 1791.

7. *St. Clair Papers*, 2:269, 271.

8. Sargent, "Sargent's Diary," pp. 253, 254.

9. Ibid., 2:254, 263; roll 6, no. 428, St. Clair Collection, Ohio Historical Society.

10. General St. Clair's First Communication, pp. 42–46.

11. Sargent, "Sargent's Diary," pp. 254, 264; roll 6, no. 429, St. Clair Collection, Ohio Historical Society.

12. General St. Clair's First Communication, p. 43.

13. Sargent, "Sargent's Diary," p. 256; *St. Clair Papers*, 2:267n, 269.

14. Sargent, "Sargent's Diary," p. 255.

15. Ibid., pp. 259, 260, 265, 269; Denny, *A Military Journal*, p. 171; McDonough to McDonough, 10 November 1791, Clements Library.

16. *St. Clair Papers*, 2:271.

17. Burton, *Michigan Pioneer*, 24:335–37.

18. *Diary of David Zeisberger*, pp. 227, 229, 230; Q 57-178, Colonial Office Records; Burton, *Michigan Pioneer*, 24:353.

19. Burton, *Michigan Pioneer*, 24:366, 401; 4 U 166, Draper Manuscripts.

20. *Minutes of Debates in Council*, pp. 6–7.

21. Ibid. pp. 7–8; Burton, *Michigan Pioneer*, 24:336.

22. Burton, *Michigan Pioneer*, 24:366.

23. Ibid., 24:366, 401.

24. Q 57-178, Q 58-1-59, Q 58-1-229, Q 58-2-240, Colonial Office Records; Burton, *Michigan Pioneer*, 24:384, 388, 423–24.

25. Burton, *Michigan Pioneer*, 24:366; *Diary of David Zeisberger*, 15 January 1792.

26. Burton, *Michigan Pioneer*, 24:366.

27. Ibid., 24:401; *Diary of David Zeisberger*, 10 January 1792.

28. Burton, *Michigan Pioneer*, 24:375–81.

29. Ibid., 24:381, 421; Q 57-181, Colonial Office Records.

30. 4 JJ 206, 217, 223, Draper Manuscripts; Guthman, *March to Massacre*, p. 247.

31. Palmer, *Calendar of Virginia State Papers*, 5:399; Sargent, "Sargent's Diary," p. 269; *St. Clair Papers*, 2:268, 279n.

32. *St. Clair Papers*, 2:256, 269–71.

33. Ibid., 2:270, 272; *American State Papers: Indian Affairs*, 1:216.

34. *American State Papers: Indian Affairs*, 1:215.

35. *Pennsylvania Archives*, 2d ser., 4:677; *American State Papers: Indian Affairs*, 1:216, 219.

36. 4 JJ 217, 224, Draper Manuscripts.

37. Denny, *A Military Journal*, pp. 174, 177; Sargent, "Sargent's Diary," pp. 256, 270; *St. Clair Papers*, 2:274.

38. *St. Clair Papers*, 2:286.

Chapter 19. A Matter of Commitment

1. Richard Rush, *Washington in Domestic Life*, pp. 65–67.

2. Denny, *A Military Journal*, p. 175.

3. *St. Clair Papers*, 2:277; Carter, *U.S. Territorial Papers*, 2:397.

4. *Writings of George Washington*, ed. Ford, 12:71–74; Flexner, *George Washington and the New Nation*, p. 302; *St. Clair Papers*, 2:275–76.

5. *St. Clair Papers*, 1:191–92, 279–86; General St. Clair's First Communication, pp. 3–10; Carter, *U.S. Territorial Papers:* 1:384–85.

6. Flexner, *George Washington and the New Nation*, pp. 301–302.

7. General St. Clair's First Communication, pp. 3, 12, 26, 52, 56; *American State Papers: Military Affairs*, 1:39; Carter, *U.S. Territorial Papers*, 1:386, 397, 398.

8. *St. Clair Papers*, 2:278; *American State Papers: Military Affairs*, 1:39–44; General St. Clair's First Communication, pp. 15–17.

9. Carter, *U.S. Territorial Papers*, 1:455; *St. Clair Papers*, 1:192, 250–52; Albert Douglas, "Major General Arthur St. Clair," pp. 455–76.

10. Burton, *Michigan Pioneer*, 24:337; Carter, *U.S. Territorial Papers*, 2:366–69.

11. Burton, *Michigan Pioneer*, 24:337; *Writings of George Washington*, ed. Ford, 12:71–73; *American State Papers: Indian Affairs*, 1:193.

12. *American State Papers: Indian Affairs*, 1:197–98.

13. Ibid., 1:199, 202.

14. Thomas H. Benton, *Abridgement of the Debates of Congress from 1789 to 1856*, 1:341–43.

15. Ibid.

16. Benton, *Abridgement of the Debates of Congress*, 1:345.

17. *Annals of the Congress of the United States, 1789–1824*, 2nd Cong. 3:343–45.

18. Ibid., 3:1350, 1730, 1392; Flexner, *George Washington and the New Nation*, p. 302.

19. *Annals of Congress*, 2d Cong. 3:1364–74.

20. *Writings of George Washington*, ed. Sparks, 12:506–512.

21. Ibid.

22. Ibid., 12:512; *Writings of George Washington*, ed. Ford, 12:138.

23. *Writings of George Washington*, ed. Ford, 12:142; Carter, *U.S. Territorial Papers*, 2:385.

24. *Writings of George Washington*, ed. Ford, 12:142; Harry Emerson Wildes, *Anthony Wayne, Troubleshooter of the American Revolution*, p. 5.

25. Wildes, *Anthony Wayne*, pp. 289–90, 329–34, 338; *Annals of Congress*, 2d Cong., 3:472, 479.

26. Wildes, *Anthony Wayne*, pp. 346, 349.

27. Ibid., pp. 5, 21, 48, 53, 169, 236; Wayne to Washington, 6 April 1789, Huntington Library, San Marino, California.

28. *Writings of George Washington*, ed. Ford, 12:142.

29. Wildes, *Anthony Wayne*, pp. 5, 305, 349; *Writings of George Washington*, ed. Ford, 12:137.

30. Q 278-187 to Q 278-189, Colonial Office Records.

31. Wayne to Berrien, 5 December 1791, Wayne Papers, Clements Library; Wildes, *Anthony Wayne*, p. 286.

32. Q 278-187, Colonial Office Records.

Chapter 20. Desultory Operations

1. Carter, *U.S. Territorial Papers*, 2:361–66; *American State Papers: Indian Affairs*, 1:198–99.

2. Carter, *U.S. Territorial Papers*, 2:362, 366.

3. Ibid., 2:366; *American State Papers: Indian Affairs*, 1:198; *Writings of George Washington*, ed. Ford, 11:134.

4. *American State Papers: Indian Affairs*, 1:226, 228; Burton, *Michigan Pioneer*, 24:370.

5. Burton, *Michigan Pioneer*, 24:367; Stone, *Life of Joseph Brant*, 2:324; *American State Papers: Indian Affairs*, 1:229–32.

6. *American State Papers: Indian Affairs*, 1:228; *Writings of George Washington*, ed. Ford, 11:507n; Burton, *Michigan Pioneer*, 24:198, 361–64; Stone, *Life of Joseph Brant*, 2:320.

7. Stone, *Life of Joseph Brant*, 2:324.

8. Ibid., 2:323; Burton, *Michigan Pioneer*, 24:416–18; *American State Papers: Indian Affairs*, 1:237.

9. Ibid., 1:228, 237; *Writings of George Washington*, ed. Ford, 12:134; Stone, *Life of Joseph Brant*, 2:328–29.

10. Burton, *Michigan Pioneer*, 24:456.

11. *American State Papers: Indian Affairs*, 1:242.

12. Ibid., 1:237.

13. Ibid., 1:227, 235, 236.

14. Ibid., 1:229–30.

15. Burton, *Michigan Pioneer*, 24:393, 413; Richard D. Knopf, *Anthony Wayne, A Name in Arms*, pp. 23, 56; Rowena Buell, ed., *The Memoirs of Rufus Putnam*, p. 296.

16. *American State Papers: Indian Affairs*, 1:243; Knopf, *Anthony Wayne*, p. 117; Burton, *Michigan Pioneer*, 24:420.

17. Knopf, *Anthony Wayne*, p. 53; Burton, *Michigan Pioneer*, 24:414–15.

18. Knopf, *Anthony Wayne*, pp. 53, 56; *American State Papers: Indian Affairs*, 1:243; Burton, *Michigan Pioneer*, 24:420; *Memoirs of Rufus Putnam*, pp. 296, 302, 311–12.

19. *American State Papers: Indian Affairs*, 1:337; Burton, *Michigan Pioneer*, 24:427; *Memoirs of Rufus Putnam*, p. 274, 311; Knopf, *Anthony Wayne*, pp. 66–67.

20. *American State Papers: Indian Affairs*, 1:237; Knpft, *Anthony Wayne*, p. 59.

21. Knopf, *Anthony Wayne*, p. 59; *Memoirs of Rufus Putnam*, p. 257; *American State Papers: Indian Affairs*, 1:234.

22. *Memoirs of Rufus Putnam*, pp. 267–74, 279, 296, 299; *American State Papers: Indian Affairs*, 1:238–40; Hamtramck to Knox, 17 June 1792, Hamtramck Papers, Burton Historical Collection, Detroit Public Library; Knopf, *Anthony Wayne*, pp. 59–61.

23. Burton, *Michigan Pioneer*, 24:274, 401, 421; G. H. Coates, ed., "A Narrative of an Embassy to the Western Indians," pp. 67, 68, 76, 78, 86, 95, 102–129; *American State Papers: Indian Affairs*, 1:233.

24. Knopf, *Anthony Wayne*, pp. 83, 84; Gunn to Wayne, April, 1792, Wayne Papers, Clements Library, Ann Arbor, Michigan; Stone, *Life of Joseph Brant*, 2:316.

25. *Writings of George Washington*, ed. Ford, 12:189; Knopf, *Anthony Wayne*, pp. 148–49.

26. Knopf, *Anthony Wayne*, p. 84.

27. Carter, *U.S. Territorial Papers*, 2:410.

Chapter 21. Toward an Uncertain Fate

1. *Memoirs of Rufus Putnam*, pp. 276, 296; Young, *Little Turtle*, pp. 35, 179; Hamtramck to Knox, 17 June 1792, Hamtramck Papers, Detroit Public Library.

2. *Memoirs of Rufus Putnam*, pp. 276, 304; *American State Papers: Indian Affairs*, 1:238; Hamtramck to Knox, 17 June 1792, Hamtramck Papers; Carter, *U.S. Territorial Papers*, 2:381.

3. *American State Papers: Indian Affairs*, 1:238, 1:238, 240, 280, 293; *Memoirs of Rufus Putnam*, pp. 277 240, 280, 293; *Memoirs of Rufus Putnam*, pp. 277–80, 295–309.

4. *American State Papers: Indian Affairs*, 1:240; *Memoirs of Rufus Putnam*, pp. 304, 333–35, 379–80.

5. *Memoirs of Rufus Putnam*, pp. 339, 366, 381; *American State Papers: Indian Affairs*, 1:235, 320.

6. *Memoirs of Rufus Putnam*, pp. 343, 354, 361–68.

7. Ibid., pp. 361–70, 381.

8. Ibid., p. 370; Burton, *Michigan Pioneer*, 24:471, 497.

9. Young, *Little Turtle*, p. 179.

10. *Memoirs of Rufus Putnam*, pp. 363n, 369, 377; Knopf, *Anthony Wayne*, p. 132; *American State Papers: Indian Affairs*, 1:338; *Journal of the Executive Proceedings of the Senate of the U.S.*, 1:128, 135, 144, 145.

11. *Memoirs of Rufus Putnam*, pp. 372–77; Knopf, *Anthony Wayne*, p. 189.

12. Wilkinson to Knox, 24 January 1792, Sargent to Knox, 9 January 1792, Knox Papers, Massachusetts Historical Society; *Memoirs of Rufus Putnam*, pp. 278, 327.

13. Sargent to St. Clair, 1 January 1792, St. Clair Papers, Ohio Historical Society; Wilkinson to Wayne, 12 July 1792, Wayne Papers, William L. Clements Library, Ann Arbor, Mich.

14. Wilson, *Fort Jefferson*, pp. 11, 12; *Journal of Captain Daniel Bradley*, p. 39.

15. Wade letter, 8 July 1792, Wayne Papers; Sargent to St. Clair, 1 January 1792, St. Clair Papers, Ohio Historical Society.

16. Sargent to St. Clair, 1 January 1792, St. Clair Papers, Ohio Historical Society; *Journal of Captain Daniel Bradley*, pp. 37–43; *Memoirs of Rufus Putnam*, pp. 273–74; Burton, *Michigan Pioneer*, 24:421, 428; Knopf, *Anthony Wayne*, pp. 55–56.

17. *Memoirs of Rufus Putnam*, pp. 268–74; Burton, *Michigan Pioneer*, 24:428; *Journal of Captain Daniel Bradley*, p. 43.

18. Wilkinson to Wayne, 12 July 1792, 4 October 1792, Wilkinson to Knox, 12 September 1792, Wayne Papers; *Memoirs of Rufus Putnam*, p. 329.

29. Wilkinson to Wayne, 4 October 1792, Wayne Papers; Quaife, *Captivity of O. M. Spencer*, p. 42.

20. Wilkinson to Knox, 12 September, 4 October, 4 November 1792, Wayne Papers; Knopf, *Anthony Wayne*, pp. 57–58, 76.

21. Wilkinson to Knox, 4 November, 6 November, 1792, Wayne Papers, Ann Arbor.

22. Quaife, *Captivity of O. M. Spencer*, pp. 115–20; Wilson, *Journal of Captain Daniel Bradley*, p. 48; Adair to Wilkinson, 7 November 1792, Wilkinson to Knox, 4 November, 6 November, 1792, Wayne Papers.

23. Adair to Wilkinson, 7 November 1792, Wayne Papers.

24. *American State Papers: Indian Affairs*, 1:335.

25. *American State Papers: Indian Affairs*, 1:335; *Journal of Captain Daniel Bradley*, p. 48. Adair to Wilkinson, 7 November 1792, Wayne Papers, Ann Arbor.

26. *American State Papers: Indian Affairs*, 1:335; Adair to Wilkinson, 7 November 1792, Wilkinson to Wayne, 12 July, 12 September 1792, Wayne Papers.

27. Wayne to Knox, 13 December, 28 December 1792, Wayne Papers.

Chapter 22. A Lack of Candor

1. Burton, *Michigan Pioneer*, 24:467, 477, 483; Coates, *A Narrative of an Embassy*, p. 86.

2. Quaife, *The Captivity of O. M. Spencer*, pp. 85, 102; Burton, *Michigan Pioneer*, 24:246, 421, 467, 468, 476–77; Coates, *A Narrative of an Embassy*, pp. 89, 96, 113–14, 122.

3. Stone, *Life of Joseph Brant*, 2:333; *American State Papers: Indian Affairs*, 1:242.

4. Burton, *Michigan Pioneer*, 24:468; Coates, *A Narrative of an Embassy*, p. 112.

5. Johnson, *Dictionary of American Biography*, 15:437; Burton, *Michigan Pioneer*, 24:235; Knopf, *Anthony Wayne, A Name in Arms*, pp. 47–48, 119, 122, 135; Wayne to Rosencrantz, 14 November 1792, Ford to Wilkinson, 12 November 1792, Wayne Papers, Ann Arbor.

6. Burton, *Michigan Pioneer*, 24:456, 467–78; *American State Papers: Indian Affairs*, 1:244.

7. Coates, *A Narrative of an Embassy*, p. 444; Burton, *Michigan Pioneer*, 24:470.

8. Burton, *Michigan Pioneer*, 24:484–85; Coates, *A Narrative of an Embassy*, p. 115.

9. Burton, *Michigan Pioneer*, 24:486–88.

10. Ibid., 24:490–91; *American State Papers: Indian Affairs*, 1:323.

11. Burton, *Michigan Pioneer*, 24:492–93.

12. Ibid., 24:493–95.

13. Ibid., 24:496.

14. Ibid., 24:492–97; *American State Papers: Indian Affairs*, 1:234; Coates, *A Narrative of an Embassy*, pp. 94, 121, 125.

15. Burton, *Michigan Pioneer*, 24:492–95, 506–16; *American State Papers: Indian Affairs*, 1:323–24.

16. *American State Papers: Indian Affairs*, 1:323–24.

17. Ibid., 1:324.

18. Ibid., 1:322, 337; Burton, *Michigan Pioneer*, 24:518; Wayne to Knox, 28 December 1792, Wayne Papers, Ann Arbor.

19. Knopf, *Anthony Wayne, A Name in Arms*, pp. 148–66.

20. Wayne to Knox, 13 December, 28 December, 1792, Wayne Papers, Ann Arbor.

21. Burton, *Michigan Pioneer*, 24:467–72, 572, 606, 614; Coates, *A Narrative of an Embassy*, p. 122; Knopf, *Anthony Wayne, A Name in Arms*, p. 207.

22. Burton, *Michigan Pioneer*, 24:460–66, 473, 481–82, 543.

23. Ibid., 24:473.

24. Ibid., 24:501, 519–23.

25. Ibid., 24:529–30; Boatner, *Encyclopedia of the American Revolution*, p. 533.

26. Burton, *Michigan Pioneer*, 24:524–30, 548; Boatner, *Encyclopedia of the American Revolution*, p. 1009.

27. Burton, *Michigan Pioneer*, 24:384, 423–26, 461, 465, 473, 479, 482, 517, 527.

28. Ibid., 24:479.

29. *The Writings of Thomas Jefferson*, ed. Albert Ellery Bergh, 4:85–86; Knopf, *Anthony Wayne, A Name in Arms*, pp. 169–70, 198.

30. Burton, *Michigan Pioneer*, 24:540–43, 549, 577–78.

31. Ibid., 24:552, 605, 614, 624.

32. Ibid., 24:545, 547; Knopf, *Anthony Wayne, A Name in Arms*, pp. 199, 232, 234; *The Writings of George Washington*, ed. Ford, 12:287.

Chapter 23. 2,500 Commissioners, Properly Appointed

1. Knopf, *Anthony Wayne, A Name in Arms*, pp. 16–17.

2. Ibid., p. 24; Wayne to Knox, 15 June 1792, Wayne Papers, Ann Arbor.

3. Harry Emerson Wildes, *Anthony Wayne, Troubleshooter of the American Revolution*, pp. 353–58, 379; Knopf, *Anthony Wayne, A Name in Arms*, pp. 17, 45.

4. Knopf, *Anthony Wayne, A Name in Arms*, pp. 118, 224–25, 232; Washington to Wayne, 12 July 1792, Wayne Papers, Ann Arbor.

5. Knopf, *Anthony Wayne, A Name in Arms*, pp. 19, 81, 144, 235; Burton, *Michigan Pioneer*, 34:352, 354, 358, 370–90, 415.

6. Knopf, *Anthony Wayne, A Name in Arms*, pp. 21, 28, 49–50, 65–68, 184–85, 220, 235; Burton, *Michigan Pioneer*, 34:351; St. Clair to Harmar, 2 May 1790, Harmar Papers, Ann Arbor.

7. Knopf, *Anthony Wayne, A Name in Arms*, pp. 121, 137, 142, 213; Wildes, *Anthony Wayne, Troubleshooter*, pp. 358, 367; *Writings of George Washington*, ed. Ford, 12:198.

8. Knopf, *Anthony Wayne, A Name in Arms*, pp. 138, 147–48; Jacobs, *Beginnings of the U.S. Army*, p. 131.

9. Knopf, *Anthony Wayne, A Name in Arms*, pp. 104, 147–48, 216; Wildes, *Anthony Wayne, Troubleshooter*, pp. 369–70; Burton, *Michigan Pioneer*, 34:382–96; Jacobs, *Beginnings of the U.S. Army*, p. 132.

10. Knopf, *Anthony Wayne, A Name in Arms*, pp. 145, 163, 183–85, 189, 235.

11. Ibid., pp. 74, 98, 144, 176, 199, 207, 208.

12. Ibid., pp. 140, 199, 212–14, 221, 222, 225, 230.

13. Ibid., pp. 232, 234; Burton, *Michigan Pioneer*, 34:411–12.

14. Wildes, *Anthony Wayne, Troubleshooter*, pp. 381–83; Knopf, *Anthony Wayne, A Name in Arms*, pp. 176, 186, 228.

15. Knopf, *Anthony Wayne, A Name in Arms*, p. 235.

16. Ibid., p. 234; Wildes, *Anthony Wayne, Troubleshooter*, p. 385.

17. Knopf, *Anthony Wayne, A Name in Arms*, pp. 234–35, 242–46, 260–62.

18. Ibid., p. 243; Burton, *Michigan Pioneer*, 24:550, 559, 561; *American State Papers: Indian Affairs*, 1:351.

19. Knopf, *Anthony Wayne, A Name in Arms*, p. 230.

Chapter 24. A Question of Unanimity

1. *Writings of George Washington*, ed. Ford, 12:257–58.

2. Boatner, *Encyclopedia of the American Revolution*, p. 635.

3. Ibid., 867; *Correspondence of Lieut. Governor John Graves Simcoe*, ed. E. A. Cruikshank, 1:400.

4. Boatner, *Encyclopedia of the American Revolution*, p. 715; *Correspondence of Lt. Gov. Simcoe*, 1:318n, 400; Burton, *Michigan Pioneer*, 24:543, 548; *Writings of George Washington*, ed. Ford, 12:258, 273–74.

5. *Correspondence of Lt. Gov. Simcoe*, 1:366, 2:26, 28; *American State Papers: Indian Affairs*, 1:340, 347; Knopf, *Anthony Wayne, A Name in Arms*, p. 218.

6. Knopf, *Anthony Wayne, A Name in Arms*, p. 242; Burton, *Michigan Pioneer*, 24:518, 559, 575; *Correspondence of Lt. Gov. Simcoe*, 1:280–83.

7. *Correspondence of Lt. Gov. Simcoe*, 1:283–84.

8. Ibid., 1:295.

9. Ibid., 1:330; *American State Papers: Indian Affairs*, 1:341–44.

10. *American State Papers: Indian Affairs*, 1:343; *Correspondence of Lt. Gov. Simcoe*, 2:25–27; Duncan Campbell Scott, *John Graves Simcoe*, p. 195.

11. *American State Papers: Indian Affairs*, 1:347.

12. *Correspondence of Lt. Gov. Simcoe*, 1:354–55.

13. Ibid., 1:365–66.

14. Ibid., 1:336, 357, 400.

15. Ibid., 1:355–57.

16. *American State Papers: Indian Affairs*, 1:342–48; *Correspondence of Lt. Gov. Simcoe*, 1:366, 2:26.

17. *American State Papers: Indian Affairs*, 1:342–49; *Correspondence of Lt. Gov. Simcoe*, 1:334, 371, 383; Burton, *Michigan Pioneer*, 24:569.

18. *Correspondence of Lt. Gov. Simcoe*, 1:371, 383, 2:5–7.

19. Ibid., 1:372–74, 2:7, 27; *American State Papers: Indian Affairs*, 1:349.

20. *Correspondence of Lt. Gov. Simcoe*, 1:383, 2:27; *American State Papers: Indian Affairs*, 1:349.

21. *American State Papers: Indian Affairs*, 1:349–51; *Correspondence of Lt. Gov. Simcoe*, 1:383, 405, 2:59.

22. *American State Papers: Indian Affairs*, 1:350–51, 359; *Correspondence of Lt. Gov. Simcoe*, 1:383, 2:28.

23. *Correspondence of Lt. Gov. Simcoe*, 1:401, 2:10–14.

24. Ibid., 2:7–11.

25. Ibid., 2:8–10.

26. Ibid., 2:12; *American State Papers: Indian Affairs*, 1:352; Rosencrantz letter, 23 September 1793, Wayne Papers, Philadelphia.

27. *Correspondence of Lt. Gov. Simcoe*, 1:393, 402–403, 2:12.

28. *American State Papers: Indian Affairs*, 1:352, 359; Paul A. W. Wallace, ed., *Thirty Thousand Miles with John Heckewelder*, pp. 315–16; Horsman, *Matthew Elliott*, p. 84.

29. *American State Papers: Indian Affairs*, 1:351–53; *Correspondence of Lt. Gov. Simcoe*, 1:353, 2:29; Horsman, *Matthew Elliott*, p. 83; Wallace, *Thirty Thousand Miles*, p. 314.

30. *American State Papers: Indian Affairs*, 1:348, 352; *Correspondence of Lt. Gov. Simcoe*, 1:400, 2:29–30; Wallace, *Thirty Thousand Miles*, p. 313.

31. *American State Papers: Indian Affairs*, 1:352–54; Burton, *Michigan Pioneer*, 17:620; Wallace, *Thirty Thousand Miles*, p. 316.

32. Wallace, *Thirty Thousand Miles*, p. 318; *American State Papers: Indian Affairs*, 1:354.

33. *Correspondence of Lt. Gov. Simcoe*, 2:12; *American State Papers: Indian Affairs*, 1:359.

34. *Correspondence of Lt. Gov. Simcoe*, 1:409n; Wallace, *Thirty Thousand Miles*, p. 319; *American State Papers: Indian Affairs*, 1:354.

35. *American State Papers: Indian Affairs*, 1:355; Wallace, *Thirty Thousand Miles*, pp. 318–19.

36. *Correspondence of Lt. Gov. Simcoe*, 2:12–14.

37. Ibid., 1:365–70, 2:15–16, 34, 36; Horsman, *Matt Matthew Elliott*, pp. 88–90.

38. *Correspondence of Lt. Gov. Simcoe*, 2:16, 47, 102.

39. Ibid., 2:16; Rosencrantz letter, 23 September 1793, Wayne Papers, Philadelphia.

40. *Correspondence of Lt. Gov. Simcoe*, 2:17–18.

41. Ibid., 2:19–20.

42. Ibid., 2:24, 33; *American State Papers: Indian Affairs*, 1:355; Wallace, *Thirty Thousand Miles*, p. 319.

43. *Correspondence of Lt. Gov. Simcoe*, 2:24, 33.

44. Ibid., 2:24, 34; *American State Papers: Indian Affairs*, 1:357–59; Burton, *Michigan Pioneer*, 17:658–59; Knopf, *Anthony Wayne*, p. 222.

45. *Correspondence of Lt. Gov. Simcoe*, 2:16–17, 47.

46. Ibid., 2:5, 59.

47. *American State Papers: Indian Affairs*, 1:341.

48. *Correspondence of Lt. Gov. Simcoe*, 2:47; Stone, *Life of Joseph Brant*, 2:358.

49. *Correspondence of Lt. Gov. Simcoe*, 2:40–59.

50. Ibid., 2:17.

Chapter 25. A Test of Initiative

1. Burton, *Michigan Pioneer*, 34:467–73.

2. Hamtramck to Wilkinson, 11 September, 13 September, 1793, Hamtramck to Wayne, 16 July 1793, Hamtramck Papers, Detroit Public Library; Knopf, *Anthony Wayne, A Name in Arms*, pp. 272–73; *Correspondence of Lt. Gov. Simcoe*, 2:217, 230; Wells deposition, 16 September 1793, Wayne Papers, Philadelphia.

3. Ibid., pp. 270–77; Burton, *Michigan Pioneer*, 34:477, 486.

4. Knopf, *Anthony Wayne, A Name in Arms*, pp. 275–76, 282; Wayne to Wilkinson, 30 September 1793, Wayne Papers, Philadelphia; Scott to Wayne, 22 September, 5 November 1793, Wayne Papers, Ann Arbor, Mich.; Richard D. Knopf, ed., "Two Journals of the Kentucky Volunteers, 1793 and 1794," pp. 93–94, 250, 255.

5. Knopf, *Anthony Wayne, A Name in Arms*, pp. 242, 246, 265, 278–79; Burton, *Michigan Pioneer* 34:491–92.

6. Ibid., pp. 256, 261, 265.

7. Ibid., p. 265.

8. Ibid., p. 261.

9. Ibid.

10. Ibid., pp. 265, 273.

11. *Correspondence of Lt. Gov. Simcoe*, 2:126; Knopf, *Anthony Wayne, A Name in Arms*, p. 301.

12. *Journal of Capt. Daniel Bradley*, p. 54; Hamtramck to Wayne, 17 October 1793, Hamtramck Papers, Detroit; Wayne to St. Clair, 22 October 1793, Wayne Papers, Ann Arbor; *Correspondence of Lt. Gov. Simcoe*, 2:126–27; Knopf, *Anthony Wayne, A Name in Arms*, p. 279; Knopf, "Two Journals of the Kentucky Volunteers," p. 252.

13. Knopf, *Anthony Wayne, A Name in Arms*, pp. 279–82; Wildes, *Anthony Wayne, Troubleshooter*, p. 399.

14. Knopf, *Anthony Wayne, A Name in Arms*, p. 277, 281, 282.

15. Wilkinson to Wayne, 14 September 1793, Wayne Papers, Philadelphia; Hamtramck to St. Clair, 22 October 1793, Wayne Papers, Ann Arbor; Knopf, "Two Journals of the Kentucky Volunteers," pp. 255, 279n.

16. Knopf, "Two Journals of the Kentucky Volunteers," pp. 255–56, 279n; Scott to Wayne, 5 November 1793, Wayne Papers, Ann Arbor, Mich.

17. Knopf, *Anthony Wayne, A Name in Arms*, pp. 276, 282–84.

18. Ibid., p. 283; *Journal of Capt. Daniel Bradley*, p. 57; Wildes, *Anthony Wayne, Troubleshooter*, p. 402; Burton, *Michigan Pioneer*, 20:323, 492; *The Diary of John Hutchinson Buell*, ed. Richard D. Knopf, 22 February 1794.

19. Wildes, *Anthony Wayne, Troubleshooter*, p. 403; *Diary of John Buell*, 15 October 1793; Burton, *Michigan Pioneer*, 20:493–94.

20. Wildes, *Anthony Wayne, Troubleshooter*, pp. 405–407.

21. Knopf, *Anthony Wayne, A Name in Arms*, pp. 278, 283; *Diary of John Buell*, 6 November 1793; Wayne to St. Clair, 22 October 1793, Wayne Papers, Ann Arbor, Mich.

22. Burton, *Michigan Pioneer*, 20:323, 34:436; *Correspondence of Lt. Gov. Simcoe*, 2:108–109.

23. *Correspondence of Lt. Gov. Simcoe*, 2:109; Burton, *Michigan Pioneer*, 34:499; *Diary of John Buell*, 13, 14 November, 2 December 1793.

24. Knopf, *Anthony Wayne, A Name in Arms*, p. 282; *Diary of John Buell*, 14 November 1793; Burton, *Michigan Pioneer*, 12:93; Thomas Robson Hay, *The Admirable Trumpeter: A Biography of General James Wilkinson*, p. 116.

25. *Correspondence of Lt. Gov. Simcoe*, 2:128.

26. Ibid., pp. 126–27; Burton, *Michigan Pioneer*, 12:89.

27. *Correspondence of Lt. Gov. Simcoe*, 2:128–29.

28. Ibid., 2:106, 128; Burton, *Michigan Pioneer*, 12:90.

29. *Diary of John Buell*, 14 November, 2–23 December 1793.

30. Ibid., 14 November 1793; Burton, *Michigan Pioneer*, 34:498, 501; *Correspondence of Lt. Gov. Simcoe*, 2:141.

31. Knopf, *Anthony Wayne, A Name in Arms*, pp. 297–98; Burton, *Michigan Pioneer*, 34:502; Wells deposition, 16 September 1793, Wayne Papers, Philadelphia; Martha Rohr, *Historical Sketch of Ft. Recovery*, p. 20.

32. Burton, *Michigan Pioneer*, 34:502; Wildes, *Anthony Wayne, Troubleshooter*, p. 408; James Ripley Jacobs, *Tarnished Warrior: Major General James Wilkinson*, p. 133; *Diary of John Buell*, 23 December 1793; Howe, *Historical Collections of Ohio*, 2:232; 16 U 124, Draper Manuscripts, Madison, Wisc.

33. Wildes, *Anthony Wayne, Troubleshooter*, pp. 408–409.

34. *American State Papers: Indian Affairs*, 1:243–44; Wayne to Burbeck, 27 December 1793, General Orders, 28 December 1793, Wayne Papers, Philadelphia; Howe, *Historical Collections of Ohio*, 2:234; Knopf, *Anthony Wayne, A Name in Arms*, p. 298; Burton, *Michigan Pioneer*, 34:503; *Diary of John Buell*, 28 December 1793, 1 January 1794.

35. Knopf, *Anthony Wayne, A Name in Arms*, pp. 299–301; Wayne to Delany, 21 January 1794, Wayne Papers, Ann Arbor, Mich.; *Correspondence of Lt. Gov. Simcoe*, 2:131–32; *Diary of John Buell*, 10 January 1794.

36. Knopf, *Anthony Wayne, A Name in Arms*, pp. 298–301; *Correspondence of Lt. Gov. Simcoe*, 2:131–32.

37. Knopf, *Anthony Wayne, A Name in Arms*, p. 301; Wayne to Delany, 21 January 1794, Wayne Papers, Ann Arbor, Mich.

38. *Correspondence of Lt. Gov. Simcoe*, 2:119, 130–31, 139–41.

39. Ibid., 138–41, 152; Knopf, *Anthony Wayne, A Name in Arms*, p. 308.

40. *Correspondence of Lt. Gov. Simcoe*, 2:138–39, 152.

41. Knopf, *Anthony Wayne, A Name in Arms*, p. 306.

42. Ibid., pp. 306–311.

43. Ibid., p. 310.

44. Knopf, *Anthony Wayne, A Name in Arms*, p. 310.

Chapter 26. Facts Are Stubborn Things

1. Boatner, *Encyclopedia of the American Revolution*, p. 183.

2. *Correspondence of Lt. Gov. Simcoe*, 2:3.

3. Ibid., 2:3, 83.

4. Ibid., 2:23, 49, 83, 136, 189, 240, 289, 295.

5. Ibid., 2:154.

6. Ibid., 2:149–50.

7. Ibid., 2:125, 188, 216; Richard Rush, *Washington in Domestic Life*, p. 49.

8. *Correspondence of Lt. Gov. Simcoe*, 2:196, 228; General Embargo, 26 March 1794, Wayne Papers, Philadelphia.

9. *Correspondence of Lt. Gov. Simcoe*, 2:188, 196, 290; Rush, *Washington in Domestic Life*, p. 50; Carman and Syrett, *A History of the American People*, 1:241.

10. *Correspondence of Lt. Gov. Simcoe*, 2:194, 234.

11. Ibid., 2:154.

12. Ibid., 2:344–45; Burton, *Michigan Pioneer*, 24:262–63, 299–301.

13. Burton, *Michigan Pioneer*, 24:301; *Correspondence of Lt. Gov. Simcoe*, 2:179, 194.

14. *Correspondence of Lt. Gov. Simcoe*, 2:179, 211, 219–21, 285, 344.

15. Ibid., 2:221.

16. Ibid., 2:211, 221, 243, 279, 309, 333, 350.

17. Ibid., 2:350, 353.

18. Ibid., 2:239; letter to Knox, 17 May 1794, Wayne Papers, Philadelphia.

19. Knopf, *Anthony Wayne, A Name in Arms*, p. 335; Carter, *U.S. Territorial Papers*, 2:487; Wayne to Belli, 26 May 1794, Wayne Papers, Philadelphia.

20. *Correspondence of Lt. Gov. Simcoe*, 2:141–42.

21. Ibid., 2:214–16.

22. Ibid., 2:194; *American State Papers: Indian Affairs*, 1:479–81.

23. *Correspondence of Lt. Gov. Simcoe*, 2:57, 103, 182, 194, 217, 257, 267; *American State Papers: Indian Affairs*, 1:522–23.

24. *Correspondence of Lt. Gov. Simcoe*, 2:275; *American State Papers: Indian Affairs*, 1:522.

25. *Correspondence of Lt. Gov. Simcoe*, 2:268, 316, 326, 391.

26. Ibid., 2:100, 103, 181–83, 189, 218, 253, 316.

27. Ibid., 2:318–19, 325–26.

28. Knopf, *Anthony Wayne, A Name in Arms*, p. 324, 334; Wayne to Elliot and Williams, 14 October 1793, 22 April 1794; O'Hara to Elliot and Williams, 23, 24 November 1793, Wayne Papers, Philadelphia.

29. Pierce to Wayne, 8 March 1794, Wayne to Elliot and Williams, 16, 24 March, 9 April, 28 May 1794, Belli to Wayne, 21 March 1794, Hunt to Wayne, 29 April 1794, Wayne Papers, Philadelphia.

30. Wayne to Elliot and Williams, 22 April, 1 May 1794, Wayne Papers, Philadelphia.

31. Wayne to Elliot and Williiams, 1, 24 May 1794, Wayne Papers, Philadelphia.

32. Ibid.; Knopf, *Anthony Wayne, A Name in Arms*, p. 324.

33. Elliot and Williams to Wayne, 16 June 1794, Williams to Knox, 24 June 1794, Smith to Wayne, 30 May 1794, Wayne Papers, Philadelphia.

34. Knopf, *Anthony Wayne, A Name in Arms*, pp. 307, 312, 323; Wayne to Shelby, 21 May 1794, Wayne Papers, Philadelphia.

35. Wayne to Shelby, 26 May, 10 June 1794, Wayne to Scott, 10 June 1794, Scott to Wayne, 21 June 1794, Wayne Papers, Philadelphia.

36. Knopf, *Anthony Wayne, A Name in Arms*, p. 312; Wayne to Delany, 10 July 1794, Wayne Papers, Ann Arbor, Mich.

37. Knopf, *Anthony Wayne, A Name in Arms*, p. 334.

38. Wilkinson to Knox, 13 March 1792, Burton Historical Collection, Detroit Public Library; Jacobs, *Tarnished Warrior*, pp. 131–32.

39. Jacobs, *Tarnished Warrior*, pp. 131, 139–40.

40. Ibid., p. 140; Hay, *Admirable Trumpeter*, p. 119; Carter, *U.S. Territorial Papers*, 2:487.

41. Knopf, *Anthony Wayne, A Name in Arms*, pp. 234–35, 280; Hay, *Admirable Trumpeter*, p. 117, 119.

42. Jacobs, *Tarnished Warrior*, pp. 137–38, 148.

43. Wayne to Wilkinson, 8 June 1794, Wayne Papers, Philadelphia.

44. Wilkinson to Elliot, 15 April 1794, Wayne Papers, Philadelphia.

45. Doyle to Wayne, 5 March, 1 May 1794; Gibson to Wayne, 24 April 1794, Hamtramck to Wayne, 13 May 1794, General Orders, 12 May 1794, Wayne Papers, Philadelphia; *Correspondence of Lt. Gov. Simcoe*, 2:249, 252.

46. Knopf, *Anthony Wayne, A Name in Arms*, pp. 307, 347; Wayne to Wells, 22 October 1793, Wayne Papers, Philadelphia.

47. Gibson to Wayne, 24 February, 23 April 1794; Wayne to Wilkinson, 14 March 1794, Wayne Papers, Philadelphia; Knopf, *Anthony Wayne, A Name in Arms*, p. 311; John McArthur, *Biographical Sketches of General Nathaniel Massie, General Duncan McArthur, Captain William Wells, and General Simon Kenton*, pp. 186–87; 16 U 128, Lyman Draper Manuscript Collection, Madison, Wisc.

371

48. *American State Papers: Indian Affairs*, 1:489: Knopf, *Anthony Wayne, A Name in Arms*, p. 340.

49. *American State Papers: Indian Affairs*, 1:489–90; Gibson to Wayne, 24 June 1794, Wayne Papers, Philadelphia.

50. Knopf, *Anthony Wayne, A Name in Arms*, pp. 340–41.

51. Wayne to Wilkinson, 8 June 1794, Wayne to O'Hara, 29 June 1794, Wayne Papers, Philadelphia.

52. Robertson to Wayne, 24 April 1794, Pierce to Wayne, 8 March, 9 June 1794, Wayne Papers, Philadelphia.

53. Knopf, *Anthony Wayne, A Name in Arms*, p. 347; Pierce to Wayne, 9 June 1794, Wayne to Gibson, 28 June 1794, Wayne to O'Hara, 29 June 1794, Wayne Papers, Philadelphia; Burton, *Michigan Pioneer*, 34:524; *Correspondence of Lt. Gov. Simcoe*, 2:306.

54. Knopf, *Anthony Wayne, A Name in Arms*, p. 345; Wayne to Gibson, 28 June 1794, Wayne to O'Hara, 29 June 1794, Wayne to Scott, 29 June 1794, Wayne Papers, Philadelphia.

55. *Correspondence of Lt. Gov. Simcoe*, 2:278.

56. Ibid., 2:234–35, 247–52, 257–59.

57. Ibid., 2:252, 262.

58. Ibid., 2:230–35, 247, 250, 294.

59. Ibid., 2:306; "Diary of an officer J. C. in the Indian Camp & Opposed to Gen'l. Wayne," 15 June 1794, Canadian Archives, Ottawa.

60. *Correspondence of Lt. Gov. Simcoe*, 2:259, 306; "Diary of An Officer J. C.," 23, 24 June 1794, Canadian Archives, Ottawa; Horsman, *Matthew Elliott*, p. 97.

61. "Diary of An Officer J. C.," 23 to 28 June 1794, Canadian Archives, Ottawa; *Correspondence of Lt. Gov. Simcoe*, 2:259, 306.

62. *Correspondence of Lt. Gov. Simcoe*, 2:306; "Diary of An Officer J.C.," 28 June 1794, Canadian Archives, Ottawa; Henry Alder, "The Captivity of Jonathan Alder and His Life with the Indians," p. 73; Potawatomie (report), 23 July 1794, Wayne Papers, Philadelphia.

63. "Diary of An Officer J. C.," 28–30 June 1794, Canadian Archives, Ottawa.

64. *Correspondence of Lt. Gov. Simcoe*, 2:230, 294.

Chapter 27. The Fortuitous Events of War

1. Wayne to Gibson, 26 December 1793, Wayne Papers, Philadelphia.

2. Knopf, *Anthony Wayne, A Name in Arms*, pp. 18, 298, 340; Gibson to Wayne, 24 February, 20, 31 March, 1 May 1794, Wayne Papers, Philadelphia.

3. Gibson to Wayne, 20, 31 March, 14, 17 May 1794, and General Orders of 28 December 1793, and 17 March, 11 May 1794, Wayne Papers, Philadelphia.

4. Gibson to Wayne, 11 May 1794, Wayne Papers, Philadelphia.

5. Gibson to Wayne, 20 March, 24 June 1794, Wayne to Gibson, 19 March 1794, Wayne Papers, Philadelphia.

6. Gibson to Wayne, 28 February, 16 March 1794, Wayne Papers, Philadelphia; "Diary of An Officer J. C.," 30 June 1794, Canadian Archives, Ottawa; Wayne to Burbeck, 22 December 1794, Wayne Papers, Philadelphia.

7. Wayne to Elliot and Williams, 24 May 1794, Wayne to Gibson, 28 June 1794, Gibson to Wayne, 24 June 1794, Wayne Papers, Philadelphia; Wayne to McMahon, 28 June 1794, Wayne Papers, Ann Arbor, Mich.; Burton, *Michigan Pioneer*, 34:523; Knopf, *Anthony Wayne, A Name in Arms*, p. 345.

8. Richard D. Knopf, ed., "A Precise Journal of General Wayne's Last Campaign," pp. 300–301; Robertson to Wayne, 26 April 1794, Wayne Papers, Philadelphia.

9. Knopf, *Anthony Wayne, A Name in Arms*, pp. 347–48; "Diary of An Officer J. C.," 30 June 1794, Canadian Archives, Ottawa.

10. Knopf, "A Precise Journal," p. 301; Gibson to Wayne, 30 June 1794, Wayne Papers, Philadelphia.

11. Knopf, "A Precise Journal," p. 301; Gibson to Wayne, 30 June 1794, Wayne Papers, Philadelphia; *Diary of John Hutchinson Buell*, 30 June, 1794, Canadian Archives, Ottawa.

12. "Diary of An Officer J. C.," 30 June 1794, Canadian Archives, Ottawa, *American State Papers: Indian Affairs*, 1:488–89; Alder, "The Captivity of Jonathan Alder," pp. 72–73, in Howe, ed., *Historical Collections of Ohio*, 2:234; Knopf, *Anthony Wayne, A Name in Arms*, p. 346.

13. Gibson to Wayne, 30 June 1794, Wayne Papers, Philadelphia; *Diary of John Buell*, 30 June, 1794; Knopf, "A Precise Journal," p. 301.

14. Gibson to Wayne, 30 June 1794, Wayne, Papers, Philadelphia; *American State Papers: Indian Affairs*, 1:488.

15. Gibson to Wayne, 30 June, 10 July 1794, Wayne Papers, Philadelphia; *Correspondence of Lt. Gov. Simcoe*, 2:306–310; "Diary of An Officer J. C.," 30 June 1794, Canadian Archives, Ottawa.

16. Gibson to Wayne, 30 June, 10 July 1794, Wayne Papers, Philadelphia; Knopf, "A Precise Journal," p. 301; *Correspondence of Lt. Gov. Simcoe*, 5:94.

17. Gibson to Wayne, 5 July 1794, Wayne Papers, Philadelphia; Drake to Wayne, 7 April 1795, Wayne Papers, Ann Arbor; Knopf, *Anthony Wayne, A Name in Arms*, p. 348.

18. Knopf, *Anthony Wayne, A Name in Arms*, p. 346; "Diary of An Officer J. C.," 30 June 1794, Canadian Archives, Ottawa.

19. Howe, *Historical Collections of Ohio*, 2:234.

20. Gibson to Wayne, 1 July 1794, Wayne Papers, Philadelphia; Knopf, *Anthony Wayne, A Name in Arms*, p. 348.

21. *Correspondence of Lt. Gov. Simcoe*, 2:306, 314, 5:94–96; "Diary of An Officer J. C.," 28, 30 June 1794, Canadian Archives, Ottawa; Howe, *Historical Collections of Ohio*, 2:234.

22. *Correspondence of Lt. Gov. Simcoe*, 2:306–310; "Diary of An Officer J. C.," 1, 2 July 1794, Canadian Archives, Ottawa; Gibson to Wayne, 5 July 1794, Wayne Papers, Philadelphia.

23. "Examination of a Potowatomie," 23 July 1794, Wayne Papers, "Diary of An Officer J. C.," 18 June 1794, Canadian Archives, Ottawa; *Correspondence of Lt. Gov. Simcoe*, 2:310–17, 326.

24. *Correspondence of Lt. Gov. Simcoe*, 2:334; "Examination of a Potowatomie," 23 July 1794, Wayne Papers, Philadelphia.

25. Examination of a Shawnee, 22 June 1794, Wayne Papers, Philadelphia; *Correspondence of Lt. Gov. Simcoe*, 2:334, 344.

26. "Diary of An Officer J. C.," 1 July 1794, Canadian Archives, Ottawa; *Correspondence of Lt. Gov. Simcoe*, 2:310, 314, 334.

27. Wayne to Gibson, 3 July 1794, Wayne Papers, Philadelphia; Knopf, *Anthony Wayne, A Name in Arms*, p. 346; Burton, *Michigan Pioneer* 34:525; 16 U 129, Lyman C. Draper Manuscript Collection, Madison, Wis.

28. Wayne to Delany, 10 July 1794, Wayne Papers, Ann Arbor, Mich.

29. Knopf, *Anthony Wayne, A Name in Arms*, pp. 349–50; Wayne to Knox, 16 July 1794, Wayne Papers, Ann Arbor, Mich.

30. Scott to Wayne, 12 July 1794, Wayne Papers, Philadelphia; Burton, *Michigan Pioneer*, 34:537, 539; Dwight L. Smtih, ed., *From Greeneville to Fallen Timbers: A Journal of the Wayne Campaign, July 28–September 14, 1794*, pp. 249–51; Knopf, *Anthony Wayne, A Name in Arms*, p. 350.

31. Wayne to Gibson, 16 July 1794, Wayne Papers, Ann Arbor, Mich.; Wayne to Gibson, 22 July 1794, Gibson to Wayne, 18, 24 July 1794, "Wells deposition," 16 September 1794, Wayne Papers, Philadelphia.

32. Burton, *Michigan Pioneer*, 34:538.

33. Smith, *From Greeneville to Fallen Timbers*, pp. 250–67; Reginald C. McGrane, ed., "William Clark's Journal of General Wayne's Campaign," *Mississippi Valley Historical Review* 1: 419–20; Wayne to Knox, 16 July 1794, Wayne Papers, Ann Arbor, Mich.

34. Burton, *Michigan Pioneer*, 34:540; Smith, *From Greeneville to Fallen Timbers*, pp. 250–54, 270; McGrane, "William Clark's Journal," p. 420.

35. Wayne to I. Wayne, 14 July 1794, Wayne Papers, Ann Arbor, Mich.

36. Ibid., Wayne to Wilkinson, 14 July 1794, Wayne Papers, Ann Arbor, Mich.

37. Smith, *From Greeneville to Fallen Timbers*, pp. 251–57; McGrane, "William Clark's Journal," pp. 419, 421; Knopf, "A Precise Journal," pp. 280–81; [John Bowyer,] "Daily Journal of Wayne's Campaign," pp. 3, 4.

38. Smith, *From Greeneville to Fallen Timbers*, p. 261; [Bowyer,] "Daily Journal of Wayne's Campaign," p. 4; Knopf, "A Precise Journal," p. 282.

39. Smith, *From Greeneville to Fallen Timbers*, pp. 261–62; "William Clark's Journal," p. 422; [Bowyer,] "Daily Journal" p. 4; Wayne to I. Wayne, 10 September 1794, Wayne Papers, Philadelphia.

40. Smith, *From Greeneville to Fallen Timbers*, p. 262; "William Clark's Journal," p. 422; Wayne to Knox, 25 January 1795, Wayne Papers, Ann Arbor, Mich.; Wilkinson to Brown, 28 August 1794, Wilkinson Papers, Chicago Historical Society.

41. Smith, *From Greeneville to Fallen Timbers*, pp. 263–65; "William Clark's Journal," pp. 422–23; Knopf, "A Precise Journal," p. 282.

42. Smith, *From Geeneville to Fallen Timbers*, pp. 240, 263–68; "William Clark's Journal," pp. 422–23; [Bowyer,] "Daily Journal," p. 5; Dwight L. Smith, ed., *With Captain Edward Miller in the Wayne Campaign of 1794*, p. 3.

43. Smith, *From Greeneville to Fallen Timbers*, pp. 259, 269; "William Clark's Journal," pp. 423–25; Wilkinson to Brown, 28 August 1794, Wilkinson Papers, Chicago Historical Society.

44. Smith, *From Greeneville to Fallen Timbers*, p. 269; *American State Papers: Indian Affairs*, 1:490; "William Clark's Journal," p. 423; [Bowyer,] "Daily Journal," p. 5.

45. Knopf, "A Precise Journal," p. 284; Smith, *From Greeneville to Fallen Timbers*, pp. 270–71; *American State Papers: Indian Affairs*, 1:490.

46. Smith, *From Greeneville to Fallen Timbers*, pp. 271–73; Knopf, "Two Journals of the Kentucky Volunteers," 8 August 1794; Knopf, "A Precise Journal," pp. 284–85; [Bowyer,] "Daily Journal," p. 5; "William Clark's Journal," p. 424; *American State Papers: Indian Affairs*, 1:490.

47. Smith, *From Greeneville to Fallen Timbers*, pp. 272–74; Smith, *With Captain Edward Miller*, p. 3; Knopf, "A Precise Journal," pp. 284–85; [Bowyer,] "Daily Journal," pp. 5–6; Burton, *Michigan Pioneer*, 34:542; Knopf, "Two Journals of the Kentucky Volunteers," 8 August 1794.

48. "William Clark's Journal," p. 424; Burton, *Michigan Pioneer*, 34:542–43; Knopf, "A Precise Journal," pp. 284–86; Smith, *From Greeneville to Fallen Timbers*, p. 274; *American State Papers: Indian Affairs*, 1:490.

49. Knopf, "Two Journals of the Kentucky Volunteers," 9 to 14 August, 1794; [Bowyer,] "Daily Journal," pp. 4–6; "Captain John Cook's Journal," p. 313, Philadelphia; Smith, *From Greeneville to Fallen Timbers*, pp. 254, 271; Wayne to Miller, 31 July 1794, Wayne Papers, Philadelphia.

50. "William Clark's Journal," p. 421; Howe, *Historical Collections of Ohio*, 2:141–43; *Correspondence of Lt. Gov. Simcoe*, 2:230, 366, 371; Smith, *With Captain Edward Miller*, p. 4; "Captain John Cook's Journal," p. 314; Knopf, "Two Journals of the Kentucky Volunteers," 12 August 1794.

51. "Examination of a Shawnee," 12 August 1794, Wayne Papers, Philadelphia; *Correspondence of Lt. Gov. Simcoe*, 2:366–67; "Captain John Cook's Journal," p. 314, Philadelphia.

52. Smith, *With Captain Edward Miller*, pp. 4–5; Smith, *From Greeneville to Fallen Timbers*, pp. 261, 278n; *Correspondence of Lt. Gov. Simcoe*, 2:349–51; [Bowyer,] "Daily Journal," p. 4; Robert Newman, Personal Military Service Records, National Archives, Washington, D.C.; "Capt. John Cook's Journal," p. 315, and Cooper to Wayne, 15 August 1794, Wayne Papers, Philadelphia.

53. *American State Papers: Indian Affairs*, 1:490; "Examination of a Shawnee," 12

August 1794, Wayne Papers, Philadelphia; *Capt. John Cook's Journal*, pp. 314–15; Smith, *With Capt. Edward Miller*, p. 5; *Correspondence of Lt. Gov. Simcoe*, 2:373.

54. *Correspondence of Lt. Gov. Simcoe*, 2:371–73; Smith, *From Greeneville to Fallen Timbers*, p. 275; Wilkinson to Wayne, 12 August 1794, Wayne Papers, Philadelphia.

55. *Correspondence of Lt. Gov. Simcoe*, 2:372.

56. Ibid., 2:372; Smith, *From Greeneville to Fallen Timbers*, p. 278; "Capt. John Cook's Journal," p. 315, Philadelphia; "William Clark's Journal," p. 425n.

57. Smith, *From Greeneville to Fallen Timbers*, pp. 270, 277–79; Knopf, *A Precise Journal*, p. 286–87; Knopf, "Two Journals of the Kentucky Volunteers," 15 August 1794; "General Orders," 15 August 1794, Wayne Papers, Philadelphia; Wilkinson to Brown, 28 August 1794, Wilkinson Papers, Chicago Historical Society; *American State Papers: Indian Affairs*, 1:490.

58. Caldwell to Scott, 1 September 1794, Wayne Papers, Philadelphia; Knopf, "A Precise Journal," p. 285; "Capt. John Cook's Journal," p. 314; Knopf, "Two Journals of the Kentucky Volunteers," 15 August, 1794.

59. Wilkinson to Wayne, 12 August 1794, Wayne Papers, Philadelphia; *American State Papers: Indian Affairs*, 1:490.

Chapter 28. Season of the Blacksnake

1. Otho Winger, *The Last of the Miamis*, p. 6; Drake, *Book of the Indians of North America*, p. 57.

2. *Correspondence of Lt. Gov. Simcoe*, 2:334; Young, *Little Turtle*, pp. 141–42.

3. Young, *Little Turtle*, pp. 136–42; Winger, *Last of the Miamis*, p. 5; Drake, *Book of the Indians of North America*, p. 55.

4. *Correspondence of Lt. Gov. Simcoe*, 2:314, 340–44, 349–52, 359, 367, 5:103; Smith, *From Greeneville to Fallen Timbers*, p. 276; Dresden W. H. Howard, "The Battle of Fallen Timbers as Told by Chief Kin-jo-i-no, *Northwest Ohio Quarterly*, 40:38–44.

5. Smith, *From Greeneville to Fallen Timbers*, p. 277; Smith, *With Capt. Edward Miller*, p. 5.

6. *Correspondence of Lt. Gov. Simcoe*, 2:367; Howard, "Battle of Fallen Timbers," p. 39.

7. Howe, *Historical Collections of Ohio*, 2:139; Leonard Covington, 31 October 1794, Covington Papers, Burton Historical Collection, Detroit Public Library; *Correspondence of Lt. Gov. Simcoe*, 2:344, 365, 371–74; *Captain John Cook's Journal*, p. 314.

8. *Correspondence of Lt. Gov. Simcoe*, 2:344–45, 367, 374–75, 377, 387, 3:13, 19; Howe, *Historical Collections of Ohio*, 2:139; *American State Papers: Indian Affairs*, 1:495.

9. *Correspondence of Lt. Gov. Simcoe*, 2:365–71; "Examination of a Potowatomie," 21 July 1794, Wayne Papers, Philadelphia.

10. *Correspondence of Lt. Gov. Simcoe*, 2:237, 362, 373–74, 389.

11. Ibid., 2:365, 377, 380, 396, 3:13–14, 315; Smith, *From Greeneville to Fallen Timbers*, p. 296; Knopf, *Anthony Wayne, A Name in Arms*, p. 354.

12. *Capt. John Cook's Journal*, p. 315n; Knopf, "A Precise Journal," p. 287; Indian "speech," 15 August 1794, Wayne Papers, Philadelphia; Burton, *Michigan Pioneer*, 25:14; Howard, "Battle of Fallen Timbers," pp. 40–42; Alder, "Captivity of Jonathan Alder," p. 72, Columbus, Ohio; Stone, *Life of Joseph Brant*, 2:387.

13. Stone, *Life of Joseph Brant*, 2:387; *Correspondence of Lt. Gov. Simcoe*, 2:283, 334, 345, 3:13, 110, 130.

14. Howard, "Battle of Fallen Timbers," pp. 42–44; Alder, "Captivity of Jonathan Alder," p. 72, Columbus Ohio.

15. Alder, "Captivity of Jonathan Alder," p. 72, Columbus, Ohio.

16. Stone, *Life of Joseph Brant*, 2:387; Howard, "Battle of Fallen Timbers," p. 44.

17. *Correspondence of Lt. Gov. Simcoe*, 2:131, 152, 387; Smith, *From Greeneville to Fallen Timbers*, p. 281; Indian "speech," 15 August 1794, Wayne Papers, Philadelphia; Drake, *Book of the Indians of North America*, pp. 41–46; *Captain John Cook's Journal*, p. 315.

18. *Correspondence of Lt. Gov. Simcoe*, 2:374; Burton, *Michigan Pioneer*, 25:14.

19. *Correspondence of Lt. Gov. Simcoe*, 2:314, 321, 324–29, 353, 3:97.

20. Ibid., 2:329, 353, 367, 369, 391, 3:98, 99, 103.

21. Ibid., 2:321–24, 3:99.

22. Ibid., 1:181n; Quaife, *Captivity of O. M. Spencer*, p. 139n; *Correspondence of Lt. Gov. Simcoe*, 2:357–59.

23. *Correspondence of Lt. Gov. Simcoe*, 2:359–60.

24. Ibid., 2:368–70, 389, 409–10; "T. Simcox deposition," September 1794, Wayne Papers, Philadelphia.

25. *Correspondence of Lt. Gov. Simcoe*, 2:362, 374–76.

26. Ibid., 2:198, 374, 377, 380, 382, 389, 394, 414, 3:7.

27. Ibid., 2:300, 332.

28. Ibid., 2:210, 290–91, 300, 322, 333, 352.

29. Ibid., 2:291, 322.

30. Knopf, "A Precise Journal," p. 287; Smith, *From Greeneville to Fallen Timbers*, pp. 281–82; Wayne to I. Wayne, 10 September 1794, Wayne Papers, Philadelphia; Smith, *With Captain Edward Miller*, p. 6.

31. Knopf, "A Precise Journal," p. 287; Smith, *With Captain Edward Miller*, p. 6; "William Clark's Journal," p. 426; Wilkinson to Brown, 28 August 1794, Wilkinson Papers, Chicago.

32. Smith, *From Greeneville to Fallen Timbers*, p. 280–84; Knopf, "A Precise Journal," p. 288; Knopf, "Two Journals of the Kentucky Volunteers," 16 August 1794; "General Orders," 15 August 1794, Wayne Papers, Philadelphia; "William Clark's Journal," p. 427.

33. Smith, *From Greeneville to Fallen Timbers*, p. 284; "William Clark's Journal," p. 427; Smith, *With Captain Edward Miller*, p. 6; Knopf, "A Precise Journal," p. 287–89.

34. Smith, *With Captain Edward Miller*, p. 7; "William Clark's Journal," p. 427; Knopf, "Two Journals of the Kentucky Volunteers," 18 August 1794; *Captain John Cook's Journal*, p. 315.

35. Smith, *From Greeneville to Fallen Timbers*, pp. 285–86; Smith, *With Captain Edward Miller*, p. 7; Knopf, *Anthony Wayne, A Name in Arms*, p. 335; Knopf, "A Precise Journal," p. 289; [Bowyer,] "Daily Journal," p. 7; Wilkinson to Brown, 28 August 1794, Wilkinson Papers, Chicago.

36. Smith, *From Greeneville to Fallen Timbers*, pp. 285–87; Wilkinson to Brown, 28 August 1794, Wilkinson Papers; Bowyer, "Daily Journal," p. 7; *Captain John Cook's Journal*, p. 315.

37. Knopf, "Two Journals of the Kentucky Volunteers," 19 August 1794; Smith, *From Greeneville to Fallen Timbers*, pp. 286–87; Wilkinson to Brown, 24, 28 August 1794, Wilkinson Papers, Chicago; 14 U 133, Lyman C. Draper Manuscripts Collection, Madison, Wis.

38. Smith, *From Greeneville to Fallen Timbers*, pp. 287–88.

39. Bowyer, "Daily Journal," p. 7; Knopf, "A Precise Journal," p. 288.

40. *Captain John Cook's Journal*, p. 315; Smith, *From Greeneville to Fallen Timbers*, p. 276.

41. *Correspondence of Lt. Gov. Simcoe*, 3:9; Alder, "Captivity of Jonathan Alder," pp. 72–73, Columbus, Ohio; Drake, *Book of the Indians of North America*, p. 56.

42. *Correspondence of Lt. Gov. Simcoe*, 2:258, 306, 317, 341, 3:8.

43. Howe, *Historical Collections of Ohio*, 2:143; "Williams' deposition," 31 October 1794, Covington Papers, Detroit Public Library; Smith, *From Greeneville to Fallen Timbers*, p. 296.

44. Alder, "Captivity of Jonathan Alder," p. 73, Columbus, Ohio; Stone, *Life of Joseph Brant*, 2:387; Burton, *Michigan Pioneer*, 12:65, 69, and 34:735, 739; *Correspondence of Lt. Gov. Simcoe*, 3:8.

45. Quaife, *Captivity of O. M. Spencer*, p. 90; Knopf, *Anthony Wayne, A Name in Arms*, pp. 390, 532; Burton, *Michigan Pioneer*, 12:65; "Diary of An Officer J. C.," 18 June 1794, Ottawa.

46. Burton, *Michigan Pioneer*, 12:65, 69, 17:606–607, 20:390, 34:739; Quaife, *Captivity of O. M. Spencer*, p. 90; *The John Askin Papers*, 1:561n; *Correspondence of Lt. Gov. Simcoe*, 2:219, 396, 3:13, 19, 99, 310; Alder, "Captivity of Jonathan Alder," p. 75, Columbus, Ohio; Howard, "Battle of Fallen Timbers," p. 45. Although it has been alleged that Blue Jacket was a white man, Marmaduke Van Sweringen, captured by the Shawnees at about age seventeen in Pennsylvania around 1769, this opinion is not substantiated by contemporary evidence (John Bennett, *Blue Jacket: War Chief of the Shawnees and His Part in Ohio's History*).

47. Knopf, "Two Journals of the Kentucky Volunteers," 20 August 1794; Howard, "Battle of Fallen Timbers," p. 45; Wilkinson to Brown, 28 August 1794, Wilkinson Papers, Chicago.

48. Alder, "Captivity of Jonathan Alder, p. 75ff., Columbus, Ohio; Howe, *Historical Collections of Ohio*, 1:321; *Correspondence of Lt. Gov. Simcoe*, 3:8, 11, 99.

49. "Williams' deposition," 31 October 1794, Covington Papers, Detroit Public Library; *Correspondence of Lt. Gov. Simcoe*, 2:396 (map), 3:8; "William Clark's Journal," p. 429.

50. *Correspondence of Lt. Gov. Simcoe*, 2:396, 3:13, 99.

51. Ibid., 2:372.

Chapter 29. Our Moccasins Trickled Blood

1. 14 U 133, Lyman C. Draper Manuscripts Collection, Madison, Wis.; Smith, *From Greeneville to Fallen Timbers*, pp. 268, 289; Knopf, "Two Journals of the Kentucky Volunteers," 20 August 1794; *Captain John Cook's Journal*, p. 316; Wilkinson to Brown, 28 August 1794, Wilkinson Papers, Chicago; "William Clark's Journal," p. 428.

2. 14 U 132, Draper Manuscript Collection, Madison, Wis.; *Captain John Cook's Journal*, p. 316; Smith, *With Captain Edward Miller*, p. 7; Smith, *From Greeneville to Fallen Timbers*, p. 288; Burton, *Michigan Pioneer*, 34:530, 545.

3. Smith, *From Greeneville to Fallen Timbers*, p. 294; "William Clark's Journal," p. 420; Knopf, *Anthony Wayne, A Name in Arms*, p. 351; Burton, *Michigan Pioneer*, 34:533–34.

4. 14 U 133, Draper Manuscript Collection, Madison, Wis.; Knopf, *Anthony Wayne, A Name in Arms*, p. 352; Knopf, "Two Journals of the Kentucky Volunteers," 20 August 1794.

5. 14 U 133, 16 U 130, Draper Manuscript Collection, Madison, Wis.

6. *Captain John Cook's Journal*, p. 316.

7. Ibid.

8. Ibid.

9. Howard, "Battle of Fallen Timbers," p. 45; *Correspondence of Lt. Gov. Simcoe*, 3:11, 99; "Williams' deposition," 31 October 1794, Covington Papers, Detroit Public Library.

10. *Correspondence of Lt. Gov. Simcoe*, 3:8, 99; "Williams' deposition," 31 October 1794, Covington Papers, Detroit Public Library.

11. 14 U 133, Draper Manuscript Collection, Madison, Wis.; "Williams' deposition," 31 October 1794, Covington Papers, Detroit Public Library.

12. Bowyer, "Daily Journal," pp. 7–8; Smith, *From Greeneville to Fallen Timbers*, p. 291; Wilkinson to Brown, 28 August 1794, Wilkinson Papers, Chicago.

13. Wilkinson to Brown, 28 August 1794, Wilkinson Papers, Chicago; *From Greeneville to Fallen Timbers*, pp. 288, 294.

14. Smith, *From Greeneville to Fallen Timbers*, pp. 290–94; Wilkinson to Brown, 24 August 1794, Wilkinson Papers, Chicago; "William Clark's Journal, p. 429.

15. "Williams' deposition," 31 October 1794, Covington Papers, Detroit Public Li-

brary; Forsyth to Beakley, 17 September 1794, Wayne Papers, Philadelphia; *From Greeneville to Fallen Timbers*, p. 292.

16. Wilkinson to Brown, 28 August 1794, Wilkinson Papers, Chicago; Smith, *From Greeneville to Fallen Timbers*, p. 292–94; Smith, *With Captain Edward Miller*, p. 7.

17. Knopf, *Anthony Wayne, A Name in Arms*, p. 352; Howe, *Historical Collections of Ohio*, 2:140.

18. Knopf, *Anthony Wayne, A Name in Arms*, p. 352; *From Greeneville to Fallen Timbers*, pp. 291–92: Wilkinson to Brown, 28 August 1794, Wilkinson Papers, Chicago; *American State Papers: Indian Affairs*, 1:492.

19. Smith, *From Greeneville to Fallen Timbers*, p. 292; Wilkinson to Brown, 28 August 1794, Wilkinson Papers, Chicago.

20. Knopf, *Anthony Wayne, A Name in Arms*, p. 352; Bowyer, "Daily Journal," p. 8; "William Clark's Journal," p. 429.

21. "William Clark's Journal," p. 429; *Correspondence of Lt. Gov. Simcoe*, 2:414, 3:8; Knopf, "Two Journals of the Kentucky Volunteers," 20 August 1794; Howard, "Battle of Fallen Timbers, p. 46; Burton, *Michigan Pioneer*, 34:482, 530.

22. "William Clark's Journal," p. 429; Knopf, "A Precise Journal," p. 290; Knopf, *Anthony Wayne, A Name in Arms*, p. 352; Smith, *From Greeneville to Fallen Timbers*, pp. 293–97.

23. Smith, *From Greeneville to Fallen Timbers*, p. 292; "Williams' deposition," 31 October 1794, Covington Papers, Detroit Public Library; Wilkinson to Brown, 28 August 1794, Wilkinson Papers, Chicago; Howard, "Battle of Fallen Timbers," p. 47; Howe, *Historical Collections of Ohio*, 2:139 (map).

24. Howard, "Battle of Fallen Timbers," p. 47; *Correspondence of Lt. Gov. Simcoe*, 2:396, 3:99, 274, 292.

25. *Correspondence of Lt. Gov. Simcoe*, 3:8; Smith, *From Greeneville to Fallen Timbers*, p. 293, 297.

26. Howard, "Battle of Fallen Timbers," p. 47.

27. Forsyth to Bleakey, 17 September 1794; "Thomas Stephenson deposition," October, 1794, Wayne Papers, Philadelphia; *Correspondence of Lt. Gov. Simcoe*, 2:396, 414, 3:13, 99.

28. *Correspondence of Lt. Gov. Simcoe*, 2:395, 396.

29. Ibid., 2:403; *American State Papers: Indian Affairs*, 1:495; Stone, *Life of Joseph Brant*, 2:390; Drake, *Book of the Indians of North America*, p. 45.

30. *Correspondence of Lt. Gov. Simcoe*, 3:14, 21; "Williams' deposition," 31 October 1794, Covington Papers, Detroit Public Library.

31. *Correspondence of Lt. Gov. Simcoe*, 3:21; Howard, "Battle of Fallen Timbers," pp. 45–47.

32. Smith, *From Greeneville to Fallen Timbers*, p. 295; Wilkinson to Brown, 28 August 1794, Wilkinson Papers, Chicago; *Captain John Cook's Journal*, p. 316; *American State Papers: Indian Affairs*, 1:492; Knopf, "A Precise Journal," p. 290.

33. "William Clark's Journal," p. 429; Knopf, "A Precise Journal," p. 290; Wilkinson to Brown, 28 August 1794, Wilkinson Papers, Chicago; Smith, *From Greeneville to Fallen Timbers*, pp. 294–95.

34. Smith, *From Greeneville to Fallen Timbers*, p. 295; "William Clark's Journal," p. 429; Wilkinson to Brown, 28 August 1794, Wilkinson Papers, Chicago; *Captain John Cook's Journal*, p. 316.

35. Wilkinson to Brown, 28 August 1794, Wilkinson Papers, Chicago; *Captain John Cook's Journal*, p. 316.

36. Wilkinson to Brown, 28 August 1794, Wilkinson Papers, Chicago; *Correspondence of Lt. Gov. Simcoe*, 2:396.

37. *Correspondence of Lt. Gov. Simcoe*, 2:397–98.

38. Ibid., 2:398, 405.

39. Ibid., 2:398, 406.

40. Ibid., 2:398–99.

41. Smith, *From Greeneville to Fallen Timbers*, pp. 298–299; Wilkinson to Brown, 28 August 1794, Wilkinson Papers, Chicago; *Correspondence of Lt. Gov. Simcoe*, 2:397.

42. *Correspondence of Lt. Gov. Simcoe*, 2:406, 3:13; Smith, *From Greeneville to Fallen Timbers*, pp. 296–99; "Wayne's notes," 21 August 1794, Wayne Papers, Philadelphia.

43. *Correspondence of Lt. Gov. Simcoe*, 2:398, 3:13; Smith, *From Greeneville to Fallen Timbers*, p. 300; Burton, *Michigan Pioneer*, 34:547; *Captain John Cook's Journal*, p. 339; "Wayne's notes," 21 August 1794, Wayne Papers, Philadelphia.

44. Knopf, "Two Journals of the Kentucky Volunteers," 22 August 1794; Smith, *From Greeneville to Fallen Timbers*, p. 301; *Correspondence of Lt. Gov. Simcoe*, 2:404–405; 3:19, 98; "Wayne's notes," 21 August 1794, Wayne Papers, Philadelphia; Knopf, "A Precise Journal," p. 291.

45. *Correspondence of Lt. Gov. Simcoe*, 2:405–407.

46. Smith, *From Greeneville to Fallen Timbers*, p. 301; "Wayne's notes," 21 August 1794, Wayne Papers, Philadelphia.

47. "Wayne's notes," 22 August 1794, Wayne Papers, Philadelphia; *Correspondence of Lt. Gov. Simcoe*, 2:404, 407; "William Clark's Journal," p. 431.

48. *Correspondence of Lt. Gov. Simcoe*, 2:408.

49. Ibid., 3:14, 98.

50. Ibid., 2:404.

51. Ibid., 2:403, 410; Smith, *From Greeneville to Fallen Timbers*, p. 302; Bowyer, "Daily Journal," p. 10.

52. *Captain John Cook's Journal*, p. 339; Smith, *From Greeneville to Fallen Timbers*, pp. 283, 305, 309; Wilkinson to Brown, 28 August 1794, Wilkinson Papers, Chicago; *Correspondence of Lt. Gov. Simcoe*, 2:403, 418.

53. Smith, *From Greeneville to Fallen Timbers*, p. 310.

54. Ibid., pp. 306–310; Wilkinson to Brown, 28 August 1794, Wilkinson Papers, Chicago; Wayne to Scott, 8 September 1794, Wayne Papers, Philadelphia.

55. *Correspondence of Lt. Gov. Simcoe*, 2:403–404, 416–19, 3:8.

56. Smith, *With Captain Edward Miller*, p. 9; Smith, *From Greeneville to Fallen Timbers*, p. 306; Wilkinson to Brown, 28 August 1794, Wilkinson Papers, Chicago; "William Clark's Journal," p. 433.

57. "William Clark's Journal," p. 433; Wilkinson to Brown, 28 August 1794, Wilkinson Papers, Chicago: Smith, *From Greeneville to Fallen Timbers*, p. 310.

58. Wayne to I. Wayne, 10 September 1794, Wayne Papers, Philadelphia; Knopf, *Anthony Wayne, A Name in Arms*, pp. 356–57; *Correspondence of Lt. Gov. Simcoe*, 3:13.

59. Burton, *Michigan Pioneer*, 34:547; Wayne to I. Wayne, 10 September 1794, Wayne Papers, Philadelphia; Knopf, *Anthony Wayne, A Name In Arms*, pp. 356–57.

Chapter 30. **The Essence of Despair**

1. *Correspondence of Lt. Gov. Simcoe*, 3:21, 30, 48, 85, 146.

2. Ibid., 2:396, 3:8, 21, 23, 48, 96.

3. Ibid., 3:96, 102, 5:110–11.

4. Ibid., 3:129, 131, 5:117.

5. Ibid., 3:5, 7, 73–77, 98.

6. Ibid., 3:76, 78, 95.

7. Ibid., 2:365, 368, 386, 411, 3:25, 114; *American State Papers: Indian Affairs*, 1:522.

8. *Correspondence of Lt. Gov. Simcoe*, 3:95, 121–25, 147, 258; Burton, *Michigan Pioneer*, 25:40–46.

9. *Correspondence of Lt. Gov. Simcoe*, 3:119–25.

10. Ibid., 3:149–51, 328, 5:119; Burton, *Michigan Pioneer*, 25:46.

11. *American State Papers: Indian Affairs*, 1:522–23; *Correspondence of Lt. Gov. Simcoe*, 2:365, 368, 3:148, 168–69.

13. *Correspondence of Lt. Gov. Simcoe*, 3:150–51, 258, 263, 293, 314, 340, 5:123; Burton, *Michigan Pioneer*, 25:64.

14. *Correspondence of Lt. Gov. Simcoe*, 2:300, 321–22, 3:79, 135, 142, 5:109.

14. Ibid., 3:174, 185, 238, 309n, 5:126, 132, 136.

15. Ibid., 3:136, 5:127, 132, 136, 142, 147–48.

16. Ibid., 3:163, 230, 234, 251, 304–307, 318, 320, 323, 324, 325, 329, 4:14.

17. Ibid., 3:307, 313–14, 348.

18. Ibid., 3:330, 335, 4:3.

19. Ibid., 3:220, 234, 305, 330, 333, 353, 5:142, 146.

20. Ibid., 3:183, 274, 279, 335; Williams to Wayne, 27 September 1794, 5 November 1794, Wayne Papers, Philadelphia.

21. *Correspondence of Lt. Gov. Simcoe*, 3:13, 166; Smith, *From Greeneville to Fallen Timbers*, p. 320; Burton, *Michigan Pioneer*, 34:546; "F. Lasselle deposition," 16 October 1794, Wayne Papers, Philadelphia; Knopf, *Anthony Wayne, A Name in Arms*, p. 361.

22. *Correspondence of Lt. Gov. Simcoe*, 3:166, 272; Hamtramck to Wayne, 15 January 1795, Wayne Papers, Philadelphia.

23. *Correspondence of Lt. Gov. Simcoe*, 3:272, 281, 282, 295, 296; "Council," 19 January 1795, Wayne Papers, Philadelphia.

24. *Correspondence of Lt. Gov. Simcoe*, 3:274–76.

25. Ibid., 3:154, 288, 294; Dorchester to Wayne, 6 October 1794, Wayne Papers, Philadelphia.

26. *Correspondence of Lt. Gov. Simcoe*, 3:197, 200, 220, 276, 287–88, 293, 5:119, 135.

27. Ibid., 3:287, 294; Burton, *Michigan Pioneer*, 34:735; "Wayne's speech," 19 January 1795, Wayne Papers, Philadelphia; Knopf, *Anthony Wayne, A Name in Arms*, pp. 271, 384–90.

28. Burton, *Michigan Pioneer*, 34:736.

29. Ibid., 34:736; Knopf, *Anthony Wayne, A Name in Arms*, pp. 389–90.

30. "Wayne's speech," 19 January 1795, Hamtramck to Wayne, 15 January 1795, Wayne Papers, Philadelphia.

31. Knopf, *Anthony Wayne, A Name in Arms*, pp. 380–81; Wayne to Hunt, 24 January 1795, Wayne Papers, Philadelphia.

32. Knopf, *Anthony Wayne, A Name in Arms*, pp. 384, 417; Wayne to Hunt, 31 January 1795, "Blue Jacket's speech," 8 February 1795, Wayne Papers, Philadelphia.

33. Knopf, *Anthony Wayne, A Name in Arms*, pp. 381, 389, 397, 418; Burton, *Michigan Pioneer*, 34:735; Hamtramck to Wayne, 15 January 1795, Wayne to Hamtramck, 25 February 1795, Wayne to Sans Crante, 25 January 1795, Wayne to O'Hara, 3 February 1795, Wayne Papers, Philadelphia.

34. "Williams' speech," 19 February 1795, "speech," 12 March 1795, White Eyes to Wayne, 9 March 1795, Wayne to White Eyes, 21 March 1795, Wayne to Hunt, 21 March 1795, "speeches" of 8 February 1795, Wayne Papers, Philadelphia; Knopf, *Anthony Wayne, A Name in Arms*, pp. 416–17.

35. *Correspondence of Lt. Gov. Simcoe*, 3:63, 95, 102, 104, 313, 314, 321, 4:1, 2, 23–24; letter from Detroit, 25 May 1795, Wayne Papers, Philadelphia.

36. *Correspondence of Lt. Gov. Simcoe*, 3:183.

37. Ibid., 3:199; Hamtramck to Wayne, 18 October 1794, Wayne Papers, Philadelphia.

38. *Correspondence of Lt. Gov. Simcoe*, 3:75, 116, 128, 155; Ingersall to Wayne, 6 October 1794, Wayne Papers, Ann Arbor, Mich.; Ingersall to Wayne, 8 October 1794, Wayne Papers, Philadelphia; Knopf, *Anthony Wayne, A Name in Arms*, pp. 362, 370–71.

39. Knopf, *Anthony Wayne, A Name in Arms*, pp. 382–93, 404–16.

40. Ibid., pp. 416, 427.

41. *Correspondence of Lt. Gov. Simcoe*, 3:347–48, 4:3–5, 15–16, 33, 45, 50, 88.

42. Ibid., 3:314, 4:33, 43, 88, 101, 177–78.

43. Ibid., 3:342–44, 4:38, 145, 164, 5:140.

44. Ibid., 3:198, 205, 4:5, 15–16, 45, 93–94, 152.

45. Hunt to Wayne, 20 April, 9 June 1795, Wayne to Hamtramck, 13 May 1795, Hamtramck to Wayne, 26 April, 7 May 1795, Williams to Wayne, 7 May 1795, letter from Detroit, 25 May 1795, Wayne Papers, Philadelphia; Correspondence of Lt. Gov. Simcoe, 4:5, 15, 29, 41, 44.

46. "Speeches" of 3 June 1795, Wayne Papers, Philadelphia; Knopf, *Anthony Wayne, A Name in Arms*, pp. 384–85.

Chapter 31. We Will Make a New World

1. "Blue Jacket's speech," 8 February 1795, "Indian speech," 3 June 1795, Wayne Papers, Philadelphia; Russell, *The British Regime in Michigan*, p. 235; Burton, *Michigan Pioneer*, 20:119.

2. "Indian speech," 3 June 1795; "Indian Council," 19 January 1795, Williams to Wayne, 4 December 1794, Wayne Papers, Philadelphia; *American State Papers: Indian Affairs*, 1:565.

3. Knopf, *Anthony Wayne, A Name in Arms*, p. 433; Hunt to Wayne, 9 May 1795, Hamtramck to Wayne, 26 April 1795, Wayne Papers, Philadelphia.

4. Knopf, *Anthony Wayne, A Name in Arms*, p. 388; Wayne to Hunt, 21 March, 19 June 1795, Wayne to Hamtramck, 1 and 13 May, 7 June, 1795, Wayne Papers, Philadelphia.

5. Knopf, *Anthony Wayne, A Name in Arms*, pp. 395, 401; Wayne to Drake, 29 June 1795, Wayne to Hunt, 19 June 1795, Wayne Papers, Philadelphia.

6. Knopf, *Anthony Wayne, A Name in Arms*, pp. 395–401, 403, 407.

7. Ibid., pp. 396–407.

8. Ibid., pp. 389–90, 394, 408, 414, 423.

9. Ibid., pp. 394, 433.

10. Ibid., p. 413; Wayne to Hamtramck, 7 June 1795, Wayne to Drake, 29 June 1795, Drake to Wayne, 30 June 1795, Wayne Papers, Philadelphia.

11. Hamtramck to Wayne, 7 May 1795, "Examination of Wm. McKee," 28 June 1795, Wayne Papers, Philadelphia; *Correspondence of Lt. Gov. Simcoe*, 4:61, 5:113.

12. Hamtramck to Wayne, 26 April, 7, 16, 25, and 27 May 1795; Drake to Wayne, 30 June 1795, "Speech of Chippewas, etc.," 3 June 1795, Wayne to Pasteur, 11 June 1795, Wayne Papers, Philadelphia; *American State Papers: Indian Affairs*, 1:564.

13. Knopf, *Anthony Wayne, A Name in Arms*, p. 427; Hamtramck to Wayne, 25, 27 June 1795, Drake to Wayne, 30 June 1795, Wayne to Hamtramck, 13 July 1795, Wayne Papers, Philadelphia.

14. *American State Papers: Indian Affairs*, 1:565–67, 582.

15. Ibid., 1:565; Knopf, *Anthony Wayne, A Name in Arms*, pp. 406, 428.

16. *American State Papers: Indian Affairs*, 1:567; Richard D. Knopf, *A Surgeon's Mate at Fort Defiance*, p. 51.

17. *American State Papers: Indian Affairs*, 1:568.

18. Knopf, *A Surgeon's Mate*, p. 39; *American State Papers: Indian Affairs*, 1:570–71.

19. *American State Papers: Indian Affairs*, 1:568–73.

20. Ibid., 1:573.

21. Ibid., 1:573–74.

22. Ibid., 1:574.

23. *American State Papers: Indian Affairs*, 1:576.

24. Ibid., 1:577–78.

25. Ibid., 1:578.

26. Ibid., 1:578, 581.

27. Ibid., 1:579; Burton, *Michigan Pioneer*, 20:418.

28. *American State Papers: Indian Affairs*, 1:579–81; Williams to Wayne, 10 August 1795, Wayne Papers, Philadelphia.

29. *American State Papers: Indian Affairs*, 1:579–82.

30. Ibid., 1:582; Davidson, "Reverend David Jones, M.A." pp. 126ff.

31. *American State Papers: Indian Affairs*, 1:583; Burton, *Michigan Pioneer*, 15:4, 5, 20:418; Winger, *Last of the Miamis*, p. 8.

32. Knopf, *Anthony Wayne, A Name in Arms*, pp. 442–43.

33. Ibid., p. 443; Wayne to Hamtramck, 13 July 1795, Wayne to St. Clair, 15 August 1795, Wayne to Hunt, 13 August 1795, Wayne Papers, Philadelphia; Wayne to Hamtramck, 14 August 1795, Wayne Papers, Ann Arbor, Mich.; *American State Papers: Indian Affairs*, 1:579; Burton, *Manuscripts from the Burton Historical Collection*, 1:36; Davidson, "Reverend David Jones," pp. 126ff.; Knopf, *A Surgeon's Mate*, p. 35.

34. DeButts to Williams, 4 August 1795, Wayne Papers, Philadelphia; Knopf, *A Surgeon's Mate*, p. 11, 22, 49, 75.

35. Knopf, *A Surgeon's Mate*, pp. 41, 53, 55.

36. Ibid., pp. 55–56; Hunt to Wayne, 22 August 1795, Hamtramck to Wayne, 13 August 1795, Wayne Papers, Philadelphia.

37. Knopf, *A Surgeon's Mate*, p. 39; Davidson, "Reverend David Jones," pp. 126ff.

Chapter 32. Epilogue: "All My Sorrows"

1. F. Clever Bald, *Detroit's First Decade, 1796 to 1805*, pp. 2, 16–19; Burton, *Michigan Pioneer*, 34:739.

2. Knopf, *Anthony Wayne, A Name in Arms*, pp. 463, 469, 512, 525–26; *Correspondence of Lt. Gov. Simcoe*, 5:341–42.

3. Bald, *Detroit's First Decade*, p. 50; Knopf, *Anthony Wayne, A Name in Arms*, p. 527.

4. Knopf, *Anthony Wayne, A Name in Arms*, pp. 463–69, 506.

5. Ibid., pp. 364, 369, 383, 495, 506, 536; Wayne letter, 14 December 1795, Wayne to Knox, 15 January 1795, Wayne Papers, Ann Arbor, Mich.; Wildes, *Anthony Wayne, Troubleshooter*, pp. 431, 453, 457–63; Davidson, "Reverend David Jones," p. 126ff.; *Correspondence of Lt. Gov. Simcoe*, 3:166–67.

6. Daniels, *Ordeal of Ambition*, p. 316.

7. Ibid., pp. 369, 411; John Edward Weems, *Men Without Countries*, pp. 184, 228; Jacobs, *Tarnished Warrior*.

8. Boatner, *Encyclopedia of the American Revolution*, pp. 183, 1009; Horsman, *Matthew Elliott*, pp. 143, 164–71; T. L. Rodgers, "Simon Girty and Some of His Contemporaries," *Western Pennsylvania Magazine of History* 8, no. 3 (July 1925); 158–59; Knopf, *Anthony Wayne, A Name in Arms*, p. 354.

9. Stone, *Life of Joseph Brant*, 2:405, 478, 481–98.

10. Young, *Little Turtle*, pp. 125ff.; Drake, *Book of the Indians of North America*, pp. 56–57.

11. Young, *Little Turtle*, pp. 29, 148–49; Burton, *Michigan Pioneer*, 14:261, 273, 486.

12. Young, *Little Turtle*, pp. 23, 25, 29; Winger, *Last of the Miamis*, p. 3.

13. Young, *Little Turtle*, pp. 158–59.

14. Ibid., p. 161.

15. Ibid., p. 169.

16. Knopf, *Anthony Wayne, A Name in Arms*, p. 532; Burton, *Michigan Pioneer*, 15:24, 25; 34:739; Hodge, *Handbook of American Indians North of Mexico*, 1:155.

17. Hodge, *Handbook of American Indians*, 1:168, 2:694; Glenn Tucker, *Tecumseh, Vision of Glory*, pp. 107, 129–30; Carl F. Klink, ed., *Tecumseh, Fact and Fiction in Early Records*, p. 89.

18. Howe, *Historical Collections of Ohio*, 2:144.

19. Klink, *Tecumseh, Fact and Fiction*, p. 89.

20. Tucker, *Tecumseh, Vision of Glory*, pp. 19, 93, 200–209, 326–27.

21. Ibid., pp. 203, 216–18, 232, 241–43, 300.

22. Ibid., pp. 284, 311–28.

23. Ibid., p. 243.

24. Knopf, *Anthony Wayne, A Name in Arms*, pp. 405, 503; Burton, *Manuscripts from the*

Burton Historical Collection, pp. 37, 68; Tucker, *Tecumseh, Vision of Glory*, pp. 81, 137, 146; Davidson, "Reverend David Jones," pp. 126ff.; Knox to Wayne, 19 August 1795, Wayne to Hamtramck, 19 August 1795, Wayne Papers, Philadelphia.

25. Burton, *Manuscripts from the Burton Historical Collection*, pp. 150–51; Knopf, *Anthony Wayne, A Name in Arms*, pp. 515, 523; Tucker, *Tecumseh, Vision of Glory*, p. 136; Burton, *Michigan Pioneer*, 20:463; McKenzie to Hunt, 26 August 1795, Wayne Papers, Philadelphia.

26. Burton, *Michigan Pioneer*, 34:738.

27. Tucker, *Tecumseh, Vision of Glory*, pp. 140, 144.

28. Ibid., pp. 144–45.

29. Knopf, *A Surgeon's Mate at Fort Defiance*, p. 77.

30. Ibid., p. 87.

31. Tucker, *Tecumseh, Vision of Glory*, pp. 87–88; Winger; *Last of the Miamis*, p. 12.

32. Winger, *Last of the Miamis*, pp. 11–14; Young, *Little Turtle*, p. 27.

33. Young, *Little Turtle*, p. 29; Deetz, *North American Indians: A Source Book*, pp. 634–35.

34. Carman and Syrett, *A History of the American People*, 1:530; Deetz, *North American Indians: A Source Book*, pp. 632–33.

35. *American State Papers: Indian Affairs*, 1:581.

Bibliography

Notes on Sources

With the exception of nominal background material, utilized primarily in the initial chapters, the vast bulk of the information for this history has been derived from primary sources. There are various large collections of contemporary documents that contain substantial amounts of information. Some of the more important of these are the Lyman C. Draper Manuscripts of the Wisconsin Historical Society, Madison; the Arthur St. Clair papers on deposit in the Ohio Historical Society, Columbus; the voluminous Anthony Wayne papers of the Historical Society of Pennsylvania, Philadelphia; and the Josiah Harmar collections of the University of Michigan's William L. Clements Library, Ann Arbor. Furthermore, the voluminous collection of British Colonial Office Records (Q Series) in the Public Archives of Canada in Ottawa is invaluable in any study of the period.

Many primary documents are published in readily accessible books. Among the most valuable sources are the *American State Papers: Military Affairs* and *Indian Affairs*; Clarence E. Carter, ed., *The Territorial Papers of the United States*; Clarence M. Burton, ed., *Michigan Pioneer and Historical Collections*; *The Correspondence of Lieut.-Governor John Graves Simcoe*, edited by E. A. Cruikshank and A. F. Hunter; William P. Palmer, ed., *Calendar of Virginia State Papers*; and Worthington C. Ford, ed., *Journals of the Continental Congress 1784–1789*.

One additional matter requiring explanation is the writer's normalizing of spelling and punctuation. In certain quotations from original sources spelling and punctuation have been corrected. Care has been taken to maintain the veracity of all quotations, and it is simply my opinion that normalization is appropriate for the sake of clarity and to eliminate reader distractions.

Manuscripts

Ann Arbor, Michigan. University of Michigan Graduate Library. Microfilm copy of Henry Knox Papers (original in New England Historic Genealogical Society Collection, Boston).

Ann Arbor, Michigan. William L. Clements Library. Josiah Harmar Papers. Anthony Wayne Papers. Michael McDonough to his brother, 10 November 1791, miscellaneous papers.

Chicago, Illinois. Chicago Historical Society. James Wilkinson Papers.

Columbus, Ohio. Ohio Historical Society. Arthur St. Clair Collection (on deposit from the state library). Henry Alder, "The Captivity of Jonathan Alder and His Life with the Indians."

Detroit, Michigan. Detroit Public Library. Burton Historical Collection. Richard
   Butler Papers. Leonard Covington Papers. John F. Hamtramck Papers. J. M.
   Howard Papers. David Jones Papers. Winthrop Sargent Papers. William D.
   Wilkins Papers. Dudley Woodbridge Papers.
Hartford, Connecticut. Connecticut Historical Society. John P. Wyllys Papers.
Madison, Wisconsin. Wisconsin Historical Society. Lyman C. Draper Manu-
   script Collection.
Ottawa, Ontario, Canada. Public Archives of Canada. Colonial Office Records, Q
   Series. "Diary of An Officer J. C. in the Indian Camp & Opposed to Gen'l
   Wayne," Manuscript Group 19.
Philadelphia, Pennsylvania. Historical Society of Pennsylvania. Anthony Wayne
   Papers.
San Marino, California. Henry E. Huntington Library. Charles Scott Papers.
Washington, D.C. National Archives. Personal Military Service Records of
   Robert Newman, William May, William Wells; Arthur St. Clair Papers;
   Record Group 94.

Published Materials, Theses, Dissertations, Newspapers

Allen, Robert S. "The British Indian Department and the Frontier in North
   America, 1755–1830." *Vocational Papers in Archaeology and History* (Ottawa,
   Canada), 1975.
Alvord, Charle Walworth. *The Mississippi Valley in British Politics*. 2 vols. New
   York, 1959.
Annals of the Congress of the United States, 1789–1824. Vol. 3, 2d Cong. (24 October
   1791–2 March 1793). Washington, D.C., 1949.
Askin, John. *The John Askin Papers*. Edited by Milo Milton Quaife. 2 vols.
   Detroit, Mich., 1928–31.
Bald, F. Clever. *Detroit's First Decade, 1796 to 1805*. Ann Arbor, Mich. 1948.
Barce, Elmore. *The Land of the Miamis*. Fowler, Ind., 1922.
Barrett, Jay A. *Evolution of the Ordinance of 1787*. New York, 1981.
Beatty, Erkuries. "Diary of Major Erkuries Beatty, Paymaster in the Western
   Army, May 15, 1786 to June 5, 1787." *Magazine of American History* (New
   York) 1 (1877).
Bemis, Samuel Flagg. *A Diplomatic History of the United States*. New York, 1965.
Bennett, John. *Blue Jacket: War Chief of the Shawnee and His Part in Ohio's History*.
   Chillicothe, Ohio, 1943.
Benton, Thomas H. *Abridgement of the Debates of Congress from 1789 to 1856*. Vol. 1.
   New York, 1857.
Boatner, Mark Mayo, III. *Encyclopedia of the American Revolution*. New York,
   1966.
Bodley, Temple. *George Rogers Clark: His Life and Public Services*. New York,
   1966.
Bond, Beverly W. Jr. *The Civilization of the Old Northwest*. New York, 1934.
[Bowyer, John.] "Diary Journal of Wayne's Campaign." In John Jacob, *A Biblio-
   graphical Sketch of the Life of the Late Captain Michael Cresap*. Cincinnati, 1866.
Boyd, Thomas. *Simon Girty, the White Savage*. New York, 1928.
Bradley, A. G. *Lord Dorechester*. Toronto, Canada, 1910.
Bradley, Captain Daniel. *Journal of Captain Daniel Bradley*. Edited by Frazier
   Ellis Wilson. Greenville, Ohio, 1935.

Brice, Wallace A. *History of Fort Wayne*. Fort Wayne, Ind., 1910.

Brymer, Douglas. *Report on Canadian Archives*. Ottawa, Ontario, Canada, 1891.

Buell, John Hutchinson. *The Diary of John Hutchinson Buell*. Edited by Richard D. Knopf. Columbus, Ohio, 1957.

Bunn, Matthew. *Narrative of the Life and Adventures of Matthew Bunn*. 1904. Batavia, Ill., 1926.

Burton, Clarence M., ed. *The City of Detroit, 1701–1922*. 4 vols. Detroit, Mich., 1922.

————, ed. *Michigan Pioneer and Historical Collections*. 2d ed. 40 vols. Lansing, Mich., 1877–1929.

Burton, M. Agnes, ed. *Manuscripts from the Burton Historical Collection*. Vols. 1–8. Detroit, Mich., 1916.

Butler, William David. *The Butler Family in America*. St. Louis, Mo., 1909.

Butterfield, Consul Willshire. *History of the Girtys*. Cincinnati, 1890.

———— *Washington-Irvine Correspondence*. Madison, Wisc. 1882.

Callahan, North. *Henry Knox, General Washington's General*. New York, 1959.

Carman, Harry J., and Harold C. Syrett. *A History of the American People*. 2 vols. New York, 1954.

Carter, Clarence E., ed. *The Territorial Papers of the United States*. 28 vols. Vol. 2, *The Territory Northwest of the River Ohio, 1787–1803*. Washington, D.C., 1934–75.

Clark, William. "William Clark's Journal of General Wayne's Campaign." Edited by Reginald E. McGrane. *Mississippi Valley Historical Review* 1:418–44.

Clift, J. Glenn. *The "Cornstalk" Militia of Kentucky, 1792–1811*. Frankfort, Ky., 1911.

Coates, G. H., ed. "A Narrative of an Embassy to the Western Indians (Hendrick Aupaumut)." *Memoirs of the Historical Society of Pennsylvania* 2 (1827).

Columbian Centinel (Boston, Mass.), 5 October 1791–6 February 1792. Burton Historical Collection, Detroit Public Library.

Cone, Stephen Decater. "Indian Attack on Fort Dunlap." *Ohio Historical Society Quarterly* 7 (1908).

Cook, John A. "Captain John Cook's Journal." *American Historical Record* (Philadelphia) 2 (1973).

Craig, Nevill B., ed. *The Olden Time*. 2 vols. Pittsburgh, Pa., 1927.

Craig, Oscar J. "Ouiatanon, A Study in Indiana History." *Indiana Historical Society Publications* 2 (1893).

Cruikshank, E. A. *Inventory of the Military Documents in the Canadian Archives*. Ottawa, Ontario, 1910.

Daniels, Jonathan. *Ordeal of Ambition*. New York, 1970.

Davidson, James A. "Reverend David Jones, M.A." *The Chronicle* 4 (1941):126.

Deetz, James J. F., Anthony D. Fisher, and Roger C. Owen, eds. *The North American Indians: A Source Book*. New York, 1967.

Denny, Ebenezer. "A Military Journal Kept by Major E. Denny, 1781 to 1795." *Memoirs of the Historical Society of Pennsylvania* 7 (1860).

De Peyster, J. Watts. *Miscellanies, By An Officer (Colonel Arent Schuyler De Peyster, B.A.), 1774–1813*. New York, 1888.

Douglas, Albert. "Major General Arthur St. Clair." *Ohio Archaeological and Historical Society Publication* 16 (1907).

Downes, Randolph C. *The Conquest*. Toledo, Ohio, 1968.

————— Council Fires on the Upper Ohio. Pittsburgh, Pa., 1940.

————— Frontier Ohio, 1788–1803. Columbus, Ohio, 1935.

Drake, Samuel G. The Book of the Indians of North America. Boston, 1834.

Eckert, Allan W. The Frontiersmen. Boston, 1967.

Edgar, Matilda, ed. Ten Years of Upper Canada in Peace and War, 1805–1815. Toronto, Ontario, 1890.

Filson, John. Filson's Kentucke. 1784. Louisville, Ky., 1929.

Finley, James B. Autobiography of Reverend James B. Finley. Edited by W. P. Strickland. Cincinnati, Ohio, 1853.

Ford, Worthington C., ed. Journals of the Continental Congress, 1784–1789. 34 vols. Washington, D.C., 1922.

Flexner, James Thomas. George Washington and the New Nation, 1783–1793. Boston, 1969.

Galloway, William Albert. Old Chillicothe: Shawnee and Pioneer History. Xenia, Ohio, 1934.

Gore, Sally. "Bluejacket, the Famous Shawnee Chief." Transactions of the Kansas State Historical Society 10 (1908).

Graymont, Barbara. The Iroquois in the American Revolution. Syracuse, N.Y., 1972.

Griswold, B. J. The Pictorial History of Ft. Wayne, Indiana. Chicago, 1917.

Guthman, William H. March to Massacre: A History of the First Seven Years of the United States Army, 1784–1791. New York, 1975.

Harvey, Henry. History of the Shawnee Indians from the Year 1681 to 1854, Inclusive. Cincinnati, 1855.

Havinghurst, Walter. River to the West: Three Centuries of the Ohio. New York, 1970.

Hay, Thomas Robson. The Admirable Trumpeter: A Biography of General James Wilkinson. Garden City, N.Y., 1941.

Heard, J. Norman. White into Red. Metuchen, N.J., 1973.

Heitman, Francis D. Historical Register and Dictionary of the United States Army . . . September 29, 1789 to March 2, 1903. 2 vols. Washington, D.C., 1903.

Helderman. Leonard C. "The Northwest Expedition of George Rogers Clark, 1786–1787." Mississippi Valley Historical Review 25:317–34.

Hildreth, S. P., ed. The American Pioneer. Vols. 1 and 2. Cincinnati, 1843.

—————. Pioneer History, Cincinnati, 1848.

Hill, Leonard V. John Johnston and the Indians in the Land of the Three Miamis. Pequa, Ohio, 1957.

The History of Darke County, Ohio. Chicago, 1880.

History of Madison County, Ohio. Chicago, 1893.

Hodge, Frederic Webb, ed. Handbook of American Indians North of Mexico. 2 vols. 1907 and 1910. Reprint. New York, 1960.

Horsman, Reginald. "The British Indian Department and the Abortive Treaty of Lower Sandusky, 1793." Ohio Historical Quarterly 70:189–213.

—————. Expansion and American Indian Policy, 1783–1812. East Lansing, Mich., 1957.

————— Matthew Elliott, British Indian Agent. Detroit, Mich., 1964.

Howard, Dresden W. H. "The Battle of Fallen Timbers as Told by Chief Kin-Jo-I-No." Northwest Ohio Quarterly 20:37–49.

Howe, Henry. Historical Collections of Ohio. 2 vols. Cincinnati, 1900.

Huber, John Parker. "General Josiah Harmar's Command: Military Policy in the Old Northwest." Ph.D. diss., University of Michigan, 1964.

Hulbert, Archer Butler. The Ohio River: A Course of Empire. New York, 1906.

Irvin, Thomas. "Harmar's Campaign." *Ohio Archaeological and Historical Quarterly* 19:393–96.

Jacob, John. *A Biographical Sketch of the Life of the Late Captain Michael Cresap.* (Daily Journal of Wayne's Campaign.) Cincinnati, 1866.

Jacobs, James Ripley. *Tarnished Warrior: Major General James Wilkinson.* New York, 1938.

———— *The Beginnings of the U.S. Army, 1783–1812.* Princeton, N.J., 1947.

Jefferson, Thomas. *The Writings of Thomas Jefferson.* Edited by Albert Ellery Bergh. Vols. 1–9. Washington, D.C., 1905.

———— *Thomas Jefferson's Writings.* Edited by Paul L. Ford. 10 volumes. New York, 1892–99.

Johnson, Allen, ed. *Dictionary of American Biography.* 20 vols. New York, 1929–36.

Johnston, Charles. *Narratives of Captivities: Incidents Attending the Capture, Detention, and Ransom of Charles Johnston of Virginia.* 1827. Cleveland, Ohio, 1905.

Johonnot, Jackson. *The Remarkable Adventures of Jackson Johonnot.* Greenfield, Mass. 1861.

Josephy, Alvin M., Jr. *The Indian Heritage of America.* New York, 1968.

Kappler, Charles, J., ed. *Indian Treaties, 1778–1883.* New York, 1972.

Katzenberger, George A. "Major David Ziegler." *Ohio Archaeological and Historical Quarterly* 21 (1912).

———— "Major George Adams." *Ohio Archaeological and Historical Quarterly* 22 (1913).

Keek, Walter W., and Thomas E. Sanders, eds. *Literature of the North American Indian.* New York, 1973.

Kenton, Edna. *Simon Kenton: His Life and Period.* New York, 1930.

Klink, Carl F., ed. *Tecumseh: Fact and Fiction in Early Records.* Cliffs, N.J., 1961.

Knopf, Richard D., ed. *Anthony Wayne, A Name in Arms.* Pittsburgh, Pa., 1960.

————, ed. "A Precise Journal of General Wayne's Last Campaign." *Proceedings of the American Antiquarian Society* 64 (1955).

————, ed. *A Surgeon's Mate at Fort Defiance.* Columbus, Ohio, 1975.

————, ed. "Two Journals of the Kentucky Volunteers, 1793 and 1794." *Filson Club Quarterly* 27 (1953).

Lossing, Benson J. *The Pictorial Field Book of the War of 1812.* New York, 1868.

Loudon, Archibald. *A Selection of Some of the Most Interesting Narratives of Outrages Committed by the Indians in Their Wars with the White People.* 2 vols. Carlisle, Pa., 1811.

McArthur, John. *Biographical Sketches of General Nathaniel Massie, General Duncan McArthur, Captain William Wells, and General Simon Kenton.* Dayton, Ohio, 1852.

McClung, John A. *Sketches of Western Adventure, Containing an Account of the Most Interesting Incidents Connected with the Settlement of the West from 1755 to 1794.* Dayton, Ohio, 1854.

Martzloff, Clement L. "Big Bottom and Its History." *Ohio Archaeological and Historical Quarterly* 15 (1906).

Meek, Basil. "General Harmar's Expedition." *Ohio Archaeological and Historical Quarterly* 20:74–108.

Metcalfe, Samuel Lytler. *Life and Travels of Colonel James Smith, 1755–1759.* Lexington, Ky., 1821.

Minutes of Debates in Council on the Banks of the Ottawa River, November, 1791. Philadelphia, 1839.

Mitchener, C. H., ed. *Ohio Annals.* Dayton, Ohio, 1876.

Morris, Richard B. *The Peacemakers: The Great Powers and American Independence.* New York, 1965.

Morse, Jedidiah. *The American Geography.* London, 1794.

"Narrative of the Journeys of Colonel Thomas Proctor to the Indians of the Northwest, 1791." *Pennsylvania Archives,* 2d ser., 4:551–622.

New York Colonial Documents. 15 vols. Albany, N.Y., 1853–87.

O'Callaghan, E. B., ed. *Documents Relative to the Colonial History of the State of New York.* Vol. 8. Albany, N.Y. 1857.

Palmer, William P., ed. *Calendar of Virginia State Papers.* Vol. 4 Richmond, Va., 1884.

Peckham, Howard H. "Josiah Harmar and His Indian Expedition." *Ohio Archaeological and Historical Quarterly* 50, no. 3 (1946).

Pennsylvania Archives. 1st ser., 12 vols., Philadelphia, 1853–56. 2d ser., 19 vols., Harrisburg, 1874–93.

Pennsylvania Colonial Records. 16 vols. Harrisburg, Pa. 1851–53.

Perkins, James H. *Annals of the West.* Cincinnati, 1846.

Preston, John Hyde. *A Gentleman Rebel: The Exploits of Anthony Wayne.* 2 vols. New York, 1930.

Prucha, Francis Paul. *American Indian Policy in the Formative Years.* Lincoln, Nebr. 1962.

Putnam, Rufus. *The Memoirs of Rufus Putnam.* Edited by Rowena Buell. New York, 1903.

Quaife, Milo Milton, ed. *The Captivity of O. M. Spencer.* Chicago, 1917.

———. "Fort Wayne in 1790 (Journal of Henry Hay)." *Indiana Historical Society Publications* 7 (1921).

Rodgers, T. L. "Simon Girty and Some of His Contemporaries." *Western Pennsylvania Historical Magazine* 8 (1925), no. 3.

Rohr, Martha. *Historical Sketch of Fort Recovery.* Fort Recovery, Ohio, 1965.

Roosevelt, Theodore. *The Winning of the West.* 6 vols. New York, 1889.

Rush, Richard. *Washington in Domestic Life.* Philadelphia, 1857.

Russell, Nelson Vance. *The British Regime in Michigan and the Old Northwest, 1760–1796.* Northfield, Minn., 1939.

Russell, Peter. *The Correspondence of the Honourable Peter Russell.* Edited by E. A. Cruikshank. 3 vols. Toronto, 1935.

St. Clair, Arthur. *A Narrative of the Campaign Against the Indians Under the Command of Major General St. Clair.* Philadelphia, 1812.

———. *The St. Clair Papers: The Life and Public Service of Arthur St. Clair.* Edited by William Henry Smith. Cincinnati, 1882.

Sargent, Charles Sprague. "Winthrop Sargent." *Ohio Archaeological and Historical Society Quarterly* 33 (1924).

Sargent, Winthrop. "Winthrop Sargent's Diary While with General Arthur St. Clair's Expedition Against the Indians." *Ohio State Archaeological and Historical Quarterly* 33 (1924).

Scott, Duncan Campbell. *John Graves Simcoe.* Toronto, Ontario, 1905.

Simcoe, John Graves. *The Correspondence of Lieut. Governor John Graves Simcoe.* Edited by E. A. Cruikshank and A. F. Hunter. 5 vols. Toronto, Ontario, 1923–31.

Smith, Dwight L., ed. *From Greeneville to Fallen Timbers: A Journal of the Wayne Campaign, July 28–September 14, 1794.* Indianapolis, Ind., 1952.

——— *With Captain Edward Miller in the Wayne Campaign of 1794.* Ann Arbor, Mich., 1965.

Smith, James. *An Account of the Remarkable Occurrences in the Life and Travels of Colonel James Smith During His Captivity with the Indians, in the years 1755–1759.* Cincinnati, 1870.

Smith, Z. F. *The History of Kentucky.* Louisville, Ky., 1886.

Stone, William L. *Life of Joseph Brant (Thayendanegea).* 2 vols. New York, 1865.

Symmes, John Cleves. *The Correspondence of John Cleves Symmes.* New York, 1926.

Thornbrough, Gayle. *Outpost on the Wabash, 1787–1791.* Indianapolis, Ind., 1957.

Thwaites, Reuben Gold, ed. *Collections of the State Historical Society of Wisconsin.* Vols. 10 and 19. Madison, Wisc., 1908, 1910.

Tucker, Glenn. *Tecumseh: Vision of Glory.* New York, 1956.

United States Congress. *American State Papers: Documents, Legislative and Executive, of the Congress of the United States. Indian Affairs*, vol. 1. *Military Affairs*, vol. 1. Washington, D.C., 1832–61.

————. *The Formation of the Union.* Washington, D.C., 1970.

————. *Journal of the Executive Proceedings of the Senate of the United States of America.* Vol. 1. Washington, D.C., 1828.

Van Every, Dale. "President Washington's Calculated Risk." *American Heritage*, June, 1959, p. 56.

Von Oppolzer, Theodore Ritter. *Canon of Eclipses.* Translated by Owen Gingerich. New York, 1962.

Wallace, Paul A. W., ed. *Thirty Thousand Miles with John Heckewelder.* Pittsburgh, Pa., 1958.

Ward, Harry M. *The Department of War, 1781–1795.* Pittsburgh, Pa., 1962.

Washington, George. *George Washington's Writings.* Edited by John C. Fitzpatrick. 39 vols. New York, 1889–93.

————. *The Writings of George Washington.* Edited by Worthington Chauncey Ford. 14 vols. New York, 1889–93.

————. *The Writings of George Washington.* Edited by Jared Sparks. 12 vols. Boston, 1858.

Weems, John Edward. *Men Without Countries.* Boston, 1969.

Wilcox, Frank N. *Ohio Indian Trails.* Cleveland, Ohio, 1934.

Wildes, Harry Emerson. *Anthony Wayne, Troubleshooter of the American Revolution.* New York, 1941.

Wilson, Frazier Ellis, *Around the Council Fire.* Greenville, Ohio, 1934.

————. *Fort Jefferson.* Lancaster, Pa., 1950.

————. "St. Clair's Defeat." *Ohio Archaeological and Historical Quarterly* 10 (1908).

Winger, Otho. *The Last of the Miamis (Me-Shin-Go-MeSia).* North Manchester, Ind., 1935.

————. "The Indians Who Opposed Harmar." *Ohio Archaeological and Historical Quarterly* 55 (1941).

————. *The Ke-Na-Po-Co-Mo-Co Eel River, The Home of Little Turtle.* North Manchester, Ind., 1934.

Withers, Alexander Scott. *Chronicles of Border Warfare.* Cincinnati, Ohio, 1895. Parsons, W. Va., 1970.

Young, Calvin M. *Little Turtle (Me-She-Kin-No-Quah), The Great Chief of the Miami Indian Nation.* Greenville, Ohio, 1917.

Zeisberger, David. *Diary of David Zeisberger: A Moravian Missionary Among the Indians of the Ohio.* Edited by Eugene F. Bliss. 2 vols. Cincinnati, Ohio, 1885.

Index

Abbott, Betsey: 102
Adair, John: 220–21, 228
Adams, George: 113, 187
Adams, John Vice-President: 282
Alder, Jonathan: 277
Alexander, William (Lord Sterling): 149
Algonquian Indians: 5, 19, 60, 72, 197, 339
Amherstburg (Fort Malden): 334
Aquenackque (Miami chief): 287
Armstrong, John: 9, 56, 106–109
Arnold, Benedict: 333
Ashby, Captain, and son Jack: 73
Asheton, Joseph: 113–14
Auglaize River: 197, 223, 269, 282–83
Auglaize villages: *see* Glaize
Aupaumut, Hendrick (Captain Hendricks): 213, 223, 227

Baby, James: 293
Barbee, Thomas: 282
Beatty, Erkuries: 92
Beaver Creek: 28, 281
Belpre, Ohio: 5, 60, 76
Bevan, John: 308
Big Bottom settlement: 129–30
Big Shawnee Ben: 110
Billy (Indian youth): 142
Blue Jacket (Shawnee warrior): 38, 85, 99, 117, 119, 122, 168, 175, 179, 186, 191, 220, 269, 271, 278, 283, 291, 297, 303, 323, 326–28, 330, 336; raid on Dunlap's Station, 126–27; changes alliance, 316–19
Blue Licks, Battle of: 39, 114, 126
Boone, Daniel: 37–39
Bowyer, John: 281
Bradley, Daniel: 219
Bradshaw, Robert: 176, 178, 180
Brant, Isaac: 321, 34
Brant, Joseph: 23, 26, 37–38, 42–43, 58, 64–68, 75, 139, 142, 158, 91, 225, 228–29, 241–45, 247–48, 250, 260,

262–63, 306, 313–14, 320–21, 334; background of, 53–55; moderate policy of, 60–61; U.S. policy toward in 1792, 209–210
Brant, Molly: 53
Brenham, Thomas: 167
British Army: Canadian militia, 280, 289, 293, 298, 303–305; Fifth Infantry, 293; Twenty-fourth Infantry, 261, 289, 293; Queen's Rangers, 230, 289, 293
Brock, Isaac: 337
Brownstown (Huron Village; Big Rock): 313ff., 320–21
Buckongahelas (Delaware leader): 242–43, 270–71, 306, 326, 330, 336
Buffalo Creek (N.Y.): 26, 55, 134–35, 208–209, 223, 225, 227, 262, 314
Builderback, Charles: 76
Bunbury, Joseph: 293
Bull, Captain: 140
Burr, Aaron: 333
Butler, Edward: 173, 185, 191, 255
Butler, Richard: 23, 29–30, 37, 121, 148, 150–52, 161, 165, 171, 173–75, 185, 187–88, 191, 255
Butler, Thomas: 173, 178, 184–85, 191

Cahokia (Ill.): 84–85
Caldwell, William: 293, 298, 303
Campbell Robert Mis: 303
Campbell, William: 289, 293, 305–311
Camp Deposit, on the Maumee River: 295, 308, 310
Campus Martius stockade near Fort Harmar: 59
Captain David (Mohawk): 65
Captain Johnny (Shawnee): 6, 243, 245, 278
Carleton, Sir Guy (Lord Dorchester): 42–43, 75, 122–24, 141, 158–59, 230, 240, 245, 258ff., 294, 313, 315, 320, 333; Indian policy of, 258–60
Carrington, Edward: 47–48

393

Miller, Christopher: 268, 272, 285, 289, 291–92, 294
Miller, Henry: 268
Mingo Indians: 137, 211
Mississippi River: 3, 19, 41, 55, 155, 198, 336–37, 339–40
Mitchell (Indian captive): 70
Mitchell, John: 11
Mohawk Indians: 24–26, 287, 313
Moluntha (Shawnee King): 37–39, 43–44, 73
Monroe, James: 206, 260
Moore, James: 33
Moore, Sherman: 299, 301
Moravian massacre, 1782: 76
Morgan, Daniel: 73, 205, 213
Morgan, Rawleigh: 169
Morris, David: 114–15
Moultrie, William: 205
Mountain Leader (Chickasaw chief): 269
Murray, Patrick: 95
Muskingum (Ohio): 120, 146
Muskingum boundary: 245, 247, 262, 325
Muskingum River: 56–57, 59–62, 66, 74, 159, 217
Muskogee Indians: 337

New Arrow (Seneca chief): 225
Newman, Robert: 284, 287–88, 296, 333
Newman, Samuel: 190
New York, state of: 26, 53, 79, 86, 94, 258, 263
Niagara: 11, 17, 19–20, 23, 83, 101, 123, 135, 195, 209–11, 225, 227, 236, 239–41, 243, 292, 313–14, 321, 332
Northwest Territory: *see* Old Northwest Territory

O'Brien, John: 301
O'Hara, James: 264, 319
Ohio Company: 45, 47–49, 58–60, 126, 129–30, 149
Ohio country: 4–5, 43, 49, 55–61, 69, 76, 81, 131, 214, 231, 337–38; Indians of, 15; black forests of, 49
Ohio River: 3–5, 27, 29, 31, 41–42, 47, 55–57, 59–60, 64–65, 69–75, 85, 121, 137–39, 148, 152, 193, 235–37, 243, 332, 337
Ohio River boundary: 24, 61, 64, 66, 74, 159, 226, 228, 241, 243, 245–46, 262
Old Chillicothe (Piqua, Ohio): 96
Oldham, William: 160, 167, 171, 174, 178, 185

Old Northwest Territory: 11, 13, 24, 27, 43, 45, 47–48, 53, 60, 85, 101, 103, 130, 196, 204, 320–21, 332, 335; Indians of, 26, 122, 225; land purchases, 50; tomahawk improvements, 55; land as asset, 324
Oneida Indians: 25–26
Oneil, John: 164
Onondaga Indians: 25–26
Ordinance of October 15, 1783: 27–28
Ordinance of 1785: 45
Ordinance of July 13, 1787: 47, 50, 58
Orr, Alexander: 136–37
Oswego, N.Y.: 11, 19, 123, 231, 332
Ottawa Indians: 6, 17, 39, 41, 111, 117, 146, 176, 223, 243, 251, 254, 256, 270, 277–78, 284, 288–89, 291, 298, 301–303, 316, 318, 326
Ouiatanon (Lafayette, Ind.): 140–41, 155–56

Painted Post (Athens, Pa.): 135, 208
Parsons, Samuel H.: 45, 47–48
Patterson, Robert: 38, 60
Paul, James: 94, 109
Pennsylvania, state of: 2, 57, 79, 92, 94–95, 199, 205–206, 235–36, 258, 325
Pennsylvania Militia: 64, 86, 92, 94–95, 134, 146–47, 263
Peters, William: 64
Philadelphia, Pa.: 55, 89, 121, 130, 133, 135, 145–46, 150–51, 156, 197, 200–202, 207–211, 226, 279, 314, 333
Piamingo (Chickasaw chief): 166
Piankashaw Indians, of Wabash Confederacy: 6, 35, 217, 339
Pickering, Timothy: 135, 238, 240, 243–44, 324–27, 330, 338
Pilkington, Robert: 262
Pinckney, Charles: 205
Pittsburgh, Pa.: 28, 82, 125–26, 134, 146, 151, 199–200, 211, 232, 234, 249, 319, 333
Point Pleasant, Ohio: 5, 70
Pond, Peter: 210
Pope, William: 31
Porter, Moses: 332
Potawatomi Indians: 6, 16, 29, 41, 88, 108, 176, 217, 223, 243, 254, 268, 272, 291, 302, 316–19, 326
Presque Isle (Erie, Pa.): 258, 263, 313–14, 325, 333
Presque Isle (Ohio country): 297, 302
Price, William: 295, 297, 299, 301, 311
Procter, Henry A.: 337

396

397

Todd, Levi: 36
Todd, Robert: 304, 310
Treaties: Falls of the Muskingum, 1788, 55, 61–62; Fort Harmar, 1788–89, 74–75, 210, 225, 244, 316, 318, 327–28; Fort Industry, Ohio, 1804, 336; Fort Knox, 1792, 215–17; Fort McIntosh, 1785, 28–30, 74, 328; Fort Stanwix, 1768, 241, 243; Fort Stanwix, 1784, 23–26, 28–30; Fort Wayne, 1809, 338; Greeneville, 1795, 320, 324–31, 335, 337, 340; Mouth of the Great Miami River, 1786, 29–30, 33, 36–38, 56; Painted Post, 1791, 208; Paris, 1783, 4, 11, 13, 25, 27, 66, 244, 263, 328; Pittsburgh, 1775, 24
Trotter, James: 37, 39, 94, 104–105
Truby, Christopher: 94
Trueman, Alexander: 181, 187, 210–12, 238, 256
Tucker, Glenn: 337
Turkey Foot (Ottawa war chief): 305
Turtle Island (mouth of the Maumee): 262, 293
Tuscarora Indians: 25–26

Underwood, Jimmy: 273
United States: Indian policy, 18, 26–28, 77, 244, 339; Revolutionary War debts of, 45; land policy of, 57, 244; treaty negotiations of, 63; Constitution of, 81; War Department, 81, 201, 210, 221; objectives in 1791, 146; Treasury, 151; consolidation policy, 324; fur trade, 325; prisoner exchanges, 331; Manifest Destiny, 340
United States Army: status of, 79, 81, 204, 248; First American Regiment, 79, 89, 147, 164, 167, 173, 190, 192–94; pay of, 82; Second United States Regiment, 145, 147, 156, 181, 184, 195; levies, 145, 147, 164, 166, 173, 184; federal militia, 205; discipline, 232; Legion of the United States, 234, 257, 262, 279–80, 288, 294ff., 302ff., 312, 332; duels in, 252; cannon recovered by, 256, 272–73, 276; First Sub Legion, 265, 282, 299, 304–305; Second Sub Legion, 265, 299; Third Sub Legion, 282, 299, 302, 304; Fourth Sub Legion, 299, 302, 304
United States Congress: see Confederation Congress; Federal Congress
Upper Canada: 229–30, 240
Upper Sandusky: 72, 102

Van Cleve, Benjamin: 182
Vermillion Villages: 85–86, 98
Vincennes, Ind.: 35–37, 57, 77, 84–86, 88, 92, 98, 101, 141, 146, 152, 158, 210, 215, 217, 219
Virginia, state of: 18, 48, 53, 70, 206
Virginia Militia: 84, 146
von Steuben, Friedrich: 13, 89, 205

Wabash Confederacy Indians: 6, 29, 33, 41, 75, 83, 84, 87, 131, 168, 196, 212, 215, 223, 239; see also tribal names
Wabash region: 45, 57, 76–77, 84, 95, 101, 139–42, 145, 269, 273, 336, 338
Wabash River: 33, 36–38, 70, 86, 98, 104, 140, 158, 175, 178–79, 182, 184–85, 188, 220, 256
Wade, John: 164
War of 1812: 336–37
Washington, George: 35, 56, 75, 81–84, 86–87, 95, 121, 130–31, 133, 146, 149, 151–52, 155–56, 209, 214, 226–27, 229–31, 234–36, 238, 244, 260, 294, 313–14, 326, 332; as surveyor, 3–4; Indian policy of, 27–28; inauguration of, 79; instructs St. Clair (1789), 84; policy guidelines of (1790), 131; instructs St. Clair (1791), 145; reacts to St. Clair's defeat, 201–203; policy revisions of (1791–92), 203–205; selects new commander (1792), 205–206
Washington, George (Delaware Indian): 63
Wasp (Wabash Confederacy chief): 141
Waterford, Ohio: 5, 60
Watkins, John: 253
Wayne, Anthony: 30, 211, 213, 216, 221, 225, 228, 230, 232ff., 241–42, 246, 249ff., 258, 260ff., 272–73, 276–78, 314–21, 324–27, 332–34, 337; appointed major general (1792), 205–206; background of, 206–207; reorganizes army, 232–35; 1794 campaign of, 279–311, 314; nearly killed, 281–82, 333; acts as "Blacksnake," 296; at Fallen Timbers, 303–305; reconnoiters British fort, 309; called "The Wind," 317; at Treaty of Greeneville, 327–31; death of, 333
Wayne, Isaac: 280–81
Wea Indians of Wabash Confederacy: 6, 35, 77, 86, 140–43, 156, 215, 217, 223, 339
Wea Towns (Ouiatanon Towns): 98, 104, 139–40

President Washington's Indian War,

designed by Bill Cason, was set in various sizes of Caslon by the University of Oklahoma Printing Services and printed offset on Glatfelter B-31, a permanized sheet, by Cushing Malloy, Inc., with case binding by John H. Dekker & Sons.